System Analysis and Design

Shih Yen Wu

Margaret S. Wu
University of Iowa

COURSE
TECHNOLOGY

ONE MAIN STREET, CAMBRIDGE, MA 02142

an International Thomson Publishing company I(T)P®

Cambridge • Albany • Bonn • Boston • Cincinnati • London • Madrid • Melbourne • Mexico City
New York • Paris • San Francisco • Singapore • Tokyo • Toronto • Washington

Systems Analysis and Design

Shih-Yen Wu

Margaret S. Wu
University of Iowa

West Publishing Company

Minneapolis/St. Paul   New York   Los Angeles   San Francisco

Production Credits

Text Design Caroline Jumper

Illustrations Kevin Tucker and Caroline Jumper

Composition The Clarinda Company

Printing and Binding West Publishing Company

On the Cover Painting by Jan Dorer of Waleska, Georgia

© 1994 by Course Technology – I(T)P®

For more information contact:

Course Technology
One Main Street
Cambridge, MA 02142

International Thomson Editores
Seneca, 53
Colonia Polanco
11560 Mexico D.F. Mexico

International Thomson Publishing Europe
Berkshire House 168-173
High Holborn
London WCIV 7AA
England

International Thomson Publishing GmbH
Königswinterer Strasse 418
53227 Bonn
Germany

Nelson ITP, Australia
102 Dodds Street
South Melbourne, 3205
Victoria, Australia

International Thomson Publishing Asia
60 Albert Street, #15-01
Albert Complex
Singapore 189969

ITP Nelson Canada
1120 Birchmount Road
Scarborough, Ontario
Canada M1K 5G4

International Thomson Publishing Japan
Hirakawacho Kyowa Building, 3F
2-2-1 Hirakawacho
Chiyoda-ku, Tokyo 102
Japan

Printed in the United States of America

ISBN 0-314-02702-5

10 9 8 7 6 5 4 3

To Jennifer and Gregory

Contents in Brief

PART V

The Design Phase   393

PART VI

The Implementation, Installation, and Post-Implementation Review Phases   607

Contents

ix

PART III

Two Real-World Projects   213

PART IV

The Modeling Tools of Systems Analysis   293

PART V

The Design Phase   393

PART VI

**The Implementation, Installation, and
Post-Implementation Review Phases 607**

Preface

This book is designed for the course dealing with the analysis, design, and implementation of computer information systems, commonly known by the title *Systems Analysis and Design*. We assume that students have already taken the introductory courses in the information systems area. Although this book does not assume prior knowledge of programming or data bases, ideally students will already have studied these topics before they tackle the systems analysis and design course. In this course, the student acquires the technical skills commonly employed by software developers in their difficult task of contructing a computer system that meets the needs of an organization. This course also obliges students to combine computer expertise with business skills in order to focus on organizational problems rather than merely building computer programs to implement standard business functions. Instructors who have taught this course know that it is demanding of both the students and the instructors. This book is designed to facilitate the teaching of this challenging mix of computer techniques with business knowledge. We hope to assist the students in the comprehension of these important topics and also to help them integrate newly acquired computer skills with their business know-how.

While several textbooks already exist for this course, in our teaching we have found that they often do not bring the real world of business decisions and uses of information systems to life for students. In our book, we have incorporated numerous practical and up-to-date business applications, two rich and illustrative cases, and have placed a strong emphasis on the analysis component including data flow diagrams, which are so crucial to successful software development. By doing so, we have strived to balance necessary technical information with an accurate picture of business needs so as to represent actual information systems planning, design, and implementation.

There are also other features that are generally unavailable in other textbooks. First, a wealth of illustrations is used to exemplify the concepts taught here. Second, ample examples are supplied to illustrate concepts rather than merely presenting an abstract idea. When appropriate, an example appears before the complete explanation of a technique is presented. By studying the example, the reader will gain familiarity with the concept before being given a detailed exposition of exactly how a software development tool is used. Because we believe that the short cases found in other texts fail to provide the student with an understanding of what software development really entails, full-length case studies have been provided as individual chapters. We have also included short projects in each chapter to enable the student to apply the relevant concepts.

Since instructors adopt different approaches to the teaching of this course, we have tried to accommodate these individual styles. Although the chapters on cost/benefit analysis and project management have been placed as Chapters 4 and 5 respectively, the material was written as separate units and may be taught in any sequence with the other topics. Similarly, the case studies in Chapters 7 and 8 can be studied anytime within the curriculum, whenever instructors feel the material best suits their purposes. In this book, the emphasis has been placed on the classical systems development life cycle; however, other methods are also fully described in Chapter 2. Charts are supplied to describe how each alternative method alters the traditional life cycle.

The book covers the entire scope of the systems development life cycle. Those instructors with only one-semester courses to cover the systems analysis and design concepts, by necessity, may find themselves unable to cover the entire text. And we can't do it, either! Instructors can make the choice of chapters to satisfy their designated objectives. However, since some colleges are now offering two-semester courses for this area, the text is also designed to supply complete coverage of all topics.

The use of a CASE tool, such as Excelerator or Visible Analyst, is recommended for this course. Many illustrations were created with the help of Excelerator. Although the topics of data flow diagrams, data dictionary, process descriptions, and structure charts have also been represented by means of Excelerator, the use of other CASE tools such as Visible Analyst or Brief-Case will not conflict with any descriptions in this book. Manually prepared data flow diagrams, data dictionary, and process descriptions may also be used in conjunction with this text.

Overview of the Text

The chapters have been organized within the framework of the well-established systems development methodology. As the reader progresses through the life cycle, the technical tools required for each stage are presented. Part I provides an introduction to the systems analysis and design area. The alternatives to the traditional development framework are described in Chapter 2. Part II deals with the Preliminary Investigation and Analysis phases. The tools of cost/benefit analysis, project management, and information gathering have been placed in this section. As we noted earlier, because some may prefer to introduce these topics at a later time, they have been written as independent units.

Part III presents two real-world projects in order to give the student the opportunity to understand how all the life cycle steps and techniques fit together to build an information system. Although we prefer to provide this overview early in the course, these chapters may be placed at a later time within the course syllabus. Chapter 7 shows the application of the traditional systems development life cycle to the problems encountered by a campus bookstore. Chapter 8 discusses a small business system for a physician's office where the best solution is a software application package. Extensive discussion of the cost/benefit trade-offs has been provided for both cases. These two complete case studies demonstrate the steps required for software development projects from start to finish. Part IV focuses on the modeling tools of systems analysis: data flow diagrams, the data dictionary, and process descriptions. The CASE tool, Excelerator, has been used to supply some illustrations, but the chapters have been structured so that other CASE tools or strictly manually prepared documents may be used in the course.

Part V deals with the Design phase, which encompasses the topics of file design, input/output design, hardware selection, and program design. Emphasis has been placed on the entity-relationship model as the diagramming tool for understanding the project data. Since structure charts continue to be the most popular tool for program design, they are explained in Chapter 16.

Part VI deals with the last three phases of the systems development life cycle: Implementation, Installation, and Post-Implementation Review. Because software quality assurance programs are now in place at many firms, this topic has been thoroughly covered. Since the Implementation phase remains a trouble spot for software projects, software engineering issues regarding coding and testing have also been included.

Questions and Projects have been provided for each chapter. The projects have been designed so that the students can investigate certain aspects of information systems by learning from real-world sources. Guidelines for the use of the projects have been given in the Instructor's Guide.

Supplements

Based on the requests submitted in our survey of potential instructors, we have provided several supplements to aid the instructor.

INSTRUCTOR'S GUIDE

The instructor's guide does more than merely outline the material in the text. It includes the following features.

Sample Course Syllabi   Because the planning for this course is really a challenging exercise in project management, sample course syllabi are incorporated into the Guide.

Lesson Guidelines   Suggestions for presenting the chapter material were written. Additional examples for class lectures are supplied.

Incorporation of Excelerator   Directions for incorporating Excelerator as the CASE tool for the course assignments are provided. Sample homework assignments in the accompanying Excelerator workbook are included.

Solutions for Chapter Questions   Solutions to the end-of-chapter questions are also furnished.

Test Bank   In response to the preferences expressed in the survey, most of the test questions are given as essay-type questions. To allow for classroom quizzes, a small test bank of multiple-choice questions is also supplied together with the answers.

Transparency Masters   Approximately 150 figures and tables from the book are provided.

PROJECTS AND CASES

Ideally, student teams should find information system projects in organizations located either on campus or in the local community. Because such projects take an extraordinary amount of time, this avenue is not always feasible. Consequently, a supplementary *Casebook* has been prepared. The casebook includes both full-length cases to be assigned to project teams and mini-cases to emphasize key points of the systems analysis and design course. An *Instructor's Guide* also accompanies the casebook to supply suggestions regarding its use and solutions to the mini-cases.

GETTING STARTED WITH EXCELERATOR

As the survey of instructors showed, many schools want to use a CASE tool but have been frustrated by the lack of good teaching materials and the problems of getting up and running. The accompanying workbook, *Getting Started With Excelerator,* should fill that vacuum. The Excelerator workbook teaches students how to use the tool to draw data flow diagrams, create the data dictionary, and produce the process descriptions. Emphasis has been placed on these three basic aspects. After the student has mastered these details, it becomes a simple matter to transfer the learning to the drawing of entity-relationship diagrams or structure charts by using the appropriate Excelerator modules. However, to ensure completeness, brief descriptions of these modules also have been incorporated into the workbook. The key features of the ANALYSIS module, which can detect errors in data flow diagrams and omissions in the data dictionary, have also been supplied.

The *Instructor's Guide* for the Excelerator workbook enables instructors to install the software, deal with students' misuse of the software, and establish projects and passwords for the students.

ORDERING EXCELERATOR

At the time of this writing, schools adopting *Systems Analysis and Design* are entitled to receive copies of *Excelerator Version 1.9,* the full-strength industrial version (not a crippled or student version) at a nominal charge. Hot-line support is included with your academic license. If you are operating in the Windows environment, you may wish to install *Excelerator for Windows,* also available for a nominal fee. Although *Getting Started with Excelerator* has been written for version 1.9, *Excelerator for Windows* has many similarities. An additional supplement for the Windows version is now in preparation. Contact Intersolv, 1 Main Street, Cambridge, MA 02142.

Acknowledgements

First, we want to express our gratitude to Harold Shipton, who has always encouraged us in our endeavors. Next, we wish to thank the many people who helped us to develop this textbook. The following individuals read and commented on some portion of the manuscript: Sarah Alexander, Martha Cronin, George Herbert, June Park, Byron Ross, Cal Siebert, V. Sridhar, Sally Staley, Jennifer Wu, and Victor Wu. Our special thanks must be given to the reviewers listed below for their diligence in scrutinizing the entire manuscript. Their suggestions and criticisms helped us to improve the initial manuscript to meet your teaching needs.

Tonya Barrier
Southwest Missouri State University

Roger Bloomquist
University of North Dakota

O. Maxie Burns
Georgia Southern College

Jane M. Carey
Arizona State University, West
Campus

Thomas L. Case
Georgia Southern College

Angela Dixon
University of Tulsa

Peter Dwyer
Sheridan College

Varun Grover
University of South Carolina,
Columbia

Dale D. Gust
Central Michigan University

Ellen D. Hoadley
Loyola College of Maryland

Geoffry S. Howard
Kent State University

Robert B. Jackson
Brigham Young University

Douglas J. Joseph
York College of Pennsylvania

Fred Lupone
Salve Regina College

Lyndon C. Marshall
College of Great Falls

Diane Miller
University of Southern
Mississippi

John M. Pearson
Kansas State University

James A. Spruell
Central Missouri State
University

Vincent Yen
Wright State University

We also wish to thank Carline Dolan, Jeanne Lambert, Ruth Ann Rich and the staff at Intersolv for facilitating our incorporation of Excelerator into this textbook. In addition, the hot-line support staff patiently answered our technical questions promptly and thoroughly.

The staff at West Educational Publishing must be credited with the production of a well-designed and edited text. Our thanks to West staff members Arnis Burvikovs, Susan Smart, and Peggy Brewington—and to Caroline Jumper—for their dedication to this project.

We also want to thank our students for their enthusaism for mastering difficult concepts in a challenging, time-consuming course. They encouraged us in our efforts to find better ways to explain the techniques for developing information systems. They invariably tackled tough projects with zeal and worked hard to become true computer professionals in the business world.

Any comments, suggestions, or criticisms are welcome and most appreciated. Please write to us in care of

West Educational Publishing
610 Opperman Dr.
P.O. Box 64526
St. Paul, MN 55164-0526

We look forward to learning from you how we can best serve you and your students in the years to come.

Margaret S. Wu

Shih-Yen Wu

An Overview of Systems Analysis and Design

CHAPTER 1

Systems Analysis and Design: An Introduction

Objectives

This chapter deals with three related topics: systems theory, the systems development life cycle, and the functions of a systems analyst. After this chapter has been completed, you will understand the following material:

■ Why systems analysis and design are essential to the creation of an information system

■ The systems approach to solving problems

■ The systems development life cycle and its role in the development of information systems

■ The tasks performed by systems analysts

■ The academic background and skills required for the position of systems analyst

INTRODUCTION

Let us begin by placing you, the reader, at the center of the stage. Today you have been summoned by the president of Greenton College to supervise the implementation of a college-wide information system. President Giorginnas tells you that the college needs this new information system because costs are out of control, enrollment is down, and information is lacking for the planning process. The Admissions Office wants to recruit more students from other geographical regions but isn't quite sure from where the present student body was drawn. It is essential that the administration lower costs, but no one really knows the breakdown of expenditures for various categories; so much information is buried in individual departmental offices that the central office just isn't informed regarding some cost issues. The basic problem is that the facts aren't available for decision making. Important data have been recorded on many types of paper documents located somewhere in the college, but the administration is unable to obtain the answers to its questions without time-consuming, tedious, and expensive manual effort. It's now *your* problem! And, if that isn't enough, the president also wants you to submit a definite schedule for system implementation, an estimate of total costs to be incurred, and a request for personnel allocation before the project can begin. Undoubtedly, you will be supervising the work of several computer professionals in order to build this system in a timely way. If the costs are too high or the project too time-consuming, the college may have to forego implementation despite its urgent need. Money is always an issue, and perhaps the administration could use the money for more advertising, student financial aid, fund-raising efforts, or maintenance of the physical facility. As desirable as the new system appears to be, there is an upper bound on what it can cost the college.

Since you have been given only this sketchy outline, you obviously require more details before you can begin to write the computer programs that will process the data. Actually, at this point, you are not even sure what data need to be processed, and you have only an inkling about the kind of output expected from this new information system. How will you start? Most likely, you will begin by formulating a list of questions, such as:

What reports are needed?

What data will enter the system?

Who will use this system?

How will the system outputs be used?

After writing down several questions, you will probably realize that many more are needed. You may even begin to feel a bit overwhelmed by the magnitude of the task. The problem is complex. It requires the collection of data from all the divisions of the college, not just the building of a simple system for a single department. Once the system is completed, many individuals will use it to obtain information and their expectations will be high. How will you really know what is wanted and how to build the final programs in the best way possible? This problem is not a well-defined homework exercise but the real thing! It's all yours—but how will the job actually be accomplished? The successful completion of this task obviously demands that detailed planning be executed before a single line of code can be written.

Now let us return to the reality of reading the words in this book. The imaginary job posed by the president of Greenton College is an assignment for a highly skilled computer professional usually identified by the title of *systems analyst.* This individual has the know-how and experience to plan and direct the building of large computer information systems. A systems analyst has the background to investigate problems that are only partially specified by management or by users of an existing information system. The analyst's toolbox contains an entire set of techniques from which the appropriate tools can be selected to solve each individual problem. Although each information system has some unique characteristics of its own, there are general procedures and analytical skills to assist the analyst in the complex work required by a software development project.

This book presents a software development methodology together with specific techniques to equip you—the future systems analyst—with the skills necessary to create a computer information system and to help you manage the project in order to achieve a satisfactory outcome in a timely fashion. Developing a computer information system is both difficult and time-consuming. Despite the advances made in the development of information systems, newspapers and computer journals still report that serious complications can arise in the creation of computer information systems. Sometimes the new system doesn't work correctly because the programmers made mistakes in writing the computer programs. Sometimes the new computerized system simply doesn't perform all its tasks in a way suitable for the organization: It just doesn't do what it is supposed to do. In the worst case, a firm may even decide that the new computer information system fails so miserably in its performance that the old system must be restored. Since developing a computerized information system may cost thousands and even millions of dollars plus months or years of effort, the failure of a system after such high expenditures of time and money is unacceptable to all concerned. If the survival of the firm depends on the proper implementation of the required information system, this failure will be intolerable.

The creation of a new information system can be divided into four major tasks:

1. Define the problem.
2. Specify the solution to the problem.

3. Frame the solution in terms of a computer information system with specific hardware and software design.
4. Code and test the computer programs.

After the system has been created, a fifth task, the installation of the new system, must be executed. Since large-scale software development demands the execution of hundreds of tasks by many different software workers, the project's activities must be carefully managed and controlled in order to achieve a successful resolution within the forecasted budgetary and scheduling requirements. Consequently, the technique of project management is a necessary component of a successful software project.

Once the programs have been written, the system will be cast into an almost irreversible mold. Although programs are not permanently embedded in concrete slabs, altering the code to reflect different requirements, while not impossible, is a formidable and error-prone process. To prevent such expensive and error-fraught activity, adequate time and resources must be allocated to the early tasks of problem definition and planning. The topic of *systems analysis and design* encompasses the work required prior to writing the program code as well as the activities necessary to install the system and thus ensure its correct operation.

As documented in Figure 1-1, **systems analysis** deals with two initial planning questions:

What is the problem?

What is the best solution for this problem?

In searching for the best solution, the analyst typically studies the existing system before formulating the requirements for the new system. Questions answered in the systems analysis stage include:

What solutions are possible, and what do they cost in money and time?

How much will it cost to implement the proposed solution?

What processing should the new system perform?

Systems design, on the other hand, creates the blueprint that guides the writing of the computer programs and the installation of the computer hardware. The general question answered in the design stage is

FIGURE 1-1

The planning activities for an information system

Systems Analysis	What is the problem?
	What is the best solution for this problem?
Systems Design	How do we transform the chosen solution into a computer information system?

How do we transform the chosen solution into a computer information system?

Specific questions answered in the systems design stage include the following:

What hardware should be used for this system?

How should the data be represented within the computer?

How should the user interface with the system?

What is the best way to organize the programming system?

While it is convenient to discuss these two major planning stages as two distinct activities, in reality they are not so clearly divided. The systems analyst who executes the planning activities must always be aware of the tasks performed in both stages. Decisions made in the analysis stage affect those to be made in the design stage.

Once an information system has been planned, coding and testing activities begin; they account for the major portion of the development time. In addition to systems analysis and design techniques, systems analysts should be skilled in other technical areas so they can adequately carry out the software development process and manage the project to its fruition. Consequently, this book also discusses guidelines for the coding and testing of software as well as the project management of these activities.

In sum, this book synthesizes various methodologies, using the term *structured systems development* (in short, *structured development*) to describe an entire set of techniques for use in planning and implementing an information system. **Structured systems development** encompasses the use of the features presented within the structured analysis and design methodology, the steps of the systems development life cycle, the available methods and software tools to assist in the software development tasks, additional formal procedures for software development, and the management techniques to control the project activities. A systems analyst should possess expertise in all of these skills.

The topics comprising structured systems development were formulated and refined by various individuals over many years. Notably, Ed Yourdon and Larry Constantine from the Yourdon consulting firm introduced the methodology known as *structured analysis and design*. As a member of the Yourdon group, Tom DeMarco wrote one of the most readable expositions of this methodology. Variations on the structured analysis and design methodology exist, such as that promulgated by Chris Gane and Trish Sarson. Barry Boehm has studied the systems development life cycle, proposed other models of the systems life cycle, and formulated techniques for estimating the time and staffing requirements of software development projects. Many others have contributed to the creation and refinement of the set of techniques discussed in this book.

The relevant course in the information systems curriculum is most often known as *systems analysis and design*. In this chapter, we begin our discussion of this topic by briefly presenting the underlying principles of general systems theory, which provides the foundation for the analysis and design of information systems. Next, we discuss the systems development life cycle, the framework by which this methodology can be implemented. Alternatives to this traditional life cycle approach are also briefly presented. In the next section, after exploring the role of the systems analyst in the development of information systems, we explain the background and skills needed for this job. Finally, we show the relationship of the remaining chapters to the various skills that are required for the systems analyst's role.

THE SYSTEMS APPROACH TO PROBLEM SOLVING

As the term implies, an information system is a *system* to which we can apply the general principles of systems theory. To understand the systems approach to problem solving, we must first learn what is meant by a system.

What Is a System?

A **system** is a set of interrelated components that function together to achieve a common goal. The components of the system are interdependent; that is, the malfunctioning of one component affects the functioning of other components. These components, called *subsystems*, interact in order to achieve the system's objectives. Ideally, to be most effective, the system produces results that cannot be provided by each component acting alone. Such a system is said to be *synergistic*—The total output of the system is greater in value than the sum of its individual parts.

As shown in Figure 1-2, a system receives inputs, which are then transformed into outputs by the processing performed within the system. The inputs of the system originate outside the system; conversely, the resulting outputs are transmitted to destinations outside the system. This general view of a system is the basis for the diagramming technique known as data flow diagrams, which will be covered in Chapter 9.

A system typically controls its operations by producing a special output known as *feedback*, which notifies the system of conditions that require special processing. The *control* mechanism consists of one or more functions that examine the system feedback in order to determine whether the system processing needs adjustment. A commonplace example of a physical system with feedback and control mechanisms is a thermostat that regulates the heat in a building. When the temperature drops below the setting on the thermostat, the control function detects this discrepancy and the system then signals the furnace to turn on. Once the proper temperature level has been reached, the control function notifies the system to stop the furnace from

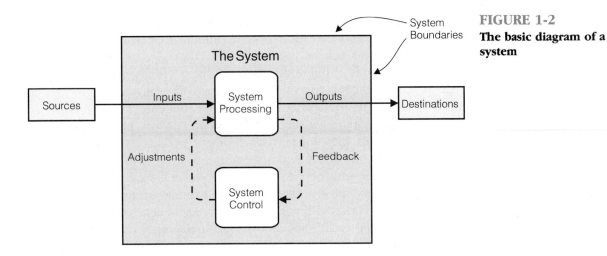

FIGURE 1-2
The basic diagram of a system

generating further heat. A supersensitive control mechanism for a thermostat would have the furnace continually turning on and off every few seconds; obviously, this would be undesirable and detrimental to the life of the furnace.

The concepts of feedback and control as applied to a data processing system can be illustrated by the example of a public library, which sends overdue notices to its patrons. Figure 1-3 shows how the circulation system at the library contains a control function in order to detect when books are overdue. Notices are then sent to the patrons. When the books are returned, the control mechanism recognizes this fact and ceases to send overdue notices. The degree of sensitivity to be placed within the control mechanism must be considered carefully. If the library sends an overdue notice as soon as a book is overdue, even by a single day, the expense to the library will be very high. Since most overdue books are returned within a week or two of the due date, most libraries delay sending overdue notices until books are

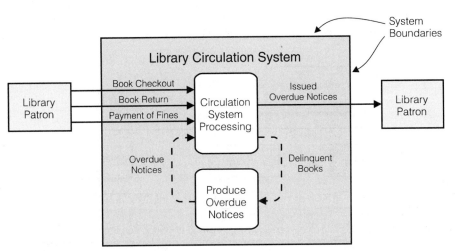

FIGURE 1-3
The circulation system at a public library with feedback and control mechanisms

at least two week late. Subsequent reminders for books still outstanding are also sent only at fixed intervals in order to minimize costs and maximize the efficiency of the system.

Systems abound in the world about us. The government on all levels—federal, state, and city—functions as a system with many subsystems. For a small municipality, the services provided are organized into subsystems such as administration, housing and inspection services, library, parks and recreation services, planning and development, police department, fire department, and public works. Another example is given by the structure chart of a business firm, which breaks it down into several subsystems. In Figure 1-4, the organizational structure chart for a manufacturing firm shows the major functions performed by the firm in order to achieve its goals. Each functional area was established as a subsystem that operates in conjunction with the other subsystems. Each subsystem receives inputs from outside the system or from other subsystems and produces outputs. The relationship between subsystems is characterized by the exchange of information among them.

When we view it as a total system, we observe that the manufacturing firm receives raw materials as inputs and, by the production process, transforms these inputs into its products, which are then sent as outputs to recipients outside the system. The subsystems of the firm work together to achieve the common goal of producing these outputs. The subsystems also interact to achieve other objectives of the system, such as increasing the firm's profits or improving quality control.

Using Systems for Problem Solving

When we encounter simple problems, we can usually solve them immediately. But when problems become complex, we are confronted with voluminous details. To solve problems of this magnitude, a series of steps is used

FIGURE 1-4 A manufacturing firm viewed as a system   Information flows among the subsystems, binding them into a system to meet the objectives of the firm.

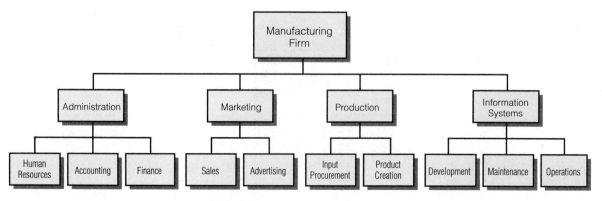

in order to reduce the problem to a manageable size more suited to our human capabilities. These steps are known as the *systems approach* to problem solving:

1. Take the original problem and decompose it into a set of smaller problems. Continue this process of decomposition until each subproblem is small enough to be solved.
2. Formulate the solution to each individual subproblem.
3. Unite the set of solutions to the subproblems into one complete unit.
4. Apply the complete solution to the original problem.
5. Verify that the solution is correct.

This approach is also called *divide and conquer*. Dividing the problem into successively smaller individual pieces enables us to conquer the problem by solving the smallest units constituting the problem.

If we look at the world about us, we observe that the systems approach is widely used. As we discussed earlier, a large organization is arranged into subsystems according to functional requirements. In this way, the overall problem of operating the firm is resolved by allocating each subproblem to the appropriate subsystem. Another example is the organizational structure of a college or university, which is composed of many academic departments. Each department performs certain functions, such as specifying the requirements for its academic majors. The course offerings for each academic term are also individually staffed by these departments. The central administration does not attempt to schedule courses or to assign instructors to teach these courses. Instead, the problems of the curriculum have been delegated to the subsystems, which are the academic departments; in effect, the problems have been subdivided into many small units. The central administration of the college serves to coordinate the activities of these departments and resolve any differences between them.

The Information System Viewed as a System

Any complex system is composed of interrelated subsystems that must share information. As we have seen, a business firm is composed of many subsystems, each of which records and exchanges information with entities outside the subsystem. Thus, a subsystem may require an information system in order to record and process information received from outside the system; for example, the Marketing subsystem needs to record information about customers and the sales of the manufactured items. In addition, the Marketing subsystem exchanges information with other subsystems. Orders from customers require that the Production subsystem be notified, so that the goods can be produced. The Finance subsystem must be notified regarding any payments received with the orders. The Production subsystem needs to track its inventory of produced goods and the raw materials received from suppliers. As discussed earlier, information flows among the subsystems. This information exchange is usually handled by appropriate computer information systems.

In building an information system, the systems approach means viewing the information system as a hierarchical arrangement of subsystems. The information system is divided into smaller and smaller parts, that is, *partitioned*. As illustrated by Figure 1-5, the information system is first broken down into a set of major subsystems, where the combined subsystems are equivalent to the entire system. Each major subsystem is further partitioned into a set of subsystems. This process continues until the desired level of refinement has been achieved. The building of the information system begins by creating the computer programs for the individual subsystems on the lowest level of the hierarchy. After the computer representations of these subsystems have been created, they are linked together (a process known as

FIGURE 1-5   **The creation of a computer information system using the systems approach to problem solving**

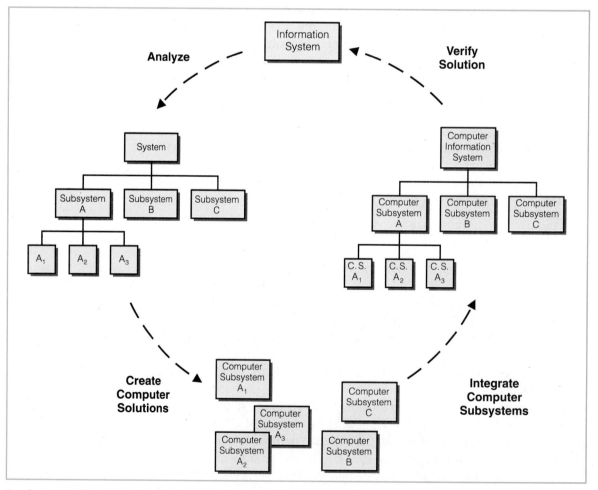

Based on Michael J. Powers, David R. Adams, and Harlan D. Mills, *Computer Information Systems,* South-Western, 1984, pp. 20–21.

integration) to form the computer information system that serves as the solution to the original problem. The completed computer information system is then reviewed to ensure that the original problem was solved correctly.

THE SYSTEMS DEVELOPMENT LIFE CYCLE

The development of an information system is accomplished according to a framework of activities and tasks known as the **systems development life cycle (SDLC)**. By defining all the major activities and individual tasks required to develop an information system, the systems development life cycle provides a detailed specification of the entire process. The SDLC can then be used to ensure that all required tasks are completed in the proper sequence. By the use of this detailed framework, the time and money required for each task can be estimated and a schedule of all tasks formulated. The entire developmental process can then be managed so that the project is successfully completed within budget and schedule constraints. Because the sequence of tasks is known, the effect of any delay in an individual task can be recognized. If possible, actions can be taken to minimize the effect of such delays.

There is no single systems development life cycle that is the standard for all organizations. The actual life cycle to be followed depends on the organization's standard for the SDLC. Each life cycle offers various features and emphasizes certain aspects of the development process. Despite these differences, each systems development life cycle contains the same basic features, possibly with different names and presented in a different structure. In this book, as shown in Figure 1-6, we divide the life of a system into two periods called *systems development* and *maintenance*. During the systems development period, the software system is created and installed as an operational system. After the system has been installed, the system continues to live on during the period of maintenance activities.

> **Warning**
>
> The systems development life cycle has many variations. Although you may have studied the SDLC in other courses, you must be careful here to observe the conventions for software development activities as given in this book.

The **systems development period** has five major phases: Preliminary Investigation, Analysis, Design, Implementation, and Installation. A sixth phase called Post-Implementation Review is also integral to the development of the system since its purpose is the evaluation of the system and the software project after the system becomes operational. However, since this phase occurs after the information system has been completed, the Post-Implementation Review phase is located within the maintenance period, as shown in Figure 1-6. These six phases constitute the systems development life cycle as presented by this book. Each phase is composed of several activities, where each activity is specified as a set of tasks. As a major component of the development process, each activity requires several weeks or months to be completed. A task requires a much shorter time span, usually about a week's duration. Figure 1-7 lists these six phases of this SDLC as well as the major activities of each phase.

After a system has been developed, it will ordinarily continue to be used for several years, the **maintenance period** of its lifetime. In order to sustain its value for a firm, maintenance is customarily performed many times to correct errors, enhance features, or adapt to new hardware. When the system can no longer be easily modified to meet the organizational needs, it is considered to have decayed and requires replacement by a completely new system. Each maintenance activity typically represents an encapsulation of the systems development life cycle. The same set of activ-

FIGURE 1-6   The life cycle of a system   This life cycle is often called the Waterfall Model because of the flow downward from one phase to the next.

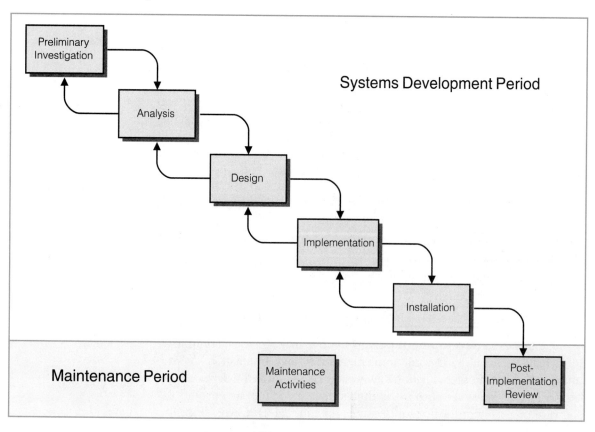

FIGURE 1-7 **The systems development life cycle** In formal descriptions of the life cycle, all activities and tasks are fully specified together with the outputs to be produced during these work units. Such descriptions occupy a book, or even volumes. Here, only major activities are listed.

I. **Preliminary Investigation**

Define the problem precisely

Estimate the time and money requirements to solve the problem

Perform a feasibility study

Determine whether to proceed with the project

Major Output: Feasibility Report

II. **Analysis**

Model the existing system:

Draw the data flow diagrams

Prepare the data dictionary and process descriptions

Model the proposed system:

Create the data flow diagrams

Revise the data dictionary

Produce the process descriptions

Major Output: Proposal for the New System

III. **Design**

Design the new system:

Select hardware and software platforms

Acquire the necessary hardware and software

Design the data files

Design the programs

Prepare training guidelines

Prepare preliminary testing procedures

Major Output: Design Specifications

IV. **Implementation**

Create the test data

Code the individual programs

Test the programs

Document the programs

Train the users

Prepare installation plans

Major Output: Set of Tested Computer Programs

V. **Installation**

Convert data files to the new system

Install new hardware and software platforms

Install the information system

Perform final testing of the entire system

Major Outputs: Performance Tests and Fully Installed System

VI. **Post-Implementation Review**

Review the development process immediately upon completion

After three to six months, evaluate the installed system

Major Outputs: System Evaluation Reports

ities is needed in order to determine whether a particular modification to the system should be carried out. If the change is considered to be very minor, the earlier phases of Preliminary Investigation and Analysis may be omitted. In the same way, coding errors discovered after system installation are ordinarily corrected without retracing the entire SDLC. If the correction of coding errors is found to affect the program design, other portions of the SDLC may be invoked. Major modifications require the same activities associated with the SDLC, from study of the problem to estimation of costs and so on. Despite the fact that maintenance activities are performed primarily to enable the same system to continue its functions, each maintenance request must be reviewed thoroughly in order to judge its impact on the entire system. The proper maintenance of a software system requires the same skills used during the software development period. To emphasize its importance the maintenance period was set apart from the development activities in Figure 1-6. Although the development period is given more physical space in this drawing, in reality, a software system typically spends most of its lifetime in the maintenance period.

FIGURE 1-8

The checkpoints in the SDLC After each phase comes a checkpoint where management decides whether the project should continue. The checkpoint also allows management to review the outputs of the completed phase before approving entry into the next phase.

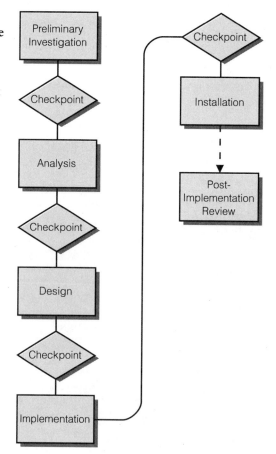

A fully specified life cycle breaks down each phase into tens of hundreds of tasks. Such detailed documentation creates several volumes of material, more than a single book can hold. Consequently, the myriad of individual tasks required for the development of an information system will not be specified here. Instead, this book will concentrate on the major activities for each phase as listed in Figure 1-7.

Figure 1-8 shows how each phase is followed by a **checkpoint** where the project's likelihood of success is evaluated. If the project is floundering and chances for a successful completion are slim, then management weighs the costs and benefits of the project and decides whether it should go forward. The decision to terminate a lengthy and expensive project occurs infrequently but it does occasionally happen. This checkpoint also allows management to verify that the preceding phase was completed satisfactorily. By examining the outputs produced by a phase, management determines whether the project is on target. The next phase will be delayed until these outputs are judged to be adequate. This prevents the new phase from being doomed to failure by the lack of properly prepared inputs. Each phase of the SDLC is described in more detail in the following sections.

Preliminary Investigation

The **Preliminary Investigation** phase is initiated when a problem has been presented to the computer professionals. The nature of the particular problem may vary from delays in processing orders to the need to compete with the other firms in the marketplace. Management may envision a complete restructuring of business procedures, in order to increase productivity while simultaneously achieving financial gains and moving ahead of the firm's competitors. The computer center director may see a problem to be solved if costs are rising due to aging computer hardware. The advent of innovative technology may be another reason for changing the current system. Whatever the problem, once it has been stated, the systems development life cycle is entered.

The main purpose of the Preliminary Investigation phase is to formulate the problem more precisely and find its best solution. A general statement of the problem and a rough estimate of the time required for further study is presented for management's approval before an extensive study of the problem takes place. After approval has been given, the systems analyst embarks on an investigation of the problem in order to conceive a plan of action. Throughout this phase and the remainder of the life cycle, the analyst turns to the users for information and for their approval of the planning activities. After studying the problem, the analyst conceives several alternative solutions to the problem. These solutions are then examined to determine the most satisfactory alternative. The selection of a final solution is accomplished by considering many different aspects, such as the system's benefits, its essential requirements, future needs of the firm, limitations on development costs, time constraints, and the availability of resources to build the system—that is, hardware, software, and personnel. It is unlikely that any single solution will be perfect. The evaluation of the trade-offs among these diverse factors leads to the choice of the best solution for the particular firm.

The major output of this phase is a report that defines the problem and proposes a solution to that problem. Known as the *feasibility study*, the report includes an evaluation of the project for its feasibility factors. The preparation of the feasibility study is discussed in Chapter 3. With the feasibility study in hand, management is able to decide whether the project meets the needs of the firm. If approved at this checkpoint, the project enters the next phase, Analysis.

Analysis Phase

In the **Analysis** phase, some activities from the first phase are performed in more depth. Now the systems analyst must truly understand the entire problem and create a final solution to this problem. To accomplish this task, the systems analyst turns once again to the users in order to gather more information on the existing system. After the existing system has been thoroughly appraised, the analyst defines the features required in the new system and creates the new system proposal. The diagramming technique known as *data flow diagrams* is the recommended method for describing the features of both the existing system and the proposed system. Chapters 9, 10, and 11 explain this technique as well as the means used to document the data and processes included within the data flow diagrams. A checkpoint occurs after this phase has been completed, and management determines, first, whether the project should continue and, second, whether the Design phase should begin.

Design Phase

The activities in the **Design** phase are executed in order to furnish the details needed for the coding of the system. The appropriate hardware and software platforms for the system's implementation are selected; these basic issues are discussed in Chapter 16. Although these issues are listed in the Design phase, they were under consideration throughout the earlier phases. The users also actively participate in the Design phase by evaluating the analyst's proposals for the user interfaces, such as screen designs and report formats. The format of the computer files is defined in this phase along with the specifications for test data needed for program testing activities in the next phase. The formats for input data and output data are also specified, the medium for the system's inputs and outputs is chosen, and any paper forms for manually recorded data are drafted. Testing procedures are formulated in a preliminary manner. The training of the users is considered in this phase, although final plans are typically deferred to the Implementation phase.

The computer programs are described in a detailed fashion, typically by a diagramming technique known as *structure charts* (discussed in Chapter 16). After this phase is completed, the details of the system have been fully specified. The system is now ready for programming to begin. Preliminary plans are also drawn up for the installation of the new system; final plans will be produced during the **Implementation** phase. Before moving into the next phase, the checkpoint occurs: Management decides whether the activities to date have progressed satisfactorily and, if so, approves continuation of the project.

Implementation Phase

With the detailed design specifications as a guide, the programmers create the test data, code the program modules, and perform testing. After testing of individual program modules is completed, these modules are integrated into the final system, which is then tested as a whole to ensure there are no inconsistencies between the modules. Chapter 17 describes testing techniques as well as the requirements for a software quality assurance program designed to ensure the development of high quality software. Final documentation of the programming system is produced, and the training of the users now takes place. The major output of this phase is the set of completed programs that comprise the information system. As with the other phases, management performs the checkpoint procedure. After the go-ahead from management, the system proceeds to the Installation phase.

Installation Phase

Before the new system can be used, it is necessary to make a transition from the old system to the new. **Installation** proceeds according to the final conversion plans formulated in the Implementation phase. Current data files are now converted and any additional data files are created. If new hardware and software are required, they must be installed. The information system is then placed on the computer and a performance test of the entire system is executed. Additional support is provided to the users to smooth the transition to the new system. The various modes of converting from the old system to the new one as well as other aspects of the Installation phase are discussed in Chapter 17.

Post-Implementation Review

Immediately upon installation of the new system, management looks back over the entire development process in a **post-implementation review**. An evaluation of the process is done to determine if the original plans for time and budget were correct. The reasons for any time or cost overruns are determined. The work performance of the systems analysts and programmers is evaluated at this time. The initial expectations for the information system are compared to the features of the installed system. After three to six months, the new system is reexamined to review its performance. Because the system has been operational for several months, it is now possible to see whether the new system fulfills the needs of the organization. Management looks into such issues as user satisfaction, response time, and problems uncovered during the actual operation of the system. The Post-Implementation Review phase is covered in Chapter 17.

The Waterfall Model

The systems development life cycle, as shown in Figure 1-6, is sometimes called the **Waterfall Model** because each major phase of the life cycle flows downward into the next phase. Although the SDLC has been defined as a neatly ordered series of steps, in reality, we have an iterative process that is not so cut and dried. As each major phase is entered, the systems analyst does not focus exclusively on the tasks in that phase. Many of the activities relegated to one phase actually must be considered in an earlier phase, even though the completion of these activities occurs later in the life cycle. For example, although the consideration of what hardware and software should be used for the information system is placed in the Design phase, the systems analyst must reflect on this issue throughout the development process until a final decision is made. The developer of a system does not put on blinders and refuse to think about issues that lie ahead. Rather, some aspects of the development process are encountered in the life cycle more than once. What the SDLC tells us is the time when final decisions must be formally made. For instance, until we decide on the hardware and software platforms for the system, we are unable to move forward to the Implementation phase, because the programmers cannot be assigned to write the code without knowing what programming language and what computer will be used. The life cycle also serves as a warning that we should not lock the system into final decisions until a particular phase has been completed.

The activities within a major phase are not necessarily sequential. For example, parallel activities within the Design phase are diagrammed in Figure 1-9. After the hardware and software platforms have been selected, their acquisition may proceed simultaneously with the remainder of the design activities. The detailed planning of systems development activities will be discussed under the topic of project management in Chapter 5.

Although the SDLC has the appearance of a sequential flow from one major phase to another, the Waterfall Model is always drawn with arrows moving backwards from each phase to its predecessor. These arrows indicate that while one phase is in progress, it may be necessary to return to an earlier phase in order to uncover additional information. In other words, although the activities in the preceding phases were completed, problems in the current phase may require that we perform some of these activities again. For example, if we enter the Implementation phase and begin programming, a programmer may raise a question that requires us to obtain more information from the users of the system. It is even possible that the

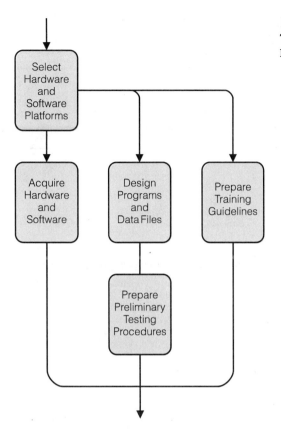

FIGURE 1-9
The activities in the Design phase

original conception of the system has some major flaws. Rather than continue to code a badly flawed system, we return to the earlier Analysis phase, revise the overall design, and then begin again to implement the system. Because of the voluminous detail essential to the construction of an information system, such backward flow in the SDLC is inevitable. When the life cycle has been rigorously followed, such backtracking is minimized. However, we should never hesitate to return to a preceding phase in order to accomplish our mission successfully.

The Problem of Software Maintenance

After an information system has become operational, the maintenance period begins. Because an information system will be used for many years, the maintenance period represents the majority of the entire system's life. As depicted in Figure 1-10, only 7% to 17% of the system's lifetime costs are allocated to the Preliminary Investigation, Analysis, and Design phases, while the coding and testing activities performed in the Implementation phase use from 13% to 33% of the total life cycle costs. In terms of total data processing expenditures, maintenance activities consume a large chunk of data processing resources, with estimates ranging from 50% to 80% of the information systems budget. Some firms have even estimated maintenance costs to be as

FIGURE 1-10

The costs associated with each phase of a system's life cycle

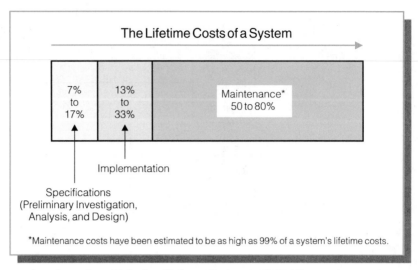

Based on data in Barry W. Boehm, "Software Engineering," *IEEE Transactions on Computers* C-25(12), December 1976, pp. 1226–1242 and Paul M. Cashman and Anatol W. Holt, "A Communication-Oriented Approach to Structuring the Software Maintenance Environment," ACM SIGSOFT, Software Engineering Notes 5(1), January 1980.

FIGURE 1-11

The sources of specification changes

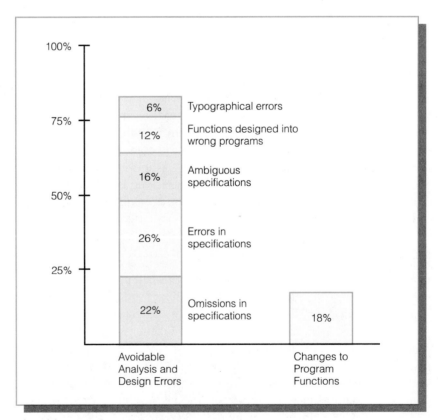

Adapted from Gopal Kapur, "Productivity Tools Betray Promises of MIS Nirvana," *Computerworld*, December 1, 1986, pp. 61–78.

high as 99% of a system's lifetime costs. Such heavy commitment of resources to maintenance activities means that new development projects essential to the firm's survival and competitiveness may be delayed or sidetracked for an indefinite period. A major concern is how to reduce the maintenance costs for a system.

Until recently, attention focused on methods to improve the coding of programs so that the number of errors in the final program would be minimized, thereby reducing maintenance costs. Although this emphasis on coding methods greatly improved the coding and testing stages, almost 50% of the programming defects in the final system are caused by errors in the Analysis and Design stages. During the coding stage, it is not uncommon to discover errors in the program specifications caused by deficiencies in the work performed during analysis and design. A study by Kapur (1986) concluded that, after the programming stage has begun, more than 80% of the changes made to programming specifications are avoidable (see Figure 1-11). A study by Boehm (1981) demonstrated that the relative cost to fix an error increases as we move through the phases of the life cycle (see Figure 1-12). The results of the analysis and design stages have a lasting effect on the

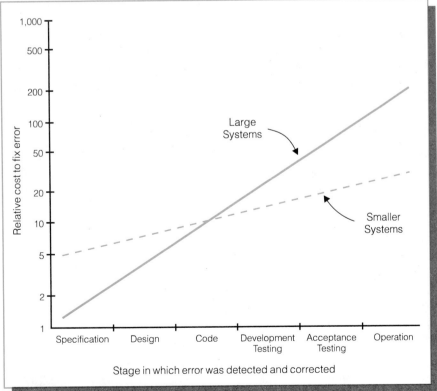

FIGURE 1-12

The relative cost to fix errors in each stage of the life cycle   As we move through the life cycle, the cost to fix errors produced by earlier stages increases dramatically.

system throughout its lifetime. For large systems, Boehm found that it costs 100 times more to correct an error in the maintenance period than in the Preliminary Investigation or Analysis phase. For smaller projects the effect is somewhat less dramatic, with a ratio of 4:1 for correcting an error in the testing stage rather than in the Preliminary Investigation or Analysis phase. The old saying, "An ounce of prevention is worth a pound of cure," has been shown to be true once again.

What do these figures mean to us as we study the topic of structured development? Because organizations are starting to recognize the importance of the early phases of the life cycle, emphasis is now being placed on the early phases of the SDLC—Preliminary Investigation, Analysis, and Design. For these same reasons, the structured development methodology offers specialized techniques to assist in the creation of complete and correct program specifications. The principles of good coding and testing are also included in the structured development methodology, as well as the concepts of successful project management. The development of information systems that meet the needs of the organization requires the proper execution of all stages in the life cycle. We are finally becoming aware that, without good analysis and design, the system is doomed to delays in the coding and testing stages, high maintenance costs, or even failure.

The Reasons for the SDLC Approach

To place the SDLC in perspective, it is necessary to know that the development of major information systems typically takes one to two years or even longer, with costs reaching into millions of dollars. For large projects, hundreds of computer professionals are engaged in the systems development process. As we discussed earlier, by providing a detailed step-by-step description of the tasks essential for systems development and the sequencing of these tasks, the SDLC supplies the framework necessary to manage this process. Because every task is measured by its specified outputs, the entire project becomes manageable. Project management techniques make it possible to detect any tasks that are running late. Since the SDLC specifies the ordering of these tasks, we can know how any delay will affect other portions of the project. Management can then take suitable action to alleviate the impacts of the delay and, if necessary, establish a new project completion date.

The SDLC also helps us to avoid any flaws in the final system. In other words, the new system will do what we want it to do. Thus, the systematic approach to solving the original problem offers the promise of a satisfactory information system that meets the users' requirements. The techniques used for the Analysis and Design phases facilitate the smooth production of working programs that perform the appropriate functions for the information system. The detailed SDLC framework provides an itemized checklist to avoid overlooking any task, no matter how small it may be. The end result should be the best system possible within the constraints imposed on the system by management and the available technology.

The Drawbacks of the SDLC Approach

There are three major drawbacks to the SDLC approach to systems development: the process is time-consuming, costly, and requires extensive documentation for each phase. Let us examine these issues one by one.

TIME REQUIRED FOR THE SDLC APPROACH

The entire SDLC process depends on properly documenting the system requirements of the users. Customarily, the systems analyst prepares detailed project specifications, which may occupy several hundred pages. After studying these written specifications, the user formally approves the project and *signs off*. However, because of the complexity of the system specifications, it is unlikely that the user actually verifies the correctness of every project detail. Despite the participation of the user in the design of the system interfaces, the remaining phases of the SDLC consist primarily of technical activities. Consequently, the systems development process proceeds to completion with little or no user involvement until the final system is presented to the user some months or years later. Meanwhile, the organization has not been static. Changes that affect the suitability of the design have probably transpired. Upon delivery of the system, the user may well take one look and find it doesn't do what is needed today. The system may be perfectly attuned to the original requirements painstakingly derived by the systems analyst—but by now the organizational environment has changed. Even if the whole development process was successfully accomplished without any flaws, the system was created in a vacuum far removed from the reality of the business firm. The lengthy time frame also means the problems to be solved by the new system must be handled in an ad hoc manner by the firm until the new system is ready and operational. Should these problems pose a threat to the firm's success or survival, the time frame necessary for the SDLC approach will be unacceptable.

HIGH COSTS OF THE SDLC APPROACH

The second drawback, high costs, is also related to the lengthy development time. Since extensive time commitments of computer professionals are required, human resource costs are high. Because of high development costs, other projects may be postponed, or *backlogged*, until more important projects are completed. If extensive delays are experienced, users may decide that it is pointless to approach management with new ideas for software development. Although such software projects might prove valuable to the firm, management is never given the opportunity to evaluate them. Because these projects were never even submitted for management's consideration, they represent the *invisible backlog* for the information systems area.

DOCUMENTATION REQUIREMENTS FOR THE SDLC APPROACH

Finally, choosing the SDLC for small projects is like using a sledgehammer to swat a fly. The SDLC is costly, time-consuming, unwieldy, and clumsy. The entire process is slowed by the requirement for voluminous documentation to be produced before the next phase is entered. The use of the SDLC approach for small projects typically causes extensive and often unnecessary documentation to be produced.

These serious drawbacks to the SDLC approach are inherent results of its detailed step-by-step approach to software development. Fortunately, other ways of developing information systems exist. These alternative approaches are briefly discussed in the next section.

ALTERNATIVES TO THE TRADITIONAL SDLC

Figure 1-13 lists seven **alternatives to the traditional SDLC** approach to project development: software packages, reusable code, prototyping, CASE tools, reverse engineering, object-oriented technology, and end-user development. An eighth alternative is simply to abandon in-house development of the system in favor of engaging an outside contractor to produce the information system. Because this alternative is not really a departure from the traditional development approach, but rather a basic choice regarding the use of in-house resources versus the hiring of an outside contractor, it is covered under design issues in Chapter 16. The first two alternatives, *software packages* and *reusable code*, are really just ways of shortening steps within the life cycle, whereas the next five approaches differ substantially from the traditional SDLC. *Prototyping* is a method that involves the user throughout the development process. *CASE tools* permit the automation of the manual effort necessary during the software development process. *Reverse engineering* uses the existing computer information system to create the new system. *Object-oriented technology* offers a completely different way of viewing the information system and creating the program structures for the software. *End-user development* places the burden of systems development on the user. In addition to these alternatives, the *multifaceted approach* incorporates various alternatives to use the best technique for each project task. Each method is briefly discussed in the following subsections; an in-depth discussion is given in Chapter 2.

```
Alternatives to the Traditional SDLC
        Software Application Packages
        Reusable Code
        Prototyping
        CASE Tools
        Reverse Engineering
        Object-Oriented Technology
        End-User Development
```

FIGURE 1-13
Seven alternatives for the development of information systems

Software Packages

A major portion of the systems development life cycle is spent in the Design and Implementation phases. The purchase of a **software application package** provides a shortcut to the SDLC by eliminating the need to design the system, to code and test the programs, and to prepare the program documentation. Both time and money are saved by selecting a software application package rather than in-house development. Because of the expanded need for information systems coupled with the rise in software development costs, software packages have become increasingly important.

Reusable Code

The time required for the SDLC is shortened by employing **reusable code**. To use this method, the organization establishes a library of routines that have been coded and thoroughly tested. Each routine is simply a set of program instructions written in a general way so that the code can be used by another program. Because the routines are thoroughly tested prior to placement in the library, the incorporation of a routine in a program does not introduce any programming errors. Thus, time and money are saved by reducing the effort required for coding and testing activities in the Implementation phase. Although this method has a measure of popularity, it requires that strict standards be imposed on the library of routines. Adequate documentation must be provided to assist programmers in selecting the appropriate routines. While this practice of reusable code is helpful, not all code is reusable. Thus, extensive coding and testing may still be required.

Prototyping

While the methods of software packages and reusable code are variations on the SDLC, **prototyping** represents a completely different approach. Prototyping allows the systems analyst and the user to join together to build the desired system. After a brief investigation into the problem, the systems analyst quickly produces a preliminary version of the information system, which is delivered to the user. The user then actually operates this preliminary version and tells the analyst what features should be changed or added. Working rapidly, the analyst refines the system and delivers it once again to the user. This process continues until the system meets the user's needs. Prototyping shortens the Preliminary Investigation phase and replaces the Analysis phase with successive refinements of each version, which are made possible by the interaction between the user and the systems analyst. Thus, less time and money for software development are needed than with the traditional life cycle approach. User satisfaction is high because the user has participated throughout the systems development process. However, it is important to keep in mind that the prototyping approach is not suitable for the development of large, complex systems.

CASE Tools

The term **CASE** stands for *computer assisted software engineering,* which means the broad category of computer programs designed especially to aid computer professionals in the systems development process. **CASE tools** range from aids for collecting information during the initial planning process to test generators that assist in creating test data. Using the appropriate CASE tools shortens the time required for software development. The systems analyst can then concentrate time and energy on the activities in the early phases of the developmental process. CASE tools also make possible the developmental approach called reverse engineering, which is discussed next.

Reverse Engineering

If the new system replaces an existing computer information system, many functions of the existing system must be replicated as computer code. For example, if the inventory system was written as a batch mode programming system, the same functions must be performed for an on-line system. Because these functions were not written as reusable code, we cannot obtain the code in that way. For older systems, serious deficiencies usually exist in documentation. It is very likely that some crucial details of the existing computer system have been omitted, or the documentation may contain some ambiguities. In the traditional approach of the full-blown SDLC, we must return to the users and determine all the features of the system again. Since the programs for the existing system are already operational and thoroughly tested, why not attempt to reuse this program code? This solution to the problem is known as **reverse engineering**.

Reverse engineering of the existing system is accomplished by means of specialized software tools known as CASE tools for reverse engineering. (The CASE tools that support the beginning steps of the life cycle are commonly known as tools for **forward engineering**.) Although reverse engineering offers great promise, the software tools are expensive and difficult to use. Lack of familiarity with this approach coupled with high costs has slowed wide adoption of this method.

Object-Oriented Technology

Object-oriented technology represents another way of analyzing and building information systems. Because the components (called *objects*) of object-oriented programs are inherently designed to be reusable, the costs for future maintenance—and even new systems development—should be less than in the traditional approach. Although this technique offers great promise, it requires software developers to view the components of an information system in a different way. Costs for retraining software workers in object-oriented development must be incurred before this technology can be used.

End-User Development

Previously, all computer programs were developed by computer professionals who programmed in third-generation languages such as COBOL and FORTRAN. Today, personal computers (PCs) perch on desks in many businesses and familiarity with spreadsheets and data base management systems is commonplace. Many other software packages are available to the user (also called the *end-user*) for performing the tasks required by firms. Because of the existence of user-friendly software, **end-user development** of a system is now possible without help from computer professionals. The end-user determines all the requirements, creates the system, performs any testing, and installs the system. Because the end-user knows the requirements of the system, user satisfaction is high. Despite the many advantages associated with end-user development, some problems arise with this do-it-yourself approach, too. They occur when the system is too complex for this type of development, the wrong software tool is chosen, testing is neglected, or documentation requirements are ignored.

The Multifaceted Approach

Although each alternative has been listed as an independent option for the traditional life cycle, a **multifaceted approach** permits the alternatives to be used selectively wherever appropriate in the SDLC in order to facilitate project development. For example, the design of input and output formats may be accomplished by the use of CASE tools. The user can then actually see the input and output screens or reports and judge whether they are acceptable. If deemed desirable, small portions of the system might be prototyped to check the design specifications before formal implementation takes place; the prototyped subsystems become the design guidelines for the coding process. In the prototyping method, the user actually has the opportunity to interact with these prototyped subsystems so as to suggest improvements to the software developers. The subsystem then continues to be refined until the user is satisfied with its design. Another option is the employment of reusable code for implementing some portion of the system. Reverse engineering offers the means to examine the structure of the existing system and may serve as an initial jump-start for the development of the system. By selecting the best technique for each task within the life cycle, the systems analyst speeds the development process and contributes to the likelihood of a satisfactory outcome.

THE JOB OF THE SYSTEMS ANALYST

In the traditional SDLC approach as well as the alternatives to the SDLC, the systems analyst plays a primary role (except for the case of end-user development). The people who will actually use the system to be developed are known as the users or **end-users**. Their expertise is directly related to the functional area in which they are engaged. On the other hand, computer professionals are trained in technical skills necessary for the creation and maintenance of computer programs. Their expertise generally involves the use of computers rather than a functional area of a business. Resolving the users' problems requires both the ability to understand the firm's objectives and its functional activities as well as high-level computer skills to develop the information system. The systems analyst is the computer professional who bridges this gap between the users and the technically oriented computer programmers.

Functions of the Systems Analyst

The role of the systems analyst is to investigate the user's problem, define the problem explicitly, and determine what solution will best meet the needs of the business. Typically, the analyst is also charged with the responsibility for implementing the problem's solution. The choice of a solution is made from the alternatives envisioned by the systems analyst. It is even possible that the solution will not be directly related to the computer area. If the analyst decides that a computer information system should be constructed, the method for systems development must also be recommended by the analyst. If the traditional SDLC approach is selected, the analyst engages in the analysis of the existing system, proposes a new system, and formulates the design of the system. The analyst strives to create design specifications in sufficient detail so that the programmers will be able to write the program code with minimal supervision. Although the coding and testing activities in the Implementation phase are usually delegated to the programming staff, these activities are typically supervised by the systems analyst. After the system has been completed and thoroughly tested, the analyst assumes responsibility for the installation of the system. The other major activities in the life cycle are either planned or directly executed by the systems analyst. Project management for the entire SDLC is typically assigned to a senior level systems analyst. After the system has been installed, ongoing support for system maintenance and enhancement is also provided by the systems analyst. These varied duties of the systems analyst require a corresponding mix of skills, which will be discussed in a later section.

Job Titles in Industry

Sometimes the title *systems analyst* is mistakenly given to a variety of jobs from the entry level programming position to the manager of all systems projects. More aptly, the entry level position should be titled *programmer/ analyst*. While it is helpful to discuss the role of systems analyst as though the job were completely separate from that of programming, oftentimes programmers do not function solely as coders. Frequently they are involved in the Analysis and Design phases and interact with both the systems analysts and the users.

As a programmer/analyst gains experience, responsibility for a larger share of the analysis and design activities is assigned in conjunction with programming activities. When programming activities have been substantially reduced, the programmer/analyst is promoted to the position of systems analyst. For each promotion in the ranks of systems analysts, the amount of programming activity further declines. A *senior systems analyst* usually spends more than 50% of the time on analysis and design activities with only a small allocation of time—perhaps 10%—to programming. The remainder of the time is devoted to supervising personnel and managing the project. A *lead systems analyst* supervises several project managers and still actively participates in the analysis and design of projects. At this level, no programming is performed.

In practice, the actual job title for the position of systems analyst varies, depending on the firm's preference. As shown in Figure 1-14, some job titles are systems analyst, systems engineer, and information analyst. Only the job description defines what the job title truly represents.

Systems Analyst

Systems Engineer

Systems Consultant

Information Analyst

Data Analyst

Business Analyst

Programmer/Analyst

FIGURE 1-14

Job titles for the systems analyst position

Requirements for the Systems Analyst Position

The basic requirements for the systems analyst position are listed in Figure 1-15. In many firms, the position of systems analyst is reserved for those who have first gained one or two years of programming experience. Individual firms may choose to make exceptions to this programming requirement. A bachelor's or master's degree in an appropriate major enables the graduate to obtain employment in an entry level programming position, most likely one with the job title *programmer/analyst*. Large firms frequently recruit graduating students for entry level positions regardless of academic major because they offer extensive training classes on site. Analytical ability and communication skills are two key factors sought in hiring such graduates.

FIGURE 1-15

The requirements for the systems analyst position

Academic Background

Bachelor's or Master's degree with a major in information systems, or computer science degree with a minor in Business. Depending on the firm, other majors may be acceptable.

Computer Skills

Programming Experience

> Typically, 1–2 years of experience in at least one major programming language; exceptions may be made by individual firms. For business applications, the primary language is COBOL; a recommended second language is C.

Familiarity with a fourth-generation language for a data base management system or an applications generator

Systems Analysis and Design Skills

> Knowledge and experience with methodologies in these areas

Data Skills

> Ability to organize data into appropriate data structures
>
> Training in one or more data base management systems

CASE Tools

> Highly desirable to have experience with CASE tools such as Excelerator, Bachman tools, and IEF.

General Skills

Verbal and Written Communications Skills

Interpersonal Skills

Problem-Solving Ability

Background in Organizational Functions

For securing an entry level position, it is advantageous to obtain data processing experience through summer and part-time jobs. The cooperative education programs offered by many colleges and universities allow students to acquire invaluable experience in the information systems area by working for a firm during the summer months or part-time during the academic year. In addition to previous experience, many firms look for a satisfactory grade point average (GPA) as proof that the student can master new material and will perform satisfactorily in this highly technical area. A mix of technical and "people" skills is necessary for promotion to the systems analyst position. We shall briefly discuss the set of characteristics most often associated with this position.

PROGRAMMING EXPERIENCE

To become a systems analyst, usually the programmer must demonstrate proficiency in programming. In business, the preferred language is COBOL; however, software firms developing software packages, especially microcomputer software, favor the language C. Because of the interest in object-oriented programming, C and C++ have gained a wider audience. For scientific and engineering applications, FORTRAN is more commonly used. Other languages with some minor share of the programming field include Pascal, Ada, and PL/1. Because the systems analyst must be able to perform prototyping, familiarity with a fourth-generation language is customarily required. A fourth-generation language may also be selected as the programming language for the traditional approach to systems development.

OTHER TECHNICAL SKILLS

To be effective, a systems analyst should know the structured development methodology as presented in this text; the mastery of a similar methodology is also acceptable. The analyst should have experience in the design of file structures and should possess a thorough understanding of data base management systems. Finally, at least one CASE tool should be present in the repertoire of the systems analyst. Because the computer field changes rapidly, the systems analyst should read technical journals in order to stay abreast of new developments.

GENERAL SKILLS

Although technical skills are indispensable for successful software development, the analyst also needs a set of general skills which include communications skills, interpersonal ability, problem-solving ability, and a background in organizational functions. Each of these skills is discussed next.

Communications Skills   Good oral and written communications skills are imperative for the role of systems analyst. Many firms express concern that some college graduates lack these invaluable skills. Computer-oriented individuals sometimes focus on acquiring technical mastery and fail to improve their oral and written communication proficiency. With hard work, it is possible to polish these skills by enrolling in classes in business communications, technical documentation, and speech. Without good communications skills, the road to success will be blocked.

Interpersonal Skills   The systems analyst engages in various tasks that demand constant interaction with others. The systems analyst is sometimes called a *people person* because he or she deals with the users, computer professionals, and management throughout the development process. Such contact requires a sensitivity to others' feelings and viewpoints. As the initiator of change in an organization, the systems analyst must be aware of people's natural resistance to change. The persuasive skills of the analyst will be called upon to convince users, and possibly even management, of the advantages of organizational changes. Finally, the systems analyst typically functions as a member of a team. The ability to cooperate and compromise with others is an indispensable characteristic that will assist the analyst in leading the team to achieve its goals.

Problem-Solving Ability   The systems analyst must be able to use the systems approach to problem solving. When a business problem is posed, the analyst must first create a precise definition of the problem. As discussed earlier, the problem is then broken down into its components, the subproblems are analyzed and solved, and then a system is designed as the solution of the entire problem. This ability to examine a complex problem by breaking it into smaller pieces—without losing sight of the whole picture—is essential for the analyst's success. Unlike problems in mathematics classes, business problems have more than one possible solution. It takes creativity to devise alternative solutions, analyze their trade-offs, and recommend the solution most suitable for the organization. In particular, the analyst must be aware that it may be necessary to discard the old methods of doing business and find a completely new approach to the problem instead. Grace Hopper, designer of the COBOL language, summed up this viewpoint when she said, "The most damaging phrase in the language is 'We've always done it that way.'" Rather than preserving the constraints of past methods, the systems analyst must look for new and innovative ways of solving problems.

Background in Organizational Functions   For systems analysts dealing with business problems, an understanding of accounting, economics, production, and marketing activities is useful in analyzing the problems posed by the users. The business curriculum offers courses covering these functional areas. College students should also strive to obtain part-time or summer jobs that provide experience in the operations of a business. If the systems analyst will work with scientific or engineering problems, a background in the appropriate discipline is highly desirable.

We close our discussion of the skills required by a systems analyst with one final observation: Be prepared to learn new ideas throughout your career! In the years to come, businesses will change and new computers, software, and methodologies will appear. The solution of problems requires more than a given set of skills; good problem solving demands that these skills continually be expanded to include current concepts and techniques. The systems analyst is a person embarked on a lifelong career of challenge and exploration.

ACQUIRING THE TECHNIQUES OF THE SYSTEMS ANALYST

The remaining chapters deal with the various techniques that belong in the systems analyst's toolkit. The alternative approaches to the traditional development life cycle also require some of these skills. Figure 1-16 identifies the tools explained in each chapter and places them within the context of the systems development life cycle. Chapters 2 through 6 cover the basic skills for the systems analyst by explaining the techniques needed for the early stages of the life cycle. Chapter 2 presents an explanation of other approaches to software development and shows how they alter the pattern of the traditional life cycle steps. Chapter 3 discusses some fundamental principles to direct the work of the systems analyst. These guidelines are pertinent throughout the life cycle. Chapter 4 shows how to determine the financial merits of an information system proposed as the solution to the user's problem. Chapter 5 offers guidelines for the estimation of time and personnel requirements in building an information system. Methods for organizing and controlling the project activities are also discussed. Chapter 6 gives an introduction to the techniques commonly used to gather information about the system. The presentation on the interviewing technique is also pertinent for exchanges between the users and the systems analyst throughout the life cycle.

In order to illustrate how the various skills of the analyst are involved in the construction of actual systems, Chapters 7 and 8 present two case studies. The first case study concerns the Campus Bookstore and its need for a new information system. The case is designed to illustrate the steps taken to create an information system by implementing custom-tailored code. The second case deals with a physician's office and demonstrates the selection and installation of a software application package as the best problem solution. Both cases include an extensive discussion of the cost/benefit analyses performed in order to select the most appropriate solution.

FIGURE 1-16 **The tools of the systems analyst**

Chapter	Title	Major Tools Covered	SDLC Phase
1	Systems Analysis and Design: An Introduction	General systems theory Systems development life cycle	All phases
2	Alternatives to the Systems Development Life Cycle	Other approaches to software development	Affects different phases
3	Discovering the Problem's Solution	Fundamental principles for systems analysts Feasibility issues for information systems	Preliminary Investigation and Analysis phases
4	Cost/Benefit Analysis	How to measure the financial worth of an information system	Preliminary Investigation and Analysis phases
5	Project Management	How to estimate time and staff requirements How to schedule the tasks	All phases
6	Information Gathering	How to collect the information needed to analyze the problem and develop the solution	Primarily Preliminary Investigation and Analysis phases
7 8	A Case Study: The Campus Bookstore A Case Study: A Small Business System	An introduction to the structured systems development methodology for two different applications	All phases
9	Data Flow Diagrams	How to model information systems	Preliminary Investigation and Analysis phases
10	The Data Dictionary	How to describe the data for an information system	Preliminary Investigation, Analysis, and Design phases
11	Process Descriptions	How to describe the processing of the data within the system	Preliminary Investigation, Analysis, and Design phases

continued

FIGURE 1-16   **Continued**

Chapter	Title	Major Tools Covered	SDLC Phase
12 13	The Logical Representation of the Data: Two Models Design of Physical Files	How to organize the system data into computer files	Preliminary Investigation, Analysis, and Design phases
14 15	Design Principles and Output Design Input Design	How to design the human interfaces to the system	Design phase
16	Hardware Selection and Program Design	How to choose the computer hardware and design the program structures	Design phase (but knowledge of computer hardware selection is always prominent in earlier phases)
17	The Final Phases of the Life Cycle	Coding and testing the software Controlling the implementation activities Installing the software Reviewing the software and developmental process after installation	Implementation, Installation, and Post-Implementation Review phases

Chapters 9, 10, and 11 explain the basic techniques customarily employed during the Analysis phase. Chapter 9 addresses the topic of data flow diagrams, a method for describing the operations of the existing information system and the functions of the proposed system. Chapters 10 and 11 deal with the documentation supporting the data flow diagrams, that is, the descriptions of the data within the system and the processing performed on that data.

After the analysis activities have been completed, the tasks of the Design phase are executed. Chapters 12 through 16 discuss the operations to be performed within the Design phase. Chapters 12 and 13 describe the procedure for organizing the system data into computer files. Chapters 14 and 15 focus on the design of input screens, output reports, and other interfaces between the computer and the users. Chapter 16 supplies a general framework for selecting appropriate computer hardware for the new system. This chapter also relates how programs are defined with regard to their overall structure and logical operations. Finally, Chapter 17 covers the last stages of the life cycle, which include the coding, testing, installation, and post-imple-

A CLASS Act for Customer-Oriented Service

The appropriate use of computer technology is a pleasure to be behold, according to the testimony of Sallie Mae, a New York Stock Exchange company. The following excerpt is from a full-page advertisement that Sallie Mae placed to sing the praises of the computer information system called CLASS.

> What CLASS demonstrates is how Sallie Mae uses modern technology to provide something that isn't modern or technological at all: Excellent customer service. Strictly speaking, CLASS is not a computer. It's a highly integrated mainframe system that automates virtually every aspect of servicing student loans. Every night it runs through our portfolio of 3.5 million student loan accounts looking for expiring deferments, loans entering repayment, past due balances, and loans nearing payoff. This nightly protocol tells us who to contact, and helps us spot situations that need our attention.
>
> For example, if a borrower has missed a payment, CLASS will identify that borrower, dial his or her number, then route the call to a service representative who will help straighten the matter out.
>
> With over a half a million calls coming in each month, providing excellent customer service in an efficient manner is obviously a high priority. So when our phone rings, we answer it promptly, usually within ten seconds. We can have a customer's complete borrowing history on the screen instantly.

The advertisement continues by relating more details regarding the interaction of the computer system, the service personnel, and the customers. The message is that Sallie Mae serves its customers using the very latest customer-oriented technology. Technology for its own sake is useless. Technology employed to fulfill the objectives of an organization is valuable.

Exerpted from "If We Taught a Course in Customer Service, . . .", Sallie Mae, *New York Times Magazine,* April 11, 1993, p. 15

mentation review of the information system. Issues such as the programming language to be used, the control of the coding and testing activities, and other tasks are considered from the analyst's position in the systems development process. The mastery of the various techniques covered within this text will assure that the analyst is equipped with the skills necessary for successful completion of software development. But remember: Only actual experience in software development supplies the missing ingredient that gives full mastery of these many skills.

SUMMARY

The focal point of this book is the structured development methodology, which consists of two major components:

1. A group of techniques to be employed for the creation of information systems
2. A framework that guides the step-by-step developmental process

The structured development methodology encompasses the areas of systems analysis and design, the systems development life cycle (SDLC), and project management. Because systems analysis is derived from the concepts found in general systems theory, a brief introduction to this area was presented.

A system is a set of interrelated components that function together to achieve a common goal. The objectives of a system are reached by transforming inputs from external sources into outputs which are then sent to persons or organizations outside of the system. A factory is an example of a system that receives the inputs of raw materials from its suppliers and converts them into finished products. Other inputs and outputs also flow to and from the factory, such as customer orders and supplier invoices. The systems approach to problem solving is given in five steps:

1. Divide the problem into a hierarchy of subproblems.
2. Create a solution for each subproblem.
3. Integrate these solutions to form a complete solution to the original problem.
4. Apply the integrated solution to the problem.
5. Check that the solution fits the problem.

The life of a software system is divided into two major periods called development and maintenance. The systems development life cycle, or Waterfall Model, is defined here to consist of five major phases in the development period—Preliminary Investigation, Analysis, Design, Implementation, and Installation—and a sixth phase, Post-Implementation Review, occurring during the maintenance period. A software system enters the maintenance period immediately after it becomes operational and continues in this period until the system is abandoned. Each phase of the systems development life cycle consists of several major activities, where an activity is comprised of many tasks. A task is a smaller unit of work, usually requiring about one or two weeks for completion. The SDLC provides a detailed step-by-step formulation of the systems development process, thereby enabling the process to be effectively managed. The checklist of tasks ensures that all tasks necessary for successful completion will be performed and accomplished in the proper sequence. After each phase, management reviews the project and decides whether it should continue.

Although the life cycle is described as a sequential process, previous phases are reentered whenever it is found in the current phase that the earlier work did not provide the necessary information. Within each phase, it may be possible to perform some tasks in parallel rather than in sequence. Because the SDLC approach is time-consuming and expensive, other alternatives to the systems development process may be appropriate, depending on the type of system to be developed. The seven alternatives to the SDLC are: software packages, reusable code, prototyping, CASE tools, reverse engineering, object-oriented technology, and end-user development. In addition, the multifaceted approach allows these alternatives to be selectively applied wherever appropriate in the SDLC.

The systems analyst is the facilitator of the systems development process. This computer professional performs the analysis of problems presented by the user and recommends the best solutions for the organization. Because no single solution is perfect, the systems analyst proposes several alternative solutions and then examines the trade-offs in order to select the best one for the organization. The requirements for the systems analyst position were summarized in Figure 1-15. The mix of skills required for the position of systems analyst includes programming experience, other computer capabilities, verbal and written communications skills, interpersonal skills, and problem-solving ability. Because the systems development process requires ingenuity in designing the best solution, creativity is an essential quality for the systems analyst. The job of systems analyst offers a challenging occupation with many rewards.

TERMS

alternatives to the SDLC

CASE tools

computer-assisted software engineering (CASE)

checkpoint

control

end-user

end-user development

feedback

forward engineering

maintenance period of the system's lifetime

multifaceted approach

object-oriented technology

prototyping

reusable code

reverse engineering

software application packages

structured systems development

system

systems development life cycle (SDLC)

1. preliminary investigation
2. analysis
3. design
4. implementation
5. installation
6. post-implementation review

systems analysis

systems analyst

systems design

systems development period

waterfall model

QUESTIONS

1. Explain what is meant by the systems approach to problem solving.

2. Assume that you have been assigned the task of writing a 30-page essay on the history of the computer industry. Outline the steps you will take before actually writing this essay. Explain how these steps relate to the steps in the traditional systems development life cycle.

3. Describe the six steps in the traditional systems development life cycle.

4. The steps of an SDLC (different from that shown in this chapter) are listed below. Explain how these steps and those of the SDLC given in this chapter are related.

An Alternative Systems Development Life Cycle

Step 1. Survey project scope and feasibility.

Step 2. Study the current system.

Step 3. Specify the requirements of the users.

Step 4. Recommend a solution from the set of alternative solutions.

Step 5. Design the new system. If any new hardware or software is required, order these products.

Step 6. Construct the new system.

Step 7. Install the new system.

Step 8. Maintain and improve the new system.

5. What alternatives to the SDLC exist for the development of information systems?

6. Professor Brown, Chair, Department of Information Systems, wants to create a computer system to track all the applicants for teaching positions now being screened. He needs to record the name, address, phone number, date the application was received, initial response date, and other details. What approach do you recommend for the creation of this information system? Give the reasons for your recommendation.

7. The Midwest State College plans to redesign its registration system, which is now handled manually. Students line up in the Field House on registration days and obtain cards for each class from faculty members at departmental tables. When all the necessary cards have been obtained, the student turns in the pile of cards. Four weeks later, class lists are available and schedules are mailed to the students.
   a. What approach to systems development do you recommend for the registration system? Why?
   b. If the registration system is currently computerized in a batch mode operation, what approaches would you also consider? Why?

8. List the skills required for a successful systems analyst.

9. Examine your own set of skills.
   a. What skills do you lack for the position of systems analyst?
   b. How do you propose to remedy these deficiencies in order to become a systems analyst?

10. Eileen Howarth is an outgoing college student majoring in the information systems area. Last summer, Eileen was employed as a programmer for a local accounting firm. She will graduate this semester with a bachelor's degree from the College of Business and a 3.1 GPA. She is seeking a position as a systems analyst. What advice do you have for Eileen in her job search?

PROJECTS

1. Visit your college placement office and inspect the listings for firms seeking Information Systems (IS) graduates.

    a. What job titles are specified by these firms? List them.
    b. Prepare a letter to these firms inquiring about the job credentials needed to obtain the position of *systems analyst*. Because this job title may indicate various positions, describe the position according to the criteria given in this chapter. Tabulate your responses.

2. Perform a literature search to find articles discussing the personality traits of systems analysts and programmers. [*Note:* If suitable articles are not available in your library, you may search for this information in books dealing with management information systems.] Read at least three of these articles, then prepare a summary of the authors' views of the following: differences between the two occupations, and the personality traits commonly found in these two categories of computer professionals.

REFERENCES

Boehm, Barry W. "Software Engineering." *IEEE Transactions on Computers* C-25(12), December 1976, pp. 1226–1242.

Boehm, Barry W. *Software Engineering Economics.* Englewood Cliffs, N.J.: Prentice-Hall, 1981.

Case, Albert F., Jr. "Computer-Aided Software Engineering (CASE): Technology for Improving Software Development Productivity." *Data Base*, Fall 1985, pp. 35–43.

Churchman, C. West. *The Systems Approach.* New York: Dell, 1981.

General Electric Company. *Software Engineering Handbook.* New York: McGraw-Hill, 1986.

Kapur, Gopal. "Productivity Tools Betray Promises of MIS Nirvana." *Computerworld*, December 1, 1986, pp. 61–78.

Martin, James, and Carma McClure. *Software Maintenance: The Problem and Its Solution.* Englewood Cliffs, N. J.: Prentice–Hall, 1983.

Alternatives to the Systems Development Life Cycle

Objectives

The goal of this chapter is to explain the alternative approaches to the traditional systems development life cycle (SDLC). After completing this chapter, you will understand the following material:

- The seven variations on the traditional systems development life cycle:

   software packages

   prototyping

   reusable code

   CASE tools

   reverse engineering

   object-oriented technology

   end-user development

- How each of these approaches is used in creating new systems
- The advantages and disadvantages of each alternative approach

INTRODUCTION

As we said in Chapter 1, the classical way of building an information system has six developmental phases: Preliminary Investigation, Analysis, Design, Implementation, Installation, and Post-Implementation Review. After the system becomes operational, maintenance activities are performed to extend the system's life. Each developmental phase is divided into major activities which are then subdivided into tasks. The traditional SDLC shows the execution of each developmental phase in its entirety. The activities in the Analysis, Design, and Implementation phases are designed to achieve the goal of a complete information system custom-tailored to meet a firm's individual requirements. Structured analysis (data flow diagrams, data dictionary, and process descriptions), structured design (structure charts and module descriptions), and custom programming are the tools recommended for the implementation of an information system under this methodology. The primary objective of the systems development life cycle and the structured development methodology is the creation of high quality information systems that fulfill the users' requirements and are easy to maintain.

As mentioned in Chapter 1, the traditional SDLC requires prolonged time and high costs to develop an information system in this classical fashion. In particular, the coding and testing of computer programs incur heavy costs in money and time, and involve extensive commitment of highly skilled computer professionals. After the information system is developed it may be used for many years, but recurring maintenance of the programs during its lifetime is usually required to meet the firm's changing needs. To resolve these difficulties, various alternatives to the classical life cycle may be chosen for the software development process (see Figure 2-1). Some alternatives shorten the time required for certain steps in the developmental process. Shortcuts are given by either purchasing a software application package or by incorporating previously written and tested code (called *reusable code*) into custom-built programs. The other alternatives represent more radical approaches to the traditional steps in the SDLC; they are pro-

FIGURE 2-1

Alternatives to the Systems Development Life Cycle

Shortcuts for the SDLC	Software Application Packages Reusable Code
New Approaches	Prototyping CASE Tools Reverse Engineering Object-Oriented Technology End-User Development

totyping, the use of CASE tools, reverse engineering (accomplished by a certain type of CASE tool), object-oriented technology, and end-user development. These new approaches are possible only because of the development of innovative software. Each approach will be discussed in the following sections.

Warning

When studying the various approaches, keep in mind the special advantages and disadvantages of each method. Because each firm has its own circumstances, there are no simple rules to guide the analyst to the right choice. Each firm must carefully weigh the cost of change in software development procedures before adopting a new approach.

SOFTWARE APPLICATION PACKAGES

The use of software application packages is based on the principle that an information system can be designed that will satisfy the needs of many businesses rather than only a single firm. By producing the software in demand by several firms, the software vendor distributes its initial cost across many buyers, thereby lowering the cost for an individual purchaser. The discussion of the selection process for **packaged software** is divided into five sections. First, the types of software packages are classified according to their purposes. Second, we explain how the traditional life cycle changes when packaged software is chosen over in-house development. Third, we discuss the trade-offs between purchased software packages and in-house development. Fourth, four major steps are recommended for selecting application software. Finally, we deal with the contract negotiations necessary for leased software.

Types of Software Packages

Software is divided into three general categories: systems software, general purpose packages, and application packages. *Systems software* refers to the programs that either support the programmers in using the computer to develop other programs or enable the computer hardware to function more efficiently for program executions. Systems software includes the operating system, the utility programs, and the compilers or interpreters necessary to translate source programs to machine language. *General purpose packages* are programs that assist programming activities or perform a specialized function. Examples of general purpose packages are spreadsheet programs and graphics programs.

In contrast, **software application packages** are designed to solve specific problems such as payroll and inventory control. The market for application packages is further split into *vertical market* applications and *generic* applications. A group of firms that perform similar functions is known as a **vertical market. Generic applications** are those that can be found in most firms. For example, payroll is a common function that all businesses perform in nearly identical fashion. By contrast, the data processing that banks require for checking and savings accounts is restricted to financial firms that execute such functions. Most firms have no use for programs that handle customer checking account transactions. Thus, banking operations form a vertical market for packaged software, whereas a bank's payroll application is a generic application performed by all firms.

The SDLC for Software Application Packages

The choice of a software application package is a shortcut measure for the traditional systems development life cycle. By purchasing the software, the firm eliminates certain activities such as the coding and testing of programs. Although the life cycle already includes the activity of selecting hardware and software, additional tasks are needed to select the software package. As shown in Figure 2-2, the use of a software application package significantly alters the life cycle. Selecting hardware and software platforms now becomes a search for a suitable software application package, which must also match the chosen hardware. The activities of designing the data files and programs are eliminated, because these components already are determined by the software package. Since the package arrives fully coded and tested, the coding step drops out of the life cycle, and detailed testing procedures to debug the program code are no longer necessary. Instead, the software package simply undergoes some testing to verify its suitability for the firm's operations. Since program documentation is already supplied by the software vendor, no resources are expended in this effort. Because coding and testing activities require a substantial amount of effort, the use of a software package typically saves both time and money.

Buying vs. In-House Development

Today many organizations turn to software application packages when they need new software rather than choosing **in-house development** by their own computer professionals. Packaged software has been estimated to account for over 40% of the major application systems in the private sector.

There are many reasons for this trend toward packaged software purchases. First, a major reason for this increased use of packaged software is the large number of versatile software packages available today. Because of this expanded market, the possibility of finding a suitable software package has been greatly enhanced. Second, the expense of packaged software is typically lower than that of in-house development. Third, when a system is

FIGURE 2-2   **How the use of packaged application software affects the SDLC**

SDLC Phase	Activities Within Each Phase		Effect of Packaged Application Software
Preliminary Investigation	⟶		Same
Analysis	⟶		Same
Design	Select hardware and software platforms	⟶	Same—tasks defined for the packaged software
	Acquire the necessary hardware and software	⟶	Same
	Design the data files	⟶	Dropped
	Prepare the training guidelines	⟶	Same
	Design the programs / Prepare preliiminary testing procedures	⟶	Dropped
Implementation	Create the test data / Code the programs / Test the programs	⟶	Dropped
	System testing	⟶	Performed to ensure acceptance of package and to give final approval of the software
	Document the programs	⟶	Dropped
	Train the users	⟶	Same
Installation	⟶		Same
Post-Implementation Review	⟶		Same

needed by a particular date, the software can be purchased and installed in a shorter time than the long period required for its development prior to installation. Fourth, a backlog of developmental work may cause managers to choose packaged software, because other applications requiring customized features can then be given higher priority for the available resources. Fifth, packaged software is a solution when the firm has no computer staff to develop software. For example, a public library may need an on-line catalog system together with an automated checkout procedure. But developing such a system necessitates great expense in time and money because highly trained computer staff must work on software development over a long period of time. The library has no desire to employ computer professionals as permanent staff, nor would the high expenditure for in-house development fit within its budget. Purchased software represents the only feasible option. A final reason for considering packaged software is that some managers believe that it is no longer necessary to "reinvent the wheel." If the system already exists, why not buy it rather than build it again?

Despite these attractions, one question remains: How do you decide whether packaged software or in-house development is better? This question is answered by examining the characteristics of the application. For instance, would in-house implementation of the system offer a strategic advantage? Even when the identical application exists at other firms, a custom-built system sometimes provides unique advantages to the firm. The possibility of doing business in a different way by breaking down the artificial barriers created by paper documents may be a compelling reason to incur the expense of in-house development. Furthermore, if the organization's requirements differ substantially from what the existing software packages offer, then in-house development is preferable. After ruling out these cases, the firm must still ask whether the choice of packaged software is really appropriate for its problem. If the problem is well defined and common to other organizations, then packaged software is most likely the better choice.

Next, the organization must determine whether its own particular way of performing this application can be adapted to fit the mold of packaged software. When the firm's procedures or data representation can be easily altered to conform to the specifications of a software package, then the savings in cost and time become meaningful. If not, a second question arises: Should the package be modified to fit the organization's specifications? The answer to this question is discussed in the following section.

Customize the Package or Modify to Fit?

The basic difficulty with application packages is that they are designed to meet the needs of most potential customers rather than the requirements of a particular firm. Although payroll is a generic function common to all firms, there may be certain operations that only occur in a small number of firms.

Consider a small firm that computes weekly paychecks for employees based on a percentage of gross sales for that week. The employees do not have a fixed salary, but are paid according to the number of hours worked and the total sales in each weekly pay period. This unusual way of calculating gross pay is unlikely to be a feature of payroll packages, which are designed to meet the common functions of payroll, namely, computing gross and net pay as well as deductions for taxes and health care benefits.

How should a firm resolve the differences between its current procedures and data formats with those dictated by a software package? There are three choices. First, the firm may request modification of the package to meet its specific requirements. This type of modification is a common practice. Even large MIS (management information systems) consulting firms may decide to modify an existing software application package rather than build the application software from scratch for an individual organization. Second, the organization may opt to change its requirements in order to conform to the specifications of the software package. Compromising its requirements saves the immediate cost of software modification as well as future maintenance costs for adapting later releases of the software package. Third, the firm may decide some in-house requirements can be altered to conform to the software package's specifications. Consequently, increased costs will be incurred only for those modifications deemed absolutely essential to the firm.

The main problem with modifying the software package is that such actions may absolve the vendor of responsibility for correcting software problems. In addition, the firm must budget for future costs incurred for modifying the package for every new release. The option to forego the adoption of a new release is seldom advisable. Because new releases typically correct software errors and offer desirable new features, the firm will want to adopt them. In general, for small companies, it is often best to change the requirements to fit the package.

How to Select the Right Package

The objective in selecting a software application package is to obtain one that fits the firm's requirements. As listed in Figure 2-3, four major steps precede the adoption of a software application package:

1. Understand the problem.
2. Study the packages.
3. Evaluate the vendor.
4. Perform the cost/benefit analysis.

The first step requires a full understanding of the existing system to ensure that the replacement system will perform the same functions. To check this, the technique of data flow diagrams, with the supporting documentation of process descriptions and a data dictionary (see Chapters 9–11), is recom-

FIGURE 2-3

**Steps for the selection
of software application
packages**

RECOMMENDED STEPS

- **Understand the problem**
   Study the existing system
   Define the new system

- **Study the packages**
   Formal presentation
   Package demonstration

- **Evaluate the vendor**
   Verify vendor's status
   Survey or interview users
   Visit other users' sites
   Determine quality of vendor service

- **Perform the cost/benefit analysis**

mended. The requirements of the new system should also be defined. In particular, response time, new reports, and other features requested by the users should be spelled out. The differences between the software packages and the firm's needs will be detected only when the details of the system are documented. What if a firm uses a 22-character inventory number but the selected software package accepts only 20 characters? Without a detailed comparison between the existing data and the software package's capability, the firm lacks the knowledge to select the best package. Complete understanding of the problem ensures that the proper software package will be selected from those available.

In the second step, the analyst reviews the available software packages. This review encompasses a formal presentation and demonstration by each vendor and a careful study of available documentation. In addition, a hands-on opportunity for the firm's staff to use a package for several hours is useful in evaluating its merits.

Having narrowed the vendor selection to a few candidates, the analyst moves to the third step: evaluation of the vendors. Not only the vendor's reputation but also its financial standing should be investigated. The users' satisfaction with these packages and their experiences with the vendor are also examined at this time. In order to judge the package's long-term merit, current users are surveyed, often by mailed questionnaires or else by telephone interviews. Finally, through visiting other sites the analyst obtains important information about the customer–vendor relationship, the users' satisfaction with the package's fit, and the vendor's response to users' problems.

The fourth step is the analysis of the potential costs incurred and benefits gained for each package under consideration. After careful execution of these four steps, the analyst is prepared to recommend a software application package. But what if the execution of these steps has caused the firm to realize that no package exists to meet its needs? Then the firm must decide whether to compromise its requirements, pay for modifications to the software, or choose to develop its own system, either in-house or by an outside contractor.

The Contract for Software Packages

The vendor typically offers a legal contract for the purchase of the packaged software together with provisions for annual maintenance. Because the software programs are supplied as machine code programs, source code is not ordinarily issued to the lessee. If the firm's projected dependence on the software package is substantial, it is advisable to safeguard the firm against the possibility of the vendor's demise. In order to avoid serious disruptions to the firm's operations, two steps are recommended. First, as already stated, prior to signing the contract, the vendor's financial standing should be investigated. Second, through contractual provision the package's source code should be placed in escrow with a third party. Should the vendor become incapable of supporting the package, the source code will be released to the lessee so as to permit future modifications. For more details on the negotiation of software contracts, consult Martin and McClure [1983].

PROTOTYPING

In terms of software development projects, **prototyping** means the rapid development of a system through constant interaction between the user and the software developer. As Figure 2-4 depicts, the user no longer stands

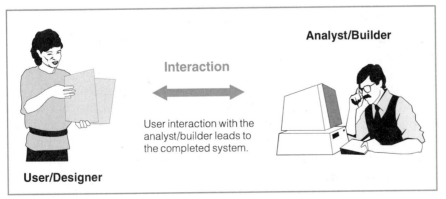

Analyst/Builder

Interaction

User interaction with the analyst/builder leads to the completed system.

User/Designer

FIGURE 2-4

The interaction between the user and the developer in prototyping

Adapted from Milton Jenkins, "Prototyping: A Methodology for the Design and Development of Application Systems," Working paper, School of Business, Indiana University at Bloomington, 1983.

outside the systems development process but is now an active participant. Assuming the role of designer, the user directs the developer to construct the software according to the user's preferences, which are uncovered during the user's trial runs with a working version of the software. In the traditional life cycle, often the user appears only at the beginning and end of the developmental process. Although the user may be actively consulted during the analysis and design stages, implementing the system requires concentrated efforts to code and test the computer programs. As discussed in Chapter 1, since these activities demand only the skills of the software developers, the user simply waits until the final system is delivered, and only then receives the opportunity to truly test the system. The coding and testing stages customarily occupy 45% of the development time. It may be many months or even years before the user receives the system—only to find that some features were omitted. Even worse, the system was so long in coming that the user's requirements have changed. Not only is the cost of correcting such problems high, but the appearance of serious deficiencies may render the system unusable. With the prototyping development method, these hazards are removed from the development process.

Prototyping for the development of an information system differs considerably from the common use of the term. In manufacturing, a prototype is developed as the master product design, which then serves as the basis for manufacturing multiple copies. In this case, the prototype is developed over a long period of time and costs much more than the actual product. The design of a new automobile illustrates this kind of prototyping. Prototyping for information systems is quite different. The initial prototype of an information system is developed in a short period of time. Consequently, the prototype system costs less to develop than the traditionally developed system. Ordinarily only one version is created, unless the system will be issued as commercial software. Because the system is developed in a short time, it will correspond closely to the organization's needs. User satisfaction will be high because, in effect, the user is the designer of the system.

The Steps in Prototyping

As shown in Figure 2-5, creating an information system by prototyping is an iterative process: Steps 4 and 5 are repeated as many times as necessary to refine the system. All steps must be executed rapidly. A typical system is created within a matter of a few weeks or months rather than the several months or years of the traditional development cycle. The first prototyping step is the Preliminary Investigation phase. Before the system can be developed, the problem must be defined. A brief statement of the user's requirements is prepared, the data elements and relationships are documented, costs for the project are estimated, and the project scope is specified. Once the problem is understood, it may be discovered that other methods are better choices for development. Whether to continue with the project and whether to use prototyping as the developmental method are decided in step 2. The most suitable developmental approach should be selected for the

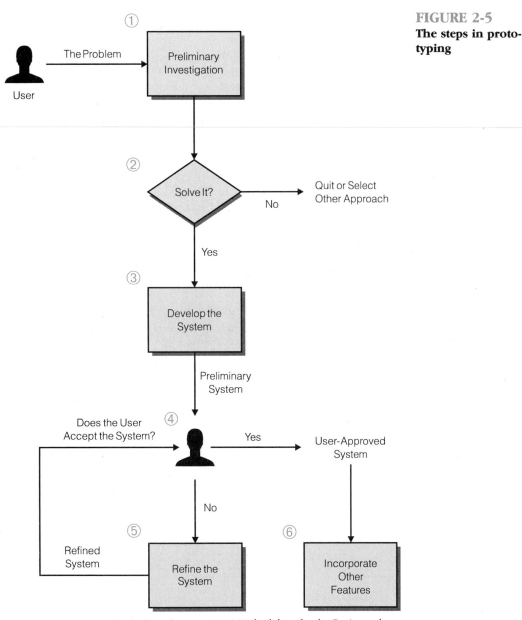

FIGURE 2-5
The steps in proto-typing

Adapted from Milton Jenkins, "Prototyping: A Methodology for the Design and Development of Application Systems," Working paper, School of Business, Indiana University at Bloomington, 1983.

problem. If the project is approved for prototyping, the analyst will construct a working prototype of the system in step 3. The interactive dialogues, menus, and commands that interface with the user are included in this working system. Some features such as data controls may be omitted in the interest of speedy development. Basically the system will appear to the user exactly as it will in its final form. The analyst now delivers the working system to the user and trains the user in its operations.

In step 4, the user is requested to evaluate the preliminary system and determine what improvements are necessary. In this way, the prototype enables the system requirements to be discovered as the system is developed. Hands-on experience with the system enables the user to decide what should be changed. The system can then be returned to the analyst so that these changes can be incorporated. In step 5, the analyst refines the system and returns the improved version to the user for evaluation. If the user's requests are unreasonable, the matter can be discussed immediately and resolved at this point in the system's development. The analyst will again alter the system according to the user's new specifications but will not introduce any other features independently of the user's requests. Steps 4 and 5 are repeated until the user approves the system. Three or four iterations are typical. If the user is persistently dissatisfied it may be impossible to continue the prototyping process. In that case an in-depth discussion of the user's requirements must be executed before continuing.

Because the interaction between the user and the analyst/builder is crucial to the success of this method, the refinements must be accomplished quickly. After the working prototype receives the user's approval, step 6 requires the analyst to insert any features that were omitted due to the speed of development. Documentation must also be completed prior to the system's release for widespread use. At the end of the prototyping life cycle, the analyst/builder will have successfully implemented a system that solves the user's problems in a satisfactory manner.

The prototyping method dramatically changes the traditional life cycle. Figure 2-6 shows the replacement of three complete phases—Analysis, Design, and Implementation—by the prototyping method. These three phases, with their extensive requirements in time and resources, have been swept aside by the rapid prototyping of the system. Although the analysis, design, and implementation of the system must still be accomplished, all three tasks are achieved simultaneously during the prototyping process. The iterative procedure allows the refinement of the working prototype through interac-

FIGURE 2-6

The effects of prototyping on the SDLC

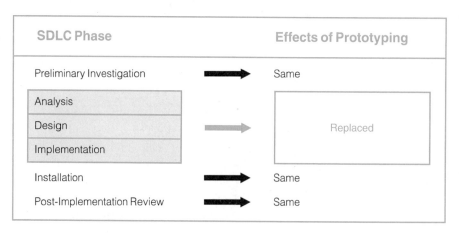

tion with the user, thereby ensuring the successful outcome of these inter-twined objectives. The remaining phases are still required for the satisfactory completion of the information system. After the system has been fully developed via prototyping, it remains to be installed and its performance reviewed by management.

Guidelines for Prototyping

Four components are essential for implementing a system via the prototyp-ing method. First, the user must be competent in the functional area. Since the user will assume the role of designer, it is crucial that this individual have sufficient knowledge to guide the system to a satisfactory completion. Oth-erwise, an inadequately defined system may be constructed. Second, the analyst assigned to build the system must be skilled in using the develop-ment tools for prototyping as well as adept in using the organization's data base. If the analyst is a novice in these matters, the prototyping process will be delayed. Long delays strain the interaction between the user and the analyst. Third, the tools available for the analyst/builder must include a **fourth-generation language** (4GL) that allows the rapid construction of the programming system. A fourth-generation language is supplied either by a special program called an *application code generator* or is associated with a data base management system (DBMS). Because one statement in a fourth-generation language is often equivalent to ten or more statements in a **third-generation language (3GL)** such as COBOL, the resultant pro-grams are more concise and programming time as well as testing time is substantially reduced. Alternatively, suitable CASE tools may be provided; the various types of CASE tools are discussed later in this chapter. The use of a conventional third-generation language would slow the development of the working prototype, making the time between user-analyst interactions unacceptably long.

Fourth, an essential component for successful prototyping is that the data required for the system be already stored and controlled by a data base management system. If the system builder must oversee the acquisition and entry of the data elements into a data base system, the project will require more time. Because the success of the prototyping technique is based upon the quick implementation of the working prototype, a lack of managed data resources will seriously handicap the system implementation and, thus, re-sult in poor interaction with the user.

Ideally, the prototyping method involves only one user and one builder. The builder is attempting to please the user, but with multiple users differ-ing requests are likely. Some requests may even contradict each other. The additional time required for communication between the users and the builder(s) will increase the time required to build the system. Documenta-tion of the users' differing viewpoints will be essential, as well as meetings to resolve the conflicts. If more than one builder is involved, similar problems arise in the control of the project. The recommendation *one user, one builder* translates into smaller systems that are more manageable. Nonetheless, some large companies have successfully switched from the traditional SDLC to prototyping for information systems with multiple users. Capitol Bankers Life Insurance Company [Warner, 1985] decided to implement projects using the prototyping technique. Because of a high growth rate of 225% annually, the company could no longer develop systems fast enough. New hardware and a relational data base management system with a 4GL were installed to permit implementation of systems via prototyping. The 6- to 8-month backlog for information systems dropped to only 3 months. In addition, new applications became possible, such as ad hoc reports and a strategic system to provide instant policy turnaround for field agents. All in all, the experiment was an outstanding success.

REUSABLE CODE

Another shortcut for the traditional SDLC is the use of *reusable code* during the Implementation phase. **Reusable code** is a unit of thoroughly tested program instructions that was previously written to perform a particular function. Since coding a program involves both writing the source code and subsequently testing it, the availability of program code already tested and documented saves considerable time and money. The concept of reusable code is not new. From the early days of computing, scientific subroutines were created as individual units of code that could be incorporated into other programs. For example, a scientific programmer never codes subroutines to compute mathematical functions such as the square root or the natural logarithm of an argument. Instead, any scientific installation maintains an extensive library of mathematical routines for use by its programming staff. Otherwise, each programmer would be obliged to spend time and energy creating these subroutines whenever needed for a program. This same principle of reusability can be applied to information systems.

The coding for a function that will be used by more than one programmer can be stored within a subroutine library. Whenever that function is needed, the coding can be placed within the calling program. No testing will be necessary for this coding; however, testing to verify that the routine was correctly incorporated must still be done. Figure 2-7 indicates how the life cycle is altered by reusable code. The program design step within the Design phase now incorporates the selection of modules already available in the subroutine library. In addition, the coding step within the Implementation phase incorporates existing code into the programs. Finally, the task of program testing is shortened, since any modules drawn from the library of reusable code do not require independent testing.

In order to establish reusable code as a standard practice for program development, several steps must be taken. The four steps for employing reusable code are listed in Figure 2-8. First, a library of reusable code is

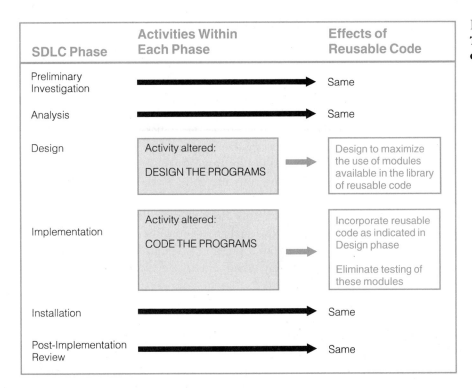

FIGURE 2-7
The effects of reusable code on the SDLC

established. To do so, the analyst inspects the functions executed by a program. If a function common to other programs is discovered, this coding should be treated as a unit of reusable code. Most likely, the code will need to be modified somewhat so that it can be used by other programs. Because descriptions for the operations on data fields, data records, and files have no universal conventions (unlike, say, mathematical functions), conventions for the routines' names and descriptions must be instituted. The library routines are useful only if programmers are able to locate the coding necessary for a function.

The second step is to design a program as a set of *modules* (see Chapter 16). During this design procedure, it is helpful if the analyst is already aware of the library routines available. After the modules have been identified, the

Step 1	Establish the library of reusable code.
Step 2	Design programs to use the reusable modules.
Step 3	Incorporate the reusable modules into programs.
Step 4	Review completed programs to uncover new reusable modules.

FIGURE 2-8
The steps for employing reusable code

analyst searches through the library of reusable routines to locate any routines that can be used. Third, when the routines have been identified, the programmer can incorporate this code into the program. The programmer should always choose to employ reusable code rather than create new code from scratch. Before coding the program, the programmer should also consider whether any newly coded modules are candidates for the subroutine library. If so, care should be taken to create these modules so that they can be stored and reused for other programs in the future. The remainder of the Implementation phase proceeds in the usual way.

The fourth step in employing reusable code is taken after the program has been completed. As standard operating procedure, another program review is executed in order to identify any new modules suitable for placement within the library. Each individual function is inspected to identify any operations potentially useful to other programs. The modules earmarked for the library are then appropriately documented and filed.

CASE TOOLS

Computer-assisted software engineering (CASE) tools are the group of programs available to aid analysts and programmers in the various activities required during the systems development life cycle. Software engineering is the discipline of software development. The term *engineering* indicates that computer professionals will execute the developmental activities and tasks as a well-structured and controlled step-by-step procedure in order to guarantee the proper completion of all tasks required for a successful programming system. **CASE tools** were created to assist the analysts and programmers in accomplishing these countless tasks efficiently and correctly. More specifically, CASE is the automation of the manual effort otherwise required to perform the methodologies recommended for implementing information systems.

CASE tools are classified with regard to the phase of the life cycle that they support. As displayed in Figure 2-9, CASE tools that facilitate the Preliminary Investigation, Analysis, and Design phases in the first portion of the life cycle are called **front-end CASE** or **upper CASE** tools. The remaining phases of the life cycle, Implementation and Installation, are supported by software programs called **back-end CASE** or **lower CASE** tools. A third category of CASE tools uses existing computer programs to define the system's design. This method is called *reverse engineering*. Because this technique is a departure from the usual way of building systems, it will be discussed in a separate section.

Effective use of CASE tools can dramatically decrease the amount of time spent in coding and testing during the Implementation phase. Figure 2-10 shows a comparison of three approaches to the development of information systems. The traditional life cycle approach did not allocate sufficient time to the early stages of analysis and design. According to McClure (1989), ap-

FIGURE 2-9 **The categories of CASE tools**

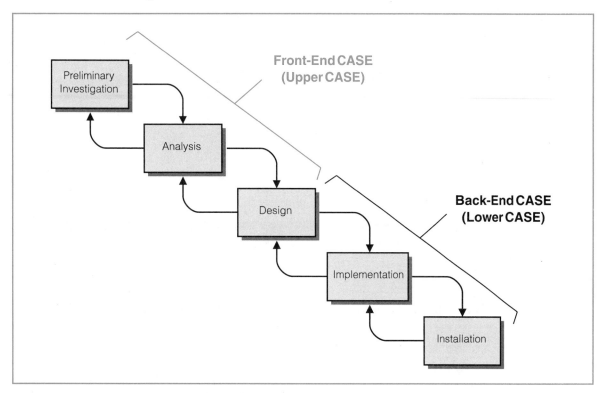

proximately 65% of the traditional life cycle was spent in coding and testing while only 35% was devoted to analysis and design. This distribution of effort led to poorly specified, high-cost systems. The lack of adequate specifications for programming resulted in systems that did not meet the users' needs. Moreover, because requirements changed in the course of the system's lengthy development, the delivered system was often unsatisfactory. The introduction of structured techniques changed this distribution of effort, placing much more emphasis on the early stages of development. When structured techniques are applied, about 60% of the life cycle is typically allocated to analysis and design activities while only 40% is assigned to coding and testing tasks.

The arrival of CASE tools changed this picture even more dramatically. Some CASE tools practically eliminate the coding step from the life cycle, thus radically shifting the distribution of effort. Now the largest amount of time is spent in the analysis and design phases, with only 15% of the life cycle needed for testing. This increased allotment to the early stages in the life cycle means that the resultant systems should truly match the users' specifications. Since CASE tools speed the development of systems, an information system can be developed without facing the inevitable change in specifications due to business transformations. Quicker implementation also

FIGURE 2-10

Comparison of three approaches to the SDLC

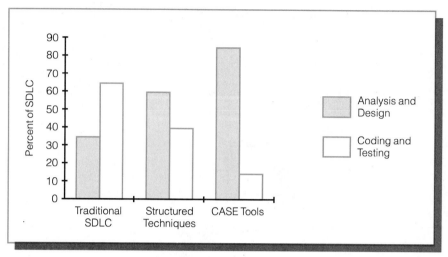

Adapted from Carma McClure, *CASE Is Software Automation,* Englewood Cliffs, NJ: Prentice-Hall, 1989, pp. 187–189.

means that the firm will be able to function more efficiently with the aid of its computer resources.

CASE tools use a central repository to store and derive information as they execute their tasks. Each tool is supported in its execution by the repository information created by CASE tools for the earlier life cycle steps. The diagram in Figure 2-11 illustrates the interaction between CASE tools and the central repository. Because the repository contains the necessary information, each task is able to retrieve its specifications automatically, complete its job and then add its own set of generated information to the central data store. The repository also assists in ensuring that all the individual components of the system are correctly described and mesh together to form a cohesive model.

Front-End CASE Tools

Although CASE is designed to support the computer professionals in their tasks, it is also used by business executives (with the assistance of computer staff) to create and adapt models relating to the company's strategic business plans. By using projections of future activities, budgetary data, and financial performance data, the executives actively participate in planning and implementing an entire information system. An example of an automated planning tool is given in Figure 2-12.

The activities in the front-end of the life cycle require the analyst to analyze and design the information system. The techniques typically used to perform these analysis and design activities are the data flow diagram methodology (including the documentation of the data dictionary and process descriptions) and the preparation of structure charts. To perform these tasks

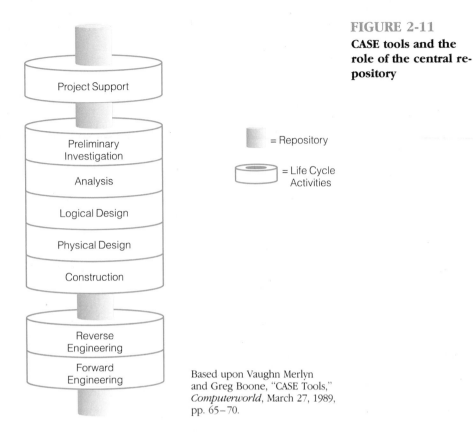

FIGURE 2-11

CASE tools and the role of the central repository

= Repository

= Life Cycle Activities

Based upon Vaughn Merlyn and Greg Boone, "CASE Tools," *Computerworld*, March 27, 1989, pp. 65–70.

FIGURE 2-12

An example of a CASE tool for business planning

Activities\Entities	Electrical	Other Than Electrical	Product	Product Category	Product Stock	Retailers Warehouse	Warehouse	Retail	Sales	Wholesale	Product History
Identify Product	C	C	C	U							
Product Management				C							
Product Ordering				U	CU	U	U				
Supplier Administration				U		C	C				
Sales Administration								C		C	
Product Administration	U	U	U								
Archive Product	U	U	U		U						C
Cancel Product	D	D	D								
Delivery Receipt	U	U	U	U							

Table courtesy of INTERSOLV.

manually, the analyst must tediously draw and redraw many diagrams. If the name for a data record or data element is changed, the analyst must search the already produced documentation to alter the name wherever it appears. When producing documentation manually, the analyst may inadvertently introduce errors into the model by failing to find all references to the revised components. In contrast, with the aid of a CASE tool, the drawing of data flow diagrams can be accomplished easily with a computer's help. But a CASE tool for the creation of data flow diagrams offers more than an easy way to draw these diagrams. It also stores the names and descriptions of all components of the model in the central repository (see Figure 2-11), so that the names assigned to data records and elements can be cross-checked automatically by using the CASE tool's special analysis features. If an element's name must be changed, the CASE tool ensures that all references will be amended.

Upper CASE tools also support the activities of the Design phase. Screens, reports, and other user interfaces can be quickly prototyped by the analyst with the use of a CASE tool. Once they have been designed, the user is asked to approve the layouts and, in the case of input screens, actually interacts with the mock-up to see if it is acceptable. The code for these screens and reports may also be generated automatically by the CASE tool. Such tools require the data elements to be described so that the screens can be painted according to this information.

Back-End CASE Tools

Back-end CASE tools are designed primarily to aid in the coding stage of the life cycle. The programming activity in the SDLC is traditionally viewed as the coding of statements in a third-generation language. To speed the software development process, a 4GL can be employed. Although we previously discussed 4GLs in conjunction with prototyping, they can also be used to reduce the time spent in coding and testing programs developed in the traditional life cycle. As discussed earlier, a 4GL is supplied either with a data base management system (DBMS) or by an application code generator. When a program is written in a 4GL supplied by a DBMS, the program is typically executed by means of an interpreter for the language. This means that each time the program is executed, the time required for its interpretation (i.e., translation) must be included in its execution time. Some exceptions to this general use of interpreters exist where compilers have been written for a DBMS-supported language. In the case of **application code generators**, the 4GL program statements are translated directly into code for a third-generation language such as COBOL or RPG III. The translated code must then be compiled to obtain a machine language program that can be executed. Once the program is ready for production runs, the program execution is performed using the machine code without repeated translation from source code to object code for each program run.

Code generator users report substantial reductions in the time required for the development of information systems. Other benefits of code generators include the high quality of code produced, ease of maintenance, standardization, performance, and portability. By *portability,* we mean that the code can be quickly generated for different hardware platforms. One reason for these advantages is the creation of 3GL code that is already correct for each statement written by the programmer in the 4GL program. Programs written in 4GL also cost less [Warner, 1985]. A major system with 90,000 lines of code was created by programmers in a 4GL for a cost of $8.67 per line. At that time, the estimated cost for a COBOL program was $25 to $35 per line. Since one 4GL line is equivalent to several lines of COBOL code, the 4GL program offers a clear cost advantage. Both time and money are saved in program development.

Testing is also much improved in 4GL programs. Since it takes only about 100 to 300 lines of 4GL code to express a comparable 5,000-line COBOL program, the programmer is testing and examining much shorter programs. The logic of the program is displayed, rather than hidden under the detailed 3GL statements. Maintenance activities also benefit because 4GL programs have fewer lines, and if changes must be made only the high-level 4GL statements are affected as opposed to the detailed 3GL code. Programmers can concentrate on the logic of the programs rather than on coding thousands of lines. Clearly, programmer efficiency is greatly improved.

Very high-level languages, sometimes called 4½ GLs, have also been developed in conjunction with code generators. These languages multiply the benefits of a 4GL because they are even more succinct than the 4GL coding statements. Some of these code generators provide a different way of writing programs by also producing the data base design; the 4½ GL program statements simply indicate the actions to be performed on the records in the data base.

The measure of a code generator's capability is its ease of use and its integration with front-end CASE tools. If the user adopts an upper CASE tool for planning, analysis, and design, then the selected code generator should interface with these tools and the methodology adopted by the firm. Many code generators are designed to draw information, especially data specifications, from a repository built by the upper CASE tools. If the code generator is incompatible with the repository, the design specifications may require substantial revision before the 3GL code can be generated by the lower CASE tool.

Code generators are designed to allow custom-built code to be inserted into the generated program code. By allowing the insertion of additional code, the code generator permits specialized operations to be included within a program. Most code generators generate 80% or more of the original code required for typical business data processing programs. The remaining 20% is custom programmed using a 3GL.

Other CASE tools exist to aid the programming task. An example is the COBOL Animator, which allows a programmer to visually observe the execution of a COBOL program. If an endless loop exists in the program, the animated display of the loop shows the programmer what is happening as each statement is executed. Such a tool provides support for program testing and helps the programmer to detect and resolve errors. There are also software tools to automatically generate test data for program testing activities. In addition to the individual tools available, integrated programming support environments (IPSE) provide an entire set of tools to support the programming activity for a particular programming language.

Integrated CASE Tools

An **integrated CASE** (**ICASE**) tool furnishes assistance to the analysis, design, and coding stages without the need for other tools. In essence, an integrated CASE tool captures the system specifications, documents the design specifications, and then generates the final programming code. The related user documentation can also be produced by using the ICASE tool. A nonintegrated approach is the use of separate software packages that operate independently of each other. When individual tools are used from different vendors, the data generated by one tool for the repository become the input data for another tool. Complications may arise when the first tool's output must be converted to the format required by the second tool. Other incompatibilities in specifications for the repository information may also be present. By coordinating all the steps, the ICASE tool offers the complete development of a system in an automated way. This linkage between the various developmental steps is achieved by the use of a central repository, which stores the specifications as they are entered for each activity in the life cycle.

REVERSE ENGINEERING

The term **reverse engineering** indicates the process by which the programs for an existing system are transformed for use in the creation of a new system which must perform many or all of the same business functions. This transformation is accomplished by using specialized CASE tools. The CASE tools discussed earlier are designed to assist in the creation of a new system. By providing superior documentation of the logical and physical program design, these tools also aid the programmer/analyst in maintaining the system. Reverse engineering CASE tools serve a different purpose. Their goal is the derivation of the existing system design from its program code.

Older systems frequently lack adequate documentation of analysis and design activities. Because modifications over the system's lifetime may not be reflected in the program documentation, the coding may represent the only unequivocal expression of the system's design. But without complete and up-to-date documentation, the programmer must attempt to reconstruct the underlying structure of the program design by tracing the program's logic through the examination of the coding. This procedure is tedious, difficult, and often impossible. Moreover, changes in the coding in one apparently isolated section may affect other portions of the program and cause serious program errors that are difficult to eliminate. Reverse engineering CASE tools address this problem by automatically providing a higher-level specification directly from the program code. As seen in Figure 2-13, reverse engineering maps backward from the implementation level of program code to formulate a higher-level specification. The resultant documents allow the programmer to design enhancements at a higher level of abstraction instead of the physical program code. The implementation of the enhancements is called **forward engineering**.

The combination of reverse engineering and forward engineering is sometimes known as **reengineering**. (Another interpretation of this term will be presented in Chapter 3.) The premise of reengineering the programs is that the proven code for the production system is already available. Why expend resources to supply new program coding that duplicates many of these functions? For example, if a batch order entry system must be converted into an on-line system, the traditional approach is to repeat the entire systems development life cycle for the new on-line system. But the batch order entry system contains many functions that also must be included in the proposed on-line system. Instead of coding these functions anew, the reengineering process allows the old order entry system to be automatically analyzed and blocks of code to be identified for the functions of the existing

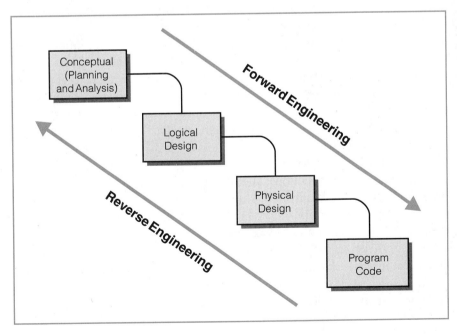

FIGURE 2-13
Reverse and forward engineering

system. Now the analyst can proceed with forward engineering. Whenever feasible, coding modules are taken from the existing system and placed into the new programs instead of being recoded. An example of such a coding block is the program code to edit the data supplied on the order form. Because these coding modules have been tested and are already operational in the current system, the analyst saves time in the analysis, design, coding, and testing activities for these modules.

In a sense, reverse engineering is a specialized case of reusable code. The problem lies in capturing the program's design and code for reuse in the new system. By using reverse engineering tools, the analyst can work forward to a new system with a better understanding of the existing programs. In addition, the use of proven modules drawn from the old system speeds the implementation of the new system.

OBJECT-ORIENTED METHODOLOGY

As we said in Chapter 1, typically a system is modeled by depicting the system using data flow diagrams. The technique of data flow diagrams and its accompanying data dictionary and process descriptions will be presented later in Chapters 9–11. The basic components of this modeling methodology (*structured analysis*) are

1. The data that move through the system (called its *data flows*) and that reside within the system (called its *data stores*)
2. The procedures performed on the data flowing through the system

Any modeling technique must deal with these fundamental aspects of a system. In this section, we explain the *object-oriented methodology* which models these two components in a completely different way.

An object-oriented methodology deals with objects that are empowered to act according to their relationship to other objects. An **object** is a module that contains both a group of data elements and the operations that can be performed upon this set of data. The *operations* are given as separate modules of code that act on the data. In essence, an object contains the code for acting upon itself. An object is said to *encapsulate* both the data and the instructions that describe the behavior and attributes of the data. Consider the production of an information system for generating a firm's quarterly report. Under the conventional methodology, we would create a COBOL program to read the data from the files and create the quarterly report. This traditional approach establishes the program and its data files as two distinct entities. In contrast, in an object-oriented system, we can define an object called *Quarterly Report*. Both the program code and the data are then contained within one object, which creates the quarterly report. Although this object, *Quarterly Report,* is a complete program, objects can vary in size down to a small routine.

Objects have the traits of **class** and **inheritance**. Similar objects are placed in the same *class* in order to share common characteristics. A class may be divided into **subclasses** that contain objects with differing attributes, but all their objects still share the same attributes of the class. As shown in Figure 2-14, the class called STUDENTS contains two subclasses, UNDER-GRADUATE and GRADUATE. By belonging to the class STUDENTS, the objects in the two subclasses are said to *inherit* the characteristics of STU-DENTS. Each object can be further assigned to its own subclass, either UNDERGRADUATE or GRADUATE, and each subclass also has its own specific characteristics. The coding for awarding scholarships to undergraduates can be defined as an operation AWARD for the subclass UNDERGRADUATE, while a completely different set of code (also called AWARD) can be associated with the subclass GRADUATE. Moreover, other operators can be assigned to each subclass. There will be no confusion because each set of code is attached to its corresponding subclass. Since the objects contained in either the UNDERGRADUATE or GRADUATE subclasses belong to the same class, they share the characteristics defined for the class STUDENTS, such as having the common attributes of STUDENT-NAME, STUDENT-CAMPUS-ADDRESS, STUDENT-CAMPUS-PHONE, STUDENT-CREDIT-HOURS, and STUDENT-STATUS.

Objects represent individual modules that can be reused. Since each object contains its own operations and data, it can function as an independent self-contained module that need not interact with other modules. When objects do interact, it is done by passing *messages* between them. An object will perform an operation after receiving a **message** that passes it any necessary arguments. (An *argument* is a data value passed to the object so that its task can be executed.) As shown in Figure 2-15, an example is the computation of federal withholding tax for an employee's paycheck. A message with the employee's gross pay as an argument is sent to the object FEDERAL WITHHOLDING and the object replies with the calculated amount. Messages are similar to the calling of a subroutine or the performing of a COBOL paragraph. We note that message passing increases the independence of the individual objects. Because any operations performed on a data

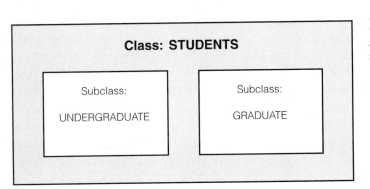

FIGURE 2-14

An example of a class and its subclasses

FIGURE 2-15

A message is passed to the object FEDERAL WITHHOLDING.

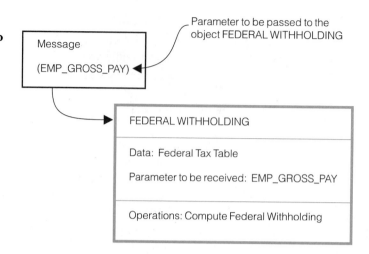

set are completely contained within the object, we say that the objects are highly *cohesive*.

Since objects are independent of each other, each object can be tested separately. After being completely tested, it is available for linking with other objects to form a complete system. The building of complex systems is simplified by the use of debugged objects. Should an error occur, it will be localized to one object rather than rippling through the system. The reuse of objects speeds the program construction activity and lessens the time required for testing.

Object-oriented programming (**OOP**) uses objects as the logical building blocks of a program rather than constructing an algorithm by means of program statements. SmallTalk and C++ are two programming languages specifically designed for object-oriented programming. However, the software design concepts of object-oriented programming can be employed in conventional languages. **Object-oriented design (OOD)** is the method by which the objects for an object-oriented program are specified on a logical and physical level. **Object-oriented analysis (OOA)** determines system requirements by constructing the system model using objects and classes as the building blocks.

While the use of **object-oriented technology** is popular among software manufacturers, most of the business community is still evaluating this issue. Object orientation is not easily grasped by programmers. Data and coding are no longer treated as separate entities; instead, they are bound together to form objects. Hence, the model of the information system must be viewed in a completely different way. The diagramming techniques for object-oriented analysis are somewhat new. The principles of object-oriented design are also a more recent development. However, object-oriented programming has been in use for many years.

Object-oriented data base technology is not well established. Many businesses, still scrambling to implement relational data bases, wonder if object-oriented data bases are worth the investment. By adopting object-oriented technology, firms hope to gain the advantages of reusability, speedy implementation, and reduced maintenance. However, object-oriented technology requires massive retraining of existing staff. In addition, some users indicate that maintenance problems are not fully overcome by the use of object-oriented technology. Because many firms today are experiencing high maintenance costs on their aging computer information systems, they are looking for better ways of developing software. The next ten years will show whether the business community will turn to object-oriented technology as the best hope for reducing both development and maintenance costs—or decide on automated software development using CASE tools. Regardless of the tools employed, the end result must be faster development and reduced maintenance costs.

END-USER DEVELOPMENT

Thus far, the discussion of other approaches to the life cycle has focused on methods to assist the computer professionals in developing systems for the users. Because hardware and software technology has progressed so dramatically in the last decade, many users now have desktop computers with much of the power and capability of the early mainframes. The availability of user-friendly software means that many workers simply choose to implement their own solutions to problems. **End-users** can use spreadsheets, data base management systems, and other personal computer (PC) tools to create new applications with little or no assistance from the computer pros. Some end-users with programming skills even code the solutions to their problems in third- or fourth-generation languages. Since the end-user functions as both the designer and developer, user satisfaction with the final system is high. While this tremendous accessibility to the computer appears to be very productive for many firms, the sunshine has some clouds. End-users often focus on solving their problems and then neglect the necessary but tedious tasks of thorough testing, program documentation, and program backup.

Anecdotes are plentiful regarding problems encountered by end-users who failed to adequately test or document their computing solutions. One contractor used a PC spreadsheet to prepare a construction bid for an office building complex. Not until the bid had been accepted did the contractor's firm discover that it had omitted a major item: $254,000 for general costs. The $254,000 was entered at the top of the spreadsheet long after the formula had been established to determine the column total. Since the amount was entered on the top line, outside the range of the formula, the spreadsheet program was unable to incorporate the additional amount into the final computation. Since this mishap appeared to the user as an error within the software, the spreadsheet maker was sued. But carelessly adding the new value at the top of the column and failing to redo the formula made the user responsible for the error, which eventually led to serious financial repercussions for the firm [Gilman and Bulkeley, 1986].

Variations of another frequently told story are about an end-user who creates a complex program to solve a problem, say, a work-in-progress report of inventory. At first, the program works well and proves very useful. However, one year later the computer's operating system is upgraded and the inventory program crashes. The program documentation is nonexistent. The program's creator, long since transferred to another division, barely remembers the program. Since the program is valuable, the user's present job is halted so that the program can be modified and documented. In yet another story the end-user constructs a number-crunching program that proves very useful to top management in the decision-making process. Much later, major discrepancies in the program output are discovered. Management is horrified to learn that its decisions had been based on erroneous information.

The moral of these stories is obvious. When people shortcut the rigorous steps required for professional computing development, disasters can happen. The results produced by a program are only useful if the program has been thoroughly tested and documented. The problem is not merely with expertise but with people. It's just easier to speed up development time and eliminate some tedium by avoiding the testing and documentation activities. Frequently, the security controls are just another hassle to most end-users. "Why back up a hard disk when nothing ever happens?" is the comment. Whenever the end-user information system is lost due to hardware or software failure, it suddenly becomes very evident why security measures are necessary.

To ensure that end-users adhere to the standards essential for effective application development, controls must be imposed on computing performed outside the computer services department. While this solution is easy to state, it is exceedingly difficult to enforce. End-user computing is, by its very nature, a free-lance activity. Too much control may diminish the productivity of the end-users, who do not wish to conform to stringent rules. Too little control means that catastrophes lurk in the future.

The controls recommended for an end-user environment, which are listed in Figure 2-16, parallel those presented in later chapters for the traditional method of system development. The suggested procedures for management controls include the training and education of all staff members with emphasis on the testing procedures for systems. Refresher courses should also be required for end-users who develop applications. Backup procedures should be automatically enforced by backing up hard disks on tape at regular intervals. If end-users work on PCs with hard disks, the computer center staff can perform regularly scheduled backups on these individual hard disks. When using a local area network (LAN), with all programs and data stored on the LAN storage device, this backup requirement is transferred from individual desktop computers to a centrally located site.

**Controls for an
end-user computing
environment**

Management Controls

Training and education for all staff

> Includes training for the verification of system results

Backup procedures automatically enforced for hard disks

Library of end-user applications controlled by a librarian

> Programs and documentation filed within the library

Verification of suitable testing and documentation *before* results are used in management projects

Design and Development Controls

Assistance to end-users available from technical support staff

Compatible hardware and software

Data security elements and audit trails incorporated into applications and fully documented

Data controls implemented within program

Restart, backup, and recovery procedures

Documentation requirements

Technical review of final application system by computer staff

Special controls for critical applications

> Approval by technical staff prior to use of results

> Post-implementation review of programs

Operations Controls

Data controls to ensure good data enters the system

Sensitive inputs and outputs safeguarded against external use

Imposition of Grandparent-Parent-Child system on data files (see Chapter 13)

Backup copies created; one copy stored at an off-site location

Security Controls

Physical security for hardware, software, and data

Access controls for software and data

Periodic reviews of security measures

Adapted with permission from *CA Magazine*, December 1987. Published by the Canadian Institute of Chartered Accountants.

An additional recommendation is the creation of an end-user application repository overseen by a technical librarian. The librarian makes sure that complete documentation is supplied with each end-user information system placed in the library. The repository both catalogs the application and prevents its disappearance due to personnel changes or other reasons.

Finally, management must assume responsibility for reviewing end-user developmental procedures prior to accepting results as accurate. This standard of review is the same condition imposed on professionally developed systems. The value of end-user computing is enormous. The potential for disaster is equally immense.

Pains and Payoffs of New Technology

The changeover to new technology can be a difficult and trying experience. Since the coding and testing portions of a software project require both large amounts of time and high costs, many firms are experimenting with the use of object-oriented technology in the hopes of lowering their development and maintenance costs. At Kash n' Karry Food Stores, a $1 billion grocery chain in Tampa, Florida, the initial move toward object-oriented technology was extremely painful. Learning to build object-oriented libraries with C++ took the company's information systems staff more than six months and boosted the $6 million IS budget by 12%. Not everyone welcomed the move. A 70% staff turnover took place in the first six months as programmers decided whether to participate in this new software development mode. Instead of writing new code, programmers are rewarded for "wiring together" objects to build a computer program. Among the results is an object-oriented warehousing system in production today which a 17-person staff built in four months. The new system processes up to 50,000 transactions a day, brought a 35% gain in productivity, and eliminated the $90,000 annual bill for the third-party vendor system it replaced. The promo-tional pricing system was built in six weeks using object-oriented technology after two mainframe programmers had abandoned a two-year effort to create the same sort of application.

The new systems produced for Kash n' Karry have much lower failure rates, programs are being created three times faster than in COBOL, and the best part is that the code can be used over and over again. A pilot C++ warehouse application boosted workers' productivity 35%. Labeling happens faster with fewer errors and better control over warehouse activity.

Kash n' Karry is only one success story. Many firms have experimented with object-oriented projects. Because object-oriented technology has the potential to substantially reduce the firm's software maintenance costs, it appears likely that more software development projects will be based on this methodology in the future.

Source: Bozman, Jean S., "Pain First, Payback Later," *Computerworld*, October 19, 1992, pp. 1, 20; and Maryfran Johnson, "Kash n' Karry Shops in New Technology Aisles," *Computerworld*, March 1, 1993, pp. 1, 24. Coyright 1992/93. Reprinted with permission from Computerworld.

SUMMARY

Serious disadvantages are associated with the traditional systems development life cycle: lengthy development time, extensive document requirements, and a high percentage of the life cycle devoted to coding and testing activities. The length of time required to develop software frequently leads to user dissatisfaction with the final system. This dissatisfaction may be caused by the inability of the user to fully express the system requirements or the failure to produce a system before inevitable changes occur in an organization. Maintenance of the system during its lifetime is difficult and costly. Despite the incorporation of structured development within the life cycle, the final system may be unsatisfactory. Nontraditional approaches to the SDLC are designed to surmount the causes for such failures.

Seven alternatives to the traditional life cycle were presented: software application packages, prototyping, reusable code, CASE tools, reverse engineering, object-oriented technology, and end-user development. Each approach offers certain advantages over the traditional approach. Software application packages *(packaged software)* are popular because they typically cost less than in-house development. In addition, packaged software offers the distinct advantage of being available immediately rather than months or years down the road. The market for packaged software is divided into two broad categories known as *generic applications* and the *vertical market.* Generic applications are those found in almost all firms, whereas applications developed for a particular industry are called vertical market applications.

Whether to buy an application package involves two questions. First, examine the role of the application: If a custom-built system will gain the firm a strategic advantage in the marketplace, then packaged software is inappropriate. The second question is whether the firm's present procedures and data formats fit the package's specifications. If not, the firm must then determine whether it is best to make changes to fit the package or pay to have the package modified to fit the firm's requirements. Modifying the package means additional future expenses, since each new software release must be similarly adapted.

The selection of the right package is a four-step procedure. First, understand the problem and its solution. Second, review the available packages to determine whether any of them fit the firm's application requirements. Third, evaluate the vendors' credentials. Fourth, study the costs and benefits of the preferred package. After a package is selected, arrange a contract to safeguard the firm's interests.

Prototyping is a methodology for rapidly building information systems by frequent interaction between the user/designer and the analyst/builder. It requires that proper software, a 4GL and a data base, must already be in place. The Preliminary Investigation phase defines the problem and determines whether prototyping is a suitable approach. The analyst then quickly constructs a working prototype but, in the interests of saving time, may omit some features not directly visible to the user during its operations. The user evaluates the system and specifies any changes that must be made. The analyst promptly refines the system and returns it for further evaluation. These last two steps are repeated until the user has no other modifications to suggest. The analyst then incorporates the additional features necessary for a production system (such as control measures) and documents the final system. The entire process should take a matter of a few months at most, rather than the many months or years required by the traditional life cycle. The prototyping method works best when only one user and one builder are involved.

Reusable code represents a shortcut in the life cycle. By storing previously tested modules of code in a library, programmers can select appropriate modules for new programs. Testing of these individual blocks of code can be eliminated. Thus, the time allocated for the coding and testing activities within the life cycle is reduced.

CASE (computer-assisted software engineering) tools are a category of programs that assist the analysts and programmers in the tasks specified by the traditional life cycle. Front-end CASE tools (also called upper CASE) support the activities of planning, analysis, and design. Excelerator is an example of a front-end CASE tool. Back-end CASE tools (also known as lower CASE) provide assistance for coding and testing. An integrated CASE tool (ICASE) is one that contributes to both front-end and back-end activities. The power of CASE tools lies in their central repository, which contains the descriptions of the system components. During the analysis and design stages, information goes into the repository for later use in such activities as the creation of input/output designs and the automatic generation of program code. These latter tasks also add further information to the repository, so that it encompasses the entire description of the system.

The production of system documentation is also facilitated by back-end CASE tools. Back-end tools include application code generators, which provide 4GLs to reduce the time and effort of coding and testing. CASE tools result in high-quality information systems that are implemented faster than with conventional tools such as hand-drawn data flow diagrams and 3GL programs.

Reverse engineering is the process by which a specialized CASE tool transforms the program code into a representation on a higher-level of abstraction. The program is mapped backwards, usually to an abstract formulation on the physical design level. The analyst/programmer can then proceed to create a new system by using the code of the existing system. This second step is known as forward engineering. The combination of reverse and forward engineering is sometimes called *reengineering*. [*Note:* This term will be given a different interpretation in Chapter 3.] Including portions of proven program code from the existing system in the new system will realize substantial time savings for coding and testing activities.

Object-oriented technology is an entirely different way of viewing the data and processes that form an information system. Instead of being considered two distinct entities, a set of data and its group of processes (operations) are combined into one unit called an *object*. Objects are the building blocks that define a system at the analysis, design, or coding stages. An object is assigned to a particular class from which it can inherit certain properties. A class may also contain subclasses of objects. The promise of object-oriented technology is the simplification of complex systems by dividing them into objects. Any error will be localized to one object rather than affecting other portions of the system. The reuse of objects speeds the program's construction and decreases the time for testing code.

End-user development permits the users to design and implement their own applications either by programming code or by using available tools such as spreadsheets. Although the wide availability of PC hardware and software has enabled end-users to create applications without the aid of computer professionals, the resultant productivity is not without problems. End-users untrained in testing strategies—or indifferent to them—may produce erroneous results that have serious adverse consequences to the firm. Controls imposed on end-user computing can prevent problems due to inadequate testing, insufficient documentation, or lack of program backup.

TERMS

application code generator	object-oriented analysis (OOA)
back-end CASE	object-oriented design (OOD)
CASE (computer-assisted software engineering) tools	object-oriented programming (OOP)
class (of objects)	object-oriented technology
end-user	packaged software
forward engineering	prototyping
fourth-generation language (4GL)	reengineering
	reusable code
front-end CASE	reverse engineering
generic applications	software application package
in-house development	subclass (of objects)
inheritance	third-generation language (3GL)
integrated CASE (ICASE)	
lower CASE	upper CASE
message	vertical market
object	

QUESTIONS

1. a. Name the seven alternative approaches to the traditional life cycle.
   b. Give a brief description of each approach.

2. For what reasons might a firm select a software application package rather than in-house development?

3. What are the disadvantages of software application packages?

4. What is *prototyping* as applied to information systems? Outline the steps required in prototyping.

5. Prepare a table listing the advantages and disadvantages of prototyping.

6. Explain the term *reusable code*.

7. Define the following terms: CASE, front-end CASE, upper CASE, back-end CASE, lower CASE, and ICASE.

8. a. What is an *application code generator?*
   b. What are the advantages of an application code generator?

9. Explain the process of creating a new system by using the methods of *reverse engineering* and *forward engineering*.

10. In object-oriented technology, what is meant by an *object?*

11. Why hasn't the business community immediately adopted object-oriented technology?

12. a. What are the problems inherent in end-user computing?
   b. What are the solutions to these problems?

EXERCISES

1. The Widget Company makes toys that are distributed internationally. Management has decided to implement a more sophisticated order processing system by purchasing a software package marketed by the Super-Whiz Software firm. Although Super-Whiz Software has just entered the marketplace, Widget's president is impressed with their sales support force, the price is right, and the software is appealing. However, since the Widget Company sells to distributors in other countries, there is a small problem with the package because it accepts the entry of monetary amounts only in U.S. dollars. Super-Whiz Software has offered to modify the package for a one-time charge of $10,000 and guarantee the results. The contract between Widget and Super-Whiz Software is now being prepared.
   a. What are your concerns about this software purchase? Is it a good investment? Justify your answer.
   b. What problems might Widget encounter after the purchase of the modified software?
   c. What special provisions do you recommend for this contract?

2. James Harrington, the division manager for a textbook publisher, wishes to implement an information system so that the college sales representatives can better track their customers' academic courses, current textbook adoptions, and stated preferences for new books. The system should also be able to issue letters addressed to individual customers to promote new offerings by the publisher.

   a. What approach do you suggest for the implementation of this information system? Justify your choice.

   b. Mr. Harrington just discovered that a sales representative, Mary Wilson, has implemented a system very similar to the one that he envisioned. Now he wishes to distribute this system for general use. What procedures do you recommend prior to adopting this system?

PROJECTS

1. Visit one of the departmental offices at your university and inquire about any information systems established by the department to handle its routine affairs. For example, inquire about the department's internal budgeting system and the handling of student records. Depending on the size of the department, information systems may also exist for tracking undergraduate or graduate student admissions, and recruiting new faculty.

   a. Document how these systems were implemented.

   b. Describe any problems that you foresee with the continuing use of these systems.

   c. Explain the procedures presently followed for backup of these applications.

   d. Evaluate the backup procedures. Are they adequate? If not, what procedures do you recommend?

2. Visit a local video rental store and observe the procedures for customer checkouts and returns.

   a. If a computer system is in use, make an appointment to meet with the manager to discuss the computer system and how it was implemented. Report on the approach taken for the implementation of this system, and discuss whether it was the most suitable approach.

   b. If a computer is not in use, what systems development approach do you recommend? Explain your reasons for choosing this approach.

REFERENCES

Anthes, Gary H. "Client/Server on Track at Railroad." *Computerworld,* September 7, 1992, pp. 59ff.

Bobrow, Daniel G. "The Object of Desire." *Datamation* 35(9), May 1, 1989, pp. 37–41.

Durbin, Gary. "Off the Rack: The Case for Packaged Systems." *Information Strategy: The Executive's Journal* 3(4), Summer 1987, pp. 11–15.

Gibson, Michael L., Charles A. Snyder, and Houston H. Carr. "Why CASE Belongs in Strategic Business Management." *Information Strategy: The Executive's Journal* 7(2), Winter 1991, pp. 17–23.

Gilman, Hank, and William M. Bulkeley. "Can Software Firms Be Held Responsible When a Program Makes a Costly Error?" *Wall Street Journal,* August 4, 1986, p. 1.

Goldmacher, Ed. "Do It Yourself: The Case for Custom Systems." *Information Strategy: The Executive's Journal* 3(4), Summer 1987, pp. 16–18.

Jenkins, Milton. "Prototyping: A Methodology for the Design and Development of Application Systems." Working paper, School of Business, Indiana University at Bloomington, 1983.

Martin, James, and Carma McClure. "Buying Software off the Rack." *Harvard Business Review* November–December 1983, pp. 32–60.

Margolis, Nell. "Re-engineering: It's Great, Whatever It Is." *Computerworld,* June 29, 1992, p. 87.

McClure, Carma. *CASE Is Software Automation.* Englewood Cliffs, NJ: Prentice-Hall, 1989.

McMullen, John. "End Users Create PC Applications." *Datamation,* December 1, 1989, p. 4.

O'Dell, Peter. "Design: Do-It-Yourself Systems." *Computer Decisions* 17, May 7, 1985, pp. 42ff.

Pfrenzinger, Steven J. "Reengineering: How High and Why?" *Database Programming and Design,* 5(7), July 1992, pp. 29–39.

Schatz, Willie. "What is Re-Engineering, Anyway?" *Computerworld,* August 31, 1992, pp. 97–98.

Snell, Ned. "Using CASE to Rebuild Software." *Datamation,* August 1, 1991, pp. 51–52.

Warner, Edward. "GTE Shuns COBOL." *Computerworld* 19(8), February 25, 1985, pp. 1, 4.

Wu, Margaret S. "Selecting the Right Software Application Package." *Journal of Systems Management* 41(9), September 1990, pp. 28–32.

PART II

The Preliminary Investigation and Analysis Phases

CHAPTER 3

Discovering the Problem's Solution

Objectives

After completing this chapter, you should know the following concepts:

- What activities are performed in the Preliminary Investigation and Analysis phases
- How to evaluate proposed information systems for technical, economic, operational, and scheduling feasibility
- The contents of a feasibility report
- The reengineering of existing systems
- The principles that guide our study of information systems

INTRODUCTION

In Chapter 1, the six phases of the systems development life cycle (SDLC) were briefly described. In this chapter, we explain the activities performed in the two phases of Preliminary Investigation and Analysis and expand on our earlier discussion. These two phases represent the stage called **systems analysis**, which takes place prior to the systems design stage. As shown by Figure 3-1, the user presents a request which must be studied by the systems analyst. The request indicates that a problem exists in the user's business area. In the systems analysis stage, the analyst must determine what the problem is and how it can best be solved.

In the Preliminary Investigation phase, the activities of analysis are performed within a short time frame because management wishes to limit its expenditures until it understands the importance of the problem and the resources required for its solution. The output of the Preliminary Investigation phase is a *feasibility report*, which recommends a solution to management as well as presenting other feasible solutions. If management decides to continue the project, the Analysis phase is entered. The Analysis phase repeats the activities performed in the first phase but in greater depth. In addition, a detailed model of the proposed system is constructed and preliminary design issues are considered. The output of the Analysis phase is a set of documents that comprise the proposal for the new system. However, before discussing these two phases and their activities, we must examine some basic principles inherent in the analyst's approach to systems analysis.

FIGURE 3-1

Systems analysis as two phases

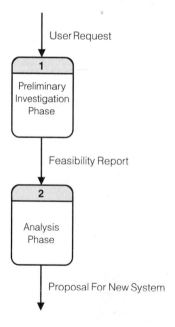

FUNDAMENTAL PRINCIPLES OF SYSTEMS ANALYSIS

The training of a systems analyst encompasses more than the acquisition of technical skills; it extends beyond the technical ability required to implement a set of computer programs for an information system. The analyst must also know how to approach the complex task of resolving the user's problem. In what follows, we shall discuss the analyst's relationship to the users of the system and then present a set of basic principles necessary to the successful solution of the user's problem.

Master Principle: The System Belongs to the Users

The purpose of an information system is to perform the tasks in the functional areas within a business. The **users** of the information system depend on the system to perform their jobs for the firm. Therefore, the information system must be developed to solve the users' problems and meet their needs. This objective must be in the forefront of the analyst's mind throughout the development of the information system. Although the analyst is responsible for the entire systems developmental process, the analyst steps aside once the system becomes operational. If the system is poorly designed, the user's work will be directly affected. Inefficient procedures, poorly designed computer screens, even program errors will not affect the actual day-to-day work of the analyst; it is the end-users of the system who suffer the consequences of the system's shortcomings or reap its benefits. Even though the analyst is the creator, the system really belongs to the users.

Because the analyst understands that the information system must be built to meet the users' needs, the importance of user involvement in the analysis and design of the system is paramount in the analyst's approach. By including the users in the design of the system, the analyst ensures that the system best suited for the users will be produced. This basic premise of user involvement is true in many disciplines. Consider the process of designing a new building to house the College of Business Administration at a major university. The architects do not retire to their offices for several months to design the building in isolation. Instead, they begin by studying the needs of the users of the facility—the faculty, staff, and students. In the systems analysis stage, the architects learn what problems exist in the current building and what functions must be provided by the new one. To gather this information, the architects may convene a planning committee composed of representatives from all three user groups. After completion of a preliminary design, the architects' proposal would be reviewed by this committee. The hundreds of details required for the building's design are studied by the users to ensure that the building will truly meet their needs. All the faculty, staff, and students can be invited to review the design and submit their criticisms. By involving the users of the building during the analysis and design stages, the planners strive to achieve the best facility for the users.

Similarly, the users must be involved in the systems analysis and systems design stages for an information system. They tell the systems analyst their needs and help to evaluate the overall design of the system. For example, the screens and the reports used by the workers and the processes performed by the system to assist the operational activities of the firm must be formulated with the users' assistance and approval. By enlisting the users' cooperation, problems encountered during the developmental process will be resolved in a more satisfactory manner and user satisfaction with the final information system will be increased.

The Triple-P Principle for Information Systems

Although the development of an information system requires the creation of computer programs coupled with an appropriate choice of computer hardware, successful realization of the system is dependent on more than computer expertise. The systems analyst must be aware of the three components—People, Policies, and Procedures—that are an integral part of any information system (see Figure 3-2). These factors are collectively called the **Triple-P principle**.

A computer information system functions by receiving inputs from people and transforming these inputs into outputs, which are then transmitted to people. How the computer system deals with **people**—that is, the *human interfaces* to the system—must be a primary consideration of the analyst. Poorly designed human interfaces interfere with the users' ability to effectively employ the system to accomplish their jobs. Operationally, the system must fit this particular group of users. For the systems analyst, human factors must rank equally with computer hardware and software issues.

The other parts of the Triple-P principle are procedures and policies. **Procedures** are the step-by-step methods that have been established for a particular operation to be performed. On the other hand, **policies** are the rules established by an organization to govern how its objectives are implemented.

FIGURE 3-2

The Triple-P principle

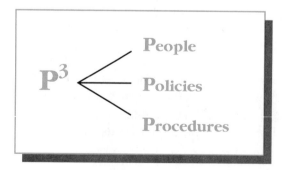

To illustrate the meaning of *procedures*, let us consider the procedure for procuring a driver's license at a state-operated license bureau. Typically, the first step in this procedure is the completion of a form by the applicant. The next step is the submission of the form to a clerk who visually checks it for any omissions. The third step may be the testing of the applicant's vision. Depending on the driver's status, additional steps such as the completion of a written test and a driving test may be included in this procedure. The required steps for issuing the driver's license must be executed in a designated order.

In order to design a new information system for the driver's license bureau, the systems analyst must study these procedures and determine which operations should be retained or modified for the new system. Paper forms could be replaced by input from a computer keyboard, electronic checks on a driver's record could be performed, and other new ways of performing the same procedures could be designed into the new system. By understanding the old procedures, the analyst can look for more efficient ways of performing the same tasks.

To illustrate the meaning of *policies*, let us examine some policies in effect at the driver's license bureau. One policy is the set of rules that govern the issuing of the driver's license to the applicant. One of these rules is that a person must have already attained a minimum age before applying for a driver's license. This minimum age is set by state law. Whenever possible, the computer information system must incorporate such policies. For this particular transaction processing system, the computer system can easily verify that the age of the applicant is acceptable according to the laws of the state.

Let us now consider another example familiar to many students. Today, some registration systems at universities and colleges permit students to register for classes at a computer terminal without the aid of any registration personnel. The Triple-P principle tells the analyst to look for the people, procedures, and policies in the system. Does it appear that the computer registration system functions without any human intervention? Actually, the system receives data—the list of classes needed by the student—directly from the student. Without the entry of data by the student, this portion of the system will stand idle. Examining this system further, the analyst sees that the registrar's office has clerks who also interact with the system by processing late registrations, which are submitted by the students on DROP/ADD slips signed by instructors. These clerks work within the information system by interacting with the computer system. Reports regarding registration are produced by the computer system and sent to various officials at the university; class lists are printed and delivered to instructors. The analyst has now identified several "people groups"—students, clerks, recipients of reports, and instructors—that must be considered in the design of the system.

The registration system's policies and procedures should also be uncovered. For example, some courses require specific prerequisites or a specified student rank such as junior or senior standing. Certain policies and procedures are followed by the registrar's office in processing registration requests for initial registration and any subsequent adding and dropping of courses. These procedures and policies must be incorporated into the computer information system where appropriate; the people performing these procedures belong to the "people" category of system users.

THE PRELIMINARY INVESTIGATION PHASE

The systems development life cycle for an information system begins with the submission of a request for computing services to solve a user's problem. As discussed earlier, before developing an information system to resolve this problem, management must understand the user's problem and the resources required to implement an appropriate solution. In addition, management needs to know the problem's impact on the current system and the overall operation of the organization. To answer these questions, a systems analyst is assigned to perform the activities of the period known as the **Preliminary Investigation phase**.

Since the users are the prime source of this information, the analyst turns to them in order to fully understand the problem submitted to the information systems personnel. Other sources of information are also used. The techniques for gathering information will be discussed in Chapter 6. The amount of time available for this study is limited, because management has not yet decided to budget any resources to service the user's request. Hence the total time devoted to this phase will be short, perhaps only three weeks or so. Due to its brevity, only preliminary analysis is possible, and an in-depth study is deferred to the Analysis phase.

To accomplish this preliminary analysis of the user's problem, the analyst embarks on an activity called the *feasibility study* and formally documents the study's findings in the *feasibility report*. As shown in Figure 3-3, the analyst performs the following steps:

1. The current system is studied.
2. The user's problem is redefined in precise terms.
3. A set of preliminary solutions is formulated.
4. The feasibility of these solutions is evaluated and one of these solutions is recommended for implementation.
5. The feasibility report is prepared.

Documentation for the feasibility report is generated during all these steps. Although the feasibility study is presented as a set of independent steps, in reality the analyst is mentally performing these tasks in an overlapping fashion. For clarity, however, each step will be discussed as an independent activity.

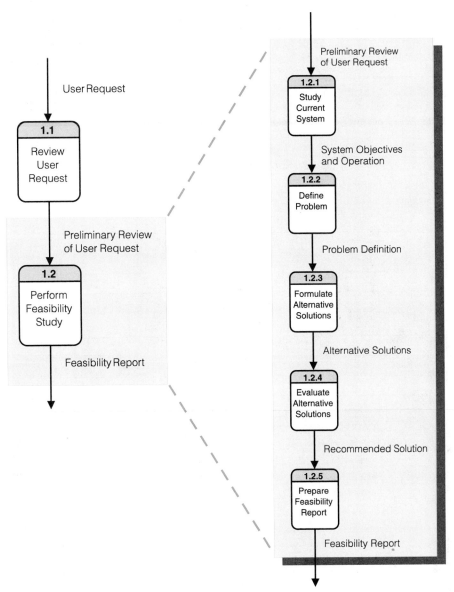

FIGURE 3-3
**The steps in the Pre-
liminary Investigation
phase**

The Submission of the User's Request

As we have mentioned, the user is the person engaged in a functional area
within the business. When problems arise in these areas, the user is the one
who sees the difficulties and requests assistance from the information systems professionals. To do so, the user submits a written request such as the
sample **user request form** shown in Figure 3-4. The user provides a brief
statement of the problem, suggests a plan of action, and furnishes other
details necessary for the processing of the request by management. The
action taken on this request will depend on several factors. Since the infor-

FIGURE 3-4

A sample user request form

REQUEST FOR COMPUTER SERVICES

SUBMITTED BY _____ DATE _____

DEPARTMENT _____ DEPARTMENTAL APPROVAL _____

TYPE OF REQUEST   [   ]   New system
                  [   ]   Modification to current system (check the type of change below)
                          [   ]   Enhancement
                          [   ]   Correction of existing error
                  [   ]   Redesign of system in progress

DESIRED COMPLETION DATE _____

PROBLEM STATEMENT (if desired, attach additional documentation)

_____

_____

_____

_____

SERVICES REQUESTED

_____

_____

_____

_____

_____

ACTION (to be completed by steering committee)
   [   ]   Request approved
           Assigned to _____ Scheduled starting date _____
   [   ]   Request to be scheduled at a later time (backlogged)
           To be reviewed by _____
   [   ]   Request rejected
           Reason for rejection _____

           _____

mation systems area typically has several requests for action on hand, the user's application must be prioritized in relation to the other requests. Each organization has a way to evaluate the user's requests and rank them in order of importance. For instance, directives for new information systems emanating from the highest level of management may be automatically awarded the highest priority. Because management must allocate the scarce resources of the software developers, sufficient information regarding the user's request must be available for consideration.

In many organizations, the allocation of computer expenditures is assigned to a Steering Committee consisting of managers who are given the task of distributing the firm's computing resources. To make appropriate decisions, the Steering Committee members must possess high levels of business expertise and an awareness of the firm's goals. They must possess the background to judge the proposed projects and determine which will best fulfill the organizational goals. Since a system typically receives inputs from and issues outputs to other systems in the organization, the proposed project may have wide-ranging ramifications on these interdependent systems, magnifying the scope of the project. The Steering Committee also considers such interdependencies. Certain projects will be more effective than others in achieving the firm's objectives. Although a proposed project may be worthy of implementation, the Steering Committee must weigh its value against other possible uses of the firm's resources. Once a project begins, the allocated computing resources are no longer available for other ventures. Other vital projects may be delayed for months or even years. The selection of the right projects for implementation is crucial to the success and survival of the firm. Such judgments require the decision-makers to have a comprehensive view of the entire organization, its functions, and its goals.

What Is the Real User Request?

Because the user's expertise exists in a functional area and not in computing services, the user's problem statement may be incomplete or inaccurate. For the same reason, the solution proposed by the user may not be the most suitable solution for this firm. It is the analyst's task to discover the actual problem faced by the user. To do so, the systems analyst begins the feasibility study by seeking the answers to three important questions:

1. What is the actual problem that the user faces?
2. How will the resolution of this problem affect the current system?
3. Does the solution to the problem affect any other systems?

Although the problem arose in the functional area of the user who submitted the request, the analyst may find that the problem also affects other business areas, so that any solution may have far-reaching consequences. If users in other departments are affected by the proposed change, they too must be consulted before a new system is designed. The analyst must put aside departmental rivalries and determine what approach is best for the firm, not merely for the user's department. To resolve these questions, the systems analyst examines all aspects of the current system and its interrelated systems, concentrating on three problem areas designated by the acronym **HIM**: Human factors, Information deficiencies, and Mistakes in the system.

HUMAN FACTORS

Even if the current information system is implemented by the means of a computer, there are always **human factors** to consider. At some point, people must interact with the system. If the system was not well designed for human interaction, the user becomes frustrated but may not realize that the problems are due to poor design. The points where the computer system interacts with the user are called *human interfaces* or simply *interfaces.* For example, computer screens interface with people. Badly designed screens may confuse the user, causing the entry of data in the wrong fields or even the omission of data from the entry procedure. The forms on which data are manually recorded represent another system component that may contribute to human error. If a form is not properly designed, then the person initially recording the data may omit items or place some items in the wrong location on the form. Poorly designed forms may result from placing the interests of the programmer over the convenience of the user. For example, a screen or report that displays only codes rather than showing their meaning is simpler for the programmer to code but makes the user's task more difficult. But when an order entry screen indicates the appropriate word RED, WHITE, or BLUE together with its corresponding color code of 40, 50, or 60, a user can process an order more easily without the need to recall the meaning of the codes.

Other human factors to be considered by the analyst include the ease of use of the system, extensive requirements for training due to poor user interfaces, and the system's failure to check for erroneous input data. A possible trouble area exists whenever the system is dependent on human faculties. The analyst studies the system with the knowledge that well-designed human interfaces facilitate the user's tasks and promote efficient use of the information system.

INFORMATION DEFICIENCIES

When examining the current system, the analyst should be looking for **information deficiencies**—places where the information supplied by the system is inaccurate, untimely, or badly presented. If a report is produced in triplicate and two copies are immediately tossed in the wastebasket while the third is stored in a file drawer without perusal, the system is not doing the right job. What the user may require is the same report produced with more timely data and in a completely different format. For example, a sales manager requested a monthly sales report listing the total sales per salesperson per division. But careful study of this 30-page report failed to give the sales manager an adequate assessment of the performance of each sales division and the individual salespersons. Although the sales manager received exactly the information requested, the true need was for the graphical display of the data and summary information by division. Moreover, because the report arrived 8 weeks after the reporting period ended, the information was too old to be valuable. The outdated information made it impossible to react quickly to poor sales. In short, the information had serious deficiencies.

Sometimes, the user requires additional information in order to handle business decisions. The capabilities of the computer information system may be limited to merely processing transactions in a routine fashion without providing the summary reports or graphical representations of data necessary for the planning functions of the firm. On-line query capability may be desirable to provide information the user needs in decision making. The sales manager who asked for a monthly sales report may have wanted to monitor the sales of a new product. Knowing the sales of the product in each geographical region would help the sales manager decide about increasing the advertising budget or initiating special marketing efforts to assist regions with low sales. If the information were not available, such steps might be taken without accurate information to guide the decision-making process. As the bridge between the user and the computer professionals, the systems analyst must identify areas where information deficiencies occur and devise plans to eliminate these trouble spots from the future system.

MISTAKES IN THE CURRENT SYSTEM

The current information system may contain **mistakes** or **glitches** which are the real reasons prompting the user's request. There are many causes for these errors. Sometimes an ambiguous specification may be interpreted by the programmer without consulting the analyst. In doing so, the programmer may unknowingly make a design choice that affects the overall system, thus causing glitches to occur. For example, inadequate space allocation for a data table internal to the program may have far-reaching consequences. If the data entered into the table exceed its physical limits and the program fails to check for such overflow, the data will spill over into another data area. The results may be erroneous output rather than the more desirable outcome of an error message followed by program termination. Errors in information could also be caused by poor file design, where data are stored redundantly in the files. The data in one file may be correct while the same data in the other files are not brought up-to-date; thus, incorrect data may be used for the production of reports. Another possible reason for the user's problem could be the use of separate files by different departments without the capability of sharing the data; such sharing of data would be available with the implementation of a data base management system. Other reasons might be found for the user's problem. Rather than simply copying the existing system, the analyst must discover why the system is failing to meet the user's needs—otherwise the new system may incorporate the same flaws. Possibly the analyst may find that the current system simply requires minor modifications to correct these glitches, rather than replacement by an entirely new system.

Study of the Current System

The goal of this activity is to build an abstract representation of the current system using a technique known as data flow diagrams, which are explained in Chapter 9. Such an abstract representation is known as a *model*. The principles by which the systems analyst operates are based on those principles found in general systems theory as discussed in Chapter 1. By dividing the information system into manageable components, the analyst is able to study each unit and focus on the details of the system at hand without losing sight of the overall system. The systems analyst examines the major aspects of the system in order to obtain the information necessary for the creation of this model. As listed in Figure 3-5, the three major features of any system—*objectives, inputs* and *outputs,* and *functions*—serve as a guide to the study of the current system. The techniques used by the systems analyst to gather information on the current system are covered in Chapter 6.

OBJECTIVES OF THE SYSTEM

Without knowing the objectives of the system, the analyst cannot determine if the system is doing what was originally intended. For example, an inventory system typically serves the objective of facilitating the procurement of supplies in order to meet the production schedule. Let us assume that, under its current system, a firm has successfully lowered its inventory costs but supplies are not readily available for production. The objective of the inventory system therefore has not been met. In an attempt to remedy the inadequacy of the inventory system, the users call for more information to be generated by the system.

It is the systems analyst's job to investigate this problem. In doing so, the analyst verifies that the production department does, indeed, frequently experience delays due to a lack of supplies. However, the analyst also finds that, because jobs are accepted without ordering the necessary supplies, the production department often fails to have the raw materials needed to execute these jobs. The real problem is that the current inventory system was

FIGURE 3-5

The steps in the study of the current system

■ System Objectives

Define the objectives of the current system. Evaluate these objectives: Do they serve the organization or only this division of the firm?

■ System Inputs and Outputs

Identify the system inputs and outputs, the origins of the inputs, and the destinations of the outputs. This information shows who will be affected by the changes to the existing system.

■ System Functions

Define the functions of the current system. Then determine how these functions are performed by identifying the components of the system: manual procedures, user interfaces, computer programs, files and data bases, and other relevant system elements.

not adequately designed to meet the requirements of the production department. By placing the system's objectives foremost in the study, the analyst is able to determine the reasons for the system's deficiencies and propose an appropriate solution.

SYSTEM INPUTS AND OUTPUTS

By identifying the inputs and outputs to the system, the analyst takes the first step in modeling the current system. The origins of the inputs and the destinations of the outputs reveal those persons or business divisions that will be affected by any modifications to the existing system. For example, the payroll department, as a user, asks for the revision of a monthly report that summarizes the salary totals by employee type. A preliminary study by the analyst reveals that the report is also used by the human resources department to prepare salary recommendations for the hiring of new employees and by management to evaluate labor costs for each company division. Any change in this report will affect all three areas of the firm, not merely the payroll department.

FUNCTIONS OF THE CURRENT SYSTEM

After determining the system objectives and identifying the inputs and outputs that flow to and from the system, the systems analyst studies how the inputs are transformed into outputs by the actions performed by the system; these actions are the functions of the system. The analyst asks several questions:

What is being done?

Is the system performance in the best interests of the firm?

Who are the users doing these functions?

What end-users of other divisions are affected by this system?

The overall interests of the business must be served, not merely the interests of an individual division of the firm. To fully comprehend the problem, the analyst must understand not only *what* but *how* functions are performed by the users and the system.

To understand the *how* of the system, the analyst studies the manual and computerized procedures, the documents created by the system, the screens that interface with the users, and the actions taken by the system. The analyst examines response time, the forms where data are recorded manually, the keying of data into the computer system, the storage of paper documents, and other procedural matters. These features often affect the user's perception of the computer system and could be the underlying causes of the problem. Further, the relationship of the computer hardware to the performance of the existing system must also be understood. In studying the system, it is important to note any records kept informally by the users. The existence of files external to the computerized system usually indicates flaws in the design of the current system; such data may in fact be the source of the problem. Finally, the analyst reviews the documentation of the system. But because only a preliminary investigation of the user's request has been authorized, all these activities must be limited in scope.

The Next Step: The Creation of Alternative Solutions

In thinking of alternative solutions, the systems analyst must be alert to the possibility of a major redesign of the system's functions by altering the way in which the work is performed. Such innovative redesign of operational procedures is known as *reengineering*. (In this chapter, reengineering is not related to the terms *reverse engineering* and *forward engineering* employed in Chapter 2.) The term **reengineering** is applied in a broad sense to the streamlining of the corporate work flow. By using the capabilities of computer and communications technology, the company redesigns its way of doing business. Rather than continuing to implement a paper-driven system, reengineering calls for a radical new approach to performing the same business functions.

As a simple illustration of reengineering, consider a bank teller's 5-step operation in servicing a customer's request to cash a check. As shown in Figure 3-6, the reengineered transaction has changed only one step in the

FIGURE 3-6

The cashing of a check: Old way and reengineered way

Step	Old Way	Reengineered Way
1	Verify that the check has been completed correctly	Same
2	Verify availability of funds from Teller Terminal	Same
3	Verify Customer Signature by the following steps: Walk to Signature File Retrieve Signature Card Verify Signature Refile Signature Card Return to Teller Window	Verify Customer Signature from Teller Terminal (signature automatically displayed on screen)
4	Validate check	Same
5	Dispense cash to customer	Same

process performed by the teller. Formerly, the teller was obliged to leave the teller window and walk over to the signature files. Then the teller located the customer's signature card and verified the signature on the check. Finally, the teller refiled the card and returned to the teller window to complete the transaction. Because the signatures were stored in a conventional card file, locating the customer's card was time-consuming—and, since tellers are only human, signature cards were occasionally misfiled. The reengineering of the system calls for the customer's signature to be stored on a document imaging system. The teller can now verify the customer's signature by simply examining the terminal screen at the teller's own window. The customer is not left waiting while the signature card is retrieved, examined, and refiled. The time spent walking to and from the central card file is eliminated. In sum, the bank gains in two ways: by improving the service offered to its customers and by increasing the amount of productive time available from the teller.

Now let us look at a more complex example, the reengineering of clerical operations at Ford. By installing a new automated system, Ford succeeded in reducing the number of staff required for ordering parts, receiving components, and issuing payments to the suppliers. Although paper forms were still being shuffled between Ford and its suppliers, the new system improved the speed and reduced the manual effort. The automated system was successful in reducing the paper-shuffling staff from 500 to 400 employees. But then Ford took a good look at Mazda, a Japanese carmaker, which had just formed an alliance with Ford. Mazda's automated system dropped paper invoices from the system. When goods are received, the shipment information is captured by waving a bar code scanner over each box. These bar codes represent all the information necessary for a shipment. The computer then automatically updates the parts in inventory, alters production schedules if necessary, and sends electronic payments to the supplier. The matching of parts to invoices was no longer needed. The shuffling of these paper documents is eliminated. Ford's managers found this to be a highly efficient way of doing business—but it also requires fundamental changes in the way people work. Before implementing this radical system, other steps must be taken. Closer relations with suppliers, warehouse communications linked directly to the finance department, and workers willing to adapt to new procedures are essential aspects of the system.

Computers, often coupled with telecommunication technology, permit a rethinking of business operations. First, the systems designer must remove the psychological barrier of considering paper documents essential to business operations. Second, the availability of information within the computer means that information can be accessed directly by users rather than through the medium of internal communications. Third, the firm can exchange information either internally or externally by allowing computers to "talk" to each other from geographically dispersed sites. Fourth, new hardware technology should be reviewed for innovative approaches to systems design. An example is the processing of document images sent electronically from one site to another. Faxed documents can be viewed immediately at a computer screen instead of being transferred to paper forms. Other types of document images can be displayed on computer screens, such as the signature cards at the bank in our earlier example. Fifth, the advancements in software technology should not be overlooked. An example is expert systems that can supplement or replace the human decision-maker. Finally, the firm must be aware of the available technology and rethink its entire business. One example is a major publisher's offer to customize textbooks by permitting professors to choose chapters from a variety of available books. For example, a professor could specify a textbook with chapters drawn from various accounting, management science, and information systems books. Because the technology exists, this publisher is using an innovative approach to publishing. These custom-tailored textbooks can be produced only because of the availability of computer technology.

Reengineering the existing system offers but one possible solution to the problem. Other solutions should also be envisioned by the analyst—the more the better. Brainstorming sessions may produce some solutions that are obviously impractical; nonetheless, such wide-ranging efforts are a good way to find the best solution for the firm. If only one solution is considered, the optimal solution may not be found. Frequently, the user already has an idea about how to solve the problem by developing a new computer system or modifying the current system. The analyst should include this proposal in the set of alternative solutions to be studied, but the user's solution must be treated with caution. Because the user typically looks to the computer for a quick solution, it is likely that other possibilities were not considered. Changes in operational procedures, improvements in manual processing, or the redesign of paper documents may be more appropriate answers to the problem. The hardware system must also be examined to determine if upgrading the equipment or even getting an entirely new computer system is what is needed to satisfy the users. After discarding the solutions that are unrealistic, the analyst studies the feasibility of the remaining solutions.

The Measures of Feasibility

There are four measures of feasibility that must be considered for a proposed solution. These **feasibility issues** are

> economic
>
> technical
>
> operational
>
> scheduling

Figure 3-7 provides a summary of these feasibility tests for a system.

FIGURE 3-7
The four measures of feasibility

■ **Economic Feasibility**

Is it worth doing here, that is, do the benefits outweigh the financial costs?

■ **Technical Feasibility**

Can we do it here?

If not, does the technology exist to do it?

■ **Operational Feasibility**

Will it work here?

■ **Scheduling Feasibility**

Will it be done in time?

ECONOMIC FEASIBILITY

Economic feasibility or *financial feasibility* is the classic method for judging the suitability of a proposal. The study of economic feasibility results in the *cost/benefit analysis*, a report that estimates the net financial gains if the proposed system is adopted. First, the costs of implementing the proposed system and its projected financial benefits (savings) are specified in detail. Then the costs are subtracted from the expected financial benefits to determine the net monetary gains to the business. If the financial benefits exceed the monetary costs, the system is deemed to be economically feasible. If the costs are more than the savings projected for the system, then other reasons must be sufficiently compelling to cause the system to be built. When costs or benefits are not directly measurable in monetary terms, they are called *intangible* costs and benefits. Such intangibles are included as factors in the analysis of economic feasibility. Because the topic of cost/benefit analysis is complex, more explanation will be found in Chapter 4. For now, we can simply summarize the issue of economic feasibility with the question: Is it worth doing here? That is, do the benefits outweigh the costs?

TECHNICAL FEASIBILITY

The issue of **technical feasibility** is embodied in two questions: Can we do it here? If not, does the technology exist to do it? The first question asks whether the hardware, software development tools, and other related equipment are available in-house to provide the technology required for the system. For example, the proposed solution may be an on-line order entry system that requires rapid response from the computer. If the examination of the current system shows that the CPU is too slow to support the on-line processing requirements, this question is answered "No." By asking the second question, we determine whether the hardware necessary to do the job exists at all. In this case, the answer is a resounding "Yes!"

Let us consider an example where the technical feasibility of a new system is doubtful. Because word processing activities have increased substantially in the past year, a firm finds that its word processing center takes 3 days or more to handle correspondence. One proposal is to acquire voice input devices, which let the computer take dictation directly from the users. The users simply dictate their letters using voice input devices attached to their own desktop computers, which then automatically print the letters. Because the keying of letters by typists is eliminated, correspondence can be processed promptly with great financial savings. On investigating the technical feasibility of this proposed solution, the analyst finds that voice input devices are not sufficiently advanced to accept such dictation. Words are sometimes misinterpreted and incorrect spelling is common. Despite the attractiveness of an automated correspondence system, the proposed system does not meet the requirements of technical feasibility and must be rejected as a possible solution.

OPERATIONAL FEASIBILITY

The question to be asked for operational feasibility is: Will the system work here? **Operational feasibility** measures the suitability of the proposed system with regard to human factors. This feasibility issue is concerned with the human aspects of the information system, not with the activities performed solely by the computer. No information system functions without some manual procedures. If the human requirements of the system are unreasonable, the system will not produce the expected results or may even be put on a back shelf and seldom used, if at all. Because computer professionals are usually convinced of the merits of computer systems, the analyst must be especially aware of this innate bias and exercise special care to ensure that the system is designed for people, not machines. Top-level management support for a system is also crucial or this essential ingredient of operational feasibility will be missing.

> ### Warning
> Operational feasibility is often difficult to see in concrete terms. Study the examples in this section closely. A simple example is a special keyboard where the keys are arranged in a nonstandard pattern in order to greatly increase the typist's speed. In fact, such a keyboard exists. Why can't a firm introduce such a marvelous device at once?

The following example of a system that resulted in poor operational feasibility is based on a true story. A major university whose payroll costs had steadily increased over the years was looking for ways to reduce these rising costs. Because employees were divided into three different pay categories—weekly, biweekly, and monthly—one proposal was to change the pay period, so that paychecks would be produced less often. Monthly paychecks were exempt from this plan because monthly pay periods were judged to be the longest time frame acceptable for the issuance of paychecks. An examination of the weekly category showed that these employees were primarily temporary employees who were assigned to jobs for at most one semester. No change was proposed for these employees. The analyst's review of the employees paid biweekly showed a stable employee group, about half of whom belonged to the union. The proposed system would change their pay period from every two weeks to twice a month. Financial savings were projected to be substantial and would quickly return the systems development costs. It appeared to be a minor change that would hardly affect the employees.

Based on the cost/benefit analysis, the university proceeded to implement the proposal. Two months before the changeover to the new system, the university announced its plans to the employees who were paid biweekly. The uproar was tremendous. The employees resented the unilateral action of the university and protested that they faced serious problems in budgeting for major items if paid twice a month rather than every two weeks. The union mobilized its forces, reviewed the university's proposal for the changeover, and then formally objected to the proposal on two grounds. First, the university planned to withhold a small portion of money from salaries during the transition from a two-week pay period to a half-month period. Second, the union's current contract with the university called for salaries to be paid on a biweekly basis. After conferring with the union representatives, the university discarded the proposed system and paychecks continued to be processed with the old pay periods. The university had failed to "sell" the system to those affected by the change in procedures. After spending substantial computing resources, management now realized that the system had failed the test of operational feasibility. The new system was junked. Although the system easily passed the tests of technical, financial, and scheduling feasibility, it lacked the support of those individuals that were most affected.

Another example of operational feasibility is provided to illustrate the case where the system is unacceptable due to its interface with the system users. A restaurant owner decided to introduce an inventory system for the liquor purchased for alcoholic drinks. The bartender was asked to record the type of cocktails prepared and the brand name of the liquor used for each drink. Two-digit codes were assigned to the 40 liquor types and 50 cocktail names available for customers at the restaurant. As each drink was prepared, the bartender was asked to ring the set of two-digit codes on the register to indicate the type of liquor or cocktail category. The register would capture the information on magnetic tape and the inventory data would then be processed automatically after business hours were over.

When the first inventory report was prepared, to the owner's surprise over 95% of the drinks used only two types of liquor and almost all the cocktails ordered were manhattans or martinis.

What was the problem with this inventory system? The bartender had quickly discovered that it was impossible to keep up with the flood of cocktail orders at busy times and also look up the code numbers for each order. There were just too many code numbers to memorize. To appease the owner, the bartender simply pretended to use the system, recording each cocktail as either a manhattan or a martini and the liquor as one of two different types. The inventory system couldn't work because it was too complicated for the bartender, who was the actual user of the system. Its design lacked operational feasibility.

SCHEDULING FEASIBILITY

Scheduling feasibility is related to the question: Will it be done in time? If the proposed information system passes all other feasibility tests with flying colors but is unavailable to handle operations crucial to the success of the firm within the time frame necessary, the system must be rejected. For example, a major firm is growing rapidly and foresees that the growth rate will continue for the next 5 years. Given the present rate of expansion, the information systems department forecasts that, within 2 years, the invoices issued to customers will require 5 months to be prepared by the present computer system. It is easy to foresee that the firm will be crippled by its inability to collect the accounts receivable necessary to sustain both its existence and its continued growth. Assigned to solve this problem, the systems analyst envisions a new information system that requires new hardware and software plus the replacement of the current billing system by an entirely new system. On studying the feasibility of the proposed system, the analyst finds that the system returns its investment within 2 years, its operational feasibility is high, and the system is technically feasible. Unfortunately, the system must be dropped from consideration because the systems development process is estimated to require 3 years. In 3 years' time, the firm will be paralyzed by its failure to bill its customers promptly, resulting in a serious lack of revenue. Other alternatives must be formulated in order to provide a feasible solution to the problem.

Selecting the Recommended Solution

Throughout the systems development process, the analyst encounters situations where no right and wrong answers exist. In selecting the best solution from the alternatives, the analyst realizes no single solution offers all the advantages desired for the system. The analyst must examine each solution and determine its relative advantages and disadvantages in competition with the other possible choices. By studying these **trade-offs**, the analyst ascertains which solution can best be recommended to management. The cost of the system and the time required to develop the system are traded off against the features provided by the system. If costs are too high, then the analyst must question whether certain aspects of the proposed system can be sacrificed.

For example, a small college may wish to provide on-line registration of its students as described earlier. After investigating this possibility, the analyst finds that the cost of software development is far less for an on-line system that operates at a central location with the assistance of clerical personnel than for an on-line system with terminals at various locations on campus. Although the centrally located registration system is not exactly what the college wants, the analyst trades off costs with the capabilities of the two systems and recommends the centralized system. Only if the college believes that the intangible benefits of the decentralized system far outweigh its actual costs will the more expensive option be implemented.

The Feasibility Report

The **feasibility report** is the formal documentation of the feasibility study performed by the systems analyst. The report represents an argument for the recommended system. As listed in Figure 3-8, several relevant documents are included; however the report should be organized so that the detailed

FIGURE 3-8

The feasibility report

Statement of the Problem

A precise statement of the problem

The Proposed Solution

Description of the proposed information system
    Forecasted schedule for implementation and total person-months required

    Estimated costs

Justifications for this proposed system

    The fulfillment of the firm's needs

    The feasibility criteria for this solution

        Cost/benefit analysis

        Technical issues

        Operational factors

        Scheduling feasibility

Other Acceptable Solutions (briefly described)

Description of each alternative solution

Feasibility criteria for the alternative solution

Reasons for rejection by analyst

information provided by the study does not interfere with the presentation of the analyst's case for the proposed system. The particulars of the cost/benefit analysis, scheduling estimates for the proposed system, and similar detailed information are treated as supporting documentation for the body of the report; this information is often relegated to an appendix. If the recommended solution was selected from among workable alternatives, these alternatives are also briefly documented in the report. After the report has been prepared and circulated to the Steering Committee, the analyst presents a summary of the report at a meeting of the committee. Questions from the Steering Committee must be fielded by the analyst and objections to the proposal rebutted. Finally, the committee decides on the best solution to the problem. Since the firm's resources are limited and many competing claims exist for these same resources, after weighing the many trade-offs, the Steering Committee may opt for a different system. Once approved by the Steering Committee, the selected information system enters the next phase of its life cycle, Analysis.

THE ANALYSIS PHASE

Although the Analysis phase greatly resembles the Preliminary Investigation phase, any activities previously executed in the Preliminary Investigation phase will now be executed in more depth. The completion of the Preliminary Investigation phase narrows the scope of the activities in the Analysis phase so that efforts will focus on the chosen solution. Now the models for the current system and proposed system can be fleshed out with more detailed specifications. Because the Steering Committee has approved the new system, work can begin in earnest. As shown in Figure 3-9, the **Analysis phase** has six basic activities:

1. Study the existing system.
2. Review the conclusions obtained by the Preliminary Investigation phase: recommended solution, feasibility issues, and rejection of alternative solutions.
3. Prepare the model of the new system.
4. Revise the preliminary design.
5. Devise the detailed schedule for project implementation.
6. Prepare the report on the Analysis phase for review by management.

The Current System Revisited

Although the systems analyst studied the current system during the Preliminary Investigation phase, the expenditure of time and effort was limited. In the Analysis phase, this study resumes with the objective of describing the current system by creating a representation of the system known as a **model**. Since ample time is now available to the analyst, a more detailed model of the current system can be produced. Once again, the users will

Study the current system

Create a model of the system showing processes, data, and boundaries.

Study the human interfaces required by the existing system.

Review the activities performed in the Preliminary Investigation phase.

Restate the problem, if appropriate.

Reevaluate the alternative solutions.

Review the feasibility issues for the new system.

Prepare a model of the new system.

Formulate a model of the new system (processes and data).

Plan the human interfaces to this system.

Estimate the storage requirements for the new system.

Examine the previously stated hardware and software requirements for the implementation of the system.

Revise the preliminary design.

Prepare a detailed schedule for project completion.

Prepare the report on these activities for management's approval.

FIGURE 3-9
The steps in the Analysis phase

assist the analyst by providing the information necessary for the creation of this model. The model includes the descriptions of the data and the processes used to transform the data. The method that will be employed in this book for creating this model is known as *data flow diagrams* (Chapter 9). The data processed by the existing system are defined explicitly by means of the supporting documentation for the data flow diagrams called the *data dictionary* (Chapter 10), and the definition of the processes is provided by *process descriptions* entered into the *project dictionary* (Chapter 11).

THE MODEL OF THE CURRENT SYSTEM

Using the technique of data flow diagrams, the analyst constructs the model of the current system, which will serve as the foundation for formulating the model of the new system. The same functions performed by the existing system—the *what* of what is being done—typically must also be executed by the new system. The *how* of the current system is also important to the systems analyst, but the means by which these functions will be performed may be substantially different in the new system. Consider a sales management system that now operates in batch mode and is being converted to an on-line system. The same functions must be incorporated into the on-line system, though new features are likely to be added to the system. The analyst reviews the specifications for the data processed by the current system to determine the data requirements for the new system. This information will be used later in the Design phase to prepare the detailed design of data files. Similarly, the detailed description of the processes permits the analyst to fully comprehend the transformations performed on the data; this information will be needed in the Design phase.

Because the analyst now knows the existing system in depth, it is possible to review the problem statement created earlier in the Preliminary Investigation phase. Armed with this additional knowledge, the analyst must ask whether the user's problem was truly understood and whether the solution chosen then was indeed the best alternative. At this stage, the analyst must rethink the plans before more time and money are invested in the project. This reexamination of previous decisions continues throughout the life cycle.

SHOULD WE STUDY THE CURRENT SYSTEM?

Although there are benefits associated with studying the existing system, this study is not always warranted. Some professionals now believe that such a study is not valuable because the thrust of the project is to create a new system, not to duplicate the old one. Bypassing this study saves a great deal of time and effort. Guidelines for deciding whether to bypass this study are:

How well does the analyst know the existing system?

Is the existing system already so heavily automated that only a few manual procedures remain, or is it primarily a manual system?

How does the user's request relate to the current system?

If the current system is already computerized with up-to-date documentation and if the analyst has great familiarity with the system, the analyst can focus on the user's difficulties and concerns, omitting an extensive study of the existing system. Otherwise, the analyst must engage in the study of the current system in order to faithfully fulfill the user's needs.

The Model of the Proposed System

By analyzing the current system, the analyst gained in-depth knowledge of what the system does and more precisely comprehends the user's problem with the system. With this combined knowledge, the analyst is now able to draw a model of the proposed system. Although this model may have been sketched out in the previous phase, a comprehensive model can now be created. As mentioned earlier, the preferred tool for drawing this model is the methodology of data flow diagrams with supporting definitions provided

Reinventing Business

When computers first began their data processing tasks, they supported the firm's traditional way of doing business by creating paper documents faster and more accurately than ever before. As computers increased their processing speeds, they turned out paper documents at even faster rates. Today firms are looking at their data processing problems and seeing whole warehouses stuffed with paper. Rather than continuing to generate more paper, organizations are reinventing business by replacing paper records with electronic data. In doing so, the entire way of doing business has been altered.

The key technology used to reinvent business procedures is electronic data interchange (EDI). Instead of paper documents, firms are using electronic forms that can travel automatically from desk to desk instantaneously without error. These "smart" forms can even be relied upon to route the information to the appropriate employees for processing.

This new technology affects how business procedures are performed. For example, discount stores such as Wal-Mart and Target exchange communications with their warehouses directly without the aid of paper. As items are sold, the bar codes are read to record the sales transactions. The computer for the retailing units communicates directly with the warehouse and orders replacements for the merchandise. The warehouse operations are also directed by the computer so that the merchandise is speedily packaged, labeled, and shipped to the retailing units. Simultaneously the computer records all these transactions for the accounting department.

Many large firms expect to handle as much as 80 percent of their business transactions with trading partners via EDI links, effectively eliminating more than 4 million business forms annually for a single firm. Organizations trying to save money by changing to electronic data include the U.S. Internal Revenue Service, through the use of electronically filed tax returns, and the Royal Bank of Canada. The substitution of electronic data for paper forms has greatly improved the productivity of businesses. As we have observed, information can be transmitted instantaneously and without error, and decisions can be executed with greater speed. For example, the Discover Card unit of Sears Roebuck formerly took six forms and two weeks to process an application. Today an automated computer process enables the work to be completed within one day. As a consequence, doing business is streamlined and its costs are substantially reduced.

Despite these gains in productivity, obstacles still remain for the adoption of this business innovation. An early prediction by the Automotive Industry Action Group was that by 1985 the production cost of a car would be reduced by $200 due to the decrease in paper flowing through the automobile manufacturing plants. But paper forms die hard and the prediction has not been realized. Instead, the automobile manufacturers are still squabbling about the standards for transferring data electronically. The paper continues to pile up while GM and Ford argue about how to change their traditional business processing into the new EDI format.

For more information, see William C. Symonds, "Getting Rid of Paper Is Just the Beginning," *Business Week*, December 21, 1992, pp. 88–89.

by the data dictionary and process descriptions. Later, this model will be used by the analyst to design the physical details of the system in the Design phase.

The Decisions of the Earlier Phase Revisited

Once the model of the current system has been prepared, further information is available regarding the problems inherent in the old system. Now the analyst is able to review the decisions previously made in the Preliminary Investigation phase and can verify that the initial understanding of the problem indeed led to the best choice. This reexamination may validate the feasibility report concerning the statement of the problem, confirm the feasibility issues regarding the proposed system, and verify the recommended solution as the most suitable one for the problem. Or, since new information may have been uncovered by exploring the existing system in greater detail in this phase, modifications may now be made to the preliminary design produced in the Preliminary Investigation phase. In particular, the cost/benefit analysis will be revised to incorporate more detailed and accurate information. Management wants no surprises when presented with the finished project! It must always be aware of how much the project will cost and what financial benefits are anticipated. The systems analyst revamps the estimates of time and money to gauge the firm's commitment to the project as accurately as possible. The preliminary schedule for the project is also studied and revised as necessary to reflect the new knowledge acquired during the Analysis phase. After management's review and approval at the checkpoint for this phase, the analyst is ready to enter the Design phase.

The line between analysis and design is not clearcut. As we have seen, the analyst sketched out a preliminary design for the information system and reevaluated it in the Analysis phase. Before moving formally into the Design phase, the analyst may further refine this general design to keep the project firmly in hand. The control of the project, however, requires drawing a line between the Analysis and Design phases and using milestones to measure the project's progress. As with all aspects of the life cycle, the boundaries between the stages of the analyst's work are artificially drawn to assist in the project management activities and to ensure that the necessary tasks have been accomplished in a timely and satisfactory manner.

SUMMARY

The systems analyst is responsible for the analysis of the system that is performed during the two phases designated as Preliminary Investigation and Analysis. As this work of systems analysis begins, the analyst is aware of two basic principles:

1. The information system under consideration belongs to the users, not to the computer professionals.

2. The Triple-P principle of people, procedures, and policies must be considered in the design of any information system.

Because the system belongs to the users, user involvement in the analysis and design of the system is crucial in creating a system that fulfills the users' needs and gives them the greatest satisfaction.

The life cycle of an information system begins with the submission of a user request for computing services. The user request is reviewed by management, which decides whether to investigate the request further. In many organizations, this decision is made by a Steering Committee of managers familiar with the goals and resources of the organization. Before the Steering Committee can decide to allocate scarce computing resources to solve the problem at hand, more information is required. Thus, the systems analyst is assigned to perform a feasibility study; this life cycle phase is called Preliminary Investigation. The feasibility study is composed of five activities:

1. A study of the current system is undertaken.
2. The user's problem is restated to reflect the real cause of the problem.
3. A set of preliminary solutions, called alternative solutions, is specified.
4. These solutions are evaluated with regard to the four feasibility issues of economic, technical, operational, and scheduling feasibility, and the best solution is selected by the analyst.
5. A report of these activities is prepared.

When searching for the best solution to the problem, the analyst is aware that reengineering the business system by the innovative use of computer technology and telecommunications should be considered. In studying the current system, the analyst remembers *HIM*, which stands for three possible sources of the user's problem: Human interfaces, Information deficiencies, and Mistakes in the system.

The alternative solutions are examined with regard to the four issues of economic, technical, operational, and scheduling feasibility. From the set of alternative solutions, the analyst recommends the best one based on the trade-offs between the alternative solutions. The findings of the analyst are then formally presented to the Steering Committee accompanied by the written documentation known as the feasibility report. After management has approved the project for development, the analyst proceeds to the Analysis phase.

The objectives of the Analysis phase are: to prepare a model of the proposed system, to review and modify the results of the Preliminary Investigation phase, and to establish a more detailed schedule for the systems development process. To meet the first objective, modeling the proposed system, the current system is studied further to deepen the initial understanding gained in the first phase. A formal methodology such as that of data flow diagrams is recommended for the creation of the model for the existing system. Yet if the analyst is thoroughly familiar with the current system and adequate documentation is already on hand, the study of the current study may be omitted. After this model has been completed, the analyst prepares a detailed model of the proposed system. The feasibility report is reviewed and more precise estimates of the feasibility issues are prepared. The schedule for the remainder of the life cycle is revised according to the new knowledge gained in this phase. These revised figures together with the models of the existing and proposed systems are submitted to management. If approved, the system enters the Design phase of the life cycle.

TERMS

analysis phase	model
feasibility issues	preliminary investigation phase
economic	reengineering
operational	systems analysis
technical	trade-offs
scheduling	triple-P principle
feasibility report	people
HIM problems	procedures
human factors	policies
information deficiencies	user
mistakes or glitches	user request form

QUESTIONS

1. Name and briefly describe the activities of the Preliminary Investigation phase.

2. Why does the Preliminary Investigation phase exist? Why not start the systems development process with the Analysis phase?

3. What is the purpose of the user request form? Why doesn't the user directly approach the systems analyst?

4. List the major steps in the Analysis phase and indicate which steps also occur in the Preliminary Investigation phase. Identify the documents produced by each major step.

5. Explain what is meant by the issue of human factors for an information system.

6. **a.** Provide an example of an information system that is not technically feasible.

    b. Describe an information system that is not operationally feasible.

c. Is it possible that the information system you described in part (b) would be operationally feasible for a different organization? Why or why not?

PROJECTS

1. The First National Bank of Fort Sumter, Illinois, has automated teller machines (ATMs) at three different locations in town. The two other banks in Fort Sumter also offer ATM service. The bank now believes that the cost of these ATMs exceeds their financial benefits. There is a major university in Fort Sumter, and the students use the ATMs frequently to withdraw very small amounts of cash—five or ten dollars at a time. Prepare a 2- or 3-page paper that discusses the following topics:
   a. The reasons that banks nationwide use ATMs
   b. The banks that provide ATM service in your local area
   c. The feasibility issues that the First National Bank should study prior to a decision about discontinuing its ATM service

   To answer these questions, you may wish to contact a local bank that provides ATM services. If there is a local financial institution that does not provide ATM services, contact that organization and ascertain its rationale for not providing such services.

2. Jane Murphy is the project leader for the development of her firm's new inventory system. Since she sees a basic need for better project management overall, she has proposed the creation of an information system that will track the development of all information systems at the firm. If such a system were in place within two months, it could control the inventory system development process. Jane thinks that the benefits to the firm will be the completion of projects within cost and schedule estimates. Unfortunately, no dollar figure can be easily placed on her beliefs. Assume the following details about Jane's proposal:

   ■ The estimated cost of building such a system in-house is $100,000 with an elapsed time of 6 months.
   ■ The system can easily be added to the local PC network, giving all managers access to the system. No special hardware costs need to be incurred.
   ■ The other project managers told Jane that they like their individually fashioned project management systems and don't want to change. Although Jane also has her own paper-and-pencil system to track project development, she really wants better documentation of the activities performed within the life cycle.

   Now discuss Jane's proposal by answering the following questions.
   a. Prepare the user request form for the project management system in the format shown in Figure 3-4.

    b. Discuss the four feasibility issues for this proposed project management system.

    c. If you were a member of the Steering Committee, would you vote for the Preliminary Investigation phase to be performed? Justify your answer.

    d. Outline the steps the systems analyst must undertake for the Preliminary Investigation phase with regard to Jane's request for the new project management system. Relate your steps directly to the information system proposed by Jane.

REFERENCES

Dykman, Charlene A., and Ruth Robbins. "Organizational Success through Effective Systems Analysis." *Journal of Systems Management* 42(7), July 1991, pp. 6–8.

Lin, Engming, and Phillip Ashcroft. "A Case of Systems Development in a Hostile Environment." *Journal of Systems Management* 41(4), April 1990, pp. 11–14.

Martin, James. *An Information Systems Manifesto.* Englewood Cliffs, NJ: Prentice-Hall, 1984.

Page-Jones, Melilir. *The Practical Guide to Structured Systems Design.* Englewood Cliffs, NJ: Prentice-Hall, 1988.

Powers, Michael J., David R. Adams, and Harlan D. Mills. *Computer Information Systems Development: Analysis and Design.* Cincinnati: South-Western, 1984.

Prescott, Jon R. "Using Structured Methodology for Project Success." *Journal of Systems Management* 42(7), July 1991, pp. 28–31.

"The Ubiquitous Machine." *The Economist* 315(7659), June 16, 1990, pp. 5–20.

CHAPTER 4

Cost/Benefit Analysis

Objectives

The issue of financial feasibility is a key factor in deciding whether an information system should be implemented. The goal of this chapter is the mastery of the techniques used to calculate financial feasibility. After you have completed this chapter, you will understand the following:

■ How to prepare a cost/benefit analysis for an information system

■ The time value of money and how to compute the present value of returns on an investment

■ The difference between tangible and intangible costs and benefits

■ The one-time and ongoing costs for an information system

■ The types of benefits that may result from implementing a new information system

■ The three methods used to compare the costs and benefits of an information system: net discounted present value, payback period, and internal rate of return

■ The role of managerial discretion in evaluating the merits of a proposed system

WHY PERFORM A COST/BENEFIT ANALYSIS?

Before management can decide to implement an information system, its costs and benefits must be estimated and compared with alternative investment opportunities. This procedure, a **cost/benefit analysis**, serves two purposes. First, it compares the costs of developing an information system with its projected benefits to see whether the expected benefits exceed the anticipated costs. If the costs are expected to outweigh the benefits, the system is not considered financially feasible. As we shall see, because the value of money is time dependent this analysis is less straightforward than it may appear to the novice. Second, the cost/benefit analysis allows us to compare the financial benefits of investment alternatives in order to identify the most desirable investment.

The following sections explain how to estimate the typical costs and benefits for an information system, and describe the three rules commonly used to assess the costs and benefits of investments. This discussion explains why the value of money is time dependent and how the present value of money is computed. This chapter concludes with the topic of managerial discretion, a crucial factor in determining whether to implement an information system.

FIGURE 4-1   **The cost/benefit items for cost/benefit analysis**

A	B
Projected System Costs	**Projected Annual Benefits**
One-time costs	Increase in cash flow
Capital	Increase in revenue
Developmental	Reduction in costs
Annual operating costs	Personnel costs
Fixed costs	Hardware costs
Administrative	Production costs
Salaries for permanent employees	Inventory costs
Maintenance–hardware and software Licensing and leasing fees	Interdepartmental communication costs
Variable costs	Intangible benefits
Depreciation	Goodwill
Supplies	
Hourly wage for temporary employees	

FIGURE 4-2
Capital costs

New Computer Hardware

Computer and related equipment

Upgrading of current equipment

Workstations

Telecommunication devices

Computer Software

General purpose software

    Data base management system

    Compilers

    CASE tools

    Other software packages

Software applications packages

    Payroll, inventory, human resources, etc.

Office Equipment

COST ANALYSIS

Regardless of the reasons for implementing a computer information system, management typically wants to know the extent of the financial investment required. All projected **costs** are classified as either *one-time* or *recurring* (that is, *annual operating costs*). Column A in Figure 4-1 lists both types of costs for a typical information system.

One-Time Costs

As their name implies, **one-time costs** occur only once during the implementation of the system. As shown in column A of Figure 4-1, one-time costs are further divided into *capital costs* and *developmental costs.*

CAPITAL COSTS

Capital costs consist of outright capital expenditures for the purchase of capital equipment or services. These costs can be estimated simply by contacting the suppliers of these items. Examples of capital cost items are listed in Figure 4-2. Three major expenses are listed under this category: computer hardware, computer software, and office equipment. Outlays incurred for buying a new computer or upgrading the current computer are examples of computer hardware costs. A new system may require additional software, such as a data base management system (DBMS) or a compiler for the selected programming language. If the decision is made to purchase a software application package rather than build a custom-designed system, its price is entered as a capital cost. Finally, if office equipment must be purchased to support the new information system, this expense constitutes a separate category of the capital costs.

DEVELOPMENTAL COSTS

Developmental costs are those incurred for the development of the new system and the subsequent activities needed for conversion from the existing system. Because each system is an individual undertaking, it is impossible to list here the precise cost items for every conceivable system. Typical developmental costs, as shown in Figure 4-3, include administrative overhead, computer time charges, consulting expenditure, personnel and training, office supplies, work lost due to disruption, communication charges, and travel.

The highest single expenditure among developmental costs is usually the wages for the computer professionals employed for the project. Building a major information system is labor intensive and requires many hours, months, and sometimes even years of effort. This cost is based on the estimated number of person-hours required to develop and implement the system. Guidelines for estimating the number of person-hours required for a project are presented in Chapter 5. Previous experience is helpful in estimating this cost as well as the remaining developmental costs.

In performing the developmental cost estimates, it is important to include all costs that will be incurred on the project. The administrative overhead for the project is a real cost that is oftentimes overlooked. When new computers or related equipment are installed, it may be necessary to hire

FIGURE 4-3
Typical developmental costs

Software Development	Conversion costs
Administrative overhead	Data base conversion
Computer charges	Training of employees
Consulting expenditure	Parallel running—personnel time, etc.
Personnel	
Training of computer personnel	
Office supplies	
Work lost due to disruption	
Communication charges	
Travel	

additional employees and to remodel the office to provide suitable space for the new equipment and personnel. For example, installing a local area network may require new electrical connections for the work stations throughout the office space. If additional employees were hired because of the new system, remodeling or acquiring new office facilities may also be needed. The costs for the expansion or remodeling of the present facilities are viewed as one-time administrative overhead.

The projected costs also include the use of computer resources required during the development of the system. A consulting firm used for any portion of the project would be listed here. Other costs are the office supplies required for the project staff, the travel costs incurred to communicate with persons off-site, and communication line charges for phone calls or computer transmission. Extensive training of the computer professionals may occur before the project is initiated, and these training costs are considered developmental costs. Finally, involving the users in the project may cause disruption and lead to work loss. Though more difficult to judge, this cost should not be forgotten.

CONVERSION COSTS

Special attention must be given to an important segment of the developmental costs—the costs incurred for converting to the new system. There are three basic categories of **conversion costs**: data conversion, training, and parallel running.

First, the data stored by the old system must be converted for processing by the new system. Prior to the installation of the new system, the analyst determines which data must be converted and how this conversion will be accomplished. A hidden cost associated with this conversion stems from the resolution of errors found in the old data. Missing or grossly inaccurate data often plague manually kept files, and tracking errors and resolving discrepancies in the data can be costly. To safeguard against introducing errors during the transcription of manual data files to the new system files, *double keying* is recommended. First the old data records are keyed by a computer operator, then the same data are rekeyed and automatically compared to the first transcription. Any discrepancies exposed can then be resolved.

Second, in preparation for implementing the new information system, time must be set aside for training the employees to become proficient in operating the new information system. New techniques need to be mastered, and new routines must be familiarized. If new employees are hired, then the personnel must learn to work with each other in an efficient and harmonious manner. During the training period, employees do not perform tasks contributing to the current revenue; hence their salaries represent an overhead cost to the firm. Even after the installation of the new system, until employees become proficient in its operation, they may commit an excessive amount of errors. The resulting cost is still considered a training cost.

Since training cost cannot be recovered from current revenues, it must be treated as a part of the development costs to be recovered eventually within the life span of the information system.

Finally, for many systems the user will insist that the old system go on operating in conjunction with the new system for an initial time period. This mode of conversion is known as *parallel running*. Since both the old and the new systems are in use simultaneously, extra staff members are temporarily needed to handle the dual operation. Other potential expenses of parallel running include supplies and communication line charges. The costs for parallel operation must be counted as part of the conversion costs for the new system.

Annual Operating Costs

The **recurring costs** of a new information system are figured on an annual basis, and are known as **annual operating costs**. These costs are divided into *fixed costs* and *variable costs.*

FIXED COSTS

Costs that are constant throughout the year, independent of how intensively the information system is utilized, are known as **fixed costs**. Examples of fixed costs are administrative costs, leasing and licensing costs, maintenance contracts, and the salaries of permanent employees. Administrative costs are those associated with the supervision of the employees who use the information system. Leasing or licensing costs refer to the expenses incurred for the computer equipment or the software acquired for the project. When hardware or software is purchased, a contract for maintaining them may be negotiated for an annual fee. Such fees are also classified as fixed costs. If maintenance of in-house software is a budgeted item, this cost also belongs here. In addition, fixed costs cover the wages of those permanent employees who will be users of the new information system.

VARIABLE COSTS

Variable costs are those costs that vary according to the intensity with which the information system is utilized. Although the variable costs incurred in each period during the year are expected to be different, these costs are nonetheless estimated on an annual basis. For example, the cost of supplies incurred in each time period during the year will depend on how intensively the information system is utilized in that period; the total cost for supplies is nonetheless estimated as an aggregate for the entire year. Other examples of variable costs are the charges for computer usage, in-house software maintenance (if not a budgeted item), depreciation, and hourly wages for temporary employees.

BENEFIT ANALYSIS

Benefits associated with increased cash flows are invariably estimated on a yearly basis. Unlike costs, benefits seldom occur on a one-time basis. A new information system may offer *increased revenue* or a *reduction of costs*. In either case, the information system leads to an increased cash flow. The specific anticipated benefits depend on what system is implemented. A category of typical benefits appears in column B of Figure 4-1.

> ### Warning
>
> Don't confuse the *benefits* of a system with its *features*. Faster processing of orders is not a benefit, but the resultant reduction in personnel requirements is definitely a tangible benefit.

An increase in revenue for a firm may occur in a variety of ways. Consider a new inventory control system that helps a firm carry adequate inventory to meet the demand for goods. Because customers no longer have to wait for out-of-stock items, sales will increase. In addition, if a new order processing system operates more rapidly and efficiently than before, an increase in revenue can be expected. Since the processing of orders must precede the shipping of merchandise and the issuing of invoices, the improved order processing system should bring in customer payments sooner than before. Revenue increases as a result.

Cost reductions also occur for various reasons. Most likely, the new information system requires fewer employees, thus leading to a direct reduction in costs. Having fewer staff positions may save some salaries per year, but management typically looks for even greater financial benefits. As computer costs steadily decline, the replacement of existing hardware with less costly equipment may provide such savings. The present trend to down-size by installing smaller computers, perhaps by employing personal computer networks rather than a mainframe, is driven by such cost considerations. Data processing costs will also decrease if the new information system requires less in-house maintenance. For example, when the new system employs techniques that facilitate software maintenance, future maintenance costs will decline.

The new system may also contribute to a cost reduction through its effect on business operations. If the new system streamlines the factory operations or reduces the carrying costs of inventory, savings will occur. Similarly, better interdepartmental communications may result from efficient reports and the on-line query capabilities of the new system, thus realizing savings through improved business operations.

An *expert system* is another cost-saving avenue the firm may use. This type of system captures the skill of a staff member who is highly proficient in performing particular tasks. If the employee's expertise can be replicated by an expert system, then other employees will be able to perform these tasks without that knowledge and skill. The value of the expert system can be appraised by judging how long it would take to train another individual to acquire the needed abilities. The more time it would take, the more valuable the expert system would be. In short, the value of an expert system is the capitalization of the costs saved in training employees to acquire the knowledge and skill needed to replace the expert system.

INTANGIBLE COSTS AND BENEFITS

Thus far, we have discussed only **tangible costs and benefits** derived from tangible assets, such as a piece of equipment or a sum of money. However, an asset need not be tangible; it can be a capitalization of some abstract earning power. For example, *goodwill* is the capitalized value of the firm's excess earning power resulting from its trademark or reputation. Conversely, a loss of goodwill may result if the firm's reputation is damaged by unfavorable publicity or a prolonged dispute with its workers.

Associated with the intangible assets are the **intangible costs or benefits**. For example, an intangible cost arises if a new computer information system leads to a loss of goodwill from the firm's employees, who are disgruntled and unhappy about the new system. Their unhappiness affects morale and productivity, which in turn increase the firm's operating cost.

There are also many intangible benefits associated with the installation of a new information system. For example, a new information system may enable the firm to supply information to customers by providing them with the capability to browse the data base using a fourth-generation language. When information is easily and quickly accessible, business decisions can be made with greater ease and confidence. The result is an improvement in the customers' business conditions, which naturally translates into goodwill towards the firm and contributes to the firm's own revenue growth.

Sometimes intangible benefits arise under the firm's strategic considerations. Suppose a rival firm has installed an information system with 4GL browsing capability. If the firm's own customers request similar services, failure to comply risks a loss of goodwill and places the firm at a competitive disadvantage. Clearly, from the strategic point of view there are intangible benefits associated with an information system.

The distinguishing feature of intangible costs and benefits is that their values are highly subjective and, therefore, cannot be assessed in an objective manner. We shall have more to say about this point later in the chapter. Here, we only wish to make clear that as a practical matter, the analyst must use a rule of thumb or a best guess method to assign a value for the intangible costs and benefits. To demonstrate, we offer an example. Under the firm's current information system, the sales volume is 20,000 orders per year with an average value of $2,000 per order. The orders are backlogged in the order processing system for an average of 2 weeks. The new information system promises to handle orders within a 3-day processing period and thus create goodwill among the customers. This increased goodwill, in turn, will cause the firm's sales to increase. Hence, the new information system offers both tangible and intangible benefits. Now, how do we set their value?

The tangible benefits of the new system are easy to compute. Note that the new information system enables the firm to save 11 days for order processing. If the invoice accompanies delivery of the merchandise, then payment from the customers will be received 11 days sooner. Since the average order is $2,000 and approximately 50 orders are received per day, the new system instantly improves the cash flow a total of $100,000 times 11 days, or $1,100,000 a year. Assuming an interest rate of 10% per annum, the annual savings in interest charges will be $110,000.

Computing the monetary value of intangible benefits of the new information system is less straightforward. To do so, the analyst generally relies on a rule of thumb or a best guess formula. A commonly used formula requires the management to state the profit margin per order and to forecast the greatest, the average, and the least increase in orders per annum due to improved goodwill. The formula for **goodwill gain** is stated as follows:

Goodwill gain = $0.2GP + 0.5AP + 0.3LP$

where G = Greatest percentage increase in sales $\times$ total volume of sales

P = Profit margin $\times$ value of average order

A = Average percentage increase in sales $\times$ total volume of sales

L = Least percentage increase in sales $\times$ total volume of sales

The management's reply to the question about the highest, average, and lowest improvement in sales is 10%, 5%, and 1%, respectively, and the profit margin is estimated to be 10% per order. Based on the above formula, the monetary value of the goodwill gain becomes

$$\begin{aligned} \text{Goodwill gain} &= 0.2(0.1 \times 20,000)(0.1 \times \$2,000) \\ &+ 0.5(0.05 \times 20,000)(0.1 \times \$2,000) \\ &+ 0.3(0.01 \times 20,000)(0.1 \times \$2,000) \\ &= \$80,000 + \$100,000 + \$12,000 \\ &= \$192,000 \end{aligned}$$

Despite the fact that a concrete value has been assigned to the goodwill gain, we again wish to remind the reader that this estimated goodwill gain is highly imprecise. There is no way to guarantee that the customers will actually order more merchandise once a system capable of processing more orders per day is installed.

Now that we have completely characterized the tangible and intangible costs and benefits, we are ready to assess the costs and benefits associated

The Proposed System (One-Time Costs)			75,000
Capital costs			
New equipment		25,000	
Software		40,000	
Office equipment		10,000	
Developmental costs			25,000
Administrative overhead		3,000	
Consulting expenditure		7,000	
Personnel		10,000	
Training of computer personnel		2,000	
Office supplies		1,000	
Work lost due to disruption		2,000	
Annual operating costs			10,000
Fixed costs		6,000	
Administrative costs	1,500		
Leasing and licensing costs	500		
Salaries and benefits of regular employees	4,000		
Variable costs		4,000	
Computer charges	500		
Supplies	500		
Maintenance	500		
Depreciation	1,500		
Hourly wages	1,000		

Annual Benefits			40,000
Increase in revenue		20,000	
Actual and tangible	18,000		
Goodwill	2,000		
Reduction in costs		20,000	
Data processing costs	10,000		
Production costs	4,000		
Inventory costs	5,000		
Interdepartmental communication costs	1,000		

with a new information system. Let the costs and benefits of such a system be given in Figures 4-4 and 4-5, respectively. With this information in hand, we can proceed to the next stage of the cost/benefit analysis.

COMPARISON OF COSTS AND BENEFITS

After the costs and benefits of a system have been calculated, the next step is to compare them and to see if the system is financially feasible. If all the costs and benefits were incurred instantaneously, this comparison would be a simple matter. The net benefits of the system could be computed immediately as the difference between the benefits and costs. In reality, however, both costs and benefits occur over time. Even the purchase costs for hardware may be distributed over time if the accounting department so decrees. Any comparison must take into account the distribution of the costs and benefits of the system over time and the *time value of money.* Three methods are commonly used to perform a cost/benefit analysis:

Net present value

Payback period

Internal rate of return

Because the value of money is time dependent and affects the analysis of costs and benefits, we will explain the time value of money before discussing the three cost/benefit analysis techniques.

Time Value of Money

By **time value of money**, we mean that money has a time dimension and its value depends on when it is received. In other words, the value of money is time dependent. If you have $100 today and place it in a bank account that pays 5% interest per annum, at the end of the year the $5 interest earned is added to the $100 principle for a total value of $105. Each year that the money remains invested, it gains in value. This example illustrates the *future value* of current money. But what is a sum of money worth when it is not available for another year? If you give me $105 a year from now, is it equivalent to the $105 that I hold in my hand today? Of course not. Because of the chance to earn a return on today's dollar in the lending market, the dollar spent or received today is not the same as the dollar spent or received tomorrow. Again assuming a market interest rate of 5% per annum, the $105 you will give me next year is worth $100 today.

Thus, given the prevailing interest rate, future monetary value can be discounted backwards to obtain its *discounted present value (DPV).* By using the discounted present values of future amounts, we can compare values of money to be received or expended at different periods of time. Note that the method for discounting forecasted future values is based on the prevailing interest rate. Assuming that the market interest rate is i% per annum, an investment of P dollars today compounded annually will grow to F dollars in t years by the following formula:

$$F = P(1 + i)^t$$

Suppose we reverse the process and assume that you are offered a contract of F dollars to be paid t years hence. Given that the market interest rate is $i\%$ per annum, how much is the F dollars to be received in t years worth to you today? The answer, of course, is P dollars. Thus, the **discounted present value (DPV)** of F dollars received in t years, with the assumption of a prevailing market interest rate of i, is given by the formula

$$P = F\left(\frac{1}{(1 + i)^t}\right)$$

For example, assuming a 5% interest rate, let us compute the present value of $20,000 to be received a year from now. By the formula, we have

$$\text{DPV of } \$20,000 \text{ in 1 year's time} = \$20,000\left(\frac{1}{(1 + .05)^1}\right)$$
$$= \$19,047.62$$

If we examine the present value of $20,000 to be received 2 years later, we have

$$\text{DPV of } \$20,000 \text{ in 2 years' time} = \$20,000\left(\frac{1}{(1 + .05)^2}\right)$$
$$= \$18,140.59$$

To simplify the computational work, a table of discounting factors for various interest rates can be used (see Figure 4-6), although today these calculations are usually performed on spreadsheets. The discounted present value for

FIGURE 4-6   The discounting factors for calculating the discounted present value

Year	Formula for Discounting Factor	Interest Rates					
		5%	6%	7%	8%	9%	10%
1	$1/(1 + i)$	0.952	0.944	0.935	0.926	0.917	0.909
2	$1/(1 + i)^2$	0.907	0.890	0.873	0.857	0.842	0.826
3	$1/(1 + i)^3$	0.864	0.840	0.816	0.794	0.772	0.751
4	$1/(1 + i)^4$	0.823	0.792	0.763	0.735	0.708	0.683
5	$1/(1 + i)^5$	0.784	0.747	0.713	0.681	0.650	0.621

FIGURE 4-7   The discounted present value for $20,000 over a 5-year period at 5% interest

Year	0	1	2	3	4	5
Initial Outlay	50,000					
Annual Benefits		20,000	20,000	20,000	20,000	20,000
Discounting Factor		0.952	0.907	0.864	0.823	0.784
Discounted Present Value		19,047.62	18,140.59	17,276.75	16,454.05	15,670.52
Cumulative DPV		19,047.62	37,188.21	54,464.96	70,919.01	86,589.53

the annual benefits of $20,000 for a 5-year period is shown in Figure 4-7. By summing the discounted present values for each year, we find that the discounted benefits total $86,589.53.

Not only must the benefits be discounted to their present values, the costs must be discounted as well. In the example of Figure 4-7, only an initial outlay of $50,000 is incurred in the present period. Since its discounting factor is equal to 1, the discounted present value of the initial outlay remains $50,000.

Now that the discounting of future benefits and costs has been illustrated by this simple example, we can discuss the net present value method of cost/benefit analysis, which uses discounted present values to evaluate the financial merits of an investment.

Net Present Value

After the discounted present values have been computed for the future costs and benefits, the net present value of an investment is obtained. **Net present value (NPV)** is the sum of the discounted present values of benefits minus the sum of the discounted present values of the costs. For an information system, NPV can be stated more simply:

NPV = (Sum of DPV for yearly net benefits) − Initial outlay

The value of the *yearly net benefits* is computed by subtracting the annual costs from the annual benefits. The *initial outlay* is the amount required for the implementation of the system prior to its operation.

The financial worth of an investment can be appraised by inspecting its net present value. Two rules govern investments under the NPV analysis:

Rule 1   The investment project is feasible if NPV > 0 within the lifetime of the system.

Rule 2   Among the feasible investment projects, choose the one with the largest NPV.

Rule 1 simply means that the initial outlay for an investment must be paid for by its net benefits during its life span. Rule 2 states that the best investment among alternative investments is the one with the greatest net present value.

When examining the financial feasibility of information systems (or any other investment), the life span of the system must also be considered. The typical lifetime of an information system for mainframe or medium range computers is 5 years, while a system built for personal computers lasts only about 3 years. The rapid changes in hardware and software affect the projected lifetime of any information system. Today, regardless of hardware platforms, many companies wish to regain their investments within a 3-year span. Thus, an information system project that would pay for itself in 6 years under current market conditions will be viewed as a poor investment, since the system will probably be obsolete before it pays for itself.

Let us illustrate the computation of NPV for an information system based on the projected costs and benefits outlined in Figures 4-4 and 4-5. The initial outlay for the system conveniently totals $100,000 and the annual benefits total $40,000. It is important to note that actual costs for a major system will be much higher, while a smaller system may cost much less. In addition, the ongoing costs and benefits may differ each year during the projected 5-year life of the system.

Given the yearly costs and benefits, we compute the value of the net benefits for each year by subtracting the yearly costs from the yearly benefits, as shown in Figure 4-8. Next we discount the net benefits for the 5-year period to obtain their discounted present values. The sum of the discounted present values of the net benefits represents the net present value for the project. Figure 4-9 shows the worksheet for the NPV. Here, a market interest rate of 5% has been assumed, and the discounting factors are displayed to clarify the calculations. After 5 years, the net present value is $29,884.30. Since the NPV is positive, this information system is deemed to be financially feasible.

FIGURE 4-8 The computation of net benefits

Year	0	1	2	3	4	5
Initial Outlay	100,000					
Annual Costs		10,000	10,000	10,000	10,000	10,000
Annual Benefits		40,000	40,000	40,000	40,000	40,000
Net Benefits		30,000	30,000	30,000	30,000	30,000

FIGURE 4-9   **The worksheet showing the computation of net present value at 5% interest**

Year	0	1	2	3	4	5
Initial Outlay	100,000					
Net Benefits		30,000	30,000	30,000	30,000	30,000
Discounting Factor		0.952	0.907	0.864	0.823	0.784
Discounted Net Benefits		28,571.43	27,210.88	25,915.13	24,681.07	23,505.78
Cumulative Discounted Net Benefits		28,571.43	55,782.31	81,697.44	106,378.52	129,884.30
Net present value = $129,884.30 − $100,000 = $29,884.30						

Although feasible, the proposed information system may still be unde-sirable. The proposed system is desirable only if its NPV exceeds the NPVs of the competing investment projects. To illustrate, let us compare the NPVs of the proposed system and the present system. Suppose the relevant cost/benefit data associated with the existing information system are as given in Figure 4-10. Comparing the information in Figures 4-9 and 4-10, we observe two major differences. First, the initial outlay for the proposed system is $100,000, while the initial outlay for the existing system is $0. The reason is that unless the already installed system has some resale value (which we do not assume), its historical initial outlay must be considered as an unrecov-erable sunken cost and should not enter into the NPV calculation. The second major difference is that the operating expenses of the existing system are higher and the benefits lower than those of the proposed system. Each year, the ongoing costs of the existing system increase while its benefits remain stable. The higher operating costs reflect the fact that the old system requires greater maintenance.

Thus there is a trade-off between the two systems. Retaining the old system saves the initial outlay but will incur higher operating costs. Con-versely, investing in the new system saves operating costs but must incur a high initial expense. Should we invest in the new system or continue with the existing system? That depends on the ranking of the NPVs associated with the two systems. The NPV of the old system, $9,080.99, is less than the NPV of the new system, $29,884.30. According to Rule 2, the new system is not only feasible but desirable. The firm should invest in the new information system.

FIGURE 4-10   **The net present value for the existing system at 5% interest**

Year	0	1	2	3	4	5
Initial Outlay	0					
Costs		14,000	15,000	16,000	17,000	18,000
Benefits		18,000	18,000	18,000	18,000	18,000
Net Benefits		4,000	3,000	2,000	1,000	0
Discounting Factor		0.952	0.907	0.864	0.823	0.784
Discounted Net Benefits		3,809.52	2,721.09	1,727.68	822.70	0
Cumulative Discounted Net Benefits		3,809.52	6,530.61	8,258.29	9,080.99	9,080.99
Net present value = $9,080.99						

The Payback Period Analysis

One characteristic of any investment program is that the capital good must be put in place before it can generate any revenue. Because the capital outlay is incurred at the outset, whereas the benefits derived accrue period by period in the future, revenues will always lag behind costs in the early periods of the capital good's life. This lag is accentuated by the fact that even after the capital good has been installed, additional operating expenses will continue to be incurred. Since the future is uncertain, the investor cannot forecast future revenues and costs with complete accuracy. Investment is, therefore, a risky undertaking. A risk averse manager naturally desires to recoup the investment as quickly as possible. This desire to recover invest-ment expenditures motivates the *payback period* analysis. By using this analysis, the manager can discover the **payback period**; that is, how much time will elapse before the accrued benefits overtake the accrued costs.

To describe how this method works, we will examine the costs and benefits for the information system initially analyzed with the NPV method. The data in Figure 4-9 are again used to generate the payback period analysis displayed in Figure 4-11, still assuming a market interest rate of 5%. To obtain the discounted net benefits of the system, the difference between the discounted present value of the benefits and costs for each year was com-

FIGURE 4-11 **The payback period analysis for the sample information system at 5% interest**

Year	0	1	2	3	4	5
Initial Outlay (IO)	100,000					
Annual Costs		10,000	10,000	10,000	10,000	10,000
Annual Benefits		40,000	40,000	40,000	40,000	40,000
Net Benefits		30,000	30,000	30,000	30,000	30,000
Discounting Factor		0.952	0.907	0.864	0.823	0.784
Discounted Net Benefits		28,571.43	27,210.88	25,915.13	24,681.07	23,505.78
Cumulative Discounted Net Benefits (CDNB)		28,571.43	55,782.31	81,697.44	106,378.52	129,884.30
Amount Repaid: CDNB − IO		−71,428.57	−44,217.69	−18,302.56	6,378.52	29,884.30
Payback period = 3 + (18,302.56/24,681.07) years = 3.74 years						

puted and then summed to find its net present value. In addition, the cumulative discounted net benefits (CDNB) for each year were listed. The last row in the table indicates the amount of the initial outlay (IO) that has not yet been repaid by the discounted net benefits. Inspecting the data in this row, we observe that until year 4 the cumulative discounted net benefits fall short of the initial outlay of $100,000. In year 4 the reverse occurs. Since the discounted net benefits overtake the initial outlay within the fourth year, we can define the payback period of the information system precisely. The calculation is performed in the following way. At the end of 3 years, the firm has made $81,697.44 and still needs $18,302.56 in order to recover the initial outlay of $100,000. Since the firm is expected to make $24,681.07 in the fourth year, we divide $18,302.56 by $24,681.07 and find that it will take about ¾ of the fourth year to accomplish this feat. Consequently, the payback period is 3.74 years.

Is a 3.74-year payback period satisfactory to the management? The systems analyst cannot say. This judgment depends on the risk attitude of the manager. Moreover, many corporations set payback period guidelines for all investments. Suppose the firm has stated that all investments must have a payback period less than or equal to 5 years. With a payback period of 3.74 years, the proposed information system looks like a good investment. However, if the lifetime of this system is estimated at only 3 years, then the investment must be rated as poor.

In general, the payback period requirement will reflect the risk attitude of the manager. The more risk averse is the manager, the more swiftly must the initial investment be recovered, hence the shorter the required payback period. Not surprisingly, the payback period is also related to the interest rate. The higher the interest rate, the longer is the payback period for any investment. This observation implies that, given any payback period requirement, the higher the discount rate, the harder it is for any investment to meet this established policy. In this sample information system, suppose the discount rate is 10% rather than 5%. The cumulative discounted net benefits for a market interest rate of 10% are given by Figure 4-12. These discounted values are less than those calculated for a market interest rate of 5% (see Figure 4-11). The decline in cumulative discounted net benefits raises the payback period to 4.26 years. Based on the 5-year payback requirement stipulated by management, this information system remains financially feasible.

FIGURE 4-12   The payback period analysis for the sample information system at 10% interest

Year	0	1	2	3	4	5
Initial Outlay (IO)	100,000					
Annual Costs		10,000	10,000	10,000	10,000	10,000
Annual Benefits		40,000	40,000	40,000	40,000	40,000
Net Benefits		30,000	30,000	30,000	30,000	30,000
Discounting Factor		0.909	0.826	0.751	0.683	0.621
Discounted Net Benefits		27,272.73	24,793.39	22,539.44	20,490.40	18,627.64
Cumulative Discounted Net Benefits (CDNB)		27,272.73	52,066.12	74,605.56	95,095.96	113,723.60
Amount Repaid: CDNB − IO		−72,727.27	−47,933.88	−25,394.44	−4,904.04	13,723.60
Payback Period = 4 + (4,904.04/18,627.64) years = 4.26 years						

As with the net present value method, caution must be taken in appraising the development of information systems. The rapid changes in hardware and software mean that information systems typically have a maximum life of 5 years, and only 3 years for personal computer systems. Consequently, a risk averse manager, knowing the volatility of the computer hardware and software markets, would want to recoup the initial project investment as quickly as possible. The shorter the payback period, the more desirable is the information system.

The Internal Rate of Return Method

A third method for evaluating the financial merits of a proposed investment is to compute the **internal rate of return (IRR)**. This method is appropriate for evaluating projects to be financed by the firm's own funds. Suppose a machine costs $100. At the end of a year, it produces a profit (total revenue minus total operating cost) of $120 and then collapses beyond repair. After deducting the initial investment of $100, $20 is left. This $20 represents the return on the initial investment, and the ratio $20/$100, or 20%, is called the internal rate of return on the investment. To put it another way, the internal rate of return on the $100 investment is defined as the value d that satisfies the equation

$$\$100 = \frac{\$120}{1 + d}$$

The value of d in this case is, of course, 20%.

Actually, because the life span of a capital good is more than 1 year, the computation of d is more involved. Suppose a capital good's expected life span is T years, its cost is x, and it is expected to generate a net return of R_t in year t, where $t = 1, \ldots, T$. The internal rate of return is defined as the largest number d that satisfies the equation

$$x = \sum_{t=1}^{T} \frac{R_t}{(1 + d)^t}$$

For our sample system with an assumed lifetime of 5 years, the internal rate of return is expressed as the largest d that satisfies the equation

$$\$100,000 = \frac{\$30,000}{1 + d} + \frac{\$30,000}{(1 + d)^2} + \frac{\$30,000}{(1 + d)^3} + \frac{\$30,000}{(1 + d)^4} + \frac{\$30,000}{(1 + d)^5}$$

To perform this calculation, the use of a computer is recommended. The computation of the internal rate of return d is available as a standard function in spreadsheet software. For this example, the value d turns out to be 15.3%.

The investment criteria under the internal rate of return regime are given by the following two rules:

Rule 1   The manager should consider projects whose internal rate of return is greater than or equal to the market interest rate and should reject projects that fail to meet this standard.

Rule 2   Among the feasible projects, the manager should choose the one that gives the largest internal rate of return.

Having obtained the internal rate of return associated with the proposed information system, we now apply the decision rules to determine whether the project at hand is feasible. Let us assume that the market interest rate is 10%. Since the internal rate of return for the information system is 15.3%, which is greater than the market interest rate of 10%, according to Rule 1 the investment project is judged to be financially feasible. Nonetheless, management must still weigh the financial merits of this project against other competing investment opportunities. Should there be another project whose IRR is greater than 15.3%, then, according to Rule 2, the superior project should be chosen for implementation.

As the reader may have suspected, the net present value method and the internal rate of return method are closely related. In fact, for the purpose of screening proposals, the screening criteria (Rule 1) of the two methods are equivalent.[1] Despite the fact that the screening rules of the two methods lead to identical acceptance or rejection of potential investment projects, the rankings of the financially feasible investments based on Rule 2 of the two methods are not always the same. To illustrate this point, consider two proposed projects, A and B, each with an initial investment of $1,000 and a life span of 3 years. Their estimated net benefits differ as shown in Figure 4-13. Project A has an annual benefit of $500 for the 3 years; project B has no

---

[1]This equivalence is easily demonstrated. First, we know that the IRR d for a project satisfies the equality

$$\sum_{t=1}^{T} \frac{(\text{Net benefits})_{\text{year } t}}{(1+d)^t} = \text{Initial outlay} \tag{1}$$

We also know that the NPV of the same project has the property

$$\sum_{t=1}^{T} \frac{(\text{Net benefits})_{\text{year } t}}{(1+i)^t} > \text{Initial outlay} \qquad \text{if the NPV} > 0 \tag{2}$$

$$< \text{Initial outlay} \qquad \text{if the NPV} < 0 \tag{3}$$

Assuming the project has a positive NPV, then equation (1) and inequality (2) together imply that the left-hand side of (1) is less than the left-hand side of (2). Since the terms $(\text{Net benefits})_{\text{year } t}$ are identical in (1) and (2), the above statement implies that $d > i$. Likewise, assuming the project has a negative NPV, then equation (1) and inequality (3) together imply $d < i$. Consequently, the IRR and NPV methods lead to the same investment selection decisions; that is, if the project is acceptable (unacceptable) by the NPV rule, it must also be acceptable (unacceptable) by the IRR rule.

FIGURE 4-13 **The comparison of two projects with different benefits**

	Initial Investment	Year 1 Net Benefits	Year 2 Net Benefits	Year 3 Net Benefits
Project A	$1,000	$500	$500	$ 500
Project B		$ 0	$ 0	$1600

benefits for the first 2 years but accrues $1600 in benefits the third year. The IRRs for the two projects are

23.4% for Project A

16.9% for Project B

Assuming the market interest rate is 5%, their NPVs are

$361.62 for Project A

$382.14 for Project B

Based on the above computation, it is evident that both projects are feasible. This is because according to Rule 1 under the IRR method, both projects A and B yield internal rates of return greater than the market interest rate, and according to Rule 1 under the NPV method, both projects A and B yield positive net present values. Project A ranks above project B by Rule 2 under the IRR method, while the opposite is true under Rule 2 of the NPV method. Thus, the ranking of the two projects under the two methods are shown to be inconsistent.

However, the difference in the rankings of these projects is sensitive to the market interest rate. Suppose the market interest rate is increased from 5% to 10%. This increase in interest rate does not affect the project ranking under the IRR method but does under the NPV method. Specifically, the NPVs now become

$243.43 for Project A

$202.10 for Project B

Based on Rule 2 under the NPV method, the ranking of the two projects is now consistent with that under the IRR method.

This simple example demonstrates that in ranking the investment projects, the IRR method does not depend on the market interest rate, whereas the NPV method does. As a consequence, under a certain range of interest rates, the two methods will render different judgments on project rankings. That internal rates of returns are independent of market interest rate is understandable, since the IRR method is designed to select investment projects financed by internal funds.

Managerial Discretion

Thus far, we have presented the objective method of selecting investment projects. The analyst uses the data available to assess whether an information system should be adopted by the business enterprise. However, not all business decisions are based on purely objective analysis. Because the business environment is highly uncertain and the information content imperfect, important decisions must be tempered with judgement. The manager who takes the analyst's cost/benefit analysis under advisement must use judgement to make the ultimate decision about whether the information system should be installed. It is not uncommon that the manager will reverse the analyst's recommendation. In this section, we shall discuss two such cases. The first case focuses on the situation where the manager disagrees with the analyst's routine assessment of the intangible benefits accrued to the information system and decides to adopt the system despite the analyst's advice against it. The second case illustrates the impact of uncertainty on investment decisions. Here the manager's aversion to risk prompts rejection of the analyst's favorable recommendation of the information system.

REVISING INTANGIBLE ASSET VALUES

As we observed earlier, the calculations of costs and benefits associated with any investment project must include intangible items. Owing to the fact that the assessment of intangible costs and benefits is highly subjective, the analyst and the manager will more often than not disagree on these assessments. The disagreement is understandable since their backgrounds and perspectives are different. The analyst, lacking knowledge about the market, must adopt a rule of thumb method to assign values to the firm's intangible assets. The manager, who knows the firm's environment and its strategic postures, will instead use personal judgement to assign values to these assets. Frequently, the manager finds that the rule of thumb method grossly undervalues the firm's intangible assets. Under these circumstances, the manager may overrule the analyst's recommendation against an improved information system and allow the system to go forward. Some concrete examples will make this point clear.

The public's image of a hospital's technological capability greatly affects the demand for its services. Not surprisingly, a hospital attempts to improve its image by reminding the public that it is equipped with state-of-the-art medical technology. Because the public often views medical technology and information technology as complementary to each other, the manager will never run the risk of damaging the hospital's public image by refusing to adopt a modern information system. The refusal to adopt a state-of-the-art information system may create a false impression in the mind of the public that the hospital is lagging on all technological fronts. Because of this concern, the manager will always value highly the intangibles associated with an improved information system.

In a similar vein, a distribution outlet advertises that its new computerized inventory system enables the firm to fill orders faster without errors. The competing distribution outlets may be forced to follow suit by adopting similar systems. The failure to take the same action will give the impression to the customers that these firms are no longer efficient. This unfavorable impression among the customers may lower the market image of these firms and dull their competitive edge. Consequently, as a competitive measure, the managers of the rival firms may have no alternative but to follow the leader by adopting new computerized inventory systems. Each manager will do so even though the analyst, based on objective calculations, does not recommend the system's implementation.

Finally, there may also exist other nonfinancial reasons that lead to the demand for a new information system. In recent years, the proliferation of government regulations heightened these demands. For example, the Equal Employment Opportunity Act, the various environmental acts, and the host of tax laws all require that detailed records be kept for accountability to the government. Should complaints by or disputes with any governmental agency occur, the ability to present defensive evidence or to use information for expedient resolution of disputes may help the firm to avoid bad publicity, damaged public image, or even costly fines. The manager will assign high intangible values to information systems in the belief that such systems can furnish the needed information that will enable the firm to avoid these unpleasant consequences.

RISK ANALYSIS

The decision of whether to invest in an information system, as we have seen before, depends on the estimated net benefits generated by the information system. Since these estimates are never perfectly accurate, the investment decisions made under any of the three decision rules are always subject to error. There are two types of error. The first type arises when the firm should not have adopted the information system but did so; the second type arises when the firm should have adopted the information system but did not. Each type of error has a different impact. The difference stems from the fact that in committing errors of the first type, actual outlays were incurred, whereas, in committing errors of the second type opportunities were foregone but no real resources expended. Owing to the fact that mistakes involving actual capital outlays may produce spillover effects and thus greatly undermine the firm's financial health, the manager is most eager to control errors of the first type. Accordingly, we shall center our attention on *sensitivity* and *risk analyses* that are designed to control the errors of the first type.

An error of the first type results whenever the estimates of the net benefits from the investment project are unduly optimistic. To avoid committing this error, the manager naturally wants to know how much decrease in the net benefits would trigger the reversal of the investment decision. The method used to obtain this information is known as the **sensitivity analysis**. Suppose an $r\%$ reduction in the estimated net benefits is just enough to reverse the investment decision. Then $r\%$ is the *safety margin* associated with this investment decision. Clearly, the larger the safety margin, the greater the manager's confidence in the decision to invest. Conversely, the smaller the safety margin, the riskier is the investment project.

Specifically, a risk exists for the investment project only if there is a positive probability that the realized net benefits will fall outside the safety margin. Naturally, we will call this probability the **risk level** associated with the investment project. In order to render a decision on the investment project, the manager must first secure from the staff an estimate of this risk level and then decide whether this level is acceptable. Clearly, the acceptability of a given risk level depends on the manager's risk attitude. The more risk averse the manager is, the less risk is acceptable and the more likely that the analyst's recommendation will be rejected.

We have briefly described the basic principle underlying the risk analysis. It is now instructive to demonstrate how this principle is applied in a concrete case. We shall do so by using the sample information system analyzed previously under the net present value method. We omit the discussion under the internal rate of return method because, as we saw earlier, the rule governing the acceptance of the investment project under the IRR method is equivalent to that under the NPV method; therefore, the risk analysis will also be the same for these two methods. We also omit the discussion of the payback period analysis because an element of risk analysis is already embedded in that method.

Recall that under the net present value decision rule the cost/benefit analysis is performed according to the formula

NPV = Total discounted net benefits − Initial investment

For the investment to be economically feasible, the value of NPV must be positive. As displayed earlier in Figure 4-9, the net present value for the proposed information system was found to be $29,884.30. Since the value of the NPV is greater than zero, the system was judged to be financially desirable.

In order to find the safety margin for the investment project, we determine the percentage reduction in the total discounted net benefits at which the NPV of the project becomes exactly equal to zero. Let this percentage be denoted by r. We find the value of r by solving the following equation:

$(1 - r)(\text{Total discounted net benefits}) - \text{Initial investment} = 0$

Again referring to Figure 4-9, we calculate $r = 0.230084$ or 23%. Thus, the safety margin is 23%. This is to say that even if the total discounted net benefits drop by 23%, the decision to invest will remain correct. Only when

The Big Pay-Off

"When should a new information system be built?" is a question for management. The practical application of the theoretical concepts applied here for financial feasibility means that the benefits brought by a new system must be measured against its costs. A concrete application of cost/benefit analysis is offered by the U.S. Department of Education and the federal loan program. As reported by an internal document, the Department of Education estimates that a simple computer match to eliminate students ineligible for federal financial support could save the government over $290 million a year. Defaulters on earlier loans are allowed to apply for financial aid regardless of their debts. The Department of Education refused to computerize a cross-check against these records because of fear that the data was not sufficiently accurate. However, auditors recently found the data records to be about 93% accurate while the erroneous records could be easily rectified. The computer matching of defaulters against new loan applicants is a relatively simple task to perform on the computer. Plans for a computer matching system have been discussed for 10 to 15 years but never implemented.

How important is this system to you, the taxpayer? Consider the benefits and costs of the planned computer matching system. Although we are unable to give an accurate estimate of its costs, let us guess at a very high figure of $10 million. Based upon the estimate of $300 million awarded to ineligible students each year, the benefits of a matching system are projected at $800,000 per day or $292 million per year. Comparing the costs and benefits, should the system be implemented? The answer is definitely yes and as soon as possible. Now the real question is: Why hasn't this system been implemented so far? That answer lies in the politics of an organization and the lack of managerial directives.

the realized total discounted net benefits fall more than 23% will the decision to invest in the information system become a financial mistake.

Suppose the research department advised the manager of a 10% probability that the realized total discounted net benefits will fall more than 23%. The risk associated with the information system is therefore 10%. If the manager's maximum tolerable risk is only 5%, then the manager will reject the analyst's recommendation and refuse to invest in the information system.

SUMMARY

The purposes of a cost/benefit analysis are twofold. First, it serves to determine whether the proposed investment is financially feasible by comparing the estimated costs to the anticipated benefits. If the costs exceed the benefits, the investment is not considered financially worthwhile. Second, the cost/benefit analysis permits us to select the most financially desirable investment among several proposed alternatives. Although the cost/benefit analysis measures the comparative worth of an investment in monetary terms, an information system may be implemented because of other compelling reasons such as the survival of the firm or strategic advantage in the marketplace.

Whether or not the financial feasibility of a system is important for its implementation, the firm typically wants to know the extent of the monetary costs for the system before authorizing its implementation. Consequently, the cost analysis for an information system should be meticulously prepared. The costs for a sample information system were illustrated in Figure 4-4. Costs are classified as either one-time or recurring costs. One-time costs are further divided into the categories of capital costs and developmental costs. Capital costs are expenditures incurred for purchases such as computer hardware and its related equipment, computer software, or office equipment. Developmental costs include the costs associated with the creation of the software programs that comprise the information system. A subcategory of developmental costs contains the costs incurred for the conversion to the new system.

Recurring costs, also called annual operating costs, are estimated for the period during which the system will be in operation. They are classified as either fixed or variable costs. Fixed costs are expenses that are independent of the level of operation during each period, thus are the same throughout the year. Variable costs, on the other hand, are dependent on the level of operation during each period, hence fluctuate over time within the year.

Costs and benefits are further identified as either tangible or intangible. The monetary value of tangible costs and benefits can be easily identified, but the monetary values of intangible costs and benefits are not so easily determined. To estimate the monetary value of costs or benefits, the analyst relies on a rule of thumb formula to compute the best guess.

Once the costs and benefits for a system have been evaluated, the cost/ benefit analysis is performed. The three ways of performing a cost/benefit analysis are the net present value method, the payback period method, and the internal rate of return method. Although it might seem easy to determine the monetary worth of a new system by subtracting the estimated total costs from the estimated total benefits, it is not that simple. Two complications arise: The costs and benefits of a system are accrued at various points during its lifetime, and the value of money does change over time. In order to determine the financial worth of a new system, it is necessary to compute the discounted present values of costs and benefits. Only when the discounted present values of costs and benefits are known will the analyst be able to use one of the three methods to perform the cost/benefit analysis. Based on this analysis, the analyst makes a recommendation to the management about the desirability of the proposed information system.

The decision whether to invest in the information system rests solely on the shoulders of the manager. In making this decision, the manager utilizes many inputs, of which the analyst's recommendation is but one. Another important input is the manager's own judgements about the market environment. The manager, who is intimately familiar with the market environment faced by the firm and strategic postures adopted by the firm, will use these information sources to adjust the various costs and benefits—especially the intangible ones—submitted by the analyst. These adjustments may lead to the rejection of the analyst's recommendation. Still another important input is the manager's risk attitude. Owing to the existence of uncertainty in the marketplace, the analyst's estimates of the costs and benefits associated with the information system are subject to error. Consequently, there is always a risk associated with investment in an information system; that is, there remains a positive probability that the firm should not have invested in the information system but did do so. The level of this risk can be estimated by using modern statistical analysis. Whether the manager is willing to accept this level of risk depends on his or her risk attitude. The more risk averse the manager is, the less risk will be considered acceptable. Consequently, an extremely risk averse manager may reject a very favorable recommendation made by an analyst to invest in an information system.

All told, it is fair to say that the decision to invest follows a complex process. The decision on an information system is a combined result of the objective analysis of the analyst and the subjective judgement of the manager. Since the manager is entrusted to chart the firm's destiny, he or she alone bears the responsibility to make the final choice. The analyst must keep in mind at all times that the analyst's role is to make recommendations, not to render decisions.

TERMS

benefits	recurring costs
intangible benefits	tangible costs
tangible benefits	variable costs
cost/benefit analysis	discounted present value (DPV)
costs	goodwill gain
annual operating costs	internal rate of return (IRR)
capital costs	net present value (NPV)
conversion costs	payback period
developmental costs	risk level
fixed costs	sensitivity analysis
intangible costs	time value of money
one-time costs	

QUESTIONS

1. What are the reasons for performing a cost/benefit analysis?

2. Define the following terms: one-time costs, capital costs, developmental costs, and conversion costs.

3. What is meant by recurring costs for an information system? Give three examples of recurring costs for an information system.

4. What is meant by fixed costs and variable costs for an information system? Give an example of each cost type.

5. What do the terms *tangible* and *intangible* mean when applied to costs and benefits? Give two examples each of tangible and intangible costs and benefits.

6. Write the formula for computing the discounted present value of money. Assuming that the market interest rate is 5% per annum, compute the discounted present value of $75,000 to be received each year for the next 5 years.

7. The cost/benefit analysis for a proposed information system shows the following data:

Total initial outlay	$250,000
Annual operating costs	40,000
Annual benefits	90,000

Assume that the operating costs and the annual benefits are constant for the next 7 years, the expected lifetime of the system is 5 years, and the market interest rate is 5% per annum. Evaluate this system to determine its financial feasibility by using each of the following methods:

  a. Net present value method
  b. Internal rate of return method
  c. Payback period method

8. Figure 8-12 (see Chapter 8) shows the cost/benefit analysis for the moderate-sized system proposed for Dr. Washington's office. The net present value method was used. What is the maximum percentage error that will still yield a favorable net present value for this proposed system?

9. What is the purpose of computing the internal rate of return for an investment when its net present value has already been calculated?

10. How does the market interest rate affect the financial feasibility of an investment?

PROJECTS

1. Tom Martinez, the proprietor of a jewelry store, wants to determine if a computer system would be helpful in recording the customers who purchase or repair jewelry. With such records, the store could mail

customers periodic notices of sales or special jewelry showings. Mr. Martinez believes that this would increase his business by 10%. The current business volume is just over $2 million. As far as he can estimate, the average amount spent by a customer for a repair or purchase is about $1,000. He is uncertain how many customers patronize his jewelry store.

a. Produce the cost analysis for the jewelry store by pricing the implementation of a PC information system. Assume that a software package will be purchased at a cost of $15,000 with an annual maintenance fee of $750. No software will be custom-built. A consultant will be hired to conduct the initial investigation. Call your local computer store to obtain the price of a PC, specifying the computer configuration with regard to memory and hard disk size. Assign dollar values to the other cost items whenever possible.

b. Prepare a benefit analysis of the proposed information system. Include an estimate for the projected benefit of increased customer sales. On further questioning, Mr. Martinez admits that at worst, sales might not rise at all; at best, sales might increase by 20%.

c. Given the cost/benefit analysis performed for parts (a) and (b), evaluate the financial feasibility of the proposed system by the three techniques of net present value, internal rate of return, and payback period.

2. Contact your local Chamber of Commerce or any civic organization and discuss the information needs of its office. For this project, you will evaluate the benefits of an office computer information system. If a system is already in place, ask the director about its financial benefits. If a system is not yet in operation, inquire about the need for such a system and the projected benefits.

Now prepare a chart listing the benefits for a computer information system at this office. Assign dollar values whenever possible. If any calculations were done to estimate the value of a benefit, define these computations on a separate worksheet.

REFERENCES

Connell, John J. "Return on Investment in Information Technology." *Information Center*, October 1986, pp. 46–51.

Lay, Peter M. W. "Beware the Cost/Benefit Model for IS Project Evaluation." *Journal of Systems Management*, June 1985, pp. 30–35.

Levy, Haim, and Marshall Sarnat. *Investment and Portfolio Analysis.* New York: Wiley, 1972.

"New Dimensions in Cost Justification." *Modern Office Technology*, May 1986, pp. 20–22.

"The New Economics of Computing." *I/S Analyzer* 25(9), September 1987, pp. 1–14.

CHAPTER 5

Project Management

Objectives

The study of this chapter will enable you to master the following concepts:

- How to use Gantt and PERT charts for scheduling and managing projects
- The determination of the tasks critical to the project schedule and the slack time available for a project
- The role of the systems development life cycle in scheduling a project
- The methods available to assist in determining the time and effort estimates for a project
- How to derive the estimates of a project's development time and effort by using the COCOMO estimation model
- The organizational structure for project implementation
- The practical problems encountered in forecasting development time and effort for a project

INTRODUCTION

When proposing a new information system, the systems analyst will be confronted with many questions from top management—in particular, "How much will it cost?" and "When will it be done?" As many project managers know, these two questions are difficult to answer correctly. Many projects experience cost overruns and finish long after their anticipated completion dates. Although we discussed cost/benefit analysis in Chapter 4, the methods of forecasting the person-months (PMs) required for software development have not been discussed thus far. Development costs are computed by multiplying the estimated person-months by an average salary for a computer professional. In this chapter, we will explain first how to forecast the costs and time requirements for a project, and second how to employ project management techniques to monitor its progress.

WHAT IS PROJECT MANAGEMENT?

The purpose of project management is threefold:

1. The scheduling of the project tasks.
2. The prediction of success or failure in meeting the schedule.
3. The estimation of time and work force requirements for the project.

The first topic will be discussed in the next section which deals with the tools for project management. Since the second topic is directly related to the methods employed for scheduling and controlling project activities, it will be discussed in connection with the scheduling of tasks. In addition, the role of the SDLC in scheduling and monitoring tasks will be presented in a separate section. The third topic will be covered in later sections.

The planning process begins with an examination of the project specifications. In order to schedule the project, project *milestones* and *deliverables* must be defined. The end points of major software activities (such as the completion of coding for a program) are designated as **milestones**. A **deliverable** is the tangible output of an activity such as the coding for a program, the results of testing a module, or the documented plans for user training. The initial work effort estimates (in person-months) and the task schedule, based on these milestones and deliverables, can then be prepared. Once the project is underway, the project manager continually monitors the progress of the tasks. This process is executed according to the steps in Figure 5-1. As more information is gained about the project, the project manager revises the schedule and cost estimates to reflect this new knowledge. Each time the schedule and cost estimates are revised, it must be asked whether the project should continue. If cost overruns are excessive and the project is months or years behind schedule, management must decide on the likelihood of ultimate success. Extra resources may be added or, despite the high investment already made, the project may be cancelled.

FIGURE 5-1
The project planning
process

Step 1	Define the initial schedule and costs.
Step 2	Review the progress of the project.
Step 3	Revise the schedule and cost estimates to match the reality of the progress.
Step 4	Decide whether the project should be continued.

FIGURE 5-1
The project planning process

THE TOOLS OF PROJECT MANAGEMENT

Gantt charts and PERT charts are two basic tools that enable the project manager to monitor and control the numerous individual tasks that must be performed for a project. Before discussing these techniques, we will illustrate them with a small project unrelated to software development. This example is designed to illustrate the scheduling of overlapping tasks, a possibility that exists for many projects. After explaining the planning and scheduling for this sample project, we will demonstrate how to prepare Gantt and PERT charts.

A Sample Project: The Lawn Maintenance Problem

Let us consider the maintenance of the exterior grounds at a university. There are six outside areas that must be maintained by mowing the lawns, clipping bushes, and trimming along sidewalk edges. For simplicity, we will assume that all six areas are squares of the same size with the same number of bushes and sidewalk edges. As drawn in Figure 5-2, each area has two sides planted with bushes and bordered by sidewalks.

Our problem is to assign the buildings and grounds staff to this task. As listed in Figure 5-3, the resources available are two riding mowers, two

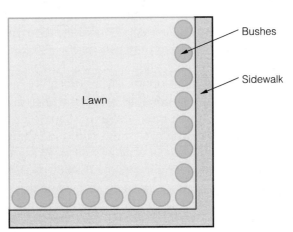

FIGURE 5-2
The diagram of a university lawn area

FIGURE 5-3

Time estimates for maintenance of a university lawn area

Tasks for One Lawn Area	Time Required (in hours)	Resources Available
		6 Staff members
		2 Riding mowers
Mowing	3	2 Hedge clippers
Clipping bushes	4	2 Electric edgers
Trimming edges	2	
Total time	9	

hedge clippers, two electric edgers, and a total of six staff members. This figure also displays the time required for each lawn, which is a total of 9 hours: 3 hours to mow the lawn, 4 hours to clip the bushes, and 2 hours to trim the edges. For safety reasons at least one third of the lawn, which is 1 hour's work, must be completed before another worker is allowed to enter the area to work on clipping bushes or trimming edges. Further, since the bush clipping interferes with edge trimming work, at least one half of the bushes, which is 2 hours' work, must be finished before edge trimming may begin.

One possible approach to scheduling the lawn maintenance project is simply to assign one person to perform these three tasks on all six lawns. The total time spent would then be 9 hours times six lawns, or a total of 54 hours. If only one person did the job and worked a standard 8-hour day, it would take 6¾ days for the entire university grounds to be completed. Our problem is to schedule this task in the most efficient manner. With unlimited machinery, we could schedule one worker for each lawn area. Since each lawn area requires 9 hours work, the entire university grounds could be maintained in just 1⅛ days. However, the reality is that machines are expensive and we have only two machines of each type for the crew of six workers. Confronted with limited equipment, we must decide how to schedule our tasks in an optimal way. The university wants to groom the lawn areas as quickly as possible before the grass and bushes become unsightly.

Since two machines of each type are available, we could assign the job to two workers who each mow, clip, and trim three lawns so that the entire job is accomplished in only 27 hours—54 hours divided by two workers. While this scheduling halves the total elapsed time, is it possible to shorten the time even further by using a schedule that maximizes the use of equipment and workers? A more efficient scheduling of these activities is pro-

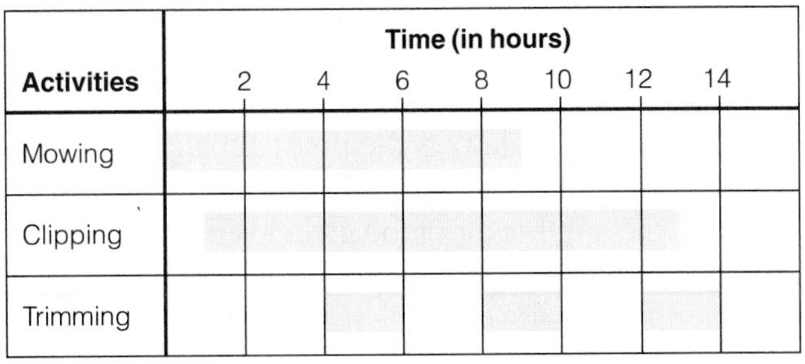

Activities	Time (in hours)						
	2	4	6	8	10	12	14
Mowing							
Clipping							
Trimming							

FIGURE 5-4

A Gantt chart for the lawn maintenance scheduling Two workers are assigned to each activity.

posed in Figure 5-4 on a diagram called a *Gantt chart*. Gantt charts will be explained more fully later on. Suppose we assign two workers to mow the lawns. This activity requires 18 working hours (3 hours times six lawns), but when divided by two lawn mowers it needs a total of 9 elapsed hours. We will schedule the mowing of the lawn area near one row of bushes, so we can permit the clipping of the bushes to start 1 hour after the mowing begins. This schedule poses no problems. Since the clipping takes longer than the mowing, the clippers will always lag at least an hour behind the lawn mowing machines. We observe that the trimming takes only 2 hours per lawn area and, for safety reasons, must lag at least 2 hours behind the bush clipping crew. Consequently, in Figure 5-4 we place the edge trimming to overlap with the fourth hour for each clipping crew. We finish the entire project at the end of 14 calendar hours (or 1¾ days) for a total effort of 54 person-hours. Regardless of the manner in which the project is scheduled, the total effort measured in number of person-hours required to complete the project will be the same. However, the total project time (the calendar time) can be substantially reduced.

In the Gantt chart the time of the trimming crew is split into small segments, with 2-hour gaps between the trimming activity for each lawn. One possible alternative, displayed in Figure 5-5, is to schedule all the lawn trimming at the very end; then the trimmers work during calendar hours 8 through 14 instead of intermittent groups of 2 hours. With this scheduling choice, we do not save any calendar time, but we do make better use of our

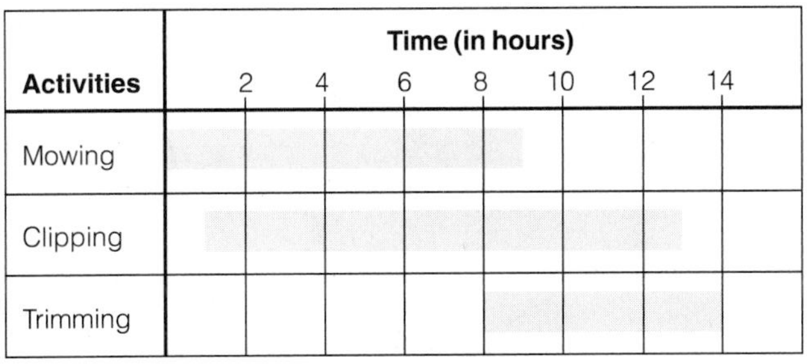

Activities	Time (in hours)						
	2	4	6	8	10	12	14
Mowing							
Clipping							
Trimming							

FIGURE 5-5

An alternative scheduling of the trimming activity

workers. We can now assign them to tasks that will occupy their time for calendar hours 1 through 8 without splitting their workload into two different tasks.

The Gantt chart allows the project manager to observe whether tasks in progress are being accomplished within the scheduled time frame. For example, the supervisor of the grounds crew can easily check that each lawn area is, in fact, mowed within the allotted time of 3 hours. At any point in the project, the supervisor is able to determine if the tasks are on schedule and will be finished within the allotted time. By knowing that the project is late, the supervisor has the opportunity to decide whether additional resources should be given to the project. For example, extra machines could be rented and additional workers hired, if necessary. The monitoring of the project also permits the other project schedules to be adjusted to reflect the slippage occurring at the present time.

Figure 5-6 illustrates the use of another project management technique called *PERT*. This diagram visually displays the scheduling of the tasks for only one lawn area. The circles or *nodes* are numbered from 1 to 7. Each node signifies the beginning or end of an activity. Node 1 indicates the start of the entire task. Node 2 represents the completion of mowing the lawn for 1 hour adjacent to a row of bushes. The line between nodes 1 and 2 indicates the execution of this task and is labeled accordingly. Similarly, node 3 stands for the completion of the last 2 hours of lawn mowing. The task of clipping the first row of bushes is indicated by the line drawn between nodes 2 and 4. Node 4 denotes the completion of this task. The dashed line between nodes 3 and 4 indicates a *dummy* activity, that is, no task is performed. This connecting line is needed to show that work cannot proceed from node 4 until node 3 has been reached; that is, the rest of the clipping (depicted by the line from node 4 to node 5) and the beginning of the edge trimming work (shown from nodes 4 to 6) cannot proceed until the mowing has been completed. We will explain the notation for PERT charts in more detail in the next section.

FIGURE 5-6   The PERT chart for the lawn maintenance project

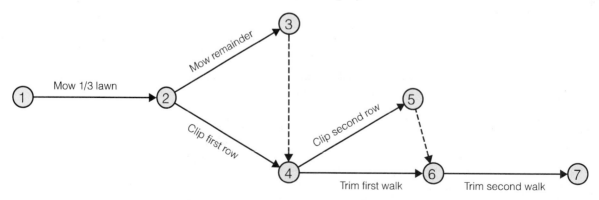

PERT Charts

The **Project Evaluation and Review Technique (PERT)** was developed in the 1950s to enable the U.S. Navy to schedule large, complex projects. At the same time a similar tool, the **Critical Path Method (CPM)**, was developed through a joint effort by the UNIVAC Division of Remington Rand and the DuPont Company. Although the two methods are closely related, CPM assumes that the time requirements for tasks are fixed and predictable, whereas PERT allows the time requirements for each task to be relatively unpredictable. To handle this situation, in PERT three different time estimates are given for each task:

the minimum time possible.
the maximum time that could be needed.
the most likely time to be spent.

The allowance for variation in time requirements is most suitable for research and development projects, whereas fixed time allotments are common in manufacturing industries. Because each new software development project has no direct precedent for the multiple operations involved, time requirements are difficult to foresee accurately. Consequently, PERT is the preferred tool for scheduling software projects.

DRAWING PERT GRAPHS

As shown in the lawn maintenance example, PERT uses a graph to show the relationships between the various project tasks. Each task is depicted in terms of what other tasks must be completed before it can be initiated. The final diagram appears as a **network** where each task is represented as the line segment between two circles on the graph. The direction of the task flow is denoted by the placement of an arrow. The circles on the graph are called **nodes**. Each node, or **event**, indicates the beginning or end points of a task. The same node may depict the starting point or end point for more than one task. The nodes are labeled with reference numbers. A task is identified by both its name and the two numbers of its beginning and ending nodes on the PERT chart. The ending node for a task may be designated as a *project milestone*.

TIME ESTIMATES FOR TASKS

As shown in Figure 5-7, the three different time estimates for a PERT task are designated as t_o, t_p, and t_m.

t_o = The **most optimistic time** estimate

that is, the least amount of time that the task could require for completion. This estimate assumes that no unanticipated events will occur and that this task will have smooth sailing.

t_o	Most optimistic time estimate	Least amount of time the task could require
t_p	Most pessimistic time estimate	Most amount of time the task could require
t_m	Most likely time estimate	Most likely time required by the task
t_e	Expected time for a task	$$t_e = \frac{t_o + 4t_m + t_p}{6}$$
t_f	Float time for a task	$$t_f = LS - ES$$
ES	Early start date	Earliest possible date a task can begin
EF	Early finish date	Earliest possible date a task can finish: $$EF = ES + t_e$$
LS	Late start date	Latest possible date a task can begin without affecting the project's final completion date: $$LS = LF + t_e$$
LF	Late finish date	Latest possible date for completing a task without affecting the project's final completion date

t_p = The **most pessimistic time** estimate

that is, the maximum time allotment required for this task. This estimate assumes that the project will experience many difficulties, some of which may seriously impede the task.

t_m = The **most likely time** that the task will take

This estimate assumes that a few things may go wrong, but only a normal number of problems will occur.

The PERT technique then asks for the calculation of t_e, the average **expected time** for the task, using these three estimates as follows:

$$t_e = \frac{t_o + 4t_m + t_p}{6}$$

This formula is based on the assumption that the most optimistic and most pessimistic times are equally likely to occur, whereas the most likely time estimate is four times more likely to really happen.

To demonstrate this formula, consider a project manager's best judgment for the completion of the coding task for a lengthy program. The time estimates are given as

t_o = 30 days

t_p = 90 days

t_m = 45 days

The application of the formula is

$$t_e = \frac{t_o + 4t_m + t_p}{6} = \frac{30 + 4(45) + 90}{6} = \frac{300}{6} = 50 \text{ days}$$

The expected time for this task is now judged to be 50 days, longer than the originally estimated most likely time of 45 days. In the following discussion, all computations will use only the expected duration for each task, t_e.

THE CRITICAL PATH

After the PERT diagram has been drawn for the project tasks, it is possible to detect the chronologically longest path through the network. The longest path represents the minimum amount of time necessary to complete the project. Since all other paths are shorter in time, they can be completed within the time allotted for the longest path. Because a delay in any task on the longest path will delay the entire project, this path is known as the **critical path**.

The identification of the critical path for a complex project is best done with the aid of computer programs expressly designed for project management. In order to illustrate the calculation of the critical path, we have created the relatively simple PERT chart shown in Figure 5-8. An alphabetical character on each line segment represents the name of the task; a number

FIGURE 5-8   A sample PERT chart   The critical path for this project follows the color line.

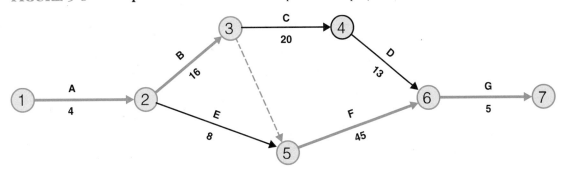

indicating the task's expected duration has been written below each line segment. Figure 5-9 lists the tasks shown on the sample PERT chart and their estimated times.

The critical path is found by first computing the length of each path through the network. In the sample PERT chart, the following three paths through the network exist:

A—B—C—D—G

A—E—F—G

A—B—DUMMY—F—G

By summing the task durations on each path, we discover that the lengths of these three paths are 58, 62, and 70 days, respectively. Therefore the last path (A—B—DUMMY—F—G) is the longest path, with a length of 70 days. This path appears on the PERT chart with a color line to indicate that it is the critical path through the network. Note, however, that it is possible for a project to have more than one critical path.

How does this knowledge assist the project manager? Any delay in a task on the critical path means that the entire project will be late. Therefore, special attention can be given to the tasks present on the critical path. Armed with the knowledge that one or more tasks on the critical path are late, the project manager has the opportunity to decide how best to deal with the delays. Since the critical path is the longest path, all other paths are shorter. Therefore, the tasks on noncritical paths in the network have **slack time** or *float*, that is, additional time may be spent on such tasks without delaying the project. The next section explains how to compute the float for each task.

FIGURE 5-9

The list of tasks for the PERT chart of Figure 5-8

Task	Location	Immediate Predecessor	Expected Duration (in days)
A	(1,2)	–	4
B	(2,3)	A	16
C	(3,4)	B	20
D	(4,6)	C	13
E	(2,5)	A	8
F	(5,6)	B, E	45
G	(6,7)	D, F	5

THE COMPUTATION OF THE FLOAT

To calculate the float for a task, we begin by examining the network graph, first moving forward from the start to the end point and then moving backward from the end to the starting point. On the forward pass, we mark the earliest date each task could be started and its earliest possible completion date. The earliest possible date for starting a task is called its **early start (ES)**. The earliest date possible for completing a task, its **early finish (EF)**, is computed by adding the expected task duration to the early start date:

$$EF = ES + t_e$$

In Figure 5-10, the sample PERT chart first shown in Figure 5-8 has been marked with the early start and early finish times adjacent to each task name. The expected time, t_e, has been indicated below the task name. For example, the early start for task A is on day 0 and its early finish date is computed by adding its duration to its start date, that is, $0 + 4$ or day 4. Task B then has an early start at day 4 and an early finish on day 20, that is, $4 + 16$. Task C can then have the earliest start on day 20 and the earliest finish on day 40, that is, $20 + 20$. This simple computation continues for all the paths in the network. We note that task F cannot begin until both tasks B and E have been finished. Thus, the longer time required for task B must be chosen to calculate the early start time for task F. After all the early finish times have been computed, the early finish time for the last task becomes the earliest finish time for the entire project. We see that task G has the early finish time of 70 days, which is also the earliest finish time for the project.

Thus far we have not identified any float. To do so, we now move backwards from the end point to the starting point of the network and mark the latest start time and the latest finish time. The **late finish (LF)** of a task is the very latest time that it can end without affecting the finish time for the project. The latest possible start time of a task, called the **late start (LS)**, is

FIGURE 5-10   The sample PERT chart   Early Start, Early Finish, Late Start, and Late Finish times are now marked. The critical path is shown in color.

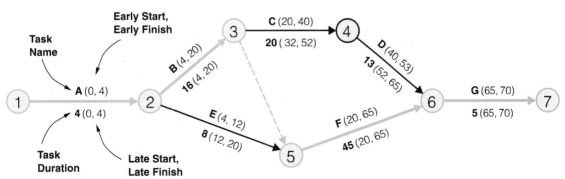

computed by subtracting the expected task duration, t_e, from the latest finish time:

$$LS = LF - t_e$$

In Figure 5-10, the LS and LF times are below the line segments for each task. As stated earlier, all tasks on the critical path have no float. Their late start and late finish times are always equal to their early start and early finish times. However, tasks C, D, and E do not lie on the critical path. By proceeding backwards from the end point, we find that task G has the late finish time of 70 days, thus its late start time is 70 − 5 or 65. We now trace the path upward to task D, which must be done before task G begins. Since task G's late start time is 65, task D has a late finish time of 65; task D's late start time is computed by subtracting its expected duration from its late finish time, that is, 65 − 13 or 52. Similarly, task C has the late finish time of 52 and the late start time of 32. Finally, we see that task E has a late finish time of 20 days and a late start time of 12 days.

The **float time**, t_f, for each task is computed by subtracting the early start date from the late start date, that is,

$$t_f = LS - ES$$

For example, task E has an early start date of 4 and a late start date of 12, giving it a float of 8 days. Tasks C and D both have floats of 12 days. The project manager now knows exactly where any float exists and will be able to forecast the final completion date for the project despite any delays that may be experienced in the tasks. Regardless of the float in the project schedule, if the tasks on the critical path are not completed within their expected time the project will run late.

THE CONTINGENCY FACTOR

While the float detected within the project network is helpful to the project manager, its value is limited since it can be consumed quickly by the delay of a single task. In Figure 5-10, if task C encounters unexpected difficulties and requires 32 days rather than the forecasted 20 days to complete, there is no longer any float left for task D to consume. In addition, any delay in a task on the critical path delays the entire project. Although the wise project manager realizes that most projects will experience delays due to unexpected difficulties, he or she also knows not to count on the float time to cover such setbacks.

Consider the problem of estimating the efforts and development time required for a project. *Effort* estimates for a project are expressed in the number of *person-months* needed to accomplish the work. *Development time* is the total elapsed time—the calendar time—required for a software project. By necessity, these estimates must incorporate some subjective ratings by the estimator, and thus may be highly biased and prone to error.

Even development time and costs predicted by modeling techniques have not proven to be highly accurate. (A modeling technique for creating these estimates for software projects will be discussed in a later section.) Some of this inaccuracy is due to having insufficient data about the project when forecasting effort and development time prior to the initiation of the project. And, as we know too well, unexpected problems frequently arise in any endeavor. As problems occur and more information is gained about the project, the schedule will undergo revision. But while prepared for discrepancies between actual task performances and the initial work schedule, top management does not really want to hear over and over again that the project is running late. Nor is it advisable to have the project's task teams readjust their schedules repeatedly because of delays encountered by interdependent tasks.

A partial solution to this problem is the commonly used tactic of allowing extra time for the project. This additional time is allotted over and above the times initially computed for the tasks. The extra time serves as a reservoir from which the project can draw time. Because this reserve addresses unforeseen difficulties, it is known as the **contingency factor**. Contractors for physical construction jobs typically incorporate contingency time into their schedules. Since this is a sensible approach to managing a project, we recommend that software project managers also allow for unexpected problems by allocating contingency time to the project.

An additional word of advice for the project manager estimating a project's development time is to consider vacation and sick time for the staff members employed on the project. While this may seem obvious, many projects are improperly scheduled because the managers failed to recognize these gaps in staff availability.

> ### *Warning*
> PERT charts are sometimes difficult to comprehend because they illustrate activities performed in parallel. Gantt charts are conceptually simpler because tasks are shown as independent activities. Be sure that you understand the relationship between the PERT chart and its corresponding Gantt chart.

Gantt Charts

After the schedule of tasks has been established, the project manager constantly monitors the progress of each individual task. *Gantt charts* are especially well suited to assist the manager in this project control activity. **Gantt charts** are bar graphs that display how much work has been done on every project task. Figure 5-11 is the Gantt chart of the schedule established for the

FIGURE 5-11   **The Gantt chart for the project displayed in Figure 5-10**   The tasks highlighted in color lie on the critical path.

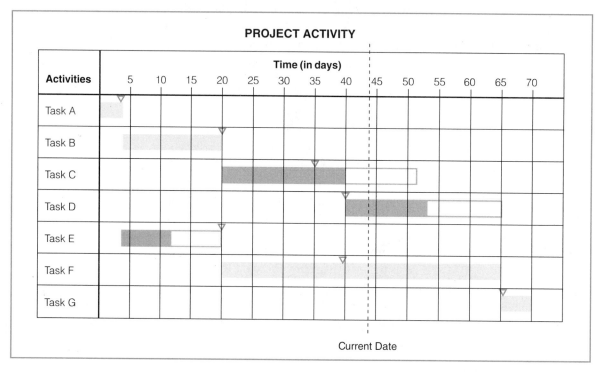

sample project depicted as a PERT chart in Figure 5-10. The top line of the Gantt chart shows the beginning of the project and every fifth day thereafter. A string or other movable marker placed vertically on the chart indicates the current date.

The tasks are listed vertically, in the order of occurrence, on the left hand side of the chart. A horizontal bar is drawn to show the length of time allocated for each task. The bar for a task begins at the date scheduled for the start of the task. Because some tasks must be scheduled sequentially, their starting dates occur after their predecessor tasks have been accomplished. The task sequence indicated by the PERT project chart must be maintained by the Gantt chart. The early finish date for a task must be indicated in some fashion on the task bar. In our figure, the bar is shaded up to the early finish date. If any float exists for the task, the bar continues unshaded to the right up to the late finish date. As a task progresses, the percentage of completion is marked in some fashion on the task bar. In Figure 5-11, an arrowhead above the bar shows the portion completed for each task.

According to the Gantt chart in Figure 5-11, tasks A, B, and E have been completed. Task C is 9 days behind schedule, but since it has some float the slippage has not affected the final project date. Task D cannot begin until Task C is done. Task F poses a small concern as it is now 4 days late. Since task F lies on the critical path, it is appropriate to authorize overtime to complete the task on schedule. Task G is not yet underway because it must follow the completion of tasks D and F. To help track the tasks on the critical path, they are highlighted in another color.

The Gantt chart is an easy-to-understand depiction of the status of project tasks. Because of its simplicity, it is popular with managers. In order for the chart to be effective, the tasks must be monitored and the Gantt chart updated at frequent intervals, usually weekly. The creation of the Gantt chart from the PERT chart can be easily accomplished, even if done manually. With a glance at the Gantt chart, the manager can quickly see if a project is on schedule.

Task Monitoring

The monitoring of a task still remains a problem in obtaining good information about the status of a task. When constructing a new building, we see the evidence of task completion; the erection of the outside walls can be viewed and the percentage completed measured by sight. But the completion of intellectual activities such as analysis, design, and programming are not so easily measured. One approach is to inquire about the status of the task from the software developer assigned to the task. When the deadline is rapidly approaching, a typical response is that the program is "90% complete." This reply often means only that the program has been compiled without errors. The testing process may still require extensive time to remove the program's other errors. The program design may be found to be faulty, and a complete rewrite may even be necessary. As many managers know, after a task is supposedly "90% complete," an equal amount of time may be spent on the "last 10%" of the programming task. If no deliverable has yet been produced, how do we know whether a program is 25% or 90% complete? Instead of asking for an estimate from the software developer, it is preferable to designate some deliverables and determine if these concrete tasks have been achieved.

A recommended procedure for the measurement of task deliverables is to use a task review sheet. An example of a task review sheet for a program module is shown in Figure 5-12. When a task deliverable is ready, it is reviewed by another computer professional who also initials the sheet. This sheet is kept in a notebook that contains the task specifications. The program code, test data, and test results are all filed appropriately and presented for review by the task evaluator. Some problems remain with this monitoring method, since individual program modules may pose particular problems. For example, one module may contain exceedingly difficult logic and require ten times more effort than any other module, or testing may uncover bugs that are time-consuming to eliminate. Nevertheless, this method of task review offers a concrete approach to evaluating the progress of a task and avoiding the "90% complete" syndrome.

FIGURE 5-12

The review sheet for an individual programming task

TASK REVIEW CHART

Project: _____   Unit: _____

Assigned to: _____   Date Assigned: _____

Section Number	Task Milestone	Due	Date Completed	Completed By	Reviewer
1	Unit Requirements				
2	Unit Design				
3	Unit Code				
4	Test Plan				
5	Test Results				
6	Problem Report				
7	Completion Report				
8	Reviewer's Comments				

Project Management Software Packages

Project management software packages are readily available to create the PERT charts from a table listing the tasks, predecessor tasks, and expected task durations (such as that given in Figure 5-9). The Gantt chart can then be directly produced from the data gleaned from the PERT chart. Tracing the critical path for a complex project is best done by means of such software.

Although project management software eases the manual efforts required for recording information, the job of scheduling and assigning personnel remains difficult. This is primarily due to the complexity of the concepts employed for project management. Not only must the tasks be scheduled, they must also be assigned to staff members who are both available and able to perform them. A *Wizard* in Microsoft *Project* for Windows™ software package walks the user through the common operations of creating a new project and resolving conflict. By asking questions, the Wizard guides the user through the various functions that must be performed. Although *Wizards* are great training tools, they can be slow and inflexible. Even the ultimate in user-friendly project management software cannot supply the knowledge required for scheduling and monitoring the project. The project manager must understand the project, how to schedule it, the importance of the critical path, the project's organization, and the capabilities of the personnel to be assigned to the tasks. Project management software is only a tool to assist the user, not an answer in itself.

THE ROLE OF THE SDLC IN PROJECT PLANNING

Before any scheduling can be performed, the project manager must be aware of all the tasks to be accomplished and the effort and time required for each task. The ordering of the tasks is also important. A successful project manager for an information system development project is cognizant of the hundreds of tasks to be performed and their scheduling sequence—which tasks must be accomplished before another task can begin. A simple example of such sequencing is coding activity, which must occur *after* the program design step has been completed and *not before*. Because the detailed description of the systems development life cycle furnishes such information, it serves as the framework for the project planning of software development projects.

In this book we have presented just a general outline of the SDLC, discussing only the major activities and their tasks in detail. Because so many tasks must be performed, many firms have developed a step-by-step list of tasks required for the development of an information system. The tasks are described and the sequencing of their execution is stipulated. It takes several volumes of documentation to describe the entire SDLC as a set of tasks listed in the appropriate sequence. But creating such detailed specifications of the software development project tasks is valuable; they can be strictly followed during the development of an information system. The detailed guide to the SDLC serves as checklist for the project manager. Because our purpose is to present the technical concepts for the implementation of an information system, we will not present the scores of details given by a fully specified SDLC methodology. Our discussion of project management is, instead, focused on how to plan, schedule, and adhere to the project deadlines.

The skill of the project manager is also demonstrated by the selection of tasks to be executed in parallel. Certain tasks clearly cannot be done simultaneously with other tasks; some must be completed before others can begin. Obviously, for instance, program testing cannot take place until the program has been written, analysis activities must precede the design activities, and so on. However, certain tasks in the SDLC can be undertaken at the same time as other tasks. Examples are preparing the plans for staff training as the programs are being written, coding and testing the program modules independently of each other, and planning the conversion to the new system while the programs are being coded.

Figure 5-13 is a PERT chart showing the major activities for an information system project. These activities with their associated deliverables are listed in Figure 5-14, which also includes the predecessor activities. For this system, a computer will be acquired and installed. As that process takes place, the design of program and data structures is scheduled to occur. Before the coding activity can begin, the installation of the computer hard-

FIGURE 5-13   **An SDLC scheduled on a PERT chart**

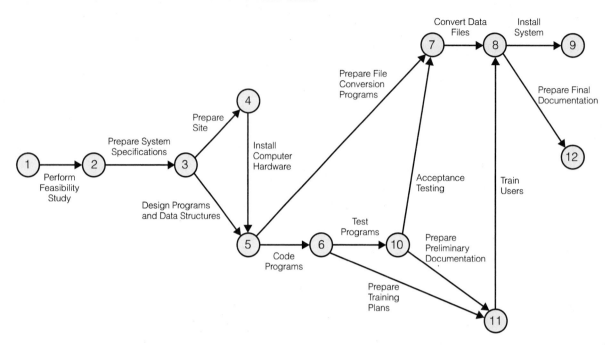

ware must be completed. Then, the program testing activity can be initiated while the training plans are prepared. The programs needed to convert the data files are scheduled concurrently with the coding and testing of the other programs. The old data files are converted only after the acceptance testing activity has been accomplished. At the same time, the tasks of training the users and preparing preliminary system documentation are scheduled. The final documentation will be prepared only after the complete system has been installed. The project manager has decided that it is best to know all aspects of the system before concluding the system documentation. Notice that the design stage has been merely sketched in the PERT chart. It is possible to specify or *decompose* this activity in terms of logical program and data design, physical program and data design, and input/output design chores (see activity E in Figure 5-14). Some design activities could be overlapped. The corresponding Gantt chart is formulated by using the information contained in the PERT chart and the activity chart, which specifies the estimated duration of each activity.

The project manager faces the additional constraint of personnel. For example, if the conversion scheme is best assigned to a particular staff member (or staffing group), that individual will not be available to work on other tasks at the same time. The planning of an information system project seldom has the problem of lack of machines, but frequently must deal with the limitation imposed by having only a finite number of highly skilled computer personnel to choose from. The project manager must select from

FIGURE 5-14 **The major activities of an SDLC** These activities match the PERT chart in Figure 5-13.

Activity Code	Activity Name	Location	Immediate Predecessor	Expected Duration (months)	Major Deliverables
A	Perform Feasibility Study	(1,2)	–	¾	Feasibility Study Report
B	Prepare Systems Specifications	(2,3)	A	2½	New System Model Hardware Requirements
C	Prepare Site	(3,4)	B	1½	Physical Site remodeled according to specifications
D	Install Computer Hardware	(4,5)	C	¼	Computer and related hardware on-site
E	Design Programs and Data Structures	(3,5)	B	8	Input/Output Designs Logical Data Design Physical Data Structures Structure Charts Module Descriptions Final Data Dictionary
F	Code Programs	(5,6)	D, E	18	Coded Programs, compiled without error
G	Test Programs	(6,10)	F	24½	Test Data, Test Results Tested Programs
H	Prepare File Conversion Programs	(5,7)	D, E	5	Conversion Plans Report Conversion Programs
I	Convert Data Files	(7,8)	H, L	¼	Converted Data Files
J	Prepare Preliminary Documentation	(10,11)	G	2¼	Preliminary Draft of System Documentation
K	Prepare Final Documentation	(8,12)	I, N	2	Final Draft of System Documentation
L	Acceptance Testing	(10,7)	G	1	Final System Version, fully tested
M	Prepare Training Plans	(6,11)	F	¾	Training Schedule User's Guide
N	Train Users	(11,8)	J, M	2½	Completion of Training Classes
O	Install System	(8,9)	I, N	¼	Operational System

among the available personnel for the various projects that will be underway at the same time. Project management software can assist in the job of tracking personnel assignments.

Defining the Project Milestones

As we stated earlier, a project *milestone* is the end point of an activity. A series of milestones must be defined for a project in order to monitor its progress. A good milestone is characterized by the delivery of tangible outputs, such as the documentation produced by a software process activity. For example, the completion of program design should be marked by the completed set of structure charts, the final data dictionary, and module descriptions. By contrast, having a deliverable simply called "program design" gives us no clue to what documents will accompany the completion of the activity. Such indefinite deliverables are unacceptable.

The systems development life cycle serves to indicate the milestones for a software development project. If an alternative to the traditional SDLC is chosen for the project, the SDLC must be modified accordingly. Each major phase is broken down into its principal activities and each activity, in turn, is then decomposed into a set of tasks. Both major and minor milestones are specified by the project manager. Because having too many milestones is burdensome to monitor, a rule of thumb is to mark milestones at 2- to 3-week intervals. Depending on the approach taken for the development of the software, this recommended interval may be varied as necessary.

SOFTWARE COST ESTIMATION

As discussed in earlier chapters, before approving a project, top management requires an estimate of the resources to be expended and the time required for project completion. In Chapter 4, we described the costs of developing an information system and analyzed these costs with regard to the forecasted system benefits. We now wish to discuss how the developmental costs of a system are estimated. As shown in Figure 5-15, the costs for software development include such items as administrative overhead, computer charges, office supplies, communication charges, travel, and personnel. This last category, human resources, is often the major expenditure in the creation of a new information system.

The cost of human resources continues to be the most difficult outlay to estimate accurately because it requires a forecast about work that has never before been performed in exactly this manner. The estimate must be made in terms of the number of person-months required—its *effort*—and the elapsed calendar time needed to complete the project—its *development time* or *scheduling time*. Unlike tract housing where the new buildings are all similar in style, the software being developed is a one-time event. The design of a house may be modified to create other housing designs, but a software design is not usually adapted for the creation of other systems.

Software Development	Conversion costs
Administrative overhead	Data base conversion
Computer charges	Training
Consulting expenditure	Parallel running—personnel time, etc.
Personnel	
Office supplies	
Work lost due to disruption	
Communication charges	
Travel	

FIGURE 5-15
Typical developmental costs

Instead, an information system typically is maintained for many years and then wholly discarded due to its replacement by a newly constructed system. Further, a builder relies on many manufactured parts and assembles a house by incorporating these parts in a suitable fashion. Because an information system often requires new processing to be constructed, we can liken its development to felling trees to get the boards needed for building a house. Such a customized approach to systems development is much to blame for the inaccuracy found in the cost and time estimates for software projects. Without manufactured components, the task of predicting the effort and time required for a software project is subject to a high degree of error.

As discussed in Chapter 2, other approaches to the traditional life cycle yield speedier systems development and some even offer plug-in components for the system. Reusable code, object-oriented methodology, software application packages, and reverse engineering let us plug in components rather than start the system from scratch. CASE tools (especially those with code generators) and fourth-generation languages also offer shortcuts for the steps in the traditional life cycle. Although no data are available, predictions for projects using such methods probably err less than with the traditional mode of development.

Although scheduling and cost overruns afflict every industry, frequently project managers for software development seriously underestimate the time required and the accompanying costs. In particular, development time for software projects is often inadequately budgeted. There are many reasons for this situation. First, the guidelines available for estimating person-months rely on information not ordinarily on hand in the early stages of development. Many estimation methods are based on the number of executable instructions to be produced for the system. Since the estimate of code size is dependent on the hardware and software selections, which are often an integral part of the project, inadequate information exists at the project's initiation. Since the code size is not known but can only be estimated based on other systems development projects, the guess will be inaccurate—possibly even grossly inaccurate.

Second, although some models exist for estimating costs and development time, none offer guaranteed success. Mohanty [1981] examined various software costing models by calculating costs for the same hypothetical project data with an assumed labor cost of $50,000 per year. The resulting estimates ranged from $362,000 to $2,766,667. When four different cost models were compared by Kemerer [1987] for business data processing applications, the predictions ranged from 230 person-months to 3,857 person-months for the same project. Obviously, these models lack consistency.

Despite the deficiencies in the estimation models, knowledge of the available modeling techniques may prove useful to the project manager. Initial cost and time estimations can be derived by use of an estimation model. As more information becomes available, better estimates can be derived and compared once again. The use of historical data from past projects is also useful in forecasting the work effort and time requirements for future projects. Further, by applying the historical project data, it is also possible to adjust some estimation models in order to reflect the firm's own experience with software development.

Three commonly used methods for estimating effort and development time are *top-down estimation, bottom-up estimation,* and *algorithmic cost modeling.* Each method has its own advantages and disadvantages. The primary disadvantage of any estimating technique is that sufficient information is not available about the project to enable the project manager to gauge the effort and development time with reasonable success. Because the estimations must be given despite this lack of knowledge, it is advisable to understand the methods currently in use.

Top-down estimation is accomplished by examining the project's functions from the top on down. The programming system is expressed as a set of functions required to implement the project's overall goals. Then the cost of each logical function is estimated. The actual components needed to perform the function are not considered. The major disadvantage of top-down estimation is that it does not deal with the low-level technical tasks that are most likely to cause difficulties. These low-level tasks include the coding and testing aspects of the system.

Bottom-up estimation is a technique that views the project as a detailed set of components which will comprise the set of final programs. After the cost of each component has been estimated, they are summed to obtain the total project cost. Typically, the estimate for an individual component is done in conjunction with the person who will actually be responsible for the task. Although bottom-up estimation does deal with the individual technical components of a project, it asks for estimates before sufficient information is available about component size, complexity, and interrelationships. Not only is it difficult to judge the cost for component testing but integration costs are hard to assess accurately until such information has been obtained.

Algorithmic cost modeling provides a method for computing the cost estimate based on historical data collected from previously developed software. Many such models exist. Two popular models are the *function point model* and the *basic COCOMO model*, both of which will be discussed below.

The Function Point Model

Because models based on code size estimates are difficult to use and yield inaccurate forecasts, the **function point model** was proposed by Albrecht [1979] and later refined by Albrecht and Gaffney [1983]. A **function point** is related to the functions performed by the software based on the following characteristics:

    External inputs and outputs

    User interfaces

    External interfaces

    Files used by the system

The complexity of each characteristic is gauged and assigned a weighting value from 3 to 15. For example, the value 3 indicates simple external inputs, whereas 15 represents complex internal files.

The raw function point count is adjusted by multiplying each raw count by the estimated weight and summing all values. Moreover, the complexity of the project is appraised by the use of separate complexity factors. This measure of complexity is found by evaluating other software features, such as on-line processing, the amount of reusable software to be employed, and the performance requirements. The adjusted function point count is then multiplied by these project complexity factors to produce a final function point count.

Since the rating of the complexity factors is an individual judgment, wide variations in estimates can occur. The project manager's judgment is crucial in this model. Because the model creates an estimate dependent on the number of files and the complexity of file manipulation, it is heavily biased towards data processing applications. A 1987 study by Kemerer showed that the model was useful in predicting efforts for such projects. By contrast, the function model is inadequate when dealing with projects that perform extensive computations without much use of input/output files or user interfaces.

The COCOMO Model

The COCOMO model was conceived by Boehm [1981] to estimate project efforts based upon a variety of factors. There are actually three versions, known as the basic, intermediate, and complete COCOMO models. Because this topic is lengthy, only the basic COCOMO model will be discussed in detail. For further information, consult Boehm [1981]. The **COCOMO model** predicts the effort in person-months required for the project during its design, programming, testing, and implementation activities. The early phases of initial investigation and analysis are not included in this estimate. The development time can also be forecasted once the number of person-months has been computed.

THE BASIC COCOMO MODEL

The Basic COCOMO model derives its estimates by using only two factors:

1. The estimated size of program code
2. The type of software to be developed

Boehm classifies software projects according to the degree of difficulty anticipated in the developmental process, forming three categories called *organic mode, semidetached mode*, and *embedded mode*. Examples of projects within each type of development mode are displayed in Figure 5-16. A large

FIGURE 5-16   Examples of the software development modes

Feature	Mode		
	Organic	Semidetached	Embedded
Degree of Difficulty in Development	Low	Moderate	High
Examples	Batch data reduction	Most transaction processing systems	Large, complex transaction processing systems
	Scientific models	New operating systems Data base management systems	Ambitious, very large operating systems
	Business models	Ambitious inventory, production control systems	Avionics
	Simple inventory, production, control systems	Simple command-control system	Ambitious command-control system
Specific example	Aircraft postflight data reduction	Aircraft flight training simulator	Aircraft on-board collision avoidance system

Barry W. Boehm, *Software Engineering Economics*, © 1981, p. 40. Reprinted by permission of Prentice-Hall, Englewood Cliffs, NJ.

software project may contain several subprojects with different developmental modes.

Organic mode projects are applications developed by small teams already familiar with the problem type and knowledgeable about the software tools. Because the team is small, communication overhead costs are low. Since all team members are already well versed in both the problem and the tool set, they can perform the job relatively quickly. An example of an organic mode project is a simple inventory or production control system.

Semidetached mode projects are projects with difficulties that fall somewhere between those of organic mode and embedded mode projects. The project team is composed of both experienced and inexperienced staff who lack familiarity with some (but not all) of the project's requirements. Communication costs are higher, and the project can be delayed due to the inexperience of the team members and the unknown aspects of the project. Most transaction processing systems (except for large, complex systems) are considered semidetached mode projects.

Embedded mode projects are those projects with the maximum amount of difficulty. The application requires the development of software that must be built within (is embedded in) a framework of hardware, software, regulations, and operational procedures. By the nature of the application, team members will ordinarily lack any prior experience with the application under development. When software problems occur for embedded software projects, it is usually impractical to alter the project requirements in order to keep the project on target because there are few, if any, extraneous functions that can be eliminated. In addition, validation costs are high. Examples of embedded mode projects are large, complex transaction processing systems and ambitious command-control systems.

The **effort** for all three types of projects is computed in person-months by the following formula:

Effort in person-months = $a(\text{KDSI})^b$

KDSI is the number of *delivered lines of source code* expressed in thousands, while a and b are constant values assigned according to the project type as follows:

	a	*b*
Organic mode	2.4	1.05
Semidetached mode	3.0	1.12
Embedded mode	3.6	1.20

A **delivered line of source code (DSI)** is defined by Boehm [1981] to be any single line of the program code regardless of how many actual programming statements appear on the line. Thus, a COBOL statement that occupies two lines counts as two lines of source code, whereas several statements written within only one line count as only one. The effort formula yields the number of *person-months* required for a project. Since Boehm defines a **person-month (PM)** to be 152 hours of working time, the final computation allows time for holidays, vacation, training, and sick leave. Figure 5-17 graphically depicts the range of effort for various project sizes and types.

The basic COCOMO model also provides for the computation of the total scheduling time required for a project, called its **development time (DT)**. The equations for the different project types are given as follows:

Organic mode $DT = 2.5(\text{Effort})^{0.38}$

Semidetached mode $DT = 2.5(\text{Effort})^{0.35}$

Embedded mode $DT = 2.5(\text{Effort})^{0.32}$

The development time required for varying sizes of organic mode projects is illustrated in Figure 5-18. Once the number of calendar months is known, the development schedule can be constructed. Note that the number of persons employed on the project cannot be computed by simply dividing the total person-months by the developmental time. The staffing requirements vary according to the project stage.

Figure 5-19 illustrates the developmental time required for all three project types according to the number of code lines to be written. Notice that the allocated development time is almost identical regardless of the project type. This similarity in scheduling time for the three project development modes reflects the increased allocation for effort in the more difficult

FIGURE 5-17
COCOMO effort estimates

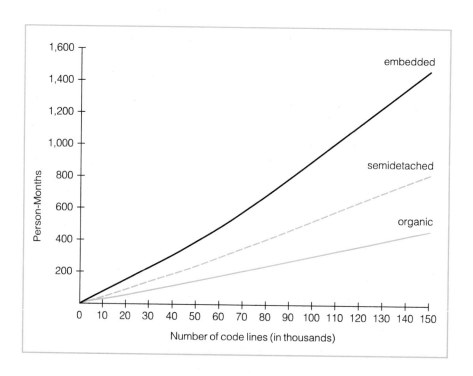

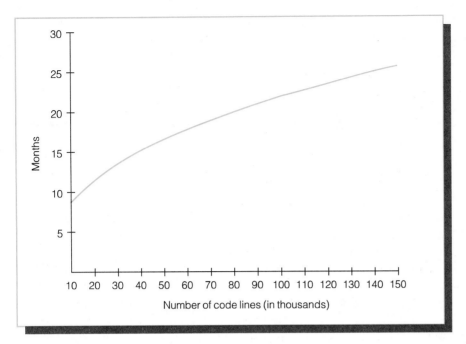

FIGURE 5-18

COCOMO development schedule for organic mode projects

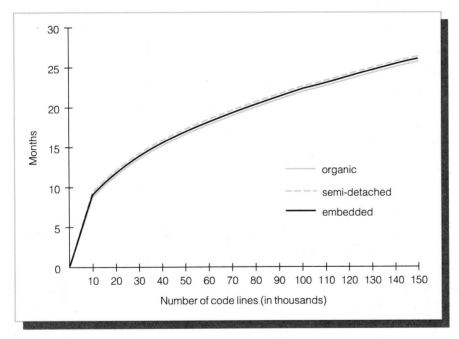

FIGURE 5-19

COCOMO development times for each project type

projects. Since more software developers are assigned, the calendar time to reach completion is nearly the same.

To illustrate the two formulas for effort and development time, let us consider a medium-size project classified as an organic mode type, which will produce an estimated 80,000 lines of COBOL code. The number of person-months needed is computed as

$$\text{Effort} = 2.4(80)^{1.05}$$

$$= 239.03 \approx 240 \text{ PMs}$$

The development time required to complete the project is calculated by

$$\text{DT} = 2.5(240)^{0.38}$$

$$= 20.06 \text{ months} \approx 21 \text{ months}$$

The values computed for effort and development time are rounded up to the next whole number on the premise that more—not less—time will be needed. Given the forecast of 80,000 lines of source code, the project will consume 240 person-months of effort and need a total elapsed time of 21 months to complete. Based on the scheduling of the tasks as previously shown for the SDLC, we know that we cannot simply assign 240 software developers to work 1 month each simultaneously. The project manager must establish the appropriate assignment of personnel to the individual tasks. Since each project has its own characteristics, there are no absolute rules to guide the personnel assignments. The time allocated per task is dependent on the project. If the estimate of 80,000 lines of source is correct, the computations from the COCOMO model tell us only that a well-planned project with adequate personnel resources assigned to the project tasks should result in a finished software product within 21 months of the project initiation date for the Design phase. However, Boehm [1981] does furnish some guidelines for allotting personnel to various project stages. As stated earlier, the estimates produced by the COCOMO model do not include the development time or person-months required for the Preliminary Investigation and Analysis phases.

THE INTERMEDIATE AND COMPLETE COCOMO MODELS

The basic COCOMO model considers only the two factors of code size and project type. The intermediate COCOMO model incorporates more variables into its computations for total effort and development time. Boehm [1981] used a set of multipliers to account for required product reliability, data base size, execution and storage constraints, personnel characteristics, and the software tools to be used for software development. But because his model was formulated prior to widespread use of structured programming or software tools, the values he established are no longer valid and will not be reproduced here.

Since a large system is composed of many subsystems with differing characteristics, classifying a complex project by only one project type is a serious disadvantage in forecasting staff and time requirements. Some subsystems may be organic, others will be semidetached, and a few may be embedded. To deal with this complexity, Boehm constructed the complete COCOMO model, which estimates each subsystem separately and sums the individual costs to obtain an overall cost for the entire project.

MODEL TUNING

In order to use the COCOMO model effectively, it is necessary to adjust the constants proposed by Boehm [1981] to reflect the organization's own experience with software development. The type of projects, the software tools in use, the staff's experience, and other factors affect the actual effort and time required for development. This means that the organization must establish a data base for the predicted and actual effort and time requirements for all software projects. The list of attributes suggested by Boehm should be modified to incorporate the firm's own developmental characteristics. The estimates and actual results are then plotted by means of appropriate software. The statistical technique known as *least squares* can then be used to obtain the best fit between the actual values and the predicted values obtained from the COCOMO model. The value of a can then be adjusted to create a formula that will compute the actual values given for the projects. The exponent value b can also be recalculated in the same fashion. However, a substantial amount of data, particularly for large projects, is necessary in order to obtain a good revised value. Since the value of b is close to 1, the difference between the new and old values for b may not be significant.

CRITICISMS OF THE COCOMO MODELS

The fundamental problem with the COCOMO model is its reliance on the number of code lines to be created as the basis for forecasting effort and time requirements. If we knew this number with reasonable accuracy at the start of a project, the COCOMO model would seem highly suitable for predicting the scope of the project. The problem is that no one really knows this figure with any degree of precision. At the start of the project, we may be able to compare it to other projects of similar magnitude and check how many lines of code they produced. From this figure, the person-months and time requirements for the new project can be computed—but the likelihood of error is immense. The variation in coding lines could easily be from 50,000 to 100,000 lines or more. The difficulty is that the project may not be outlined in sufficient detail to provide enough information for valid estimates.

Another problem with the COCOMO model is that its foundation rests on old software development projects executed before the widespread use of the structured programming methodology and of such tools as the structured analysis and design methodology, CASE tools, and other development support software. The type of applications included is another source of criticism. Of the 63 projects in Boehm's study, only five employed COBOL and seven were data processing applications. This sample size for data processing applications is very small, making the resulting estimates of these coefficients imprecise. Consequently, the coefficients in the COCOMO model require adjustment to reflect each firm's own environment.

The Realist's Approach to Project Estimations

Given this abysmal situation in modeling the project estimates, what should the project manager do? Because the situation will never improve without more information on actual projects, historical data should be kept on all software projects. Estimates can then be based on experience. After completion, the actual project effort and time requirements can be compared to the predicted efforts forecasted with the function point model and the CO-COMO model. The historical data should be identified by the particular phases in which the effort and time were spent. As suggested by Boehm [1981], the COCOMO model should also be refined for the organization's environment. Amassing several years of project data should sharpen the project manager's forecasting tools.

These models require much more information than a manager will ordinarily have on hand when the cost estimates must be made. Because of this inherent difficulty, there remains no substitute for experience when forecasting projects. Even at an early stage, an experienced project manager is able to judge certain aspects of the project. The new project can be mentally compared to past projects; the previous performance of the systems analysts and programmers available for each software development task will be rated. Figure 5-20 lists the eight steps of cost estimation. This approach combines a bottom-up estimation technique with the COCOMO model.

In step 1, the project manager estimates the total number of subsystems and their relative difficulty. After doing so, step 2 requires the manager to appraise each subsystem with regard to the factors of logical code complexity and reliability requirements. In step 3, the ability of the team members is assessed. Previous experience with this type of application, training, expe-

FIGURE 5-20

Guidelines for estimating software development projects
Estimates exclude the activities for the Preliminary Investigation and Analysis phases.

Step 1	Determine the number of subsystems.
Step 2	Appraise the characteristics of each subsystem.
Step 3	Assess the ability of the team members.
Step 4	Rate the software development environment.
Step 5	Estimate the project effort manually.
Step 6	Use the COCOMO model to estimate effort.
Step 7	Estimate the total development time manually and via the COCOMO model.
Step 8	Create the best estimates.

rience, and overall technical capability should be considered. Step 4 specifies that the project manager rate the software development environment with regard to programming language, CASE tools, and other productivity aids to be employed. In step 5, the effort in person-months for each subsystem is estimated manually. The total project effort is computed by summing the person-months for each subsystem. Step 6 involves the computation of the total project effort by using the COCOMO model. First, the project manager judges the total number of deliverable source code lines. Then the project features already appraised in steps 2, 3, and 4 are used to choose the project type—organic, semidetached, or embedded— and the proper coefficients for the COCOMO model.

Finally, in step 7, further computation is performed to yield two estimates of the total development time for the project by first using the COCOMO model and second, bottom-up estimation. In step 8, the project manager decides on the best effort and time estimates. The larger estimates are selected unless other considerations prevail. Such factors as previous experience with similar applications and exceptionally capable software personnel may overrule the choice of the larger estimate. Consider, however, that large-scale software projects are often seriously underestimated with regard to person-months of effort and time required. Although the COCOMO model incorporates contingency time, if especially difficult circumstances prevail it is advisable to add extra time. For example, a shift to a new programming language or a new software methodology would be reasonable cause to add extra time to the estimates.

Dealing with Late Projects

Once the project is underway, what should the project manager do if the project is not meeting the schedule requirements? Although adding more software personnel seems an easy way to speed up the project, this view is now recognized as erroneous. Adding more professional staff to the project is actually more likely to hinder its progress! This inability to speed up the work is caused by the need for the new team members to learn about the project and communicate with co-workers. In short, communication demands will impede the project.

As shown in Figure 5-21, adding two more members to a three-member team multiplies the time expended on communication among the workers. If each team member communicates with the remainder of the team, a five-person team has nine communication paths versus only three paths for a three-person team. Moreover, the time needed to educate additional team members about the project reduces the time available to actually work on the project tasks. There is one exception to the rule against adding more software personnel to late projects: the appointment of a person with very high levels of expertise in both the software environment and the application under development. Because this person already has some familiarity with the project, the initial costs of communication may well be repaid in the

FIGURE 5-21

The communication requirements for two projects The lines show the communication network among the team members.

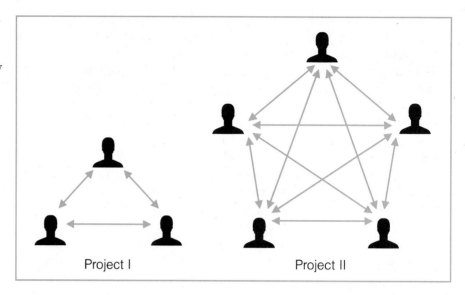

Project I   Project II

long run. Obviously, before adding any new workers, it is preferable to request overtime for the present team members, if possible.

Given that it is not feasible simply to add more persons to the team, the recommended solution to project overruns is to reduce the project specifications to a level that can be implemented within the estimated costs. This means that negotiations must be undertaken between the users and the project manager. Unfortunately, such modifications to the project specifications will most likely necessitate extensive changes to the partially completed programming tasks and may delay an already late project even more. The project manager can request a formal technical review to determine what new schedule is acceptable to the users and how the project specifications can be adapted to allow the project schedule to be met. This technical review includes discussing the option to cancel the project. Even though project termination is an extraordinary option, a project that will cost far more than the firm can afford must be dropped.

SOFTWARE MANAGEMENT STRUCTURES

Because a software project entails substantial interaction among the software personnel, the computer professionals are typically organized into small team structures managed by team leaders. The leaders then report to the project manager. If the project is very large, the hierarchical structure can be increased but the work continues to be performed by small teams. The two team structures in use are known as the *project team* and the *chief programmer team*.

Project Teams

Ideally, a project should be assigned to a small group of software developers, known as a **project team**. Naturally, more workers are needed for large projects. However, because of the nature of software development, it is inadvisable to manage large teams; instead, the project should be divided among several small teams. A typical organizational structure for a large-scale project is depicted in Figure 5-22. Except for the clerical staff, personnel have been organized into teams according to functional areas.

Small programming teams offer several benefits. First, they can work closely together and share their knowledge freely. Large teams inhibit such interchange. Second, *egoless programming* can be encouraged among small groups. Many times, a programmer works alone and "owns" the code. Since it is impossible to write error-free code, the programmer independently debugs the code to remove these errors, but avoids revealing his or her fallibility to others. **Egoless programming** means that the programmer no longer "owns" the code. Instead, the team members function as a unit and help each other to detect the errors in the program code. Since all programmers freely admit making mistakes, the team functions without any hurt egos. A third benefit of small teams is that the team interaction allows its members to learn about all aspects of the project.

A team is headed by a team leader, who typically also performs programming tasks. Work is discussed in team meetings and tasks are allocated according to ability. The program design is executed by senior team members, and programming tasks are assigned to junior staff members. The most

FIGURE 5-22   **The organizational structure for a large-scale project**

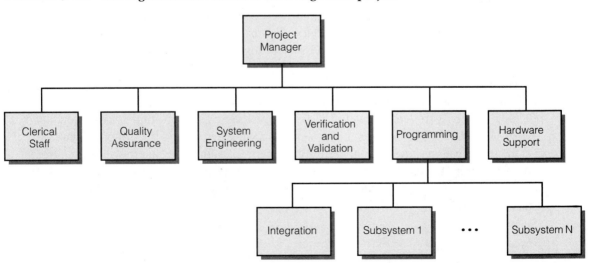

Barry W. Boehm, Software Engineering Economics, © 1981, p. 106. Reprinted by permission of Prentice-Hall, Englewood Cliffs, NJ.

Just Over the Horizon:
The FAA's Air-Control System

The problem of estimating projects correctly is a perennial one. Examples abound of projects that aren't delivered on time or within the original cost estimates. Even worse are the stories of projects that drag on for years with success always just over the horizon and that sometimes, as a last resort, are cancelled. The U.S. air-traffic control system offers an example of the quandary that can develop from project management problems. By January 1982, the computer system used to guide planes safely through the air had become prone to breakdowns. The increased volume of air traffic due to deregulation would soon exceed the capacity of the aging computer hardware, much of which was built in the 1960s. The Federal Aviation Administration (FAA) needed a solution to this problem in time to handle the anticipated increase in air traffic. The development of a new multi-billion-dollar system to provide both faster and safer trips was proposed by the FAA. The plan was to install a new highly automated air traffic control network in Seattle by 1992 with a complete phase-in of the system throughout the U.S. by the year 2000.

Today the project is nine years late with a $1.5 billion budget overrun, due to errors admitted by both the contractor and the FAA. First, the FAA took four years to select the final two bidders, who then took three years and $500 million of FAA funds to build the prototypes. IBM was awarded the contract on the basis of a fixed-price bid of $3.6 million despite the warning from the General Accounting Office (GAO) that the project would cost much more. Several more months elapsed while Hughes protested the award. In March 1989, IBM and the FAA finally began the task of writing nearly 2 million lines of code for the system that needed to be absolutely correct because passengers' lives were at stake. A key requirement was that downtime be restricted to only three seconds a *year*. To make matters even more difficult, the FAA demanded that all programming be accomplished in Ada, a computer language unknown to most commercial programmers but required by the Department of Defense for all "mission-critical" software.

When coding finally began, hundreds of changes to the original specifications appeared within a two-year period; deadlines became impossible to meet as programmers were forced to rewrite coding in order to meet revised requirements. Rather than dispute the changes and face the time-consuming delays of the FAA formal procedures, IBM chose not only to accept the revisions, but also to save time by abandoning software quality review procedures. The end result was serious coding errors and even more delays. At last, the specifications have been frozen. IBM now predicts that the system will be finished some time after the year 2000. Meanwhile Congress may choose to review the FAA fiasco and determine whether to abandon the system or continue to sink more millions into an already-late project.

For more information, see Mark Lewyn, "Flying in Place: The FAA's Air-Control Fiasco," *Business Week,* April 26, 1993, pp. 87, 90.

successful teams work together with good lines of communication and respect for each member.

Chief Programmer Teams

An alternative team organization, the chief programmer team, is advocated by Harlan Mills and Terry Baker [1973], who headed an extensive software development project for the *New York Times* in the early 1970s. The **chief programmer team** consists of a small group of subordinate programmers directed by a chief programmer, who is responsible for the project. Both a **backup lead-programmer** and the chief programmer must be thoroughly familiar with every aspect of the project at all times. If the chief programmer leaves the project for any reason (such as illness or resignation), the backup lead-programmer is capable of assuming its leadership. The code written by the programmers is reviewed by the entire group for errors prior to compilation. Egoless programming is an inherent feature of this organizational style. Prior to the initiation of testing, the code is examined once again for errors. Since the code will be studied by the entire team, easy-to-read code has high value and programmers are more likely to strive to achieve this goal.

During the *New York Times* project, programmers submitted compilation or program jobs for batch processing. Thus, their team structure also included a **program librarian** to document the progress of the team. The source code and test data were submitted to the librarian for filing prior to program execution. A record of all compilations and executions was maintained by the librarian. This process could be easily controlled under batch processing because the librarian was assigned the responsibility for submitting the job to the computer center.

Today, programming practices have changed substantially. Most programmers type their programs at their own terminals and can directly request program execution to take place. Nonetheless, the function of the program librarian remains an important one. By monitoring the different versions of the program, the librarian exercises control. Should the disaster of introducing new errors into a program occur, the return to earlier versions will be easier because the librarian has been performing the clerical chore of recording versions and test data. The required filing of the test data allows the team to examine the testing and decide whether all cases were adequately validated. The control of the program modifications and test data also provides complete information if a staff member should have to leave the team.

SUMMARY

The purpose of software project management is threefold: (1) to predict the work force and time requirements for the project, (2) to schedule the project, and (3) to control the project by forecasting the degree of success or

failure in meeting the established schedule. The planning process for a project begins by decomposing the project into major activities and the individual tasks required for each activity. The milestones and deliverables for the project activities are then identified. A milestone is the end point of a software activity, such as the completion of the training plans for the users. A deliverable is the tangible output of a milestone, such as the written plans for user training or the compiled code for a program module. The costs of the effort in terms of person-months (PMs) are then estimated. Once the project is initiated, the manager must monitor its progress to know if any slippage has occurred. As more information is gained about the project, the manager will revise the schedule and cost estimates to reflect the new data.

If delays occur, the project manager has several options. First, the work force may be expanded by adding software personnel. However, unless they are exceptionally qualified professionals, adding more workers may actually cause even more delays by complicating communications among the project staff. The second option is the reduction of the project scope by revising the project specifications. Such modifications must be negotiated with the users. Third, the manager may call for a formal technical review to determine whether steps should be taken to meet the schedule or the project should be terminated.

Gantt and PERT charts are two techniques useful in scheduling and controlling a project's many tasks. The sample project for the maintenance of the university lawns demonstrated how tasks can overlap to reduce the total time required. The Gantt and PERT charts for this sample project illustrated the general principles of these techniques.

PERT charts graphically depict the relationship between project tasks and their interdependence. Each task is represented by an arrow between two circles (called nodes) on the graph. The arrow indicates the direction of the work flow. A dummy task may be drawn from the end point of one task to the beginning of another task. PERT allows for each task time to be estimated at three different levels: t_o, the most optimistic time; t_p, the most pessimistic time; and t_m, the most likely time. The expected time for a task is then computed as

$$t_e = \frac{t_o + 4t_m + t_p}{6}$$

The longest path through the network graph is known as the critical path. To find the critical path, the total lengths of all paths through the network are computed; then the longest path is selected as the critical path. More than one critical path may exist for a PERT chart.

Gantt charts are designed to permit the project manager to easily ascertain the status of each task. They are drawn as bar charts where each task is depicted by a bar with an appropriate physical length to indicate the time required for the task. The tasks are placed on the chart in the sequence in which they will be executed. The float time for a task is shown in some fashion, such as an unshaded portion of the bar.

Since the systems development life cycle specifies the major activities and tasks performed for a software development project, it can be used as the framework for managing these projects. Project milestones are identified by the tangible outputs resulting from the life cycle's major activities. In order to better manage software projects, many firms have constructed volumes of detailed step-by-step specifications for the SDLC activities.

Software cost estimation is primarily concerned with the problem of predicting the amount of effort, expressed in person-months, and the total time required for the project. Because the project is ill defined in early stages, these models do not yield reliable information until much later in the project. Despite these deficiencies, knowledge of modeling techniques may benefit the project manager in estimating project costs and time requirements. Toward that goal, three popular techniques—*top-down estimation*, *bottom-up estimation*, and *algorithmic cost modeling*—were presented. Top-down estimation requires the project to be decomposed top-down into the logical functions to be performed. The cost of each function, but not its individual components, is then estimated. Bottom-up estimation is based on the decomposition of the project into its detailed components. The cost of each component is estimated in order to find the total project cost. Algorithmic cost modeling provides a method to compute the costs by using information regarding the project's attributes. The computational method is based on historical data collected from past projects. The algorithmic cost models known as function point and COCOMO were discussed.

The function point model offers a cost estimate computed with function points. A function point is related to the software's external inputs and outputs, user interfaces, external interfaces, files used by the system, and other features. The model relies heavily on the use of files and complexity of file manipulation, and it has been shown to be effective for projects with these characteristics.

The COCOMO model produces effort and time estimates that are dependent on the total deliverable source lines of code expressed in thousands (KDSI). A delivered line of source code (DSI) is defined to be any single line of the program code regardless of how many actual programming statements it contains. Effort is measured in the number of person-months required for the project during its design, programming, testing, and implementation activities. Documentation is included in this estimate. The effort for the initial feasibility study and the Analysis phase must be estimated independently of the COCOMO model. Total development time (also called scheduling time) is the number of calendar months required for the project duration. The COCOMO model classifies projects according to their characteristics of complexity, problem type, requirements for reliability, and the project staff's experience level with similar applications. The three categories of projects ranked according to difficulty are organic mode, semidetached mode, and embedded mode projects.

In the basic COCOMO model, the effort and time estimates are computed as shown in Figure 5-23. The intermediate version of the COCOMO

FIGURE 5-23

Effort and time esti-mates for the basic COCOMO model

Type of Project	Effort in Person-Months	Total Development Time
Organic mode	Effort = $2.4(\text{KDSI})^{1.05}$	DT = $2.5(\text{PM})^{0.38}$
Semidetached mode	Effort = $3(\text{KDSI})^{1.12}$	DT = $2.5(\text{PM})^{0.35}$
Embedded mode	Effort = $3.6(\text{KDSI})^{1.20}$	DT = $2.5(\text{PM})^{0.32}$

model incorporates more project characteristics into the formulas for effort and development time. The complete COCOMO model estimates the total project by dealing with each subsystem separately. The effort and development time figures for the subsystems are then summed to furnish estimates for the overall project. It is advisable to tune the COCOMO model by computing new coefficients based on the firm's own historical project data.

An eight-step approach to software cost estimations (except for the Preliminary Investigation and Analysis phases) was proposed as listed in Figure 5-20. These steps combine the knowledge of the project manager's experience with past projects and the results of the COCOMO model. A software development project is typically implemented by means of a small project team. If the project is too large for a single team, additional teams are formed rather than adding more members to the same unit. An alternative team structure is the chief programmer team, which consists of the chief programmer, a backup programmer, two or three more programmers, and a program librarian.

TERMS

algorithmic cost modeling	function point
backup lead-programmer	function point model
bottom-up estimation	Gantt chart
chief programmer team	late finish (LF)
COCOMO model	late start (LS)
contingency factor	milestone
critical path	most likely time, t_m
critical path method (CPM)	most optimistic time, t_o
deliverable	most pessimistic time, t_p
delivered line of source code (DSI)	network
	nodes

development time (DT)	organic mode projects
early finish (EF)	person-month (PM)
early start (ES)	program librarian
effort (in person-months)	project team
egoless programming	project evaluation and review technique (PERT)
embedded mode projects	
expected time, t_e	semidetached mode projects
event	slack time
float time, t_f	top-down estimation

QUESTIONS

1. What are the objectives of project management?

2. Explain the following terms:

project milestone

deliverable

critical path (in a PERT chart)

3. Why should a project manager use the techniques of Gantt and PERT charts to schedule a project?

4. What actions can a project manager take if a software project is late?

5. What problem(s) may arise if more members are added to the team for a software development project?

6. Why should the float time for a project be computed?

7. Why are software development costs harder to estimate than those of a physical construction task such as building a house?

8. Explain the following terms used for the COCOMO model:

delivered line of source code (DSI)

organic mode project

semidetached mode project

embedded mode project

development time

9. What criticisms of the COCOMO model were discussed in this chapter?

10. How can the software project manager ensure that the progress of each task is measured with some degree of accuracy, that is, deal with the "90% complete" answer from software personnel?

11. Explain the structure of the chief programmer team. What are its advantages over the typical project team structure?

PROBLEMS

1. The tasks of lawn mowing, clipping bushes, and edge trimming for the university lawn maintenance project were discussed in this chapter. Times were estimated as shown in the accompanying table.

Tasks for One Lawn Area	Time Required (in hours)
Mowing grass	3
Clipping bushes	4
Trimming edges	2
Total time	9

    The project schedule was constructed assuming only two machines of each type. The Gantt chart and PERT diagram for the lawn maintenance project appear as Figures 5-4 and 5-6, respectively.

    The lawn maintenance department has now purchased one additional machine of each type. Draw the new Gantt chart. Be sure to incorporate the assumption that one third of a lawn (1 hour's work) must be mowed before clipping can occur and that one half of the bush clipping (2 hours' work) must be done before edge trimming can start on the same lawn.

2. Compute the estimates for effort and development time by using the basic COCOMO model for the following projects.

    a. An on-line inventory system will be implemented. The reliability requirements for the communications module are high. The software personnel to be assigned to the project are inexperienced in this applications area. The staff will write in C++ and use object-oriented methodology; both are new project characteristics just adopted by the firm for all future software development. The estimated size of the final system is 100,000 delivered lines of source code. This estimate is really just a guess based on other large systems developed by the firm in past years.

    b. A system to perform sales tracking will be implemented in order to measure the effectiveness of various advertising media. The software personnel to be assigned to the project are experienced with data processing tasks and have high levels of expertise in the programming language to be used. The estimated size of the final system is 10,000 delivered lines of source code. However, the team will use a program generator and write in a fourth-generation language. The most difficult portion of the project is the program design, but even there, the project team has good credentials.

PROJECTS

1. Make an appointment with the director of the physical plant at your university to discuss the project management techniques, if any, in use. Prepare the following report on your discussion.
   a. Describe how the effort and time requirements for tasks such as grounds maintenance and painting are determined.
   b. Explain how the director is aware of the status of tasks underway.
   c. Suggest how the present project management methods could be improved for the physical plant area.

2. Visit the director of the data processing center at your university and explain your interest in software cost estimation problems. Inquire about the scheduling of new projects and how the projects are controlled. Prepare a report containing the information that you obtain. Be sure to include the following material:
   a. How the initial effort and time estimates are made
   b. Why Gantt and PERT charts are or are not used for scheduling any activities
   c. What remedial actions are taken by the data processing director when a project is found to be late

REFERENCES

Albrecht, A. J. "Measuring Application Development Productivity." *Proceedings SHARE/ GUIDE IBM Application Development Symposium*, 1979, pp. 83–92.

Albrecht, A. E., and J. E. Gaffney. "Software Function, Lines of Code, and Development Effort Prediction: A Software Science Validation." *IEEE Transactions on Software Engineering* 9(6), June 1983, pp. 639–647.

Boehm, Barry. *Software Engineering Economics.* Englewood Cliffs, NJ: Prentice-Hall, 1981.

Duncan, William R. "Projects from the Ground Up." *Computerworld*, March 7, 1988, pp. 85, 90.

Excelerator Reference Guide, Version 1.9 Facilities and Functions. Rockville, MD: Intersolv, 1990.

Kemerer, C. "An Empirical Validation of Software Cost Estimation Models." *Communications of the ACM* 30(5), May 1987, pp. 416–429.

Mills, Harlan, and Terry F. Baker. "Chief Programmer Team." *Datamation*, December 1973, pp. 58–61.

Miller, Michael J. "Project Management for the Real World." *PC Magazine* 11(12), June 30, 1992, pp. 81–82.

Mohanty, S. N. "Software Cost Estimation: Present and Future." *Software—Practice and Experience* 11(2), 1981, pp. 103–121.

Phan, Dien, Douglas Vogel, and Jay Nunamaker. "The Search for Perfect Project Management." *Computerworld*, September 26, 1988, pp. 95–100.

Sommerville, Ian. *Software Engineering*, 4th ed. Reading, MA: Addison-Wesley, 1992.

CHAPTER 6

Information Gathering

Objectives

In this chapter, we discuss the techniques that are employed by systems analysts to gather information from users. After completing this chapter, you will understand

- The characteristics of users and of analysts
- The principal ways of gathering information: interviews, questionnaires, observation, work sampling, and joint application design
- How to conduct interviews
- The advantages and disadvantages of each information gathering technique

INTRODUCTION

As we discussed in Chapters 1 and 3, the systems analyst is responsible for understanding the user's request and formulating a solution to the user's problem. To do so, the analyst must study the user's problem within the context of the current system, determine the problem's relationship to other aspects of the organization, and recommend the best solution to the problem. Without proper study, the analyst will be unable to judge whether a new information system or modification of the existing system is the best choice. Careful study may even discover that the best resolution of the problem lies in the improvement of manual procedures, the redesign of forms, or other refinements within the computer information system but external to the actual computer programs. In order to resolve the user's difficulties, the analyst needs more information than merely the user's problem statement.

Instead, as we discussed in Chapter 3, the systems analyst needs to become familiar with various aspects of the current system. An outline of the information typically sought by the analyst was presented earlier in Figure 3-5; this itemized list is repeated here for your convenience as Figure 6-1. The acquisition of this knowledge requires that the analyst gather information from the available sources in the organization. In order to gather this information, the systems analyst must be skillful in the use of various information gathering methods. The appropriate method must be selected to match the individual circumstances of each problem. The analyst is also confronted with collecting information directly from the users, who work with the existing system and experience its difficulties firsthand. In the first portion of this chapter, we will explain the role of the users in the infor-

FIGURE 6-1

The list of information sought by the analyst

- **System Objectives**

  Define the objectives of the current system. Evaluate these objectives: Do they serve for the organization or only this division of the firm?

- **System Inputs and Outputs**

  Identify the system inputs and outputs, the origins of the inputs, and the destinations of the outputs. This information shows who will be affected by the changes to the existing system.

- **System Functions**

  Define the functions of the current system. Then determine how these functions are performed by identifying the components of the system: manual procedures, user interfaces, computer programs, files and data bases, and other relevant system elements.

mation gathering process and the relationship between the users and the systems analyst. In the second portion, the information gathering techniques employed by systems analysts will be presented.

UNDERSTANDING THE USERS

Throughout the systems development process, the systems analyst must turn to the users as the primary source of information about the current system and its problems. In order to secure the best quality information, the analyst must enlist their cooperation. As shown in Figure 6-2, there are several obstacles to securing this much needed cooperation. Systems analysts often lack empathy for the users' problems, freely employ computer jargon in their discussions with the users, and exhibit poor listening skills. These problems arise because of one major barrier—the analysts forget that their function is to assist the users. In turn, the users frequently recall past system failures and are reluctant to engage in another systems project that may also fail. But problems primarily arise due to a second major barrier: Users may be fearful of the changes that will result from the implementation of a new system. These two barriers to the information gathering process are discussed below.

Assisting the Users

As we said in Chapter 3, the information system truly belongs to the users. Nonetheless, systems analysts and other computer professionals often do not act as though they believe that fact. As a consequence, the relationship between the analysts and the users may become strained and hinder the information gathering activities. Sometimes, users have sad tales to relate about the so-called assistance of information systems personnel. The users' requests for improvements in the existing system may have been seriously delayed or even dismissed from consideration by the information systems

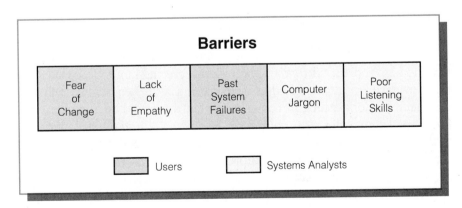

FIGURE 6-2
Obstacles to user cooperation

department. The suggestions of the users, during the investigation stage for the system now in use, may have been ignored. From the users' viewpoint, the current system may be less than satisfactory and it seems the information systems professionals are to blame for the flaws in the system. On top of these unfavorable experiences, users may also have encountered conceited systems analysts who rated themselves as superior on the basis of their computer skills. By acting in a patronizing way, these analysts stirred the users to righteous indignation. Besides the natural resentment of such treatment, the users may also regard the information systems personnel as incompetent because, in the past, they failed to understand the users' business problems and could communicate only in computer jargon. As a result of these unhappy episodes, the users consider the systems analyst to be an intruder rather than an agent who will assist them in performing their jobs. Such negative experiences on the part of the users explain why the much needed cooperation may not be present during the analyst's investigation of the existing system and its problems.

Why Users Fear Change

The systems analyst is the agent who causes changes to take place in the user's environment through the installation of a new system. Users often resent change in procedures—in particular, change that is imposed from outside. A new system typically means that the users must adjust to new screen designs, different reports, and altered procedures. The initial learning period is disruptive to their work and causes them to be somewhat uncomfortable with their work environment. The need to learn new procedures for a computer information system is frequently considered an unpleasant prospect.

Users not only may resent the new system but may be apprehensive about the changes accompanying its installation. Figure 6-3 lists some reasons why users fear change. Clerks may worry that they are too old to master new concepts; supervisors may believe that they cannot acquire the skills necessary for computer information systems. The workers may also be apprehensive about the effects of the new system on their work assignments. A line manager may be reluctant to change because she presumes that her position will be diminished by a new system. Another manager may think that the new system will require fewer clerks, causing him to lose status. A third manager may fear that decisions previously in her domain will be delegated to clerks acting in conjunction with the proposed computer information system. All these concerns are justified, because the introduction of a new information system can result in the realignment of authority with a corresponding loss of power and prestige by some users.

Finally, some users may be concerned that a new system will cause them either to lose their jobs or to be transferred to different and less satisfying positions. If a new system can perform the same job functions with fewer

FIGURE 6-3
Why users fear change

How the Computer Affects the Work Place	Possible Effects on the Worker
Changes in the job	Elimination of job, resulting in employee termination Employee transfers to less interesting tasks Job becomes less satisfying Computer may monitor job performance Decrease in job prestige Loss of decision making
Skills needed for the job	Inability to learn new skills Job performance levels become too high

people, then it is reasonable to assume that some employees will be terminated or moved to other locations within the firm. Change is not easy for most people. If the fear of job loss is coupled to change, users are likely to place obstacles in the analyst's search for information.

Winning the Users' Cooperation

If, for whatever reasons, analysts are confronted by unfriendly users, they must strive to change the situation. When serious difficulties are encountered due to concerns about job security, the assistance of management must be sought. The analyst does not have the authority to allay these fears. If job security is not at stake, management must communicate the much needed assurances to the employees. The analyst should be careful not to overstep the boundaries of authority by attempting to reduce the users' concerns in such matters.

In seeking the users' cooperation, the systems analyst should recognize that the users possess the business expertise with the existing system; their judgment and opinions must be respected. To display a condescending attitude is a mistake on the part of the analyst. The analyst must also recognize that the users own the system and acknowledge the importance of their role throughout the systems development process. This stance will ensure the users' involvement in the systems analysis and design activities. Such involvement not only enables the users to guide the system to a successful completion but also generates the enthusiasm that is needed to overcome the difficulties faced by the users in making the transition to the new system.

Despite these cautionary remarks, systems analysts must also be confident of the fact that they bring objectivity, technical expertise, and analytical skills to bear in solving the users' problem. By building rapport with the users, the systems analyst fosters the users' appreciation for the expertise and contributions of the computer staff.

METHODS OF INFORMATION GATHERING

Although the systems analyst must acquire information throughout the systems development process, the bulk of the information is collected during the early phases of the life cycle, that is, the phases of Preliminary Investigation and Analysis. During these phases, the analyst focuses on understanding the users' problems in the context of the existing system. Although the users are the prime source of such information, the study of the current system should commence with an examination of the organization charts, annual reports, departmental documents regarding goals and functions, and similar documentation. By doing so, the systems analyst acquires certain basic knowledge regarding the business enterprise and gains familiarity with the firm's structure, its long-range goals, its objectives, and its functions. The systems analyst also studies any documentation regarding the current system and its procedures and policies. Properly prepared to understand the current system within the context of the organization itself, the systems analyst can now continue the investigation of the current system by obtaining further information from the users. In this undertaking, the systems analyst employs one or more of the following methods (also listed in Figure 6-4):

> interviews
>
> questionnaires
>
> observation
>
> work sampling
>
> joint application design

Before starting the information gathering process, the analyst ensures that permission has been granted to contact the users and solicit information

FIGURE 6-4
Methods of information gathering

> Interviews
>
> Questionnaires
>
> Observation
>
> Work Sampling
>
> Joint Application Design

from them. Management must formally approve the investigation and grant the necessary time from the users' work schedule for this activity. Only with proper authorization can the analyst proceed on the information gathering task. In turn, the analyst is responsible for informing management about these activities and gaining their approval of the information gathering methods to be followed. An appropriate data gathering method must be chosen for the project. It is important to seek information in an efficient manner in order to minimize the disruption of the jobs performed by the users.

INTERVIEWING

An **interview** is a structured question and answer session between two persons, the interviewer and the interviewee. Interviewing is an important skill for the systems analyst because this is the most common way in which to obtain information from the users. Although other methods may be used once or twice during the life cycle, interviews will take place many times during the various phases of the systems development process. In an interview, the systems analyst attempts to learn the details concerning the current system by asking the users to supply this information. If the interview is conducted poorly, little or no information—or even an incorrect understanding of the system—may be gained.

A successful interview depends on the following steps:

1. Prepare for the interview.
2. Schedule the interview.
3. Open the interview.
4. Conduct the interview.
5. Close the interview.
6. Perform a follow-up interview, if needed.

As shown in Figure 6-5, two additional steps are performed outside the formal interview process. The documentation of the information acquired

1. Prepare for the interview
2. Schedule the interview
3. Open the interview
4. Conduct the interview
5. Close the interview
6. Perform follow-up interview for clarification

7. Document the interview
8. Send written appreciation and thanks to the interviewee

FIGURE 6-5

The interview method
Six steps form the actual interview process, followed by documentation of the interview and acknowledgement of the interviewee's contribution.

during the interview is listed as the seventh step. The eighth step is the recognition of the user's contribution to the systems development process by participation in the interview. These steps are explained in the subsequent sections.

Preparation for the Interview

An interview requires adequate preparation on the part of the systems analyst so that appropriate questions are asked and time is not wasted on matters not pertinent to the investigation. To plan the interview, the systems analyst seeks certain basic knowledge regarding the business. As stated earlier, the analyst first examines the documents available regarding the firm's goals, functions, and long-range objectives. Documentation of the current system is also perused. Following the documentation review and after securing permission, the analyst observes the current system in operation and examines the screens and reports produced by the system. Any manual procedures and records are also inspected. After this overview of the system has been acquired, the analyst composes the set of questions to be asked. These questions are tailored to the individual user's knowledge of the current system.

Scheduling the Interview

Before scheduling any interviews, the systems analyst must determine who should be contacted and in what sequence. For a large organization, several persons must be interviewed. By consulting the organization chart, the analyst decides on the particular individuals to interview. The order of interviews within a department is typically arranged in hierarchical fashion with the top executive interviewed first, the next level of managers, and so on. The higher level managers will contribute their evaluation of the system and its problems, the forecasts of future needs, the objectives of a new system, and its projected performance goals. However, the operational details of the system are ordinarily best known by lower echelon personnel. Consequently, all staff levels usually require the attention of the analyst.

The interview is a formally arranged event and must be scheduled. When scheduling the interview, the analyst specifies the format of the interview, the types of information being sought, the length of the interview, and its location. After the interview has been arranged, it is advisable to confirm the appointment with a letter or memorandum. Figure 6-6 illustrates a memorandum confirming the appointment of a systems analyst, George Kubal, with a store manager, Maria Lopez. The length of the interview should be between 30 minutes and an hour; if the interviewer is well prepared, this time is adequate in most cases. The interview is held in the user's work place providing that some privacy is possible. If the user's area is too noisy or offers no opportunity for uninterrupted conversation, a nearby conference room should be reserved for the interview. For example, the interview of an office manager, who is constantly dealing with phone calls and pop-in visi-

FIGURE 6-6

DATE: January 12, 1993

TO: Maria Lopez, Store Manager, The Georgeson Department Store, Highland Park, IL

FROM: George Kubal, Systems Analyst, IS Division, GDS Administrative Offices, Springfield, IL

SUBJECT: Interview Appointment on January 20

This memorandum confirms my appointment for an interview on next Wednesday, January 20, at 2:00 p.m. at your office. The interview should require no more than an hour and will cover the features desired for the new sales processing system.

As you are aware, the Information Systems Division has been directed to develop a new sales processing system. Henry Thomas, President, GDS, has expressed a need for better information in order to handle the growth requirements of the next five years. In addition, serious concerns have been raised regarding customer satisfaction and the apparent inability to restock items on a timely basis.

During the next two weeks, I will be meeting with all the managers of the Georgeson Department Stores located in Illinois. The supervisors of the ordering processing activities and a select group of sales clerks at each store will also be interviewed. The purpose of these discussions is to gain a fundamental understanding of the existing sales system, its inventory control procedures, and the ordering process.

To aid us in the proper definition of the new system, your assistance is requested in the following subjects:

1. Handling of sales transactions with payment by cash, external credit card, or GDS credit card.
2. Credit verification procedures.
3. Order processing system. Problems with stock-outs and backorders.
4. Evaluation of management reports now generated by the sales system; requirements for additional reports.
5. Problems now experienced with the current system.

It would be greatly appreciated if examples of reports, sales slips, and so on could be supplied to illustrate your points.

If you have any questions regarding the interview topics, please feel free to call me at (314) 555-9801. I look forward to meeting with you.

A sample memorandum to confirm a scheduled interview
The interviewer also uses the memorandum to outline the topics to be covered.

tors, is difficult at best and should be conducted in a more suitable location such as a conference area.

Opening the Interview

The opening of an interview establishes the way in which the body of the interview will proceed. The interviewer must project a friendly but businesslike demeanor. In opening an interview, the analyst begins by introducing himself or herself by full name. Some general introductory comments are appropriate, but a good interviewer is careful not to waste the interviewee's time with idle chitchat. Sometimes, the users feel ill at ease because they mistakenly believe that analysts are on a faultfinding mission. Since the users have the expertise in the system, the analyst can begin by acknowledging that fact and explain the need to learn about the system.

Confidentiality in any personal matters discussed during the interview should be guaranteed to the interviewee. If the user lambastes the boss or complains about co-workers, the analyst listens but never repeats such remarks. By winning the user's trust, the analyst can establish a solid foundation for the exchange of information. However, the interviewer should remain neutral during any criticisms. For example, the analyst can respond to the user's description of bad working conditions and an overbearing boss with the comment, "You certainly have problems here. Perhaps this study of the system will help to solve some of them." This response is sympathetic but avoids taking sides in the battle of the worker against the boss. The analyst must remain objective throughout the information gathering process and not allow biased viewpoints to influence his or her judgment.

Although the format of the interview was explained to the user at the time of scheduling, it is appropriate to review the format for the interviewee at this time. If a set of questions was previously sent to the interviewee, the analyst can proceed to the body of the interview with the first question. Otherwise, the analyst initiates the interview with a broad question designed to make the user feel comfortable with the interview process.

FIGURE 6-7

Standardized form for taking notes

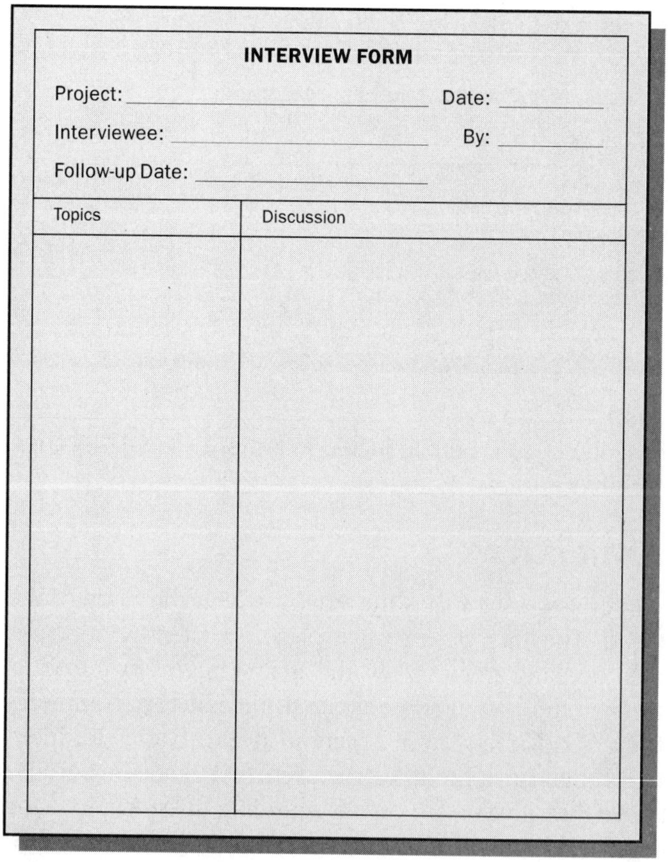

```
                    INTERVIEW FORM

    Project: _____   Date: _____

    Interviewee: _____   By: _____

    Follow-up Date: _____

    | Topics        | Discussion                      |
```

For most interviews the analyst records information by taking notes. If notes are omitted, important details may be lost and confusion may result later. Since note taking may disconcert the interviewee, it is performed as unobtrusively as possible. Because the use of an itemized list of topics can interfere with the flow of the interview, most analysts either employ broad categories for note taking (see Figure 6-7) or simply jot down notes on a blank sheet of paper.

Even though the easiest way to record information is by taping the entire interview, most people are uncomfortable with this method and do not want their every word permanently on tape. If the interviewee becomes self-conscious and reluctant to speak freely, the informality of the interview may be destroyed. Building rapport between the analyst and the user is also hampered under these circumstances. An equally serious disadvantage to taping interviews is the amount of time the analyst later spends listening to the tapes and summarizing the information in written form. For these reasons, the taping of interviews is not recommended.

Conducting the Interview

The body of the interview is conducted by the analyst posing questions to the interviewee. Questions can be classified into two categories, *open-ended* and *closed-ended*. **Open-ended questions** invite answers that are comprehensive discussions of the topic under consideration. **Closed-ended questions** are those that require only a short answer of one or two words. Figure 6-8 provides examples of both open-ended and closed-ended questions.

Because no boundaries have been established for the discussion, open-ended questions provide an opportunity for the user to speak candidly and straightforwardly. Since the analyst cannot possibly know all the right questions to ask the user, open-ended questions encourage the user to contrib-

Open-Ended Questions	Could you tell me how you process an order? Why do you send the yellow form to the Shop Floor? What do you do when the customer's account is overdue?
Closed-Ended Questions	How often do you review the customers' accounts in order to issue overdue notices? When is the blue form sent to the bank? Do you ever bypass this procedure?

FIGURE 6-8
Examples of open-ended and closed-ended questions

ute to the analyst's understanding of the issues on hand. Examples of open-ended questions are

"Would you tell me what happens after a salesperson submits the sales contract to your office?"

"Would you explain to me what information is lacking in the reports now produced by the system?"

"Why is the year-end report printed in triplicate?"

The words *what, how,* and *why* are good beginning words for open-ended questions. The preliminary words "would you tell me" or "would you explain to me" are extra words of courtesy, to prevent the interview from becoming an interrogation.

Closed-ended questions automatically constrain the dialogue between the analyst and the user by limiting the reply to only a few words. Some samples of closed-ended questions are

"How many times a day do you call the main office for reports?"

"Can you track the sales figures by individual salespersons?"

"Are all salespersons identified by a unique code?"

Closed-ended questions often start with the words *does, can,* or *when.* In answering these questions, the interviewee tends to reply with a short answer, often simply "yes" or "no." In doing so, the user provides an answer but gives only a minimum of information.

It is unlikely that an interview will contain only open-ended questions; some closed-ended questions should be included, as needed. The balance between closed-ended and open-ended questions is important. An interview without any open-ended questions is an unpleasant experience for the interviewee and elicits insufficient information for the systems analyst. Because a steady stream of closed-ended questions may cause the user to feel interrogated rather than a partner in the analysis process, it is best to mix closed-ended and open-ended questions whenever feasible. However, jumping back and forth between discussion topics to create an alternating pattern of such questions is inappropriate.

In formulating the questions to ask the user, the analyst maintains a neutral attitude regarding the current system by avoiding words that show bias or that may confuse the user. By refraining from such expressions as "awkward method," "messy area," and "badly designed report," the analyst allows the users to freely state their own views of the system. Restricting the analyst's vocabulary to commonplace words ensures good communication with the users and avoids any appearance of disdain for the users. Computer jargon should be avoided at all costs. By using computer terminology, the analyst conveys a sense of elitism rather than demonstrating interest in the user's area. Moreover, the analyst should not expect the user to make decisions regarding the computer aspects of the information system. For example, the question "Does the data file need to contain this information?" is asking for a decision regarding the data file rather than asking about the importance of the information to the user. "What data are necessary to obtain this information?" is a legitimate inquiry for the systems analyst, but how and where the data should be stored are not matters for the user to decide.

In a successful interview, the interviewer regularly indicates that the user's comments have been understood. One effective device is to restate the user's responses in different words. The purpose of restatement is to encourage further comments and provide feedback to the user. The interviewer should avoid exact repetition or too frequent use of restatement. Repeating the user's remarks too often will quickly make the user uncomfortable with the interview. Instead, the interviewer makes restatements occasionally in order to acknowledge the interviewee's information and encourage the imparting of further information.

Suppose the interviewee replies to a question by saying, "Ordinarily, I key in all the customer's data as soon as I get it by phone, but if there is a backlog of orders, I put the phoned-in data aside until much later. In that case, the customer's credit sometimes isn't checked." The analyst shows that this comment has been understood by observing, "I understand that the system requires manual checking of the customer's credit, but it's sometimes omitted when too many orders are backlogged." When using this method, the analyst cannot merely parrot what was just said. For example, an ineffective restatement of the user's remark is, "You key in all the customer data as soon as it's received, but when orders are backlogged, you put the phoned-in data aside. In that case, you will omit the check of the customer's credit." Not only is this statement merely echoing the interviewee's statement, but it even distorts it by the failure to include the word "sometimes."

Body cues, such as a nod of the head, also convey that the interviewer is paying attention to the conversation and continues to be interested in the interviewee's words. In a like manner, the interviewer avoids the appearance of indifference, which is evidenced by slouching in a chair, turning the face away from the interviewee, or folding the arms. All indicate lack of enthusiasm for the subject matter. Good posture, courteous manners, and other appropriate body cues set the stage for the discussant to enjoy the interviewing process as well as to disclose the information sought by the interviewer.

During the interview, it is also important that the interviewer use silence so that the interviewee has time to frame the answers to the questions. In the American culture, there is an innate desire to sustain conversation without any gaps of silence. In ordinary conversations, such gaps are indeed awkward. But in an interview the analyst should be prepared to be silent. When a question is only half-answered, the interviewee should be allowed sufficient time to formulate a full response. The interviewer who interrupts this thought process breaks the flow of the interview. Showing attentiveness to the interviewee with appropriate silences helps the interview proceed smoothly. However, long silences should not be ignored. If the question has not been answered within a reasonable time, the interviewer should either rephrase the question or inquire why the question was not answered. Perhaps the question was directed to the wrong individual and the user is reluctant to confess ignorance of the matter. Or, the question may simply need to be restated or amplified in order to clarify its meaning for the interviewee. During an interview, a good interviewer is an active participant, who continually acts to assist the interviewee in the disclosure of the information sought.

Closing the Interview

After all topics on the interview outline have been discussed, the analyst closes the interview with one or two questions that allow the interviewee to discuss any topics pertinent to the new system. An example of such a question is

> "What changes would you like to see so that you
> can do your job more effectively?"

This question provides an opening for the user to add valuable comments about the proposed system. Other good final closing questions are

> "Is there anything else about the system you want to
> tell me before we break off?"

> "Before we finish up, let me check on this. Have I left
> any topics out of our discussion?"

Most of the time, such questions will not elicit more information, but they demonstrate that the analyst respects the user's knowledge and they create goodwill.

Before terminating the interview, the analyst briefly summarizes the information obtained from the user. This synopsis demonstrates that the analyst listened attentively to the discussion and it permits the user to clarify any matters. The summary is a straightforward accounting of the discussion that took place. The conclusions of the analyst should not be stated here. Finally, the analyst closes the interview by thanking the interviewee for the discussion and asking permission to schedule a follow-up interview in order to clear up any details at a later date, if needed. At this time, the interviewee is also requested to review the written summary of the interview after it is prepared by the analyst, so its accuracy can be confirmed.

Follow-up Interview

After the interviewer has documented the highlights of the interview, a few matters may still be unclear. Ambiguities may exist, or information from a subsequent interview with a different user may have raised additional questions. The interviewer then exercises the prerogative of a follow-up interview to clarify these matters. Because permission for a follow-up interview was requested at the closing of the first interview, the analyst simply needs to arrange a suitable time and place with the interviewee. Since only certain matters need to be covered, the follow-up interview may be composed of only closed-ended questions. To save time, a telephone call may be enough to resolve simple questions.

Documenting the Interview

Shortly after the interview, the facts obtained are recorded and the report is submitted for approval by the interviewee. The written summary includes all the pertinent facts the user supplied. The interview can be documented in memorandum form, or a standard form for documenting interviews may have been devised. A sample format is displayed in Figure 6-9. If several

INTERVIEW SUMMARY

Project: The Georgeson Department Stores
Date: January 20, 1993
Prepared By: George Kubal
Interviewee: Maria Lopez, Store Manager, Highland Park, IL

Project Scope: Ms. Lopez wishes to change the existing sales transaction system in the store in order to speed up customer checkout, improve tracking of inventory, automate the reordering of merchandise, and obtain up-to-date information on sales revenue and the profits yielded each month. Although the present system uses an OCR system to scan merchandise tags, prices of sale merchandise or special coupon discounts must be entered manually. The OCR wand appears to have a high error rate, causing the sales clerk to manually key in data for each item purchased. Even when the wand is working, the clerks prefer to use the manual entry method. The handling of credit cards such as VISA and MasterCard is also very slow and requires the clerk to manually key in all pertinent information. The credit transaction then requires a separate slip to be written manually by the clerk. The use of the store's own credit card requires the same lengthy process. Whenever the store offers a special sale with discounts on selected merchandise, the clerks must manually enter the discount rate. If one item is wrong on a sales slip, the entire sales slip must be manually rekeyed.
    The inventory tracking portion of the present system is not working to her satisfaction; merchandise runs out frequently. Sales forecasting is desirable but can be delayed until the sales transaction system has been improved.

System Objectives
1. To improve speed and ease of sales transactions.
2. To reduce manual keying of sales data.
3. To produce current information regarding sales volume, revenue, and profits per monthly period, preferably by the 5th of each month. On demand queries are also desired.
4. To automatically create the orders for restocking merchandise and do so in a timely fashion. Note: Individual items require a separate lead time for goods.

Required System Features
1. Speedy and accurate customer transaction procedure.
2. Monthly sales reports (prepared no later than the 5th of each month).
3. Reorder of merchandise on an as-needed basis.
4. Sales forecasting to be installed later.

FIGURE 6-9

A sample format for documenting an interview

users were interviewed about the same matters, their interviews may all be summarized in one report. Using standard formats facilitates the study of the documentation as well as the synthesis of this information into a document stating the current system's operations and the requirements of the new system. Diagrams such as systems flowcharts or data flow diagrams are created whenever appropriate. Forms used in the current system are collected and appended to these documents. Although blank forms provide the general layout, it is better to obtain forms containing real data. If confidential data such as salary information exist on these forms, dummy data are substituted. An important consideration for documentation is the proper tracking of the individual items produced during the study of the existing system. An up-to-date index to this material should be maintained to allow quick retrieval of particular information.

Acknowledging the Interviewee

After suitable documentation has been prepared, a copy is sent to the interviewee for two reasons. First, it is important to acknowledge the productivity of the interview session with this participant, who contributed time and knowledge to the project development activity. As a courtesy to the interviewee, a written appreciation of the interviewee's contributions should accompany the interview summary; if the interview summary is given in memorandum form, this acknowledgement can be the opening statement. Second, the facts gleaned from the interview should be reviewed by the contributor so that any errors can be rectified as soon as possible. This early review of the information provides the systems analyst with immediate feedback, ensuring that misinformation is not carried forward into the next phase of the project. As mentioned earlier, when several related interviews are performed, the pertinent details may be condensed into one summary report. Each interviewee then receives a copy of this synopsis and comments on its accuracy.

Guidelines for the Interviewer

Although each interview has its own characteristics, we have presented several recommendations applicable to the deportment of the analyst during any interview process. As displayed in Figure 6-10, these various recommendations can be summarized by the following basic guidelines:

1. Be aware of the interviewee's individuality.
2. Show good listening skills.
3. Choose appropriate words and phrases.
4. Remain objective.

The analyst must always remember to function in a manner that strengthens communication links between the users and the software developers. The need to respect the user as a unique person should be the principle governing any interaction between analyst and user. As discussed

Be aware of the interviewee's individuality.

Change is difficult for most people.

Differing backgrounds and job tasks should be respected.

Show good listening skills.

Use appropriate body cues.

Restate responses.

Use silence where appropriate.

Choose appropriate words and phrases.

Use a balance of open-ended and closed-ended questions.

Avoid computer jargon.

Avoid emotionally charged words.

Remain objective.

Don't comment on the strengths or weaknesses of the current system.

Stay neutral regarding office politics.

Don't make claims regarding a new system.

FIGURE 6-10

Guidelines for the interview process

earlier, the analyst must be aware that many users fear change and have serious reservations regarding a new system. The technique of good listening furnishes the proper atmosphere to enable the user to impart the necessary details to the analyst. The choice of suitable words and phrases as well as a balance of open-ended and closed-ended questions also help to establish the proper meeting ground for the user to feel comfortable in assisting the analyst in the information gathering task. Finally, the analyst must remain objective to avoid antagonizing the user. Neutrality about office politics and problems with the existing system is the best policy. The analyst must also refrain from making any claims about the new system, such as its not yet

Warning

If you are assigned to interview for a project, always obtain permission from the proper individual: the owner, the director, or the manager. Also, be sure to approach the right person for the information needed. The individuals who perform the routine work are usually the best source of detailed information. When asking for information, remember that you ordinarily do not need access to the firm's financial records; the general format of the data as written on forms is usually sufficient for your purposes.

specified capabilities or its ramifications for the employees' jobs. Such matters must be handled by management and do not fall into the analyst's realm.

Advantages of Interviews

The major advantage of the interview method is its flexibility. Because the systems analyst has personal contact with the user, the interview is not locked into a rigid framework. Although the systems analyst prepares a list of questions, the disclosure of new information during the interview can lead the analyst to shift the focus of the interview to other areas. Any question can be explored in greater depth depending on the interviewee's response. This opportunity to adapt to unforeseen situations is always available to the interviewer. By using these chances to gain information, a skilled interviewer is able to obtain information of higher quality than possible through more structured methods.

Interviews also build rapport between the systems analyst and the users. If the analyst has maintained good posture and listening skills throughout the interview, it is likely that the user will have positive feelings about the proposed system. The direct involvement of the users in the systems development process gives them a sense of control over the development of the new system. A further advantage of the interview method is that a fruitless session can be quickly terminated by the analyst, saving time and effort.

Disadvantages of Interviews

Despite their many benefits, interviews have the serious disadvantages of being time-consuming and costly. Because interviews require time from both highly paid systems analysts and from employees and keep them from their usual tasks, the technique is costly. Ordinarily, managerial employees are also interviewed, adding to the expense. Other disadvantages result from the unstructured nature of the interview. The quality of the information obtained depends on the skills and objectivity of the interviewer. If the interviewer is biased and unable to be open to the interviewee's responses, then the interview will result in insufficient or incorrect facts. The interpretation of the information given by the interviewee likewise depends on the systems analyst's ability. If the interviewer fails to ask suitable questions, lacks objectivity, or has poor interpersonal skills, the interview session may be unsuccessful or only minimally productive. Thus, the success of the interview technique rests almost entirely on a single individual, the systems analyst.

QUESTIONNAIRES

A **questionnaire** is a specially prepared document designed to obtain a specific body of information. As an example, a portion of a questionnaire is shown in Figure 6-11. Preparing the questions in written form renders the

FIGURE 6-11

An example of a questionnaire This excerpt is from a questionnaire designed to survey a textbook publisher's sales personnel about a proposal for portable computers to be used to speed up orders and to provide information on new books more efficiently.

1. When making your sales calls, how many minutes do you generally spend with each faculty member?
    a. Less than 10 minutes
    b. 10 to 20 minutes
    c. 20 to 30 minutes
    d. Over 30 minutes

2. What are your major difficulties when making a sales call? Circle all that apply.
    a. Can't locate the textbooks in the catalog
    b. Unable to locate brochures on newly issued textbooks
    c. Instructor becomes impatient due to time needed to locate book titles
    d. No matching textbooks available for course
    e. Other problems (please explain below)

    _____

    _____

3. If the main office supplied you with a computer and appropriate software to look up titles by topics and authors, would you use this system?
    a. Yes, definitely
    b. Uncertain but very likely to do so
    c. Uncertain but very unlikely to use it
    d. Not at all

4. What are your concerns about the use of a computer with your work?
    a. Too complicated to use quickly
    b. Will cause delays in answering the instructor's questions
    c. Too heavy or bulky to carry with me on my calls
    d. Instructor may respond unfavorably to the computer
    e. Other (please specify below)

    _____

    _____

information gathering process impersonal. Unlike the interview method, questionnaires are a rigidly structured means to obtain answers to preselected inquiries. They offer no opportunities for in-depth questioning when new facts are uncovered. Because of the impersonal nature of the technique, users do not feel genuinely involved with the systems development process.

The preparation of a good questionnaire requires adequate time be spent on selecting questions, designing their format, and arranging the document for the ease of the respondents. As indicated in Figure 6-12, a good questionnaire has four characteristics: *validity, reliability, face validity,* and *ease of use*.

Validity

Reliability

Face validity

Ease of use

FIGURE 6-12

The characteristics of a good questionnaire

Validity

Validity of a data collection method means that it obtains accurate information that fulfills the investigator's needs. The validity of a questionnaire is judged by whether it asks the right questions from the right people. In order to authenticate the validity of a questionnaire, the document undergoes a pilot test with only a sampling of potential respondents prior to its mass distribution. The questionnaire is then revised to remove ambiguities and include additional questions if necessary. The pilot test may be repeated to guarantee that the revised questionnaire meets the goals of the study. Depending on the complexity of the questionnaire, it may have to be refined and tested several times. After the questionnaire has been administered to the entire survey population, the results should be verified by other methods. Interviews with a selected group of users, observation of the existing system, or comparison of the results with managerial projections are all avenues by which the questionnaire's findings can be validated.

Reliability

The **reliability** of the questionnaire is measured by the consistency of the responses. To ensure that the responses were correctly given, more than one question may be used to elicit the same information. The answers to these redundant questions are checked to see if identical data were obtained. If not, the information collected by the questionnaire should be considered unreliable and an unacceptable basis for any decision-making regarding the new information system.

Face Validity

A data collection method has **face validity** whenever it provides the appearance of eliciting valid data to those viewing the data collection procedure. For instance, if the respondent thinks that the questionnaire asks the right questions in the right way, the document is said to have face validity. Questions that seem meaningless to the respondent may evoke answers that are given without sufficient thought. If poorly prepared, the entire questionnaire may be dismissed as a waste of time and tossed aside or answered carelessly. As mentioned earlier, testing the questionnaire with a small group of users should eliminate such problems.

Ease of Use

A good questionnaire features **ease of use**. This means it is easy for the respondent to complete in a reasonable length of time and the information it supplies is easy to synthesize into a comprehensive description of the existing system. Accordingly, the questions should be clearly stated and simple to answer. As a general rule, a questionnaire contains closed-ended questions such as multiple choice or short answer questions, so that the answers can be quickly tabulated. Open-ended questions are usually avoided because of the difficulties in accurately summarizing the responses. The number of questions is limited so that excessive time is not required by the respondent. The overall appearance of the questionnaire also affects the user's ability to understand the questions fully and issue a suitable response. Similarly, if the questions are badly organized, the user may experience difficulty in comprehending the questions and formulating appropriate responses. Questions are grouped by subject area to allow the user to follow the questionnaire's overall purpose. This aids the user in determining the correct response and also contributes to the face validity of the document.

Advantages of Questionnaires

Despite the fact that good questionnaires require the investment of large amounts of time and effort, they are a popular way to elicit information. Once the questionnaire is validated, information from large groups can be procured conveniently and economically. Moreover, when the questionnaire is properly designed, the information supplied by the respondents can be quickly tabulated into a cohesive document. When used appropriately, the questionnaire is a valuable tool.

Disadvantages of Questionnaires

As we have said earlier, designing a good questionnaire can be time-consuming. Although multiple choice or short answers typically have high face validity, the proper construction of such questions is often difficult. If a multiple choice question does not offer a suitable choice to the respondent, the final tabulation of responses will be flawed. Badly worded questions can quickly mislead the respondent and yield incorrect information. If open-ended questions are used, the analyst faces the laborious task of interpreting the responses and tabulating the answers. At best, questionnaires supply only the information requested. The opportunity to discover new information in areas unfamiliar to the systems analyst is not available here. The advantages of flexibility and adaptability associated with the interview method are also not attainable with this technique.

OBSERVATION

In some projects, it is advisable to obtain additional information about the existing system by observing the daily activities performed in the actual work place. This is called the **observation** method of information gathering. It is especially valuable when tasks require a relatively short time span and occur repeatedly throughout the work period. For example, the processing of a claim by an insurance firm is a task that is performed continuously in the claims processing work area. To observe the work flow and detect problems, the systems analyst simply obtains a bird's-eye view of the work place and studies the performance of the task for a portion of the work shift. It is insufficient to observe only one execution of the task. Only by seeing the task performed several times will the analyst be able to draw conclusions regarding the problems of the user.

The primary advantage of the observation method is the acquisition of firsthand knowledge of the system-related tasks. The analyst is able to directly judge the performance of the system and see the problems encountered by the users without any intermediaries. Because the analyst observes the system in operation, any bias or failure by the user to accurately describe system details is avoided. Despite this obvious advantage, the analyst must also be aware that bias may be introduced by the mere act of observation. Knowing that their work performance is under scrutiny may affect the behavior of the users. They may perform tasks more precisely and rapidly than usual. On the other hand, it is also possible that the users will slow down and make more mistakes because of the presence of an observer. This phenomenon, the **Hawthorne effect**, was first described in a study of factory workers [Roethlisberger and Dickson, 1939].

Since the users' activities were directly observed, the conclusions drawn by the analyst are automatically accorded high validity. Others assume that the analyst has the ability to understand the system features through the act of observation. However, good results from this technique require a highly observant individual who has familiarity with similar systems and the ability to analyze the system's activities during their actual performance. If the analyst lacks the necessary skills and experience, then observation will yield information that may appear valid but lacks authenticity. A third disadvantage of observation is that some tasks are performed infrequently or at inconvenient times. For example, the observation of shipping problems may be difficult if products are shipped only in the early hours of the morning. Another example is found in an insurance firm where the special processing required for exceptionally large insurance claims occurs infrequently. If the observation period chosen by the analyst does not include such claims, the handling of special cases will not be observed.

WORK SAMPLING

Work sampling means that the appropriate information is gathered from a small group, called a *sample*, drawn from the entire population. The technique of work sampling is useful when interviewing, questionnaires, or observation of all users is unsuitable due to the large size of the work force. Instead, the analyst must rely on the selected work groups to be representative of the entire population. This method has its dangers. If only high performance work units are chosen for study, the problems of other workers may be ignored or dismissed as unjustified. In the same way, if only workers with poor performance records are selected for the sample, the knowledge to be gained from the other workers will not be available. In addition, the work flowing through the selected employee groups may not be truly typical of the overall body of tasks performed by the firm. Consequently, work sampling must be used with great care. Appropriate statistical methods should be used to select the sample so that it truly represents the entire population. Otherwise, erroneous conclusions will result from the study.

JOINT APPLICATION DESIGN

Developed by IBM, **joint application design (JAD)** represents an alternative to interviewing users. Instead of separate interviews, a work session lasting two to four days is scheduled with information systems personnel and a representative group of qualified users. The purpose of the group work session is to collect the pertinent information within a short time frame, thereby reducing the calendar time required for the analysis activities. The total time required for software development may be shortened by 15%, thereby lowering overall costs for the project. Since the JAD method is more successful in eliminating systems specification errors than the other traditional information gathering techniques, development costs are reduced and user satisfaction is high. As with the interview method, the users who attend a JAD session feel that they have guided the design of the system, so they gain a sense of system ownership. Their direct involvement in the systems development process also helps the users to understand the difficulties faced by the information systems (IS) professionals who will build the system.

Since a JAD session has a high commitment of employee time and requires wholehearted participation in the process, the firm's top management must fully support the activity. To demonstrate that sponsorship, typically a high-ranking executive of the firm launches the JAD session with a short introduction stating the firm's endorsement of the software project and the JAD information gathering session. Near the close of the JAD session, this same executive returns to commend the participants for their contributions to the project's ultimate successful conclusion.

The Organization of the JAD Session

As depicted in Figure 6-13, everyone attending a JAD session plays one of four roles: the *leader*, the *active participants*, the *observers*, and the *recorders*. The **active participants** are a representative group of the users, who know the necessary facts and details regarding both the current system and the objectives of the future system. An IS professional serves as the **leader** of the group work session. This person is responsible for guiding the participants to an accord on the requirements for the new system. Because the JAD session must provide the opportunity for a free exchange of ideas, it is

FIGURE 6-13

The participants in a JAD session

Session leader	Chairs the session
	Leads participants to consensus
Active participants	Furnish the information sought regarding the future information system
Observers	Provide technical assistance when needed
	Observe the session
Recorders	Document the session

not a highly structured meeting. The session leader presides over the meeting to aid the participants in openly expressing their ideas. In this forum, all contributions from the speakers are valued. Because the success of the JAD session is dependent on the skills of the session leader, this person must be chosen with great care. Ideally, the session leader should be a top-ranking IS professional who has a wide-ranging knowledge of technical and business areas. The session is not chaired in the classical sense; rather, the leader promotes open discussion and plays a neutral role in decision-making. Issues must be resolved by the participants. The session leader's responsibility is to assist the group in arriving at decisions mutually agreeable to both the users and the IS personnel.

Since the session leader will be fully occupied in leading the group discussion, other IS professionals must attend the meeting in order to act as either observers or recorders. A systems analyst from the project team attends but maintains a listening role as an **observer**. Because the session leader alone has the responsibility of guiding the users towards realistic requirements, the analyst must refrain from comment even if impossible expectations are expressed by the users. Depending on the project, it may be necessary to assign additional IS personnel to the session as observers to provide technical support. For technical areas outside of the IS area, other technical personnel may be invited to attend the session. These people serve primarily as observers rather than participants, joining in only when needed to resolve specific technical issues. To provide further support to the session leader, one or more IS personnel are designated as **recorders**, who document the discussions and the conclusions of the session. This record is formally published and distributed to the participants shortly after the session has been completed.

Disadvantages of JAD

Although the JAD method has been shown to be a time-saving technique which yields high quality information on the requirements for the new system, it does have some drawbacks. The JAD session requires the full participation of a large number of employees for a period of two to four days. This is a major investment of human resources in time and cost. However, because the use of JAD results in higher quality systems with fewer design changes in the Implementation phase, its costs are quickly recovered. If management fails to give whole-hearted support to the JAD method or if its endorsement is not communicated to the firm's employees, the IS professionals will be hindered in their efforts to encourage the free exchange of

What Users Want

Users and computer personnel frequently have different priorities for system features. As we have said, it is not enough simply to upgrade a system according to a computer professional's viewpoint. An example is given by the Air Force Materiel Command, which planned to revamp its communications and computer support organization. Air Materiel Command (AMC) is responsible for the procurement, deployment, and maintenance of weapons systems for the Air Force. To find out what its users really wanted, AMC performed a six-month survey and also dropped in on its users. Major Hal Ellis, who is in charge of the customer support project, admits, "We thought we knew what users wanted. We had good intentions, but we were all focusing on the internal processes, on buying the right product to make it easier for IS managers to do the job." He found out the users had a different agenda. "They wanted an instant connection to the data; and when there was a problem, they wanted one source, one phone call, to get it solved."

Sometimes a crucial part is missing from a parts warehouse even though the computer says it is on the shelves. Although AMC has a phone line for help in such cases, the users prefer to call a local programmer. They saw the AMC phone line as a "trouble ticket" rather than a solution to their problems. The survey found that calling AMC was useful at logging and tracking problems but not at getting the parts any faster. The project team, led by Major Ellis, then put together a strategy to flip the priorities. An overhauled system was needed to focus on serving the command's "core business functions" of supporting the Air Force's weapons systems. Rather than concentrating on specific products, the software developers decided that the users needed support in the basic areas of accounting, configuration, performance, and fault management.

Ellis found a pivotal strategic tip in Eliyahu Goldratt's *The Goal* [1986]. Goldratt's thesis is that an organization should focus on its "throughput." Ellis' group defined throughput for IS customer services as client connectivity and also set the objectives of decreasing operating expense and inventory costs. AMC hopes to fulfill its users' needs by installing a new customer service center at each base by October 1993.

Source: Horwitt, Elisabeth, "Basic Instinct," *Computerworld*, January 11, 1993, pp. 75, 77. Copyright 1992/93. Reprinted with permission from *Computerworld*.

information. Since it is not possible to invite all users to the JAD session, the sense of system ownership may be limited to only those employees participating in the session. If the attendees do not include those personnel who potentially could obstruct the new system, the systems development process could be hindered. Finally, the diplomatic skills of the session leader must be superb in order to foster the open exchange of ideas and obtain the participants' agreement upon realistic goals and plans for the system.

SUMMARY

In the information gathering process, the users are the principal source of information regarding the operations and problems of the existing system. In their dealings with the systems analyst, the users may be unwilling to reveal the required information about the system. This lack of cooperation may be due to a variety of reasons. The users may fear for the loss of their jobs, they may resent the changes that will come with the new system and the necessity to learn new procedures, or they may have previously encountered IS personnel who provided poorly designed systems. By acknowledging the users' ownership of the system, the analyst takes the first step in enlisting the cooperation of the users. The analyst continually seeks to build rapport with the users and gain their involvement in the systems development process. Doing so helps to increase user satisfaction.

There are five information gathering methods typically employed in the systems development process: interviews, questionnaires, observation, work sampling, and joint application design. Before the information gathering process begins, management must approve the method selected and grant permission to contact the users. An interview is a formally arranged session in which the interviewer asks questions of the interviewee. Six steps compose the successful interview process: preparing for the interview, scheduling the interview, opening the interview, conducting the interview, closing the interview, and the follow-up interview. Two additional steps, outside of the interview process, are the documentation of the interview and the written expression of appreciation to the interviewee.

Because the interview allows direct interaction between the participants—the user and the analyst—great flexibility is offered to the interviewer to adapt the interview according to the circumstances that occur. A skillful interviewer is able to build rapport with the user. The interview's main drawbacks are its expenditure of time and resulting costs. Despite these disadvantages, the interview method is the most commonly used information gathering technique.

Questionnaires are documents especially designed to collect information from large groups rapidly and efficiently. Closed-ended questions are preferred because of the difficulties in tabulating responses to open-ended questions. A good questionnaire has four characteristics: validity, reliability, face validity, and ease of use. Validity means that the questionnaire collects the information required for the investigation; that is, it asks the necessary questions. The reliability of the questionnaire is gauged by the consistency of the responses. Face validity means that the respondent simply accepts the questionnaire as an instrument that collects valid information. To be effective, a questionnaire must be easy to use by the respondent and permit quick and accurate tabulation of the responses. To ensure that a questionnaire meets these four criteria, it is pretested on a small group of users. Typically, a large investment of time and effort must be expended to create a suitable questionnaire. The disadvantages of questionnaires are the time required to design an appropriate instrument, the difficulties in tabulating the responses (especially for open-ended questions), and the lack of the flexibility and adaptability that the interview method features.

Observation is a method whereby the analyst observes the functions of the users performed in the work place. Although the conclusions drawn from this activity are frequently accepted without question, the users' behavior may change due to the act of observation (the Hawthorne effect). The interpretation of what the analyst sees may be biased or incorrect due to the observer's own expectations or lack of knowledge. In addition, some tasks that are performed only at inconvenient times or infrequently may be inadvertently omitted from the study.

In work sampling only a small group, called a sample, is used for the investigation. Usually, this means selecting a group of users or work sites from the entire population because it is not feasible or economical to study the existing system in its entirety. If the sample is not carefully selected to be representative of the whole population, then the study will be biased.

Joint application design (JAD) is an information gathering technique developed by IBM to improve the quality of the requirements definition while also reducing the calendar time needed for this activity. The method relies on a joint session of selected users and IS personnel, lasting two to four days. The session leader must be a highly skilled IS professional who endeavors to lead all participants to mutual agreement on a set of specifications for the new system. To assist the session leader, a systems analyst acts as an observer but does not participate. One or two other IS professionals serve as recorders to provide complete documentation of the discussion. Technical personnel from information systems and other areas of the firm may attend to supply any technical details required by the participants. Because of their intimate participation in the systems development process, the users in the JAD session acquire a sense of system ownership and an understanding of the limitations faced by the IS personnel in building the system.

TERMS

closed-ended questions   open-ended questions

interview   questionnaire

Hawthorne effect   ease of use

joint application design (JAD)   face validity

   active participants   reliability

   leader   validity

   observer   work sampling

   recorder

observation

QUESTIONS

1. For what reasons might a user feel hostile towards the systems analyst during the information gathering activities?

2. **a.** Name the five information gathering methods discussed.
   b. Explain each method briefly.

3. **a.** Outline the eight steps recommended for a successful interview.
   b. Briefly describe each step you listed.
   c. Explain the advantages and disadvantages of the interview as an information gathering technique.

4. **a.** What are closed-ended and open-ended questions?
   b. Give two examples of each type of question.

5. What is the purpose of a follow-up interview?

6. What is the Hawthorne effect? Give an example of it from your own experience.

7. **a.** Explain the information gathering method known as observation.
   b. Explain the method known as work sampling.
   c. What are advantages and disadvantages of each method?

8. Describe the joint application development (JAD) method.

9. Classify each of the following questions as closed-ended or open-ended.
   a. How do you process the shop floor's requisition of parts?
   b. When do you turn over your reports to the vice-president of finance?
   c. Could you tell me how often errors occur in the data received from the main office?
   d. What procedure is followed for granting credit to a customer?
   e. After you key in the individual sales transactions, do you ever find that data have been omitted?

10. Susan Adams, systems analyst, has been assigned to collect information regarding the problems experienced by the sales division of the Super-PC Software Company. Criticize the following interview between Susan Adams and Douglas Herrington, manager of the sales division, by writing each improper statement made by the interviewer and stating why it is unacceptable.

> Susan: Hello, I'm Susie from IS and I just came by your office to see if you were free to talk with me.
>
> Douglas: I happen to free at the moment. Come in for a few minutes before my conference with the lead sales people.
>
> Susan: Well, I have so many questions. How many sales reports are produced by IS for your office each month?
>
> Douglas: Ten.
>
> Susan: How many of these sales reports do you find useful?
>
> Douglas: Only one.
>
> Susan: Which report is that and could you tell me why it is useful to you?
>
> Douglas: Sorry, it's almost 9:30 now and I'm due at the conference. Good-bye.
>
> Susan: Thanks for your time. Good-bye.

PROJECTS

1. a. Prepare a questionnaire to survey students to determine if the computers and software available in the college computer lab facility are adequate for their use. If no computer lab is available, attempt to determine what types of computers and software should be placed in a future facility.

b. Administer the questionnaire to at least 25 students. Tabulate your results and prepare a summary report of your findings.

2. Investigate what information on job opportunities is needed by students majoring in the information systems area. Interview at least five students. Summarize your findings in a two- to three-page report. There are three major questions in this study:

a. What information from what sources is currently available to the graduating seniors?

b. What other information do they desire?

c. From the students' perspective, what information should have been provided to them before the senior year?

3. Request an interview with at least three department chairs to investigate their needs for information systems to process their budgetary data during the year. Prepare a report that documents the results of your interviews.

REFERENCES

Corbin, Darrell S. "Team Requirements Definition: Looking for a Mouse and Finding an Elephant." *Journal of Systems Management* 42(4), May 1991, pp. 28–30.

Gane, C. *Rapid Systems Development.* Englewood Cliffs, NJ: Prentice-Hall, 1989.

Gildersleeve, Thomas R. *Successful Data Processing System Analysis.* Englewood Cliffs, NJ: Prentice-Hall, 1978.

Goldratt, Eliyahu M. *The Goal: A Process of On-going Improvement.* New York: North River Press, 1986.

Lucas, Mark. "The Way of JAD." *Database Progamming and Design* 6(7), July 1993, pp. 42–49.

Palmer, Richard J., Martin W. Tucker, and James B. King II. "A Diagnostic Approach to Information Management Problems in the Organization." *Journal of Systems Management* 42(4), May 1991, pp. 23–27.

Pitman, Ben. "Technical and People Sides of Systems Project Start-Up." *Journal of Systems Management* 42(4) April 1991, pp. 6–8.

Ramsgard, William C. *Making Systems Work: The Psychology of Business Systems.* New York: Wiley, 1977.

Roethlisberger, F. J., and W. J. Dickson. *Management and the Worker: An Account of a Research Program Conducted by the Western Electric Company, Chicago.* Cambridge: Harvard University Press, 1939.

Schultz, Duane, and Sydney Ellen Schultz. *Psychology and Industry Today* 4th ed. New York: MacMillan, 1986.

Two Real-World Projects

CHAPTER 7

A Case Study: The Campus Bookstore

Objectives

After reading this chapter, you will understand the concrete application of each step in the systems development life cycle:

- Preliminary Investigation
- Analysis
- Design
- Implementation
- Installation
- Post-Implementation Review

By studying the overview of the systems development process for the Campus Bookstore information system, you will be better equipped to implement an information system that solves the various problems posed by users.

INTRODUCTION

In the previous chapters, we discussed the steps performed in the systems development life cycle (SDLC) and focused our presentation on the theoretical aspects of the methodology. Now we will demonstrate these steps by describing how a systems analyst implements a solution to the problems encountered at a bookstore. While this narration is a combination of fact and fiction, the problems in this account are realistic. Each step of the life cycle must be executed in any real-world system in order to obtain a successful solution to the problems experienced by the users. In this portrayal of the bookstore's difficulties, the major phases of the life cycle are clearly delineated. In reality, the individual tasks in these phases recur and the phases overlap. The boundaries of the phases are actually just guidelines for project management. Although the technical details of the project will be discussed, you should focus on the overall view of the systems development activities. The case studies presented here and in Chapter 8 illustrate how various techniques are used to create a computer-based information system. These techniques will be explained in later chapters. Now we will begin our saga of the Campus Bookstore and the hardworking systems analyst, Maria Lopez. The cast of characters is listed in Figure 7-1.

THE BOOKSTORE'S PROBLEMS

After Midwestern College's enrollment surged in the 1970s, a group of entrepreneurs saw the need for a second bookstore to supply the textbooks required for the college classes. They opened the Campus Bookstore in a location convenient to the college and gained immediate success in the student market. Today the Campus Bookstore sells over 80,000 textbooks to the college students annually as well as supplying paper, pencils, pens, and other office supplies. Competition is keen between the two rival bookstores,

FIGURE 7-1   **The cast of characters**

Campus Bookstore	George Howard, manager
	Susan Adams, textbook manager
	Don Papke, shipping room clerk
	Sam Henderson, assistant to the textbook manager
	Tom Havel, assistant manager
Computer Consultants	Maria Lopez, systems analyst
	John Sabatini, chief programmer
	Vice-President (unnamed)

but the market is sufficiently large to provide both stores with adequate profit margins.

George Howard, the manager of the Campus Bookstore, is rather pleased with the overall operation of the bookstore. Since he took the position two years ago, the profits of the store have risen, customers appear to be generally satisfied, and new merchandise has been added to the shelves. But one pesky problem remains: how to improve the efficiency of the ordering system for textbooks. Somehow all his efforts have been ineffective. The old card file system was revised, but it is still nearly impossible to quickly answer telephone inquiries such as:

Have the books come in yet for my course?

How many copies did I order this semester?

How does that total compare to last time?

Was this book used in any courses last year?

It takes so long for Susan Adams, the textbook manager, to search the card files that she cannot answer these questions promptly. Sometimes Susan has to look through the stack of purchase orders or pull out the original textbook order. And then, of course, there is that old problem of manually keeping the records up-to-date. Sometimes, the cards are not updated for days. Even worse, a card can be misfiled and Susan may hunt for hours to find the information.

Before the purchase order forms can be typed, the book titles must be arranged by publisher so that only a single set of purchase orders is sent to each publisher. Reordering the book cards is a major task requiring many hours of clerical effort. Last year, they experimented with recording the data in two card files, one with the complete information in order by course number and the second with partial information in order by publisher. But somehow there were just too many errors even with that system. It was easy to make a mistake in recording information, and the final preparation of the purchase orders to send the publishers became even more difficult. All in all, it remains a tedious, time-consuming process to collect the textbook orders, record them on cards, order the books from the publishers, and then keep track of shipments received.

This year, Mr. Howard has resolved to initiate a new system. He has been concerned about the continued prosperity of the bookstore. It is easy to become complacent, but there is another bookstore available to the faculty and students. If enough students complain about problems buying textbooks at the Campus Bookstore, the instructors could transfer their future orders to Midwest Book and Supply. Then, too, the instructors sometimes feel frustrated with the long delays in answering their inquiries. Even worse, when the record-keeping system fails to keep up with orders, the textbooks may not arrive on time for the opening of the term. Mr. Howard is very aware that if a textbook is shipped late or not at all because of a clerical error, the instructor can simply switch to his competitor. To survive in this business, Mr. Howard realizes that it is important to offer the best possible service. He knows that a computer could handle all these records efficiently. In fact, he has planned for a computer system since his first day on the job. To sustain its position in the marketplace, the Campus Bookstore clearly needs a better way to process textbook orders.

Unfortunately, Mr. Howard lacks the expertise to implement a computer-based information system and none of his staff are trained in computers. To solve this problem, he has decided to engage the firm of Computer Consultants. This firm has performed consulting services for several businesses in town and has excellent recommendations. Today, he will contact them to obtain an estimate on the costs to implement the much-needed computer system for the textbook area.

THE INITIAL DEFINITION OF THE PROBLEM

Computer Consultants is delighted to undertake the investigation of the bookstore's problems and arranges for Maria Lopez, one of their leading systems analysts, to meet with George Howard. After a lengthy discussion with Mr. Howard, Maria proposes that a feasibility study be performed. The feasibility study will enable her to better understand the bookstore's problems and propose a solution for them. By commissioning a careful study of the problem, Mr. Howard can avoid the implementation of a system that does not meet his needs or that will be obsolete in a short time. Maria also points out that the preliminary work performed for this study will be beneficial again later to develop any computer information system that she might recommend.

Mr. Howard responds that he is already convinced that a computer-based system is absolutely necessary. "Why can't you just begin to implement the system without wasting time on a feasibility study?" he protests. Having heard this argument in the past, Maria smiles and replies, "If something is worth doing, it's worth doing right the first time." To elaborate on this point she describes the dangers of building a system without sufficient knowledge of the problems facing the bookstore. The feasibility study represents the opportunity to do the job right, to install the system needed today and for the next five years. By contrast, rushing into building a system before the requirements are fully specified risks leaving Mr. Howard with a system that will not meet the bookstore's needs. Even if the system proved adequate for the moment, it might become obsolete within a year. Money would have been wasted; the Campus Bookstore would have to either operate with continuing problems or pay once again to replace a brand-new system.

Maria concludes her remarks by asking, "Isn't it worth taking the time to do it right?" Mr. Howard smiles back. "Yes, it certainly is worth doing it right the very first time," the bookstore manager agrees, and he adds, "Turn in your proposal as soon as you can, so that I can approve the cost figures." The next day Maria submits a written bid for a three-week study with corresponding costs.

The initial proposal from Computer Consultants is shown in Figure 7-2. Notice that Maria was careful to state the problems faced by the bookstore without committing herself to a particular solution to the problems. Mr. Howard's concerns regarding the textbook system were expressed, but the final approach was left open. The scope of the problem was stated in terms of time and money, that is, a maximum expenditure of $100,000 and 12 months time. The terms of the contract were given explicitly so that Mr. Howard will know what results the feasibility study will produce.

After reviewing the time and cost figures, Mr. Howard decides to approve the proposal and to give the go-ahead for the feasibility study. His hopes for a computer solution to the bookstore's difficulties remain strong, but Maria's explanation of the Preliminary Investigation phase makes sense to him. It is better to take time now to look at the problem than to leap into a system that will fail to meet his needs. With his approval, Maria begins the feasibility study by investigating the current system.

FIGURE 7-2

The initial project definition prepared by Computer Consultants

DATE: January 15, 1994

PROJECT: Campus Bookstore Textbook System

THE PROBLEM: The present method of processing textbook orders is slow and
                   error-prone. Queries regarding orders are difficult or impossible
                   to answer.

SCOPE OF THE PROBLEM: The solution should require no more than 12 months
with a maximum expenditure of $100,000.

OBJECTIVES: To investigate the potential for installing a new system to efficiently
handle textbook orders for college courses. The new system must be able to respond
quickly to inquiries regarding orders and the status of textbook inventory.

SCOPE OF THIS PROPOSAL: Three weeks at a total cost of $6,000

PROJECT OUTPUT: The report of the feasibility study will include

1. Statement of the problems in the current textbook system
2. Preliminary design of a computer-based information system, if deemed feasible,
   or specifications for an improved manual record-keeping system
3. Estimated costs and time requirements to implement the proposed system
4. Tentative schedule for system implementation

This report will be delivered no later than five weeks (35 days) after the signing of the
contract.

THE FEASIBILITY STUDY

Before contacting any employees of the bookstore, Maria phones Mr. Howard and asks him to authorize the interviewing and observation activities she is planning for her information gathering activities. She also requests that Mr. Howard inform the staff about her study and encourage their co-operation. After taking these steps Maria returns to the bookstore to begin her study of the existing system.

The Study of the Existing System

Before concentrating on the textbook system, Maria wants to obtain an overview of the bookstore's operations. Mr. Howard is glad to discuss the current and future operations of the bookstore during the hour-long interview Maria had requested. He explains that all the record-keeping operations in the store are performed manually. "What about the payroll system? Is that a problem in any way?" asks Maria. Mr. Howard replies that paychecks and W-2 forms are prepared by an accounting firm. The firm charged $15,000 last year and has just announced a price increase of 10% starting in May. However, their work has always been satisfactory and Mr. Howard is reluctant to investigate other accounting firms or start his own system. The cost is based on the number of checks prepared; because bookstore employees are paid once a week, the cost is high.

The scheduling of employees is a minor problem. The work schedule is prepared so that the part-time employees can attend their classes at the college. Once again, although it takes some time, it has always been accomplished satisfactorily. Most of Mr. Howard's record-keeping problems are associated with the textbook system and the general merchandise sold in the bookstore. Maintaining the appropriate levels of inventory is a difficult task. Maria inquires about future plans. "Yes," Mr. Howard says, "We are arranging to sell software packages for the IBM PC and the Macintosh computers. The sales of software packages should begin in July this year." He continues by explaining that the general trade book area will not be expanded for a long time. There are already several bookstores competing for the trade of the general reading public. He reiterates his interest in automating the textbook system. Maria ends the interview with a summary of Mr. Howard's comments and requests a follow-up interview, if needed. Mr. Howard offers his assistance at any time.

Maria now begins her study of the textbook system. She has arranged an appointment with Susan Adams, the assistant manager in charge of textbooks. Because Susan has worked in the textbook area for the last two years, she has the necessary background to answer Maria's questions fully. Susan hands Maria samples of the forms currently in use. Textbook order forms are sent to all faculty members ten weeks before the semester ends. Orders can be written on these forms and mailed to the bookstore or they can be phoned in. When a textbook order is called in, the information is recorded on a blank order form. A sample order form received from an instructor is shown in Figure 7-3.

New textbook orders are transferred to cards at the beginning of each working day. The information from the textbook order forms is typed on the cards; each book title is placed on a separate card. Occasionally, Susan just handwrites the cards whenever that appears more convenient than using the typewriter. The card file is organized by book title. The original form filled out by the instructor is placed in a file arranged by department and by course number. Because some courses are cross-listed, errors in filing can occur; for example, a course on Asian Civilization may be listed as a course in both the Asian Studies and History Departments. Since only one form is submitted by the instructor and placed in the textbook file, the staff has to refer to the course schedule issued by the college to answer queries about these courses. It usually takes a long time to answer such a question. Some-

FIGURE 7-3 A sample order form for textbooks

CAMPUS BOOK STORE

555-3874

PLEASE TYPE OR PRINT CLEARLY

INSTRUCTOR: Seimer

LIST OF BOOKS FOR

OFFICE ADDRESS: 374 LC

DEPT. 7P COURSE # 075 SECTION # all Spring SEMESTER, 19 94

PHONE # 555-5570

(THIS FORM COVERS ONE SEMESTER ONLY)

EST. NO. OF BOOKS NEEDED	AUTHOR	TITLE	OPTIONAL ISBN # Edition, year	PUBLISHER
350	Woolfolk	Educational Psychology	0132364281	Prentice-Hall

RECOMMENDED, BUT NOT REQUIRED

THIS ORDER GIVEN TO CAMPUS BOOK STORE ONLY? YES ☑ NO ☐

WILL SOME STUDENTS ALREADY HAVE THIS TEXT FROM A PREVIOUS SEMESTER? NO

INSTRUCTIONS

1) MAIL OR DELIVER ALL THREE COPIES TO:

Campus Book Store, 540 Main St., Dalton City, MD

2) YELLOW COPY WILL BE RETURNED AS CONFIRMATION OF YOUR ORDER.

M W Seimer

INSTRUCTOR SIGNATURE

12/2/93

DATE

12154/3-90

Based on the order form in use at the University Bookstore, University of Iowa.

times, the clerks forget about cross-listed courses and conclude that the books inquired about do not exist. "We just get confused," admits Susan.

As the beginning of the semester draws near, the bookstore receives a flood of textbook order forms. These orders must be processed quickly so that the books can be obtained in time for the opening day of the semester. As a general rule, each publisher's book titles are grouped together to go on a single purchase order. The purchase orders are manually prepared from the grouped cards by the clerical staff. If there is insufficient time for a written purchase order to be prepared and sent by the instructor, a phone order is placed. Notations made on the book order cards indicate any order that requires "express service."

In addition to new books, the bookstore deals with used books, which are purchased from used book distributors and from students. Used books are much more profitable for the bookstore; consequently, every attempt is made to secure used books. If an instructor orders the same book as the previous year, the bookstore can buy back the used copies from students. These books are then sold for next semester's classes. As Susan points out, "This buyback operation is really important for the bookstore, because our greatest profits come from used book sales." The students also like the buyback system, because they can make some money reselling their books.

Now, Maria asks Susan for a guided tour of the bookstore. She learns that the arrival of each carton of books is recorded by Don Papke, the shipping room clerk, on a checklist form. Then the carton is opened and the books are counted to ensure that the specified number was received. Don marks the packing slip as approved or short and forwards it to Susan so that her records can be updated. When the number of books is short, Susan phones the publisher and the call is noted on the order card.

When a textbook shipment is received, the instructor is not notified. Hence the faculty members often call up to be sure their texts have arrived in time for the opening day of class. When asked about the textbooks ordered for a particular course, Susan has to look for the original order form to identify the book titles. Then she searches through her stack of more than 3,000 cards to check the desired information. Many courses have more than one textbook, and it is easy to get cards out of order or not see all the information on the order form. It is also difficult to handle the file of original paper forms arranged by course number. Susan frowns, "I really want to be able to retrieve information in a number of different ways."

As the tour continues, Susan explains about the pricing of the textbooks. A label indicating the selling price is put on each book. The clerk at the cash register uses this price to tally the sale. The checkout lines are short today as Maria studies the store's operations, but Susan warns her that the first two weeks of classes are hectic. The store always hires extra clerks for that period. Maria observes the other merchandise sold by the store, including pencils, pens, paper, and other school supplies; general reading books are also available. Although no problems exist with these merchandise areas, the employees think it would help to install an automatic checkout system with bar scanning equipment to speed up the checkout process. Those first two weeks of school demand everyone's utmost endurance and agility. "Can't we put in a really fast system?" Susan questions Maria. "We need some help here, and the number of textbooks has just grown too large. Since the college's enrollment boomed, we are constantly behind in the clerical work of tracking the textbook orders." Maria acknowledges Susan's expectations of the new system but refrains from endorsing any particular system design.

Maria spends the next several days inspecting documents and records in the bookstore's business office and the textbook ordering division. Once she fully comprehends the flow of data through the system, she is ready to draw a preliminary sketch of the textbook system as a set of data flow diagrams. Her overview of the textbook system is shown in Figure 7-4. This type of diagram is called a level 0 data flow diagram. The submission of the textbook order by a faculty member is the data input that triggers the system activities. Maria calls the textbook order the *driving force* of the system.

FIGURE 7-4 The overview of the textbook system The level 0 data flow diagram

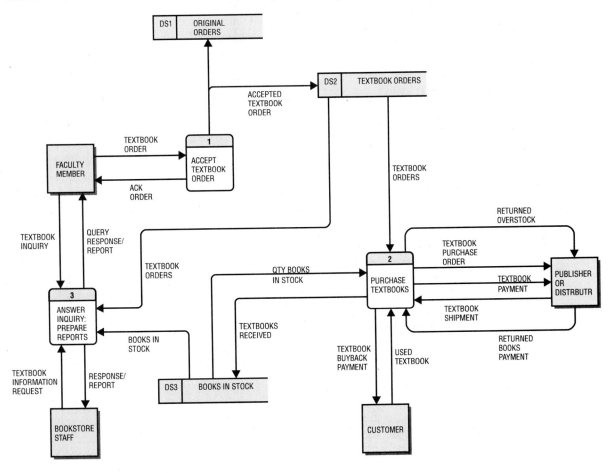

The data flow diagram represents the movement of data through the textbook system. For the sake of readability, Maria has omitted the error data flows. Such details of error handling would complicate her report without improving the overall picture of the textbook system. Of course, Maria's final specifications will indicate all the error data flows and error handling processes.

Warning

Study the data flow diagrams given in the figures by walking your way through them. Try to understand what the diagrams represent, but don't worry yet about how to draw them.

Now, let us inspect the diagram in Figure 7-4, starting with the faculty member who sends (or calls in) a textbook order to the bookstore. Process 1, ACCEPT TEXTBOOK ORDER, first checks the textbook order for errors or omissions before filing it in the files—the *data stores* called TEXTBOOK ORDERS and ORIGINAL ORDERS. Because textbook orders are sent by each instructor individually, process 1 takes place many times before the textbooks are ordered from the suppliers. Five weeks before the new semester begins, the bookstore orders the textbooks (process 2, PURCHASE TEXTBOOKS). Process 2 occurs more than once because some textbook orders arrive after the bookstore's cutoff date for orders. Finally, the bookstore must answer questions about the book orders and the availability of the books for purchase (process 3, ANSWER INQUIRY; PREPARE REPORTS). Maria does not indicate the date or time when any process actually takes place. These dates change each semester and the time frames can be altered as needed by the bookstore. By convention, whenever diagrammed inputs are received the processes are ready to be executed; thus, no time indication is needed.

Because process 2 (PURCHASE TEXTBOOKS) contains several steps, Maria decomposes it into a separate data flow diagram, shown in Figure 7-5. The process is said to be *exploded* into further detail. To facilitate its reading by the end users, she again uses the conventions of the level 0 type of data flow diagram. Later, in Chapter 9, we will follow slightly different conventions. In Figure 7-5, the data flow TEXTBOOK ORDERS enters process 2.1, ORDER TEXTS, which prepares the TEXTBOOK PURCHASE ORDER. Before placing a book title on a purchase order, the clerk checks whether any copies are in stock by consulting the file BOOKS IN STOCK. The TEXTBOOK PURCHASE ORDER is sent to the publisher or distributor (PUBLISHER OR DISTRBUTR) and also placed in the TEXTBOOK PURCHASE ORDERS file. Process 2.1 also sends the textbook title to the BUYBACK LIST, which is used to approve the purchase of used textbooks from students. The PUBLISHER OR DISTRBUTR sends the shipment of textbooks (TEXTBOOK SHIPMENT)

FIGURE 7-5   The explosion of process 2 (PURCHASE TEXTBOOKS)   The conventions of a level 0 diagram have been followed.

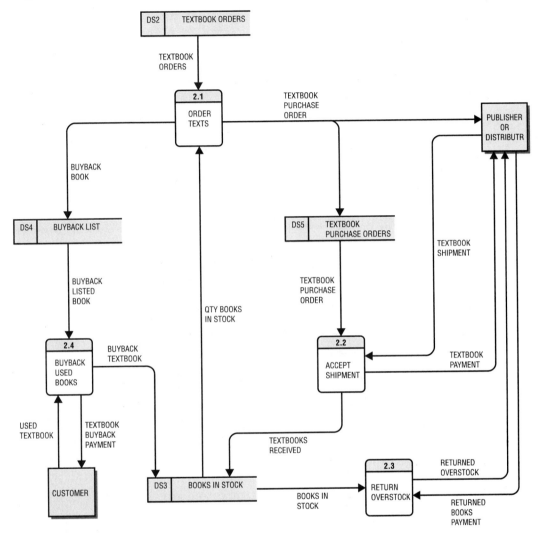

which is received by process 2.2, ACCEPT SHIPMENT; the payment is issued to the supplier as shown by the data flow TEXTBOOK PAYMENT. The receipt of the textbooks is recorded as shown by the issuing of the data flow TEXTBOOKS RECEIVED to the file BOOKS IN STOCK. Process 2.3, RETURN OVERSTOCK, represents the return of unsold textbooks at the end of the term. Process 2.4, BUYBACK USED BOOKS, shows the purchasing of used books that appear on the BUYBACK LIST, from the students (CUSTOMER).

An *organization chart* giving an overview of the bookstore's operations is also created (see Figure 7-6). The bookstore has four major subsystems: Accounting, Sales, Acquisitions, and Human Resources. The Acquisitions

FIGURE 7-6   The organization chart of the Campus Bookstore

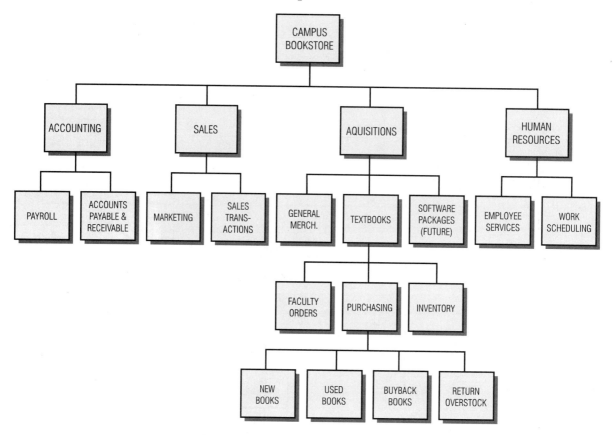

subsystem has three subdivisions: General Merchandise, Textbooks, and Software Packages. Although the sale of software packages is still in the future, it may affect decisions regarding a new system; thus, it is shown here. The major aspects of the textbook subsystem are described as Faculty Orders, Purchasing, and Inventory. The Purchasing area is decomposed further into four areas: New Books, Used Books, Buyback Books, and Return Overstock.

To verify that she has not neglected any aspect of the bookstore system, Maria returns to George Howard to have him inspect her model of the current system (Figure 7-4) and the organization chart of the bookstore (Figure 7-6). She asks about any new reports that might be desirable with a computerized system. Mr. Howard tells her about the problems of deciding what quantity of books to order for a course. Sometimes an instructor grossly overestimates the number required. Because the bookstore usually has to pay shipping costs for returning books and normally is not reimbursed for the full amount paid, it is unprofitable to buy books that will not be sold. Such overruns could be minimized with a new system. Mr. Howard wants some way to determine an appropriate quantity based on previous history with the course and, if possible, the instructor. By examining the records of the previous years, he could make a more intelligent purchasing decision. Maria decides to incorporate this additional feature in the model for the new system. Consequently, a historical file must be included in the textbook system. Because the use of this file will affect the ordering of the textbooks, Maria modifies process 2, PURCHASE TEXTBOOKS, in the model of the existing system to show the creation of the data store HISTORICAL BOOKS IN STOCK and indicates its subsequent use by process 2.1, ORDER TEXTS. This revised diagram illustrating the activities associated with purchasing textbooks in the new system is displayed in Figure 7-7.

Next, Maria documents the data required for the system by creating descriptions of the data flows and data stores shown in the data flow diagram. These descriptions are stored in the *data dictionary*, a collection of data about data. Every data flow and each individual component (an *ele-*

FIGURE 7-7   The data flow diagram for process 2 (PURCHASE TEXTBOOKS) in the new system   The conventions of a level 0 diagram have been followed.

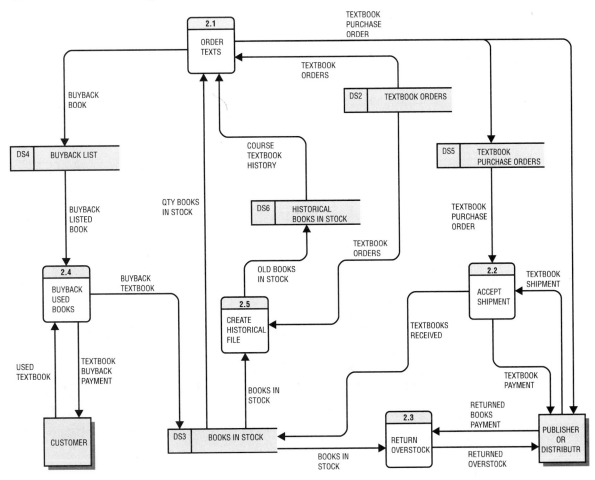

ment) within each data flow is described by a data dictionary entry containing information about its name, meaning, format, source, and use. This information is the "data" stored in the data dictionary. By creating the data dictionary, the systems analyst organizes the information about the data that exists within the system. The data dictionary entries serve to fully explain the data flow diagram. For now, the analyst needs the data dictionary primarily to facilitate communication with the user. The data dictionary will also provide a basis for estimating file storage requirements, which will be discussed subsequently. Later, in the Design phase, Maria will rely on the data dictionary entries in order to incorporate all the necessary data into the system's computer files and to design them appropriately. The data dictionary will also assist the programmer in creating the programs for the computer information system. In Figures 7-8 and 7-9, two sample entries, the data flow TEXTBOOK ORDER and the data element INSTRUCTOR, are displayed by means of the screens provided by the CASE tool, Excelerator, for keying this information. The word Record in the Excelerator screen for Figure 7-8 indicates that a group of data elements, rather than a single data element, is described; this is not the documentation of an actual data record for a computer file.

Based on the data dictionary descriptions, Maria prepares a rough estimate of the total disk space required for all the data files. This calculation will be useful in selecting the computer hardware for the textbook system. The processes performed by the bookstore personnel also require further documentation in order to support the set of data flow diagrams for the textbook system. Each process on a data flow diagram is exploded in greater

FIGURE 7-8

The data dictionary entry for TEXTBOOK ORDER

Record		TEXTBOOK ORDER			
Alternate Name BOOK ORDER FORM					
Definition					
Normalized N					
Name of Element or Record	Occ	Seq	Type	Sec-Keys	
INSTRUCTOR	1	0	E		
OFFICE ADDRESS	1	0	E		
PHONE#	1	0	E		
DEPT	1	0	E		
COURSE#	1	0	E		
SECTION#	1	0	E		
SEMESTER	1	0	E		
YEAR	1	0	E		
REQUIRED BOOK	8	0	R		
RECOMMENDED BOOK	3	0	R		
ONLY TO US	1	0	E		
PREVIOUS USE	1	0	E		
ORDER DATE	1	0	E		
	1	0	e		PgDn

Screen shot produced using INTERSOLV's Excelerator solution for Requirements Analysis and System Design.

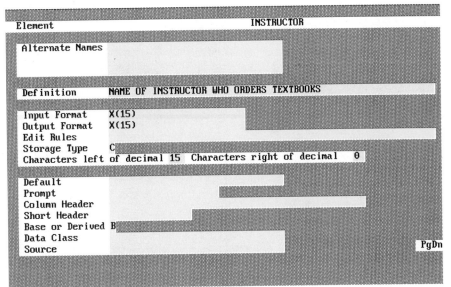

FIGURE 7-9

The data dictionary entry for the data element INSTRUCTOR

Screen shot produced using INTERSOLV's Excelerator solution for Requirements Analysis and System Design.

detail by means of its own data flow diagram until the processes on a diagram can be described by simple procedures. The explosion of process 2.2 is displayed in Figure 7-10. Because the processes in Figure 7-10 are not exploded further, they are called *primitive processes* and are documented by process descriptions. In Figure 7-11, the partial description of the primitive process 2.2.2 is shown by its Excelerator screen. By recording the steps performed by the staff, Maria is able to communicate with the users with greater precision. Instead of relying on her memory, Maria records the users' descriptions. These process descriptions will be useful later in the Design phase.

Alternative Solutions

After completing this rough model of the bookstore system, Maria considers the possible solutions to Mr. Howard's problems. A full-blown system automating the major record-keeping systems at the bookstore could be installed. All merchandise—textbooks, software packages, and items of a general nature—would be handled by such a system. Textbook orders would still require a separate system because of the special nature of their origin and processing. The cash registers could be tied to bar code scanners, the unique bar code on each merchandise item read by the scanner, and the prices rung up on the register. The computer system could also be designed to automatically reduce the quantity in stock listed in the inventory records by the quantity sold.

FIGURE 7-10   **The explosion of process 2.2 (ACCEPT SHIPMENT)**

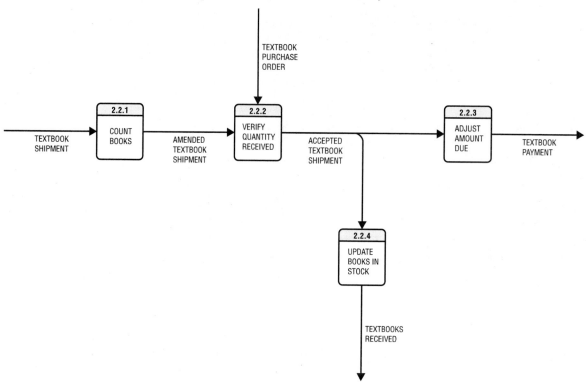

The scheduling of the employees is one of the problems mentioned by Mr. Howard. Because the bookstore makes a point of employing students, almost all the staff are part-time workers. The work schedules are arranged around their classes; the less favored weekend hours are rotated among the employees. Occasionally, several hours are spent manipulating the schedule in order to satisfy the requirements of the student workers. Yet Maria observes that most of the time it is a simple adjustment to trade the hours for one worker with those of another. She notes that Mr. Howard has expressed satisfaction with the work scheduling system. The payroll system is also acceptable to Mr. Howard, who does not wish to change it. Overall, the bookstore is working quite efficiently. Maria concludes that Mr. Howard is right; the problem truly is the handling of textbook orders. She can now move to the next step: formulating a set of alternative solutions.

Maria sketches out the preliminary specifications of four proposals:

1. Improve the manual system by using redesigned cards. Supplement the system with other record-keeping devices.
2. Implement a textbook system using a personal computer system. Basically, this system would support the textbook system but would not be adequate for automated checkout. The checkout procedure would re-

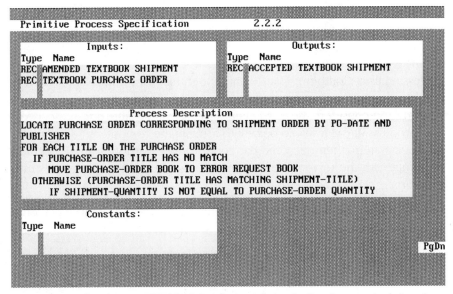

FIGURE 7-11
The partial description of primitive process 2.2.2 The screen scrolls to show the remainder of the process description.

Screen shot produced using INTERSOLV's Excelerator solution for Requirements Analysis and System Design.

main a manual system and the other functions—payroll and work scheduling—would continue as before.

3. Purchase a minicomputer with a network of three or four personal computers or terminals and also tie in the cash registers using bar code scanners to ring up sales of textbooks and general merchandise. This alternative not only includes the textbook system but also requires that labels with bar codes be affixed to the textbooks. The sale of a textbook would cause the sales transaction system to adjust the inventory record for that book title.

4. Redo the entire bookstore system as stated in alternative 3 but include the payroll function, automate the employee scheduling system, automate the functions of the general merchandise system, and update the inventory records using the bar code checkout system.

The first alternative, the improvement of the existing manual procedures, represents only a slight upgrading of the current system. Since this type of system is rather clumsy compared to a computer system, Maria doubts it would satisfy Mr. Howard. Many firms using such systems are now phasing them out. Consequently, Maria deletes the first alternative from her list. Maria also has serious reservations about the second alternative, the small computer system, because of the projected growth of the bookstore. The textbook file would be extensive and would require at least 80 megabytes of hard disk storage. The historical files requested by Mr. Howard would need another 300 megabytes. Although a PC upgrade would be possible later on when needed, it seems unwise to select a computer that cannot handle the anticipated growth of the bookstore's data records. The recommended computer must have sufficient disk capacity and adequate response times to meet the bookstore's needs. The technical feasibility of this second alternative is questionable. Maria decides to check with more experienced professionals at Computer Consultants about this plan. Until disproved, it is a viable alternative.

As Maria considers the third alternative, she looks ahead to the conversion process. Maybe it would be best to bring in the computer and install the textbook system, then delay the bar code scanner portion until all is going smoothly with the textbook procedures. Thus, she splits alternative 3 into two parts:

3a. Purchase a minicomputer (or supermicrocomputer) and three personal computers or terminals. Implement a local area network to handle the textbook system.
3b. Purchase the cash registers and bar scanners for the four checkout lanes and have them controlled by the minicomputer. This portion of the system would automate checkout of all merchandise with bar codes, not just the textbooks, and update the inventory list of textbooks.

Then Maria studies alternative 4, which automates all the data processing. With this alternative, the bookstore would reap substantial financial benefits. Payroll is presently handled by an accountant who charges a fixed rate on each check prepared for the employees. Bringing payroll under the control of the bookstore means saving that expense. Is that worth doing? Financially, it might be worthwhile. But Mr. Howard said that he is satisfied with the payroll system and does not want to change. Maria decides to investigate this alternative further and discuss it with Mr. Howard again.

Preliminary Plans for the Recommended System

To select the most desirable alternative, each alternative must be evaluated with regard to its technical, operational, financial, and scheduling feasibility. For easy reference, the four alternatives have been summarized in Figure 7-12. First, Maria considers the issue of financial feasibility.

FINANCIAL FEASIBILITY

To measure financial feasibility, the costs and benefits of each system must be estimated. To calculate the costs of a system, it is necessary for Maria to decide on the best approach for implementation of the proposed system as well as the computer and its associated equipment. She wonders if a similar information system has been implemented at other bookstores and if such a system is available for purchase. If a suitable software application package exists, some steps in the systems development life cycle (SDLC) can be eliminated, saving time and money. It is an option that should be investigated. By calling several bookstores at major universities, Maria finds that

FIGURE 7-12

The four alternative solutions

Alternative 1. Improved Manual System

Improve the manual system by using redesigned cards and other record-keeping devices.

Alternative 2. Small System (Textbook System Only)

Implement a textbook system using a personal computer system. This system would support the textbook system but would not be adequate for automated checkout. The checkout procedure would remain a manual system and the other functions—payroll and work scheduling—would continue as before.

Alternative 3. Medium-size System (Textbook System and Automated Checkout)

a. Purchase a minicomputer with a network of personal computers or terminals and implement the textbook system.

b. Later, add the cash registers and bar scanners for automated checkout and inventory control. Includes the placement of bar codes on textbooks.

Alternative 4. Full System

Redo the entire bookstore's system as stated in alternative 3 but include the payroll function, automate the employee scheduling system, automate the functions of the general merchandise system, and update the inventory records using the bar code checkout system.

none has implemented such a complete system. A few bookstores have implemented simple systems, but none has all the necessary features. Moreover, none of these systems is available for purchase. Despite its desirability, a software application package must be removed from the list of alternatives. Another approach has to be chosen.

Maria reviews the other approaches for implementing her proposal and selects the traditional approach of design, programming, testing, and installation. There is no reusable code to draw on, and prototyping is unsuitable because of the complexity of the system. Guided by her previous experience in software development, Maria decides to use a completely integrated CASE tool, which would allow her to generate the program code from her design specifications. She has already used this tool to assist her in the Preliminary Investigation phase. The automatic generation of code will greatly reduce the development time.

Now that the hardware and software platforms have been selected, Maria is ready to draft the project schedule and the cost/benefit analysis for each alternative. Figure 7-13 shows the preliminary project schedule for alterna-

FIGURE 7-13

The preliminary project schedule for the textbook system, alternative 3a

Project Schedule	Personnel Requirements (in person-months)	Elapsed Time (in months)
Feasibility Study	0.75	0.75
Analysis	1.5	1.5
Design General Detailed	 1.0 2.0	3.0
Implementation	3.0	2.0
Totals	8.25	7.25

tive 3a. Figure 7-14 illustrates its estimated costs and benefits. The total cost of developing the system is a one-time outlay of $106,000. The operating costs per year for the new system are estimated as $13,500. The savings due to the new system are found in the reduction of clerical staff (estimated at $12,000 per year), the reduction in overtime by Susan Adams and her assistants (estimated at $3,000 per year), and the reduction in shipping costs and lost revenue due to overstock returns (estimated at $5,000).

The question of financial feasibility is whether the financial benefits outweigh the costs. To perform this cost/benefit analysis, Maria subtracts the costs of the system from the benefits accrued during the life of the system. The life of a computer information system on a minicomputer or mainframe is typically estimated to be 5 years. Because of rapid technological changes, personal computer system longevity is now estimated at 3 years. Consequently, Maria is interested in the costs and benefits of the system for at most a 5-year-period of operation.

In order to compute the actual benefits of the system, Maria first computes its net benefits for each year as

Net Benefits = Annual Benefits − Annual Costs
= $20,000 − $13,500
= $6,500

As discussed in Chapter 4, money changes in value over time. Consequently, the net benefits for each year from using the proposed system must be adjusted to reflect this difference, so that the net benefits are stated in terms of present value. The discounted net benefits are computed by multiplying the discount factor (at 5% interest) times the net benefits. The table in Figure 7-15 provides the discounted net benefits for each year. The net present

One-Time Costs	
Analysis	$ 6,000
Software development	60,000
Computer hardware and supporting systems software	40,000
Total one-time costs	**$106,000**
Annual Operating Costs	
Maintenance	$ 6,000
Utilities	500
Supplies	1,000
Weekly backup for system (staff hours)	6,000
Total annual operating costs	**$ 13,500**
Annual Benefits	
Reduction in clerical staff	$ 12,000
Reduced overtime	3,000
Reduction in shipping costs	5,000
Total annual benefits	**$ 20,000**

value is then computed as the cumulative discounted net benefits for 5 years minus the initial outlay for the system:

$$
\begin{aligned}
\text{Net Present Value} &= (\text{Sum of the discounted present values for yearly} \\
&\qquad \text{net benefits}) - \text{Initial outlay} \\
&= \$28{,}141.60 - \$106{,}000 \\
&= -\$77{,}858.40
\end{aligned}
$$

Because the net present value is negative, the proposed system will not pay for itself during its projected lifetime. A complete explanation of cost/benefit analysis and the computation of savings in terms of present value was provided in Chapter 4. Looking at the negative net present value, Maria knows that alternative 3a is not financially worth doing.

But what will Mr. Howard think? Perhaps he still would want to proceed with this approach for the textbook system despite a negative return on his investment. Maria now turns to the other possible approaches for implementing the textbook system. Because Mr. Howard will want to know their financial feasibility too, she prepares cost/benefit analyses for the other alternatives on her list. After calculating the net present value of the complete textbook system given by alternative 3b, Maria finds it is similarly an unprofitable investment for Mr. Howard. However, alternative 4, the full-blown system, proves to be financially viable. Its estimated costs and benefits

FIGURE 7-15   **The cost/benefit analysis for alternative 3a**

Year	0	1	2	3	4	5
Initial Outlay	106,000					
Annual Costs		13,500	13,500	13,500	13,500	13,500
Annual Benefits		20,000	20,000	20,000	20,000	20,000
Net Benefits		6,500	6,500	6,500	6,500	6,500
Discount Factor		0.952	0.907	0.864	0.823	0.784
Discounted Net Benefits		6,190.48	5,895.69	5,614.94	5,347.57	5,092.92
Cumulative Discounted Net Benefits		6,190.48	12,086.17	17,701.11	23,048.68	28,141.60

Interest rate assumed to be 5%.
Net Present Value = \$28,141.60 − \$106,000 = −\$77,858.40
Payback period is over 20 years.
Internal rate of return = −29.78%

are displayed in Figure 7-16. Largely because the accounting firm no longer prepares the paychecks, Maria finds that the net present value of the system is estimated at \$101,251. She further computes the payback period and the internal rate of return and finds similar favorable outcomes. Consequently, she believes that Mr. Howard will find this alternative more satisfactory than alternative 3. Before recommending a solution, however, she must continue her tests of feasibility for these alternatives.

THE OTHER MEASURES OF FEASIBILITY

The remaining three measures of feasibility—technical, operational, and scheduling—must also be considered. From her study of the system, Maria knows that it is possible to acquire the appropriate hardware and develop the software for all three alternatives. Thus, the system passes the test of *technical feasibility*. Next, Maria examines the *operational feasibility* of the three alternatives. The bookstore's employees are eager to install a new system. Susan Adams, the textbook manager, is more than willing to learn a computer system. With her help, the manual procedures can be carefully designed and the human interfaces formulated for ease of use. The book-

FIGURE 7-16 **The full-blown system for the Campus Bookstore, alternative 4**

ONE-TIME COSTS		
Developmental costs		
Textbook system: development costs		$66,000
Analysis	6,000	
Development	60,000	
Payroll (software package)		10,000
General Ledger (software package)		20,000
Sales Subsystem (software package)		15,000
General merchandise subsystem (modified textbook system)		10,000
Bar code registers: inventory hookup (customized)		8,000
System Costs: hardware and software		
Computer hardware and supporting systems software		45,000
4 bar code registers and laser readers		4,000
Total one-time costs		**$178,000**
ANNUAL OPERATING COSTS		
Maintenance		8,000
Utilities		500
Supplies		1,000
Weekly backup for system		6,000
Total annual operating costs		**$15,500**
ANNUAL BENEFITS		
Accounting services eliminated		$15,000
Reduction in clerical staff		40,000
Reduced overtime		20,000
Reduction in shipping costs		5,000
Total annual benefits		**$80,000**

Net present value = $279,251.25 − $178,000 = $101,251.25
Payback period = 3.04 years
Internal rate of return of 23.75%

store's customers and the faculty should receive better service but will have little or no direct contact with a new system. No, Maria does not foresee any *operational* difficulties. *Scheduling* is also not a problem. Her preliminary schedule shows that any of the alternatives can be accomplished in less than

12 months; Mr. Howard is agreeable to that schedule. All the alternatives have passed the remaining three feasibility measures.

THE FINAL PROPOSAL

Now Maria is ready to select a recommended system from the alternatives already examined. The financial feasibility of the full-blown system (alternative 4) is excellent. The second and third alternatives do not offer any financial return and require substantial resources for development. Maria decides to recommend the full-blown system. The smaller system (alternative 3) is also desirable despite its lack of financial feasibility. As her second choice, it will be fully presented to Mr. Howard. At last, Maria is ready to prepare the report of the feasibility study.

The Approval of the Recommended Plan

The final report for the feasibility study is reviewed by the vice-president of Computer Consultants and then submitted to George Howard for his evaluation. Based on the negative net present value shown by the cost/benefit analysis, alternative 3a should not be accepted. But Mr. Howard questions the cost/benefit analysis for alternative 3a, pointing out that there are intangible benefits for the textbook system. If the system is not installed, he risks losing a substantial portion of the textbook orders from the college faculty. Maria realizes that she has been negligent in failing to inquire about possible intangible benefits. Further discussion with Mr. Howard reveals that the intangible benefits are significant. In Mr. Howard's opinion, these benefits amount to $25,000 per annum. Maria now works out a revised cost/benefit analysis for the alternatives. The new computations for alternative 3a now give a net present value of $30,378.52 (see Figure 7-17).

Based on this revised evaluation, Mr. Howard decides to build the new system incrementally as suggested by Maria in alternative 3a and 3b. At this time, he does not want to change the other subsystems for the bookstore. In Mr. Howard's judgment, the textbook system is a necessity. He simply does not want to expend resources on the full-blown system even with the promise of tangible financial benefits. Estimates can be wrong and his bottom line is the $106,000 one-time cost. Although that amount exceeds his original financial boundary of $100,000, the additional $6,000 could be managed without much difficulty. But financial resources are needed for other areas of the business; there is a remodeling project already scheduled for the fall months. Unlike the textbook system, the rest of the data processing activities can wait for a more opportune time.

Looking at the cost figures, Mr. Howard questions the high cost of implementing the system and wonders about hiring a programmer instead as a temporary staff member. That is also an expensive route, but perhaps more economical. "Maybe," he suggests, "a graduate student in information systems would be willing to undertake the project." In fact, Maria has already

The model of the *existing physical system* will show how processing is performed now. The actual paper forms and card files will be represented and even the textbooks themselves can be represented. Maria has made a good start on the physical model (as we saw in Figure 7-4) but needs to add more detail by representing each process with its own data flow diagram. For example, process 2.2 has been shown in more detail by the data flow diagram in Figure 7-10. The physical handling of the books, such as counting them, has been included here. To be certain that the model accurately reflects the current system from the staff's viewpoint, these manual procedures are incorporated into the diagram. Maria also wants to support the model by completing the data dictionary and process descriptions.

After completing the documentation of the physical system, Maria begins work on the *logical model of the existing system*. She removes any physical items such as references to paper documents, actual books, or physical processes (such as COUNT BOOKS) and creates a new data flow diagram that shows only the logical data passing through the system. The data dictionary and process descriptions are modified to support her new diagrams.

Now Maria is ready to create the final *logical model of the proposed system* with all its details. After a careful review, the completed model is ready for a walk-through with Mr. Howard. George Howard is delighted with the logical model of the new system. Maria cautions him that the final system is still in the future. His scrutiny of the systems model ensures that all the desired features have been incorporated.

With the logical model for the new system in hand, Maria checks over her original projections for the project and finds them to be accurate. With that final step, Maria exits the Analysis phase and enters the next phase of the SDLC. But she recognizes that the topics in the phases still ahead have already occupied her thoughts in the Analysis phase. The SDLC guidelines serve as checkpoints and enable her to know that all the necessary documentation and decisions have been accomplished.

THE DESIGN PHASE

Maria once again turns to the guidebook for Computer Consultants and reviews the major steps in the Design phase, shown in Figure 7-18. Her preliminary investigation of the bookstore indicates that a minicomputer is the best hardware choice. Maria has also considered the possibility of a network of PCs. Because of the file storage requirements and the need for expansion in the future, the minicomputer is the preferred hardware platform. Before contacting various computer manufacturers, she verifies her projected requirements for file storage, outlines the programs required, and specifies the response time required from the system. Maria prepares the final draft of the hardware specifications and submits them with a cover letter requesting a price quotation from the minicomputer firms; such a request is known as an RFP (request for proposal). She also formulates the plans for the installation of the hardware. Maria has recommended that Sam

FIGURE 7-17   **The revised cost/benefit analysis for alternative 3a**

Year	0	1	2	3	4
Initial Outlay	106,000				
Annual Costs		13,500	13,500	13,500	13,500
Annual Benefits		45,000	45,000	45,000	45,000
Tangible Benefits		20,000	20,000	20,000	20,000
Intangible Benefits		25,000	25,000	25,000	25,000
Net Benefits		31,500	31,500	31,500	31,500
Discount Factor		0.952	0.907	0.864	0.823
Discounted Net Benefits		30,000.00	28,571.43	27,210.88	25,915.1
Cumulative Discounted Net Benefits		30,000.00	58,571.43	85,782.31	111,697.4

Interest rate assumed to be 5%.
Net Present Value = \$136,378.52 − \$106,000 = \$30,378.52
Payback period is 3.78 years.
Internal rate of return = 14.84%

considered this possibility but rejected it. The consulting firm has experience and can guarantee its work. Any modifications to the original scheme in the future will cost extra—but so would retaining a professional programmer/analyst. After some reflection, Mr. Howard chooses to have the consulting firm perform the entire task of system implementation.

THE ANALYSIS PHASE

Maria checks the SDLC chart developed by Computer Consultants and finds that the Analysis phase requires the following three steps:

Model the existing physical system.

Model the existing logical system by revising the model of the physical system.

Model the proposed logical system.

1. Select and acquire the hardware and software platforms for the new system
2. Specify the human interfaces: screens, reports, and forms
3. Design the data files
4. Design the programs
5. Prepare training guidelines
6. Create preliminary testing procedures

FIGURE 7-18

The major activities in the Design phase

Henderson, the assistant to the textbook manager, be trained to deal with minor hardware issues. Major matters will be handled by Computer Consultants as part of the maintenance agreement. Sam will attend training sessions prior to the delivery of the computer. Backup for the files and controls on the data are two other issues on which Maria has deliberated and for which she has drafted plans.

Using the data dictionary prepared for the new system, Maria proceeds to design the data files. First, she models the data by means of an *entity-relationship diagram*. Then she organizes the data according to the rules of *normalization*. The next step is to design the screens and reports with the objective of making good human interfaces. Because Maria has employed a CASE tool throughout the project, she begins the screen and report designs using this tool. The CASE tool allows her to paint the screen easily and immediately show the designs to Susan Adams for her comments. Once the screen and report formats are satisfactory, the corresponding COBOL program code will be generated by the use of this CASE tool. A sample screen design is shown in Figure 7-19. Susan is given the opportunity to review the screens and reports during the design stage and makes several suggestions which are easily incorporated.

The next step is the design of the programs. The logical model is reviewed for the number of programs required. With the data flow diagram as a guide, a hierarchical diagram is drawn; see Figure 7-20. The process descriptions are now carefully formulated by Maria. The completed specifications for the screens and reports, the process descriptions, the hierarchical chart, and the data file formats are turned over to John Sabatini, the chief programmer at Computer Consultants. John will be responsible for the coding and testing activities. Maria continues to work on the project to prepare the testing guidelines and the preliminary training schedule.

THE IMPLEMENTATION PHASE

The programming for the project advances on schedule. Using the CASE tool, John generates the programs and begins testing according to the testing guidelines. Maria helps prepare the test data, assists in writing the program

FIGURE 7-19   **A sample screen design**

```
Textbook Adoptions:  Find Next Previous Items Update Reports ...
Show and modify books on this adoption.

Dept:Crse [ 7P]:[075]    Instructor [SEIMER       ]   Ordered [12/02/1993]
Section   [ALL  ]        Address    [374 LC  ]        Entered [12/04/1993]
Session   [914]          Phone      [  5-5570]        Exclusive  [Y]
[Spring, 1994   ]        Notes      [                                    ]
======================================================================

                                                        First    Addtl
------- Title ------    --Author-    -- ISBN  --   -Pub--  Quant  Quant  Req
[EDUCATIONAL PSYCHOLO]  [WOOLFOLK ]  [0132369281]  [PH   ] [  350] [    0] [#]
[                    ]  [         ]  [          ]  [     ] [     ] [     ] [ ]
[                    ]  [         ]  [          ]  [     ] [     ] [     ] [ ]
[                    ]  [         ]  [          ]  [     ] [     ] [     ] [ ]
[                    ]  [         ]  [          ]  [     ] [     ] [     ] [ ]
[                    ]  [         ]  [          ]  [     ] [     ] [     ] [ ]
[                    ]  [         ]  [          ]  [     ] [     ] [     ] [ ]
[                    ]  [         ]  [          ]  [     ] [     ] [     ] [ ]
[                    ]  [         ]  [          ]  [     ] [     ] [     ] [ ]
[                    ]  [         ]  [          ]  [     ] [     ] [     ] [ ]
[                    ]  [         ]  [          ]  [     ] [     ] [     ] [ ]
```

Based upon sample screen, University Bookstore, University of Iowa.

documentation, and continues her participation in the project as lead analyst. The training of personnel is now scheduled with Mr. Howard. A systems manual for the users is written as well as formal documentation of the programs. To the user, the entire system is just one major program rather than a series of programs. After thorough testing of the system by the programmers, Maria performs final system testing to verify the system's performance. The system is now turned over to Susan Adams for *acceptance testing*, which is a battery of tests formulated by the system users rather than the software developers. Since Susan was asked much earlier to be prepared to approve the new system, she has several sample tests ready to be executed. Her assistants have also participated in formulating the sample cases. These tests by the users demonstrate that the system does indeed function according to their expectations. At last, the system is ready for installation.

THE INSTALLATION PHASE

Prior to installing the system, the data files for the current system must be converted. Although it is possible to convert the data files as soon as the new system files are fully specified, Maria knows that the timing for file conversion is crucial. If the files are converted too soon, new data records entering

FIGURE 7-20   The hierarchical chart for the textbook system

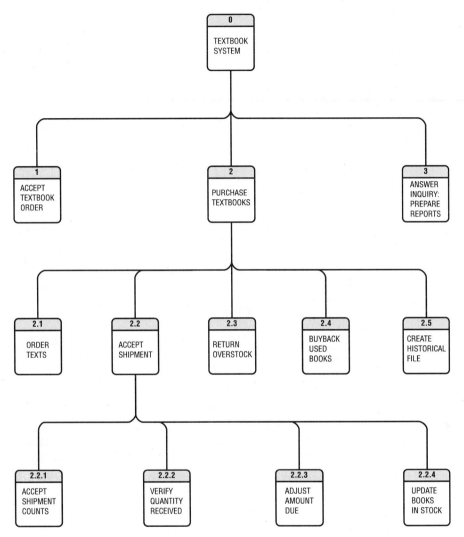

the old system will need special handling to ensure that they will be placed on the converted files prior to the installation date. Because file conversion efforts should be minimized, it is advisable to convert only those data records essential to the new system's operations. Since Mr. Howard decided not to convert the textbook card files for previous semesters, the file conversion activity is simplified. Only current textbook orders will be entered into the new system. The old textbook orders are no longer needed by the bookstore. Since the new system will be installed at a time when few new orders will enter the system, Maria schedules data entry of the textbook orders for the day preceding the formal installation of the new system. The card file on publishers, containing their addresses and phone numbers, also requires manual data entry, using the first program finished by John Sabatini. Work continues on the system with activities overlapped as much as possible.

At last, the day for system installation arrives. Maria has decided that the new system will simply replace the old system, that is, it will be a *direct cutover* to the new system. The scheduled date is 8 weeks before the opening day of the semester. Training has already been performed, but Maria plans to spend the next two days in the bookstore to supervise the transition to the new system. Because the flurry of inquiries just prior to the first day of classes may require some guidance for the users, she will also be present for a few hours each day that week. The transition proceeds smoothly, except that one staff member suddenly quits to accept a job at the rival bookstore. Since the training manual is available, the replacement staff member quickly masters the details of the new system with only minimal assistance from Susan.

THE POST-IMPLEMENTATION REVIEW

As agreed in the contract, Mr. Howard participates in a post-implementation review the week after installation. The meeting commences with Susan Adams, John Sabatini, Maria Lopez, George Howard, and Tom Havel, the bookstore's assistant manager, present. Maria chairs the meeting and invites comments regarding the performance of the system. Mr. Howard begins by congratulating Maria and John on a job well done. He then asks Susan and Tom to describe any problems with the system. Susan mentions the difficulty in answering inquiries when a student knows only a few words of the title. If the opening words are incorrect, it is impossible to locate the book. While it is possible to find a book by author, title, course number, or instructor's name, sometimes students completely muddle that information as well. "Can anything be done?" is her question. Maria replies that Susan's request represents a modification to the original system and will require a separate bid. Before engaging in an additional expense, Maria suggests that the bookstore evaluate the need for this procedure. Mr. Howard nods. "Only if it were cost-effective and desirable to meet the competition would we want such a modification undertaken," he firmly states.

The discussion moves on to other suggestions. Overall, Computer Consultants has performed well and Mr. Howard would confidently recommend the firm to his associates. Maria requests an additional review of the system in 3 months so that any problems covered by the original contract can be quickly remedied. Adding new features would require the negotiation of another contract.

SUMMARY

This case study presents an overview of the systems development life cycle where the traditional approach of building a system has been chosen. In

The Promise of CASE Fulfilled

Computer-aided software engineering (CASE) serves to close the gap between business requirements and computing solutions by involving end users directly in the development process. CASE tools also offer the promise of automating the entire software development process. The traditional steps of the systems development life cycle are now supported by individual tools. An integrated CASE package allows the entire development of a system to be supported and automated as much as possible. Typically, the end product of integrated CASE is a set of fully generated source code produced without syntactical errors. Systems analysts are able to concentrate on the analysis and design of the system without the necessity of writing and testing thousands of lines of code.

Examples of the successful adoption of CASE tools are abundant. The CASE tools sold by a Seattle-based developer, FourGen Software, Inc., have proved successful in saving money and increasing productivity. Paging Network, Inc., a firm supplying paging services, chose the general ledger, accounts payable, and CASE tools marketed by FourGen rather than develop software the conventional way by coding COBOL programs. It took only a month and a half to modify eight general ledger and 45 accounts payable applications. A system to track the help calls from the firm's 2,500 users was created in only six weeks. The firm estimates that productivity has increased two or three times over the previous COBOL development environment.

The BDM Corporation, Kettering, Ohio, employed a CASE tool for the development of an information system designed to track and order parts for aircraft and weapons systems. In this case, Excelerator was used to provide the diagramming and documentation required during the crucial analysis and design phases. The final systems specifications occupied 7,000 pages. The diagram of the system drawn by Excelerator depicts 60 separate software programs with a total of 4,000 processes. Combined with desktop publishing tools, Excelerator allowed BDM to reduce system and documentation errors by more than 50 percent. Since Excelerator has improved both productivity and documentation quality, BDM staff can spend more time on analysis and design activities and reduce errors in the earlier part of the developmental phase when errors are less costly to fix.

For more information, see Mary Emrich, "75,000 Spare Parts Flying in Close Formation," *Manufacturing Systems*, December 1988, pp. 14–15 and pp. 18–19; Thomas Hoffman, "When Smaller Really Is Better," *Computerworld*, September 13, 1993, pp. 83, 86.

large firms with their own information systems personnel, an outside consulting service would not be employed. Despite the differences between in-house development and outside consulting services, the steps in the life cycle remain unaltered when the creation of the system from ground up is undertaken.

The case study of the Campus Bookstore was designed to illustrate the situation where management chooses to implement an information system that lacks tangible financial feasibility. As envisioned here, the Campus Bookstore will spend the $106,000 required for the textbook system without any hope of direct financial benefit. George Howard, the manager, makes this decision because he must successfully compete with the other textbook store in the community. If customers are dissatisfied with the services provided by the Campus Bookstore, students may complain and the faculty may send their textbook orders to his competitor. Mr. Howard believes that he has little choice but to pay the costs for a new system. When Maria uses his estimates of intangible loss in textbook sales volume if the textbook system were not built, she discovers that the recomputed cost/benefit analysis justifies Mr. Howard's decision to go forward with implementation.

This case study also demonstrates the step-by-step process performed by Maria Lopez, the systems analyst. She faithfully follows the systems development life cycle established by her consulting firm in order to ensure that no detail is omitted. The life cycle also indicates the sequence of activities. By adhering to the life cycle's specifications, Maria hopes to guarantee that the final system will be completed on time, will be within budget, and will meet the requirements of the users—Mr. Howard, Susan Adams, and the clerks who use the textbook system. Throughout the systems development process, we have shown how Maria turns to the users, first for information and later for approval of the designs she creates. At each step, Maria acts according to the principle that the users are the ultimate judges of the system, rather than the software developers.

The development of the Campus Bookstore system was described with an emphasis on the early stages of the life cycle. As shown in Figure 7-21, Maria employs various techniques to accomplish her multitude of tasks throughout the systems development process. Her expertise in areas such as project management, cost/benefit analysis, and communication skills is needed over and again. Her previous experience in developing information systems also plays a role in her work for the Campus Bookstore system.

For the Preliminary Investigation phase, Maria initially applies her knowledge of project management as well as her interviewing skills to draw up the initial project definition given in Figure 7-2. After the system has been approved for implementation, Maria models the existing system by creating a model using the technique of data flow diagrams with their accompanying data dictionary and process descriptions. Then she carefully creates the model of the new system by incorporating the added functions desired by Mr. Howard. She formulates several alternatives for systems implementation, examines them for financial, operational, technical, and scheduling feasibility, and recommends the best approach to Mr. Howard. With his approval, she begins to design the new system according to the chosen means of implementation. Maria designs the screen and report mock-ups, the logical and physical file structures, and the program structures, and she describes the individual modules to be coded. She then turns her design over to the chief programmer, John Sabatini, for coding and testing. By using a CASE tool, John is able to develop the system quickly and also use the COBOL

FIGURE 7-21   **The techniques employed during the development of the Campus Bookstore system**

The Phase in the SDLC	Techniques	Deliverables
Preliminary Investigation	SDLC guidelines* Cost/Benefit analysis* Project management* Interviewing* Data flow diagrams Data dictionary	Initial problem definition Feasibility study report
Analysis	Interviewing Data flow diagrams Data dictionary Process descriptions CASE tool skills	Models of the existing system and the proposed system
Design	CASE tool skills for screen and report mock-ups Normalization technique Structure charts Module description methods	Design of user interfaces and program structures Logical and physical file designs Testing plans Training plans
Implementation	This technique was chosen by the analyst to be used by the programmer: CASE tool for code generation	Coded and tested programs Trained personnel Conversion plans
Installation	Project management*	Converted files Installed system
Post-Implementation Review	Communication skills*	Critique of installed system Proposal for modifications Performance evaluation of software developers

*These techniques are used throughout the life cycle phases

code generated by Maria for the screens and reports. After all testing has been completed, the users approve the system by performing further tests; these tests are called acceptance testing.

During the Implementation phase, the users are trained and plans are made for conversion of the manually recorded data. The system is now ready for installation. The manual files are transferred into computer files and the carefully planned cutover to the new system takes place. Maria remains on site for a short time to assist the users with any problems due to unfamiliarity with the system. At a later time, Mr. Howard and his staff review the system with Maria and mention some ideas for improvement. These modifications will be handled by a separate contract for system maintenance. Throughout all these activities, Maria employs her communication skills to interview·Mr. Howard and his staff and obtain the users' input into the decision making that occurs at various points in the life cycle.

This case study demonstrates how Maria, the systems analyst, uses her repertoire of professional skills to accomplish the successful implementation of an information system. While the task may appear somewhat daunting to novice systems analysts, well-trained analysts are able to confront a problem with confidence in their ability to apply these many techniques.

TERMS

Since the case study for the Campus Bookstore was intended to illustrate the activities of the entire life cycle, terms are not listed for this chapter. The technical aspects of software development activities are covered in other chapters.

QUESTIONS

1. In this case study, Mr. Howard wants to forego the feasibility study and begin the implementation of a computer-based system immediately. Justify the time and money required by Computer Consultants for the feasibility study.

2. **a.** Why did George Howard, the bookstore manager, decide on an evolutionary building of the proposed system, that is, the incremental approach discussed in this chapter?

   b. Present an argument for implementing the automated cash registers together with the textbook ordering system.

3. Why does George Howard want to implement the textbook system by means of a computer system? Are his reasons realistic?

4. Maria briefly considers the purchase of a software package for the textbook system. Explain why she would prefer such a system to the custombuilt system ultimately selected.

5. During the post-implementation review, Susan raised the issue of re-trieving textbook records by any combination of words in the book title.
    a. Explain why Maria refused to implement this change.
    b. Do you believe this feature to be valuable for the bookstore? Ex-plain.

6. Maria chose to install the new system using the direct cutover method.
    a. What is meant by direct cutover conversion?
    b. What risks exist with the direct cutover method?

7. Mr. Howard decides to contract with Computer Consultants to imple-ment the proposed system rather than hiring his own programmer. What are the reasons for and against hiring a programmer rather than the consulting firm for implementation?

8. After Mr. Howard states that payroll and work scheduling are not oper-ations to be implemented in the new system, why does Maria nonethe-less consider the alternative of a full-blown system (all data processing systems implemented on the computer)?

9. During the feasibility study, Maria inquires about future plans for the bookstore. Why are future plans important to the design of the textbook system requested by Mr. Howard?

PROJECTS

1. Visit your local bookstore and investigate how textbook orders from instructors at your college are processed. Prepare a short report de-scribing the textbook system. Include the following information:
    a. A copy of a textbook ordering form used by instructors
    b. The method of recording these orders (manual files or computer system)
    c. A description of the process by which orders are assembled into purchase orders to be sent to the publishers
    d. A statement of the problems encountered in the current system

2. Arrange to discuss the ordering of office supplies with the secretary of a departmental office of your university or a local business firm. Write a short report that gives the following details:
    a. A copy of the purchase order used to order supplies
    b. A statement of the problems the secretary faces in maintaining an adequate supply of all items for use by the department or firm
    c. Your recommendation for or against the implementation of a com-puter information system to automate the ordering of supplies
    d. The evaluation of your recommendation in terms of the four mea-sures of feasibility

CHAPTER 8

A Case Study: A Small Business System

Objectives

In this chapter, we present the problems a physician confronts in managing her office. By studying this chapter, you will comprehend the following material:

- How the steps in the systems development life cycle guide the implementation of a system
- The reasons for selecting a commercial software application package instead of developing a custom-built information system
- The criteria for choosing an application package from those available in the marketplace
- The planning necessary to implement a software application package

INTRODUCTION

The previous chapter presented a case study of the Campus Bookstore and the problem of the textbook ordering system. By choosing to build a system tailored to the bookstore's needs, the Campus Bookstore provided us with an illustration of the traditional approach to the implementation of a computer-based information system. All the steps in the systems development life cycle were executed, including the design, implementation, and installation of an information system especially designed to meet the needs of the textbook processing system. The implementation phase was shortened by the use of a CASE tool. Now we want to examine the situation where the systems analyst finds that a different method of systems implementation will best solve the problems of the user.

A physician's office is the case study that will demonstrate the issues leading to the selection of a software application package rather than a custom-built system. As in the Campus Bookstore case study, the systems analyst methodically executes each step in the systems development life cycle in order to achieve a satisfactory resolution of the user's problems. The reasons for installing a software package are explained in detail. Since the latter phases of the SDLC are altered by this approach to the systems development process, these phases have been given more emphasis in this chapter. Once again, certain technical aspects are included in this presentation to show their relationship to the entire systems development process, although these techniques will not be fully explained until later chapters. Now we begin our story of the problems encountered in Dr. Claire Washington's office with a brief overview of her medical practice. The cast of characters for this case study is listed in Figure 8-1.

DR. WASHINGTON'S OFFICE

After completing her residency, Dr. Claire Washington entered an established dermatology practice with an older physician in a suburban community of a major metropolitan city. Over the last 3 years, she has gradually

FIGURE 8-1
The cast of characters

Dr. Washington's Office	Dr. Claire Washington, dermatologist
	Dr. Halwell, retired
	Dr. Frank Jefferson, soon to join the practice
	Mrs. Teresa Liu, office manager
	Ms. Jennifer Carrington, receptionist
	The nurses
Computer Consultants	Mr. Ron Czalka, systems analyst

taken over most of Dr. Halwell's patients as well as seeing new patients. On an average day, she sees 25 to 30 patients. Her clientele numbers about 5,000, but most of them see her only occasionally. Dr. Halwell retired a month ago and Dr. Washington bought the practice. To serve Dr. Halwell's patients, she has arranged for Dr. Frank Jefferson to join the practice this month. Dr. Jefferson recently completed his residency in dermatology at a nearby hospital. He will be paid a salary plus a percentage of his billings.

The gross income of Dr. Washington's practice averages about $35,000 per month (excluding Dr. Halwell's share). Although that amount is large, the income must cover the office expenses and the salaries of her office staff—an office manager, a receptionist, and two nurses. Other expenses include the rental of the office, equipment and supplies, malpractice insurance, subscriptions to medical journals, and attendance at medical conferences and other symposiums.

When Dr. Washington entered Dr. Halwell's practice, his longtime office manager Mrs. Teresa Liu was running the office to perfection. Mrs. Liu long ago devised her own way of doing things. The system is still completely manual, using forms purchased from a medical records firm. Everything runs smoothly except when Mrs. Liu is absent from the office due to illness or vacation. A few minor problems have come up, such as filing Medicare forms and learning the new rules for some insurance companies, but all in all Mrs. Liu has done a fine job. Now she plans to retire, but she has consented to work a few more months until Dr. Washington finds a suitable replacement. The receptionist, Jennifer Carrington, has worked in the office only 6 months. Although Ms. Carrington is a capable receptionist, she has no experience in preparing bills and recording receipts. When asked, she insists that she has no interest in taking over the office manager's position. The nurses are not likely candidates, either, since both want to practice nursing, not take up accounting or record management.

Dr. Washington has no wish to spend her time on business matters. The management of the day-to-day financial details of the medical practice would take away time she needs for reading medical journals to keep up with the latest research. If she becomes occupied with the bills, payroll, and other paperwork, surely her medical practice will suffer. No, what she wants is a solution to her dependence on a single employee. Whenever Dr. Washington examines the financial records, she must struggle to decode Mrs. Liu's notations. But even when someone else takes over, will such problems persist? Mrs. Liu's replacement may also have an individualized system, leaving Dr. Washington with the same difficulties as before. The manual system has worked for Mrs. Liu, but Dr. Washington knows many medical colleagues who have already invested in computer systems. The paperwork for Medicare appears to be worsening. The private health insurance paperwork has changed, too. Mrs. Liu confided that she spends hours of unpaid overtime work doing the insurance forms. A new employee could not be expected to be so unfairly overburdened. What can Dr. Washington do to alleviate her office problems?

Recently, when attending a medical conference, she discussed her problem with several colleagues. One physician suggested that she get some expert advice from a consulting firm, Computer Consultants. Upon her return, Dr. Washington called the consulting firm to talk about her problem. A breakfast meeting with Ron Czalka, a senior systems analyst, has been set for tomorrow to explain her predicament.

THE PRELIMINARY INVESTIGATION

Over breakfast, Dr. Washington outlines the problems existing in her office. She sees a need to automate the office so that billing can be easily handled without overtime hours for the office manager. A uniform system—well documented and easily learned—would let anyone, even an outsider, fill the role of office manager. "Absolutely no more personalized systems," she decrees.

The doctor's main concern is billing. Over 85% of her billing is sent to insurance companies or Medicare, rather than the individual patient. With such *third-party billing*, besides filing the insurance forms, it is necessary to bill the patients and show what amount was collected from their insurance companies. Sometimes a patient is billed over and over again until the insurance payment reaches the office. Patients sometimes complain that the office wastes time and energy on these redundant bills, when everyone knows it is only a matter of time until the claims are paid. The worst case is when a claim is filed incorrectly. Then it usually takes an extra 6 weeks until the claim is paid.

Dr. Washington has been notified by Blue Cross/Blue Shield that electronic claim filing is now possible. She wonders, "Can't my office use that method, instead of being snarled up in all this paperwork?" Although she has never experienced a serious problem in claim processing, she worries that a less experienced person than Mrs. Liu could make mistakes and delay claim processing. Any error on the form, such as adding the individual charges incorrectly or transposing two digits on the account number, causes delays and entails a corresponding reduction in revenue. Should Medicare requirements change, processing time would probably increase. Her main concern is the escalation in burdensome paperwork with no obvious way to improve the situation.

During the interview, Ron notices that Dr. Washington has focused on one problem. "Are there other problems in your office or medical practice?" he inquires. "How about payroll, accounts payable, drugs, and so on? Is all the paperwork there acceptable?" Rather than solve one problem and leave others for the future, Ron wants to understand Dr. Washington's entire practice in order to identify all the difficulties in the office procedures. If he solves one problem and ignores the others, the chosen solution might prove incompatible with future solutions. In addition, Dr. Washington will be dissatisfied if she discovers that billing is proceeding smoothly but everything else remains a problem. Billing is her immediate concern, but the other aspects of the medical practice must also be reviewed. Dr. Washington agrees and decides to continue their discussion tomorrow at 5:00 P.M. Meanwhile, she will check with her staff to collect their comments.

On the next day, Dr. Washington is able to provide some additional information. The nurses report that the patient history files are another problem area. To locate any information, the nurses have to scan a patient's entire folder, so when a patient has a long medical history it is difficult to retrieve the desired information. Dr. Washington has also checked with the receptionist. Appointment scheduling is routine except when a patient calls to cancel an appointment. Sometimes Ms. Carrington has to search the appointment ledger over and over again because the patient gives the wrong date and time. Whenever Dr. Washington has an emergency case, it is a truly formidable task to shift appointments, because the phone numbers for the patients are in their file folders; before the receptionist can call the patients, the list of phone numbers must be compiled. She also sometimes has trouble fitting in the longer appointment periods required for complete exams. Patient follow-up visits are another problem. Typically, after the initial patient visit, Dr. Washington wants a follow-up visit after 1, 3, or 6 months, or even a year later. Ms. Carrington has noticed that some patients forget to show up because their appointments were scheduled so far in advance. Naturally, that wastes the doctor's time. A patient recall system could reduce the rate of no-shows by reminding patients about a week before their appointments. That is another area for consideration.

"What about payroll?" Ron asks next. "Is payroll a responsibility of the office manager, or is it hired out to an accounting firm?" "No, payroll is not a problem area," Dr. Washington replies. The office manager manually prepares the checks and Dr. Washington reviews them before signing them. Payroll is a tedious task but not overwhelming, since everyone is on a monthly salary rather than an hourly wage. The entry of Dr. Jefferson into the practice might pose more of a problem, however, because a percentage of his billings must be added to his salary. Also, the staff size may need to increase. Dr. Halwell had cut back on his practice over the last 5 years, so the present staff has been adequate up to now. If the staff does increase, then payroll would be a good area to automate. For now, payroll can still be prepared manually by the office manager.

Another trouble spot in the financial management system of any small business is accounts payable. "Are there any problems that need attention in this area?" prompts Ron. Dr. Washington remarks that accounts payable seem to be under control. Since not many supplies are used, the office manager can process payments quickly and easily maintain good records. Although the new office manager will need as much help as possible, accounts payable can wait for a few years. "If the cost is low enough, put accounts payable in the new system. Otherwise, it can be done some other time," Dr. Washington concludes.

Finally, Ron considers the aspects of this small business that are unique to a medical practice. Patient histories have already been discussed. "Are there any other medical functions that should be included in the new system?" he inquires. Dr. Washington explains that pharmaceutical firms frequently distribute free samples to her. She also stocks some drugs required for in-office treatment of patients. When a patient requires hospital care, whether in-patient or out-patient, the hospital is responsible for drugs administered within its facility. So far, the nurses have kept accurate drug records manually. They do not view the maintenance of the drug records as burdensome; it is a routine task with no difficulties.

When Ron asks at the end of the interview for any further information, Dr. Washington stresses again the importance of an office that runs smoothly. If the office operations yield erroneous bills, late insurance payments, or irate patients, her practice will suffer. She emphasizes that she needs to be free from worry about the financial management of the office. Dr. Washington wants assurance that the absence of one staff member will not cause a major breakdown in the office operations. The requirement for accurate records is obvious. But the new system also must be easy to use with minimum training and independent of any one person's expertise. The computer system should insulate her from any unpleasant ramifications of employee turnover. If not, she will be back to square one with an indispensable employee problem. Before installing a computer system, she needs some guarantees about reliability and continuing support for the system. Training must be accessible for new employees in the future, even years after the system starts up. These issues are crucial to the choice of any computer system. When Ron asks about total costs for the system, she replies that a new system should not cost more than $100,000. "Now, what can you do to solve these problems?" Dr. Washington wants to know.

The Initial Proposal

Ron returns to his office with a basic understanding of Dr. Washington's problems and her convictions about their solution. First he prepares a written summary of the interview, and then he drafts an initial proposal for Dr. Washington's approval (see Figure 8-2). The new system will be designed to perform the following office functions:

Billing (that is, accounts receivable)

Appointment scheduling

Patient recalls

Patient histories

Accounts payable (depending on price considerations)

Since Dr. Washington is eager to see a new system in place, she immediately signs the contract with Computer Consultants. Ron formally starts the feasi-

FIGURE 8-2
The preliminary proposal for Dr. Washington's office

DATE: February 7, 1994

PROJECT: Office Management System for Dr. Claire Washington

PROJECT SCOPE: The total cost of the project will not exceed $100,000.
                   This cost includes that of the feasibility study.

PROJECT OBJECTIVES:
  1. To improve record keeping for the following subsystems:
     Billing (that is, accounts receivable)
     Appointment scheduling
     Patient histories
     Accounts payable (dependent on price considerations)
  2. To institute a system for patient recalls
  3. To improve the collection of bills sent to third-party accounts
  4. To provide clear and detailed specifications for office procedures

CRITERIA FOR THE PROPOSED SYSTEM:
  cost
  ease of use
  availability of training
  high reliability with minimal or no downtime; provision for processing to continue
     despite any downtime
  maintenance of hardware and software included in the contract for the system
  support services available for a period of five years from the date of installation

PRELIMINARY PLAN:
To implement commercially available software on suitable hardware.

SCOPE OF THIS PROPOSAL:
Three weeks for a total cost of $6,000

INITIAL PROPOSAL:
In order to recommend a suitable solution, a feasibility study is suggested with a cost
of no more than $6,000. The report resulting from the feasibility study will include the
following materials:
  1. Statement of problems in the current office management system
  2. Preliminary design of a computer-based information system, if deemed feasible
  3. Recommendation regarding the best approach to implement a computer-based
     information system
  4. Estimated costs and time requirements to implement the proposed system
  5. Tentative schedule for the implementation of the system

This report will be delivered no later than five weeks (35 days) after the signing of
the contract.

bility study on the following day, as Dr. Washington introduces him to her office staff.

The Feasibility Study

Ron embarks on the feasibility study with the premise that all previous information is subject to review. He must examine the details of the existing system in order to fully understand how the office is managed now. As he performs the feasibility study, he will be searching for any reason to revise the initial proposal. Are there other problems to be solved as well as those stated by Dr. Washington? This is the question foremost in his mind.

Although Ron already has conceived a plan for implementing a system, he must measure this plan against the reality of the work actually performed in the office. As he studies the existing system, he will be formulating other alternatives for solving Dr. Washington's problems.

STUDY OF THE EXISTING SYSTEM

The study of the existing system begins with Ron's interview of the office manager, Mrs. Liu. After some preliminary remarks, Ron opens the interview with the open-ended question, "Would you explain to me how the billing system works?" Mrs. Liu responds with a detailed explanation of the billing process. When a patient arrives for an appointment, the appointment schedule is annotated with a circle to indicate that the appointment was kept. After each patient visit, the doctor completes the form shown in Figure 8-3 to indicate the diagnosis and what services were performed. Two copies are placed in the current week's stack for subsequent processing. The original white copy is filed as a permanent record of the office visit. The pink copy together with the third-party insurance form is mailed to the insurance company. The patient gets the remaining yellow copy.

At this time, a patient is requested to pay in full for the office visit unless the patient is covered by health insurance. The amount charged for each service is determined by locating the procedure in the Charge Reference Book. Once insurance claims are filed by the office, the payments are sent directly to Dr. Washington. There is, however, a delay in receiving most payments. Many patients simply do not pay at this time; they prefer to wait to see if their medical expenses will be paid by the insurance company, especially when the amount is large. Since most claims are only partially reimbursed by the insurance, the patient must be billed later for the remaining amount. Frequently, 10 to 12 weeks elapse before insurance claims are paid and another 6 to 8 weeks expire before the patient remits the outstanding portion of the bill.

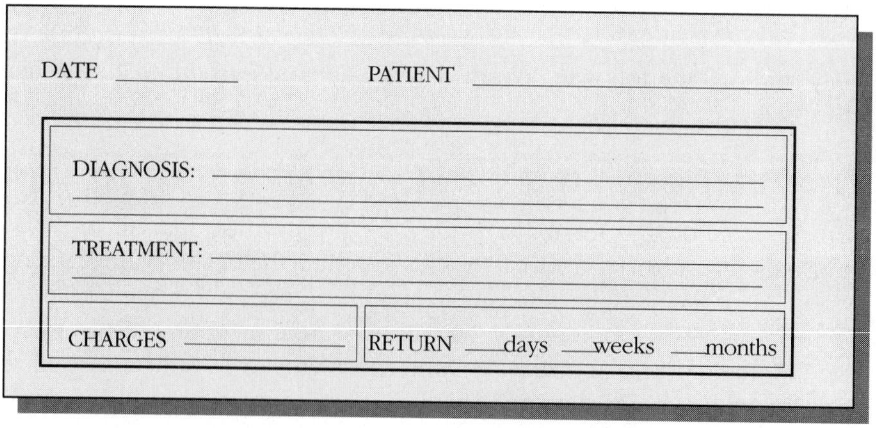

FIGURE 8-3

The form completed by Dr. Washington for a patient visit

DATE _____   PATIENT _____

DIAGNOSIS: _____
_____

TREATMENT: _____
_____

CHARGES _____   RETURN ___days ___weeks ___months

At the start of each week, Mrs. Liu prepares patient invoices for the patients treated during the previous week. Regardless of the patient's insurance coverage, the invoice (Figure 8-4) is prepared for the full amount and mailed to the patient. After the invoices are completed, the ledger card (Figure 8-5) for each patient is pulled from the file to record the same information. Until full payment is received, the ledger cards are maintained in a separate file. This enables the office manager to review these cards and issue follow-up notices. Then the invoices are ready to be mailed to the patients.

When services are billed to a third party, such as an insurance firm or Medicare, an additional form must be completed. Each insurance company requires that its own claim form be filed. Since most patients are insured by one major insurance company, its forms are always on hand for use by the office manager. A supply of Medicare forms is also stocked. Should a different form be required, Mrs. Liu must phone the insurance company to request it. Lack of the proper insurance form can delay the payment of the claim, sometimes by 2 or 3 months. As Ron inspects Mrs. Liu's records, he

Claire Washington, M.D.
Dermatology and Dermatologic Surgery
Park Plaza Building, Suite 201
Greenton Grove, Illinois 69911

Invoice Number: **1402**

Date: 1/26/94

Patient: Gregory Waldstein
          3030 West Park Avenue
          Greenton, IL 69910

Total Due: $28.00

Date of Visit	Services Rendered	Amount Due	Payment Received
1/19/94	Office Visit CLAIM FILED WITH INSURANCE CARRIER	28.00	
	TOTAL DUE	28.00	

FIGURE 8-4

The patient invoice

FIGURE 8-5

The ledger card for a
patient

PATIENT NO. 0249			PATIENT:	Gregory Waldstein	
				3030 West Park Avenue	
				Greenton, IL 69910	
				Phone: (708) 599-0011	

Date	Invoice	Billed to Insurance	Billed to Patient	Payment Received	Balance Due
6/11/93	0456		35.00		35.00
6/20/93	A2789	35.00			35.00
7/30/93	BC/BS			31.50	3.50
8/25/93	0675		3.50		3.50
9/7/93	P/P			3.50	0.00
1/19/94	1402		28.00		28.00
1/19/94	A2851	28.00			28.00

sees the same information being copied over and over again. Payments are recorded directly on the ledger card. The source of the payment is annotated directly on the card. In addition, a duplicate copy of the third party payment form is filed.

Duplication of data is definitely a problem. Entering the same data in different places leaves the door open for recording errors. There is no check on errors except for the patients themselves. The office manager also seems to be unclear about the follow-up for unpaid patient charges. The standard procedure is simply to bill the patient repeatedly if a bill is not paid. Sometimes patients become annoyed when they are dunned for the payment because the claims still have not been paid by their insurance company.

The office manager continues her discussion with an explanation of the payroll system. Payroll requires a concentrated effort on her part to prepare the checks for payday. Since all the employees are on monthly salary rather than hourly wage, it is not too difficult to check over all the figures. But every time the tax laws change, she faces extra work until she understands the new regulations. Mrs. Liu warns that the real burden may be the computation of Dr. Jefferson's salary plus the percentage of fees billed to his patients. "Well, I'm leaving and don't have to deal with that problem," she says with evident relief.

After the interview, Ron realizes that another problem in the billing system is the lack of controls. The same person sends the bills and receives payments. Although there is no doubt about Mrs. Liu's integrity, it is unwise for such procedures to exist. It is always better to guard against possible fraud than to permit such loopholes to remain. Ron adds that item to his list of problems in the current system.

The next problem areas on Ron's list are appointment scheduling and patient recalls. In order to understand these activities, he arranges to meet with the receptionist early the next day. Jennifer Carrington is glad to answer Ron's questions about the appointment scheduling system. She is familiar with the procedure for booking appointments. Certain types of appointments require more time than others. For some patient visits, Dr. Washington marks on the form that the patient should return in a certain length of time. These appointments, perhaps several months ahead, are usually scheduled before the patient leaves the office.

Dr. Washington tried to establish a patient recall system, but the receptionist was just too busy to notify patients about their appointments in advance. Ideally, patients should be called and reminded about appointments scheduled so long ago. Unfortunately, most patients are never called, so many of them simply forget about their appointments. Later on, they usually call to reschedule their appointments, often because the condition has recurred. Dr. Washington is particularly concerned about this situation because timely intervention can often prevent serious medical problems. Ms. Carrington is all too aware that Dr. Washington wants the patient recall system to be improved. But she does think that the appointment scheduling is working as well as possible. Although the scheduling of lengthy appointments remains a problem, she somehow manages. However, rescheduling patients is another matter. Whenever Dr. Washington is called away due to a medical emergency, Ms. Carrington must reschedule appointments for several patients. Before the patients can be contacted, their phone numbers must be located by searching the file records. It is a laborious task, but she asserts that she always accomplishes the appointment rescheduling in a satisfactory way.

Finally, Ron investigates the record-keeping system for patient histories. A file folder exists for each patient. After each patient visit, Dr. Washington enters her own notes about the ailment and the treatment prescribed. Unless the patient has a long medical history, this system seems to be satisfactory for Dr. Washington. Patients with complicated histories are troublesome because Dr. Washington needs to review the entire file to be sure that no vital information is overlooked. The nurses express a different view of the patient history system. When patients call, they have to pull the correct file folder, search for the information, and answer their questions. Both nurses have worked in other offices where computer systems retrieved the patient's record for them. "It is so much easier. Can't something be done here?" one comments to Ron.

Having obtained an in-depth view of the various systems pertinent to Dr. Washington's practice, Ron also examines the accounts payable system and the drug records. Ron knows that he must understand the entire office system. If any problems are uncovered after the new system is installed, it may be difficult or even impossible to incorporate their solutions into the new system. Although the accounts payable system is functioning well, Ron becomes concerned about controls in this area, too. He discovers that an audit has never been performed on accounts payable. Mrs. Liu has the authority to pay bills without any supervision from Dr. Washington, since these amounts are relatively small compared to the monthly salaries. Mrs. Liu writes checks on a separate checking account designated for this purpose. The receipts from the patients are deposited in a second checking account from which only Dr. Washington is authorized to withdraw funds. Since Mrs. Liu can draw funds only from the first checking account, Dr. Washington believes that the patient receipts placed in the second checking account are secure from fraud. Ron is not satisfied with the controls in this area, however, and marks this matter for discussion with Dr. Washington.

Ron then interviews the nurses about the procedures for issuing drugs. The nurses both agree that the record-keeping system is adequate. The distribution of controlled substances, drugs that are strictly regulated by law, are recorded in a special book. The inventory of other drugs is simply checked once a week by one of the nurses; drugs are reordered by writing the drug name and quantity on an order form. From there Mrs. Liu takes over, ordering the drugs and paying the bills. There have never been any problems in this area. The quantity of each drug to stock is written in the Drug Book. The nurses are emphatic in their disapproval of any change to this system. Having gathered all the necessary information, Ron returns to his office to draw a data flow diagram to represent an overview of the system (Figure 8-6). Each process is specified in more detail by further data flow diagrams, called explosions. The explosion of process 3 is shown in Figure 8-7.

THE PROPOSED SOLUTION

Using the technique of data flow diagrams, Ron prepares a model of the new system. First, he inspects the original data flow diagram (Figure 8-6) showing the data flowing through the current system. Because any new system could use other means to process the data, Ron checks that this diagram shows only *what* is being done rather than *how* the process is actually performed. A diagram that shows the logical activities, the *what* rather than *how* of the system, is called a logical data flow diagram. In this instance, Ron has already concentrated on the logical aspects of the system and does not need to modify his diagram. Next he prepares the data dictionary entries to ensure that all data flowing through the system have been fully documented. Sample descriptions of the data elements are shown in Figure 8-8. The process descriptions are also written.

After the model of the current system has been completed, Ron meets again with Dr. Washington for a critique of his system model. Ron explains that the design of a new system will be based on his knowledge of the old

FIGURE 8-6   **The data flow diagram for Dr. Washington's office**

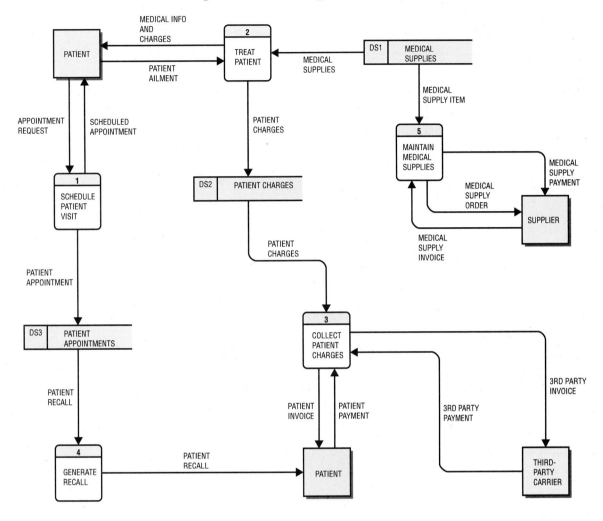

one; it is important to be certain that his model and the reality of the existing system are the same. Dr. Washington agrees to review his model and finds that she quickly understands his diagrams and notations. After a careful examination of Ron's report, Dr. Washington approves the work thus far. Following the approval of the model for the current system, Ron determines that no additional functions are needed for the new system. He now begins the process by which the recommendation for the new system will be formulated.

THE ALTERNATIVE SOLUTIONS

Ron has already decided that any new system must include improved third-party billing by Dr. Washington's staff to produce better cash flow. Now the question becomes *how* rather than *what*. Specifically, how can the problems

FIGURE 8-7   The explosion of process 3

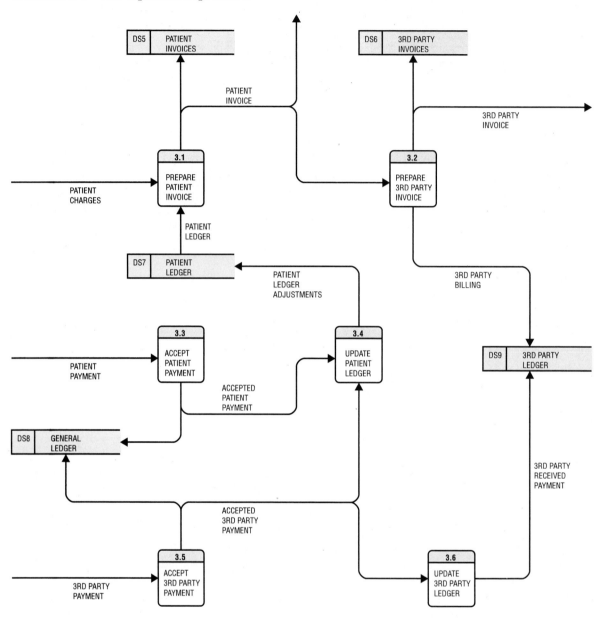

best be solved for Dr. Washington? Before proposing a solution to Dr. Washington, Ron formulates several possible solutions. Some solutions are immediately discarded as impractical. The most likely solutions are studied further. Finally, the three solutions listed in Figure 8-9 are judged to be worthy of additional study:

1. Modification of the current manual system with revised forms and well-defined procedures

FIGURE 8-8   **Sample data dictionary entries for data records**

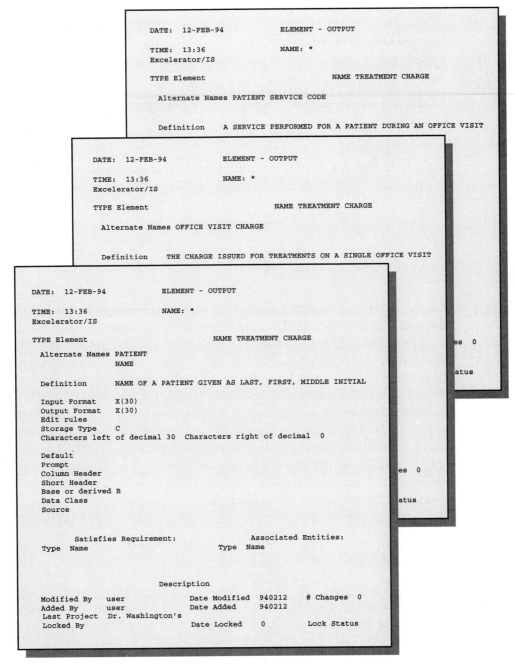

Courtesy of INTERSOLV.

2. A medium-size computer-based information system that processes billing, appointment scheduling, patient histories, and patient recalls
3. A full-blown computer information system that incorporates all the subsystems in alternative 2 plus payroll and accounts payable

FIGURE 8-9
**The three alternative
solutions**

> **Alternative 1**
>
> Modification of the current manual system with revised forms and well-defined procedures
>
> **Alternative 2**
>
> A medium-size computer-based information system that processes billing, appointment scheduling, patient histories, and patient re-calls
>
> **Alternative 3**
>
> A full-blown computer information system that incorporates all the subsystems in alternative 2 plus payroll and accounts payable

To evaluate these solutions, Ron applies the feasibility tests: economic, technical, operational, and scheduling.

The Revised Manual System   The first alternative, an improved manual system, is clearly technically feasible. There are better manual systems available and the office procedures could be clearly documented. Ron's consulting firm could supply the training of new employees. Controls could be imposed on the financial aspects of the office, even with the manual system. Operationally, the staff would have no difficulty in adapting to a revised manual system. Because it can be quickly installed, it poses no scheduling feasibility problems. The one-time cost is also low (estimated at $25,000), well within Dr. Washington's budget. But the annual net benefits are only $7,000. Although the savings over a 5-year period will total $35,000, Ron also has to consider the time value of money and compute the net present value of this system. This computation is shown in Figure 8-10. The net present value at a 5% interest rate is calculated as

$$\text{Net Present Value} = \text{(Sum of the discounted present values for yearly net benefits)} - \text{Initial outlay}$$
$$= \$30,306.34 - \$25,000$$
$$\doteq \$5,306.34$$

The positive value of savings indicates that the manual system is financially feasible. The investment pays for itself in less than 5 years with a return of $5,306.34 at the end of the 5-year period. Financially, the manual system is a sound investment.

The first solution is very attractive because it is low in initial outlay. What about the future? Will the manual system meet Dr. Washington's needs for the next 5 years? Dr. Washington expects a computer system, so should Ron recommend one or opt for the least expensive solution that passes the financial feasibility test? Looking ahead to the future, Ron is aware that

FIGURE 8-10   The cost/benefit analysis for the manual system

Year	0	1	2	3	4	5
Initial Outlay	25,000					
Annual Costs		5,000	5,000	5,000	5,000	5,000
Annual Benefits		12,000	12,000	12,000	12,000	12,000
Net Benefits		7,000	7,000	7,000	7,000	7,000
Discount Factor		0.952	0.907	0.864	0.823	0.784
Discounted Net Benefits		6,666.67	6,349.21	6,046.86	5,758.92	5,484.68
Cumulative Discounted Net Benefits		6,666.67	13,015.87	19,062.74	24,821.65	30,306.34

Interest rate assumed to be 5%.

Net Present Value = \$30,306.34 − \$25,000 = \$5,306.34

manual systems in physicians' offices are being phased out. Dr. Jefferson's entry into the practice will create additional work for the office manager. Another full-time staff member will soon have to be hired to process the extra bills and perform other clerical work. This salary would quickly wipe out any savings from this bargain alternative. Ron also knows that manual processing costs grow as volume increases. If his projections for the anticipated future workload were increased the calculations would most likely produce other results. Ron revises his estimates to allow for a larger volume of billing and finds that the net present value turns negative. Once Dr. Jefferson's patient load equals Dr. Washington's clientele, the manual solution will be a poor investment. This solution will be documented, but he cannot recommend it as the final choice.

The Medium-Size Computer System   The alternative of a computer-based information system would provide Dr. Washington with all the functions specified in the original proposal. Although Ron is aware that there are already many software packages on the market to handle the processing required in a medical practice, he decides to explore the ramifications of a custom-built system before opting for a software package. He uses Computer Consultant's standard estimation techniques to discover that the development of a custom-built system will occupy 15 months of development time with total costs forecasted at $240,000. Since the consulting firm has never dealt with this type of application, extensive analysis time must be budgeted in order to permit an in-depth study of the detailed requirements for a physician's office.

When Ron evaluates the custom-built system for scheduling feasibility, he finds that it fails this test. Dr. Washington wishes to resolve her office management problems before Mrs. Liu retires. If a new system isn't installed soon enough and a new office manager is hired, Dr. Washington fears that she will need to take time from her medical practice in order to supervise her business affairs. She has already emphasized that she has no desire to manage the day-to-day operations of her practice. Mrs. Liu has agreed to continue working for a few more months—but an additional 15 months hardly seems to be a reasonable request. Given the lengthy time required to custom build a system, a commercial software package appears to be the only option. The business procedures necessary for a medical practice are well known and the standard business functions should be adequately handled by such software. Although a software package will probably mean some compromises with some details of the current office practices, its total cost should be far less than the $240,000 estimated for developing a custom-built system. Ron elects to pursue that line of investigation and to price the available packages. If the packages are too expensive, he can always return to the alternative of a custom-built system.

Ron begins his search by phoning several software vendors and hardware companies in order to evaluate the costs for his cost/benefit analysis. In all his cost/benefit analyses, he chooses the most conservative approach by employing the highest priced software package on the market. The actual package to be installed will be selected later by using other criteria, which are discussed in a later section. The estimated development costs for the medium-size system, shown in Figure 8-11, are only $97,000, just below the upper bound of $100,000 set by Dr. Washington. This cost is $143,000 less than the estimate for a custom-built system. The recurring costs per year are reasonable at $13,500.

The benefits of the system are two-fold. First, the reduction in staff will yield a savings of $25,000 per year. Second, because both third-party and patient invoices will be issued more rapidly, payments will be received in much less time. Thus, the increase in cash flow can be estimated at $60,000. This benefit is accrued only for the new system's first year of operation. The calculations show that the net benefits for the first year are ample at $71,500:

$$(\$60,000 + \$25,000) - \$13,500 = \$71,500$$

After the first year, accounting principles dictate that only the interest on the increased cash flow can be counted. The interest on $60,000 at a short-term rate of 10% is $6,000. The total annual benefits for the following years are

$$\$6,000 + \$25,000 = \$31,000$$

One-Time Costs	
Analysis	$ 6,000
Implementation costs	6,000
Computer system and related equipment	40,000
Software package—four modules	45,000
Total one-time costs	**$ 97,000**
Annual Operating Costs	
Maintenance	$ 5,000
Utilities	500
Supplies	4,000
Daily backup (staff time)	4,000
Total annual operating costs	**$ 13,500**
Benefits for Year 1	
Increased cash flow	$ 60,000
Reduction in staff	25,000
Total benefits for year 1	**$ 85,000**
Benefits for Year 2 and on	
Interest on increased cash flow (based on 10% short-term interest rate)	$ 6,000
Reduction in staff	25,000
Total annual benefits after year 1	**$ 31,000**

FIGURE 8-11

The estimated costs and benefits for the medium-size system

The net benefits for the second year and thereafter are computed to be

$31,000 − $13,500 = $17,500

Ron also proceeds to compute the net present value of the system as displayed by the cost/benefit analysis in Figure 8-12. After calculating the discounted net benefits, Ron discovers that the net present value (for a long-term interest rate of 5%) is $30,194.41 for the 5-year life span of the system; this sum is judged to be very good. In addition, the other financial estimates of payback period and internal rate of return are quite favorable. Financially, this system appears to be an excellent investment. Because of increased cash flow and reduced personnel costs, the medium-size system pays for itself in 2.86 years. "What a great investment," thinks Ron. Still, the system must be evaluated for the other three feasibility issues.

Inspecting the system for operational feasibility, Ron concludes that the staff can easily be trained to operate a computer system, provided it is sufficiently user-friendly. The patients would also be satisfied with the improved billing and appointment systems. Technical feasibility is an issue

FIGURE 8-12   **The cost/benefit analysis for the medium-size system**

Year	0	1	2	3	4	5
Initial Outlay	97,000					
Annual Costs		13,500	13,500	13,500	13,500	13,500
Annual Benefits		85,000	31,000	31,000	31,000	31,000
Net Benefits		71,500	17,500	17,500	17,500	17,500
Discount Factor		0.952	0.907	0.864	0.823	0.784
Discounted Net Benefits		68,095.24	15,873.02	15,117.16	14,397.29	13,711.71
Cumulative Discounted Net Benefits		68,095.24	83,968.25	99,085.41	113,482.71	127,194.41

Long-term interest rate assumed to be 5%.

Net Present Value = $127,194.41 − $97,000 = $30,194.41

Payback Period = 2.86 years

Internal Rate of Return = 20.22%

quickly resolved; there are many software packages for physicians' offices on the market and the computer hardware is available. The issue of scheduling feasibility is answered by the speed with which the software can be purchased and installed. There are no problems with this medium-size system. In fact, it is very promising. Nonetheless, Ron is obliged to continue his study of the alternatives by inspecting the feasibility of the full-blown system in order to see how that system stacks up.

The Full-Blown System   Ron first examines the financial feasibility of the full-blown system. The estimated costs and savings for this system are given in Figure 8-13. The development costs are calculated to be $136,000. The yearly costs are appraised at $20,750, while the estimated benefits for the first year are $95,000. As before, the benefits for the second year and thereafter decline because only the interest on the increased cash flow can be included, not the cash flow itself. Consequently, starting with the second year, the annual benefits are $41,000. The net present value (again, at the long-term interest rate of 5%) is computed to be $3,100.47, as shown in Figure 8-14. Since the net present value of the full-blown system ($3,100.47)

FIGURE 8-13
The estimated costs and benefits for the full-blown system

One-Time Costs	
Analysis	$ 12,000
Implementation costs	9,000
Computer hardware and related equipment	40,000
Software package—eight modules	75,000
Total one-time costs	**$136,000**
Annual Operating Costs	
Maintenance	$ 8,000
Utilities	750
Supplies	6,000
Daily backup (staff time)	6,000
Total annual operating costs	**$ 20,750**
Benefits for Year 1	
Increased cash flow	$ 60,000
Reduction in staff	35,000
Total benefits for year 1	**$ 95,000**
Benefits for Year 2 and on	
Interest on increased cash flow (based on 10% short-term interest rate)	$ 6,000
Reduction in staff	35,000
Total annual benefits after year 1	**$ 41,000**

is less than that of the medium-size system ($30,194.41), financially this system is less satisfactory. (For a detailed discussion of this point, you may wish to review the appropriate portion of Chapter 4.) The remaining three feasibility issues similarly pose no problems since the system is identical in nature to the medium-size system. The full-blown system does provide for the removal of payroll from the hands of the office manager, and that feature is highly desirable. Dr. Washington must be persuaded that controls are necessary for her financial well-being. Cases are regularly reported of trusted office managers embezzling the funds of private businesses, despite close friendships of many years. Ron will do his best to ensure that Dr. Washington is safeguarded against such theft.

Selecting the Recommended System   Reviewing the three systems, Ron opts for the medium-size system but decides to include the full-blown system in his presentation to Dr. Washington. Regardless of his recommendation, Ron knows that the final decision rests with Dr. Washington. The system belongs to the user and the user must be the satisfied person, not the

FIGURE 8-14 **The cost/benefit analysis for the full-blown system**

Year	0	1	2	3	4	5
Initial Outlay	136,000					
Annual Costs		20,750	20,750	20,750	20,750	20,750
Annual Benefits		95,000	41,000	41,000	41,000	41,000
Net Benefits		74,250	20,250	20,250	20,250	20,250
Discount Factor		0.952	0.907	0.864	0.823	0.784
Discounted Net Benefits		70,714.29	18,367.35	17,492.71	16,659.73	15,866.40
Cumulative Discounted Net Benefits		70,714.29	89,081.63	106,574.34	123,234.07	139,100.47

Long-term interest rate assumed to be 5%.
Net present value = $139,100.47 − $136,000 = $3,100.47
Payback Period = 4.8 years
Internal Rate of Return = 6.09%

systems analyst. With that decision made, Ron turns to the feasibility report he must prepare for Dr. Washington.

At the formal presentation of Ron's feasibility study, Dr. Washington concurs with his recommendation of the medium-size system. The cost is within her budgetary framework and the financial benefits appear to be outstanding. Since the full-blown system automates the entire office, she might consider that possibility for the following year. But at this time, she does not want to spend more than $100,000. "Can you arrange that the upgrading of the office system to include the other functions will be easy to implement when I'm ready to pay for them?" she inquires. "No problem," Ron reassures her. He explains that the functions in most medical software packages are sold as separate modules; thus, upgrading at a later date will pose no difficulties.

ANALYSIS

The Analysis phase follows the feasibility study. With the solution to the problem now in hand, the next step is to determine exactly what the proposed system must do. Because the feasibility study is limited in nature, it is

now time to flesh out the earlier model with more detail, by completing the data dictionary entries and composing the entire set of algorithms for the processes in the data flow diagram. To collect this additional information, Ron asks more questions about the current system and the procedures required for the new system. After examining the logical data flow diagram and its associated data dictionary, Ron sees that there must be an automatic way of determining the service charges on the patient bills. It is evident that a code for each patient service must be developed or, more likely, the list of service codes supplied by the software package must be inspected.

Ron also has several other questions about patient billing. Should patients be individually tracked, that is, each patient considered a separate entity, or should patients of the same family be billed to a common name, such as the insurance subscriber? Does Dr. Washington have any preference with regard to this form of billing? Are there any peculiarities about patient histories that are crucial in selecting the best software package? These issues are individual matters of preference; only Dr. Washington can make certain decisions once she knows what choices are available. Ron formulates a list of questions regarding the handling of the billing data and patient histories. He also documents the controls necessary for the various computer files that will be created. The transfer of funds to and from bank accounts must be monitored. All funds received must be recorded properly and withdrawals for accounts payable and salaries must be controlled.

To assist in the analysis of the system, Ron draws a model called an *entity-relationship diagram* describing the data and the relationships among the data. The entity-relationship diagram for the billing subsystem is shown in Figure 8-15. This model depicts the data but does not show how the data are processed within the system. The objective of this model is to define the data that will be stored within the new system's files. Although verbal phrases are given, this diagram depicts only the relationships between the various data elements, not the flow of data through the system. The diagram provides a simple and readily understood picture of the primary features required for the data design to be implemented for the computer. If custom software had been the choice for Dr. Washington's office, Ron would have used this diagram to help design the computer files. Since a software package will be selected, Ron plans to use this diagram to verify that the data requirements of Dr. Washington's office functions are fully met by the available software packages. The data associated with the entity-relationship diagram will also be described by entries in the data dictionary. In that way, Ron can check the detailed data specifications of the available packages against those necessary for the new system.

Before moving to the Design phase, Ron asks Dr. Washington and Mrs. Liu to review the logical model of the proposed system. "Does the model really represent what happens here?" Ron wants to know. After Dr. Washington examines the model, she confirms that it truly reflects how data flows through her office. Mrs. Liu adds her approval but asks impatiently when Ron will begin work on the actual system. "Why are we still bothering with

FIGURE 8-15   The entity-relationship diagram for Dr. Washington's office

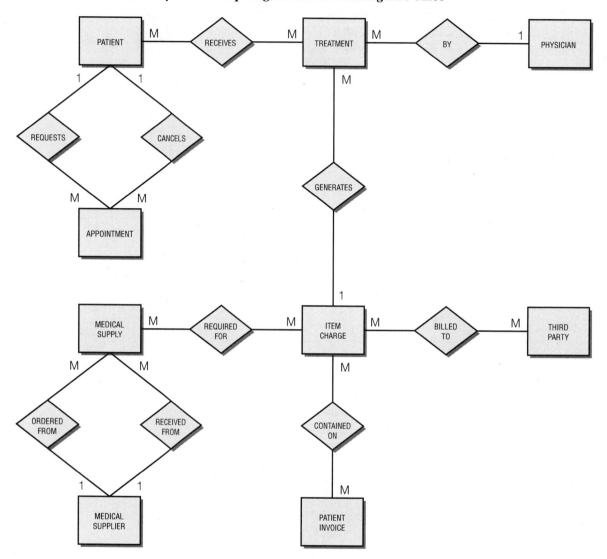

models?" she demands. Ron explains that his complete understanding of the current system is essential to the proper formulation of a new system. "Say that you don't know the dimensions of a room and the locations of its windows and doors. How can you decorate it?" Ron offers as an analogy. "Maybe you'll wallpaper over a window, or place a desk to block the door." This time, Mrs. Liu nods and gives her support to the planning activities. She is still eager to move ahead but grasps Ron's justification of his preliminary investigation and systems analysis activities. Now, Ron assures her, they can move into the Design phase and initiate the selection process for the software package to fulfill the needs of Dr. Washington's office.

DESIGNING THE SYSTEM

The decision has already been made to purchase a software package. Dr. Washington endorses the argument "Don't reinvent the wheel." Time and money will also be saved by purchasing the software. The development of a custom-tailored system would be much more costly and time-consuming. The "perfect" system for Dr. Washington clearly cannot be built within a short time frame. Some special detail common to a physician's office but not found in the typical business firm could be easily overlooked by an analyst unfamiliar with the operations in a medical office, especially if rapidity is demanded. For example, recording patient histories is a feature not present in other types of businesses. Additional examples are the treatment codes for services performed and the billing of medical services to third parties. None of these activities are found in nonmedical businesses. If the systems analyst is not familiar with medical offices, fine details of the activities may be missed. While it is obvious that a patient must be billed, the processing requirements for third-party invoices require specialized knowledge. Ron would need to spend valuable time acquiring such detailed information. By purchasing an appropriate software package, Ron will cut the time required for the system specifications substantially.

The logical data flow diagram will be helpful in gaining the understanding of the proposed system. By documenting the procedures to be followed, that is, creating the process descriptions, Ron ensures that the selection of a software package will be guided by what is truly needed rather than by vague assumptions about the operations to be performed.

> **Warning**
> It is unwise to assume that the software application packages for a physician's office system will be almost identical except for price. The packages will differ in many aspects, such as the handling of patient billing by individual or family and the restrictions on data formats. Thorough inspection of each package is essential before the right selection can be made.

Now that the logical model has been completed and his many questions have been answered, Ron prepares a request for proposal (RFP). The request will be sent to various vendors asking them to submit a proposal for the computer system required for Dr. Washington's office. Because there are no plans to hire a computer professional for the physician's office, it is necessary to ensure that the computer hardware will pose no difficulties. Thus, Ron opts for a complete *turnkey system*—a system that offers both user-friendly software and the computer hardware platform from a single vendor. If hardware or software problems occur, only one vendor call will be needed. Such a turnkey system works as easily as turning a key in a lock; the software is especially easy to use and the hardware is merely the facility by which the system works. Using a single vendor for hardware and software will provide additional ease of use for the staff once the system has been installed and Ron is no longer involved.

The Request for Proposal

What constitutes a request for proposal (RFP)? Its specifications are general in nature and yet detailed enough to spell out the requirements of the system. The essentials are stated but the reports and other documents are described at a functional level. The issue is what has to be done rather than the details of how to do it. The RFP must be specific enough to elicit appropriate bids from vendors and sufficiently broad so that vendors are not discouraged from bidding.

Since a wide range of formats for the computer files, reports, and other features will be acceptable to Dr. Washington, these physical specifications are not specified by the RFP. However, the proposal must be precise regarding the logical aspects of the system. Specific concerns over hardware problems should be included. For example, since excessive downtime cannot be tolerated or the office will be at a standstill, ways to handle the patient records and appointment scheduling during downtime periods must be included. Although the billing and accounts payable can be deferred until the system is operational once more, it must always be possible to record patient charges, either manually or on a backup system such as a PC.

Because the study of the current system has been completed, Ron is now prepared to write the RFP. The data processing performed by most physicians' offices is similar, so it is very likely that a good fit with Dr. Washington's requirements can be found. At the same time, the packages on the market probably do not exactly match how Dr. Washington's office presently operates. A summary of the technical specifications contained within the RFP is shown in Figure 8-16. The example shown in this figure is really an abbreviated version of the RFP which must be prepared. Information is furnished regarding the nature of Dr. Washington's requirements. Any special way of doing business is specified. Yet Ron knows that compromise is likely to be necessary. No system is likely to satisfy Dr. Washington's wishes in every regard.

THE PHYSICAL SPECIFICATIONS

Since the turnkey system will provide both the hardware and the software, the physical specifications here differ substantially from those at the Campus Bookstore. Instead of preparing the detailed specifications for designing files and programs, Ron must define what the system does; how the functions are performed is not his concern. The data required for the system and the functions needed to process the data are the heart of the matter. The

FIGURE 8-16 **The technical specifications contained in the RFP**

Background Information   Dr. Claire Washington, M.D., Inc. has fewer than ten employees. This is a single practice but another physician will join in September.

Medical specialty: dermatology

Estimated number of patients for two-physician office: 15,000 per year

Average number of patient visits per day: 25–30 per physician

Minimum Requirements   **1.** Patient billing and accounts receivable
                                        2. Patient scheduling
                                        3. Patient histories
                                        4. Patient recall

Optional Features   Accounts payable, drug inventory, and word processing.

Minimum Data Requirements   Billing and medical histories maintained for all patients. Retention of records:

    All medical histories kept for 20 years after decease.

    Billing data must be retained for 3 years after issue.

    Patient scheduling up to 1 year in advance.

Type of System   A complete turnkey system with hardware and software from one vendor is desired, but alternatives will be considered. Adaptation of the software by custom programming is unacceptable. The following support features are required:

1. Documentation written for the nontechnical user
2. Training support
3. Maintenance support from a single source:
    a. Guarantees of minimum downtime
    b. Hot-line support during normal working hours
4. Backup procedures
5. A two-level security system: (1) gives access to the system; (2) gives access to a specific file.
6. Shielding of electronic signals to prevent interference with medical equipment.

Processing Requirements

Patient invoices   The patient charges must be computed based on the fees associated with the diagnostic codes. User needs option to override the standard fees. Invoices must be prepared for each patient.

Third-party invoices   Invoices for third-party billing, including Medicare, must be provided. Direct billing via communication lines is desired.

Patient histories   These records must be retrievable on request, by patient or by date.

Reports and Forms   Patient invoices, third-party invoices, appointment scheduling, patient histories, and various patient and financial reports are required. The ability to query files on an ad hoc basis is desired. The format of the reports and forms is open.

Estimated Budget   The total cost of the system should not exceed $85,000, including initial installation and training. Continuing costs for maintenance of hardware and software, training, and new software versions should be no more than $5,000 per annum.

Installation Schedule   State the estimated delivery schedule once an order is placed.

Demonstrations   Please state your policy on prepurchase demonstrations. Demonstration of the system is required prior to its purchase.

Recommendations from Other Users   Please state name, address, phone number, and length of use for at least three current users of your system.

Conditions for Purchase or Lease   Dr. Washington wishes to pretest the system in her office prior to final purchase. Please state the conditions for in-office pretesting prior to the final purchase agreement. Pretesting is a necessary condition for purchase. If a lease is available, please specify its terms.

exact format of data files, reports, and forms is not pertinent here except for third-party requirements. During the Analysis phase, the data dictionary entries were created for the data records and data elements required for the files; the entity-relationship diagram was also prepared. Using this information together with the logical model of the system (the set of data flow diagrams), he can evaluate the specifications of the software packages. The number of patient visits per day and the specification of a two-physician office permit the software vendors to determine whether their software packages are designed to meet these needs. The essential functions have been specified. The additional statement regarding the retention of data records indicates the individual requirements of Dr. Washington's office and the legal requirement for medical records.

The portion labeled Type of System provides minimum specifications for the kind of system to be supplied by the vendor. The supporting features are also enumerated. Notice that a guarantee of minimum downtime has been clearly stated as well as hot-line support during normal working hours. If help is just a phone call away, any difficulties can be quickly overcome. Security of the system is crucial here because of the confidentiality of medical records and the need to safeguard financial transactions. Consequently, a two-level security system is specified. A brief statement regarding the processing requirements for the billing and patient history subsystems is given. As discussed earlier, the format of reports and forms has been left open. Because the ability to query the data files on an ad hoc basis appeals to Dr. Washington, it has been included. The upper bound of Dr. Washington's capital resource allocation for the computer system is stated explicitly so that the vendors know whether their system would be financially feasible. The delivery schedule is important, because a system that cannot be installed shortly after purchase would delay the conversion. Dr. Washington also feels strongly about the credentials of the vendor. She wants to see the system demonstrated, check recommendations from other users, and have a trial period in her office. All these validation procedures have been stipulated.

SOLICITING THE BIDS

After the completion of the RFP, the request for bids must be sent to the various sources that provide this specialized software. To identify the potential bidders for this RFP, Ron consults a list of vendors who have displayed their wares at medical conferences. Such listings can be obtained from the conference organizers. During the investigatory activities, he already examined the computer information systems at several medical offices; vendors for these systems can also be contacted. A search of the medical journals reveals additional sources, and the local medical association is another source of contacts. Finally, technical information services such as *Datapro reports* may offer him referrals to appropriate vendors.

The mailing or delivery of the request for a bid must be accompanied by a cover letter stating the deadline for the receipt of proposals. The cover

FIGURE 8-17
The cover letter for the RFP

Claire Washington, M.D.
Dermatology and Dermatologic Surgery
Park Plaza Building, Suite 201
Greenton Grove, Illinois 69911

February 28, 1994

Medical Software, Inc.
777 Second Street, N.W.
Washington, DC 20009

Dear Sir or Madam:

Enclosed is a request for proposal for a medical software system for my office. The general objectives and requirements of the medical practice have been included to assist you in gaining a better understanding of my requirements.

My objective is to obtain a complete data processing package (hardware and software) that will satisfy my needs without software modifications.

Your proposal should be submitted no later than April 5, 1994. Please send your proposal to Ron Czalka, Computer Consultants, 89 Pulaski Boulevard, Wheatonville, Illinois 68891. Mr. Czalka has been engaged to assist me with this selection process.

If you desire additional information or have any questions regarding this request, please contact Ron Czalka at Computer Consultants, phone (708) 555-9999.

Very truly yours,

Claire Washington

Claire Washington, M.D.

letter written by Dr. Washington for the RFP is shown in Figure 8-17. The vendors are given a month to respond to the RFP. This time frame is adequate because the solicitation is for a turnkey system that already exists. Vendors who do not respond promptly presumably lack the appropriate system or are not interested in obtaining this contract.

Selecting the System

Once bids are received, Ron will review them to see if they match the stated requirements. Bids over the stated limit will be set aside. Only if suitable bids within the price range are not received will these higher-priced bids be considered. Bids that pass the financial hurdle will be reviewed for the office functions outlined by Dr. Washington. The criteria for the system will also be examined: ease of use, training, high reliability, provision for manual processing during downtime, backup, security, maintenance, and support services for a period of 5 years. These factors cannot be stated with the numerical precision of the financial criterion (but we must remember that the financial data are *estimates*, not facts). For example, the characteristic, ease of use, will be appraised subjectively. The skill of the analyst is the deciding factor in evaluating the merits of the system. Further, there will be trade-offs among the criteria. A system judged extremely easy to use may not have training and maintenance options. Weighting each criterion is the responsibility of the systems analyst, with the ultimate decision made by Dr. Washington. While it is simple to eliminate bids that fail to meet the minimum standards, no system will be perfect.

Finally, the analyst is confronted with the reality that the software packages to be reviewed were designed to serve all kinds of physicians. This means that some aspect of Dr. Washington's procedures and data may have to be altered to conform to the particular specifications of the canned software. It is possible to customize the software and pay the custom programming costs, but each time a new version is released the customizing would have to be repeated, adding to the costs. Since many software vendors do not offer customization, Dr. Washington would be dependent on free-lance programmers for future modifications. Vendors may refuse to support software that has been altered, because software errors may have been introduced by the modifications. If any problems were encountered after modifications were done, the vendor would blame the free-lance programmer and Dr. Washington's office would be caught in the middle.

Dr. Washington has already expressed her desire for reliable software. Because customization risks a frustrating situation with added expenses, Ron advises Dr. Washington to alter her procedures to fit the canned software. Would a fair-to-middling software package with a close fit to the proposed system be better than a superior package that requires substantial changes in her business practices? This trade-off is another gray area for the analyst. A clear-cut decision is unlikely. After examining the documentation supplied by the vendors and viewing the demonstrations, Ron is able to narrow the field to a few packages. Any vendors who refused to demonstrate the software features were dropped from consideration.

Ultimately, Dr. Washington is responsible for the selection of the software. Ideally, the demonstrations will allow her to key in data, access the files, and obtain reports. By getting the feel of the system, she will gain insight into its workings. Ease of use has now been established as the primary criterion for selection. But how can anyone measure this factor? Ease of use is judged subjectively by the individual user. The analyst, as a technician, may overlook small nuances of the system. Given his knowledge of how most systems work, Ron can quickly adapt to different software systems. Since Dr. Washington's staff members will be the users of the system, they should attend the demonstrations. Their comments regarding the potential systems will contribute to the selection process.

A free trial period for the system is also requested in the RFP. Because the system's costs are high, it is advisable to have the option to return a system that just does not work out. But such an option may not be offered by the vendor. Instead, a lease/buy arrangement may be proffered. By leasing the system for 6 months, Dr. Washington could gain experience with the system and then make a purchase decision. However, once the system is operational and files are converted, it would be awkward to return to the manual system. Similarly, replacing the system by a different software package would most likely require new file formats, changes in manual procedures, different computer screens and reports, and other alterations in user interfaces. To install an inadequate system would have serious consequences, even if the system were free for a 6-month trial period. Reversion to the old system would mean a major upheaval in the office procedures, confusion among the staff, and poor morale. Switching to a different software package would have similar unpleasant consequences. Aware of these ramifications, Ron works to ensure a good choice the first time around.

THE IMPLEMENTATION PHASE

Before the new system can be installed, Ron must carefully plan and execute many tasks. Nothing must be overlooked or the new system will have to sit in a corner while the employees scramble to get things in place. Fortunately, Computer Consultants has prepared a chart of the activities in the systems development life cycle for the implementation of a software package. This chart serves as a checklist for Ron's planning. He plans all the activities and devises a detailed schedule for them. Wherever possible, activities are overlapped. Conversion of the data files can occur while the physical site is altered to accommodate the computer equipment. At the same time, training can begin. The checklist shows Ron that computer supplies, forms for patient charges, diskettes, printer cartridges, and other items must be ordered. The acceptance testing dates are established; the entire process of implementation and installation must be planned and controlled. By using the Computer Consultants' checklist, Ron makes sure that all will proceed on schedule and that the installed system will meet Dr. Washington's expectations.

Acceptance Testing

The selection process performed in the Design phase included a demonstration of the combined hardware and software system. Acceptance testing means executing some of the typical work for this office so that the system's capabilities are verified. By performing both samples of routine work and test cases requiring error handling, the system proves that it conforms to the stated specifications. If the system fails to perform as required by the original specifications, either it will be rejected or compromises with the initial requirements must be made.

Training the Staff

Training of the office workers precedes conversion to the new system. Sample record processing is performed, and the staff members learn the manual processing procedures required by the new computer system. How to handle errors must be mastered. For example, if the receptionist keys in the wrong name for a time slot, she must know how to change the data. Everyone makes mistakes, and the error-correction procedures must be mastered for the computer system. In turn, the system needs safeguards against errors that the software can detect.

Training manuals written especially for the users are supplied by the vendor. For simple questions, the employees can simply turn to these manuals for the answer. The hot-line phone number is another feature the staff must learn to use. With these two activities underway, Ron checks that the plans for the equipment have been completed.

Installing the New System

Immediately after selecting the software package in the Design phase, Ron formulates plans for the installation of the system. There are two major concerns: space for the computer equipment and the power supply. The space for the computer and its work stations was determined earlier. Except for large-scale computers, most computers today tolerate the standard air-conditioned environment of office buildings. However, the computer does generate heat; ideally, the room for the computer needs its own thermostat to regulate temperature and humidity. Printer paper wilts in humidity, which can affect the printer. Since Dr. Washington's office building was constructed with temperature controls in each room, Ron sees no problems in this area. Otherwise, depending on the computer manufacturer, remodeling might have been necessary. Ron draws a layout of the office suite and plans where telephones, workstations, desks, and other furnishings will be placed.

The power supply for the computer hardware must be adequate. If the physical site is not adequately wired, problems with the power source will occur. In Dr. Washington's case, the building is new and the architects allowed for the installation of computer equipment in the offices. Another concern is the continuity of the power supply. A computer is not just another electrical device, and it is important to ensure against sudden loss of power. In that event, the processing being performed will be lost and the integrity of the data files will be damaged. An uninterruptible power supply (UPS) can be placed between the computer and the electric company's lines. If the electric power should fail, the UPS will switch the computer to battery power, which permits operations to continue for a short period. If the power outage continues, there can be an orderly shutdown of the system. Depending on the battery, the computer may continue working for several hours, thus avoiding any downtime. Ron also orders a power surge suppressor to prevent computer failure due to sudden surges or slumps in the power supply sent by the electric lines. Careful planning can keep the downtime to a minimum. Any telecommunication lines installed will be tested prior to the arrival of the hardware. Ron works diligently to identify problems before the equipment arrives at Dr. Washington's office.

Conversion of Data Records

Before the switch to the new system, the paper files must be transcribed as computer files. Earlier, Ron prepared the schedule for this conversion process and determined which records must be converted to the new system. In discussing this problem with Ron, Dr. Washington decided that medical histories for all patients treated in the past 18 months will be converted to computer files; all others will be retained as paper documents. Old medical history records will be converted for every returning patient on an as-needed basis. For the accounts receivable system, only patient ledgers with an outstanding balance will be converted. New entries will be created with each new patient visit after the new system is installed. Similarly, the appointment book must be entered into the system. All data records essential for the efficient functioning of the office must be available to the staff.

Dr. Washington expresses her concern over the data records. What if errors in the patient charges or patient history file creep into the system during the conversion process? That would be a serious problem for her medical practice. Ron reassures her that all data will be double keyed: After the first entry of the data, the same data will be rekeyed and compared by the computer program to the first entry. If there is a discrepancy, the keying operation will be halted and the operator required to choose the correct entry. The chance of any keying errors is almost nonexistent under this double keying method of data conversion. In addition, cross-checking of gross totals can be used to compare the old records with the new computer data. There should be no problems here.

Planning the Backup Procedures

At present, Dr. Washington's office operates without any backup procedures. Since all data records are paper documents, maintaining duplicate copies would mean great expense and considerable difficulty. If the office were destroyed in a fire, the records would simply be lost. The notion of backup is new to Dr. Washington. After all, she never had the capability to back up her records under the current manual system. "Why bother now?" she queries. Ron explains that records will now be stored within the computer and the paper documents will no longer be up-to-date. Periodically, printouts of the data will be produced and filed, but meanwhile only the computer files will hold the latest information. While plans have been made to prevent failure of the computer, hardware failures and even software failures do sometimes happen. Then, too, other disasters such as fires or floods might destroy all the information stored within the computer. If the information were lost, it would be necessary to reenter all the data to get her office operations up and running again. "Isn't it better to be prepared for disasters than to spend days or even weeks unable to process the office data records? Good backup procedures mean your office could open soon after a major problem. Since your patients' medical records will still be there, you will be able to continue to provide excellent medical services. Isn't that worth a good deal of money?" Ron argues. By explaining the advantages of backup procedures, Ron persuades Dr. Washington of their importance.

The contingency plans for Dr. Washington's office include a fixed schedule for backing up the files stored on hard disk, storing one copy of all files off-site, and having guaranteed replacement of the computer equipment within 48 hours. Backup procedures must be rigidly followed. Ron stresses how easy it is for the busy staff to delay performing the backup tasks until a "better time." There is never a convenient time for backup, he knows. If the office is fortunate the backup files will never be required. But if things ever break down, the backup files will allow operations to continue and avoid a lengthy delay. Backup procedures are like an insurance policy against disasters; maybe the insurance claim will never come due—but then again, it just might. "Be prepared," is Ron's professional advice.

Converting to the New System

In making the plans for the new system, Ron also must decide on the method of conversion. Should the old system be executed initially in parallel with the new system? If both systems are active at the same time, any problems with the new system can be detected without affecting the office records. That is a possibility, but it means double work for the staff. Can the new system be phased in, function by function? The appointment scheduling and patient recall systems could be installed first, then the patient charge system, and finally the patient history system. A third possibility is a direct cutover, achieved by switching to the new system completely as of a particular date. The old system would simply be discontinued and the new procedures would take over. Is that the best plan? Because the new system is modular, a step-by-step conversion procedure seems best. This approach gives the receptionist experience with the computer appointment scheduling system before she has to deal with patient charges the new way. The phased-in approach is Ron's preference but Dr. Washington's approval is necessary. She must be involved in this decision, since it is her office system. After a brief discussion, she agrees with Ron and the conversion planning goes forward.

INSTALLING THE NEW SYSTEM

As planned, the installation goes smoothly. The extensive planning allows the system to be phased in without incident. The staff members like the advantages of the new system. They feel a sense of ownership since Ron consulted them about many facets of the system. The excellent training has given them confidence and Ron's presence during the early days helped them master the new ways of entering data and accessing the files. The hot-line support personnel have been helpful, too. Even when the staff members call with a "dumb" question, the technicians are patient in guiding them to the right keying sequence. Although the training manuals are on the bookshelves, the staff members never look up information. It is much faster and easier to call the hot-line with a question. "A few questions every day isn't too bad," they remark.

By the end of the second week, the staff members have mastered the computer operations and the hot-line questions stop. For events that rarely happen they are still uncomfortable with the system, but the on-line help and easily understood menus enable them to deal with these infrequent occurrences. The staff members are not expected to remember procedures for events that happen only once or twice a year. The easy to use criterion means that they can handle exceptional occurrences as well as the daily routine without frustration. Overall, the installation is a success.

THE POST-IMPLEMENTATION REVIEW

As arranged earlier, Ron meets with Dr. Washington to conduct a post-implementation review. Dr. Washington opens the meeting with a concern. She has recently read about the bankruptcy of a software vendor. What if her vendor closes up shop, leaving her office without software and hardware support? Ron responds that her medical software vendor is prospering and the firm's management displays a good understanding of the market. This vendor now holds a 35% market share and sales are increasing. With that success, rather than closing the business, it is more likely that the vendor will be acquired by another firm. To safeguard their interests in the software, the software users' group has already arranged for the source code to be placed in escrow; that is, a third party holds the source code for the programs and the technical documentation. In the event of the firm's failure, the software users' group can contract with another vendor to continue the maintenance of the software. The large market share of the vendor, the strong software users' group, and the escrow arrangement for the software are sound reasons for confidence in the future of the software package. Dr. Washington is satisfied with this reassurance.

She continues the post-implementation review meeting by saying that the new system has met her expectations. The morale of her staff is high, and

Finger-Pointing at Computerworld

As wonderful as new software and hardware may appear, problems with them still arise, even at such presumably savvy businesses as the publication headquarters for *Computerworld*. If yours is an aging computer system, there is no choice but to change. But the changeover may bring unforeseen problems. Contract for hardware and software from different vendors and you risk having every system failure evoke the frustrating reply, "Not me, call the other guy." Making that crucial mistake has left *Computerworld* still operating on an antiquated Digital Equipment Corporation PDP-J11 with dumb terminals instead of their problem-ridden "state-of-the-art" system of personal computers tied to a network. Although the new system has been installed, numerous technical and reliability problems remain unresolved.

Using the new system is an adventure with no guarantee of success. Staff writer Lynda Radosevich suffered the infamous "network connection lost" problem when her PC froze without warning during an important telephone interview. Even the new file structure contributes to the difficulties of staffers trying to write stories. Multiple files have identical names and are scattered throughout a variety of subdirectories. The file naming convention fails to prevent the wrong version of a story from slipping through to publication. Rather than place the responsibility on the software, the staff writers will be trained in new procedures for file naming.

Because the software vendor changed ownership three months ago, its support department has been slow to answer questions about specific bugs or software problems; delays as long as six weeks have been encountered. The engineers who were once available to answer customers' questions have now been prohibited from customer contact. Since *Computerworld* turned off the RS/6000 servers in case of power failure during a March blizzard, certain disk functions controlled by the software are no longer operable. Although the software vendor, Atex, and the hardware vendor, IBM, have worked hard to find the cause, neither can discover why the system is failing. Finger-pointing is an easy solution.

Alas, the story in *Computerworld* bemoaning these troubles had to be written on a dumb terminal connected to the old publishing system. So many months have elapsed since the writers were trained on the new PCs that, if the new system finally becomes operational, retraining will almost certainly be necessary. Though the staff writers continue to use the creaking PDP-J11, Paul Gillin, *Computerworld*'s executive editor, still hopes to gain the advantages of open systems and take the publication into a new era of computing.

Source: Johnson, Maryfran, "Client/Server Medicine Can Be Bitter Pill," *Computerworld*, April 12, 1993, p. 49. Copyright 1992/93. Reprinted with permission from *Computerworld*.

only small problems, easily solved, have occurred. The employees are happy because the hours of overtime have stopped. They would rather spend time with their families than with the paperwork of the office. The replacement for Mrs. Liu, Juanita Garcia-Tomas, who has had previous experience with medical software, rates the system as excellent. In general, Dr. Washington is pleased with the new system. In another year, she will consider the conversion of the payroll system to the computer. "Definitely, Computer Consultants is the group I'll call to perform the job," she declares. The time spent in investigating the old system and in the detailed planning has paid off. The conversion to the new system was well executed. Dr. Washington congratulates Ron on a job well done. Ron takes a few more minutes to check that procedures are being followed, especially the backup operation. He will stop back in three months and evaluate the system again. "Following established procedures is crucial, and a checkup by 'Dr. Ron' would be a good idea," smiles Dr. Washington, and adds, "It's always better to practice preventive care than to need major surgery." Agreeing to that comment, Ron shakes hands and departs for Computer Consultants to take on another challenging assignment.

SUMMARY

The case study of Dr. Washington's office was designed to illustrate several major points:

1. a situation where only tangible benefits exist for a system
2. the implementation of a new system by means of commercially available software
3. the problem of the "indispensable employee," which is resolved by the introduction of a computer system

The physician's office provides the setting in which to explain these issues.

Dr. Washington was faced with the loss of a valued employee, the office manager, who had designed her own way of handling the billing system. The manual system of keeping records was time-consuming and slow. She believed that the moment had come to acquire a computer system in order to provide efficient, accurate processing of patient billing. With that idea in mind, she engaged Computer Consultants to implement a computer system for four functional areas: patient billing, appointment scheduling, patient recalls, and patient histories. The activities performed by the systems analyst, Ron Czalka, for each phase of the SDLC are outlined in Figure 8-18.

During the Preliminary Investigation phase, the analyst performed a cursory study of the problems in Dr. Washington's office and presented the initial proposal for the project. After approval, Ron executed the feasibility study in order to find a solution to these problems. First, he endeavored to fully understand the functions that must be implemented in the new system. Then he reviewed various alternatives and measured the financial, technical, operational, and scheduling feasibility of each possible solution. Choosing the best system from this review, Ron recommended a medium-size computer system to Dr. Washington. The purchase of a software application package represented a major savings over the development of custom software designed explicitly for Dr. Washington's needs. Since software pack-

FIGURE 8-18

**The SDLC Activities for
Dr. Washington's Office**

The Phase in the SDLC	The Activities of the Systems Analyst
Preliminary Investigation	Prepare initial proposal Perform feasibility study
Analysis	Create logical model of future system Understand the data by drawing the entity-relationship diagram

Design	Prepare request for proposal (RFP)
	Investigate packages through:
	    vendor demonstrations
	    study of documentation
	    review of other customers
	    vendor stability
	Select best software package

Implementation	Site preparation General testing Acceptance testing User training Installation plans
Installation	Convert data files Cutover to new system
Post-Implementation Review	Attend the review of new system performance Request appraisal of software development activities

ages are created to meet the needs of diverse customers, it was likely that Dr. Washington would have to change some aspects of her office procedures to fit a package's requirements. Customization of the package by altering the code was judged to be inappropriate in this situation.

After obtaining Dr. Washington's agreement for the recommended system, Ron prepared a request for proposal (RFP) and sent it to vendors who market medical software. The resulting proposals were examined by studying the documentation, attending demonstrations, contacting the vendors' customers, and investigating the vendor's financial stability and general reputation. The office staff and Dr. Washington were asked to study the package for its compatibility with current procedures and to rate its user-friendliness, or ease of use. Although Ron rated the software packages and endorsed the purchase of a particular software package, the final decision was made by Dr. Washington.

Several tasks still remained to be accomplished prior to the package's installation at Dr. Washington's office. Ron planned and supervised the following activities: site preparation for the computer facility, general testing of the software package, acceptance testing by the users, user training, and preparations for conversion tasks. Following the successful completion of these tasks, the manual files were converted to computer files and the new system was gradually phased in. Dr. Washington was then requested to evaluate the software implementation activities and to appraise the performance of the newly installed system. A second review of the system's performance was scheduled in another three months' time.

TERMS

Because the case study of Dr. Washington's office was designed to illustrate the activities of the entire life cycle, terms are not listed for this chapter. The technical aspects of these activities are covered in other chapters.

QUESTIONS

1. Why did Dr. Washington want to install a computer information system in her office?

2. Explain why Dr. Washington chose to engage the services of a consulting firm rather than to acquire her system directly from a software vendor who could install the software.

3. Describe the three alternatives formulated by Ron Czalka, the systems analyst, for Dr. Washington's office.

4. Assuming the cost/benefit analyses performed by the systems analyst were correct, which alternative was the best financial investment? Why?

5. Explain why an improved manual system would have been unsatisfactory for Dr. Washington.

6. **a.** What is a complete turnkey system?
   b. Why was a complete turnkey system desirable for Dr. Washington's office?

7. What factors regarding a software vendor should be evaluated before buying or leasing from that vendor?

8. Since Mrs. Liu was a woman of unquestionable integrity, why was Ron Czalka concerned about the lack of controls for financial matters?

9. In the detailed planning for installation, the systems analyst scheduled training prior to the installation of the computer system. Was this feasible? Explain.

10. **a.** Why did Ron Czalka not expect to find a software package that exactly fits Dr. Washington's existing data processing methods?
    b. How did he propose to overcome this difficulty?

11. Why did Ron Czalka, reject customization of the software package in order to meet the requirements of Dr. Washington's office?

12. Dr. Washington expressed concern about the software vendor's continuing presence in the marketplace. Assuming that the software vendor closes and no other firm purchases the company, what will be the consequences to Dr. Washington's office system?

PROJECTS

1. The criteria for selecting the best software package for Dr. Washington are listed as ease of use, training availability, high reliability, provision for processing during downtime, backup, security, maintenance, and support services for a 5-year period. The accompanying table ranks each criterion from 1 to 10, where 10 indicates the highest quality. Assuming that the systems analyst has evaluated three software packages by assigning the values shown in the table, which package would you recommend? Justify your answer.

Selection Factor	Vendor 1	Vendor 2	Vendor 3
Ease of Use	5	9	7
Training	8	3	7
Reliability	8	8	9
Downtime Provisions	5	5	7
Backup	8	9	8
Security	3	3	9
Maintenance	9	7	9
Support Services	9	8	3

2. Visit a local physician's office and observe the appointment scheduling and method of recording a patient's visit; or visit your Student Health Center and observe these functions. Prepare a short paper describing

   a. The procedures for entering and cancelling a patient's appointment

   b. The procedures for recording a patient's visit and treatment

   If possible, obtain samples of the forms used to record the patient visits. Point out any differences between this real-world medical office and the office of Dr. Washington.

3. You have been engaged by the local bakery to evaluate the installation of a computer information system for recording bakery orders, payroll processing, and general ledger functions. How will you locate the names of vendors that sell software packages suitable for use by bakeries? *Suggestion:* Visit the local bakery and discuss this matter with the manager.

The Modeling Tools of Systems Analysis

CHAPTER 9

Data Flow Diagrams

Objectives

This chapter explains data flow diagrams, which are one of the primary means of modeling information systems. After studying this chapter, you will be able to:

- Describe the role that data flow diagrams play in systems analysis

- Understand the symbols used to construct data flow diagrams

- Draw simple data flow diagrams

- Detect errors and critique the depiction of information systems represented by data flow diagrams

INTRODUCTION

The Analysis phase of the systems development life cycle requires that we understand and document the user's needs that must be met by the new system. A widely accepted procedure is to first construct a *model* of the existing system, and then, by using this model as a reference point, produce a model of the new system. Models enable the systems analyst to communicate with the users of the current system and ensure that the new system will meet their requirements. The term **model** simply means a representation of a real-world object by some means other than the object itself. In manufacturing automobiles, one step in the design of a new car is to create a model of the car prior to its actual production on the assembly line. Many details of the new car are given by drawings produced by the designer. These drawings represent a theoretical view or model of the proposed automobile. In addition, a miniature replica of the new car is produced so that decision-makers can fully understand the design of the car before any are produced by the factory. Such a replica is also called a model. These representations of the new car are created to ensure that the design is completely specified and error-free. The cost of producing an automobile with flaws or unmarketable features far outweighs the time and expense required for such detailed specification. Because an information system deals with data and with processes performed on the data, we build our models by using abstractions to represent the actual data and the processes within the system.

In building a model of the existing information system, we gain an understanding of what the system presently accomplishes. We are also able to demonstrate to the users that we comprehend the capabilities of the current information system as well as its deficiencies. Typically, the data and processes within the existing system are incorporated into the design of the new system. For example, if we examine the existing sales and inventory system for a retail store, we know that any new system must provide the same functions. An information system for the store must be able to process customer transactions, send bills to the store's credit customers, verify shipments from suppliers, and perform the myriad of tasks necessary to support the store's operations. The existing system presently performs these same tasks. When we represent the existing system by a model, we can clearly see what changes must be made and what new features should be added. By using a model of the system, we are studying a representation of these many tasks and are better able to concentrate on the important aspects of the system without becoming lost in the details. Consequently, the model of the existing system serves as the foundation for the design of a new information system.

To model an information system, we employ a diagramming technique known as *data flow diagrams*. Data flow diagrams are the most commonly used tool—and the one employed in this book—for the creation of such models. By using data flow diagrams, we can represent all or any portion of an information system. Before turning our attention to the methodology of data flow diagrams, it is important to note that this modeling technique is only a means to an end, not the end itself. We should not lose sight of our final objective: the design and implementation of an information system to meet the user's needs.

In this chapter, we explain the principles governing the creation of data flow diagrams. The first section defines the four components required for the modeling of an information system. The second section explains how the details of an information system are depicted by a hierarchy of data flow diagrams. The third section presents the rules that should be followed for the drawing of these diagrams. The fourth section defines the characteristics of physical and logical data flow diagrams. The fifth section presents the major steps required to model the proposed information system.

THE COMPONENTS OF INFORMATION SYSTEMS

An information system accepts data from a person or organization outside of the system, performs several tasks to change the data into output data, and sends the final transformed data to a person or organization that is, once again, outside the system. Within the information system, the input data is transformed by one or more processes in order to create the output data. The basic components needed to describe an information system are

> The data
>
> The entities outside the system that are the sources or final destinations of the data (called *external entities*)
>
> The processes that transform the data

When we look at the data passing from one process to another process within the system, we observe that not all data immediately enter a process; some are instead recorded temporarily or permanently. Consequently, data are viewed in two different ways:

1. Data flowing within the system, represented by *data flows*
2. Data resting temporarily or permanently in a medium such as computer files, represented by *data stores*

With these basic components, we can construct a model of any information system by using a technique called *data flow diagrams*.

A **data flow diagram (DFD)** furnishes a graphical description of the data and processes within an information system by using only four basic components (or *elements*): *external entity, process, data flow*, and *data store*. As shown in Figure 9-1, each element is depicted by a symbol according to the conventions of either Gane and Sarson [1979] or Yourdon [1989].

FIGURE 9-1   **The four elements of data flow diagrams**

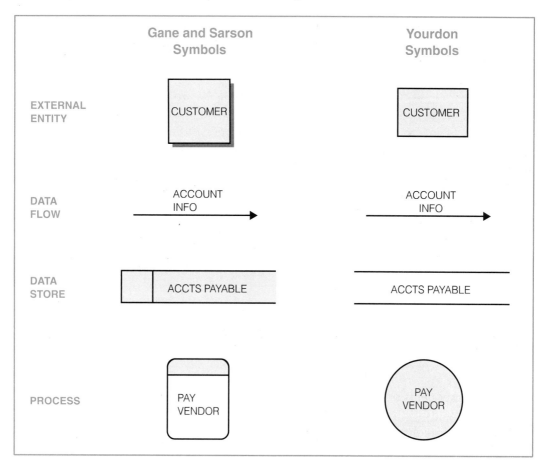

We use as many of these elements as necessary to diagram the system. In this text, we have chosen to use the symbols popularized by the Gane and Sarson methodology for data flow diagrams. There are some differences in the actual diagramming techniques between these two methodologies. Although this book employs the Gane and Sarson notation, the methodology presented is similar to the Yourdon view of data flow diagrams.

> **Warning**
>
> Don't confuse data flow diagrams with flowcharts. The flow on a data flow is not necessarily sequential. In fact, we strive for parallelism in DFDs rather than the sequential display given by flowcharts.

To demonstrate the use of data flow diagrams, the model of an information system that processes customers' orders is displayed in Figures 9-2

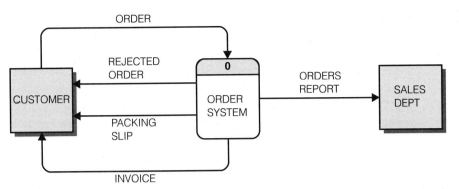

FIGURE 9-2

The context level data flow diagram for the ORDER information system

and 9-3. In Figure 9-2, we have the *context level data flow diagram* for the ORDER information system. A context level diagram shows only the external entities and the data flowing into and out of the system. Consequently, in Figure 9-2 the ORDER system itself is represented by a single process, labeled ORDER SYSTEM. In Figure 9-3, the model now shows the information system at its topmost level, with the many individual tasks grouped into

FIGURE 9-3   The level 0 data flow diagram for the ORDER information system

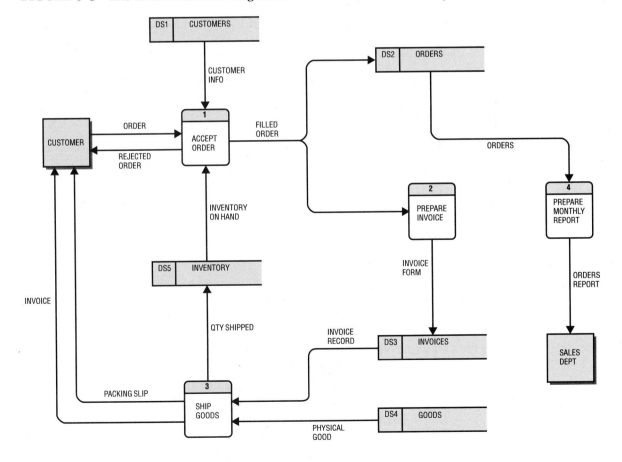

major activities—the processes. As in the context level diagram, there are two external entities, CUSTOMER and SALES DEPT. The five data stores here labeled CUSTOMERS, ORDERS, INVOICES, GOODS, and INVENTORY did not appear in the context level diagram. The four major activities are given by the processes labeled ACCEPT ORDER, PREPARE INVOICE, SHIP GOODS, and PREPARE MONTHLY REPORT. The processing of the input data flow ORDER received from a customer causes the data to be finally transformed to either REJECTED ORDER, INVOICE, PACKING SLIP, or ORDERS REPORT. You can easily see the flow of data through this system and the processes are clearly labeled. This graphical view of the system allows us to see the major activities of the system and to identify the data necessary for the operation of the system.

Data flow diagrams (DFDs) are models of how data are processed by a system. Despite its name, the data flow diagram is process-oriented rather than data-oriented. We are interested in how the data are transformed by the various activities within the system. A data-oriented methodology focuses on the data and does not emphasize the flow of data through a system. However, it is important to understand that in a data flow diagram we are really attempting to depict both the data and the processes that alter the data. We must know what data moves in and out of each process and what data is placed in or retrieved from a data store. An information system is processing data and we must be constantly aware of the data and how they are transformed by the processes within the system.

Before proceeding further with the topic of data flow diagrams, it is necessary to understand that a data flow diagram by itself is incomplete. The details of data flows and data stores must be documented by entries in a **data dictionary** (covered in Chapter 10). The data dictionary is stored within the **project dictionary**. Similarly, each process must be defined by a process description which is also stored in the project dictionary; this topic is covered in Chapter 11. Now we will continue our discussion of data flow diagrams with the details of their components and the rules for their construction.

External Entity

Any person, organization, or division of an organization that supplies data to the information system or receives data from the system is called an **external entity**. We represent an external entity by a square labeled with an appropriate noun. In Figure 9-3, we saw that CUSTOMER was written within a square to indicate an external entity, the customer. Although a business undoubtedly has many customers, an external entity is always named with a singular rather than plural noun. When a customer orders a product, the person is an external entity that sends data to the ordering system. The customer may also receive data from the system in the form of an invoice, a shipping document, and so on. There may be customers who order by mail and others who phone in their orders. All these customers are usually represented in a DFD by only one external entity labeled CUSTOMER.

An external entity does not handle or process the data in any way; consequently, an external entity resides outside of the actual system. Many times an external entity is an actual person, but we always represent this person by title rather than by personal name. Examples of external entities that may send or receive data from an information system are the manager, the director of the marketing department, or the customer. By generating a query for information and receiving the report, the manager functions as both a source and destination of data. The director of the marketing department serves as a destination of data by receiving the summary report of sales for the quarter.

An organization such as a bank or a department within an organization (for example, the accounting department) may also serve as an external entity for a system. Rather than identify the individual in the organization who is the source or destination of the data, we simply name the organization. For example, the bank may receive the deposits of customer payments. The accounting department may be the recipient of a report that lists the payments for the month. The sales department may request reports and receive these reports.

Since the people who work within the system merely perform the processing required by the system, they are not external entities. These individuals are represented by the processes on the data flow diagram. For example, a clerk who receives a phone order from a catalog customer and records the order using an on-line order entry system is acting within the system by recording the data. The clerk has not generated the data entering the system but executes the operations necessary to accept and record the data. Consequently, the clerk is not an external entity for the system; instead, the clerk's actions are viewed as a process within the system. Occasionally, an individual within the system plays a dual role by performing a process and also sending data to or receiving data from the system. A manager who approves each customer's request for credit is performing a process. The same manager may be the recipient of a report listing the customers who are 30 days overdue on their payments. In the latter case, the manager receives data from the system and so would be represented as an external entity.

Data Flows

A **data flow** represents data being conveyed to or from an external entity, a process, or a data store. We also say that a data flow is *data in motion*, because the data move or flow to or from a data entity, a data store, or a process. A line with an arrow indicating the direction of the flow together with a noun naming the data contents flowing on the line depicts the data in motion. In Figure 9-3, three examples of data flows are given by the customer's order (called ORDER), the monthly report for the Sales Department (called ORDERS REPORT), and the invoice (called INVOICE). In this figure, we also can see that the data flow ORDER is flowing from the external entity CUSTOMER to the process called ACCEPT ORDER. The data flow FILLED ORDER flows from the process ACCEPT ORDER to the data store ORDERS and also to the process PREPARE INVOICE. The third data flow from the process ACCEPT ORDER is called REJECTED ORDER and is represented by a line with an arrow pointing to CUSTOMER, the recipient of the data.

A data flow is typically depicted as only one set of data. In other words, the external entity CUSTOMER sends only one order into the system. The many orders that actually flow through the information system are implicit in the data flow diagram. The information system is always operational; thus the next order placed by a customer will be processed in the same way in the system. Even if a customer is allowed to send more than one order at a time, we still view the data flow as a single order because each of the orders will be processed in the same way.

A data flow is labeled by a descriptive noun that may be modified by an appropriate adjective, for example, VERIFIED ORDER, PAYCHECK, ACCOUNTING MONTHLY REPORT, ACCOUNT INFORMATION, and SALARY. The detailed description of the data contained on a data flow is entered in the data dictionary, which must accompany the data flow diagram. As we stated earlier, this topic will be covered in Chapter 10.

Data Stores

A **data store** is a repository for data that are temporarily or permanently recorded within the system; such data are known as *data at rest*. Easily discerned data stores are any files used by an organization, for instance, the university's payroll file, the student master file showing all courses and grades for every student at the university, and the accounts receivable file containing all the billing information for the university. Data that are recorded manually are also considered to be data at rest and, thus, are represented by a data store. For example, recording the receipt of each customer order in a daily log is a process that transmits data to a data store. Another example is an IN/OUT box with documents to be processed daily; these data are temporarily not in motion and thus represent a data store. Other examples are a binder containing a list of customers, a deck of 3″ × 5″ cards listing the customers of a retail firm, and a file folder containing the bills that will be paid at the end of the month.

It is important to notice that a report is rarely created from only a single data record. Instead, several data records must be processed in order to produce a report. Consequently, the data necessary to produce a report reside in a data store. For example, a report listing all customer accounts that are past due requires the processing of the appropriate file containing this information. The examination of only one customer account record could not produce the desired report.

The direction of a data flow *to* or *from* a data store designates respectively whether data are written into or read from the data store. A data flow that travels *to* a data store indicates the writing of data into the data store. This type of data flow is labeled with the name indicating the actual data to be written into the data store. A data flow *from* a data store means that data are only read from the data store while the contents of the data store remain unaltered. We note that whenever a computerized file is read an entire record must be retrieved from the data store. But in depicting an information system, it is desirable to show only the information that is necessary for the process. Consequently, an appropriate name is given to the data flow from a data store. The actual contents of the data flow are documented in the accompanying data dictionary. The updating of a data store—the addition, deletion, or modification of a record—is shown by a data flow *to* the data store. We show only an input data flow *to* the data store despite the fact that the deletion or modification of a record on a computer file requires the reading of that record. Otherwise, the diagram would quickly become too cluttered. In Figure 9-3 we saw examples of data flows to and from data stores; for example, the data flow FILLED ORDER is an input flow to the data store labeled ORDERS.

Processes

A **process** is a task or set of tasks that must be performed on data by a person, a machine, or a computer. The task or set of tasks transforms the input data flows to the data, which are emitted from the process as output data flows. A process is represented by a special symbol, as we saw in Figure 9-1. Except for *context level diagrams*, each process is named in a shorthand manner by a strong verb and a noun. The name is descriptive and designates what the process actually does to the input data flows in order to produce the output data flows. Examples are COMPUTE NET PAY, ACCEPT PAYMENT, and BILL CUSTOMER. The exception to this convention, context level diagrams, have only one process labeled with the name of the information system, such as PAYROLL SYSTEM, ACCOUNTS RECEIVABLE SYSTEM, and so on. Context level DFDs are described in a later section.

Four types of transformations may occur within a process:

1. The input data flows may be used by the process to create a set of data flows that are outputs from the process. In Figure 9-4, the input of payroll information for an employee into the process COMPUTE PAYCHECK is shown. The two input data flows HOURS WORKED + EMPLOYEE ID and SALARY RECORD have been transformed to create the employee's paycheck, called PAYCHECK, a data flow that is completely different from either of the input data flows.

2. We may gain new knowledge of the input data while the same data serve as the output data flow. For example, we wish to verify a customer's account number as shown in Figure 9-5. The input data flows are ACCT

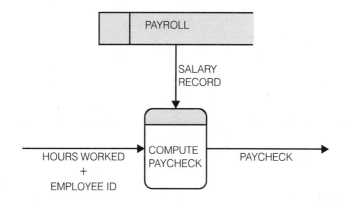

ID and ACCOUNT INFO, the process is VERIFY ACCT ID, and the output data flow is VERIFIED ACCT ID. The process has simply performed various checks on the input data flow ACCT ID, and it sends out the identical data as the output data flow now called VERIFIED ACCT ID. However, our knowledge of the data has changed, since we now know that the account number was verified and is ready for further processing. Consequently, the data flow is renamed VERIFIED ACCT ID to indicate our new knowledge about this data.

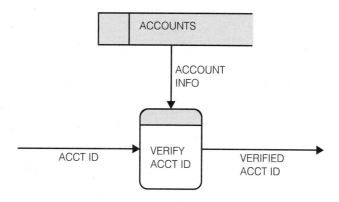

3. A process may reorganize the incoming data in some way. The input data may be rearranged in a different order (that is, sorted), reformatted in some way, or screened. By screening, we mean that only a portion of the input data is selected by the process and transmitted as output. As shown in Figure 9-6, the sorting of employee records by job type prior to creating the paychecks is accomplished by a process labeled SORT BY JOB TYPE. Because the process sorts a group of data records, its primary input comes from a data store. The output data flow, SORTED EMPLOYEES, contains all the data records for the data store EMPLOYEES but they are now rearranged in order by job type.

4. The process may not change the data at all but may simply send the data to other processes. The input data flow may be split into several output

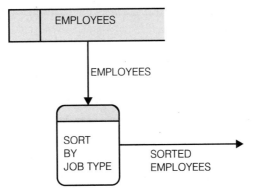

FIGURE 9-6

Data are reorganized or dispersed to other processes.

data flows; the incoming data flows may be combined into a single data flow; or the input data flow may be directed to the appropriate process. An example in Figure 9-7 shows the data flow STUDENT INFORMATION

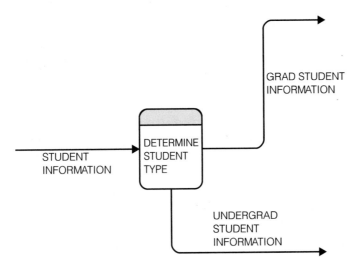

FIGURE 9-7

Data are examined and distributed to different processes.

being directed by the process DETERMINE STUDENT TYPE. The two output data flows are labeled UNDERGRAD STUDENT INFORMATION and GRAD STUDENT INFORMATION. Only one of these data flows is produced each time the process is executed. The data flow STUDENT INFORMATION must flow either to a process that handles undergraduate student data or to a separate process for graduate student data. The process DETERMINE STUDENT TYPE is required to direct the data flow STUDENT INFORMATION to the appropriate process.

A process should receive only the data needed for that process. Because a data flow diagram is not a diagram of sequential processing such as displayed by a program flowchart, a data flow can be drawn directly to the process that needs it. Only the data needed by a process should be sent to that process. The parallel execution of processes is a characteristic of data flow diagrams. If all processes on a data flow diagram execute in sequence, one after another, it is most likely that the diagram needs to be redrawn.

THE HIERARCHY OF DATA FLOW DIAGRAMS

The documentation of an information system by means of data flow diagrams requires the drawing of several data flow diagrams organized in a hierarchical framework. As we proceed through the hierarchy, further details of the processing performed by the system are revealed to us. The model of the information system begins with a *context level diagram*. The **context level DFD** contains only one process labeled with the name of the system and numbered 0 (see ORDER SYSTEM in Figure 9-2). In addition, external entities and the data flows to and from these entities are drawn on the context level DFD. Data stores are not shown on the context level diagram.

The single process of the context level diagram, representing the entire information system, is then described in more detail by the next level data flow diagram, called level 0. Each process on this data flow diagram is also portrayed with more detail by a data flow diagram at a deeper level, called level 1. The process is said to be *exploded* to its next level. This decomposition of processes into successive levels of DFDs (called level 2, 3, and so on) continues until the system has been described in sufficient detail. The entire collection of DFDs called a *leveled set* represents the model of the system. The processes on the bottom-most level of DFDs are called *primitive processes*; they are described by detailed process descriptions (see Chapter 11).

Number of Processes and Levels

How many processes should appear in a data flow diagram? Except for the context level diagram, the recommended number is from five to nine. If fewer than five processes are shown, we should question whether the diagram shows sufficient detail but if more than nine processes are depicted, probably too much detail has been given. When more than nine processes are present on a DFD, it is likely that some processes can be combined into a single process in order to better display the system's operations. The process is then exploded into greater detail on its next level. This rule is only a recommendation, however, and not an absolute standard.

The reader will observe that some examples in this text use fewer than the preferred minimum of five processes. The DFD modelling technique is not meant to decompose a system artificially into a certain number of processes. Rather, the art of drawing data flow diagrams requires us to recognize how individual tasks are executed within a system to accomplish a particular function. Any major function typically requires the execution of several steps. The leveled set of DFDs represents a model of the system, and its goal is to provide an overall view of the system. By focusing first on major functions and then decomposing each function successively in greater detail, we achieve a complete picture of the system in an easily comprehensible set of diagrams.

How many **levels of DFDs** are desirable? When documenting a complex system, another guideline is to create no more than seven levels of DFDs. For a simpler system, a rule of thumb is to model the information system with at least three levels of DFDs: context level, level 0, and level 1. The more complex the system, the more levels will be required to explain the system fully.

The Leveled Set of DFDs

To illustrate our discussion on the leveled set of DFDs, Figure 9-8 displays a payroll system as a set of DFDs for three levels. The context level diagram in Figure 9-8a shows a single process bubble labeled with PAYROLL SYSTEM and numbered 0. This single process bubble is *exploded* into a level 0 DFD which depicts the major processes performed by the system (see Figure 9-8b). As a general rule, the level 0 DFD contains the identical external entities and data flows shown on the context level diagram; exceptions to this rule will be discussed later on. Within the level 0 DFD, the process bubbles are numbered sequentially using the integers 1, 2, 3, and so on. Data stores are also drawn whenever needed by more than one process. In Figure 9-8b, the data stores have been numbered according to the convention of DS1, DS2, and so on. To prevent the crossing of data flow lines, the symbols for an external entity or data store may be duplicated within a data flow diagram. This should be done as sparingly as possible. Such duplication occurs for the data entity EMPLOYEE in Figure 9-8b. The boxes for EMPLOYEE are notched with a diagonal line to indicate this duplication.

Let us further explain the explosion of a context level DFD to a level 0 DFD by once again studying the DFDs for the payroll system (Figure 9-8). Notice that, according to the rule, the input data flow TIME SHEET and the output data flows, PAYCHECK, W-2 FORM, and PAYROLL REPORT occur on both Figures 9-8a and 9-8b. Furthermore, the same external entities appear on both DFDs. The explosion of process 2 (COMPUTE PAYCHECK) in the level 0 DFD is given by Figure 9-8c. Here the explosion of process 2 (COMPUTE PAYCHECK) has resulted in the data flow PAY RECORD entering process 2.1. The output of process 2 is PAYCHECK, which is also the output of process 2.3. There can be no other open-ended inputs or outputs on the diagram exploded from process 2. In other words, the explosion of process 2 yields the same inputs and outputs as the initial input data flows and final

FIGURE 9-8   **Three levels of DFDs for a payroll system**

a. **Context Level DFD**

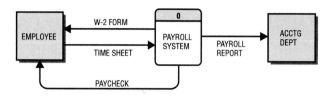

b. **Level 0 DFD**

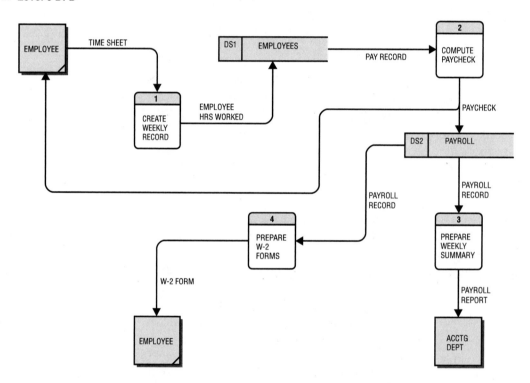

c. **Level 1 DFD**

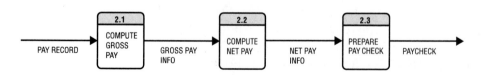

output data flows on the exploded level. (The exception to this rule is discussed in the section on *Level Balancing.*)

If the level 0 DFD contains an excessive number of data stores, we choose to hide these data stores by showing them only on a lower level of the diagram. Thus, in general, the rule for depicting a data store within a DFD is stated as:

A data store appears on the first level where it is connected by data flows to more than one process.

Since the objective of the data flow diagram is to present a drawing that communicates the details of the system to both the user and the systems analyst, overly complex drawings must be avoided. Instead the complexity of the system is documented by adding further levels to the set of DFDs.

Each process on a level 0 DFD is exploded to a separate DFD on level 1, called its *child.* The process in the upper level DFD is known as the *parent.* In Figure 9-8b, process 2 is the parent of the lower-level diagram given in Figure 9-8c. The external entities shown on both the context level and level 0 diagrams no longer appear on level 1 and subsequent levels of DFDs. As we see in Figure 9-8c, the data flows that flow to or from external entities on the level 0 DFD are now drawn open-ended. When a process is exploded, it creates a set of processes numbered with the parent's number appended with a single digit. The digits within a process number are separated by decimal points. Thus, the processes in Figure 9-8c are numbered as 2.1, 2.2, and 2.3.

The numbering convention for processes on the leveled set of DFDs is further illustrated by Figure 9-9. For example, the explosion of process 3 on level 0 results in four processes on the level 1 DFD numbered as 3.1, 3.2, 3.3, and 3.4. In Figure 9-10, we see that the explosion of process 3.1 yields five processes numbered 3.1.1, 3.1.2, 3.1.3, 3.1.4, and 3.1.5. This numbering scheme is continued for all subsequent levels. For example, the explosion of process 3.1.5 will have processes numbered 3.1.5.1, 3.1.5.2, 3.1.5.3, and so on.

Now observe how the diagrams in Figures 9-9 and 9-10 show the same data flows throughout the leveled set of DFDS for a system. In Figure 9-9, we saw that the data flows X, Y, and Z are present on the context level DFD. The next DFD (level 0) has the data flow X as its initial input and Y and Z as its final output flows. We also see that the explosion of process 3 shows the data flows B and C entering the level 1 DFD and the data flow D exiting from it; these flows are identical to those entering and leaving process 3 on level 0. Similarly, in Figure 9-10, the inputs B and C to process 3.1 on the level 1 DFD are likewise the only inputs to its level 2 DFD. In the same way, the final output data flow (labeled J) from process 3.1 is identical to the output data flow from process 3.1.5. The exception to this consistency of data flow names between levels is discussed later.

FIGURE 9-9   The explosion of the context level DFD to three levels

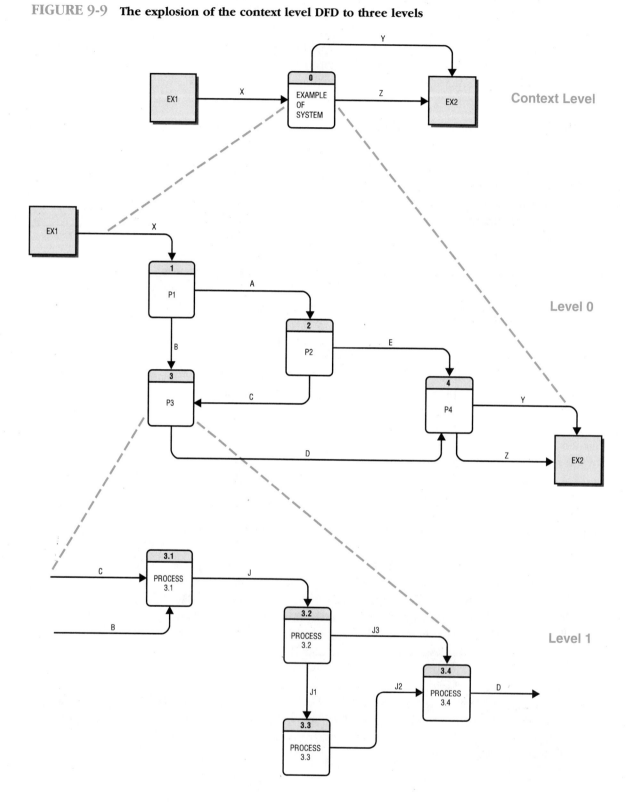

FIGURE 9-10   **The explosion of process 3.1 to its level 3 DFD**

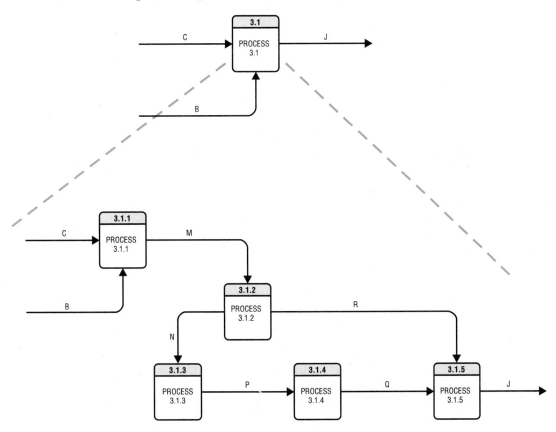

RULES OF THE GAME

There are several rules that must be followed for the drawing of data flow diagrams. If any rule is violated, the data flow diagram is considered to be incorrect. You should remember that mere adherence to the rules does not guarantee that you have accurately represented an information system in your data flow diagram. Some of these rules have already been presented in our earlier discussions but are repeated here for completeness. All of the rules are explained in this section. The **consistency** of a set of data flow diagrams is assured by strictly following the rules for drawing these diagrams.

Rules for Data Flows

Rule 1   A data store must always be connected to a process; similarly, an external entity must always be connected to a process. The violation of this rule is illustrated in Figure 9-11.

FIGURE 9-11

**Violation of Rule 1:
Data stores and exter-
nal entities must be
connected to a process.**

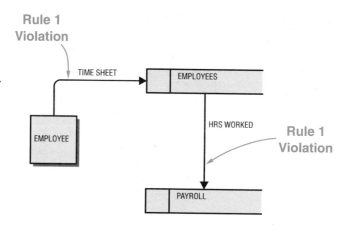

Rule 2   Data flows must be named. If a data flow is not named, we cannot know what data are used by a process. An output data flow from a process cannot have the same name as the input data flow. Because a process transforms the input data, the output data needs a different name. In Figure 9-5, the process VERIFY ACCT ID receives the input ACCT ID and emits the output VERIFIED ACCT ID. These two data flows have the same contents. However, the names of data flows to or from data stores may be the same.

Rule 3   A data flow must be named with a noun. A verb or verbal phrase is unacceptable. For example, the data flow name VERIFIED ORDER is a noun but the verbal phrase VERIFY ORDER is not an acceptable name for a data flow.

Rule 4   Data that travel together should be one data flow. For example, if both ORDER and PAYMENT are sent at the same time to a process, the data flow line can be named ORDER AND PAYMENT. This practice makes the diagram clearer to the user of the diagram.

Rule 5   Data should be sent only to the processes that need the data. If necessary, a data flow line can be split to create two or more data flows, each of which contains only the data needed by the process receiving that data. For example, the data flow CUSTOMER ORDER can be split into the data flows CUSTOMER ID and ORDER INFO. In Figure 9-12, the data flow CUSTOMER ID is sent to process 1.1 and ORDER INFO flows to process 1.2. Since the data flow ORDER INFO is not needed by process 1.1, which approves the customer's credit, it is sent directly to process 1.2.

For clarity, data flows may also be combined to create one data flow line. The example in Figure 9-13 combines the data flow DEPOSIT SLIP produced by a process with the data flow CHECK produced by another process, to create the single data flow DEPOSIT TRANSACTION.

Rule 6   If a data store within the data flow diagram never has an input data flow, it is questionable whether the information system is properly repre-

FIGURE 9-12
An example of Rule 5: Data should be sent only to the processes that need the data.

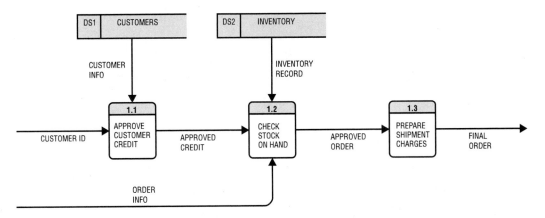

sented. Sometimes, such a data store was created elsewhere by another system, and the data flow diagram does faithfully describe the system now under study. For example, the data store CUSTOMERS in the ORDER information system shown in Figure 9-3 is only read by the system; there is no arrow flowing to CUSTOMERS because no new records are added to the data store by this system. We must ask whether there is a flaw in the system as diagrammed here and we must determine where data are initially placed into this data store. It is possible that the diagram is correct, but only further investigation of the information system will answer this question for us.

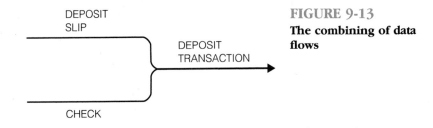

FIGURE 9-13
The combining of data flows

Rules for Processes

Rule 7   A process must have at least one input and one output data flow. If a process has only input data flows, we say that the process is a *black hole*. Data flows into the process but it disappears into the black hole and never reappears in its transformed state. The black hole is illustrated by Figure 9-14.

If a process creates only output data flows without receiving any input data flows, it is a *miracle process*, as shown in Figure 9-15. It is always necessary for a process to receive input data in order to create output data. However, a process may send its only output data flow to a data store; we say

FIGURE 9-14
The black hole

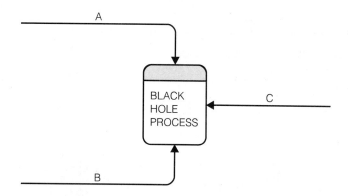

that the process dead-ends at the data store. This is perfectly acceptable. A data store may also serve as the only source of input data to a process; this, too, is acceptable.

FIGURE 9-15
The miracle process

Let us return to Figure 9-8b, where the level 0 DFD for the payroll system of a small business is shown. Process 1, labeled CREATE WEEKLY RECORD, has the input data flow TIME SHEET; the process has only one output data flow, EMPLOYEE HRS WORKED, which is sent to the data store EMPLOYEES. Notice that none of the processes is connected by data flows to other processes. Instead, process 2, COMPUTE PAYCHECK, begins with the input data flow PAY RECORD from the data store EMPLOYEES. We also observe that both processes 3 and 4 receive input data flows only from the data store PAYROLL. Although the four processes in this DFD are not directly connected to any other process, the rules for DFDs have been obeyed.

Rule 8   A process begins to perform its tasks as soon as it receives the necessary input data flows. The task performed is always the same task; thus the same data flows are possible outputs each time. Even if all the output data flows are not created each time as in our diagram in Figure 9-7, nonetheless the process has the possibility of creating these data flows each time it is executed.

Rule 9   A process on the lowest level of the data flow diagrams performs a single well-defined function. If we have exploded the DFD to three levels, this means that a process on level 1 must execute one and only one function. For example in Figure 9-16a, there is a process that verifies a bill and issues the payment for that bill. The correct representation of this process is shown in Figure 9-16b.

a.   **Violation of Rule 9: a process that performs two functions**

FIGURE 9-16

Rule 9: On lowest level of DFD a process performs only one function.

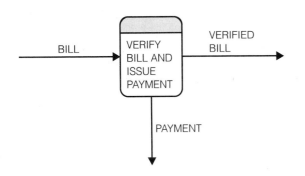

b.   **The correct representation of the process shown in part a**

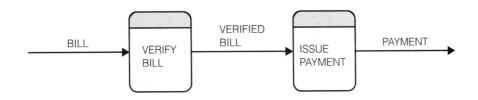

Rule 10   A process with a single input or single output may or may not be partitioned enough. As a rule of thumb, the presence of one input data flow and one output data flow usually indicates that the process describes only a single well-defined function.

Rule 11   Never label a process with an IF–THEN statement. The conditions that must be dealt with are documented in the process description, but not stated within the process name. An example is the situation where we must recognize what type of invoice is flowing into the system. Figure 9-17a is incorrectly labeled IF TYPE BUSINESS, GIVE DISCOUNT. Figure 9-17b correctly names the process DETERMINE DISCOUNT; the detailed explanation of what occurs within this process is given in the process description placed within the project dictionary.

Rule 12   Never show time dependency directly on a data flow diagram. Many processes are executed only at certain time intervals. An example is the production of paychecks on a weekly basis or the creation of W-2 forms by the payroll system at the end of the year as illustrated earlier in Figure 9-8b. The exact time a process takes place is not important on the data flow diagram. This information can be included in the overall specifications for the information system. Time dependent processes are typically initiated by a data flow from a file. As we saw in Figure 9-8b, the production of W-2 forms after the end of the year is diagrammed by showing a flow directly from the

FIGURE 9-17
Process Rule 11: Never use IF–THEN labels.

a. The incorrect use of IF within a process

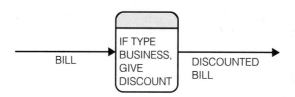

b. The correct representation of the process shown in part **a**

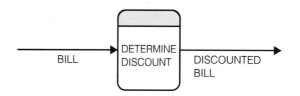

data store PAYROLL. The actual time intervals are independent of any process because a process is always ready to go once it receives the necessary input data flows. Thus, the same data flow diagram can be used to show that W-2 forms are produced every week, every month, or on a specific date such as annually on January 15.

Level Balancing

The twelve rules stated for data flows and processes address the mechanics of drawing data flow diagrams. These rules help to ensure that an information system depicted by a DFD will be easily understood by both the analysts and the users. *Level balancing* conventions also govern the explosion of a data flow diagram. **Level balancing** refers to the requirement that, as successive levels of data flow diagrams are created, the child diagram must maintain a *balance* in data content with its parent process.

There are two ways to achieve this balance. First, if exactly the same data flows of the parent process enter and leave its child diagram, then level balancing has been achieved. The payroll system we saw in Figure 9-8 offers an example of level balancing in this way; so do the levels of DFDs in Figure 9-9.

The second way to balance levels compares the net data content. If the same net data contents from the parent process serve as the initial inputs and final outputs for the child diagram, level balancing has been achieved. Similarly, if a data flow from the parent process splits into two data flows for its child diagram, these lower-level data flows taken together must contain exactly the same data as given by the parent's data flow. We say that their net data contents are equivalent.

Let us examine the parent DFD in Figure 9-18a, which shows process 1 with the input data flow VENDOR INVOICE. In Figure 9-18b, the child diagram, the data contents of VENDOR INVOICE have been distributed and sent to two different processes; two data flows called VENDOR ID and INVOICE are now displayed. In this instance, the data elements contained within the two lower-level data flows VENDOR ID and INVOICE must be equivalent to the data elements found in the upper-level data flow VENDOR INVOICE. Although duplicate data elements are permitted to exist, no additional data elements may be given; the net data contents must be the same. In the same way, an output data flow may be represented by two or more data flows in the subsequent explosion of a process. In all such instances, the data flow

a. **Process 1 with only one input data flow**

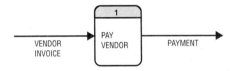

FIGURE 9-18

Balancing levels by net data contents

b. **Explosion of Process 1 showing two input data flows**

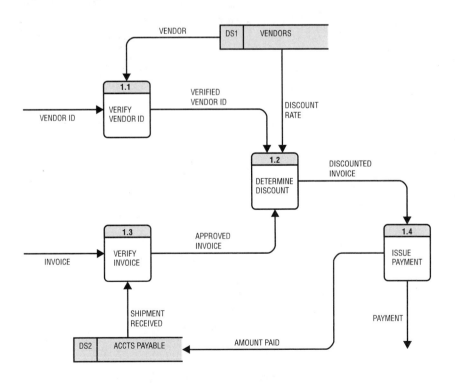

diagrams are said to balance because the combined data flows comprise the same data elements as the single data flow.

In Figure 9-18b, we also see that two data stores were hidden from view in the level 0 DFD. As we explained earlier, data stores may be concealed from upper layers of the system's DFDs for the sake of simplicity. Too many data stores make a DFD overly complex, and the DFD may lose its ability to communicate the system overview to the analyst and the user.

PHYSICAL VERSUS LOGICAL DFDS

Our objective in drawing the DFDs for an information system is to model the flow of data through the system. In drawing the DFDs, we often include physical objects or physical processes that are not really necessary for the understanding of the system's processing but help us to initially model the system's activities. When any physical object or physical process is present, the DFD is called a **physical DFD**. A DFD that has no physical components is called a **logical DFD**. A physical DFD tells us *how* the system functions, whereas a logical DFD illustrates *what* the system does. If we limit our view of a system to how things are done, we may fail to understand what is actually happening within the system. If we can model the necessary functions of the system, we will be better equipped to design a new system that not only performs the essential functions but also incorporates the new functions needed to solve the problems found within the existing system. Consequently, we strive to concentrate on what is being done rather than the actual physical details of how it is being accomplished. However, since the physical aspects of the system are immediately apparent, the analyst may prefer to model the system initially by including its physical components. Once drawn, the physical DFDs are easily modified to reflect a logical view of the system.

Physical Processes

A **physical process** is a process that is not necessary for the implementation of the information system. Instead of the physical process stated in a DFD, other possibilities may exist for the implementation of the information system. Four categories of physical processes exist:

1. The process uses a physical object.
2. The process performs the entry of data into a data store.
3. The process sends data to a destination but does not accomplish any other processing.
4. The process simply rearranges the data in another form.

1. THE PROCESS USES A PHYSICAL OBJECT

If the process names a physical object, such as a book circulated by a library, we must determine whether the object BOOK is treated as data or as merely a physical object. Because we are interested in the data flowing through the system, the data flow BOOK must represent data such as the title, author, edition, call number, and copy number linked together in order to identify each book. The actual object, the book itself, should not appear in a data flow diagram.

2. THE PROCESS PERFORMS DATA ENTRY

The preparation of data is also a purely physical process. In batch systems, it is usually necessary to transform the data to computerized form as the first step in the information system. For example, the keying of payroll data may be represented by a process named KEY-IN PAYROLL DATA as shown in Figure 9-19, where the process sends an output data flow PAYROLL DATA to

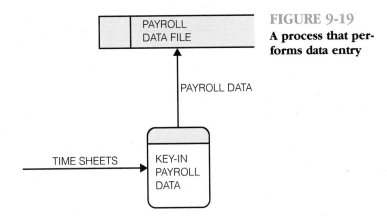

FIGURE 9-19

A process that performs data entry

a data store PAYROLL DATA FILE. Such a process is not directly relevant to us in the construction of the new system because the data could be entered in other ways; thus, the process KEY-IN PAYROLL DATA should not appear in the logical DFD of the PAYROLL SYSTEM.

3. THE PROCESS ONLY TRANSMITS DATA

Sending data is also a physical process and should not be shown as a separate process on the logical DFD. For example, after the paychecks are created, we may show a process SEND PAYCHECK as in Figure 9-20, with an output flow to the external entity EMPLOYEE. This process is physical because we have limited the system to sending the paychecks and mailing them directly to the employees. The data flow MAILED PAYCHECK is also a physical element. The information system has not been modeled to allow for

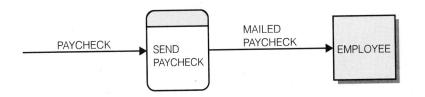

FIGURE 9-20

A physical process that only transmits data

other means of transmission, such as electronic funds transfer directly to the employees' banks. The mailing of a customer invoice is another physical process that should not be shown. Instead, we can draw the data flow INVOICE directly to the CUSTOMER and eliminate the process MAIL CUSTOMER INVOICE. Processes that only transmit data flows are physical and are eliminated in order to create the logical DFD.

4.   THE PROCESS REARRANGES DATA

The rearrangement of data is another type of process that does not transform the data or change our understanding of the data. The sorting of data such as the process SORT PAYCHECKS BY EMPLOYEE NAME in Figure 9-21 is

FIGURE 9-21

A physical process that acts only to rearrange the data

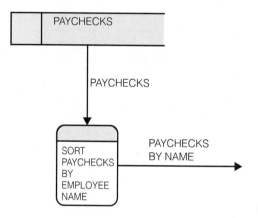

purely physical. Since a different implementation of the information system may not require this process, such a process is not shown on the logical DFD. Another example of a process that rearranges data is the process ORDER BY BUSINESS TYPE. Once again, in a different implementation of the system, such a physical process might be eliminated.

Physical Data Flows and Data Stores

Data flows and data stores may also be represented in a physical way. A data flow that names a physical object rather than data is a **physical data flow**. An example is a data flow called ITEM that is defined not by its data but only as a physical object. We may choose to define such a data flow logically by entering its data description in our data dictionary. Consequently, there is no objection to using the noun ITEM, but we must ensure that the data dictionary defines ITEM by its associated data elements and not as a physical object.

A **physical data store** often can be recognized by its name, which signifies a physical collection of data. For example, an In/Out box is clearly physical and the use of its name IN/OUT BOX for a data store does not describe what data records reside within it. Other examples of physical names for data stores are FILE DRAWER, HOLDING BIN, and COMPUTER FILE. We must remember that the names assigned to components within a DFD should communicate what is happening. A name such as COMPUTER FILE tells us nothing about what is contained in the computer file. For a logical DFD, we rename a physical data store such as IN/OUT BOX with an appropriate name indicating its contents, such as ORDERS, EMPLOYEES, or PARTS.

Example of a Physical DFD

An example of a simplified physical DFD on level 0 is shown in Figure 9-22. Several processes have been omitted from this DFD in order that we may concentrate on the physical aspects of the system. The customer's request for a merchandise item and the filling of that request have been shown as two processes for this level 0 DFD of a simplified sales system. But this view of the sales system fails to consider the data that flow through the system. The output data flow PURCHASED ITEM from process 1 (SERVICE REQUEST) is defined to be the actual physical merchandise item purchased by the customer. Instead, this data flow must be viewed as the data associated with the physical merchandise item; the data flow is really PURCHASED ITEM ID (or a similar label) rather than the physical item.

We also see that the input data flow to process 2 is labeled MONEY to represent the customer's payment, which may be provided as cash, check, or credit card. Because the term MONEY implies only cash, it restricts our understanding of the system. The process seems to accept only cash rather than other forms of payment. Even if the system presently handles only cash, still our attention should be on the cash as an amount paid by a customer instead of the actual dollars and coins given to the sales clerk. A more appropriate name for the data flow would be PAYMENT, which includes all

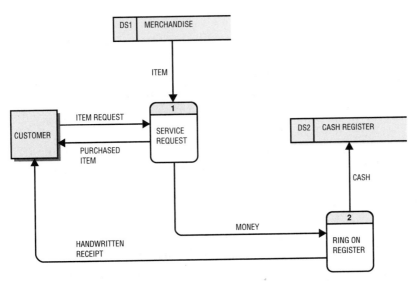

FIGURE 9-22

A physical DFD for a simplified sales system

forms of payment, even those we have not mentioned such as electronic funds transfer. Process 2 itself is also poorly named as RING ON REGISTER because the physical device CASH REGISTER is included and the whole process is a physical action. Modeling the system in this physical way limits us severely. We are unable to substitute other methods for processing the customer's payment. A suitable logical name for process 2 would be ACCEPT PAYMENT.

Depending on the data dictionary, the data store MERCHANDISE may be physical or logical. The data associated with the merchandise items must be documented in the data store MERCHANDISE; in a logical DFD, it cannot be considered as a collection of physical items existing on the shelves of the store. The data store CASH REGISTER has also been given a physical name and should be renamed with a logical name such as PAYMENTS. The data flow HANDWRITTEN RECEIPT contains a physical component so it should be renamed simply RECEIPT. Since the data flow RECEIPT should contain the ITEM ID for the item purchased, the output data flow PURCHASED ITEM is no longer needed.

The revised DFD is shown as a logical DFD in Figure 9-23. The data store MERCHANDISE has been renamed INVENTORY to indicate a detailed list of merchandise items, giving the code number and quantity on hand of each

FIGURE 9-23

A logical DFD for a simplified sales system

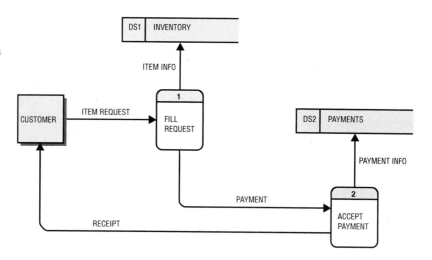

item. The data flow ITEM INFO is now correctly moving to the data store INVENTORY in order to indicate an updating operation.

MODELING THE PROPOSED SYSTEM

As we stated earlier, the use of DFDs enables us to build a model of an information system. Our ultimate goal is to build a model of a new system that resolves the problems now found in the existing system. How do we best reach our goal of the new system? The recommended plan of attack is to study the existing system and then model the new system. When using the data flow diagram technique, we follow these five steps:

1. Model the existing system—incorporating the physical features of the system—and produce a set of physical DFDs. If possible, eliminate this step and immediately draw the logical DFDs for the existing system. But if the system functions are not immediately visible, the system is complex, or the application type is unfamiliar, modeling the physical DFD is advisable in order to gain an accurate understanding of the system's operations.

2. As far as possible, remove the physical aspects from the physical DFDs and obtain a set of logical DFDs.

3. Modify the logical DFDs as necessary to depict the new system. If the existing system is performed manually—that is, a computer information system does not exist—switching to computers would make it possible to provide new information to the users. Because of the existence of computerized data, new information could be generated. The systems analyst should always be looking for ways to supply new information for decision making; this may be done by adding new reports or query capabilities to the system.

4. Examine the new system and determine how each portion will be physically implemented. For instance, decide which parts will be batch or on-line systems. To illustrate this step, Figure 9-24 shows the payroll

FIGURE 9-24   **The payroll system divided into functional units**

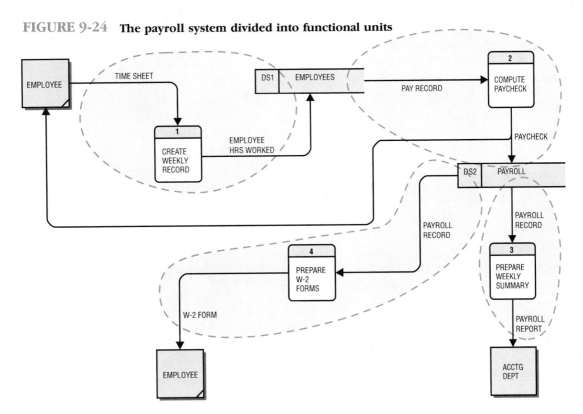

system previously given in Figure 9-8b, except that dashed lines now indicate boundaries dividing the system into functional units. Process 1 (CREATE WEEKLY RECORD) is one such unit and will be implemented as a single program. Process 2 (COMPUTE PAYCHECK) is another unit to be implemented as a batch program. Similarly Processes 3 and 4 each constitute separate programs. Thus we see that the payroll system must be implemented as four separate programs and not as a single complex program.

5. Produce a physical set of DFDs for the new system by modifying the logical DFDs. This step is often omitted, however, and a systems flow-chart is created in its place.

Breaking Down Physical Barriers

In this chapter, we have emphasized modeling the logical functions of a system rather than the physical way of doing business. It is important to remember that there may be other technologies available to solve a particular problem. Although the familiar paper documents may still be necessary, other methods of storing and retrieving such material are possible through imaging systems. Document imaging systems require good planning, however, to ensure proper integration with other systems.

The need for regulatory compliance spurred the introduction of an imaging system in the chemical industry. After the chemical disaster in Bhopal, India, the chemical industry, the Environmental Protection Agency, and the Occupational Safety and Health Administration (OSHA) changed their rules about safety and information relating to hazardous materials. OSHA wanted immediate access to crucial information stored in various formats such as paper, blueprints, regulatory guides, company memoranda, maintenance logs, and data in online data bases. Immediate access meant that electronic retrieval was now required for data not available in computerized form. Previously separate systems somehow had to be integrated into a single document management system.

Another example is the cost-effective solution found by Lockheed Advanced Development Co.—an integrated imaging, optical character recognition and full text-retrieval software package. Using a standard Touch-Tone phone, field personnel can dial into the imaging system and have a document faxed to the number they specify. This system allows fast remote access to images and documents with little training for end-users. Because costs have declined for imaging equipment, we can expect more firms to adopt this technology for their problems of information retrieval.

Source: Koulopoulos, Tom, "User Demands Force Old-Guard Changes," *Computerworld*, April 5, 1993, p. 91. Reprinted with permission from Tom Koulopoulos.

SUMMARY

Data flow diagrams are an important tool for the systems analyst. By modeling the existing information system by means of data flow diagrams, the systems analyst achieves a thorough understanding of the functions currently performed by the system users. The data flow diagrams also serve to communicate this understanding to the users.

Any data flow diagram is constructed by using only four basic elements: external entity, process, data flow, and data store. We stated twelve rules for drawing data flow diagrams. The consistency of a data flow diagram is determined by verifying that data stores and external entities are directly connected to processes. Level balancing means that the net data contents of the initial inputs and final outputs for a process are equivalent to those given on its child diagram.

DFDs are frequently drawn showing physical components; such a DFD is called a physical DFD. Our objective in modeling an information system is to produce a logical DFD, which illustrates the flow of data through the system. We may choose to draw a physical DFD first and then modify the DFD to contain only the logical data flows, data stores, and processes. The recommended approach to modeling the new information system is: (1) document the existing system with physical DFDs, (2) modify the DFDs to obtain a set of logical DFDs, (3) using the logical DFDs for the existing system, modify the DFDs as necessary and incorporate new features in order to obtain the DFDs for the new system, (4) determine how the new system will be implemented, and (5) document the physical aspects of the new system with either a physical DFD or a systems flowchart.

TERMS

consistency of DFDs	logical DFD
context level DFD	model
data flow	physical DFD
data flow diagram (DFD)	physical components of DFDs
data dictionary	physical data flow
data store	physical data store
external entity	physical process
level balancing	project dictionary
levels of DFDs	process

QUESTIONS

1. Why are data flow diagrams useful?
2. Name the four components of a data flow diagram.

3. **a.** What numbers would be assigned to the five processes in the child DFD for process 8.4?

   b. What numbers would be assigned to the four processes in the child DFD of process 5.8.6?

4. Mr. Burlington owns a small business that repairs household appliances. When Mr. Burlington accepts a service order, he records it in a looseleaf book. At the end of each month, he prepares a report showing the number of orders processed, the amount charged for each order, and the cost of the parts installed in the appliances. This report also shows summary information such as the total orders processed for the month.

   a. Name the external entities for this small business system.

   b. What data stores exist for this system?

   c. What processes are performed within this system? Give each process a brief descriptive label, as required for a data flow diagram.

5. There are six errors in the data flow diagram shown in Figure 9-25. Name them and explain what is wrong.

FIGURE 9-25   A data flow diagram containing six errors

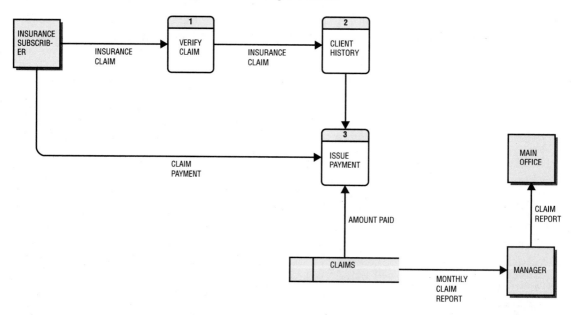

6. Figure 9-26 shows three partial data flow diagrams. Critique these partial DFDs; do not look for violations of the rules but analyze each DFD to determine whether it might be improved by altering or adding information to the diagram.

7. Explain the differences between physical and logical data flow diagrams.

8. Describe the recommended steps in modeling a new information system.

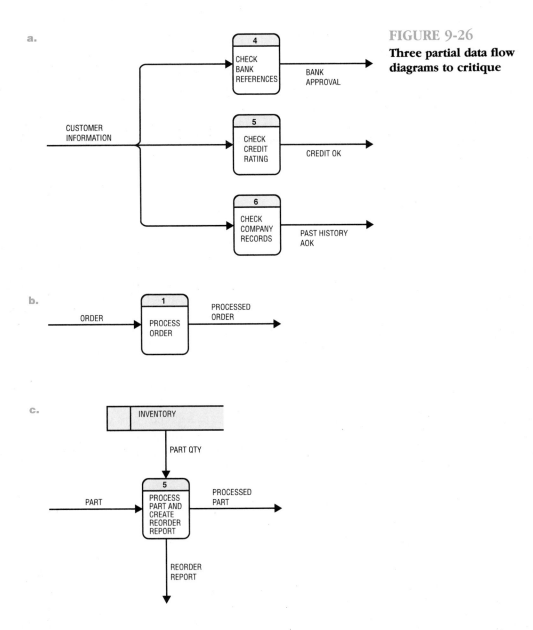

FIGURE 9-26

Three partial data flow diagrams to critique

9. Draw both the context level and level 0 data flow diagrams for the following information systems.

   a. When parts are received from VENDORS, they are accompanied by an INVOICE. Mrs. Gauron in the Receiving Department checks the INVOICE against the ORDER FILE to be certain that the correct parts were delivered. If the parts were not ordered or the order was incorrectly filled, the parts are returned. If the parts are correct, the INVENTORY FILE is updated to reflect the new quantity for these parts. This is done by increasing the data element QUANTITY ON HAND by QUANTITY RECEIVED for the PART ID. Mrs. Gauron then prepares the PAYMENT for the VENDOR. She also enters the payment transaction in the GENERAL LEDGER, which is maintained as a bound accounting ledger. A worker on the factory floor who needs a part requests it by submitting a REQUISITION to the Parts Clerk. The information on this form is used to update the INVENTORY FILE. Each week, the Parts Clerk uses the INVENTORY FILE to prepare a REPORT listing all parts whose QUANTITY ON HAND has fallen below the REORDER POINT. For parts listed on the REPORT, a PURCHASE REQUEST FORM is prepared and sent to the Purchasing Office. [*Hint:* Don't confuse the processes being performed with the people performing the processes.]

b. The student chapter of the Data Processing Management Association (DPMA) plans to sponsor a conference on management information systems in April. It is necessary to establish a computerized system to handle the registration process. Participants may register before the day of the conference, but the payment must be made at the time of registration. Each student will submit a REGISTRATION FORM with the PAYMENT to the club's conference coordinator. The information on the REGISTRATION FORM will be recorded in the CONFERENCE FILE. The PAYMENT will be recorded in the CHAPTER LEDGER. A RECEIPT will be prepared and issued to the student. The day before the conference, a LIST of all paid attendees will be prepared by the chapter's secretary and given to the Conference Coordinator. After the conference is over, an ADDITIONAL MAILING LIST of all nonmembers who attended the conference will be prepared using the CONFERENCE FILE and the MEMBERSHIP LIST. This ADDITIONAL MAILING LIST will be retained by the Club Secretary in the club's files. [*Hint:* As before, be sure to understand which persons function as external entities and which persons only perform processes.]

c. The customer of the Super-Deal Video Store obtains a MEMBERSHIP by completing an APPLICATION FORM. The APPLICATION FORM is reviewed for completeness by the store's clerk and then recorded in the MEMBERSHIP FILE. PAYMENT is then accepted from the customer; the amount of PAYMENT is recorded in the LEDGER. A MEMBERSHIP CARD is then issued to the customer. On the first of each month, a FINANCIAL STATEMENT is prepared from the data recorded on the LEDGER and sent to the Store Manager.

PROJECTS

1. Study your college's registration system. To simplify your project, consider only the standard registration process and omit any details about dropping and adding classes after registration has been completed.
   a. Name the inputs and outputs of the registration system.
   b. Draw the data flow diagrams for the context level and level 0.

2. Study the procedures of the automated teller machines (ATMs) for the deposit and withdrawal of money by performing these transactions yourself. If you do not have an ATM card, ask another student to show you how to perform these procedures. Then draw the context level and level 0 data flow diagrams for the ATM system. Assume that all data are transmitted to and received from only one file called the ATM MASTER FILE.

REFERENCES

Davis, William S. *Systems Analysis and Design: A Structured Approach.* Reading, MA: Addison-Wesley, 1983.

DeMarco, Tom. *Structured Analysis and System Specification.* Englewood Cliffs, NJ: Prentice-Hall, 1979.

Gane, Chris, and Trish Sarson. *Structured Systems Analysis: Tools and Techniques.* Englewood Cliffs, NJ: Prentice-Hall, 1979.

Keller, Robert. *The Practice of Structured Analysis: Exploding Myths.* New York: Yourdon Press, 1983.

Martin, James. *Diagramming Techniques for Analysts and Programmers.* Englewood Cliffs, NJ: Prentice-Hall, 1985.

Yourdon, Edward. *Modern Structured Analysis.* Englewood Cliffs, NJ: Yourdon Press, 1989.

CHAPTER 10

The Data Dictionary

Objectives

A data flow diagram provides a model of an information system but it is an incomplete description without the documentation of the data flows, data stores, and processes depicted within the set of data flow diagrams. In this chapter, we introduce the topic of the data dictionary, which contains the detailed descriptions of the data flows and data stores shown within a data flow diagram. Process descriptions are discussed in Chapter 11. After completing this chapter, you will know the following material:

- The reasons for the creation of the data dictionary
- How to describe the data flows and data stores of data flow diagrams in a data dictionary
- How to define data fields that contain coded information
- The way in which the data representations are stored in the data dictionary of the CASE tool Excelerator

INTRODUCTION

After an information system has been modeled by a set of data flow diagrams (DFDs), an overview of the entire system has been created. Although this overview is useful, it will not directly assist us in the creation of the programs needed to perform these system activities using the computer. The DFDs do not contain any detailed description of the data occurring in the data flows or data stores. Also missing from the data flow diagrams is the explicit description of how each process transforms its input data flows to create the resulting output data flows. In fact, the data flow diagrams taken alone represent only a superficial view of the information system. To amplify this description, we create a **project dictionary** to contain the DFDs and the related documentation for the system. The inner workings of each process must be described by process descriptions stored in the project dictionary; the methods used to describe processes will be discussed in Chapter 11. The data flows and data stores are described by entries in a **data dictionary**, which is also incorporated within the project dictionary.

In this chapter, the data definitions are first described by means of an informal notational system that can be used for a manually prepared data dictionary. Later, the data descriptions are presented in the notation required by a software package, Excelerator. Excelerator is a computer-assisted software engineering (CASE) tool that provides the capabilities of drawing DFDs as well as documenting the data flows, data stores, and processes depicted within the DFDs. Excelerator stores these data definitions and process descriptions in a project dictionary, which is associated with the information system under development. Other information regarding the project, including the system's data flow diagrams, is also placed within this project dictionary. Since each information system is considered to be a separate project, each system has its own project dictionary.

This chapter is divided into the following sections. First, the reasons for a data dictionary are discussed. Second, the components of the data dictionary are defined. Third, methods for preparing the data dictionary are explained. Finally, two real-world examples are presented to illustrate how actual data are transformed into entries for the data dictionary.

THE REASONS FOR A DATA DICTIONARY

As we have already explained, the data dictionary is necessary to document the data flows and data stores shown in a DFD. In addition, the processes in a DFD are documented by descriptions that depict the actions performed on the input data flow(s) in order to create the output data flow(s). The data named in the process descriptions must have corresponding entries in the data dictionary associated with the project. This requirement ensures that each process will be defined precisely enough to be translated into the appropriate instructions for a computer program, regardless of the programming language chosen for implementation. Consequently, the data dictionary is the means to communicate crucial information not only among the software developers but also between the software developers and the users.

There are four additional reasons for describing the data for the information system in a detailed fashion. First, the data dictionary furnishes a primary avenue for communication between the software developers who are working to construct the computer information system. During the systems development process, many programs and subprograms may be required. Since the data dictionary provides explicit documentation of the system's data, misunderstandings about the data can be avoided—or resolved early in the SDLC, thus preventing costly software modifications later. Consider the data element called TOTAL ENROLLMENT for a university. It must be explicitly defined by its entry in the data dictionary, since the total student enrollment has several possible meanings: undergraduates only, full-time students in all the colleges except the colleges of law and medicine, all students including part-time students for all colleges including law and medicine, all students in all colleges except those enrolled in off-campus programs, and so on. The data definition field in the data dictionary entry should provide us with a clearly stated definition of what TOTAL ENROLLMENT really means.

A second reason for a detailed description of the data is to avoid duplicate data names. By using the data dictionary, the systems analyst can quickly check if a name is already in use and then assign a unique name. Third, a CASE tool such as Excelerator includes the capability to relate each process to the data dictionary descriptions of its input and output data flows. Identifying the data used by a process allows subsequent changes to the design of the information system to be incorporated more easily. Errors introduced into the system design due to alterations in the data items and processes are minimized by this provision. Fourth, even without a CASE tool, the data dictionary serves as the first step towards an automated data dictionary. Moreover, the implementation of data base technology requires unambiguous naming and definition of all data elements. Thus, the data dictionary prepared for a project facilitates the creation of the data dictionary needed for a data base management system.

THE COMPONENTS OF THE DATA DICTIONARY

Each data flow and data store within the set of DFDs for a project is represented by a **data dictionary entry**. Each entry itself is a type of data record. We sometimes say that the data dictionary is "data about data" because it uses data to describe data. Data dictionary entries are divided into four types: *data records, data elements, data stores,* and *code tables.* The first two types, data records and data elements, begin our discussion of how to formulate the data dictionary.

Definitions

A **data record** is composed of either data elements, subrecords, or a combination of data elements and *subrecords*. Every subrecord and data element is also defined by an entry in the data dictionary. The reader should note that the term *data record* has a special meaning in this chapter: It indicates a data dictionary entry that describes a data structure rather than indicating a physical record in a computer file.

A **data element** is the smallest unit of data that has meaning as a separate piece of data. The term data element has basically the same meaning as the more commonly used term **field**. Examples of data elements are an employee's social security number, an employee's last name, the grade received by a student in a class, and the color of an item sold in a retail store.

A **subrecord** has the same definition as a data record; that is, it consists of data elements, data subrecords, or some combination of data elements and subrecords. When a subrecord contains other subrecords, we say that these subrecords are *nested* within the first subrecord. Each nested subrecord is defined until the final group of nested subrecords has been described as containing only data elements. The definition of a subrecord causes related data elements to be grouped together as a unit, either for convenience or in order to properly define the format of the data record.

Example of a Data Record

Before proceeding with the detailed specifications for entries in the data dictionary, we will use the data flow STUDENT INFORMATION to illustrate the format of the data records, subrecords, and elements. The data flow STUDENT INFORMATION is represented by a data record within the data dictionary, as shown in Figure 10-1. The data record has been assigned the

FIGURE 10-1

An example of a data record within a data dictionary

DATA RECORD NAME: STUDENT INFORMATION
ALTERNATE NAME: None
COMPOSED OF:

NAME	TYPE	NUMBER OF OCCURRENCES
STUDENT ID	E	1
STUDENT NAME	R	1
STUDENT SEX	E	1
STUDENT CAMPUS ADDRESS	R	1
STUDENT CAMPUS PHONE	E	1
STUDENT HOME ADDRESS	R	1
STUDENT HOME PHONE	E	1
STUDENT MAJOR	E	2

same name as the data flow STUDENT INFORMATION. The field ALTERNATE NAME is shown as "None" for this data record. An **alternate name**, also called an **alias**, is another name for exactly the same data. Any alternate names are documented in the data dictionary description to prevent confusion between data records that contain exactly the same data. The data record STUDENT INFORMATION consists of three subrecords (STUDENT NAME, STUDENT CAMPUS ADDRESS, and STUDENT HOME ADDRESS) and five data elements (STUDENT ID, STUDENT SEX, STUDENT CAMPUS PHONE, STUDENT HOME PHONE, and STUDENT MAJOR). The column TYPE indicates whether the data name represents a data subrecord or data element. The letter E is used to indicate a data element, while the letter R indicates a data subrecord. Of course, R really stands for a data record because a data subrecord is defined in exactly the same way as a data record. The column NUMBER OF OCCURRENCES shows how many times each data element or subrecord occurs within this data record. All of the data subrecords and data elements occur only once, except for STUDENT MAJOR.

Each subrecord and element within STUDENT INFORMATION must also be fully defined by a data dictionary entry. The data dictionary entry for a subrecord is given in the same format as the original data record. As shown in Figure 10-2, the data subrecord STUDENT NAME is composed of three data elements: STUDENT LAST NAME, STUDENT FIRST NAME, and STUDENT INITIAL. To illustrate the data dictionary entry for a data element, we show the data dictionary entry for the data element STUDENT LAST NAME in Figure 10-3. The ALTERNATE NAMES field for STUDENT LAST NAME is shown to contain only one alternate name, STUDENT LN. This means that other areas at the university or perhaps a computer program or data file refers to STUDENT LAST NAME as STUDENT LN.

The TYPE of data stored in STUDENT LAST NAME is listed as "Character" with a LENGTH of 30 characters. The various data types that may be used for data elements are discussed in a later section. The PICTURE fields present a shorthand notation to illustrate how the data element appears. Both the INPUT PICTURE and OUTPUT PICTURE fields for STUDENT LAST NAME have been defined as X(30); X denotes an alphanumeric character and (30)

FIGURE 10-2

Definition of the data subrecord STUDENT NAME

DATA RECORD NAME: STUDENT NAME

ALTERNATE NAME: None

COMPOSED OF:

NAME	TYPE	NUMBER OF OCCURRENCES
STUDENT LAST NAME	E	1
STUDENT FIRST NAME	E	1
STUDENT INITIAL	E	1

FIGURE 10-3

Definition of the data element STUDENT LAST NAME

DATA ELEMENT NAME: STUDENT LAST NAME

ALTERNATE NAMES: STUDENT LN

DEFINITION: The last name of a student entered on the registration form

DATA TYPE: Character   LENGTH: 30 characters

INPUT PICTURE: X(30)

OUTPUT PICTURE: X(30)

EDIT RULES: None

means that there are 30 alphanumeric characters in this data element. For numeric data elements, the PICTURE fields indicate the number of digits on each side of the decimal point, the appearance of a comma in the number, and so on. In this book, the symbols used for the PICTURE fields are the same as those used by Excelerator; they are specified later in the subsections on INPUT PICTURE and OUTPUT PICTURE within the detailed information on the data dictionary. The field for EDIT RULES documents the checks that a computer program should perform in order to prevent the entry of erroneous data into a computer file. Because any alphanumeric characters will be accepted, no edit rules have been shown for STUDENT LAST NAME. Now that the general format of the data dictionary entries for data records and elements has been illustrated by this example, we will begin our explanation of how data elements and subrecords are organized within a data record.

DATA RECORDS

As we stated earlier, a data record is composed of data elements, data subrecords, or a combination of data elements and subrecords. The **data structure** of the data record is determined by the arrangement of its data elements and subrecords and by the number of times these elements and subrecords appear within the record. A data element within the data record may occur only once, or it may be repeated a specified number of times. A data subrecord may also occur either singly or more than once within the structure of a data record. In addition, certain data elements or subrecords are *optional*; that is, they may not take on values for every occurrence of a data record. For example, we could choose to include the name of the student's spouse as the data element SPOUSE within the data record STUDENT INFORMATION in Figure 10-1. Since not all students are married, the data element SPOUSE will not always contain a value; thus, the element SPOUSE is considered to be optional. It is also desirable to document the possible values that may be stored within each data element. A data element may be defined to contain a value that must be selected from a set of predetermined values called *codes*. These three characteristics of components within data records — repetition, optional occurrence, and selection of predetermined values — are discussed in the following sections.

Repetition

Frequently, a data element or subrecord must occur more than once in order to properly represent the data structure as stored within the data dictionary. In Chapter 12, we will discuss the design of the data structures for the computer files. Here, we are concerned only with documenting the data structure as it appears on a business form, on a screen, or in some other means of representation. In the data record for STUDENT INFORMATION in Figure 10-1, the data element STUDENT MAJOR represents the information regarding the student's major and its number of occurrences is marked as 2. The reason for this repetition is that we are assuming that any student may have two major areas of study recognized by the university. Consequently, the data element STUDENT MAJOR may occur twice within the data record STUDENT INFORMATION. Some students may not yet have declared a major area of study or may have only one major area. But it is more important to document the maximum number of times that the data element STUDENT MAJOR may occur within the data record rather than indicate whether it may occur zero, one, or two times. We must know the maximum number of occurrences when we design the physical data files (see Chapter 13).

Data subrecords may also occur more than once. Whenever a group of data elements occurs more than once, it is important to determine whether the data elements should be grouped together as a subrecord. Let us consider the following information required whenever a student registers for a course: STUDENT ID, STUDENT NAME, COURSE NUMBER, and SECTION NUMBER. We place this information into a data record called STUDENT REGISTRATION as shown in Figure 10-4. Because a student may register for more than one course (and usually does so), COURSE NUMBER and SECTION NUMBER are repeated for a maximum of 12 times. Since a student

DATA RECORD NAME: STUDENT REGISTRATION

ALTERNATE NAME: None

COMPOSED OF:

NAME	TYPE	NUMBER OF OCCURRENCES
STUDENT ID	E	1
STUDENT NAME	R	1
COURSE-SECTION INFO	R	12

FIGURE 10-4

The data record STUDENT REGISTRATION

FIGURE 10-5

The definition of the data subrecord COURSE-SECTION INFO

DATA RECORD NAME: COURSE-SECTION INFO

ALTERNATE NAME: None

COMPOSED OF:

NAME	TYPE	NUMBER OF OCCURRENCES
COURSE NUMBER	E	1
SECTION NUMBER	E	1

FIGURE 10-6

The data record STUDENT REGISTRATION fully described

DATA RECORD NAME: STUDENT REGISTRATION

ALTERNATE NAME: None

COMPOSED OF:

NAME	TYPE	NUMBER OF OCCURRENCES
STUDENT ID	E	1
STUDENT NAME	R	1
COURSE-SECTION INFO	R	12
COURSE NUMBER	E	1
SECTION NUMBER	E	1

registers for a section of a particular course, the data elements COURSE NUMBER and SECTION NUMBER must be grouped together as a single unit in order to convey this information. Thus, in Figure 10-4, COURSE NUMBER and SECTION NUMBER are represented by the subrecord COURSE-SECTION INFO which is shown as occurring a maximum of 12 times.

The subrecord COURSE-SECTION INFO is then documented by the data dictionary entry shown in Figure 10-5. The data elements COURSE NUMBER and SECTION NUMBER occur only once within the group of data elements forming the subrecord COURSE-SECTION INFO. In general, we will find that data elements do not repeat within a subrecord; however, there are always exceptions to this rule. After documenting the subrecord COURSE-SECTION INFO, an automated data dictionary typically will provide us with a listing of the data record STUDENT REGISTRATION, which also shows the individual data elements contained within the subrecord; this complete listing is shown in Figure 10-6.

Optional Occurrence

A data element or subrecord may also be an *optional* member of a data record (or subrecord), that is, a value for the data may not always be present for every occurrence of the data record. An example of optional data is a

DATA RECORD NAME: COURSE-SECTION INFO

ALTERNATE NAME: None

COMPOSED OF:

NAME	TYPE	NUMBER OF OCCURRENCES
COURSE NUMBER	E	1
ALTERNATE COURSE NUMBER	E	1
SECTION NUMBER	E	1

FIGURE 10-7

The revised definition of the data subrecord COURSE-SECTION INFO

course that is listed by more than one department within the college. Such a course has an alternate course number, but most courses will not have such alternate course numbers. For example, the course 016:005, Civilizations of Asia, taught by the Department of History is cross listed as course number 039:055 for the Department of Asian Languages and Literature. As shown in Figure 10-7, the alternate course number may be defined as the data element ALTERNATE COURSE NUMBER, which occurs as a data element within the revised subrecord COURSE-SECTION INFO. Because we are adhering to the conventions of Excelerator, no provision has been made in the data dictionary entry for the distinction between optional and required data. As stated earlier, for the physical file design, we need to document the maximum number of occurrences for the data.

Selection of Predetermined Values

In this section, we discuss the definition of data elements whose values are drawn only from a *predetermined* set of values. This type of constraint does not affect the structure of the data record in which the data element appears. Most data elements do not have such constraints. For example, in the data record STUDENT INFORMATION, the data element STUDENT LAST NAME (Figure 10-3) was defined with no editing rules. Any possible combination of alphabetic, numeric, or symbolic characters could be accepted as a value to be stored as the student's last name. We say that the **domain** of values for this data element is the set of all alphanumeric characters. Data elements that contain only numeric values will be defined with domains that are more restrictive. For example, the data element AGE could be defined to have the domain "positive numbers from 1 to 150."

But some data elements have domains restricted to a set of predetermined values. An example of a data element with predetermined values is the zip code assigned by the U.S. Postal Service. Certain five-digit numbers have been defined to geographical regions in the United States. This means that some other five-digit numbers do not represent valid zip codes. When the set of values is large, such as that for zip codes, a *code table* is created to store the values (called *codes*) and the meaning of each value. Thus, the data element ZIP CODE will be defined with the following statement entered under EDIT RULES:

Values are from "ZIP CODE TABLE"

The complete code table ZIP CODE TABLE within the data dictionary must be described as an entry called a code table within the data dictionary. The use of double quotes is optional for a manually prepared data dictionary. Figure 10-8 shows the beginning portion of a code table for the five-digit zip code. This table is arranged alphabetically by state and then by the postal regions within each state. By sorting the ZIP CODE TABLE on the coded values, we can obtain another code table ordered by the zip code values.

Another example of a data element with a predetermined set of values is SEX. We know that the data element SEX may contain only one of two possible values representing either male or female. The designer of the data files decides on how this representation will be stored. Here, we will choose the characters M for male and F for female. Because there are only two values, a code table is not necessary. The characters M and F are easily related to the actual meaning of the values. In Figure 10-9, we have shown

FIGURE 10-8

The beginning portion of the ZIP CODE TABLE

TABLE OF CODES: ZIP CODE TABLE

ALTERNATE NAME: None

DEFINITION: Five-digit zip codes ordered by state, then by postal region

CODE	MEANING
36310	AL ABBEVILLE
35440	AL ABERNANT
35004	AL ACMAR
35005	AL ADAMSVILLE
35540	AL ADDISON
35006	AL ADGER
35441	AL AKRON
35904	AL ALABAMA CITY, STA.GADSDEN
35007	AL ALABASTER (1ST)
36720	AL ALBERTA
35950	AL ALBERTVILLE (1ST)
35008	AL ALDEN
35010	AL ALEXANDER CITY (1ST)
36250	AL ALEXANDRIA

FIGURE 10-9

The definition of the data element SEX

```
DATA ELEMENT NAME:  SEX
ALTERNATE NAMES:  None
DEFINITION:  The sex of a student entered on the registration form

DATA TYPE:  Character        LENGTH:  One character

INPUT PICTURE:  A
OUTPUT PICTURE:  A

EDIT RULES:  Values are M or F
```

the data dictionary entry for the data element SEX. The description given under the edit rules is sufficient to indicate the possible values of SEX. When the assigned codes are less apparent, a code table should be defined for the data element.

DATA ELEMENTS

In this section, we will formally define the fields contained within the data dictionary entry for a data element, as previously illustrated by Figures 10-3 and 10-9. The following fields will be explained: data element name, alternate names, definition, data type, length, input picture, output picture, and edit rules.

Data Element Name

Each data element must be assigned a unique name that symbolizes the data element. A maximum of 30 characters is advisable. Hyphens or underlines may be used to join words within the names. Since an ample number of characters is permitted, we can avoid shorthand names that obscure what the data element denotes. Care must be taken when naming data elements that appear to be similar. For example, if the information system must process both the names of employees and the names of customers, there must be two uniquely identified data elements: EMPLOYEE NAME and CUSTOMER NAME. If both are called NAME, we cannot tell what NAME represents. Similarly, if there are two dates, such as DATE ORDERED and DATE SHIPPED, assign two different names rather than give them both the designation DATE. Although DATE ORDERED and DATE SHIPPED both describe calendar dates, they must be given unique names to distinguish them from each other.

Alternate Names

A data element may be known by more than one name—its alternate name or alias. For example, the data element SOCIAL SECURITY NUMBER may be called EMPLOYEE ID by another division of a firm. The field ALTERNATE NAMES lists such alternate names in order to fully identify the data element. Any confusion due to different names for the same data element is thereby avoided.

DEFINITION Field

The DEFINITION field contains a brief explanation of what the data element represents. The description should be precisely stated so that those using the data dictionary will understand exactly what the data element denotes within the information system. Since the process descriptions will explain the actions performed on the data elements, only a short statement is given here, not a lengthy explanation.

DATA TYPE Field

The **data type** of a data element indicates how the data will be stored within a computer file. The codes for the DATA TYPE field—C, B, P, F, and D—are defined in Figure 10-10. The best representation of a data element is determined by its usage and its range of values. The data type C (for character data) may be used for any type of data, including numeric data. Each character—alphabetic, numeric, or symbolic—is represented by an 8-bit code that occupies one storage position (or byte). The choice of C for numeric data is appropriate only if the data is never used in computation. The data type P (for packed decimal) offers a more compact way than the character

FIGURE 10-10

The codes for the DATA TYPE field

These data types are a subset of those offered by the CASE tool Excelerator.

Data Type	Explanation
C	Character (used for alphanumeric data, that is, data that contain letters, numerics, or symbols)
B	Binary (used for numeric data that contain only integers)
P	Packed decimal (used for numeric data)
F	Floating point (used for data that are numeric and contain a fractional portion, such as the number 345.6789)
D	Date (used for data that represent a calendar date, such as BIRTHDATE)

data type for storing numeric data within the computer. Each digit in packed decimal representation requires only 4 bits; thus, two digits are placed in each storage position (or byte) except for the rightmost byte. A 4-bit code for a digit as well as a 4-bit code indicating either a plus or minus sign is stored in the rightmost byte. The packed decimal data type is useful for those computers which offer machine instructions to perform computations on this type of data.

Two other data types available for numeric data are the data types B and F. Both types—B and F—are used for numeric data to which computations are applied. The data type B (for binary data) is used only to represent integers. The data type F (for floating point) is used to represent either integers or numbers with fractional portions. Floating point representation is also suitable for representing numbers with a decimal exponent such as 1.2435×10^8. Finally, the data type D indicates the representation of a calendar date required for fields such as INVOICE DATE.

LENGTH Field

The LENGTH field contains the total number of bytes to be occupied by the data element within computer storage. The value of this field should correspond to the information given by the element's INPUT PICTURE, described next.

INPUT PICTURE Field

The input data format of the data element is described by its **INPUT PICTURE**, which uses notations similar to those employed by COBOL. The INPUT PICTURE field consists of one or more *input characters* selected from the set of input characters defined in Figure 10-11. The repetition of an input character can be shown by placing the number of repetitions in parentheses. For example, the data element STUDENT LAST NAME (displayed earlier in Figure 10-3) was defined by the INPUT PICTURE X(30) to indicate 30 alphanumeric characters. The choice of X allows for the storage of symbols, such as the apostrophe or hyphen, within a person's last name. To define the INPUT PICTURE for the data element STUDENT INITIAL, we would simply write a single A for one alphabetic character. Another example, the INPUT PICTURE for the data element EMPLOYEE SALARY with data type P, can be stated as

999,999.99

Here, the INPUT PICTURE is clearer by writing all the characters for its expression.

The PICTURE field for a date (D data type) often appears as YYMMDD or YYYYMMDD; this order of year, month, day permits the records to be sorted in the proper sequence.

FIGURE 10-11

The characters for the INPUT PICTURE field

Character	Explanation
X	Alphanumeric character
9	Numeric character
A	Alphabetic character
B	Blank position
S	Positive or negative sign
Y	Year
M	Month
D	Day
,	Comma
.	Period
( )	Used to indicate a repeating character

Y (Year), M (Month), D (Day) only when combined to represent a date, i.e., YYMMDD

OUTPUT PICTURE Field

The **OUTPUT PICTURE** field defines the format of the data element as it will appear on output screens or printed reports. The characters possible in the OUTPUT PICTURE field are the same allowed for the INPUT PICTURE field, plus the four additional characters of $, +, −, and Z (see Figure 10-12). The symbols $, +, and − are self-explanatory. The symbol Z specifies a nonzero blank that can be used as a filler. Except for the use of these additional characters, the definitions for the INPUT PICTURE and OUTPUT PICTURE fields should be the same. In our example of EMPLOYEE SALARY, we defined the INPUT PICTURE to be

999,999.99

For the OUTPUT PICTURE, we will describe the value of EMPLOYEE SALARY as

$ZZZ,ZZ9.99

FIGURE 10-12

The four additional characters available for the OUTPUT PICTURE field

$	for a dollar sign
+	for a plus sign
−	for a minus sign
Z	for a nonzero blank that is used as filler

The character $ indicates the dollar sign preceding the number; the use of the character Z causes any leading zeros to be suppressed and displayed as blanks.

Edit Rules

The editing requirements for a data element are listed in the field called EDIT RULES. By **edit rules**, we mean the checks that should be performed on a value before it is accepted for placement in the data record. The EDIT RULES field specifies the edit checks to be included in the computer programs implemented for the information system. As a general rule, if input screens are designed with the aid of a CASE tool, these edit rules are automatically invoked for any input data entered on the screen. The topic of input data screens will be discussed further in Chapter 15.

To illustrate the purpose of edit rules, let us consider the data dictionary entry for the data element STUD-HOME ZIP CODE, shown in Figure 10-13. The description of the data element STUD-HOME ZIP CODE in the data dictionary provides a guide to the programmer for the creation of the necessary edit checks on the data values that will be entered into the data records. INPUT PICTURE informs the programmer that STUD-HOME ZIP CODE must contain five digits. But it is also necessary that the value for STUD-HOME ZIP CODE be one of the values specified by the U.S. Post Office. The list of valid zip codes and their corresponding geographic locations has been entered in the code table called ZIP CODE TABLE, as shown earlier in Figure 10-8. Consequently, the edit rules for the data element STUD-HOME ZIP CODE may be concisely stated as

Values are from "ZIP CODE TABLE"

where all valid zip codes have been stored in this table. The double quotes are optional for a manually prepared data dictionary.

FIGURE 10-13

The data dictionary entry for the data element STUD-HOME ZIP CODE

```
DATA ELEMENT NAME:   STUD-HOME ZIP CODE

ALTERNATE NAMES:   None

DEFINITION:   Zip code for student's home address


DATA TYPE:   Character        LENGTH:   5 characters


INPUT PICTURE:   99999
OUTPUT PICTURE:   99999


EDIT RULES:   Values are from "ZIP CODE TABLE"
```

DATA STORES

As we stated earlier, a data store may be described in the data dictionary by simply expressing it as a data record in the data dictionary. It should be noted that the design of the computer files is not specified by the data dictionary entries for the data stores. At this time, the data structures are merely documented as they now exist, and the final design of the computer files is deferred until the Design phase; the logical and physical design of the data files will be covered in Chapters 12 and 13.

In addition to the detailed description provided by its corresponding data record, the estimated size and anticipated growth rate of the data store—the data file—should be documented. Figure 10-14 illustrates the

FIGURE 10-14

The data dictionary entry for the data store STUDENTS

DATA STORE NAME: STUDENTS

ALTERNATE NAME: None

COMPOSED OF:

NAME	TYPE	NUMBER OF OCCURRENCES
STUDENT ID	E	1
STUDENT NAME	R	1
SEX	E	1
STUDENT CAMPUS ADDRESS	R	1
STUDENT CAMPUS PHONE	E	1
STUDENT HOME ADDRESS	R	1
STUDENT HOME PHONE	E	1
STUDENT MAJOR	E	2
CURRENTLY ENROLLED	E	1
DATE FIRST ENROLLED	E	1

LOCATION: DISK F

MANUAL OR COMPUTER: Computer

TOTAL NUMBER OF RECORDS: 110,000

AVERAGE NUMBER OF RECORDS: 1,800 per year

INDEX ELEMENTS: STUDENT ID

STUDENT LAST NAME

FURTHER DESCRIPTION:

Estimated size in 1995—75,000 records

Conversion of paper records to begin in July 1994.

data dictionary entry for the data store STUDENTS. The data dictionary entry is given in the same format as that of a data record except for the following additional fields: LOCATION, MANUAL OR COMPUTER, TOTAL NUMBER OF RECORDS, AVERAGE NUMBER OF RECORDS, INDEX ELEMENTS, and FURTHER DESCRIPTION.

The LOCATION field for the data store STUDENTS has been specified as DISK F. Because the data store is a computer file, the field MANUAL OR COMPUTER contains "computer." The total number of records has been estimated as 110,000. The average number of records per year has been designated as 1,800. The listing of the data elements STUDENT ID and STUDENT LAST NAME as index elements means that the computer file will be established with two indexes to speed the retrieval of records by either of these two data elements. In the field FURTHER DESCRIPTION, the analyst has written supplementary information regarding the file. No formatting rules apply for this field. The analyst has stated that the data store STUDENTS will contain 75,000 records in 1995 and the conversion of the paper records will begin in July 1994.

CODE TABLES

As previously discussed, if a data element may contain a value only from a predetermined list of values, it is necessary to define a **code table** that documents these values (*codes*) and the meaning of each code value. A code table for zip codes was shown in Figure 10-8. Another illustration of a code table is provided by Figure 10-15. The codes 01, 02, 03, 04, and 05 are values that indicate the color of a catalog item. The meaning of each code value is shown in the adjoining column. The EDIT RULES given for the data element CATALOG COLOR can now be expressed succinctly as

Values are from "CATALOG COLOR"

FIGURE 10-15
The code table for the data element CATALOG COLOR

TABLE OF CODES: CATALOG COLOR

ALTERNATE NAME: None

DEFINITION: Code table for catalog item colors

CODE	MEANING
01	red
02	blue
03	brown
04	purple
05	black

The convention of quotes surrounding the code table name is recommended but not essential for a manually prepared data dictionary.

> **Warning**
>
> Be aware that different formats for describing the data dictionary entries for your project may be required from those shown in this chapter. The formats required for a manually prepared data dictionary can be specified using other headings that are arranged in a different order. Slightly different formats for the data dictionary entries may also be specified by CASE tools other than Excelerator. Despite any superficial differences, the basic principles for describing the data dictionary entries remain the same as those presented in this chapter.

PREPARING THE DATA DICTIONARY

If you prepare the data dictionary by manual methods, you are advised to follow the format shown earlier for data elements, data records, data stores, and code tables (see Figures 10-1, 10-3, 10-14, and 10-15). To shorten the laborious work required for a manual data dictionary, you can describe the contents of a data subrecord immediately below its name within a data record (see the subrecord COURSE-SECTION INFO in Figure 10-6) and then omit the documentation of any subrecords by individual dictionary entries. If using a word processor, you can prepare a formatted page for each type of dictionary entry and copy the formatted page before recording the values of the fields. Another approach is to photocopy the blank forms and simply write the information directly on these forms. The recorded information should correspond to the guidelines given for each field.

In order to use a manually prepared data dictionary efficiently, the entries should be alphabetized within the individual categories of data record, data element, data store, and code table; a CASE tool will automatically order the entries appropriately. Although the preparation of a data dictionary is somewhat tedious, the successful development of the information system requires a faithful rendering of all the data to be processed. Because manual preparation is time-consuming and error-prone, it is recommended that you employ a CASE tool such as Excelerator. The conventions used in this chapter closely correspond to those followed by Excelerator; however, Excelerator specifies additional conventions for some fields as well as including other fields in the data dictionary descriptions. Following these rules precisely allows the project dictionary to be checked by Excelerator for the consistency of the DFDs, data dictionary, and process descriptions. In addition, the data dictionary entries enable the analyst to create mock-ups of input and output designs. Although it is easy to use Excelerator to create the data dictionary entries, the instructions are too long to cover here; we offer the detailed discussion of the Excelerator data dictionary operations in a separate workbook.

THE DESCRIPTION OF REAL-WORLD DATA

Now that we have explained how data records and elements are described in a data dictionary, we want to show how real-world data are translated into such descriptions. Two examples will be presented: the Reader Service Card from the journal *Computer* and the textbook order form for the Campus Bookstore. Although these examples will be demonstrated by the use of Excelerator, the screens easily translate into the format required for a manually prepared data dictionary. The same fields explained for data record and data element entries are shown on the Excelerator screens.

Reader Service Card

As shown in Figure 10-16, the Reader Service Card polls the reader of the journal *Computer* regarding the most interesting articles in the issue and permits the reader to request further information on products and advertisements in the issue. Our problem is to identify the data elements and subrecords on this card and to prepare its description for the data dictionary. The completed data dictionary entry for Excelerator is shown in Figure 10-17.

By examining the card, eight data fields—either elements or records—are easily identified: NAME, TITLE, COMPANY, ADDRESS, CITY, STATE/ZIP, COUNTRY, and PHONE. Because the card does not provide for subdividing NAME into last name, first name, and middle initial, NAME will be defined as a data element rather than a subrecord. For the same reason, the fields ADDRESS and STATE/ZIP will be classified as data elements. The remaining five fields are easily identifiable as data elements.

Now consider the middle portion of the card labeled READER INTEREST. This portion also contains the instruction "Circle what you liked." Because the reader can circle as many items as desired, this field contains 17 possible responses. Since all 17 responses may be circled, this field corresponds to a data element that repeats 17 times. This field is represented in the data record for READER SERVICE CARD by the data element READER INTEREST, which occurs 17 times. We also observe that this data element is a coded value drawn from a code table containing the letters A through Q. Because it is necessary to document what each letter represents, a code table is required.

Next, we examine the right-hand portion of the Reader Service Card, the area labeled PRODUCT INFORMATION. We see that the journal allows the

FIGURE 10-16   The Reader Service Card from the journal *Computer*

COMPUTER

FREE INFORMATION!

READER SERVICE CARD
February 1993 Issue
(Card void after August 1993) Print address below.

Name _____

Title _____

Company _____

Address _____

City _____

State/Zip _____

Country _____ Phone _____

READER INTEREST
(Circle what you liked)

A Optical Networks
B Checkpoint and Rollback
C Cataloging Framework
D Object-Oriented Systems
E Wormhole Routing Techniques
F Editor-in-Chief's Message
G Hot Topics
H Standards
I CS News
J Update
K New Products
L IC/Micro Announcements
M Product Reviews
N Conferences
O Calendar/Call for Papers
P Media Reviews
Q Open Channel

PRODUCT INFORMATION
(Circle the numbers for products and advertisements on which you want more information)

1	2	3	4	5	6	7	8	9	10
11	12	13	14	15	16	17	18	19	20
21	22	23	24	25	26	27	28	29	30
31	32	33	34	35	36	37	38	39	40
41	42	43	44	45	46	47	48	49	50
51	52	53	54	55	56	57	58	59	60
61	62	63	64	65	66	67	68	69	70
71	72	73	74	75	76	77	78	79	80
81	82	83	84	85	86	87	88	89	90
91	92	93	94	95	96	97	98	99	100
101	102	103	104	105	106	107	108	109	110
111	112	113	114	115	116	117	118	119	120
121	122	123	124	125	126	127	128	129	130
131	132	133	134	135	136	137	138	139	140
141	142	143	144	145	146	147	148	149	150
151	152	153	154	155	156	157	158	159	160
161	162	163	164	165	166	167	168	169	170
171	172	173	174	175	176	177	178	179	180

(Side tab: READER SERVICE CARD)

Reprinted with permission from Computer Magazine.

reader to circle up to 180 numbers designating the products and advertisements contained within this issue. We will call this field PRODUCT INFORMATION and classify it as a data element occurring 180 times.

There are also two data elements on the Reader Service Card that do not request data values from the sender of the card. Notice that the meanings of the letters A–Q for READER INTEREST and the numbers 1–180 for PRODUCT INFORMATION are dependent on the issue of the journal. The date of the issue is February 1993, as shown on the fifth line at the left-hand side of the card. The information "Card void after August 1993" follows on the next line. These two fields contain values that will change depending on the issue of the magazine. Thus, we create two data elements called DATE OF ISSUE and CARD VOID DATE for the data record READER SERVICE CARD.

But is the data element CARD VOID DATE really necessary? If the journal has a stated rule that all Reader Service Cards expire after 6 months, the element CARD VOID DATE may not be necessary. Instead, the expiration of the Reader Service Card can be explicitly stated in the process description that treats the rejection of expired cards. The managerial staff of the journal should be consulted regarding this matter.

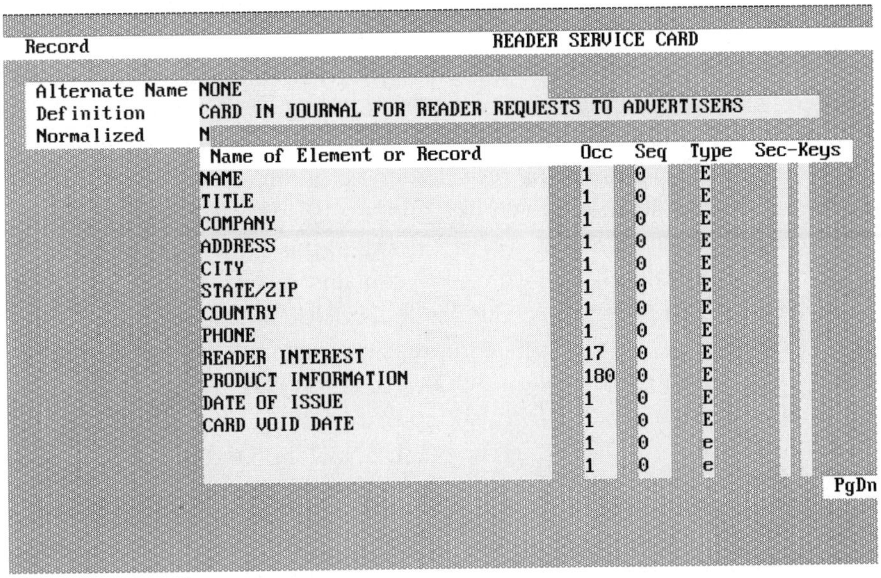

FIGURE 10-17
The Excelerator data
record READER
SERVICE CARD

Screen shots produced using INTERSOLV's Excelerator solution for Requirements Analysis and
System Design.

Although we have not done so here, each data element in the data record READER SERVICE CARD must be defined by its own entry in the data
dictionary. To illustrate the requirements for the data dictionary, the data element READER INTEREST is shown as an Excelerator data dictionary entry in
Figure 10-18. The field names correspond to those discussed for a manually
prepared data dictionary. The edit rules specify that the value for READER
INTEREST must be one of the values listed in the code table INTEREST
CODES.

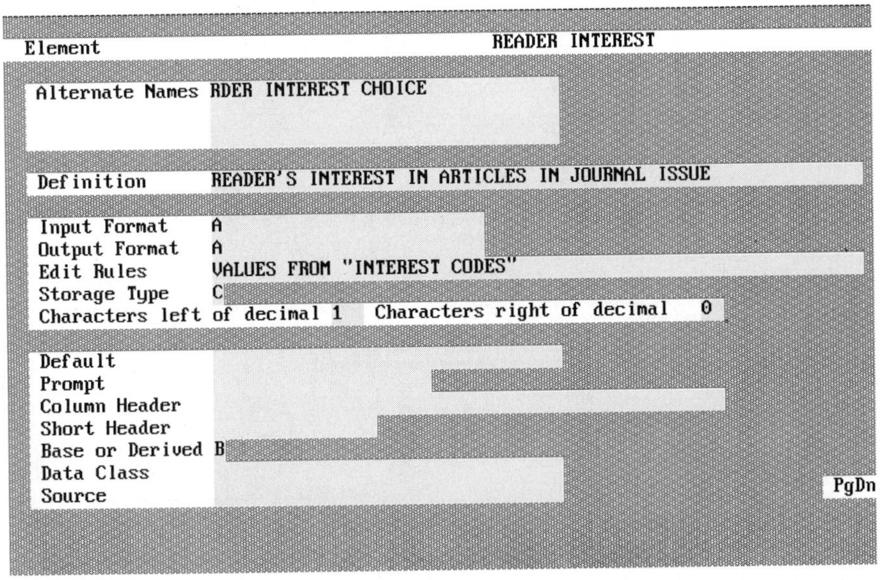

FIGURE 10-18
The Excelerator screen
for the data element
READER INTEREST

Screen shots produced using INTERSOLV's Excelerator solution for Requirements Analysis and
System Design.

The Campus Bookstore Order Form

In this example, we will create the data dictionary record for an order form that contains a repeating subrecord. The Campus Bookstore provides an order form to be used for ordering textbooks for classes held at the college. Provision is made for ordering required books and recommended books. A copy of the order form is shown in Figure 10-19. The data dictionary entry named BOOK ORDER FORM corresponding to this form appears in Figure 10-20. The top portion of the order form contains the following fields: DEPT, COURSE#, SECTION#, SEMESTER, YEAR, INSTRUCTOR, OFFICE ADDRESS, and PHONE#. Each of these fields represents a separate data element to be placed in the data record called BOOK ORDER FORM.

The next portion of the form shows five columns labeled EST. NO. OF BOOKS NEEDED, AUTHOR, TITLE, OPTIONAL ISBN# Edition year, and PUBLISHER. By examining the column labeled OPTIONAL ISBN# Edition

FIGURE 10-19 The order form for the Campus Bookstore

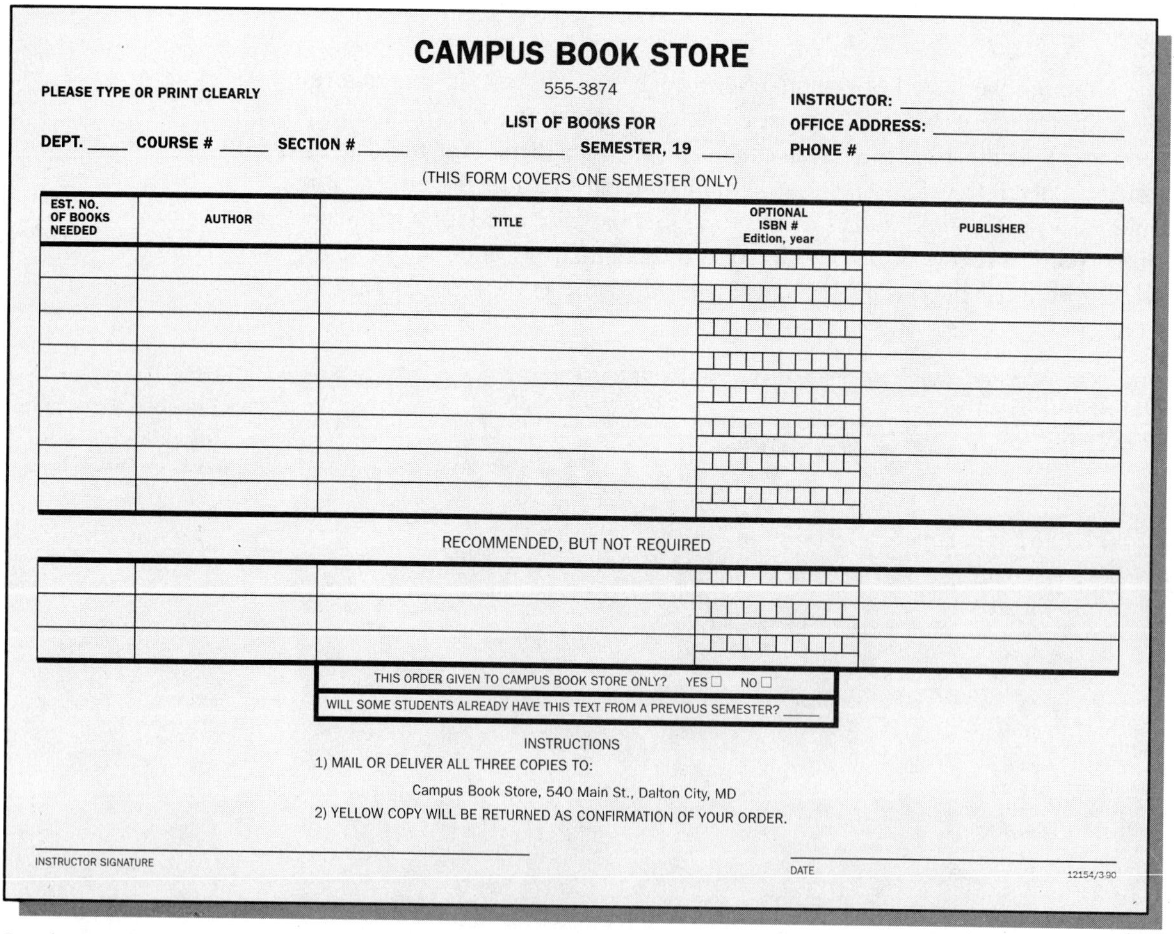

CAMPUS BOOK STORE

555-3874

PLEASE TYPE OR PRINT CLEARLY

LIST OF BOOKS FOR

INSTRUCTOR: ______

OFFICE ADDRESS: ______

DEPT. ____ COURSE # ____ SECTION # ____ ______ SEMESTER, 19 ___

PHONE # ______

(THIS FORM COVERS ONE SEMESTER ONLY)

EST. NO. OF BOOKS NEEDED	AUTHOR	TITLE	OPTIONAL ISBN # Edition, year	PUBLISHER

RECOMMENDED, BUT NOT REQUIRED

THIS ORDER GIVEN TO CAMPUS BOOK STORE ONLY? YES ☐ NO ☐

WILL SOME STUDENTS ALREADY HAVE THIS TEXT FROM A PREVIOUS SEMESTER? ____

INSTRUCTIONS

1) MAIL OR DELIVER ALL THREE COPIES TO:

Campus Book Store, 540 Main St., Dalton City, MD

2) YELLOW COPY WILL BE RETURNED AS CONFIRMATION OF YOUR ORDER.

INSTRUCTOR SIGNATURE

DATE

12154/3.90

Based on the form in use at the University Bookstore, University of Iowa.

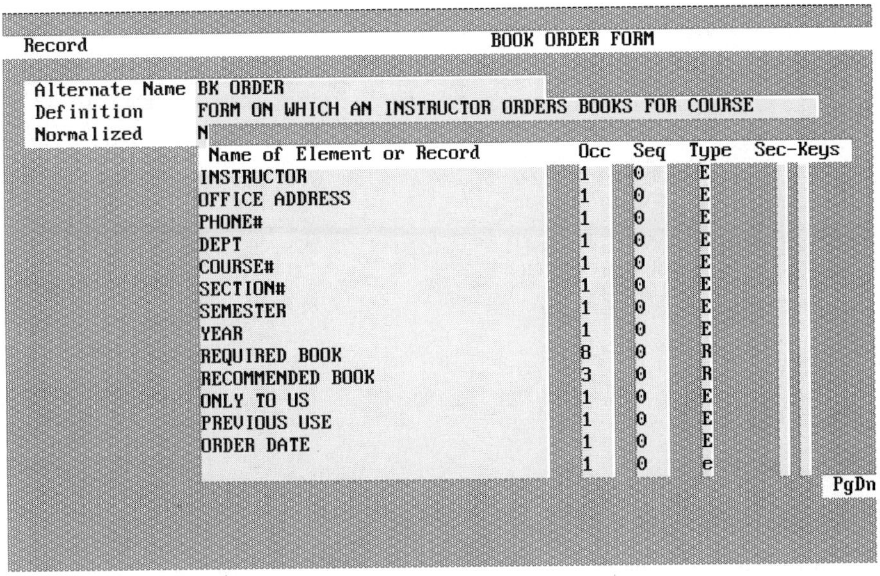

FIGURE 10-20

The Excelerator screen for the data record BOOK ORDER FORM

Screen shots produced using INTERSOLV's Excelerator solution for Requirements Analysis and System Design.

year, we observe that this column really represents three separate fields, which we will call ISBN#, EDITION, and YEAR. ISBN# means the International Standard Book Number, a number uniquely assigned to each edition of a book and usually printed on the copyright page. The top eight lines on the order form are available to list the required books for a course, while the last three lines are labeled RECOMMENDED, BUT NOT REQUIRED. Each line contains a group of data elements that specify a required or recommended book for the course. We place the group of data elements for a required book into the subrecord REQUIRED BOOK, which is shown to occur eight times in the record BOOK ORDER FORM by the 8 placed in the column Occ. The individual data elements are not repeated eight times within the subrecord REQUIRED BOOK (see Figure 10-21); rather, each data element occurs only once within the subrecord. Each data element in the subrecord REQUIRED BOOK is named with the leading characters BOOK RQ to show its association with the data record BOOK ORDER FORM. Similarly, for the last three lines on the order form, which represent the recommended books for the course, each line contains the same group of data elements as the subrecord REQUIRED BOOK. Because this group of data elements represents a recommended book, we will call the subrecord RECOMMENDED BOOK. The occurrence of the subrecord RECOMMENDED BOOK is indicated by the number 3 in the Occ column of Figure 10-20. The data elements for the subrecord RECOMMENDED BOOK are identical to those for the subrecord REQUIRED BOOK except that each element name is preceded by the characters BOOK RC, for example, BOOK RC EST NO OF BOOKS (see Figure 10-22). This naming convention ensures unique names

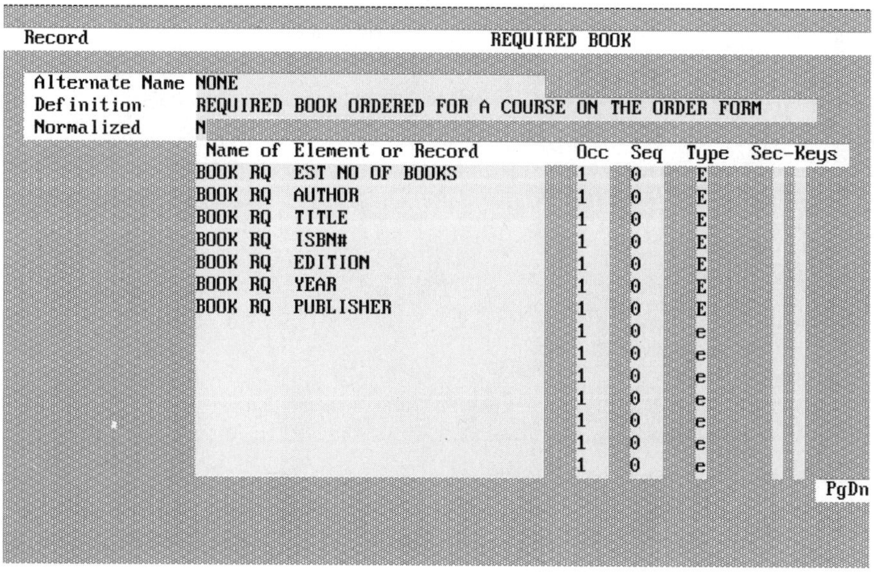

FIGURE 10-21

The Excelerator screen for the subrecord REQUIRED BOOK

Record		REQUIRED BOOK

Alternate Name	NONE
Definition	REQUIRED BOOK ORDERED FOR A COURSE ON THE ORDER FORM
Normalized	N

Name of Element or Record	Occ	Seq	Type	Sec-Keys
BOOK RQ EST NO OF BOOKS	1	0	E	
BOOK RQ AUTHOR	1	0	E	
BOOK RQ TITLE	1	0	E	
BOOK RQ ISBN#	1	0	E	
BOOK RQ EDITION	1	0	E	
BOOK RQ YEAR	1	0	E	
BOOK RQ PUBLISHER	1	0	E	
	1	0	e	
	1	0	e	
	1	0	e	
	1	0	e	
	1	0	e	
	1	0	e	
	1	0	e	

PgDn

Screen shots produced using INTERSOLV's Excelerator solution for Requirements Analysis and System Design.

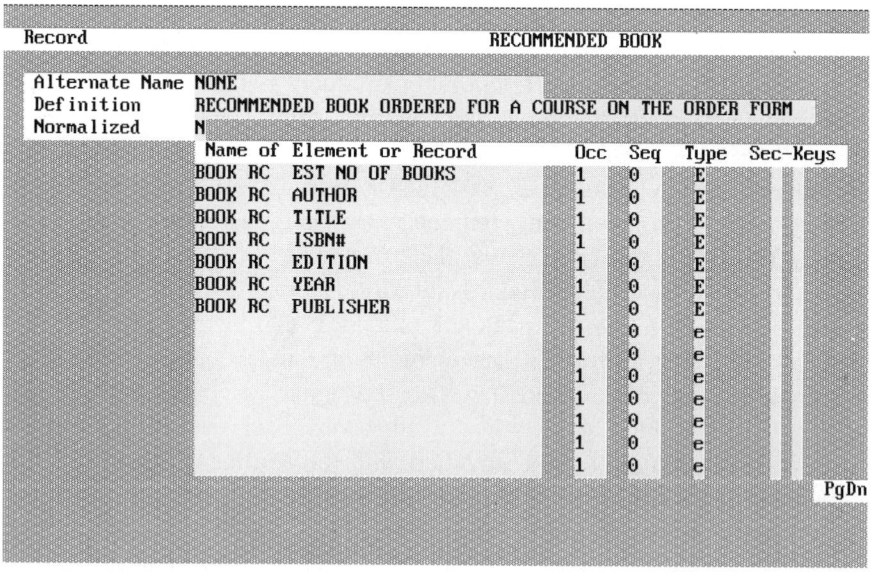

FIGURE 10-22

The EXCELERATOR screen for the sub-record RECOMMENDED BOOK

Record		RECOMMENDED BOOK

Alternate Name	NONE
Definition	RECOMMENDED BOOK ORDERED FOR A COURSE ON THE ORDER FORM
Normalized	N

Name of Element or Record	Occ	Seq	Type	Sec-Keys
BOOK RC EST NO OF BOOKS	1	0	E	
BOOK RC AUTHOR	1	0	E	
BOOK RC TITLE	1	0	E	
BOOK RC ISBN#	1	0	E	
BOOK RC EDITION	1	0	E	
BOOK RC YEAR	1	0	E	
BOOK RC PUBLISHER	1	0	E	
	1	0	e	
	1	0	e	
	1	0	e	
	1	0	e	
	1	0	e	
	1	0	e	
	1	0	e	

PgDn

Screen shots produced using INTERSOLV's Excelerator solution for Requirements Analysis and System Design.

and also indicates the elements' association with the data record BOOK ORDER FORM.

The final fields that appear on this order form are in the lower third of the form. The two boxed questions represent data fields. The first question asks "THIS ORDER GIVEN TO CAMPUS BOOK STORE ONLY" and may be answered only by "YES" or "NO." This field is designated in Figure 10-20 as the data element ONLY TO US. The second question is "WILL SOME STUDENTS ALREADY HAVE THIS TEXT FROM A PREVIOUS SEMESTER?" which also elicits only a "YES" or "NO" (even though the form does not specify these responses). This field is represented by the data element PREVIOUS USE.

The last line on the form contains the "INSTRUCTOR SIGNATURE" and the "DATE." We will rename the field DATE as ORDER DATE and enter it as a data element in Figure 10-20. Because the computer information system will not store a facsimile of the original form, how should we handle the data element INSTRUCTOR SIGNATURE? Either we may store the data element INSTRUCTOR SIGNATURE as an indicator that the form was signed or unsigned, or we may rely on the person who visually checks the form to ensure that the instructor signed the form. Doing the latter means we simply ignore this field and do not store it within the data record. After consultation with the bookstore manager, we learn that a textbook order is not accepted without the instructor's signature or the signature of the clerk who handled the order by phone. Therefore, we pick the second option and will not show the field at all.

An alternative way of dealing with the subrecords RECOMMENDED BOOK and REQUIRED BOOK is to create a single subrecord to represent the two types of books ordered by the instructor. This alternative subrecord called ORDERED BOOK is shown in Figure 10-23. The seven data elements to represent the five columns—EST NO OF BOOKS, AUTHOR, TITLE, OPTIONAL ISBN# Edition year, and PUBLISHER—are placed into the new

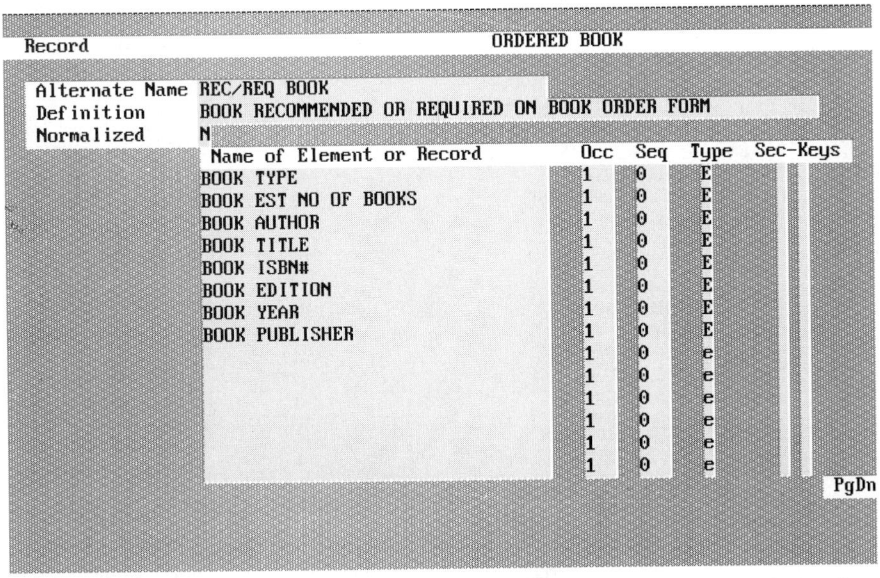

FIGURE 10-23

The subrecord ORDERED BOOK This single subrecord replaces the two subrecords REQUIRED BOOK and RECOMMENDED BOOK in the data record BOOK ORDER FORM.

Screen shots produced using INTERSOLV's Excelerator solution for Requirements Analysis and System Design.

subrecord ORDERED BOOK; the added data element BOOK TYPE indicates whether the book is recommended or required. The element BOOK TYPE is a coded field designated to contain only one of two possible values: RC for a recommended book or RQ for a required book. By using the subrecord ORDERED BOOK, we simplify the data record BOOK ORDER FORM, as shown in Figure 10-24. The final choice between having a single subrecord ORDERED BOOK or two subrecords, RECOMMENDED BOOK and RE-QUIRED BOOK, is a fundamental decision in the design of the computer data file. Because the bookstore must order all books, whether required or recommended, and must answer inquiries regarding all books for courses regardless of type, the choice of a single subrecord is preferable. The designation BOOK TYPE associated with each book allows the bookstore to distinguish between required and recommended books but avoids creating two distinct computer files, one file for recommended books and another file for required books. The design of data files depends on the view of the data fields to be stored in the data record. The systems analyst must be alert to the various ways in which to represent data and then decide on the most suitable representation.

Thus far, we have ignored the problem of the *primary key*. A **primary key** is the element or group of elements that serves to uniquely identify each data record. For the BOOK ORDER FORM record, no single data element may serve as the primary key. However, the two data elements COURSE# and SECTION# together form a suitable primary key. Consequently, the indicator in Figure 10-24 for the TYPE of these two data elements shows the numeral 1, which means that both elements are required

FIGURE 10-24

An alternative representation of the data record BOOK ORDER FORM

Record				BOOK ORDER FORM – REVISED VER.	

Alternate Name BOOK ORDER FORM
Definition   FORM ON WHICH AN INSTRUCTOR ORDERS BOOKS FOR COURSE
Normalized   N

Name of Element or Record	Occ	Seq	Type	Sec-Keys
INSTRUCTOR	1	0	E	
OFFICE ADDRESS	1	0	E	
PHONE#	1	0	E	
DEPT	1	0	E	
COURSE#	1	0	1	
SECTION#	1	0	1	
SEMESTER	1	0	E	
YEAR	1	0	E	
ORDERED BOOK	11	0	R	
ONLY TO US	1	0	E	
PREVIOUS USE	1	0	E	
ORDER DATE	1	0	E	
	1	0	e	
	1	0	e	

PgDn

Screen shots produced using INTERSOLV's Excelerator solution for Requirements Analysis and System Design.

What's in a Name?

When it absolutely positively had to get there overnight—but it didn't—Federal Express faces a daunting systems challenge: how to search through 56 billion bytes of information to find the airbill for Robert Jones at XYZ Co. while Jones waits on the telephone. Federal Express adds 2 million airbills to its files every working day. Generating the indexes for those airbills and subsequently retrieving information from the gargantuan data base is made possible by software from Search Software American, Inc. (SSA).

SSA specializes in servicing organizations where failing to locate a file record by name quickly enough means a lost sale or an angry customer. To handle the problems of data retrieval by name, the software generates multiple keys for names. For example, the name Robert Jones has the additional search keys of Bob Jones, Jones Robert, and Jones Bob. Because organizations can also be wrongly identified by the inquirer, XYZ Co. is also known by XYZ Inc. and XYZ Corp. The algorithms for keys can be adapted for the user's unique data.

Federal Express runs its airbill data through the software to generate multiple 5-byte search keys for each airbill—for the sender's name, sender's company, recipient's name, and recipient's company. These numbers become the indexes for the files. When a query is executed, the program employs these keys to locate the record in the data base. If the first attempt fails, the user can

widen the search window, by getting a list of possible matches, until the desired record is found.

The algorithms in SSA-Name3 fine-tune the searches for international addresses. Common but useless words such as "mailroom" are ignored in addresses. Greatest weight is assigned to the right-hand portion of a name (that is, the area for the last name) when a person's name is being sought, while the left-hand portion of a company name is weighed more heavily. An exact match is just not good enough. If there is an exact match and another that is very similar, it may be uncertain which one is the desired record. A single keying error will leave the correct entry unfound if only exact matching is used.

Another organization using the SSA-Name3 software is the state of Georgia's Department of Revenue. In Georgia, the records for a business's income tax, the business's sales tax, and the withholding tax for the employees can all be linked even though they are maintained in separate systems with differing conventions for names and addresses. Instead of refunding money with one hand and dunning the firm for unpaid sales tax with the other hand, the state of Georgia now sees the entire tax picture for each firm.

Source: Anthes, Gary H., "It's All in the Name," *Computerworld*, December 14, 1992, pp. 77, 80. Copyright 1992/93. Reprinted with permission from *Computerworld*.

to form the primary key. In other cases, such as when a firm imprints each order form with its own unique number, the single data element ORDER NUMBER can then serve as the primary key. Another option for forms not imprinted with a unique number is to assign a unique number during processing. For example, when you reserve a room by phone at a major motel chain you are assigned a confirmation number. This confirmation number is a unique number created by the information system to serve as the primary key for the data record representing your room reservation. The topic of primary keys will be discussed in detail in Chapter 12.

SUMMARY

The data dictionary exists for several reasons. Primarily, the data dictionary ensures complete communication between all computer personnel and users working on the project. Process descriptions are written using the names of the data elements and subrecords that have been fully defined by entries in the data dictionary. Confusion and errors during the development of the information system are prevented by the use of the data dictionary. The use of a CASE tool for creating and modifying a data dictionary helps to alleviate the burden of recording the detailed data descriptions and also assists in maintaining consistency in the model of the information system. The data dictionary also serves as a preliminary step for the implementation of a data base management system.

In this chapter, we explained how to describe the data flows and data stores appearing on a data flow diagram by entries in a data dictionary. A data flow or data store is represented by a data record, which is composed of data elements or data subrecords, or some combination of elements and subrecords. The description of a data subrecord has the same format as a data record. A data element is another name for a data field, the smallest unit of data that has meaning. Within a data record (or subrecord), a data element or subrecord may occur more than once; the maximum number of repetitions is defined by the data dictionary entry. If a data element may contain only a specified set of values, edit rules indicate such a restriction. To document such a set of restricted values or codes, a table of codes showing each value and its meaning is defined by an entry in the data dictionary. We described the data dictionary entries for data records, subrecords, elements, and code tables according to the conventions of the CASE tool Excelerator. If another CASE tool is in use, its syntax should be followed. If no CASE tool is available, the format shown in Figures 10-3, 10-6, 10-14, and 10-15 should be employed.

TERMS

alias	data element
alternate name	data record (for a data dictionary)
code table	
data dictionary	data structure
data dictionary entry	data subrecord

data type	INPUT PICTURE
domain	OUTPUT PICTURE
edit rules	primary key
field	project dictionary

QUESTIONS

1. As discussed in this chapter, what is a data dictionary?
2. Why is a data dictionary necessary for the documentation of data flow diagrams?
3. Define the following terms: data element, data record, data subrecord, data structure.
4. Give examples of three data elements that illustrate each of the following characteristics: repetition, optional occurence, and predetermined values. To show the first two characteristics, you will also need to provide a data record containing the data element. You may use the data records described in this chapter.
5. Why is the use of a CASE tool such as Excelerator advantageous for the preparation of the data dictionary?
6. Explain the meaning of *alternate name* or *alias* for a data record or element. Why do alternate names exist?

For questions 7–9, use Excelerator to prepare your solutions if you have already mastered the mechanics of the module XLDICTIONARY. Otherwise, prepare your answers using a word processor in the format shown in Figures 10-3 and 10-6.

7. Describe the data record for the subscription card shown in Figure 10-25. Show the data dictionary entries for all subrecords and for any two data elements.
8. Prepare the data record for the order form shown in Figure 10-26. Show the data dictionary entries for all subrecords and for any two data elements.
9. Describe the data record for the FREE PRODUCT INFORMATION card shown in Figure 10-27. Prepare the data dictionary entries for all subrecords and for at least one data element. [*Hint:* A data element may be repeated and also contain a coded value.]

FIGURE 10-25

The subscription card for the journal *Database Programming & Design*

Copyright © Database Programming & Design. Reprinted with permission of Miller Freeman, Inc.

FIGURE 10-26 **The order form for the Lands' End catalog**

Reproduced by permission of Lands' End, Inc.

FIGURE 10-27

The FREE PRODUCT INFORMATION card

Copyright © Database Programming & Design. Reprinted with permission of Miller Freeman, Inc.

PROJECTS

1. Obtain a cash register receipt from a grocery store, then describe the data appearing on this receipt in the form of a data record. If you have already mastered the mechanics of XLDICTIONARY, use Excelerator to prepare your description; otherwise, use the format shown in Figure 10-6.

2. If you have a checking account, examine your monthly checking statement; otherwise, see Figure 14-19. Describe the monthly statement as a data record using Excelerator or in the format given by Figure 10-6. If using Excelerator, also provide the data dictionary entries for any sub-records.

REFERENCES

DeMarco, Tom. *Structured Analysis and System Specification*. Englewood Cliffs, NJ: Prentice-Hall, 1979.

Excelerator Data and Reports Reference Guide. Cambridge, MA: Intersolv, 1990.

Excelerator Facilities and Functions User Guide. Cambridge, MA: Intersolv, 1990.

Gane, Chris, and Trish Sarson. *Structured Systems Analysis: Tools and Techniques*. Englewood Cliffs, NJ: Prentice-Hall, 1979.

Stern, Nancy, and Robert A. Stern. *Structured COBOL Programming*. New York: Wiley, 1991.

CHAPTER 11

Process Descriptions

Objectives

As we have discussed in Chapters 9 and 10, the data flow diagrams that represent an information system require the supporting documentation of a data dictionary and process descriptions. The definitions of data flows and data stores entered into the data dictionary were explained in Chapter 10. This chapter discusses the techniques by which process descriptions are documented. By the conclusion of this chapter, you will have learned:

- How to incorporate the names of the data dictionary entries within process descriptions
- The three ways of describing processes: structured English, decision trees, and decision tables
- The advantages and disadvantages of these three methods
- How process descriptions are entered into the Excelerator project dictionary

INTRODUCTION

A data flow diagram (DFD) is typically exploded to several levels. Although the processes on each level of the DFD could be documented by process descriptions, such descriptions are not necessary. The processes on the DFDs at the higher levels are considered to be adequately documented by the explosion of each process to a lower level DFD. Each process on the lowest level DFD is called a **primitive process** and must be documented by a process description. For example, if an information system has been documented by DFDs on the context level as well as on levels 0, 1, 2, and 3, process descriptions must be prepared for only the processes on the bottom level, level 3. These primitive process descriptions are stored in the project dictionary associated with the information system under development.

The primitive process descriptions are designed to serve two purposes. First, we must be certain that the DFDs truly reflect the actions of the information system on the data that travels through the system. By formally describing the processes in a manner easily understood by the users of the information system, it is possible to request the users to verify that the systems analyst has accurately modeled the system. By tracing the model with the users, the analyst can check the correctness of the process descriptions and remedy any mistakes early in the life cycle. Secondly, the process descriptions are the means to communicate the system's policies and procedures to the programmers, who will code the computer programs.

Because process descriptions are designed to communicate with both the users and computer professionals, they must be specified in a way that is precise, unambiguous, and easily understood by persons unfamiliar with computer programming. Further, since at this stage in the system's development it is too soon to decide which programming language will be used to implement the software, the process descriptions must be expressed in such a fashion that any programming language may be chosen. There are three methods that satisfy these dual objectives: *structured English, decision tables*, and *decision trees.* Each method will be discussed in the following sections and illustrated by a sample problem that computes the surcharge for an automobile insurance policy. The last section explains the use of Excelerator for preparing the process descriptions for a project. If Excelerator or a similar CASE tool is not available, processes may be prepared as handwritten descriptions or by the use of a word processor.

POLICIES AND PROCEDURES

Each process in the lowest level DFDs represents a well-defined task that transforms input data flows into output data flows. The user defines these tasks to the systems analyst by describing the policies and procedures followed by the organization. A **policy** is a set of rules that determines what actions should be performed by the firm. Policies are the means by which decision making has been codified so that routine decisions can be made in a consistent manner by all employees. For example, credit may be extended to a customer according to the following set of rules:

> If the customer has a checking account with a good record at a local bank and the customer owns his/her own home, extend credit. Otherwise, check the employment record of the customer.

> If the customer has worked for more than 2 years at the present position and the credit bureau issues a good rating, then extend credit.

> If the customer is a student but underage, the application must be signed by the parents or guardian. Otherwise, reject the application.

This set of rules is called the policy for credit approval. If we examine this policy carefully, we immediately see that we do not know what is a "good record" at the local bank, the meaning of a "good rating" by the credit bureau, or the definition of "underage." These terms must be precisely defined before the systems analyst can describe the policy for a computer information system. We do so by requesting more information from the user, the person who knows and works with this policy.

Procedures are the step-by-step actions that implement a policy. In our example of the credit approval policy, several steps are required to approve a credit application. The user may explain to us how the local bank is called to verify the customer's standing or the means by which the credit bureau is contacted to determine the customer's credit rating. There may be several steps performed before the information is available to approve or reject the credit application. These steps comprise the procedure by which the retail store approves the customer's application for credit. The systems analyst must study the policies and procedures relevant to the information system model so that they will be correctly expressed in the primitive process descriptions.

GENERAL RULES FOR PROCESS DESCRIPTIONS

Before proceeding to a detailed explanation of each technique, we wish to discuss the overall requirements for preparing process descriptions. As we have said, process descriptions are designed to be read in conjunction with the data flow diagram and the data dictionary. A **process description** should tell us exactly how the input data flows are transformed by the process into the output data flows. This transformation is expressed by stating the actions performed on the data that enter the process. The data are identified by the names for the data elements, subrecords, and records as stored within the data dictionary. Because the input and output data flows have been fully described by their entries within the associated data dictionary, this detailed information should not be repeated in the process description. Since the DFD also shows the origin of the input flows and the destinations of the output data flows, this information is not customarily included within the process description. However, process descriptions in Excelerator (version 1.9) do allow for this information to be specified.

To illustrate these principles, we will once again present the data flow diagram originally displayed in Chapter 9 as Figure 9-18b and duplicated here as Figure 11-1. Because this DFD exists on the lowest level of the DFDs representing the vendor payment system, the processes appearing here will be documented by primitive process descriptions placed within the project dictionary. We will discuss only the process description for process 1.1, VERIFY VENDOR ID. As shown by the DFD, the data flows VENDOR ID and VENDOR (from the data store VENDORS) enter process 1.1, which then creates the output data flow VERIFIED VENDOR ID. Because the process description will tell us how VERIFY VENDOR ID transforms the data flows VENDOR ID and VENDOR into the output data flow VERIFIED VENDOR ID, only these names (or the names of the data elements and subrecords comprising these data flows, or the name of the data store VENDORS) will appear in the process description. Within process descriptions, we will use the convention of capital letters for the names of data flows, data stores, data elements, subrecords, and records.

In Figure 11-2, process 1.1 has been described by the use of statements in the language called structured English. The procedure for verifying the

FIGURE 11-1

A DFD on level 1 for the Vendor Payment System

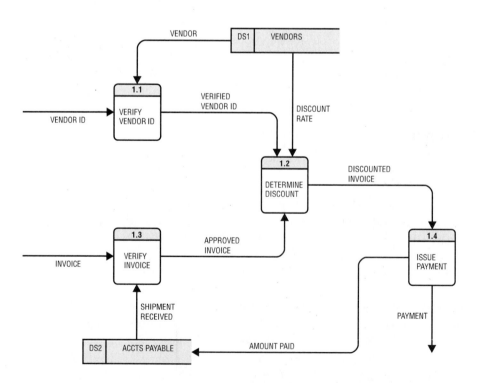

FIGURE 11-2

The process description for process 1.1

Find record on VENDORS file with matching VENDOR ID.

If not found, Then

Reject VENDOR ID.

vendor's identification number (VENDOR ID) has been clearly stated. If requested, a programmer could prepare the program code to implement this procedure without further questions. The user can also quickly grasp this description of the process. The steps have been explicitly stated and the data identified by the corresponding data dictionary names. This example illustrates the basic principles for the preparation of process descriptions. We will now explain the three techniques for preparing process descriptions, beginning with the most popular method, structured English.

STRUCTURED ENGLISH

Structured English is a somewhat free form language which bears many similarities to high-level programming languages such as Pascal or COBOL. As its name implies, structured English imitates these languages by adopting the structures of high-level programming languages while using ordinary English statements. Because structured English is designed to communicate with the user as well as the computer professional, ordinary words and expressions are used to express the tasks to be performed. The syntax of structured English is rather loosely defined, and such matters as semicolons and periods—significant for programming languages—are not important. Since the mixture of freely expressed statements must be balanced with the need to properly define a process, certain syntactical requirements exist; they will be presented in the following material.

The same types of logical constructs provided for programming in high-level languages are also available in structured English: *sequential statements, decision constructs*, and constructs for the *repetition* of instructions. These three constructs are sufficient to express the actions of any process. As in structured programming, structured English requires each process to have only one entrance and one exit. The requirement of one entrance means that the first statement in the process is where the process always begins. To ensure there is only one exit, the process must not contain any statements that exit from the process, such as a GO TO statement. If you find that you cannot write the description for a primitive process without violating this rule, you probably have not exploded the process to a sufficient depth of DFDs. We will now define the logical constructs for structured English in the following sections.

Sequential Statements

A **sequence construct** is composed of one or more simple statements. Examples of such statements are

> Set DEPRECIATED AMOUNT to CURRENT CAPITAL VALUE.
>
> Let NET PAY equal GROSS PAY minus TOTAL DEDUCTIONS.
>
> Write VERIFIED CHECK to CHECK FILE.

Each statement is precise and unambiguous. The names of data elements, data records, or data stores in the data dictionary are used. Statements may be written in a free form as long as the action to be performed is clearly specified. Any imperative verb may be used, but vague verbs such as *process* and *handle* are not permitted.

Decision Constructs

A **decision construct** is a statement that tests a condition, usually the value of a data element, and determines which set of instructions should be performed. We say that the decision construct chooses among *paths* based on a condition. There are two ways of expressing a decision in structured English: the If-Then-Otherwise statement and the Case statement.

IF-THEN-OTHERWISE STATEMENT

The If-Then-Otherwise statement is similar to the If-Then-Else statement more commonly found in high-level programming languages. Structured English relies on proper indentation of statements to indicate the end of the If-Then-Otherwise statement rather than explicitly stating an ENDIF termination clause. The word "Then" may be omitted. The use of the word "Otherwise" is designed to be more akin to ordinary conversational English. The formal definition of this statement is given in Figure 11-3. When an If-Then-Otherwise statement is executed, the condition specified by the If statement is tested. If the condition is true, the statements indented below the If-Then clause are performed. If the condition is false, the statements indented below the Otherwise clause are performed. The statements must be indented as shown; improper indentation will cause the statements to be interpreted incorrectly.

FIGURE 11-3
The format of the If-Then-Otherwise statement

> If *condition*, Then
>   *statements for Then policy.*
> Otherwise (*negated condition is stated*),
>   *statements for the Otherwise policy.*

In structured English, the negation of the specified condition is given in parentheses following the word Otherwise. By stating the negation of the condition being tested, we hope to avoid any confusion about the actions performed by the process. For example, when "X less than 0" is stated as the condition for the If-Then clause, the condition is restated for the Otherwise clause as "X greater than or equal to 0." Because these process descriptions are read by the user, it is best to avoid mathematical notation such as <, =, and > symbols. For instance, rather than stating a condition as "ACCT BALANCE > 0" the expression should be written as "ACCT BALANCE greater than zero."

To illustrate the use of the If-Then-Otherwise statement, let us examine the policy for awarding bonuses, stated next in narrative form.

> The Super-Sale Company wishes to award annual bonuses based on the number of years of service by each employee regardless of salary. If an employee has worked 25 years or more, the bonus will be 5% of the annual salary. Otherwise, the employee will receive a bonus of 2.5% of the annual salary.

In Figure 11-4 we show this process, COMPUTE BONUS, as a fragment of a data flow diagram. Before documenting the process, the data flows EM-PLOYEE YEARS OF SERVICE, ANNUAL SALARY, and BONUS should be described by entries in the data dictionary. As shown in Figure 11-5, the process description COMPUTE BONUS uses the data dictionary names so that the process is fully specified. The If-Then clause specifies the condition to be tested as "EMPLOYEE YEARS OF SERVICE is 25 or greater." The negation of this condition is stated after the word "Otherwise" to ensure that the process description is complete. The indentations of the Then and Otherwise clauses are crucial for the proper interpretation of the actions to be performed by the statement.

Let us now consider a more complicated process which calculates the surcharge for an automobile insurance policy. The insurance company has stated the policy in narrative form.

> If a driver of the automobile is under 25 years and male, charge 15% more for the automobile insurance policy. But if this driver has success-

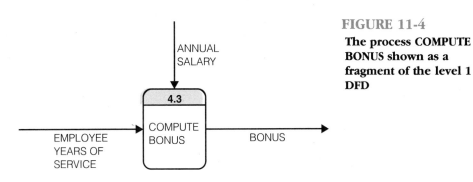

FIGURE 11-4

The process COMPUTE BONUS shown as a fragment of the level 1 DFD

FIGURE 11-5

An example of the If-Then-Otherwise statement The policy for awarding bonuses to employees

If EMPLOYEE YEARS OF SERVICE is 25 or greater, Then
 Compute BONUS = .05 times ANNUAL SALARY.
Otherwise (EMPLOYEE YEARS OF SERVICE is less than 25),
 Compute BONUS = .025 times ANNUAL SALARY.

fully completed a driver's education course and is a good student, charge only 10% more. If the driver is under 25 and female, charge only 7% more. Otherwise, charge the normal rate.

This description is imprecise because we do not know what constitutes a "good student." After consultation with the user, we learn that a "good student" means a student with a high school grade point average of 3.0 or above. Now we can write the complete process description in structured English, as shown in Figure 11-6. The process requires the use of several If-Then-Otherwise statements which are nested within each other. Notice that each Otherwise clause contains the negation of the condition stated in the matching If clause. The terms—DRIVER AGE, DRIVER SEX, DRIVER EDUCATION, DRIVER HS-GPA, and SURCHARGE—represent data elements that exist in the input or output data flows to the process. These data elements have already been defined within the corresponding data dictionary.

The If-Then-Otherwise statement provides for a *binary decision*, a choice made between two paths. In many instances, multiple paths are present; this is the case with the process COMPUTE SURCHARGE. Although the logic has been correctly stated by means of several If-Then-Otherwise statements, the process description is somewhat confusing and not easily understood. To avoid the entanglement caused by nested If-Then-Otherwise

FIGURE 11-6

The automobile insurance policy process expressed in structured English

If DRIVER AGE is less than 25, Then
 If DRIVER SEX is "Male", Then
  If DRIVER EDUCATION is "Yes", Then
   If DRIVER HS-GPA is greater than or equal to 3.0, Then
    SURCHARGE is 10 percent.
   Otherwise (DRIVER HS-GPA is less than 3.0),
    SURCHARGE is 15 percent.
  Otherwise (DRIVER EDUCATION is "No"),
   SURCHARGE is 15 percent.
 Otherwise (DRIVER SEX is "Female"),
  SURCHARGE is 7 percent.
Otherwise (DRIVER AGE is 25 or older),
 SURCHARGE is zero.

statements, the analyst may choose to express the same logic more straight-forwardly by employing the Case construct. The next section defines the general format of the Case construct and shows an example of its usage.

CASE STATEMENT

When a choice must be made among several possible paths, the Case state-ment offers a direct way to state the various alternatives or *cases*. The general format of the Case statement is shown in Figure 11-7. The Select line is a general statement that simply declares that one of the possible cases will be picked for execution. Each Case clause defines the condition to be tested; if the condition is found to be true, then the statements below the Case clause will be executed. Once a case has been found to be relevant and its corre-sponding statements executed, the remaining cases are skipped over. More-over, the selection of a particular case must be independent of the fact that preceding cases were not selected. This means that the conditions for each case must be mutually exclusive so that the cases can be listed in any order. An example will be given later.

Select the appropriate case:
    Case 1. (*condition 1*):
           statements for condition 1.
    Case 2. (*condition 2*):
           statements for condition 2.
           .
           .
           .
    Case n. (*condition n*):
           statements for condition n.

FIGURE 11-7
The general form of the Case statement

The earlier problem of defining the surcharge for an automobile policy has been restated for your convenience in Figure 11-8. This procedure is now expressed with the use of the Case statement in Figure 11-9. As with the If-Then-Otherwise statement, indentations are important for understanding the process description. An examination of all the Case clauses shows that all

If a driver of the automobile is under 25 years and male, charge 15% more for the automobile insurance policy. But if this driver has successfully completed a driver's education course and is a good student, charge only 10% more. If the driver is under 25 and female, charge only 7% more. Otherwise, charge the normal rate.

FIGURE 11-8
The automobile insur-ance policy process

FIGURE 11-9

The automobile insurance policy expressed by the Case structure

Select the appropriate case:

Case 1.   (DRIVER AGE is 25 or older):
          SURCHARGE is zero.

Case 2.   (DRIVER AGE is less than 25 and DRIVER SEX is
          "Male" and DRIVER EDUCATION is "Yes" and
          DRIVER HS-GPA is 3.0 or greater):
          SURCHARGE is 10%.

Case 3.   (DRIVER AGE is less than 25 and DRIVER SEX is
          "Male" and [either DRIVER EDUCATION is "No" or
          DRIVER HS-GPA is less than 3.0]):
          SURCHARGE is 15%.

Case 4.   (DRIVER AGE is less than 25 and DRIVER SEX is
          "Female"):
          SURCHARGE is 7%.

possible situations for determining the value of SURCHARGE have been specified. Once again, the names of the data elements—DRIVER AGE, DRIVER SEX, DRIVER HS-GPA, DRIVER EDUCATION, and SURCHARGE—are used here in the process description to ensure that the process is explicitly defined.

The Select statement simply tells us to select the case that applies. The first Case clause is associated with the condition that the data element DRIVER AGE is the value 25 or more. If this condition is true, the resulting action is to place the value zero in the data element SURCHARGE. The Case statement is then terminated. If DRIVER AGE contains a value of less than 25, we proceed to the next Case clause which covers the case where the data element DRIVER AGE is less than 25, DRIVER SEX equals the value "Male," DRIVER EDUCATION contains "Yes," and DRIVER HS-GPA is 3.0 or greater. The values stated for DRIVER SEX, DRIVER EDUCATION, and DRIVER HS-GPA must be included in the possible values listed within their respective data dictionary entries. If all four conditions are true, the value "10% " is stored in the data element SURCHARGE. Otherwise, the condition for the next Case clause is tested. This mode of execution continues until one of the cases is found to apply or all cases have been exhausted. The confusion of the nested If statements in the process description shown in Figure 11-6 has been prevented by using the concise Case statement. We also note that Case 3 has been precisely stated by the addition of the words

and [either DRIVER EDUCATION is "No" or DRIVER HS-GPA is less than 3.0]

Because these words have been included in the conditions for this case, the order of the cases is immaterial. If, however, we omit these words and move

FIGURE 11-10
An example of a Case statement incorrectly stated

Select the appropriate case:

Incorrect Case Statement

Case 1.   (DRIVER AGE is 25 or older):
          SURCHARGE is zero.

Case 2.   (DRIVER AGE is less than 25 and
          DRIVER SEX is "Male"):
          SURCHARGE is 15%.

Case 3.   (DRIVER AGE is less than 25 and
          DRIVER SEX is "Male" and DRIVER EDU-
          CATION is "Yes" and DRIVER HS-GPA is
          3.0 or greater):
          SURCHARGE is 10%.

Case 4.   (DRIVER AGE is less than 25 and
          DRIVER SEX is "Female"):
          SURCHARGE is 7%.

Case 3 before Case 2, as shown in Figure 11-10, all male drivers under the age of 25 will pay the surcharge of 15%. Because the conditions for Case 3 are tested only after Cases 1 and 2 are examined, Case 3 will never be selected.

Repetition Constructs

Structured English offers three constructs for expressing the repetition of statements: While-Do, Repeat-Until, and For-Each statements. The continued repetition of the loop is governed by whether or not a specified condition is true. The particular situation and your own preference determine which repetition construct should be used to describe a policy.

WHILE-DO STATEMENT

The general format of the While-Do statement is shown in Figure 11-11. The While-Do statement first tests whether the specified condition is true. If the condition is true, the group of indented statements is performed. If the condition is not true, none of the indented statements is executed. Although computer professionals are accustomed to the syntax of the While-Do state-

FIGURE 11-11
The general form of the While-Do statement

While *condition* Do the following steps:
    statements for condition being true

ment, users may more easily understand the Repeat-Until or For-Each statements discussed later.

We will illustrate the While-Do statement for the procedure stated informally as:

Check the EMPLOYEE file and issue a letter about retirement options to all employees who are 62 or older.

In Figure 11-12, this procedure is expressed with the aid of the While-Do statement. Because the retirement letter must be issued only to those employees who are 62 or older, the If statement is employed to check the data element EMPLOYEE AGE. The process locates all such employees and issues the required letter represented by the data record RETIREMENT LETTER in the data dictionary. According to the While-Do statement, the process will terminate after the last record in the data store EMPLOYEES has been tested and a retirement letter sent, if appropriate.

FIGURE 11-12

The policy for sending the retirement letter

> While there are records in the EMPLOYEES file, Do:
>   Get a record from the EMPLOYEES file.
>   If EMPLOYEE AGE is 62 or older, Then
>   Send RETIREMENT LETTER.

REPEAT-UNTIL AND FOR-EACH STATEMENTS

The Repeat-Until and For-Each statements represent two other ways of expressing the While-Do statement. These modes of expression are closer to plain English than to the syntax of a computer programming language. The general format for these two statements is illustrated in Figure 11-13. The style of indentation shown in this figure should be followed so that the structure of the statements is clearly shown. Both the Repeat-Until and For-

FIGURE 11-13

Two alternatives to the While-Do statement

> a. The Repeat-Until statement
>   (We note that the convention is that the statements will always be executed at least once.)
>
>   Repeat the following steps:
>   *statements to be executed while the condition is false*
>   Until *condition is true.*
>
> b. The For-Each statement
>
>   For each record in *the named data file*:
>   *statements to be performed on each record in the data file*

Each statements are typically used to indicate the repetition of actions performed on records contained in a data file.

In Figure 11-14, a Repeat-Until statement has been used to control a sequence of statements that first reads a record from the INVENTORY file and then decides whether to reorder an inventory item. The Repeat-Until statement indicates that the designated group of statements is executed *until* no more records remain in the data file. The data acted on by these statements are identified by their names in the data dictionary.

Repeat the following steps:

    Get a record from the INVENTORY file.

        If REORDER POINT is greater than the sum of QUANTITY-ON-HAND and QUANTITY-ON-ORDER, Then

            Create the REORDER INFO record.

            Write REORDER INFO to the REORDER REPORT file.

Until there are no more records on the INVENTORY file.

FIGURE 11-14

The reorder policy expressed by the Repeat-Until statement

The For-Each statement achieves the same effect as the Repeat-Until statement by indicating that the designated statements are executed *for each* record in the data file. Whereas the Repeat-Until construct is a general type of repetition construct, the For-Each statement is especially designed to control the repetition of actions for file processing. Figure 11-15 shows an example of a For-Each statement, which commands the set of indented statements to be executed for each record in the INVENTORY file until the file has been exhausted. This process description is equivalent to the reorder policy described by the Repeat-Until statement shown earlier in Figure 11-14.

For each record in the INVENTORY file:

    If REORDER POINT is greater than the sum of QUANTITY-ON-HAND and QUANTITY-ON-ORDER, Then

        Create the REORDER INFO record.

        Write REORDER INFO to the REORDER REPORT file.

FIGURE 11-15

The reorder policy expressed by the For-Each statement

Guidelines for Structured English

The constructs of structured English permit the actions of a process to be informally expressed in English. Although a programming language requires strict adherence to a formal syntax, structured English permits a less restrictive format for expressing program logic. There is a wide range of approaches for the description of any particular process. Despite this freedom, certain restrictions apply. The guidelines for writing structured English are summarized next.

1. Verbs can be selected from the set of active verbs except for nondescriptive verbs such as "process" and "handle."
2. Nouns must be the names of data elements, subrecords, records, data flows, or data stores all of which are defined by entries in the data dictionary.
3. The qualifying values of a data element must be taken from the set of values specified in its data dictionary definition. For example, to write the conditional statement, IF EMPLOYEE TYPE is "PT," the value "PT" must be one of the values listed for EMPLOYEE TYPE in its data dictionary entry.
4. Only conjunctions (such as If, Then, and Until) defined for the logical constructs may appear in a structured English statement.
5. A condition is stated by using any combination of the following reserved words: equal, less than, greater than, and, or.

These limitations on the vocabulary of structured English enable us to write descriptions clearly and concisely. Words that are not well defined are prohibited. Although the vocabulary has been somewhat restricted, try to avoid overly stilted English; strive for an informal style that precisely states what is being done.

The Pros and Cons of Structured English

Structured English offers several advantages for writing process descriptions. First, because structured English is independent of any particular programming language, the selection of the programming language can be deferred until later in the project when more is known about the project requirements. Any subsequent revisions to the system will be more easily accomplished because the process descriptions are precisely but generally stated. Second, textual descriptions can be efficiently prepared and maintained either by the use of a word processor or a CASE tool such as Excelerator. Third, process descriptions in structured English are concise, precise, and readable. Fourth, if properly written they are readable by the users who are not computer professionals. Because of this readability, the accuracy of the process descriptions can be checked by those who are most familiar with the policies and procedures of the existing information system. Fifth, employing the data dictionary names allows the consistency of the data flow diagrams, data dictionary, and process descriptions to be verified. Finally, it is relatively easy and quick to write process descriptions in structured English. Since the format is similar to standard English with an added framework of rules, computer professionals adapt quickly to writing process descriptions in structured English.

Although structured English is a highly regarded method for process descriptions, there are some difficulties in using this method. First, as with any new skill, it takes time to gain proficiency in writing structured English descriptions. You must learn to follow the guidelines, use only the limited vocabulary of words, and express the actions of the process correctly. Second, the use of structured English (or any other technique) does not guarantee that the process has been stated correctly. We cannot execute a computer program and examine the results. After we do our best to express the actions of a process, we then must turn to the user to ask for verification. Third, the user may not appreciate the carefully wrought statements in structured English. He or she may find the structure and rigor too foreign and removed from everyday English. The analyst should help the user by explaining each process description, step by step. If the user still balks at the strange-looking statements, the systems analyst may try to continue to use structured English by removing the indentations and making the description look purely narrative. If you fail in your attempt to disguise structured English, rewrite your descriptions in narrative form and incorporate the narration as comments in your process description. Then ask the user to verify the narrative form of the process description; retain the structured English statements for the programmer's use in writing code. Above all, avoid computer jargon in your discussions with users. Just say that you are using English to write down what they have told you; the term structured English should never be mentioned. You can explain that the indentations are your own special style for writing down these descriptions and accept the blame for having a strange writing style. The users may be willing to deal with a humble systems analyst, even one who writes in a funny style of English.

DECISION TABLES

Decision tables are another way to specify the logical structure of a process. A **decision table** is composed of conditional statements and program branches arranged in tabular form. Since the conditions that determine decisions are given in English, decision tables can be quickly understood by managers, engineers, programmers, and others. When a decision table is used, it is a simple matter to check whether all the options related to a decision were documented. Because a decision table is constructed with English statements, any symbols, shorthand notation, and computer jargon can be avoided. With the advent of compilers that translate the tables into computer programs, decision tables gained some popularity; however, this initial success has faded. Today it is more likely that the programmer will code directly from the decision tables.

A decision table is divided into four quadrants: condition-stub, condition-entry, action-stub, and action-entry (see Figure 11-16). The **condition-stub quadrant** contains a list of conditional statements or questions, called

FIGURE 11-16
The structure of a decision table

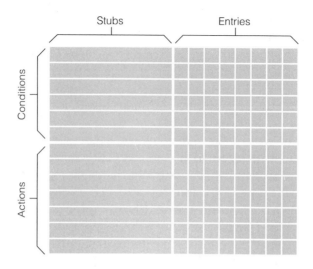

stubs. For example, the conditional statement "Y = 0" in the condition-stub quadrant means "Does Y equal 0?" The **condition-entry** quadrant shows the possible replies to the questions listed in the condition-stub quadrant. The **action-stub** quadrant contains a list of actions, or *action stubs,* while the **action-entry** quadrant designates whether an action will be executed. An x indicates that the action specified in the stub will be executed; a blank means that it will not be performed.

Decision tables are classified according to the rules governing the entries placed in the condition-entry quadrant; in turn, the notation possible for the condition-entry quadrant also determines how the statements in the condition-stub quadrant are phrased. The three basic categories of decision tables are known as *limited entry, extended entry,* and *mixed entry.* Although other variations on decision tables exist, such as reduced and multiple-page tables, the more complex features of decision tables are not needed for process descriptions. If a process description requires these complex features, the process undoubtedly is too complex and should be represented by two or more processes; that is, the process should be exploded to another level. Consequently, only the three basic categories of decision tables are discussed in the following sections.

Limited Entry Tables

In **limited entry tables**, the condition-entry quadrant contains the replies to the questions posed in the condition-stub quadrant. A condition entry may be Y for YES, N for NO, or a dash (–) to indicate an irrelevant factor. As explained earlier, the action-entry quadrant shows whether an action will be executed. An x indicates that the action specified in the stub will be executed; a blank indicates that the action will not be performed. The more rules that are added, the more complex the decision table becomes. A general rule is to limit a decision table to no more than 16 conditional statements in the condition-stub quadrant. This ensures that the decision table will be comprehensible to the reader.

Figure 11-17 provides an example of a limited entry decision table that gives all possible replies to these three questions:

1. Is condition A met?
2. Is condition B met?
3. Is condition C met?

Each column in the decision table indicates a logical path that may be chosen, depending on the status of the conditions A, B, and C. The columns in the upper right quadrant (the condition-entry quadrant) are numbered sequentially, starting with the numeral 1. We say that each column represents a **rule** to be followed by the process. For example, rule 1 (represented by column 1) states that if conditions A, B, and C are true, then action 1 will be executed; rule 2, denoted by column 2, states that if condition A is false and conditions B and C are true, then action 2 will be executed; and so on.

Process Name	1	2	3	4	5	6	7	8
Condition A	Y	N	Y	N	Y	N	Y	N
Condition B	Y	Y	N	N	N	N	Y	Y
Condition C	Y	Y	Y	Y	N	N	N	N
Action 1	X							
Action 2		X						
Action 3			X					
Action 4				X				
Action 5					X			
Action 6						X		
Action 7							X	
Action 8								X

FIGURE 11-17

A sample decision table

A rule may specify that several actions are to be performed; we show this by placing an x in each row corresponding to the desired actions.

If all possible combinations of Y and N are shown, there will be 2^n rules, where n is the number of statements in the condition-stub quadrant. Using this computation, the creator of the decision table is able to check that all possible outcomes have been tabulated. Since all possible combinations have been listed for the decision table in Figure 11-17, the total number of rules is 2^3 or 8.

Another example of a limited entry table appears in Figure 11-18. This table contains three items in the condition-stub quadrant but only four possible combinations of responses. If condition A is met, conditions B and C are irrelevant. This reduces the number of responses to five and eliminates the need for the combination of Y and N responses in rules 3, 5, and 7 in the decision table shown in Figure 11-17. Because condition C becomes irrelevant whenever condition A is false *and* condition B is met, rules 2 and 8 are the same. Thus, one more rule can be eliminated, leaving only four rules as shown in Figure 11-18.

Since the implementation of a decision table is ordinarily left to the discretion of the programmer, it is advisable to take care when employing a dash (–) to indicate the irrelevancy of any condition-stubs within a rule. Otherwise, the translation of the decision table into programming statements may result in erroneous code. The clarity of the decision table is compromised when dashes are intermixed with Y's or N's within a rule. Since a rule is read from top to bottom, the recommended practice is that any dashes be placed at the end of the rule; this, in turn, means that the

FIGURE 11-18

A limited entry decision table

Process Name	1	2	3	4
Condition A	Y	N	N	N
Condition B	–	Y	N	N
Condition C	–	–	Y	N
Action 1	x			
Action 2		x		
Action 3			x	
Action 4				x

condition-stubs must be arranged appropriately. Y and N entries may precede a dash but they should never follow any dash in a rule. Adherence to this advice unfortunately means that some decision tables cannot be shortened by using the dash (–).

Extended Entry Decision Tables

Extended entry tables permit the items in the condition-stub quadrant to extend into the condition-entry portion of the decision table. Let us consider the following items in the condition-stub quadrant for a limited entry table:

$Y < 0$

$Y = 0$

$Y > 0$

As shown in Figure 11-19, the extended entry table combines these three conditional statements into the single condition stub, "Compare Y to zero." The three possible conditions of $Y < 0$, $Y = 0$, and $Y > 0$ are shown by placing the symbols $>$, $=$, and $<$ in the action-stub quadrant. Because the number of items in the condition-stub quadrant have been reduced, the table is more concise and simpler to understand. Whenever it is necessary to test a data element for multiple values, an extended entry table is most likely to be the best choice.

Policy for Y	1	2	3
Compare Y to zero	>	=	<
Action 1	X		
Action 2		X	
Action 3			X

FIGURE 11-19
An extended entry decision table

Mixed Entry Decision Tables

Mixed entry tables combine the features of the limited entry and extended entry table. Each item in the condition stub may assume either the limited entry or the extended entry form. This combination permits the decision table to be as concise as possible. A mixed entry decision table is shown in Figure 11-20. The limited entry feature allows us to state whether overtime pay should be given to the employee; the use of the extended entry feature

FIGURE 11-20

A mixed entry decision table

Policy for Overtime Pay	1	2	3	4	5
HOURS WORKED greater than 40	N	Y	Y	Y	Y
EMPLOYEE RANK	–	F	P	T	R
Pay Overtime		X	X	X	X
Set OVERTIME RATE equal to 1½ times BASE RATE			X	X	X
Set OVERTIME RATE equal to 2 times BASE RATE		X			

permits us to express the employee's rank directly. Each rule is succinctly stated. If we examine rule 2, we quickly see that when employees with a rank of F work more than 40 hours per week, they receive overtime pay at an overtime rate of two times the base rate. If a conventional limited entry table were given for this same policy, the table would require 32 rules rather than only the five rules given for the mixed entry table.

An Example of a Decision Table

As we said earlier, a decision table is especially well suited to express a process that contains several conditions to be tested before a set of actions will be executed. The answers are tabulated as rules, and the appropriate actions are marked with an x for each rule. For instance, consider the example of the automobile insurance policy previously written in structured English (see Figures 11-6 and 11-9). The decision table for computing the surcharge for the automobile insurance policy is shown in Figure 11-21. Dashes (–) indicate when a "Yes" or "No" answer is irrelevant. If the driver is not under 25 years of age, the other questions regarding the driver can be disregarded. For example, rule 3 states that if the driver is a male under 25 without driver's education and with a high school GPA of 3.0 or more, the insurance rate is computed with a surcharge of 15%. Rules 1 and 2 correspond respectively to cases 1 and 2 in Figure 11-9. Rules 3, 4, and 5 are equivalent to case 3; rule 6 expresses case 4. The decision table clearly states the policy for the insurance surcharge and avoids any possible confusion arising from the conjunctions, "and" and "or" in the conditions for case 3. By using separate conditional statements (in the condition-stub quadrant) and unequivocal answers of Y or N to each condition (in the action-stub quadrant), the decision table has provided an unambiguous expression of all possible cases and their corresponding actions.

Surcharge Policy	1	2	3	4	5	6
DRIVER AGE less than 25	N	Y	Y	Y	Y	Y
DRIVER MALE	–	Y	Y	Y	Y	N
DRIVER with DRIVER'S EDUCATION	–	Y	N	Y	N	–
HIGH SCHOOL GPA greater than or equal 3.0	–	Y	Y	N	N	–
SURCHARGE is 15%			x	x	x	
SURCHARGE is 10%		x				
SURCHARGE is 7%						x
No SURCHARGE	x					

FIGURE 11-21
The decision table for the insurance surcharge policy

DECISION TREES

A **decision tree** is a graphical representation of a decision table. Because complex logic may be more easily understood when shown graphically, the use of a decision tree helps us to ensure that all possible choices have been stated for the process description. Unlike decision tables, decision trees are valuable when only a small number of conditions and actions must be described. Because of the graphical depiction of conditions, a decision tree may quickly become unwieldy and unreadable. However, for a given set of conditions, a decision tree may be the best choice.

Unfortunately, we are faced with the reality that most CASE tools do not provide for drawing decision trees. For that reason, we suggest limiting the use of decision trees to a preliminary description of the processes. Then a formal description by means of structured English should be entered into the project dictionary for a CASE tool. If the systems analyst finds that the decision tree is the best vehicle to express the process, the process description can simply refer to the decision tree as a document outside of the project dictionary.

General Form of a Decision Tree

The general form of a decision tree is shown in Figure 11-22. The name of the policy is placed at the tree's beginning, which is called its *root*. The root

FIGURE 11-22   The general form of a decision tree

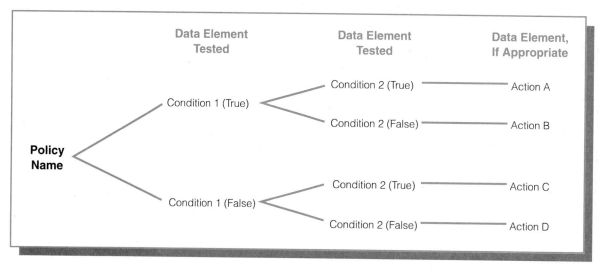

immediately branches into two or more lines to indicate the possible choices for the data element. Each conditional statement is then tested further and the appropriate path is selected. Finally, a conditional statement is terminated by a horizontal line followed by one or more action statements. The data dictionary name of the data element tested by a conditional statement is placed directly above its possible values, as shown in Figure 11-22.

The Decision Tree for the Surcharge Rate

To make this general format clearer, let us examine Figure 11-23, which shows the decision tree for the automobile insurance policy presented earlier in structured English and as a decision table. The root has been called "Insurance Surcharge Policy" and is immediately followed by two lines that branch outward. At the top of the chart we see the names of each data element being tested. The first data element name appears directly above the point where the tree splits by testing the value of the data element DRIVER AGE. The first branch is labeled "under 25" and the second branch, "25 or older." The words "under 25" are followed by a second set of branches labeled "Male" and "Female" for the two values of DRIVER SEX. The word "Male" is the start of a third set of branches labeled "Yes" and "No" for the values of the data element DRIVER EDUCATION. The "Yes" for DRIVER EDUCATION then splits into a fourth set of branches labeled "3.0 or above" and "less than 3.0" for the data element HS-GPA.

Since all the required conditions have been tested in order to establish the surcharge, horizontal lines are drawn from the last label of each branch, terminating at the column for the data element SURCHARGE (far right column in Figure 11-23). The values of SURCHARGE corresponding to the various paths are displayed in this last column. Notice that the response of

FIGURE 11-23 The insurance surcharge policy expressed by a decision tree

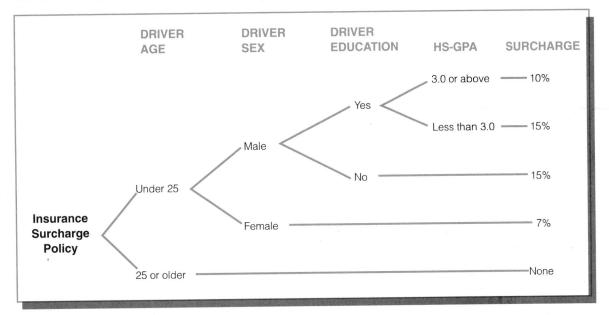

25 or older for DRIVER AGE is followed by a long horizontal line leading to the word "None." This line was drawn across the page in order to align the word "None" under the label SURCHARGE. Similarly, the horizontal lines from the terminations of other branches are extended to align the values for the surcharge rate in the column labeled SURCHARGE.

Multiple Branches on Decision Trees

The insurance policy example in Figure 11-23 illustrated a decision tree that branched repeatedly but always split into exactly two branches. Some decision trees must be drawn with three or more branches in order to represent the paths inherent in the problem posed. For example, in Figure 11-24 we see that the decision tree contains an initial three-way split to determine the number of hours for which a student is enrolled. Then each branch splits two ways, because the data element STUDENT TYPE has only two possible values: "Grad" and "Undergrad." Finally, the appropriate value for TUITION CHARGE is shown as the action to be taken.

WHICH TECHNIQUE TO USE FOR A PROCESS?

Structured English is the preferred choice for all process descriptions. The mechanics of using a CASE tool or preparing process descriptions by a word processor dictate that process descriptions be prepared in a format suitable

FIGURE 11-24   The decision tree for the tuition charge policy

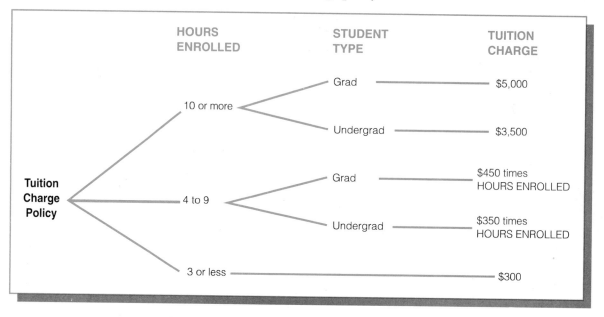

for typing on a screen or paper. However, we also know that the proper use of decision tables ensures that all possible combinations of conditions will be linked with appropriate actions. If any combination of conditions has been omitted, the omission can be detected by the use of a decision table. Decision tables remain a valuable mode for documenting a process even though only some CASE tools offer the means to enter them in the project dictionary. The entry in an automated project dictionary could state that the process has been described by a manually prepared decision table. Because decision tables may be prepared by a typist, they remain a viable choice for process descriptions.

Since we know that "a picture is worth a thousand words," we cannot lightly dismiss decision trees from our choices for process descriptions. The pictorial statement of a decision tree allows the viewer to easily understand the internal workings of a process. Research by Vessey and Weber [1985] has shown that programming code is more efficiently written if the specifications were expressed by a decision tree rather than a decision table or structured English. Consequently, the hand-drawn decision tree is useful and should be retained with the project documentation. However, with a CASE tool the process description should be prepared in structured English for entry into the project dictionary or else an appropriate reference to the decision tree documentation should be made. The descriptive method should be selected according to the structure of the process and the preference of the systems analyst.

PROCESS DESCRIPTIONS IN EXCELERATOR

In this section, we will explain how to enter process descriptions into the project dictionary in Excelerator. As with the data dictionary, there are two ways of placing process descriptions into the project dictionary:

1. Direct entry from the data flow diagram
2. Entry through the XLDICTIONARY module

Only the first approach will be explained here. Because of the difficulty in aligning the label field, it is preferable to label the process by means of the LABEL function available on the drawing screen for the data flow diagram. The process is then described by the use of the DESCRIBE function. Invoking the DESCRIBE feature causes a blank screen for the process to appear on the monitor. Figure 11-25 displays the screen for process 3.4.2, labeled COMPUTE SURCHARGE, already filled by the Excelerator user. Excelerator automatically places the process label COMPUTE SURCHARGE in the field Label, and shows the process number 3.4.2 across from the word Process on the screen's top line. The Type field has been filled by the analyst with the code PPS to indicate that the process will be described by a primitive process specification. The analyst has also placed the same label, COMPUTE SUR-CHARGE, in the Name field. The depression of the F3 key causes Excelerator to save the screen and return to the data flow diagram.

A second step is required in order to complete the process description. On the DFD drawing screen, the analyst must select the function EXPLODE from the list of available operations. The screen for the primitive process

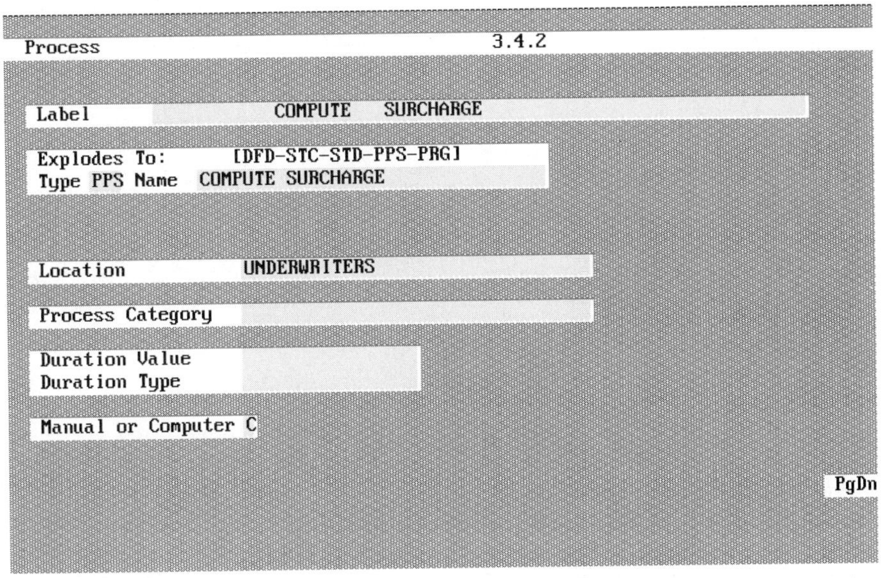

FIGURE 11-25

A completed Excelerator screen for the process COMPUTE SUR-CHARGE This screen results from the operation DESCRIBE.

Screen shots produced using INTERSOLV's Excelerator Solution for Requirements Analysis and System Design.

FIGURE 11-26

A completed Excelerator screen for the process 3.4.2   This screen is filled by the user after the function EXPLODE is called for the process COMPUTE SURCHARGE.

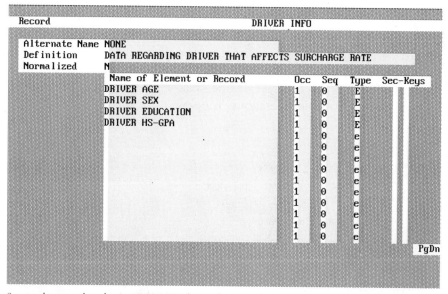

```
Primitive Process Specification                    COMPUTE SURCHARGE

            Inputs:                                   Outputs:
Type  Name                               Type  Name
REC DRIVER INFO                          ELE SURCHARGE



                         Process Description
SELECT APPROPRIATE CASE FOR SURCHARGE:
CASE 1.   (DRIVER AGE IS 25 OR OLDER):
          SURCHARGE IS ZERO.
CASE 2.   (DRIVER AGE IS LESS THAN 25 AND DRIVER SEX IS 'MALE' AND
          DRIVER EDUCATION IS 'YES' AND DRIVER HS-GPA IS 3.0 OR GREATER):
          SURCHARGE IS 10 PERCENT.
CASE 3.   (DRIVER AGE IS LESS THAN 25 AND DRIVER SEX IS 'MALE' AND

             Constants:
Type  Name



                                                                    PgDn
```

Screen shots produced using INTERSOLV's Excelerator solution for Requirements Analysis and System Design.

FIGURE 11-27

The data dictionary entry for the data record DRIVER INFO

```
Record                              DRIVER INFO

Alternate Name  NONE
Definition      DATA REGARDING DRIVER THAT AFFECTS SURCHARGE RATE
Normalized      N
              Name of Element or Record        Occ  Seq  Type  Sec-Keys
              DRIVER AGE                        1    0    E
              DRIVER SEX                        1    0    E
              DRIVER EDUCATION                  1    0    E
              DRIVER HS-GPA                     1    0    E
                                                1    0    e
                                                1    0    e
                                                1    0    e
                                                1    0    e
                                                1    0    e
                                                1    0    e
                                                1    0    e
                                                1    0    e
                                                1    0    e
                                                1    0    e
                                                                    PgDn
```

Screen shots produced using INTERSOLV's Excelerator solution for Requirements Analysis and System Design.

specification is then displayed on the monitor. The completed process description is given by Figure 11-26.* Excelerator automatically enters the contents of the Name field (not the Label field) from the previous DESCRIBE screen as the name of the Primitive Process Specification on the top line. The

---

*This screen format is associated with Excelerator, version 1.9. Version 1.8 does not include the areas for listing inputs, outputs, or constants.

inputs to the process are listed in the area labeled Inputs; either data record or element names are indicated, with the Type field given by the code REC or ELE, respectively. Since the process on the DFD has the input DRIVER INFO, comprising the four data elements, DRIVER AGE, DRIVER SEX, DRIVER EDUCATION, and DRIVER HS-GPA (see Figure 11-27), the input is specified as Type REC and the Name is DRIVER INFO. The outputs from the process are described in a similar fashion on the upper right of the screen. If more space is needed to list the inputs or outputs, the screen scrolls down. The entire process description is then typed in the area labeled Process Description. Once again, the screen scrolls if more space is needed. This screen is saved and exited by depressing the F3 key. You are reminded that only the bottom level processes are described by process descriptions. The processes on higher level DFDs—context level, level 1, and so on—are exploded into other DFDs.

Moving Government into the Computer Age

When building an information system, it is easy to simply duplicate the old way of doing business, with the clerks keying in data and the computer spewing out paper documents. The old system becomes the foundation for the new computerized system, and the same old paper documents are printed faster than ever. But the problems of the old system may not be overcome merely by turning it into a set of computer programs.

In Maryland, administrative costs for processing welfare checks rose to $5.10 per client under its traditionally structured computer system. Because of soaring costs, it was decided that a radical change in business operations was necessary. The solution was to change the way in which welfare payments were distributed to recipients.

In April 1993, all Maryland residents eligible for welfare and food stamps began to receive their benefits electronically, by drawing their allotments from 1,800 automated teller machines and point-of-sale terminals at 3,000 grocery stores across the state. This system of electronic benefits transfers nearly eliminates the proverbial "waste, fraud, and abuse" involved in mailing checks and food coupons to recipients. Officials expect the new system to save the state $1.2 million a year.

Even as Maryland became the first to rebuild its welfare system by using information technology, other states began moving towards new systems. The New Jersey Department of Motor Vehicle Services, for example, completed a pilot test of teller machines for vehicle registrations and plans statewide installation in late 1993. As we move toward the 21st century, government is reconsidering how to perform its basic functions by using electronic filing, kiosks for two-way data transfers, and the existing network of automated teller machines.

For more information, see Mitch Betts, "States Redefining Public Service," *Computerworld*, April 19, 1993, pp. 1, 20

Either structured English or decision tables may be entered as process descriptions in Excelerator; however, decision tables cannot be documented directly using the DESCRIBE and EXPLODE functions. Because decision trees are graphical, they cannot be entered directly into the Excelerator project dictionary. If you wish, decision tables and decision trees can be converted into equivalent statements in structured English and then entered as process descriptions. Since some CASE tools do not permit the entry of decision tables, the documentation of the particular CASE tool in use should be consulted.

SUMMARY

In this chapter, we discussed the description of processes by three methods: structured English, decision tables, and decision trees. The general format for each method was presented. The data elements, subrecords, and records referenced within a process description must be entries in the data dictionary associated with the data flow diagram. An example of determining the surcharge for an automobile insurance policy illustrated the use of each technique.

Structured English is the most popular technique for describing processes. As its name implies, English words are used within a structured form. The vocabulary of structured English is restricted to transitive verbs, data dictionary names, and conjunctions (such as If, Then, and Otherwise) defined for the language. To avoid the complexity of nested If statements, the Case statement should be used. Although decision tables and decision trees are most useful in describing processes with multiple conditions, they are not suitable for a project dictionary prepared by most CASE tools; some CASE tools, such as Excelerator, do provide for the entry of decision tables. However, decision tables and decision trees are helpful to the systems analyst in formulating the statement of the process; they can then be translated into structured English statements. The preparation of process descriptions in Excelerator is accomplished by either requesting a process description screen directly from the process on the data flow diagram or by entering the XLDICTIONARY module.

TERMS

action-entry quadrant	condition-stub quadrant
action-stub quadrant	decision tree
condition-entry quadrant	decision table

decision construct	procedure
extended entry table	process description
limited entry table	rule
mixed entry table	sequence construct
policy	structured English
primitive process	stub

QUESTIONS

1. What are the three ways of describing processes? Which is the most convenient method?

2. What are the advantages and disadvantages of each method used for process descriptions?

3. What is the preferred method for process descriptions entered into a project dictionary by means of a CASE tool? Why?

4. The Super Software Company has established the following guidelines for the payments made by customers:

    > If the payment is received within 10 days, the customer is given a 5% discount. The customer is also recorded as a good credit risk if the amount paid is more than $500 and the payment is received within 30 days. If the payment is received within 30 days, there is no penalty. If the payment is received after 30 days and within 60 days, there is a 3% penalty on the amount due. If the payment is received after 60 days but within 1 year and no special arrangements were made, there is a 10% penalty on the amount due. If the payment is received after 60 days but within 1 year and special arrangements were made with the chief financial officer, there is a 6% penalty on the amount due. If the payment is overdue more than 1 year, there is a 20% penalty on the amount due.

    Provide the algorithm for the company penalty policy for customer billing in three different representations:
    a. Structured English
    b. A decision table
    c. A decision tree

5. A tuition charge policy was displayed by a decision tree in Figure 11-24.
    a. Express this policy in structured English.
    b. Prepare the decision table for this policy.

6. The policy for the computer lab fees for undergraduate and graduate students in the College of Business Administration is stated as follows in the *Schedule of Courses*:

Computer lab fees for undergraduate students admitted to the College of Business Administration and graduate students in business will be:

Undergraduate Semester Hrs.	Graduate Semester Hrs.	Amount/Session
1–5	1–3	$15
6–11	4–8	$25
12 or more	9 or more	$35

The fee for nonbusiness (including prebusiness) students is $7 per business administration course taken, except for 6A:1, 6A:2, 6E:1, and 6E:2, for which no fee is assessed.

a. Prepare the decision tree to express this policy.

b. Express this policy in structured English.

c. Which method do you prefer for the description of this policy? Explain the reasons for your choice.

PROJECTS

1. Obtain the grading policy for one of your classes and express it as a policy in the form of structured English, a decision table, and a decision tree.

2. Call on the loan officer at a local bank and inquire about the policy for lending $1,000 to a customer. After you have learned the specifics of this policy, express this policy in three ways: structured English, a decision table, and a decision tree.

3. Visit the admissions office of your college and determine the policy for admitting students with regard to GPA, ACT or SAT scores, and high school standing. Create a decision table to denote this policy.

REFERENCES

DeMarco, Tom. *Structured Analysis and System Specification.* Englewood Cliffs, NJ: Prentice-Hall, 1979.

Excelerator Facilities and Functions Reference Guide. Cambridge, MA: Intersolv, 1990.

Excelerator Data and Reports Reference Guide. Cambridge, MA: Intersolv, 1990.

Excelerator Application Guide. Cambridge, MA: Intersolv, 1989.

Keller, Robert. *The Practice of Structured Analysis.* New York: Yourdon Press, 1983.

London, Keith R. *Decision Tables.* Princeton: Auerbach, 1972.

McDaniel, Herman. *An Introduction to Decision Logic Tables.* New York: Wiley, 1968.

Pollack, Solomon, Hicks, Harry T., Jr., and Harrison, William J. *Decision Tables: Theory and Practice.* New York: Wiley-Interscience, 1971.

Vessey, Iris, and Ron Weber. "Structured Tools and Conditional Logic: An Empirical Investigation." *Proceedings of the Sixth International Conference on Information Systems,* Indianapolis, IN, December 16–18, 1985.

The Design Phase

The Logical Representation of the Data: Two Models

Objectives

After completing this chapter, you will have a fundamental understanding of the method by which data are organized into files. The individual topics to be covered are:

- Organizing data according to the requirements of the relational model
- Drawing an entity-relationship diagram
- Using the entity-relationship diagram to organize data according to the specifications of the relational model

INTRODUCTION

In Chapter 10, we saw how data are documented in the data dictionary, which supports the data flow diagrams constituting the model of an information system. The data stores in the data flow diagrams for the system represent the data items that must be placed in computer files for the new information system. The first step in designing these files is to construct a data model that provides a logical view of the data rather than depicting the physical structures of the computer files, which will ultimately be placed in the computer's secondary storage such as disk storage or magnetic tape. The logical model of the data provides us with a data representation which can serve as the basis for designing the physical computer files. In addition to allowing us to understand the data and their relationships in order to design the appropriate data files, the logical data model enables us to delay the decision regarding the final physical representation of the data. The logical data model provides us with an abstract view that is divorced from any particular means of physically storing the data. This independence from a physical design allows us to define the data representation without restricting the final design to any particular physical implementation.

In this chapter, we discuss two popular data models: the *relational* model and the *entity-relationship* model. These two models complement each other. The relational model supplies a precise set of rules by which the data can be organized into two-dimensional tables called **relations**. Each row in the table represents a record and each column signifies a data field or data element (also called an *attribute*). The entire table is roughly equivalent to a file. The arrangement of the data elements into relations is performed according to certain formally defined constraints called *normal forms*. The resulting relations can be used as the basis for arranging the data into files, which must conform to other criteria such as hierarchical or network data base management systems. The topic of file design is covered in Chapter 13.

The second data model is the entity-relationship model. This model organizes the data according to two broad categories called *entities* and *relationships*. Entities are things about which data are collected. For example, in the payroll system, an employee is an entity about which we collect the data elements EMPLOYEE-ID, EMPLOYEE-NAME, EMPLOYEE-ADDRESS, and SALARY. A relationship is an association between two entities that is stated as either one to one, one to many, many to one, or many to many. For example, the relationship between the entities EMPLOYEE and DEPARTMENT is many to one because we have assumed that an employee is assigned to only one department in a firm, but a department has more than one employee. After the entities and relationships have been identified, a graphical representation of the data called an *entity-relationship diagram* is drawn. Although the entity-relationship model lacks the formal definitions of the relational model, the diagram produced by this technique is useful as an aid to the design of the data base.

To explain these two data models, the chapter has been organized as follows. The first section discusses the relational model and its guidelines for data organization. The second section describes the entity-relationship model. In the third section, we present a technique by which a set of data elements can be represented by an entity-relationship diagram and then organized in the format specified by the relational model. We now begin our discussion with a description of the relational model and the reasons for following its guidelines.

THE RELATIONAL MODEL

When designing the data files, the basic problem is to decide which data elements should be grouped together to form a file record in order to provide the best file structures for both current and future data processing needs. The relational model for data bases offers a set of specific rules that tell us exactly how to perform this organizational task. We note that the final design of the data files may be different because of the physical requirements for the hardware or software. By offering a logical representation of the data independent of any physical restrictions, the relational model provides a flexible structure to accommodate the physical design of the files later on. In order to understand why we follow the guidelines given by this model, we will explain two problems commonly encountered when organizing data into files: data redundancy and repeating groups.

Data redundancy means that the same data value for a data element will be stored more than once in the data base. For example, if a data element such as CUSTOMER ADDRESS occurs in several different files, all these files must be modified whenever a customer's address changes. Too often, some files are updated at once while others are not updated until a later time. This leads to inconsistencies in the data and confusion in the use of the data records. Because the data value exists in multiple locations, control over the information is diminished. Thus, a primary objective is to organize the data so as to minimize or eliminate data redundancy. Avoiding redundancy means that the modification of a data value will require a minimum number of updating operations to alter the value throughout the data base.

To avoid redundancy of data, we wish to create the file record design so that the value of a specific data element does not require duplication within the same data file or in other files. For example, as shown in Figure 12-1a, the order form for a product includes information regarding the product's description and price. Because any product may be ordered by more than one customer, the product's description and price are likely to appear on many order forms. If each order form represents a record on the ORDER file, then redundant data will stored on the file. If the product's description or price changes, we must locate every order for this product and alter the data appropriately. Instead, if we store this product information only once in

FIGURE 12-1   **The representation of the order form as a set of data elements**

a. The data elements on the order form

b. The abstract representation of the data values on the order form

ORDER NO. 1234	DATE	12/20/93

ORDERED BY:	Bays Produce Co.
	1811 DeForest Avenue
	Chicago, IL 60612

CUSTOMER ID:	33091

Qty Ordered	Product No.	Description	Price
25	067809A	mixers	$ 10.95
25	010523C	balers	$ 22.95

ORDER-NUMBER

ORDER-DATE

CUSTOMER-ID

CUSTOMER-NAME

CUSTOMER-ADDRESS

ORDER-LINE (repeated 9 times)

    PRODUCT-#

    PRODUCT-DESCRIPTION

    PRODUCT-PRICE

    QTY-ORDERED

a separate file, only one data record must be modified in order to change the description or price of a product.

When the product information does not exist on a separate file, two other problems also occur. First, if a particular product has not been ordered by a customer, the information regarding its description and price simply disappears; it is not available on any other file. Second, if we wish to describe a new product that has not yet been ordered by a customer, we are unable to do so. Since no customer has ordered the new product, the product information cannot be retained in the computer file. These two problems are called *modification anomalies*, because when the data are modified, irregularities may occur.

Another problem with files is how to treat **repeating groups**, that is, groups of data elements that occur more than once within each record on a file. For instance, if we choose to organize the data for the customer's order within one record type, the information on items ordered will be repeated several times within the record. For example, in Figure 12-1b, the data on the order form are displayed abstractly as a set of data elements. The order line is given as a repeating group consisting of PRODUCT-#, PRODUCT-DESCRIPTION, PRODUCT-PRICE, and QTY-ORDERED. Because of physical design constraints, we must decide how many times to repeat this information. Since the order form allows for nine lines, it makes sense to allocate storage space in the record type for nine groups of this data. But once this limit has been established, it is difficult—and sometimes almost impossible—to increase this dimension in order to store more data groups in the physical records representing the order forms. Whenever a repeating group occurs, the maximum number of occurrences becomes a restriction on further expansion. Hence, to provide for the uncertainties of the future, a common practice is to assign more space for repetitions than is actually needed at the time; this "wasted" space ensures that future expansion will be possible. Even with this extra allocation, changes in the future may cause serious problems with files designed in this fashion and the programs that process these files.

The relational model was designed to allow files to be structured so that these problems are avoided. A primary objective of the relational model is to formally specify the file structures so that redundancies are minimized and the number of repeating groups is unrestricted. This model also provides the greatest flexibility for the future, in case the firm decides to place additional data elements into its data base. In the past, the systems analyst who performed the file design drew on skills acquired through years of experience. Now the rules of the relational model give us a precise way of organizing the data into record types. To make our explanation of this procedure easier to understand, we have chosen to omit a detailed discussion of the concepts of the relational data model. Instead of using the specialized terminology of the relational model we will employ the generally accepted terms of record type and data element. A **record type** is a list of the data elements that comprise a file record. Because of this informality, some technical details may be imprecise; a more comprehensive treatment of this topic is provided by Date [1990].

In order to avoid modification anomalies and data inconsistencies, the data are transformed or normalized into record types according to the constraints called **normal forms**. A record type is said to be in a particular normal form if it satisfies the constraints for that normal form. The first step requires the data elements to be arranged according to the constraints for *first normal form*. The record type in first normal form is then transformed into progressively higher normal forms. The process of transformation is called **normalization**. There are five normal forms, known as first through fifth normal form, as well as the *domain-key* normal form. The original definition of third normal form has been essentially superseded by that for *Boyce–Codd* normal form. At any step in the normalization process, a record type may satisfy the constraints for all higher normal forms. For the practical purpose of organizing the data elements into record types, we need to deal with only the definitions for first, Boyce–Codd, and fourth normal forms.

Before discussing the definition of normal forms, let us consider the order form again by showing its representation as a set of normalized record types. In Figure 12-2, the data elements for the abstract representation of

FIGURE 12-2   The record types for an order form

a. The abstract representation of the
data elements on the order form

b. The group of data elements rearranged into
four record types called ORDER, CUSTOMER,
PRODUCT, and PRODUCT-ORDERED

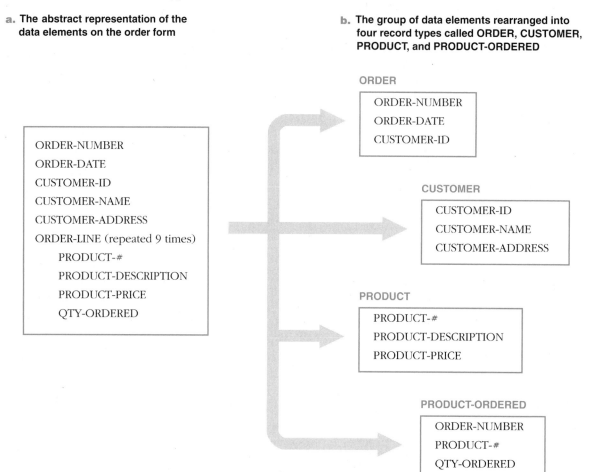

the order form are rearranged into four record types called ORDER, CUS-TOMER, PRODUCT, and PRODUCT-ORDERED. The repeating group has been eliminated. The product and quantity ordered for each order are now represented by the record type called PRODUCT-ORDERED. An order may list any number of products because there is no limitation on the number of times the record type PRODUCT-ORDERED may occur for each order. Thus, the group of data elements ORDER-NUMBER, PRODUCT-#, and QTY-ORDERED may be repeated as many times as necessary. The record design allows for the direct representation of as many requests for products as a customer wishes to order at any time. Since the data elements for the customer and the product have been placed into separate record types, the problems of data redundancy and modification anomalies have also been avoided.

Now we begin our explanation of normalization and the definition of normal forms. To illustrate the normalization process, we will examine the following set of data elements:

STUDENT-ID, STUDENT-NAME, STUDENT-HOME-ADDRESS,
STUDENT-CAMPUS-ADDRESS, MAJOR, STUDENT-ORGANIZATION,
COURSE-#, COURSE-TITLE, GRADE, INSTRUCTOR-SSN,
INSTRUCTOR-NAME, INSTRUCTOR-OFFICE, INSTRUCTOR-PHONE

For reference purposes, the sample set of data elements has been listed in
Figure 12-3. The relationships among the data elements are given by the
following statements.

Students may enroll in more than one course.

A course may have more than one student.

A student may have more than one major.

A course is taught by only one instructor.

An instructor may teach more than one course.

A student may receive a grade in a particular course only once; that is,
a second grade option is not permitted.

A student may join more than one student organization.

To illustrate the appearance of these data elements for actual values, several
occurrences of this sample group are displayed in Figure 12-4. Because of
space limitations, the data elements STUDENT-HOME-ADDRESS, STUDENT-
CAMPUS-ADDRESS, INSTRUCTOR-SSN, INSTRUCTOR-NAME, INSTRUCTOR-
OFFICE, and INSTRUCTOR-PHONE are not shown.

First Normal Form

The definition of first normal form is given in the box.

Definition: First Normal Form

A record type is in first normal form (1NF) when all occurrences
of the record type contain the same number of elements.

An *occurrence* of a record type is a set of values assigned to its data elements.
At this time, the *primary key* of the record type should be identified. The

---

STUDENT-ID	COURSE-TITLE
STUDENT-NAME	GRADE
STUDENT-HOME-ADDRESS	INSTRUCTOR-SSN
STUDENT-CAMPUS-ADDRESS	INSTRUCTOR-NAME
MAJOR	INSTRUCTOR-OFFICE
STUDENT-ORGANIZATION	INSTRUCTOR-PHONE
COURSE-#	

FIGURE 12-3

The sample set of data elements to be normalized

FIGURE 12-4   **Several occurrences of the sample set of data elements**

STUDENT-ID	STUDENT-NAME	MAJOR	STUDENT-ORGANIZATION	COURSE-#	COURSE-TITLE	GRADE	...
354899	White Curt	MIS	MIS ASSN	A022	ACCTG I	A−	...
		ACCTG		M001	Bus. Policy	A+	...
102893	Wong James	ACCTG	BETA ALPHA PHI	C098	COBOL	B+	...
			ACCTG ASSN	M001	Bus. Policy	C−	...
				A022	ACCTG I	B−	...
178903	Dias Anna	MIS	MIS ASSN	A022	ACCTG I	A	...
			STUDENT COUNCIL REP	C098	COBOL	B+	...
			INTERNATIONAL CLUB	L002	Bus. Law	B	...
			STUDENT SERVICE ORG.	M001	Bus. Policy	A−	...

primary key is the minimal set of elements that uniquely identifies each record occurrence. In other words, given the value of the primary key, the values of all the other data elements in a record are explicitly known with only single values. For example, the social security number of an employee unequivocally identifies the name, address, and other pertinent data for this employee. Consequently, the social security number is frequently selected as the primary key for this set of data elements.

To transform the sample set of data elements to first normal form, it is necessary to eliminate any repeating groups by duplicating data values. To meet this requirement, the values for the data elements are duplicated as necessary for each record occurrence. In order to preserve the relationship between the data elements, additional records may be required. Although the record type in first normal form contains much redundancy, further normalization arranges the data elements to eliminate this repetition of values. The record type in 1NF for this data sample is expressed as

FIRST   (<u>STUDENT-ID</u>, STUDENT-NAME, STUDENT-HOME-ADDRESS,
          STUDENT-CAMPUS-ADDRESS, <u>MAJOR</u>,
          <u>STUDENT-ORGANIZATION</u>, <u>COURSE-#</u>, COURSE-TITLE,
          GRADE, INSTRUCTOR-SSN, INSTRUCTOR-NAME,
          INSTRUCTOR-OFFICE, INSTRUCTOR-PHONE)

This record type has been named "FIRST" and the data elements comprising the primary key have been underlined. INSTRUCTOR-SSN is not included in the primary key because the value of COURSE-# will immediately determine the value of INSTRUCTOR-SSN and all the other data elements associated with INSTRUCTOR-SSN. The data element MAJOR is part of the primary key because there may be more than one value for MAJOR associated with any particular value of STUDENT-ID. Similarly, since the data element STUDENT-ORGANIZATION may have more than one value for any particular student, it also is included in the primary key. We also note that individual names may not be unique. Consequently, STUDENT-NAME is not a suitable choice for inclusion in the primary key. Because the primary key contains more than one data element, it is known as a *composite key*. Strictly speaking, the relational model states that the data elements MAJOR and STUDENT-ORGANIZATION should not be included in the primary key since their values may be null, for a student may not have selected a major area of study or belong to any student organization. We have chosen to violate this rule for two reasons:

1. The steps required for normalization become clearer to the novice.
2. The normalization process proceeds correctly despite their inclusion in the primary key.

Sometimes, there may exist more than one data element that is suitable for use as the primary key. For example, an organization may choose to assign a unique company identification number to each employee. Because social security numbers already exist, we now have a choice between the use of company identification numbers and social security numbers for the primary key. A data element or group of elements that is suitable for use as the primary key is known as a **candidate key**. The primary key for a record type is picked from the available candidate keys. As discussed earlier, a primary key may also be composed of a group of data elements; in this case, it is known as a **composite key**.

Boyce–Codd Normal Form

Because it is simpler, the normalization process can transform the 1NF record type directly to Boyce–Codd normal form without passing through the intermediary normal forms. In order to explain **Boyce–Codd normal form (BCNF)**, we will use the notions of *single-valued facts* and *determinants*. Y is a single-valued fact about X if there is one and only one value of

Y associated with each value of *X*. In this case, *X* is called a **determinant** of *Y*. For example, as shown in Figure 12-5, STUDENT-ID is a determinant of STUDENT-NAME because each value of STUDENT-ID is associated with exactly one value of STUDENT-NAME. As shown, the STUDENT-ID 354899 belongs to the student named Curt White. As we know, a person's name may not be unique. It is conceivable that the college population contains another student with the name Curt White, and a different value for STUDENT-ID must then be assigned to this student. Only one student can be assigned a particular value for the data element, STUDENT-ID.

The definition of Boyce–Codd normal form is given in the box.

Definition: **Boyce–Codd Normal Form**

A record type is in Boyce–Codd normal form (BCNF) if and only if every determinant is a candidate key.

The transformation of the 1NF record type FIRST to BCNF (and finally to 4NF) is shown in Figure 12-6. The method of obtaining the set of record types in BCNF is as follows. First, the data elements that are determined by any single data element are identified. It is easily seen that STUDENT-ID determines STUDENT-NAME, STUDENT-HOME-ADDRESS, and STUDENT-CAMPUS-ADDRESS. Thus, the record type R1 in BCNF is formed as

R1   (<u>STUDENT-ID</u>, STUDENT-NAME, STUDENT-HOME-ADDRESS,
       STUDENT-CAMPUS-ADDRESS)

Next, we see that the data element COURSE-# is the determinant for the elements COURSE-TITLE, INSTRUCTOR-SSN, and INSTRUCTOR-NAME. As

FIGURE 12-5

An example of a determinant

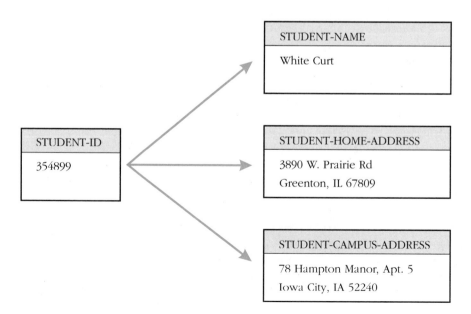

FIGURE 12-6 **The transformation of the 1NF record type to BCNF and then to 4NF**

First Normal Form	Boyce-Codd Normal Form		Fourth Normal Form
STUDENT-ID	STUDENT-ID		STUDENT-ID
STUDENT-NAME	STUDENT-NAME		STUDENT-NAME
STUDENT-HOME-ADDRESS	STUDENT-HOME-ADDRESS	SAME	STUDENT-HOME-ADDRESS
STUDENT-CAMPUS-ADDRESS	STUDENT-CAMPUS-ADDRESS		STUDENT-CAMPUS-ADDRESS
MAJOR	COURSE-#		COURSE-#
STUDENT-ORGANIZATION	COURSE-TITLE	SAME	COURSE-TITLE
COURSE-#	INSTRUCTOR-SSN		INSTRUCTOR-SSN
COURSE-TITLE	INSTRUCTOR-SSN		INSTRUCTOR-SSN
GRADE	INSTRUCTOR-NAME		INSTRUCTOR-NAME
INSTRUCTOR-SSN	INSTRUCTOR-OFFICE	SAME	INSTRUCTOR-OFFICE
INSTRUCTOR-NAME	INSTRUCTOR-PHONE		INSTRUCTOR-PHONE
INSTRUCTOR-OFFICE	STUDENT-ID		STUDENT-ID
INSTRUCTOR-PHONE	COURSE-#	SAME	COURSE-#
	GRADE		GRADE
	STUDENT-ID		STUDENT-ID
	MAJOR	SPLIT	MAJOR
	STUDENT-ORGANIZATION		STUDENT-ID
			STUDENT-ORGANIZATION

an interim step to BCNF record types, this observation yields the record type R2A:

R2A (COURSE-#, COURSE-TITLE, INSTRUCTOR-SSN,
INSTRUCTOR-NAME, INSTRUCTOR-OFFICE,
INSTRUCTOR-PHONE)

Each element in record type R2A must be checked to see if it is a determinant of other data elements. We observe that INSTRUCTOR-SSN determines the value of INSTRUCTOR-NAME; that is, if we know a value for the data element INSTRUCTOR-SSN, then the value of INSTRUCTOR-NAME is also known. Consequently, the record type R2A is decomposed into two record types in BCNF:

R2 (COURSE-#, COURSE-TITLE, INSTRUCTOR-SSN)

R3 (INSTRUCTOR-SSN, INSTRUCTOR-NAME, INSTRUCTOR-OFFICE,
INSTRUCTOR-PHONE)

The data element INSTRUCTOR-SSN is placed within record type R2 because it is necessary to know who teaches a course, that is, the INSTRUCTOR-SSN. Because INSTRUCTOR-SSN is the primary key for the record type R3 and also a nonkey element in the record type R2, it is called a **foreign**

key in R2. We will defer the discussion of foreign keys until the end of this section.

In a similar fashion, the record type R4 in BCNF is created as shown below:

R4   (<u>STUDENT-ID</u>, <u>COURSE-#</u>, GRADE)

Both data elements STUDENT-ID and COURSE-# are needed to determine a single value for the data element GRADE. If we choose to use only the data element STUDENT-ID, we will have a list of values for GRADE. We know this statement is true because each student may complete more than one course for which a grade will be assigned.

We now inspect the data element MAJOR, which was included in the primary key of the 1NF record type. Because each student may have more than one major, there is no determinant for the data element MAJOR. This is easily seen by testing whether the data element MAJOR can be placed within any other record type. A single value for MAJOR is not determined by any data element (in particular, it is not determined by STUDENT-ID). We also see that we cannot combine MAJOR with any other data element to serve as a determinant. However, we observe that, given any particular value for STUDENT-ID, multiple values for MAJOR could be associated with that value of STUDENT-ID. We say that MAJOR is a *multivalued* data element. Temporarily, we group MAJOR and STUDENT-ID together to form the record type R-TEMP:

R-TEMP   (<u>STUDENT-ID</u>, <u>MAJOR</u>)

Both data elements must form a composite key since no determinant exists.

The data element STUDENT-ORGANIZATION is also multivalued. Since each student may join more than one student organization, there is no determinant for the data element STUDENT-ORGANIZATION. Similarly, the multiple values of STUDENT-ORGANIZATION are associated with a single value of STUDENT-ID. Consequently, we place the element STUDENT-ORGANIZATION into the same record type as STUDENT-ID and MAJOR, to obtain the record type R5 in BCNF:

R5   (<u>STUDENT-ID</u>, <u>MAJOR</u>, <u>STUDENT-ORGANIZATION</u>)

As mentioned earlier, the incorporation of foreign keys within a record type provides the link between the record types that are logically associated with each other. The placement of foreign keys within a record type is defined in the following way. After the record types have been decomposed to BCNF, inspect the relationships among all the primary keys specified for the BCNF record types and determine the foreign keys. To make this procedure clearer, we show a list of three record types in Figure 12-7. What can we say about the relationships among their primary keys? If the primary key K1 of record type R determines the primary key K2 for record type S, then the data element K2 is placed as a foreign key into the record type R. We will

Unnormalized Record Types	Assumptions about the Primary Keys	Normalized Record Types
R (K1, . . .)	K1 determines K2	R (K1, . . . , K2)
S (K2, . . .)	none	same
T (K3, . . .)	K3 determines K1	T (K3, . . . , K1)

FIGURE 12-7

The identification of foreign keys

assume that K1 does, in fact, determine K2 and consequently have placed K2 as a foreign key in the record type R (column 3) of Figure 12-7. Next, we will examine the primary keys K1 and K3 to decide if K3 should be placed as a foreign key in record type R. This process continues until each pair of primary keys has been examined and the record types modified accordingly.

> ### Warning
> Foreign keys are sometimes confusing. Remember that a foreign key is a nonkey element in a record type that also acts as a primary key in another record type. A foreign key is essential for designating the relationship between two record types.

Fourth Normal Form

As shown by Wu's research [1992], the need to normalize to *fourth normal form* does occur in real-world data. Whenever a record type in BCNF has all its data elements in its primary key, further normalization to fourth normal form may be needed. The definition of **fourth normal form (4NF)** rests on our understanding of **independent multivalued facts**. We say that Y is a **multivalued fact** about X if, for any value of X, there may exist more than one value of Y. For example, a student may enroll in more than one course. This implies that the value for the data element STUDENT-ID may determine more than one value for the element COURSE-#. Conversely, we say that STUDENT-ID is a multivalued fact about COURSE-#. A multivalued fact is not necessarily independent. Informally, we say that a multivalued fact Y is independent if the value of Y is determined by the value of only a single element (or group of elements) and the values of any other elements are immaterial. For example, the multivalues for the element COURSE-# are said to be *multi-determined* by the value given in the data element STUDENT-ID, and the values of other elements such as STUDENT-HOME-ADDRESS or COURSE-TITLE are not needed.

Fourth normal form is designed to limit the number of multivalued facts in a record type. For all practical purposes, the definition of fourth normal form can be expressed as stated in the accompanying box. The formal definition of fourth normal form is more precise [Fagin, 1977].

Definition: **Fourth Normal Form**

A record type R is in fourth normal form (4NF) if R is in BCNF and contains at most one independent multivalued fact.

To illustrate the application of fourth normal form, consider the record type R5, presented earlier:

R5   (STUDENT-ID, MAJOR, STUDENT-ORGANIZATION)

We observe that both MAJOR and STUDENT-ORGANIZATION are independent multivalued facts about STUDENT-ID. Because the values of MAJOR associated with a particular STUDENT-ID are not required in order to find the values of STUDENT-ORGANIZATION associated with that student, the two data elements are independent of each other. In other words, if you tell us that the value of STUDENT-ID is 55609, then we can tell you the values of MAJOR and STUDENT-ORGANIZATION for this student. There is no need to first learn the values of MAJOR for student 55609 before finding the associated values for STUDENT-ORGANIZATION.

To obtain 4NF, the record type R5 is decomposed into two record types:

STUDENT-MAJOR   (STUDENT-ID, MAJOR)

STUDENT-ORG   (STUDENT-ID, STUDENT-ORGANIZATION)

It is important to note that some record types consisting only of keys do not require further normalization to 4NF. The factor of the *independence* of the data elements is crucial in deciding whether to split the BCNF record type in order to obtain record types in 4NF. An example of a BCNF record type that may already be in 4NF is

STUD-PROJECT-SKILL   (STUDENT-ID, PROJECT, SKILL)

We will make the following assumptions:

When a student is a member of a project team, we want to know what skills are used by the student during that project.

A student may work on more than one class project.

A class project is worked on by a team of students.

A student may possess more than one skill.

In this case, PROJECT and SKILL are not independent of each other. Since it has been decided to track which skills a student uses for each class project, there is a relationship between the data elements PROJECT and SKILL. Consequently, the record type STUD-PROJECT-SKILL is already in 4NF and requires no further normalization.

THE ENTITY-RELATIONSHIP DIAGRAM

The **entity-relationship diagram** is a graphical depiction of data entities and the relationships between them. A data flow diagram shows data moving through a system in order to portray how they are transformed by the system functions; that is, the data flow diagram shows data in motion. In contrast, the entity-relationship diagram displays data that exist within the data stores of the data flow diagram—data at rest. By diagramming the relationships between the data, we create a static model of the system. This model can also be used to design the data files for the new system.

The entity-relationship diagram serves three purposes. First, the diagram provides a logical data model, which is independent of the physical data files. Since this model does not impose any bias towards a particular physical organization, the designers gain the freedom to view all possible data structures without prejudice. Second, the entity-relationship diagram serves to show what the firm actually does. Although the diagram does not depict the processing performed by the system, the graph shows the links between the various entities about which data are collected. Because the entity-relationship diagram offers this top view of the organization, it is also called an *enterprise model.* Third, the set of record types in fourth normal form can be derived directly from the entity-relationship diagram by following well-specified rules, bypassing the traditional normalization procedure discussed earlier.

The Components of an Entity-Relationship Diagram

An entity-relationship diagram has three basic components:

Data entities

Relationships

Supertypes or subtypes

Before discussing these components, we will illustrate the diagramming technique by explaining the entity-relationship diagram given in Figure 12-8. This diagram shows the relationship between the data entities STUDENT, COURSE, INSTRUCTOR, ACADEMIC MAJOR, and CAMPUS ORGANIZATION. The relationships are represented by diamond-shaped symbols labeled with verbs or verbal phrases such as ENROLLS IN for the relationship between

FIGURE 12-8

The entity-relationship
diagram for the sample
data set

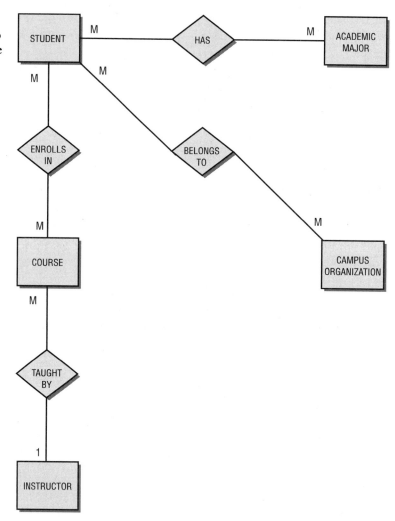

FIGURE 12-8

The entity-relationship
diagram for the sample
data set

the data entities STUDENT and COURSE. The diagram can be read from top
to bottom or left to right in the form of abbreviated sentences. For example, STUDENT ENROLLS IN COURSE forms a sentence and illustrates the
connection between STUDENT and COURSE. Similarly, the sentence that
describes the relationship between the data entities COURSE and
INSTRUCTOR reads: COURSE TAUGHT BY INSTRUCTOR. The remaining
two sentences in this diagram are STUDENT HAS ACADEMIC MAJOR and
STUDENT BELONGS TO CAMPUS ORGANIZATION. The labels M and 1
located near each data entity symbol supply further information about the
relationship between the data entities.

DATA ENTITIES

A data entity is represented by a rectangular box labeled with its name. In the
formal description of the model, this representation is known as an *object*

type. The object is the actual "thing" that exists in the material world, whereas the object type is the logical representation of the object. A **data entity** is a person, location, physical object, or event about which data are collected for the information system. Examples are employees, travel destinations, parts in a factory, and business trips. A group containing data entities of the same type is called an *entity class*. The same set of facts is collected about the entities within a data entity class; these are called the characteristics or *attributes* of the data entity. For example, the attributes for the entity class EMPLOYEE may be the employee's social security number, name, address, and phone.

The data entities shown on an entity-relationship diagram are not the same as the external entities shown on a data flow diagram. The word *entity* simply means *thing* and does not necessarily represent the external entities that appear on data flow diagrams. As you will recall, external entities are things that either send data to or receive data from the system. In contrast, data entities are things—persons, events, places, or objects—about which we collect data.

In the example discussed earlier, the students at a college constitute a single category (or class) about which data are collected. The college maintains files that contain names, addresses, telephone numbers, course enrollment listings, and other data items that pertain to students. The category of students is, thus, a data entity class which can be called STUDENT. In Figure 12-8, the data entity class has been indicated by the singular noun STUDENT, which designates its logical concept rather than its actual occurrences. An *occurrence* (or *instance*) of a data entity class is a physical object that is represented by the values of its attributes. For example, an occurrence of the data entity class STUDENT is given by the values for the data elements STUDENT-ID, STUDENT-NAME, STUDENT-HOME-ADDRESS, and any other data elements defining the entity STUDENT. Thus, the value of the data element STUDENT-ID, say 354899, indicates a particular student who actually exists in the real world; as shown in our sample data (Figure 12-4), this person is named Curt White. Henceforth, we will simply use the term *data entity* rather than data entity class.

To be included in the data model for the system, a data entity must fit two basic constraints. First, each data entity must be described by one or more data elements. For example, the data entity STUDENT is described by such data elements as STUDENT-ID, STUDENT-NAME, STUDENT-HOME-ADDRESS, and STUDENT-CAMPUS-ADDRESS. Second, the data entities shown on the entity-relationship diagram must be necessary for the information system under construction. For example, if we are building a student registration system, the data model will include the essential data entities but should not display any data entities outside the system. The data entity STUDENT is necessary for the student registration system for a college, whereas the payroll system requires information about the data entity EMPLOYEE but not the data entity STUDENT.

RELATIONSHIPS

A **relationship** is a logical association between two or more data entities. For example, a CUSTOMER places an ORDER, a STUDENT enrolls in a COURSE, an EMPLOYEE works for a DEPARTMENT. For the purpose of data modeling, the important fact about a relationship is the number of entities that are possible at either end of these statements. In other words, to know the relationship between CUSTOMER and ORDER, two questions must be answered:

1. A single customer is connected to how many orders?
2. A single order is connected to how many customers?

When answering these questions, we must answer in the broadest possible way. We want to know how many orders any customer could place rather than how many orders a particular customer places. By our knowledge of the world, we know that at any given time a customer may place many orders. But since a customer may still be a member of the category CUSTOMER and not currently have an order on file, a more precise description is "zero or more orders." The use of "zero" rather than "one" as the minimum ordinarily does not affect the final organization of the data elements. Consequently, we will ignore whether an optional data element is ("zero or more") and consider "zero or more" to be the same as "one or more." The answer of "zero or more" and "one or more" will be stated simply as "many." As an aside, we note that the computer program processing this data must be aware whether a data element is optional. Again, drawing on our knowledge of the real world, we determine the relationship between CUSTOMER and ORDER, namely, a single order is placed by one and only one customer. Consequently, we say that the degree of the relationship of CUSTOMER to ORDER is **one to many** (or **1:M**). Its converse is a **many to one** or **M:1** relationship. The relationships of **one to one** and **many to many** are defined in an analogous manner; they are written as **1:1** and **M:M** respectively.

Since the relationships between the data entities will determine how the data elements are organized into data files, it is very important that these relationships be accurately documented. In our earlier example about students, courses, and instructors, we hypothesized that a course will have only one instructor. In reality, a course may be taught by a team of instructors. But any change to this relationship alters how the relevant data elements will be organized into data files. For the purposes of our example, we will continue to ignore the real world and consider a course to be taught by only one instructor.

SUPERTYPES AND SUBTYPES

If the set of attributes for a data entity can differ, then the object type may be best represented by a **supertype** composed of **subtypes**. Consider a firm where the object type EMPLOYEE has these attributes:

EMPLOYEE-ID

EMPLOYEE-NAME

EMPLOYEE-ADDRESS

EMPLOYEE-SALARY

The firm wishes to maintain additional information on certain categories of employees. For instance, the firm wants to know which clerical staff members have typing skills, their speed of typing, and other data pertinent to its clerical personnel but not to other employees. For its engineers, the firm wants to track the professional licenses held by individual engineers, their membership in professional societies, and other information available only for this employee category. Rather than create three data entities called CLERICAL STAFF, ENGINEER, and OTHER EMPLOYEES, the entity-relationship model provides for the creation of a supertype called EMPLOYEE with two subtypes called CLERICAL STAFF MEMBER and ENGINEER. Since the category OTHER EMPLOYEES has no special data requirements, it does not constitute a subtype. The supertype EMPLOYEE is indicated by the addition of a diamond labeled TYPE; the subtypes are connected to this diamond, as shown in Figure 12-9.

The attributes of the entities in the supertype share the same characteristics. For example, each employee has the attributes of employee number, employee address, employee phone, and salary. The attributes of the subtypes differ. The clerical staff members have the attributes of typing speed, word processor mastery, and dictation capability while the engineers have the attributes of professional societies and engineering licenses. In addition to the record type for the supertype, separate record types will be created for each subtype.

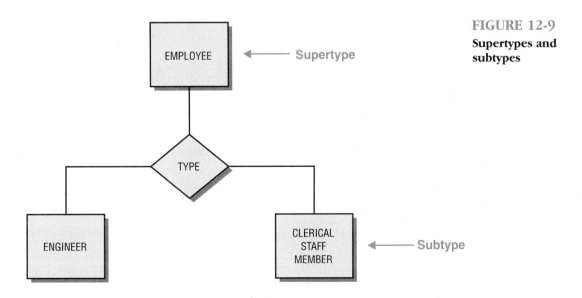

FIGURE 12-9
Supertypes and subtypes

SEVEN STEPS TO NORMALIZATION

If an entity-relationship diagram is drawn in a suitable fashion, it is possible to normalize the associated data elements to record types in 4NF by following precise steps. Since an entity-relationship diagram is now a popular method for modeling the system data, we recommend this approach to the problem of normalization. But how do we draw a suitable entity-relationship diagram? Since it is sometimes difficult to identify data entities and draw a correct diagram, a method based on the work of Teorey, Yang, and Fry [1986] has been developed to assist this process. After normalization has been performed, it is advisable to check the resulting record types against the formal definitions for BCNF and 4NF normal forms (presented in the first section).

There are seven steps to the normalization procedure described in this section. The outline of these seven steps appears in Figure 12-10. An entity-relationship diagram is the product of step 5. The sample set of data elements for the data entities student, course, and instructor will also be used to illustrate these steps (see Figure 12-3). The relationships assumed between the data elements are the same as stated earlier; for your convenience,

FIGURE 12-10   **The seven-step method for normalization**

Step 1   Divide the data elements into three columns.

Column 1	Determinants Only
Column 2	Data Elements Determined by the Determinants in Column 1
Column 3	Data Elements That Don't Belong in Either Column 1 or 2

Step 2   Reorganize the third column.
   a.   Identify the data elements that are determined by two or more determinants.
   b.   If a data element is not determined by any combination of data elements, consider it to be a determinant and place it in the first column.

Step 3   Name the data entities.

Step 4   Diagram the relationships between the data entities.

Step 5   Convert the diagram to an entity-relationship diagram.

Step 6   Create the unnormalized record types.

Step 7   Normalize the record types by applying the four rules.

FIGURE 12-11
The assumptions regarding the data entities

Students may enroll in more than one course.

A course may have more than one student.

A student may have more than one major.

A course is taught by only one instructor.

An instructor may teach more than one course.

A student may receive a grade in a particular course only once.

A student may join more than one student organization.

they have been summarized in Figure 12-11. There are also commonsense rules that are obvious; for example, a student organization may have more than one member. The seven steps are presented in the following sections.

Step 1: Divide the Data into Three Columns

In step 1, we take all the data elements and organize them into three columns according to the following rules:

Column	Contents
1	The determinants contained within the set of data elements
2	The data elements uniquely determined by each data element in column 1.
3	Any data elements not placed in the first two columns

The name of a data element can occur only once and will appear in only one of these columns.

As defined earlier, a determinant is a data element (or group of elements) whose value uniquely determines a single value for another data element. In step 1, we will only consider determinants that are single data elements. To find the determinants in a list of data elements, we examine the relationship between the value of a data element and the values of any associated data elements. Given any value of a determinant, the values of its associated data elements are uniquely determined and contain only single values. For example, STUDENT-ID is a determinant because if you provide any existing value for STUDENT-ID, we can immediately reply with a single set of values for the data elements STUDENT-NAME, STUDENT-HOME-ADDRESS, and STUDENT-CAMPUS-ADDRESS. However, the value of STUDENT-ID does not uniquely determine a single value for MAJOR, COURSE-#, GRADE, or INSTRUCTOR-SSN for every student. Some students have two academic majors, most take more than one course, and so on.

How many possible values of MAJOR, COURSE-#, GRADE, or INSTRUC-TOR-SSN can be associated with any particular value of STUDENT-ID? Although a student may not have a double major at present, a double major is possible. Another case is a student who has not yet selected a major area of study. Thus, for any particular student, either zero, one, or two values for the data element MAJOR will exist. Because a student may enroll in more than one course, multiple values are possible for COURSE-#. Multiple values are also possible for STUDENT-ORGANIZATION, GRADE, and INSTRUCTOR-SSN.

The execution of step 1 creates the table shown in Figure 12-12. Examining each data element in turn identifies three determinants: STUDENT-ID, COURSE-#, and INSTRUCTOR-SSN. These determinants are placed in the first column. The data elements associated with each determinant are written in the second column to correspond with their determinants. Because the data elements MAJOR, STUDENT-ORGANIZATION, and GRADE are not uniquely determined by any single data element, they appear in the third column. For now we disregard any relationship between two determinants; that situation will be handled by step 7.

Step 2: Reorganize the Third Column

In step 2, the data elements in column 3 are rearranged. Each data element is reviewed to see if it is determined by a combined group of data elements. If not, the data element is removed from column 3 and placed at the bottom of column 1; for the purposes of normalization, we view this data element as a determinant. If a data element is found to be determined by some com-

FIGURE 12-12   Step 1: The set of data elements organized according to determinants

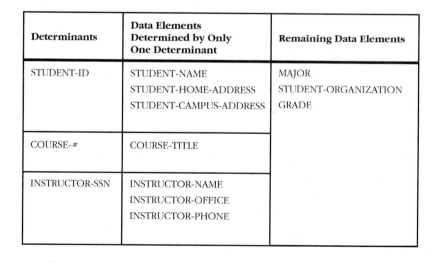

The Original Set of Data Elements
STUDENT-ID
STUDENT-NAME
STUDENT-HOME-ADDRESS
STUDENT-CAMPUS-ADDRESS
MAJOR
STUDENT-ORGANIZATION
COURSE-#
COURSE-TITLE
GRADE
INSTRUCTOR-SSN
INSTRUCTOR-NAME
INSTRUCTOR-OFFICE
INSTRUCTOR-PHONE

Determinants	**Data Elements Determined by Only One Determinant**	**Remaining Data Elements**
STUDENT-ID	STUDENT-NAME STUDENT-HOME-ADDRESS STUDENT-CAMPUS-ADDRESS	MAJOR STUDENT-ORGANIZATION GRADE
COURSE-#	COURSE-TITLE	
INSTRUCTOR-SSN	INSTRUCTOR-NAME INSTRUCTOR-OFFICE INSTRUCTOR-PHONE	

bination of determinants already listed in column 1, it remains in the third column, which is now renamed "Data Elements Determined by Multiple Determinants."

To illustrate this procedure, let us examine the data elements appearing in column 3 of Figure 12-12, in order to create the table shown in Figure 12-13. Because the data elements MAJOR, STUDENT-ORGANIZATION, and GRADE are not determined uniquely by any single data element given in the first column, they were put in column 3. Now we check to see if any combination of determinants will determine them. A simple way to start is to take all the determinants together to check if they can determine the value of the data element MAJOR. If they do, we then look for the minimum set of data elements that can serve as the determinant. Because MAJOR can have more than a single value for any particular student, we observe that it cannot be determined by any combination of data elements. Whenever a student has a double major, there will be two values for MAJOR. Thus, we remove MAJOR from column 3 and place it in column 1. A similar situation exists for STUDENT-ORGANIZATION and it, too, is relocated to column 1.

We continue by examining the data element GRADE. Although GRADE is not determined by any single determinant, it is uniquely determined by the combination of the data elements STUDENT-ID and COURSE-#. In fact, if we were to state how a grade is determined, we would say, "A student receives a grade in a particular course." We quickly spot the key words *student* and *course* and then simply need to identify these words in terms of the determinants listed in column 1. Neither the value of STUDENT-ID nor that of

FIGURE 12-13   **The modified list of determinants and nondeterminants**

Determinants	Data Elements Determined By Only One Determinant	Data Elements Determined By Multiple Determinants
STUDENT-ID	STUDENT-NAME STUDENT-HOME-ADDRESS STUDENT-CAMPUS-ADDRESS	GRADE (determined by STUDENT-ID and COURSE-#)
COURSE-#	COURSE-TITLE	
INSTRUCTOR-SSN	INSTRUCTOR-NAME INSTRUCTOR-OFFICE INSTRUCTOR-PHONE	
MAJOR	none	
STUDENT-ORGANIZATION	none	

COURSE-# alone will determine a single value for GRADE, because a student may enroll in more than one course. Similarly, the value for COURSE-# is associated with many values for GRADE. But we do know that a single value for GRADE is defined by any combination of valid values for STUDENT-ID and COURSE-#. We say that GRADE is dependent on the relationship between STUDENT-ID and COURSE-#. Thus, GRADE remains in column 3, which is now renamed as shown in Figure 12-13.

Step 3: Name the Data Entities

As we said earlier, a data entity is a person, location, physical object, or event about which we collect data. A determinant is a data element that uniquely denotes each occurrence of a data entity. For example, a particular value of the data element STUDENT-ID represents an individual student who has been assigned that value for his or her student identification number. We say that the particular student is an occurrence of the data entity class called STUDENT. The name of the data entity class is also used as the name of the data entity.

In step 3, we identify the data entities to be used in the entity-relationship model. In the table of Figure 12-13, each determinant and its associated data elements represent a data entity; only a data entity name is lacking. In Figure 12-14, we assign names to the data entities: STUDENT for the deter-

FIGURE 12-14   Step 3: The table of data entities and associated data

Data Entity	Determinant	Data Elements Determined By Only One Determinant	Data Elements Determined By Multiple Determinants
STUDENT	STUDENT-ID	STUDENT-NAME STUDENT-HOME-ADDRESS STUDENT-CAMPUS-ADDRESS	GRADE (determined by STUDENT-ID and COURSE-#)
COURSE	COURSE-#	COURSE-TITLE	
INSTRUCTOR	INSTRUCTOR-SSN	INSTRUCTOR-NAME INSTRUCTOR-OFFICE INSTRUCTOR-PHONE	
ACADEMIC MAJOR	MAJOR	none	
CAMPUS ORGANIZATION	STUDENT-ORGANIZATION	none	

minant STUDENT-ID, COURSE for the determinant COURSE-#, INSTRUC-TOR for the determinant INSTRUCTOR-SSN, ACADEMIC MAJOR for the determinant MAJOR, and CAMPUS ORGANIZATION for the determinant STUDENT-ORGANIZATION. Despite the lack of attributes for ACADEMIC MAJOR and CAMPUS ORGANIZATION, they will be regarded as data entities. Although it is possible to use the name of the determinant as the name of the data entity, choosing a different name prevents confusion. We also note that the data entities are named by singular nouns rather than plural nouns.

Step 4: Diagram the Relationships

In step 4, the relationships between the data entities are diagrammed in a manner very close to that of the entity-relationship diagram. First, for each data entity, we draw a rectangular box labeled with the data entity name. Second, we show the relationship between two data entities by drawing a line with arrows connecting the two boxes.

To determine the relationship between any two data entities X and Y, we ask two questions:

1. How many values of the determinant for data entity Y are associated with a single value of the determinant for the data entity X?
2. How many values of the determinant for data entity X are associated with a single value of the determinant for the data entity Y?

The answers to the above questions must be expressed as either ONE AND ONLY ONE or ONE OR MORE. For the purposes of normalization, the answers NONE OR AT MOST ONE and NONE OR POSSIBLY MORE THAN ONE are viewed as equivalent to ONE AND ONLY ONE and ONE OR MORE, respectively. If the answer is NONE AT ALL, there is no relationship between the two data entities. Otherwise, a double arrow is drawn for the relationship ONE OR MORE and a single arrow for the relationship ONE AND ONLY ONE.

Let us consider the data entities STUDENT and COURSE. The first question can be posed as a fill-in-the-blank statement:

A single value of STUDENT-ID is associated with _____ values of COURSE-#.

The answer is ONE OR MORE because a student may enroll in more than one course. Consequently, in Figure 12-15, a line is drawn from the box for STUDENT to the box for COURSE, and a double arrow pointing to COURSE is placed on this line.

Now the order of the sentence is reversed:

A single value of COURSE-# is associated with _____ values of STUDENT-ID.

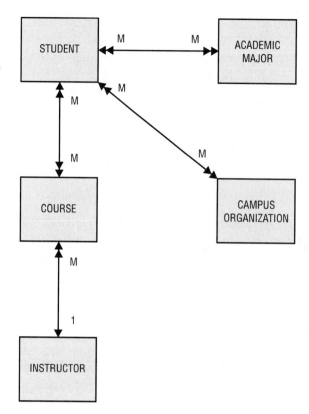

Because any course may enroll more than one student, the answer is ONE OR MORE. Thus, a double arrow pointing to STUDENT is drawn on the line connecting the data entities STUDENT and COURSE.

This procedure continues with the remaining combinations of data entities. Consider the entities COURSE and INSTRUCTOR. Because we assume each course is taught by only one instructor and each instructor may teach more than one course, the line connecting COURSE and INSTRUCTOR is drawn with a double arrow pointing to COURSE and a single arrow pointing to INSTRUCTOR.

We now examine the relationship between the data entities STUDENT and INSTRUCTOR. Because the box for STUDENT is connected to the box for COURSE and the COURSE box is already connected to the INSTRUCTOR box, the relationship between STUDENT and INSTRUCTOR has been given implicitly. It is not necessary to directly connect the data entities STUDENT and INSTRUCTOR.

From the assumptions regarding the data, we know that a student can have ONE OR MORE academic majors. To show this relationship a line is drawn from the STUDENT box to the ACADEMIC MAJOR box with a double arrow pointing to ACADEMIC MAJOR. We also know that each value for the determinant MAJOR may be identified with ONE OR MORE values for the determinant STUDENT-ID. Consequently, a double arrow pointing to the STUDENT box is drawn on the line to the ACADEMIC MAJOR box.

In Figure 12-15, the data entity ACADEMIC MAJOR is drawn to depict a relationship with only the data entity STUDENT. Although we can conjecture a relationship between COURSE and ACADEMIC MAJOR via STUDENT, we are not interested in this relationship. We also are aware that finding a relationship between INSTRUCTOR and ACADEMIC MAJOR serves no purpose. The relationship would be extremely remote. Although a student with a particular major will enroll in a course taught by an instructor, the instructor has no direct effect on the student's major; therefore no significant relationship exists between these two data entities. Our only concern is knowing which students have what major, and such remote relationships with other entities are not meaningful in the real world. Thus, the only line connecting the data entity ACADEMIC MAJOR to another data entity is the line to the data entity STUDENT. In a similar fashion, the data entity CAMPUS ORGANIZATION has only the many to many (M:M) relationship with the data entity STUDENT. In the diagram, a line with double arrows at both ends connects the two boxes labeled STUDENT and CAMPUS ORGANIZATION.

Finally, we label all the double arrows in Figure 12-15 with the letter M (for many) to indicate ONE OR MORE and the single arrow with the numeral 1 to indicate ONLY ONE. The relationship indicated by a set of two double arrows is called many to many (M:M); a double arrow and a single arrow indicates many to one (M:1); and two single arrows depict a one to one (1:1) relationship. The converse of an M:1 relationship is a 1:M (or one to many) relationship.

Step 5: Convert the Diagram to an Entity-Relationship Diagram

Step 5 performs a simple translation of the diagram drawn in step 4 to the conventional entity-relationship diagram displayed in Figure 12-16. First, a diamond is drawn on each line connecting two data entities. Then each diamond is labeled with a suitable verb to connect the names of the two data entities in a meaningful shorthand sentence. The sentences are read from left to right or from top to bottom. For example, we can use the words "enrolls in" to name the relationships between STUDENT and COURSE, forming the shorthand sentence STUDENT ENROLLS IN COURSE. ENROLLS IN is written within the diamond-shaped box as shown in Figure 12-16. Other words could be chosen, such as "takes" to obtain the sentence STUDENT TAKES COURSE.

The data entities COURSE and INSTRUCTOR are connected by the phrase TAUGHT BY. Either "has" or the phrase "has chosen" could serve to create a sentence between the data entities STUDENT and MAJOR. No verb or phrase is the sole correct choice. However, a verb or phrase should appear only once in the entity-relationship diagram. The single and double

FIGURE 12-16
Step 5: The entity-
relationship diagram

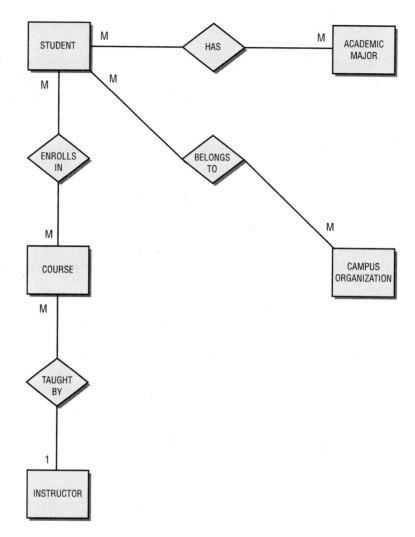

arrows of step 4 are removed from the connecting lines, but the symbols M and 1 remain on the diagram. The final diagram conforms to the conventions of an entity-relationship diagram. The alignment of lines and diamonds is comparable to that produced by the CASE tool Excelerator.

Step 6: Create Unnormalized Record Types

Before deriving the set of normalized record types, we first create an *unnormalized* record type for each data entity. First, the data entity name is used as the name of the record type. Then the data element name for its determinant and the associated data elements (column 3 of the table formed by step 3) are placed within parentheses; the element names are separated by commas. Because the determinant is the primary key for the record type, its name is underlined. The set of unnormalized record types for our example is created by using the table provided earlier in step 3 (see Figure

12-14). For example, the unnormalized record type associated with the data entity STUDENT is

STUDENT   (<u>STUDENT-ID</u>, STUDENT-NAME,
                    STUDENT-HOME-ADDRESS, STUDENT-CAMPUS-ADDRESS)

The entire set of unnormalized record types is displayed in Figure 12-17.

Step 7: Normalize the Record Types

To normalize the unnormalized record types created in step 6, we apply one of the four rules given in this section. The rule to be applied is selected according to the type of relationship between the two data entities shown on the entity-relationship diagram created in step 5. The application of the rules ensures that the relationship between data entities will be preserved either by inserting an additional data element into one of the unnormalized record types or by creating an entirely new record type. The proper application of the rules will result in a set of record types normalized to fourth normal form. The four rules for normalization follow.

Rule 1   If the relationship between two data entities is 1:1, place the primary key of the record type for one data entity into the record type for the other data entity. It does not matter which record type is used from the standpoint of normalizing the data.

Rule 2   If the relationship between two data entities is 1:M or M:1, place the primary key of the record type for the data entity on the 1 side into the record type for the data entity on the M side.

Rule 3   If the relationship between two data entities is M:M, their record types are already normalized. In addition, now create a new record type with its primary key composed of the determinants of the two data entities, and place any data elements that are determined by both determinants into this

STUDENT   (<u>STUDENT-ID</u>, STUDENT-NAME, STUDENT-
                    HOME-ADDRESS, STUDENT-CAMPUS-ADDRESS)

COURSE   (<u>COURSE-#</u>, COURSE-TITLE)

INSTRUCTOR   (<u>INSTRUCTOR-SSN</u>, INSTRUCTOR-NAME,
                    INSTRUCTOR-OFFICE, INSTRUCTOR-PHONE)

ACADEMIC MAJOR   (<u>MAJOR</u>)

CAMPUS ORGANIZATION   (<u>STUDENT-ORGANIZATION</u>)

FIGURE 12-17
Step 6: The set of un-normalized record types

new record type. The data elements to use for these new record types are found in column 4 of the table formed in step 3.

Rule 4   Discard any record type that contains only one data element. This data element has already been placed into another record type by one of the preceding rules.

THE NORMALIZATION PROCEDURE

To begin this process of normalization, the relationship between any two data entities is examined. To make this procedure clearer, we have created Figure 12-18 by placing the unnormalized record types adjacent to the data

FIGURE 12-18
The enhanced entity-relationship diagram
The unnormalized record types are displayed adjacent to the data entity types.

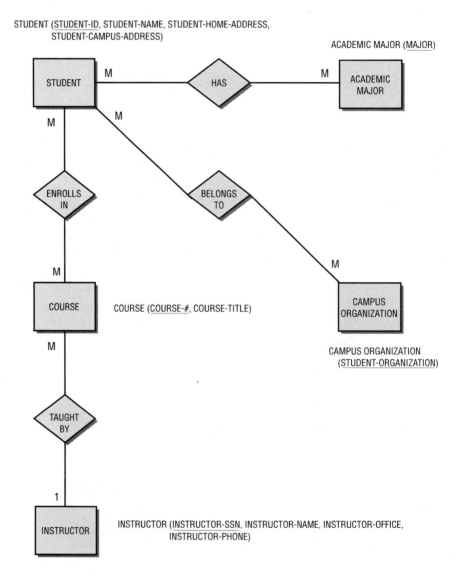

STUDENT (<u>STUDENT-ID</u>, STUDENT-NAME, STUDENT-HOME-ADDRESS, STUDENT-CAMPUS-ADDRESS)

ACADEMIC MAJOR (<u>MAJOR</u>)

COURSE (<u>COURSE-#</u>, COURSE-TITLE)

CAMPUS ORGANIZATION (<u>STUDENT-ORGANIZATION</u>)

INSTRUCTOR (<u>INSTRUCTOR-SSN</u>, INSTRUCTOR-NAME, INSTRUCTOR-OFFICE, INSTRUCTOR-PHONE)

entity types on the entity-relationship diagram created in step 5. Since the relationship between COURSE and INSTRUCTOR is M:1, Rule 2 is applied by placing the primary key for the record type INSTRUCTOR, that is, INSTRUC-TOR-SSN, into the record type for the data entity COURSE. In Figure 12-19, the unnormalized record type

COURSE   (<u>COURSE-#</u>, COURSE-TITLE)

has been transformed into the normalized record type

COURSE   (<u>COURSE-#</u>, COURSE-TITLE, INSTRUCTOR-SSN)

The relationship between the record types COURSE and INSTRUCTOR has been expressed by placing the data element INSTRUCTOR-SSN as a foreign key within the record type COURSE. Since INSTRUCTOR-SSN is not included in the primary key, it is not underlined. The so-called unnormalized record type for INSTRUCTOR is now considered normalized and, thus, it is now placed in the set of normalized record types.

STUDENT   (<u>STUDENT-ID</u>, STUDENT-NAME, STUDENT-
          HOME-ADDRESS, STUDENT CAMPUS-ADDRESS)

COURSE   (<u>COURSE-#</u>, COURSE-TITLE, INSTRUCTOR-SSN)

INSTRUCTOR   (<u>INSTRUCTOR-SSN</u>, INSTRUCTOR-NAME,
             INSTRUCTOR-OFFICE, INSTRUCTOR-PHONE)

ENROLLS IN   (<u>COURSE-#</u>, <u>STUDENT-ID</u>, GRADE)

HAS   (<u>STUDENT-ID</u>, <u>MAJOR</u>)

BELONGS TO   (<u>STUDENT-ID</u>, <u>STUDENT-ORGANIZATION</u>)

FIGURE 12-19

Step 7: The set of normalized record types

Next, we see that the relationship between STUDENT and COURSE is M:M. By the application of Rule 3, we place both record types STUDENT and COURSE (as modified earlier) in the set of normalized record types. In addition, Rule 3 requires that a new record type be formed with the name of the relationship as shown on the entity-relationship diagram. Thus, EN-ROLLS IN is used as the name of the new record type. Since the data element GRADE is determined by the two data elements STUDENT-ID and COURSE-#, as documented in Figure 12-14, the new record type is created as

ENROLLS IN   (<u>STUDENT-ID</u>, <u>COURSE-#</u>, GRADE)

Because the relationship between STUDENT and ACADEMIC MAJOR is M:M, by Rule 3 a new record type is formed. In this case, no data are determined by the determinants of STUDENT-ID and MAJOR. Thus, the new record type is given as

HAS   (<u>STUDENT-ID</u>, <u>MAJOR</u>)

Since the data element MAJOR has been placed within the new record type HAS, the record type ACADEMIC MAJOR serves no purpose and, by Rule 4, it is discarded. We say that the record type ACADEMIC MAJOR has been subsumed by the record type HAS. Similarly, by Rule 3, the relationship BELONGS TO between STUDENT and CAMPUS ORGANIZATION produces the normalized record type

BELONGS TO   (<u>STUDENT-ID</u>, <u>STUDENT-ORGANIZATION</u>)

By Rule 4, the unnormalized record type

CAMPUS ORGANIZATION   (<u>STUDENT-ORGANIZATION</u>)

is subsumed by the record type BELONGS TO.

Now that all the relationships have been examined and the appropriate rule applied in each case, normalization to fourth normal form has been accomplished. The complete set of record types is presented in Figure 12-19. To double-check that all the rules were followed correctly and no exceptional cases exist, the record types should be examined according to the formal rules for Boyce–Codd and fourth normal forms.

Additional Cases for the Procedure

Unfortunately, there are several situations not illustrated by our discussion of the seven-step normalization procedure. These special situations are covered next.

TWO OR MORE RELATIONSHIPS BETWEEN ENTITIES

Data entities often have more than one relationship existing between them. An example is the sale of an item to a customer and the return of an item by a customer. This is easily shown by drawing two relationships labeled SOLD TO and RETURNED BY between the entities STOCK ITEM and CUSTOMER (see Figure 12-20). Both relationships require the application of Rules 1 through 3 to form the normalized record types. Employing a prefix for the names of the data elements will ensure the uniqueness of the data element names. In this case, the data element CUSTOMER-ID may be called SOLD-TO-CUSTOMER-ID for the record type formed for the M:M relationship SOLD TO and RETURNED-CUSTOMER-ID for the record type formed for the M:M relationship RETURNED BY. Similarly, other data elements for the record types formed for the relationships SOLD TO and RETURNED BY should be prefixed by the appropriate word.

RECURSIVE RELATIONSHIP

A data entity may have a relationship to itself. An example is the representation of a manager who supervises employees. Because the manager is also

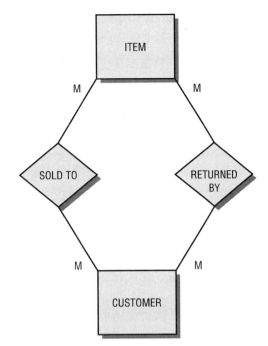

FIGURE 12-20

**An example of two re-
lationships between
two data entities**

an employee, this circular relationship is called *recursive*. Rather than diagram a **recursive relationship** and introduce additional rules for normalization, we can diagram it as a relationship between two distinct data entities,
that is, a **binary relationship**. Once again, unique names should be created
to handle the data elements properly. In this example, if the determinant is
called EMPLOYEE-ID for the data entity EMPLOYEE, the name MGR-EM-
PLOYEE-ID can be used for the determinant that corresponds to the data
entity MANAGER. This relationship is diagrammed in Figure 12-21.

TERNARY RELATIONSHIP

A **ternary relationship** occurs when three data entities are connected by
the same relationship. Whenever possible, the relationships should simply
be drawn as two binary relationships. However, if depicting a ternary relationship is really necessary, the three data entities are connected to the same
diamond-shaped symbol. A ternary relationship occurs only when the rela-

FIGURE 12-21

**The recursive relation-
ship for MANAGER and
EMPLOYEE** Diagrammed
as a binary relationship to
avoid the introduction of
additional rules for nor-
malization.

tionship between at least two of the data entities is many to many. Two types of ternary relationships are possible and each has its own normalization rule, as we see next.

Case 1   The relationships between the entities are all M:M. To normalize the unnormalized record types, form a new record type with the primary key consisting of the determinants of all three data entities. Place any data elements determined by all three determinants into this new record type. The so-called unnormalized record types for the three data entities are already normalized and are also included in the set of record types in 4NF.

Case 2   The relationships between two of the data entities are M:M and the remaining relationship is M:1. To normalize, form a new record type with the primary key consisting of the determinants of the data entities for the M:M relationship. Place the determinant of the data entity on the 1 side of the relationship into the new record type as a nonkey element. As in Case 1, the unnormalized record types for the three data entities are already normalized (unless the entities have additional relationships requiring the application of one of the four rules) and are included in the set of record types in 4NF.

An example of a ternary relationship is given by these statements:

A student may have more than one major.

For each major, the student has been assigned an advisor.

An advisor advises several students.

Because the data elements ADVISOR-ID, ADVISOR-NAME, and ADVISOR-PHONE will be stored in the data base, there exists the data entity called ADVISOR. This ternary relationship has been diagrammed in Figure 12-22. The unnormalized record types have been placed adjacent to the data entity symbols.

The record type formed for the ternary relationship appears as

STUDENT-MAJOR-ADVISOR   (<u>STUDENT-ID</u>, <u>MAJOR</u>, ADVISOR)

The record types for the data entities STUDENT and ADVISOR are also included in the set of normalized record types. The record type ACADEMIC-MAJOR has been subsumed because the data element MAJOR was placed within the newly created record type for the ternary relationship.

LACK OF A DETERMINANT FOR A DATA ENTITY

Sometimes a data entity is not identified by a determinant. If a determinant, that is, a primary key, cannot be found among the set of its associated data elements, or the so-called determinant is not truly unique, there are four possibilities: create a determinant, use a pseudo-determinant, include a time-stamp, or accept a nonunique determinant.

FIGURE 12-22   An example of a ternary relationship

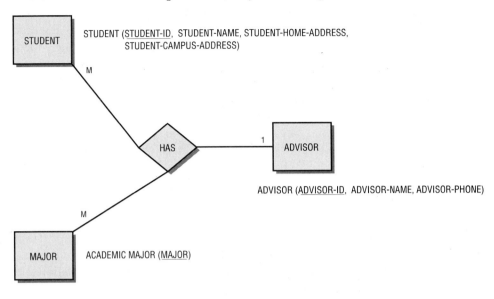

NORMALIZED RECORD TYPES

STUDENT (STUDENT-ID, STUDENT-NAME, STUDENT-HOME-ADDRESS, STUDENT-CAMPUS-ADDRESS)

ADVISOR (ADVISOR-ID, ADVISOR-NAME, ADVISOR-PHONE)

STUDENT-MAJOR-ADVISOR (STUDENT-ID, MAJOR, ADVISOR-ID)

Creation of a Determinant   Frequently, we simply choose to create a unique data element to serve as the determinant for the data elements collected about a data entity. Examples of such created determinants are the student identification numbers assigned by a college, the social security numbers obtained from the Social Security Administration, and the order numbers affixed to customer orders either by preprinted forms or by computer generated numbers. As we will see next, it is not always appropriate to create a new data element to identify a set of data elements for an entity.

Pseudo-Determinants   In other instances, a determinant really does not exist to uniquely identify the occurrence of a data entity. Instead, there may exist a data element that could almost function as a determinant because it can be combined with another data element to form a unique identifier. An example is a person's name. Because two or more persons with the same name may exist within any data entity class, the name of an individual is not an acceptable choice for the determinant of the data entity EMPLOYEE. Instead, firms typically use the employee's social security number or assign a payroll number to uniquely identify each employee.

In some cases, it is undesirable to create a new data element to serve as a determinant, so a **pseudo-determinant** is adopted. All relationships between a data entity with a pseudo-determinant must be given as many to many (M:M), because the pseudo-determinant alone does not uniquely identify the record type. The data elements "determined" by this pseudo-determinant belong to the relationships between the data entity using the pseudo-determinant and the other data entities.

To illustrate the case of a pseudo-determinant, consider how a firm might record the names of each employee's children. The relationship between an employee and an employee's child is, of course, one to many (1:M). We assume that all children of a particular employee bear different names within the family. To ensure a unique determinant for each employee, we assign an identification number to each employee. Because a person's name cannot be guaranteed to be unique, we know that a child's name cannot be used as a primary key. But creating unique identification numbers for each employee's child is impractical. Instead, we may choose to consider each child's name to be a pseudo-determinant. The relationship between the values of EMPLOYEE-ID and CHILD-NAME is now many to many rather than one to many, because the data entity CHILD lacks a unique determinant. If any information about each employee's child (such as the child's birth date) will be retained in the data base, this information is placed in the record type formed for the M:M relationship between EMPLOYEE and CHILD. The data entity CHILD does not have its own record type because

FIGURE 12-23   The use of a pseudo-determinant   Because the data entity CHILD lacks a determinant, the relationship between EMPLOYEE and CHILD must be given as many to many (M:M).

a. The Entity-Relationship Diagram

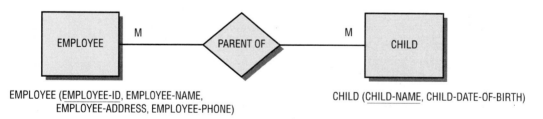

EMPLOYEE (EMPLOYEE-ID, EMPLOYEE-NAME,
        EMPLOYEE-ADDRESS, EMPLOYEE-PHONE)

CHILD (CHILD-NAME, CHILD-DATE-OF-BIRTH)

b. The Set of Normalized Record Types

EMPLOYEE (EMPLOYEE-ID, EMPLOYEE-NAME, EMPLOYEE-ADDRESS, EMPLOYEE-PHONE)

PARENT OF (EMPLOYEE-ID, CHILD-NAME, CHILD-DATE-OF-BIRTH)

Note: If the child's name is not unique within the family, the element
CHILD-DATE-OF-BIRTH must be included in the primary key.

there is no primary key for such a record type. The entity-relationship diagram and the set of normalized record types for these data elements is shown in Figure 12-23.

Time-Stamping   To obtain a unique identifier for a data entity, the inclusion of a **time-stamp** (the appropriate date and, if necessary, the clock time) may be desirable. For example, many colleges have second grade options. Consequently, the date enrolled in a particular course becomes a third data entity related to both COURSE and STUDENT. Any relationships with time—temporal relationships—may increase the complexity of the entity-relationship diagram. In general, the use of time-stamping will result in ternary relationships. A diagram showing time-stamping for the data entity COURSE is shown in Figure 12-24.

It is possible to avoid time-stamping by using a determinant that also uniquely identifies the date associated with the data entity. For example, the data entity ORDER could be assigned the determinant ORDER-NUMBER. In that case, the data element ORDER-DATE is determined by ORDER-NUMBER and time-stamping is not required.

ACCEPTANCE OF NONUNIQUE DETERMINANTS

Finally, in some isolated situations, it may not be possible to guarantee the uniqueness of the key, but the organization may still desire to organize the

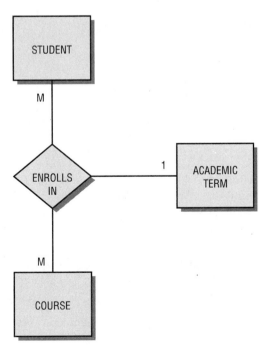

FIGURE 12-24
An entity-relationship diagram showing time-stamping

data in this way. Since the primary key for the record type will not be unique, great care must be taken to handle the data correctly. In essence, the entire set of data elements in the record type comprises the primary key. Since the uniqueness of the data record occurrences cannot be guaranteed, it is best to assign a unique identifier to each record. Otherwise, the rules for normalization are violated and the possibility exists of corrupting the data base by such practices.

Using the Seven-Step Method

Despite the simplicity of the seven-step method for normalization and for drawing the entity-relationship diagram, the analysis of real-world data is much more difficult. The systems analyst will be confronted by many more data elements as well as data entities with complex relationships. The meaning associated with each data element must be defined and the relationship between the data elements must be fully understood for the correct modeling of the data base. Consequently, the drawing of a real-world entity-relationship diagram may require several days rather than the hour spent to solve a textbook exercise.

During the construction of the data flow diagrams, the data stores were fully documented in the data dictionary. To begin the data modeling process, assemble all the data elements from the data stores and immediately arrange them into determinants and the elements determined, employing the format of the table created in the first step (see Figure 12-12). Before continuing with the data modeling, three actions are performed:

1. Remove any duplicate data elements.
2. As a general rule, remove any data elements that are computed from existing data elements.
3. Review the data element names and rename as needed.

Let us examine the reasons for each of these preliminary actions.

ACTION 1: REMOVE DUPLICATE ELEMENTS

If the same data element exists in more than one data store, remove the duplicates. However, do not remove any data elements that require renaming. For example, let us assume that the data element PRODUCT-ID appears in the data stores NEW ORDERS and BACKORDERED PRODUCTS. In this case, PRODUCT-ID really has two meanings. For the data store NEW ORDERS, PRODUCT-ID indicates a product ordered by the customer. But for the data store BACKORDERED PRODUCTS, PRODUCT-ID means a product that is on backorder from the supplier. When drawing the entity-relationship diagram, two M:M relationships between CUSTOMER and PRODUCT will be shown. With the seven-step method, step 3 requires giving the data element PRODUCT-ID, the determinant for PRODUCT, a unique name when it is placed in a record type specifically created for a relationship. Consequently, we will name two new data elements: ORDERED-PRODUCT-ID and BACKORDERED-PRODUCT-ID. The same prefixes are also placed on the other data elements in the record types associated with these two relationships. It is also possible that these two distinct data elements were created earlier, when the data elements were documented in the data dictionary.

ACTION 2: REMOVE COMPUTED VALUES

If a computed value is retained in the data base, any modification to the data means that the value must be recomputed and updated. If the values can be easily calculated, it is best to omit them from the files and compute them whenever they are retrieved. Having a program that alters data values but omits the updating of the computed values means the data base becomes flawed. For example, the grade point average of a student can be quickly computed each time a transcript is printed. Otherwise, the addition or alteration of a grade in a student's record will require both recomputing and updating the grade point average immediately.

ACTION 3: RENAME ANY ELEMENTS, IF NECESSARY

The data elements must be inspected to ensure that no two data elements have the same name but different meanings. For example, the element STUDENT-ADDRESS may appear in two different data stores but not have the same meaning in both stores. In the data store STUDENTS and the data store ENROLLED STUDENTS, does the data element STUDENT-ADDRESS mean the permanent address or the campus address? The definitions of the data elements must be checked to verify that they have the same meaning.

Data element names may also be erroneous if the same data item has two different names. Suppose the student's permanent address was named FAMILY-ADDRESS in the data store STUDENTS and PERMANENT-ADDRESS in the data store ENROLLED STUDENTS. Two data elements with identical meanings introduce inconsistencies into the data base. Consequently, we should rename the element FAMILY-ADDRESS as PERMANENT-ADDRESS in the data dictionary and place only this single data element in the data base. When more than one relationship exists between two data entities, the renaming of data elements is also necessary, as we discussed earlier.

A Real-World Example

To provide an example of a real-world data model, Figure 12-25 shows the entity-relationship diagram for a clinic that tests patients for hearing aids. The diagram shows several data entities and many relationships. The list of normalized record types is given by Figure 12-26. The data entity PATIENT

FIGURE 12-25   An example of a real-world data model   The entity-relationship diagram for a clinic that dispenses hearing aids to patients

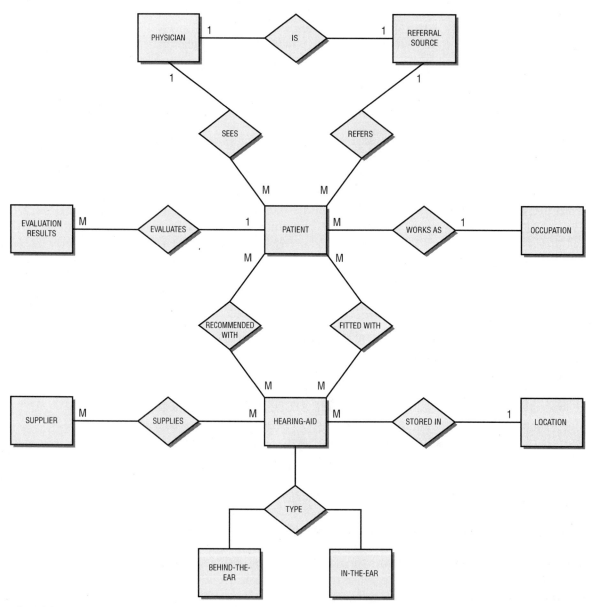

Adapted from From Robert Ngu, Master's Thesis, "A Logical Database Design Methodology Using the Extended Entity-Relationship and Relational Models," University of Iowa, August 1988, p. 99

is linked to HEARING-AID by two M:M relationships. The record type REC-OMMENDED WITH provides the information that the clinic recommended that a patient be fitted with a particular hearing aid. Over time, a patient may be seen by the physician several times and another type of hearing aid recommended for use, so the data element RECOMMENDED-DATE contains

FIGURE 12-26   **The set of normalized record types derived for the hearing aid clinic**

PATIENT   (<u>HOSPITAL-NUMBER</u>, REFERRAL-NAME, PATIENT-NAME, PATIENT-ADDRESS,
   PATIENT-PHONE, PATIENT-SSN, . . .)

PHYSICIAN   (<u>PHYSICIAN-NAME</u>, REFERRAL-NAME, PHYSICIAN-NAME, PHYSICIAN-OFFICE,
   PHYSICIAN-PHONE, SPECIALTY, . . .)

REFERRAL SOURCE   (<u>REFERRAL-NAME</u>, REFERRAL-ADDRESS, REFERRAL-PHONE, . . .)

EVALUATION RESULTS   (<u>EVALUATION-FORM-NUMBER</u>, HOSPITAL-NUMBER, DEAFNESS-
   LEVEL, DATE-SEEN, . . .)

SUPPLIER   (<u>SUPPLIER-NAME</u>, SUPPLIER-ADDRESS, SUPPLIER-PHONE, . . .)

CHARGES   (<u>CHARGE-FORM-NUMBER</u>, HOSPITAL-NUMBER, CONSULTATION,
   EVALUATION-DATE, . . .)

WORKS AS   (<u>HOSPITAL-NUMBER</u>, <u>TITLE</u>)

SUPPLIES   (<u>SUPPLIER-NAME</u>, <u>TYPE</u>, <u>MODEL</u>)

RECOMMENDED WITH   (<u>RECOMMENDED-HOSPITAL-NUMBER</u>, <u>RECOMMENDED-TYPE</u>,
   <u>RECOMMENDED-MODEL</u>, DATE-RECOMMENDED)

FITTED WITH   (<u>FITTED-HOSPITAL-NUMBER</u>, <u>FITTED-TYPE</u>, <u>FITTED-MODEL</u>,
   DATE-FITTED)

HEARING-AID   (<u>TYPE</u>, <u>MODEL</u>, ROOM, SHELF, COST, STOCK-COUNT, . . .)

BEHIND-THE-EAR   (<u>TYPE</u>, <u>MODEL</u>, DIRECT-INPUT, NOISE-SUPPRESSION, . . .)

IN-THE-EAR   (<u>TYPE</u>, <u>MODEL</u>, COMPRESSION, APPROPRIATE-TONE, . . .)

Note: Because the attributes of the entities LOCATION and OCCUPATION have been subsumed by other record
   types, they do not appear as normalized record types.

the date of recommendation for a particular hearing aid. A second record
type FITTED WITH furnishes the information regarding the actual hearing
aid fitted to the patient. Once again, the date of the fitting is needed as a data
element called DATE-FITTED. Since the behind-the ear and in-the-ear hearing aids have different characteristics and thus are associated with dissimilar
data elements, HEARING-AID is shown as a supertype with the subtypes
BEHIND-THE-EAR and IN-THE-EAR. The data design specifies two separate
record types, BEHIND-THE-EAR and IN-THE-EAR; otherwise, the use of a
single record type would mean that each record for a hearing aid would
contain several fields with no value because they pertain only to the other
type of hearing aid. It should also be noted that the data entity EVALUATION
RESULTS has been assigned a unique identifier, EVALUATION-FORM-NUM-
BER, to ensure that a single data element can be used as the primary key.

The Strength of the Data Base Structure

The importance of a system's data organization is highlighted by the example of the Royal Mail, the letter delivery branch of the British post office. Royal Mail required a complete overhaul of its payroll and personnel software to deal with its 160,000 employees across the country. Like many U.K. public agencies, Royal Mail was behind the times, lacking a centralized system. Instead, each of its 64 districts operated independently. Payroll and personnel systems were functioning separately on outdated computer equipment.

Processing requirements are very strict because most staff paychecks are issued for the current week rather than the week before. Personnel time sheets are completed on Monday for the pay run on Wednesday. John Harriman, project controller for the Royal Mail, decided that the data base structure would be crucial to a successful reform and chose a software package featuring a single relational data base design from a U.S. firm, Software 2000. By inputting data only once

and maintaining it in one place, the mail service could improve productivity and reduce duplication of effort. Additional computer programs were easily custom built by Royal Mail since Software 2000 features the flexibility needed for in-house application development. The U.S. software product had also been thoroughly translated to meet the requirements of the U.K. market.

Next year, the new system will be fully operational and Royal Mail expects a $14 million savings in administrative costs. It also expects a payback on the system in less than 3 years—well below the usual 5-year requirement in Great Britain. Since the relational structure of the data files offers great flexibility, it is anticipated that several million dollars in maintenance costs will also be saved.

Source: Black, George, "U.K.'s Royal Mail Boosts HR Efficiency," *Software Magazine*, April 1993, pp. 107–108. Reprinted with the permission of *Software Magazine*, Sentry Publishing Company, Inc., 1900 West Park Drive, Westborough MA 01581.

SUMMARY

The data elements for a proposed system are described in the data dictionary, which supports the logical model of the information system. Before designing the information system, the systems analyst must gain a complete understanding of the data and the relationships between the data elements. Two data models—the relational data model and the entity-relationship model—are used to define the data in a logical framework. By formulating a model of the data, the systems analyst produces a logical data design independent of its physical aspects. The data model then serves as the foundation for the physical design.

The relational data model offers precisely stated rules for the organization of the data into two-dimensional tables called relations. The logical description of a relation is also known as a record type. These constraints are specified by the definition of normal forms. Normalization can be performed by moving from first normal form (1NF) directly to Boyce–Codd normal form (BCNF) and then to fourth normal form (4NF).

The set of data elements is normalized to a record type in 1NF by (1) the elimination of any repeating groups by the simple duplication of these groups as many times as necessary, and (2) the identification of the primary key. A primary key is the minimal set of data elements that uniquely identify each record on a file. The definition of BCNF is based on the notion of single-valued facts. If Y is a single-valued fact about X, then X is called a determinant of Y. Any data element (or group of data elements) that could be chosen as the primary key is called a candidate key. A record type is in BCNF if every determinant is a candidate key. To achieve BCNF, the 1NF record type is decomposed into record types where every determinant is a candidate key.

If a record type is composed of only data elements forming a composite primary key, it may require further normalization to 4NF. A record type R is in 4NF if R is in BCNF and contains at most one independent multivalued fact.

The entity-relationship model depicts the data for an information system graphically by describing the system's data entities and the relationships between these data entities. The three components of an entity-relationship diagram are (1) data entities, (2) relationships between these entities, and (3) supertypes and subtypes. A data entity is an object about which data values are gathered. The relationships between data entities are defined by the maximum number of times a data entity is associated with another data entity. Relationships are described as one to one, one to many, many to one, and many to many.

A seven-step technique is presented to derive both an entity-relationship diagram and a set of normalized record types. Because real-world data are much more complex, several situations are not included in the seven-step procedure. These additional cases are: two or more relationships between data entities, recursive relationships, ternary relationships, and lack of a determinant for a data entity.

The chapter closes with a discussion of how to establish the set of data elements to be placed into the files for the new system. Duplicate data elements must be eliminated. Computed values, as a general rule, are not stored on data files and should be eliminated, too. A review of the data elements should verify that each data element is required and there is no confusion of names or definitions.

TERMS

binary relationship	primary key
candidate key	pseudo-determinant
composite key	record type
data entity	recursive relationship
data redundancy	relation
determinant	relationship
entity-relationship diagram	one to one (1:1)
foreign key	one to many (1:M)
independent multivalued fact	many to one (M:1)
multivalued fact	many to many (M:M)
normal forms	repeating groups
first normal form (1NF)	subtype
Boyce–Codd normal	supertype
form (BCNF)	ternary relationship
fourth normal form (4NF)	time-stamp
normalization	

QUESTIONS

1. Discuss the problems of file organization that led to the development of the relational data model.

2. Define the terms primary key, candidate key, and composite key.

3. Consider a list of data elements:

     PART-NUMBER

     PART-DESCRIPTION

     WHOLESALE-PRICE-OF-PART

     RETAIL-PRICE-OF-PART

    a. Name the data entity represented by these data elements.

    b. Given this set of data elements, what is the primary key? Why?

    c. If we place these data elements in a record type called RP, is the record type in first normal form? In Boyce–Codd normal form? In fourth normal form?

4. What is meant by the term determinant?

5. Define the terms data entity and relationship as applied to an entity-relationship diagram.

6. The State College wants to implement an information system to assign classrooms for scheduled courses. A classroom is defined to be a room within a campus building. A building contains many rooms that can be used as classrooms. A classroom is scheduled for a particular period designated by the time of day and the days of the week required for the class. All classes listed on the semester schedule of classes must have a classroom assigned.

a. Define the relationship between the data entities listed.

CLASSROOM and BUILDING

CLASSROOM and SCHEDULED COURSE

b. Draw an entity-relationship diagram showing only the three data entities CLASSROOM, BUILDING, and SCHEDULED COURSE.

7. A university's Division of Sponsored Research stores information about the grants offered by various private and governmental organizations. Each funding organization sends a document regarding each grant now being offered. On receipt of a document, a unique ten-digit number is assigned to the document. The document is then read by a clerk who assigns up to ten keywords to the document. A keyword is a 5-digit code. A description of up to 80 characters provides the meaning of each code. A list is also maintained of the faculty members who require information from the Division of Sponsored Research. Each professor has filled out a form listing his or her social security number, name, campus address, campus phone, and five keywords indicating research interests. The research interests are indicated by keyword codes, which are the same codes assigned to the documents.

The Division now wishes to define the data by creating a set of record types in fourth normal form. The data collected are

Faculty Social Security
    Number

Faculty Name

Faculty Campus Address

Faculty Campus Phone

Faculty Research Interests
    (given by keyword codes)

Document Identification
    Number

Document Title

Document Keywords
    (given by keyword codes)

Keyword Code

Keyword Description

Funding Organization Name

Funding Organization Address

Funding Organization Phone

Use the seven-step procedure to obtain the entity-relationship diagram and the set of record types in 4NF for this data base.

8. The TRY Yogurt Company sells many products. Each product is composed of several raw ingredients that are supplied by various vendors. A particular ingredient is always supplied by the same vendor; however, a vendor may supply more than one ingredient. The product line is divided up so that only one department is responsible for a particular

product. However, each department is responsible for more than one product. Each manager manages exactly one department. The following data fields must be stored in the TRY Yogurt Company's data base:

Product Number	Employee ID of the Manager
Product Name	Manager's Name
Ingredient Number	Department Identification Code
Ingredient Name	Department Name
Quantity of the ingredient required for each product	Department Office Address
	Department Phone Number
Vendor ID	
Vendor Name	
Vendor Address	

By using the seven-step procedure, derive the following models of the data:

a. The entity-relationship diagram

b. The set of record types in 4NF for this data base

PROJECTS

1. Visit a local business and obtain a copy of the various forms used to record information. Create an entity-relationship diagram for the data elements on only one of these forms. Then list the data elements as a set of record types in fourth normal form. If time permits, perform this exercise for each business form.

2. Arrange an appointment with the librarian at either the public library or a college library. Ask the librarian to explain the checkout procedure for books and the check-in procedure for returned books. Then prepare an entity-relationship diagram for the library system that records the loan and return of books. List the data elements that will be placed in the computer files for this system.

REFERENCES

Date C. J. *An Introduction to Database Systems*, 5th ed. Reading, MA: Addison-Wesley, 1990.

Fagin, Ronald. "Multivalued Dependencies and a New Normal Form for Relational Databases." *ACM Transactions on Database Systems* 2, 1977, pp. 262–278.

Kent, William. "A Simple Guide to Five Normal Forms in Relational Database Theory." *Communications of the ACM* 26(2), February 1983, pp. 120–125.

McFadden, Fred R., and Jeffrey A. Hoffer. *Data Base Management*, 2nd ed. Menlo Park, CA: Benjamin/Cummings, 1988.

Ngu, Robert. "A Logical Database Design Methodology Using the Extended Entity-Relationship Diagram and Relational Models." Master's thesis, University of Iowa, August 1988.

Teorey, T. J., D. Yang, and J. P. Fry. "A Logical Design Methodology for Relational Data Bases Using the Extended Entity-Relationship Model." *Computing Surveys* 18(2), June 1986, pp. 197–222.

Wu, Margaret S. "How to Normalize in Seven Easy Steps." *Proceedings of the International Academy for Information Management,* December 1989, pp. 290–305.

Wu, Margaret S. "The Practical Need for Fourth Normal Form." *Twenty-Third SIGCSE Technical Symposium on Computer Science Education—SIGCSE Bulletin* 24(1), March 1992, pp. 19–23.

CHAPTER 13

Design of Physical Files

Objectives

In this chapter, the techniques for designing the physical data files for an information system are presented. After completing this chapter, you will understand the following material:

- The types of computer files that may be created by an information system
- The specifications for physical records
- Three methods for physical file organization: sequential, indexed sequential, and direct
- The internal controls for computer files
- The trade-offs between the options available for physical file design

INTRODUCTION

This chapter deals with the physical design of the data files, rather than the logical design discussed in Chapter 12. *Logical design* covers the theoretical representation of the data. *Physical design* of data files means how the actual data will be organized on physical devices such as magnetic disk or tape. In this chapter, we show how the logical design of data is carried forward to create the structure of the computer files to be processed by the information system.

An information system can be divided into two components:

1. The processing to be performed
2. The data to be processed by the system

As we saw in Chapters 9 and 11, the processing component of the system is described by the data flow diagrams and process descriptions stored in the project dictionary. In Chapter 10 we explained how the second component, the data, is documented by the data dictionary. Which component is more important? Obviously, both parts are inextricably linked to form a whole unit, the information system. Processing performed without any data to be processed is, of course, an absurdity. But the heart of any information system is the files that contain the data to be processed by the system.

If the files are poorly organized without careful planning for the future, the performance of the information system will be inadequate. In the worst case, it may even be impossible to write the programs to perform the necessary processing because the file design is so inadequate. An example is the creation of a file where records are stored for retrieval in physical sequence, one after another. Suppose that the file design requires every record to be read, one after another, until the desired record is located. If the program is supposed to perform on-line processing, it must be able to retrieve records from the file in any order. Hence the system cannot be implemented with the chosen file design.

Once the files have been designed and stored on the physical computer devices, any change in the data organization is usually difficult and costly to implement. A change ripples through the system, causing modifications to many programs as well as other files. To correct mistakes, the files may need to be completely rewritten in new formats. Translating voluminous files into another format is time-consuming and expensive. Consequently, it is essential to understand the data fully, execute the logical data design, learn the processing requirements of the system, and only then proceed to design the physical files.

Before explaining how to produce a physical file design, we will discuss the technical concepts involved. This discussion includes the various types of files that may be required by an information system, the ways of retrieving data from files (called *access methods*), three file organization techniques, and the requirements for good physical design, including the issue of internal controls. The chapter closes with a presentation of ten steps for designing files. These steps will be illustrated by using the sample data set for students, courses, and instructors discussed in Chapter 12.

TECHNICAL CONCEPTS

Although some technical terms were explained in Chapter 12, they are repeated here for completeness. Because the technical concepts for file design are taught in other courses, only those concepts relevant to the system analyst's role in designing an information system are reviewed here. If additional information is required, a data base textbook such as McFadden and Hoffer [1991] should be consulted.

Fields

For most practical purposes, *field* has the same meaning as the term *data element* (defined in Chapter 10). In this chapter, we reserve the term field for our discussion of the physical file design and refer to the logical data unit as the *data element*. A **field** is the smallest named unit of data that has meaning. As shown in Figure 13-1, examples of fields are EMPLOYEE NUMBER, EMPLOYEE NAME, HOURLY WAGE, HOURS WORKED YTD (year-to-date), and SICK LEAVE YTD. Each field corresponds to a data element, with its length and data type defined by its data dictionary entry. However, the data type chosen for the data element may not be available in the programming language selected for the project. In that case, the field will be defined with a data type closely related to the data type designated by the data dictionary entry.

Employee Number	Employer Name	Hourly Wage	Hours Worked YTD	Sick Leave YTD
428728901	Chang, Amy Lou	8.75	160	0
478092314	Arnaz, Juan	9.50	240	5
479981560	Anderson, Joseph	9.50	98	0

FIGURE 13-1
Some examples of data fields

FIGURE 13-2
**The record type
EMPLOYEE**

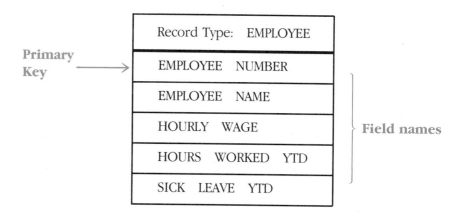

Records

A **logical record**, or simply *record*, is a named collection of data values that are grouped together to describe a particular object or entity. A **record type** is a list of the fields within the record. The physical organization of the data fields within each record is called the **record format**, or the *file format.* The record format includes a description of the length and data type of each field as well as its physical position within the record. For example, the employee number could be the first physical field of the EMPLOYEE record. The data fields within each record on the EMPLOYEE file are organized in the same way. An *occurrence* of a record is given by the set of values assigned to the fields within a record. For example, Figure 13-1 displays three occurrences of the record type EMPLOYEE that is documented in Figure 13-2. A **file** is a named collection of record occurrences with the same record type.

A **physical record** or **block** is the group of data written as a single data unit on a physical device such as a hard disk or magnetic tape. Because of the physical requirements of such devices, a physical record is followed by a blank area that marks the end of the block; this space is known as the **interrecord gap** or *interblock gap.* A physical record contains one or more logical records. The number of logical records placed within a single physical record is called the **blocking factor** for the file. Suppose each EMPLOYEE record contains 250 bytes; then we can group ten records together to form a physical record with 10 times 250 bytes, that is, 2,500 bytes. In this case, the blocking factor is defined as 10.

It is important to group logical records into physical records in order to improve the efficiency of the processing. Each access to the file storage device can then retrieve several logical records at once rather than only a single record. In addition, the amount of blank space forming the interrecord gaps is minimized by grouping the logical records in blocks. It would be most efficient for data transfer to and from the disk to set the blocking factor equal to the size of the entire disk track; however, the blocks transferred to or from the disk must be held in the computer's main memory. For that reason, the blocking factor chosen is usually ¼ or ⅓ of the maximum number of bytes on the disk track.

Subrecords

As you will recall from Chapter 10, a *subrecord* consists of two or more data fields grouped together. Besides data fields, a subrecord may also contain other subrecords; we say that these subrecords are *nested* within the first subrecord. Each nested subrecord is defined until the final group of nested subrecords has been described as containing only data fields. Defining a subrecord permits related data fields to be grouped together as a unit, in order to properly define the structure of the data record or just for convenience.

Keys

A **key** is a field that is used to retrieve the records from a file. There are two types of keys: primary and secondary. A *primary key* is a field (or group of fields) that uniquely identifies each record in a file. Regardless of the file organization method, using the value for a primary key ensures that one and only one record in the file will be retrieved. There may be more than one field (or group of fields) that could serve as the primary key for the file. If so, one field is selected as the primary key and the other possible fields are called *candidate keys.*

A **secondary key** is a field that may be used to retrieve from a file the group of records that share a common characteristic. More than one record may be retrieved for any given value of a secondary key. For example, if we wish to retrieve the records of all employees who are division managers, the secondary key will be the field called JOB-TYPE; multiple records will be retrieved—one record for each division manager presently employed.

File Storage Medium

The **file storage medium** is the secondary storage device on which the data file is stored. Two types of devices are commonly used for the storage of files: magnetic tape and magnetic disk. The latter device is further divided into hard disks and floppy disks. Magnetic tape offers the advantages of being a relatively inexpensive medium that can be easily extended to contain more data by adding another tape reel. Its primary disadvantage is that retrieving a record, say the 10,000th record, from a file requires the preceding 9,999 records to be physically passed over; not until the 10,000th one is reached can it be transferred into the main memory. In short, all data records must be read in physical sequence. The modification or deletion of any record means that the entire tape reel containing the record must be rewritten to another tape reel in order to obtain an updated file.

Magnetic disk is a more expensive medium (except for the low cost floppy disks) but offers the advantage of *direct access* (also called *random access*) to the data records. Instead of physically moving over all the data records on a file, we only need to know the address of the block (physical record) that contains the required data record. A disk unit is composed of one or more disks, which resemble phonograph platters. Each disk surface contains concentric circles called **tracks**, which constantly revolve under the read/write arms. A **cylinder** is a logical designation of all the tracks that have the same radius; they exist in layers above each other as shown in Figure 13-3. The access mechanism of the disk moves the arms from one cylinder to another. Because the movement of the arms is mechanical, it is much slower than the internal speed of the computer. Consequently, a primary objective of physical file design for disks with movable heads is to minimize arm movement. In order to achieve this objective, we store the data records for a file in cylinders located adjacent to each other and limit the number of accesses required for locating a record to as few cylinders as possible.

FIGURE 13-3
The physical characteristics of a disk unit

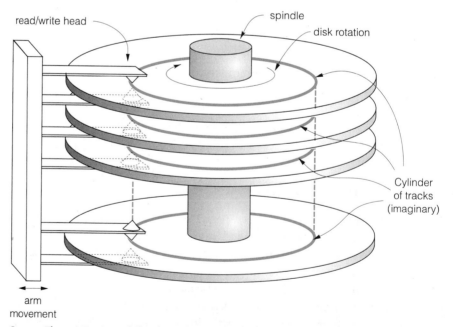

Source: Elmasri, Ramez and Shamkant B. Navathe, *Fundamentals of Database Systems.* Redwood City, CA: Benjamin/Cummings Publishing Co. 1989, p. 68. Reproduced by permission of Benjamin/Cummings Publishing Co.

Record Lengths

Two types of record lengths exist for files: *fixed length* and *variable length* record types. Unless an application has a compelling need for variable length records, fixed length records will be chosen for the file design. Each type is briefly described in the following sections.

FIXED LENGTH RECORDS

With a **fixed length record**, all records on the file have the same number of bytes. If a record contains any repeating groups, then the number of groups to be repeated is the same for all records. For example, in Figure 13-4, the analyst has decided that the vendor information for the product will occur exactly three times. For some products, there may be only one vendor. In that event, the record will contain blanks for the fields 9 through 14. Notice that there is no provision for storing information on a fourth vendor. If the firm decides that it must carry information on additional vendors for certain products, the entire physical file must be rewritten in order to create a file with a fixed length record large enough to contain the additional information. Programs that reference this file will also have to be modified in order to process the new file structure.

Field Number	Field Name
1	PRODUCT NUMBER
2	PRODUCT DESCRIPTION
3	QUANTITY IN HAND
4	QUANTITY ON ORDER
5	REORDER POINT
6	VENDOR NUMBER
7	VENDOR PRICE
8	VENDOR DISCOUNT QUANTITY
9–11	Repetition of Fields 6, 7, 8
12–14	Repetition of Fields 6, 7, 8

FIGURE 13-4

The fixed length record PRODUCT contains a repeating group for VENDOR INFORMATION. Fields 6, 7, and 8 are a repeating group that occurs three times. If only one or two vendors supply the product, the physical record will have blank spaces.

VARIABLE LENGTH RECORDS

A **variable length record** varies in the number of bytes that it may contain. Instead of allocating a fixed amount of storage space, the number of fields or the length of individual fields is allowed to vary. There are different ways of indicating the beginning and end of such variable groups of fields or individual field lengths. For example, if we want the number of vendors to vary for the record PRODUCT, we must somehow indicate how many times the three fields VENDOR NUMBER, VENDOR PRICE, and VENDOR DISCOUNT QUANTITY will occur. Thus, in Figure 13-5 we introduce a new field (field 6) that indicates the number of times the repeating group will occur. Although variable length records can be useful in certain circumstances, they are more difficult to process and are not supported by some software packages that perform file processing operations. Because of these constraints, only fixed length records will be discussed in this chapter.

File Access Methods

There are two types of **file access method**: *sequential* and *direct* (also known as *random access*). In **sequential access** a particular data record is retrieved by scanning the file from the beginning until the desired record is encountered. Sequential access is like searching for a word by reading a

FIGURE 13-5
The variable length record PRODUCT-V contains a repeating group for VENDOR INFORMATION. Fields 7, 8, and 9 are a repeating group that occurs a variable number of times. If five vendors are to be shown, the repeating group will occur five times.

Field Number	Field Name
1	PRODUCT NUMBER
2	PRODUCT DESCRIPTION
3	QUANTITY IN HAND
4	QUANTITY ON ORDER
5	REORDER POINT
6	Number of times that fields 7, 8, and 9 occur within this record
7	VENDOR NUMBER
8	VENDOR PRICE
9	VENDOR DISCOUNT QUANTITY

book from the first word on page one until the designated word turns up. To ensure efficient processing of a file using the sequential access method, we arrange the records on the file in ascending order by the primary key. Any data processing must then be executed according to this established pattern. For example, before updating a sequential access file, the desired modifications must first be placed in sequential order by primary key.

The **direct access** method can be compared to searching for a particular word in a book by using the index. To locate the term *data flow diagram*, we simply turn to the index of this book and find which page lists this term. Then we can open the book directly to the page rather than scanning the book from the beginning. However, we must still scan the page to locate the reference to the particular term. For files, the direct access of a specified record means that the address of the block holding the desired record can be somehow determined so that the file need not be read sequentially until the desired record appears. Instead, the block containing that particular record will be retrieved and scanned until the record is located. The direct access method can be used only for files placed on random access devices such as disks.

File Organization

File organization is the technique by which the data records are physically arranged on the storage medium. The ability to retrieve data records from the file efficiently and rapidly is directly related to how the records have been organized on the storage medium. The three most common file organizations are *sequential, direct*, and *indexed sequential*. Which type of file organization to choose is directly linked to the access method prescribed for data retrieval. We use either sequential or indexed sequential file organization if the records in the file will be retrieved sequentially—the first record of the file followed by the second record, and so on. We choose either indexed sequential or direct file organization if the file records will be retrieved at random—any record in the file followed by any other record.

SEQUENTIAL FILE ORGANIZATION

In **sequential file organization**, records are physically arranged on the storage medium, one record after another, so that they can be retrieved in the same way in which they were created. The first record written for the file is immediately followed by the second record written for the file, and so on. The efficient processing of records organized as a sequential file requires the records to be maintained in a particular sequence, such as ascending order by the primary key. If the data records are always processed in the same order as arranged in the file, sequential file organization is most suitable. Each record can be accessed only by reading all the records that physically precede it on the file storage medium. For example, to retrieve the record with the primary key 06891 in the file shown in Figure 13-6, it is

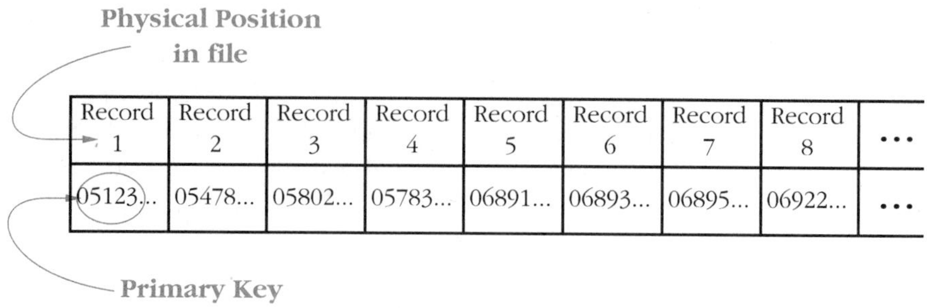

FIGURE 13-6

An example of a sequential file organization   The file is ordered by its primary key, PRODUCT-NUMBER.

necessary to physically pass over records 1 through 4. For recording data on magnetic tape, only sequential file organization is practical.

INDEXED SEQUENTIAL FILE ORGANIZATION

In **indexed sequential file organization**, the data records are written on the file storage medium in physical sequence according to the primary key. An index (or set of indexes) is maintained so that it is possible to retrieve any data record by its primary key without accessing other data records. Because the file is preserved in sequential order by primary key, it is also efficient to perform sequential processing of the data records. This type of file organization thus facilitates both sequential and random access of the data records.

The file systems called *Indexed Sequential Access Method* (ISAM) and *Virtual Sequential Access Method* (VSAM) implement the indexed sequential file organization method. The sequential ordering of the file records is maintained in somewhat different ways by ISAM and VSAM. A fundamental concern in using the technique of indexed sequential organization is how to deal with the addition and deletion of file records. Because existing records are modified and replaced into the same block on the disk by both ISAM and VSAM, modifications pose no difficulties in either file system. In ISAM, deleting a record is also accomplished within the same physical block by inserting a special symbol into the record to indicate its deletion from the file. To accommodate new records in ISAM some free space is left on each track, and occasional insertions can then be managed by placing them on the appropriate track. However, if a new record can no longer be accommodated in the track's allocated free space, it is written into one of the specially assigned overflow areas on other tracks. The retrieval of records from these extra overflow areas is slower because additional accesses to the disk are required to search these tracks. Periodic rewriting of the entire file is required to avoid lengthy retrieval times.

VSAM differs from ISAM in the handling of addition and deletion of records. A mechanism in VSAM automatically rewrites the portion of the file affected by either adding or deleting a record so that the records are always in sequential order on the disk. Since VSAM is constantly maintaining the indexes and the physical file arrangement, periodic rewriting of the file is unnecessary. Because of its design, VSAM also offers independence from the physical specifications of the hard disk. If an installation were to change hardware, the file could simply be rewritten on the new hard disk without altering the file's internal information that documents the arrangement of the data records. For these reasons, many firms prefer to use VSAM rather than ISAM.

To illustrate the indexed sequential file organization method, a simplified diagram of accessing a record is shown in Figure 13-7. Three indexes were built by the file system: a master index, a cylinder index, and a track index. Each entry in an index contains the highest key to be found in a physical location and a pointer to that disk location. A *pointer* is a data value associated with one piece of data used to identify the location of another piece of data. The file system is now requested to retrieve a record with the primary key of 610. First, the master index is read and the value 610 is compared to the list of keys. Since 1231 is the smallest value greater than 610, the pointer from 1231 is used to locate the cylinder index. Using this second index, since 812 is the smallest value greater than 610 the file system uses the pointer for the number 812 in order to obtain the proper track index. The track index contains the numbers 438, 667, and 812 together with

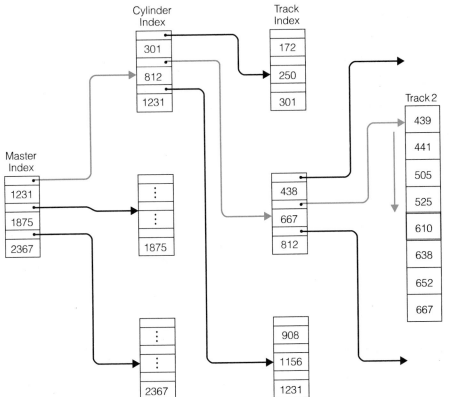

FIGURE 13-7

Indexed sequential file organization The record with primary key 610 is reached via the search path (shown in color) which moves through the three levels of indexes. For each index, the pointer for the least number that is also greater than 610 is followed to the next level. The final track is searched until the desired record is found.

Based on F. R. McFadden and J. A. Hoffer, *Data Base Management*, Menlo Park, CA: Benjamin/ Cummings, 1985, p. 103.

their corresponding pointers. Selecting the pointer for the number 667, the system locates track 2 and then searches the track to find the block containing the record with the key 610. By employing these three abbreviated indexes, the indexed sequential file technique reduces the time required to find each record. The addition and deletion of records is more complex. For more information, consult any data base textbook.

DIRECT FILE ORGANIZATION

In **direct file organization**, to retrieve or update a record requires just one access to the disk. For some applications, there is little or no need to retrieve records in sequential order, and the speed of retrieval is the most important factor in the physical file design. Airline reservations provide an example of an information system where it is crucial to retrieve information rapidly in order to answer questions from potential customers. In the 24 hours before a flight, an airline processes many cancellations and reservations. In the 1960s, as the number of flights increased, the airlines were confronted with a data processing problem that demanded a minimal response time. For such a system, both updating and retrieval are best accomplished in the direct mode. The need for multiple accesses to the disk to retrieve a record and the extra time required to maintain file records in sequential order make the indexed sequential method an unacceptable choice. Since the airlines need a way to retrieve any record as quickly as possible, direct file organization was chosen for the airline reservation system.

In order to reference any data record on the file directly, the system must quickly determine the disk address for the *bucket* containing that record. A **bucket** is a physical area that provides storage for one or more records. Since we are discussing the storage of records on a disk, a bucket represents a physical block on the disk. By a computational procedure, the primary key of a record is transformed into the relative address for its storage block; the computation is called **hashing**. Various methods (hashing routines) can be used to compute the *relative address* for a bucket. A **relative address** is a value that gives the position of a data unit relative to the first data unit in a data structure. The relative address is then used to compute the *physical address* of any data unit.

One popular hashing routine is the **division-remainder method**. First, we choose the number of buckets to be allocated to the file. Each bucket has one or more *slots* where records may be stored. Second, we pick a prime number such as 19 to be the divisor; then we divide the primary key of each record by this prime number. Each remainder is employed as the relative address of the bucket that will contain the record. By adding the disk address for the first bucket in the file to the remainder, we obtain the bucket address for the data record to be stored. Retrieval is performed in the same fashion. Once the bucket address is known, the bucket is retrieved and scanned for the desired record.

To demonstrate this division-remainder method, let us choose 19 as a divisor. For simplicity, assume that the file contains only 15 records and each bucket can hold only one record. At least 15 buckets must be allocated. For efficiency, it is best to allocate extra buckets so that no more than 80% of the storage space will be actually used. Consequently, we allocate 19 buckets to the file with relative addresses 0 to 18. To store a data record with a primary key of 1000, we compute the relative bucket address for this record: Dividing 1000 by 19 yields the value 52 and the remainder 12. The remainder becomes the bucket's relative address for this record (see Figure 13-8).

The problem with hashing arises from the number of buckets and their limited size. What if a new record has a primary key that "hashes" to a bucket already filled with records? Various solutions are possible. One solution is to

Relative Address	Bucket Contents
0	2755
1	
2	2529
3	
4	1904
5	4451
6	2381
7	
8	2060
9	1890
10	1663
11	
12	1000
13	2122
14	1705
15	
16	1764
17	2544
18	5281
Overflow Area	1894

Storage for record with primary key 1000

Pointer to overflow area

FIGURE 13-8

A hashed file with 19 buckets For this example, each bucket contains at most one record indicated only by its primary key. The record with primary key 1894 hashes to bucket 13, which is already filled.

place any records that do not fit into their assigned buckets (the *home buckets*) into a separate overflow area. A pointer placed in the home bucket indicates the overflow location for records unable to fit in the bucket. Judicious selection of the divisor and bucket size will keep the references to overflow areas at a minimum. The hashed file for a file containing only 15 records is shown in Figure 13-8. Each bucket contains at most one record and only the primary key has been displayed for each record. Some buckets are empty. Since the primary key 1894 hashes to bucket 13, which is already filled, the record is placed in the overflow area.

The hashing method offers the most rapid retrieval of records in a random pattern. The main disadvantage of the direct file organization method is that, because the records are stored randomly, it is inefficient to retrieve records in sequence by primary key.

Types of Files

The processing for an information system may require the use of different types of files. As listed in Figure 13-9, there are seven types of files: master files, transaction files, archive files, table files, intermediate files, log files, and backup files.

MASTER FILES

When a file contains data records that must be maintained for a long period of time, the file is known as a **master file**. Even though the data fields may change within individual records over time, the file is really a permanent register for this set of data. Examples of master files are: (1) a student file where each record contains information about an individual student such as name, address, and phone number; (2) an inventory file where each record includes the part number, quantity on hand, and quantity on order; and (3) a payroll file that stores each employee's social security number and current salary as well as other appropriate fields within each record.

FIGURE 13-9
Seven types of files

Master Files

Transaction Files

Archive Files

Table Files

Intermediate Files

Log Files

Backup Files

TRANSACTION FILES

The collection of data records indicating deletions, additions, and changes to data records in a file is called a **transaction file**. Each transaction record includes a field that designates the type of transaction to be performed by the data processing program. The transaction file is a temporary file that is retained for a period of time according to the policies of the computer center. To update a sequentially accessed file, the transaction file must be organized by the same key as the master file. For on-line processing, no formal transaction file exists. Instead, the modifications to the master file are stored in a separate file that serves as an audit trail of the transactions.

ARCHIVE FILES

In order to maintain an audit trail, the transaction records and the master records, prior to alteration by these transactions, are retained in off-line files known as **archive files**. These files are rarely changed. Subsequent analysis can be accomplished by using these historical records of modifications performed to the master files.

TABLE FILES

A **table file** is a file of tabular information such as code tables, tax tables, and other relatively permanent data. As we discussed in Chapter 10, data values in a field may exist in coded form. The codes and the code meanings for a coded data field are stored in a code table. An example of a table file is provided by a payroll system that must calculate the amount to deduct for FICA tax, state income tax, and federal income tax. Since these percentage amounts vary depending on the tax laws in effect, it is wise to place such information in a table file, which can then be referenced by the payroll program. Similarly, actuarial tables, student fees, and other semipermanent information can be placed in table files.

INTERMEDIATE FILES

It may be necessary or desirable to create temporary files that hold information only during program execution; we designate such a file as an **intermediate file** or *scratch file*. After the program has terminated, the file is no longer needed and the area on the file storage medium can be freed for other use.

LOG FILES

A **log file** is used to record modifications to master files. Prior to updating a record on the master file, we write the master record (the *Before* image) to the log file. After the update has been performed, the modified record (the *After* image) is also placed in the log file. The log file is then available to assist in data recovery operations if errors occur due to hardware or software failure.

BACKUP FILES

A **backup file** is a copy of a file that is essential for the successful operation of the information system. Backups of master files and transaction files are maintained so that, in the event of system failure, the duplicate file can be placed into service (but only after first being copied to create a new backup file). If the master file exists on magnetic tape, the file is copied after each update run. For on-line files, the file is written on magnetic tape periodically on an established backup schedule. Backups of transaction files are also maintained, so that an update processing run can be repeated, if necessary.

Backups should be retained according to the **grandparent-parent-child method**. As shown in Figure 13-10, the current file is always called the *child*. After the current file (file 1) has been updated, the new master file (file 2) is the new child file, and the previous master file (file 1) becomes the *parent* file. A second update transaction causes the *parent* file (file 1) to become the *grandparent* file, while file 2 becomes the *parent* file. The new master file (file 3) is now the *child* file. This backup scheme requires that the grandparent, parent, and child files for any master file be retained at all times. The transaction files applied to the grandparent, parent, and child files are also retained in case the now-obsolete files need to be updated.

In addition to the grandparent-parent-child scheme, copies of the current master file should be made. Typically, three copies of the master file are placed in storage. One copy is stored in an off-site secured location; this removal provides protection in the event of a disaster at the computer site. Although disasters are rare, it is best to be prepared for such occurrences.

On-line master files require a different solution to secure their information against loss due to hardware or software failure or natural disasters such as fire or earthquakes. Periodically, the entire file must be transferred (*dumped*) onto magnetic tape. Thereafter, the log file serves as the means to supply the master file with the updates performed since the master file copy was made. For on-line files, safeguards against disasters that might destroy the computer center require storing copies of the master file and log file off-site, a good distance away from the firm's locale. Should the off-site location suffer the same disaster, the computer records will not be recoverable. If the firm has more than one site, another approach is possible: Update the local computer files but also transmit the data for storage by the second computer. For example, after the 1989 earthquake, one San Francisco firm decided that it was essential to protect its data by electronically transmitting all data to a second site in the eastern United States.

FIGURE 13-10   **The grandparent-parent-child scheme for backup files**

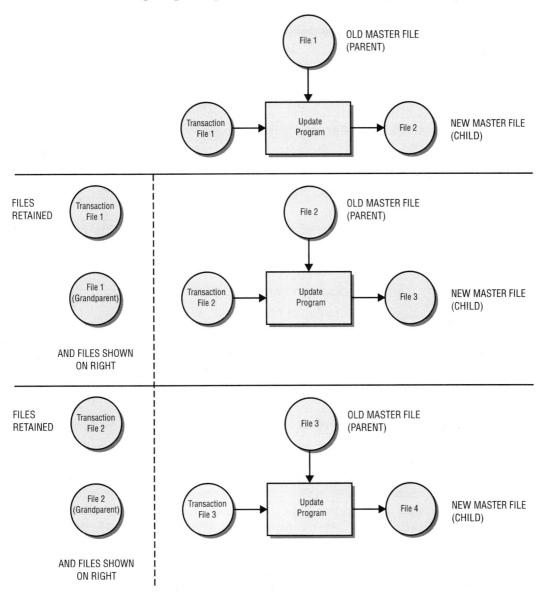

TEN STEPS FOR PHYSICAL FILE DESIGN

The ten steps outlined in Figure 13-11 are guidelines to the design of physical data files. Although each step will be discussed as a separate task, in reality an analyst considers the design issues for one step while making the decisions required in another step. The foundation for the physical file design is given by the data dictionary (see Chapter 10) and the logical data

FIGURE 13-11

Ten steps for physical file design

Step 1	Choose data base or conventional files
Step 2	Review the logical data design

Step 3	Specify the system requirements:
	    response time
	    future growth
	    type of processing required

Step 4	Define the files to be designed

Step 5	Describe the record layout:
	    variable or fixed length
	    data types and lengths
	Choose the blocking factor

Step 6	Select:
	    file access
	    file organization
	    storage medium

Step 7	Determine the file conversion procedures

Step 8	Design the file controls:
	    backups and backup storage site
	    log files
	    file recovery
	    security

Step 9	Choose the secondary keys for the files
Step 10	Compute the file storage requirements

structures (see Chapter 12). As we discuss the ten-step design of physical files for an information system, the sample data set for students, courses, instructors, and academic majors in Chapter 12 will be used here to illustrate the execution of these steps. To be more realistic, we have enlarged this data set to include the elements SESSION-DATE, DEPT-#, DEPARTMENT-NAME, and ASSIGNED-COURSE-# as shown in Figure 13-12. The actual set of data elements required for a student registration system would be much larger. For the purpose of understanding the basic concepts covered in the following material, this smaller subset is preferable.

Step 1: Choose Data Base or Conventional Files

Before embarking on the physical design of the computer files, the analyst must first answer a fundamental question: Should the system files be created for a data base management system or for a conventional file system? This

FIGURE 13-12   **The expanded sample data set**

Data Entity	Determinant	Data Elements Determined By Only One Determinant	Data Elements Determined By Multiple Determinants
Student	STUDENT-ID	STUDENT-NAME STUDENT-HOME-ADDRESS STUDENT-CAMPUS-ADDRESS	GRADE· (determined by STUDENT-ID, COURSE-#, and SESSION-DATE)
Course	COURSE-# (composed of DEPT-# and ASSIGNED-COURSE-#)	COURSE-TITLE	
Instructor	INSTRUCTOR-SSN	INSTRUCTOR-NAME INSTRUCTOR-OFFICE INSTRUCTOR-PHONE	
Academic Major	MAJOR	none	
Campus Organization	STUDENT-ORGANIZATION	none	
Academic Session	SESSION-DATE	none	
Department	DEPT-#	DEPARTMENT-NAME	

design decision cannot be made simply by examining the logical data design. The system processing requirements, the installation's standard operating procedures, and the available software all influence the analyst's recommendation. If a data base management system (DBMS) is already in use for other information systems, very likely this system, too, will be implemented with files placed within the data base. If no DBMS is in use, the analyst by now will have considered the possibility of acquiring such software and the trade-offs between a conventional file system and data base files.

A **data base** system provides many advantages not offered by a conventional file system. These benefits include the creation of data files that have minimal data redundancy, data consistency, and adherence to installation standards. Further, the data base allows for sharing data fields among various application systems without the necessity of creating additional computer files. However, the response time for the system could be slowed excessively because the program must request the DBMS to retrieve the data records from the data base before processing can be performed. The serious disadvantage of the high cost to purchase a DBMS and maintain it on a mainframe computer may also deter the analyst from recommending a data base system. Because the advantages of data base systems are significant, most firms will choose to establish a data base. For our sample data set, however, we will assume that a conventional file system will be used. Except for the handling of repeating fields, the discussion also applies to files designed for a relational data base system.

Step 2: Review the Logical Data Design

The analyst has already created the logical data design by producing the entity-relationship diagram and the set of normalized record types (Chapter 12). In step 2, the analyst reviews the logical data design prior to designing the physical files. At this point, it is still relatively easy to include new data elements and alter the design. But once the physical files are formulated and the programs written to process the data, changes will be extremely costly. Now is the time to modify the logical data design so that no mistakes are made in the physical file design. As shown in Figure 13-13, the entity-relationship diagram for the expanded sample data set contains seven entities and six relationships. The entity ACADEMIC SESSION, represented by the data element SESSION-DATE, was added to create a more realistic set of data elements. To avoid crossing lines, we draw the box for ACADEMIC SESSION twice on the diagram. In addition, Figure 13-12 now shows COURSE-# as a subrecord composed of two distinct data elements: DEPT-# and ASSIGNED-COURSE-#. (To avoid complexity, we have omitted the section number for a course offering from the sample set of data elements.) The revised set of normalized record types for the expanded sample data is displayed in Figure 13-14. The definition of each data element has been previously documented by an entry in the data dictionary. The data dictionary descriptions will be used in step 4 to formulate the record layout. The normalized record types are the basis for deciding which files to define in step 3 and how the record layouts should be specified in step 4.

Step 3: Specify the System Requirements

Before designing the physical files, the analyst must understand the system's requirements for processing, the future growth of the data files, and the relationship of this system to existing or projected information systems. Two basic aspects of the system processing are the *response time* and the *type of processing* required. **Response time** means how fast a system function can be performed; typically, the response time indicates how fast a record can be retrieved for on-line processing. Also involved is how quickly an on-line system can update a record after new data fields are entered by the operator.

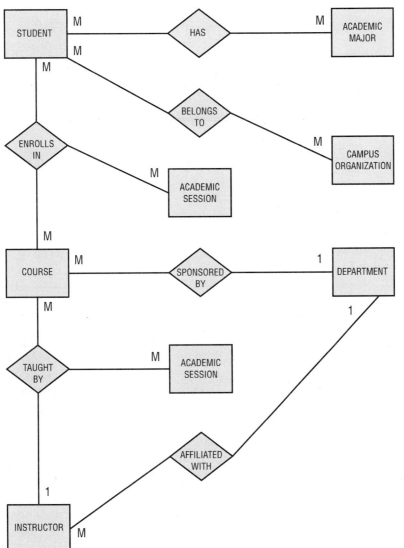

FIGURE 13-13
**The entity-relationship
diagram for the ex-
panded sample data set**

If the system is too slow in responding, the user will become frustrated. Often the user is addressing an inquiry from a person external to the system, so delays also frustrate anyone who interacts with the system. Unacceptable delays may cause loss of revenues, loss of customer goodwill, and higher processing costs due to employees obliged to wait idly for system responses and customers intolerant of these holdups. For batch systems, the total amount of time required for processing by a system executing in batch mode is considered to be its response time. In batch systems, response time can also be a matter for concern. For example, if it will take 24 hours to print paychecks for a firm, problems may be caused by the slow response time. The security necessary to safeguard the checks will be difficult to enforce for 24 hours, delays in printing may be excessive, and the computer hardware

FIGURE 13-14

The set of normalized record types for the expanded sample data set

STUDENT   (STUDENT-ID), STUDENT-NAME, STUDENT-
           HOME-ADDRESS, STUDENT-CAMPUS-ADDRESS)

COURSE   (COURSE-#*, COURSE-TITLE)

TAUGHT BY   (COURSE-#*, SESSION-DATE, INSTRUCTOR-SSN)

INSTRUCTOR   (INSTRUCTOR-SSN, INSTRUCTOR-NAME,
              INSTRUCTOR-OFFICE, INSTRUCTOR-PHONE,
              DEPT-#)

ENROLLS IN   (COURSE-#*, SESSION-DATE, STUDENT-ID,
              GRADE)

HAS   (STUDENT-ID, MAJOR)

BELONGS TO   (STUDENT-ID, STUDENT-ORGANIZATION)

DEPARTMENT   (DEPT-#, DEPARTMENT-NAME)

*COURSE-# is composed of the subfields DEPT-# and ASSIGNED-COURSE-#

may fail during such a lengthy run. The analyst must know what bounds are acceptable for the system's response time.

Next, the analyst must anticipate future growth of the file. The choice of file storage medium is influenced by the size of the file. A firm that decides to implement a system on a personal computer with only an 80-megabyte hard disk may be surprised to find that the data files grow rapidly and require much more space in only a year's time. Proper planning ensures that the file storage medium will be adequate for several years.

Finally, the analyst must be concerned with the relationship of the data elements required for the proposed system and those elements processed by the existing systems at the organization. Although the analyst has carefully documented the data elements in the data dictionary for the proposed system, the design of separate files for these data elements may be unnecessary or unwise. If a data base system is in use, the data base administrator should inspect the data elements to be added to the data base and determine the best arrangement of the data.

For conventional files, if the same data elements appear in different files the *integrity* of the new files may be at risk. To preserve *data integrity*, any change in a data value for a data field in one file must be carried out for all the files containing that data field. However, it is unlikely that all such files will be updated simultaneously. *Referential integrity* must be enforced when a value for a data field on a file must also exist within a record on another file. For example, a value for STUDENT-ID that exists in a record in the ENROLLS-IN file and indicates a particular student enrolled in a course must have a corresponding record in the STUDENT file with the same value for STUDENT-ID.

For our sample data set, the analyst reviews the files already existing in the registrar's office at the university. The analyst observes that an office directory of the instructors is maintained, listing their offices and phone numbers as well as their department affiliation. The directory is created from a computer file called INSTRUCTOR-ADDRESSES, which is ordered by the primary key <u>INSTRUCTOR-ID</u>. After checking the contents of this computer file, the analyst finds that it is not necessary to create a file for the record type INSTRUCTOR (described earlier in Figure 13-14). These data fields already exist and are updated by another system. To ensure that a correct INSTRUC-TOR-ID is placed in the TAUGHT-BY file records, the IDs can be verified by means of this existing file.

Step 4: Define the Files

In this step, the analyst must decide what files should be designed for the system. If a relational data base management system will be used, the nor-malized record types could be used to directly specify the files to be imple-mented. For a relational data base, it may be necessary to violate the normalization rules (that is, denormalize the data) in order to achieve better performance for the retrieval and updating of records. The recommenda-tions of the DBMS should be followed in this regard. Even if the DBMS is not based on the relational data model, the set of normalized record types is useful as the starting point for the design of the record structures.

For conventional files, the analyst must decide how many files should be implemented and what data fields should be placed in each file. The output requirements during the system's lifetime, the access type, and the file or-ganization all play a role in this decision. Although a data base system will not be used, the files must be designed to achieve the same goals as the data base system as much as possible. The primary goal of the analyst in design-ing conventional files is to minimize redundancy—the appearance of the same field in more than one file. Redundancy is undesirable because, when a field appears on more than one file, any change to its value will require changes to all the files containing that field. Since it is rare for all the pertinent files to be updated immediately, various values for the same data field may exist on the files, leading to inconsistencies in the data.

If we consider the field called STUDENT-CAMPUS-ADDRESS, we know that for some students its value will require frequent updating. If this field appears on both the STUDENT file and the ENROLLS-IN file, each time a student changes his or her campus address, an updating run will be neces-sary for both files rather than only one. This updating of multiple files causes additional programming effort (since each update program must be pre-pared to alter this duplicated field); it risks inconsistency of data values (when all the files are not updated at exactly the same time); and it uses extra computer time to perform the updating runs. All in all, it is best to avoid redundancy. In reality, the analyst knows that redundancy is very likely to be necessary in a conventional file system because the system must also work efficiently. The trade-offs between redundancy and the system's processing requirements mean that some redundancy may be necessary. However, every attempt should be made to reduce the degree of redundancy in the system files.

Using the entity-relationship diagram, the analyst determines which data entities and relationships to include within each file. It is decided that the fields MAJOR and STUDENT-ORGANIZATION really belong to the information about an individual student. This conclusion is also reached by examining the set of normalized record types and observing that STUDENT-ID is included in the primary key for the record types HAS and BELONGS TO. The analyst now takes the entity-relationship diagram and circles the data entities and relationships to be included within each file, as shown in Figure 13-15. In Figure 13-16, we see that six conventional files have been defined for this information system. The analyst has also included the DEPARTMENT-CODE file so that the value in the DEPT-# field can be translated to its corresponding value for DEPARTMENT-NAME. The design of the INSTRUCTOR file is not required because in step 3 the analyst discovered that these same fields are contained in the existing file INSTRUCTOR-ADDRESSES.

The analyst must also consider what data fields will be referenced as a group by the users and what reports must be produced. The system outputs, as defined by the logical model (the data flow diagrams and data dictionary), will provide this information. A major system output is the class lists sent to each instructor. The designer knows that class lists, giving each student's name and identification number, must be produced four times during the term for each instructor. A sample class list is depicted in Figure 13-17. Class lists are distributed to the department that offers the course; the department then sends the class lists to the instructors. We observe that the data element DEPT-# is a subfield within COURSE-#, as shown in the data dictionary description in Figure 13-18. The remainder of the field COURSE-# represents the number assigned to the course by the department, now named ASSIGNED-COURSE-#.

To illustrate the planning necessary in the design of the physical files, we will consider the production of the COURSE-LIST output. If the normalized record types were simply converted into physical files, the program that creates the course listings would have to reference six files. As shown in Figure 13-19, the TAUGHT-BY file serves as the guiding file for the creation of the course listing. After a record is obtained from the TAUGHT-BY file, the fields COURSE-# and INSTRUCTOR-SSN are used to build the record for the COURSE-LIST output file. The field COURSE-TITLE is retrieved from the COURSE file, the field INSTRUCTOR-NAME from the INSTRUCTOR-ADDRESSES file, the DEPARTMENT-NAME from the DEPARTMENT-CODE file, and the fields STUDENT-ID from the ENROLLS-IN file and STUDENT-NAME from the STUDENT file for each student enrolled in the course. Each

FIGURE 13-15   The entity-relationship diagram marked with possible file designations

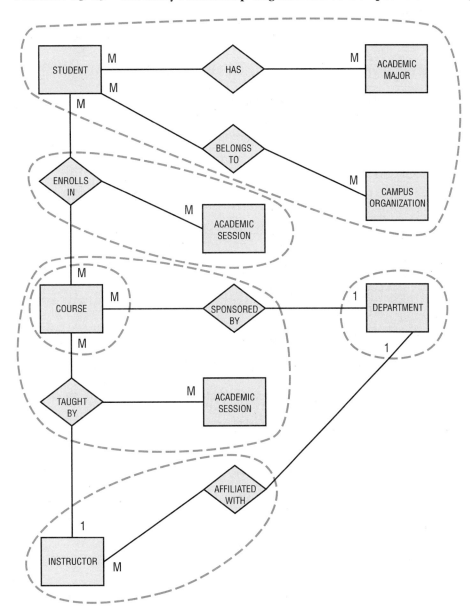

reference to the STUDENT file must be done randomly, since the previous record retrieved has no influence on the next record retrieved from the file.

After careful reflection, the analyst sees it is best to arrange the data records on some files in order to reduce the number of record retrievals. The records on the ENROLLS-IN file will be placed in sequence first by SESSION-DATE, second by COURSE-# and last by STUDENT-ID, while the TAUGHT-BY file will be rearranged in sequence by SESSION-DATE followed

FIGURE 13-16

The first draft of the file templates

STUDENT File

    <u>STUDENT-ID</u>   ←——— **Primary Key**

    STUDENT-NAME

    STUDENT-HOME-ADDRESS

    STUDENT-CAMPUS-ADDRESS

    MAJOR   Occurs two times

    STUDENT-ORGANIZATION   Occurs ?? times

COURSE File

    <u>COURSE-#</u>

    COURSE-TITLE

TAUGHT-BY File

    <u>SESSION-DATE</u>

    <u>COURSE-#</u>

    [DEPT-# + ASSIGNED-COURSE-#]   } **Primary Key**

    INSTRUCTOR-SSN

ENROLLS-IN File

    <u>SESSION-DATE</u>

    <u>COURSE-#</u>

    [DEPT-# + ASSIGNED-COURSE-#]   } **Primary Key**

    <u>STUDENT-ID</u>

    GRADE

INSTRUCTOR File   Not required since the
                           INSTRUCTOR-ADDRESSES
                           contains the same fields

DEPARTMENT-CODE File

    <u>DEPT-#</u>   ←——— **Primary Key**

    DEPARTMENT-NAME

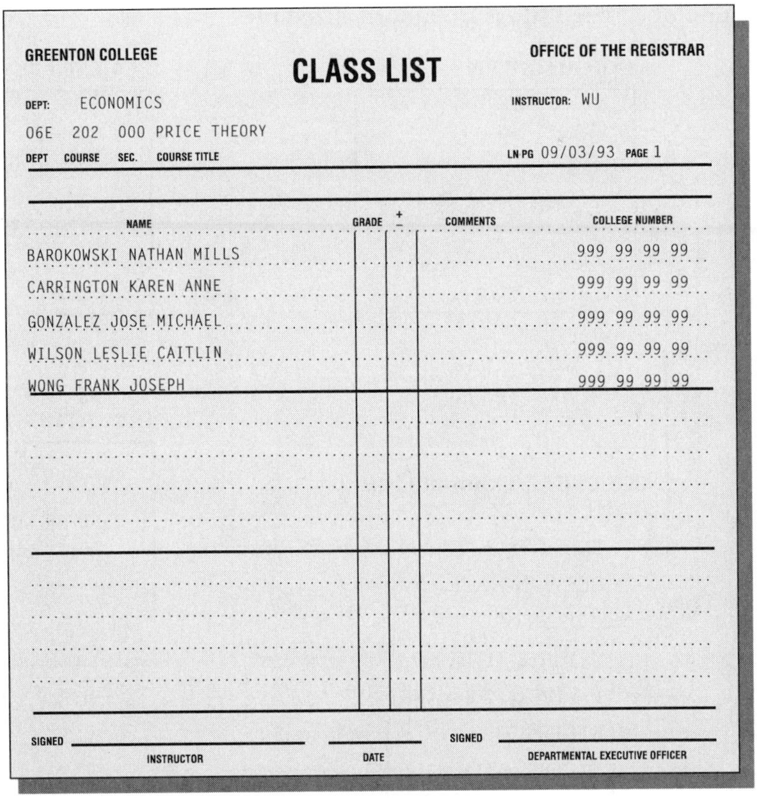
GREENTON COLLEGE

CLASS LIST

OFFICE OF THE REGISTRAR

DEPT: ECONOMICS

INSTRUCTOR: WU

06E 202 000 PRICE THEORY

DEPT COURSE SEC. COURSE TITLE

LN PG 09/03/93 PAGE 1

NAME	GRADE	+ −	COMMENTS	COLLEGE NUMBER
BAROKOWSKI NATHAN MILLS				999 99 99 99
CARRINGTON KAREN ANNE				999 99 99 99
GONZALEZ JOSE MICHAEL				999 99 99 99
WILSON LESLIE CAITLIN				999 99 99 99
WONG FRANK JOSEPH				999 99 99 99

SIGNED ______ INSTRUCTOR ______ DATE SIGNED ______ DEPARTMENTAL EXECUTIVE OFFICER

FIGURE 13-17
A sample class list to be produced by the student registration system

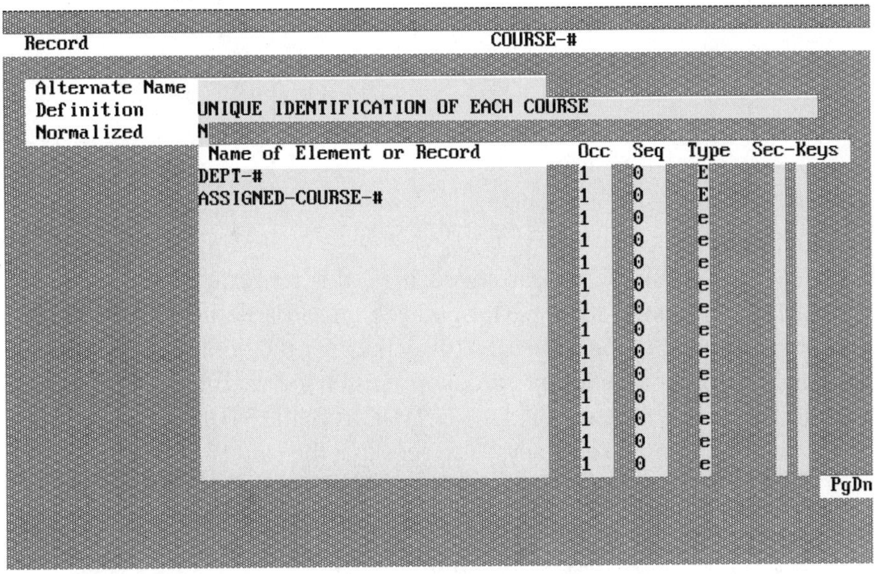

FIGURE 13-18
The revised data dictionary entry for COURSE-#

Screen shots produced using INTERSOLV's Excelerator solution for Requirements Analysis and System Design.

FIGURE 13-19   The creation of course listings from normalized files

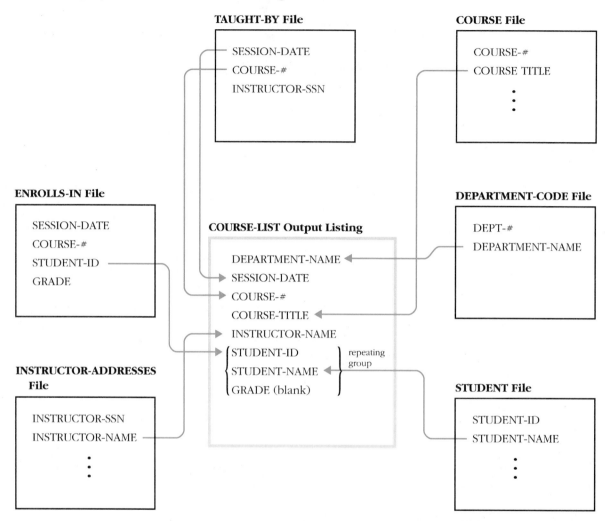

by COURSE-#. Using the rearranged files, the retrieval of the value for DEPARTMENT-NAME can be performed just once for all the courses offered by a department. But the retrieval of the values for the field STUDENT-NAME remains a problem. Different students register for each class, and the retrieval of the value for each STUDENT-NAME from the STUDENT file must be performed randomly. The analyst also sees that the value for COURSE-TITLE will require the matching record for COURSE-# from the COURSE file. The creation of COURSE-LIST in this way means that the listing for a single course with only 20 students could require as many as 43 disk accesses, even with direct access file organization. Using indexed sequential access organization means as many as 129 accesses. What should be done?

> **Warning**
>
> Although this chapter discusses denormalization, do not use this technique for files unless absolutely necessary. Because redundancy occurs in denormalized files and the use of repeating groups restricts changes in file design, denormalization should be used only when essential for system performance.

The solution to this problem is to denormalize the data files. The analyst designs a physical file called COURSE-GRADE, which will be maintained in ascending sequence by COURSE-#, and then by STUDENT-ID. The field STUDENT-NAME will be included in the physical record in the COURSE-GRADE file (replacing the ENROLLS-IN file) to avoid the frequent disk references demanded by strictly normalized data files. To eliminate the problem of retrieving the instructor's name and the course title, the fields INSTRUCTOR-NAME and COURSE-TITLE have been incorporated into the COURSES-TAUGHT file (replacing the TAUGHT-BY file). Figure 13-20 illustrates the final design of the physical files needed for producing the course listings. The design of the repeating fields MAJOR and STUDENT-ORGANIZATION is decided in Step 5. The creation of the course listings from the denormalized files is depicted in Figure 13-21. Using the denormalized files streamlines the program by eliminating the need to retrieve the instructor names and student names randomly from their respective files.

Another role for this information system is recording the grades for the students in each course. After the grades are placed in the final course listings by the instructors at the end of the academic session, they will be stored in the COURSE-GRADE file. If we stored this file in sequential order by its primary key (SESSION-DATE, COURSE-#, and STUDENT-ID), the updating procedure could retrieve the first record for a particular course and then update the remainder of the records for that course in sequence. Alternatively, the grade reports could be rearranged in this way prior to the computer updating procedure so that sequential access of the file could take place. Because it is necessary to produce academic reports for each student at the end of the session, the completed COURSE-GRADE file can be sorted in sequence by the fields STUDENT-ID, SESSION-DATE, and COURSE-#, in order to create the file STUDENT-GRADE. The student grade reports can then be produced sequentially according to the STUDENT-ID field by separate processing programs as diagrammed in Figure 13-22.

FIGURE 13-20

The final physical files displayed as record types   The number of repetitions for MAJOR and STUDENT-ORGANIZA-TION is determined in Step 5.

STUDENT file
    STUDENT-ID   ←——— **Primary Key**
    STUDENT-NAME
    STUDENT-HOME-ADDRESS
    STUDENT-CAMPUS-ADDRESS
    MAJOR   Occurs two times
    STUDENT-ORGANIZATION   Occurs five times

COURSES-TAUGHT File
    SESSION-DATE
    COURSE-#   } **Primary Key**
    [DEPT-#+ASSIGNED-COURSE-#]
    COURSE-TITLE
    INSTRUCTOR-SSN
    INSTRUCTOR-NAME

redundant data fields

COURSE-GRADE File
    SESSION-DATE
    COURSE-#   } Primary Key contains
    STUDENT-ID   these three fields
    STUDENT-NAME
    GRADE

INSTRUCTOR File   Not required since the file INSTRUCTOR-ADDRESSES contains the same fields

DEPARTMENT-CODE File
    DEPT-#   ←——— **Primary Key**
    DEPARTMENT-NAME

Step 5: Describe the Record Layout and Choose the Blocking Factor

The analyst must now answer the following questions:

Should the records be fixed or variable length?

What data type and number of bytes should be allocated to each data field?

What blocking factor should be used?

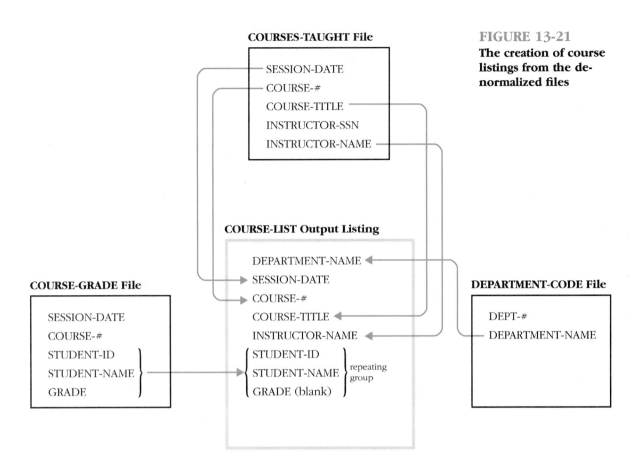

FIGURE 13-21

The creation of course listings from the denormalized files

As we saw in Figure 13-20, MAJOR and STUDENT-ORGANIZATION are repeating fields. Should the STUDENT file be designed with a variable length record, so no space is wasted within the records for students with only one major and no membership in student organizations? But, as we noted earlier, variable length records are more difficult for the programmer to process. Hence variable length records are used only in special circumstances. Is this a special circumstance that warrants the extra difficulties of dealing with variable length records? The programmer may face much additional work. Further, using other software packages to process the file, such as the sort/merge program, could be a problem. Given these drawbacks, and since the amount of wasted space for students without double majors or membership in campus organizations is not excessive, the analyst selects fixed length format for the STUDENT file record.

After the analyst decides to include the fields MAJOR and STUDENT-ORGANIZATION in the STUDENT file record, the maximum number of occurrences for each field must be established by consulting the users. When the analyst asks the university staff members about the number of campus organizations to be recorded for each student, it is found that five organizations is ample. Most students join only one or two student organizations; few join as many as five. The analyst cautions that the fixed length

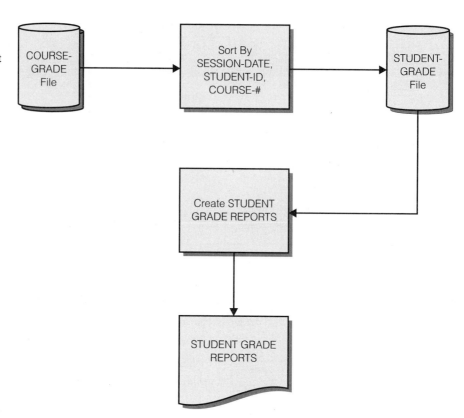

record format means that the users cannot easily change their minds later on. After some discussion, the users agree that future changes seem extremely unlikely. Nonetheless, the analyst chooses to pad the record with additional space to allow for future data fields. This additional space is added to the record just as insurance against change. Padding the records is customary for conventional files because the future is uncertain and the physical record format is rigid and difficult to change. It is better to waste a little space over the lifetime of the file than to modify every program whenever an unforeseen increase in record size occurs. Rewriting a voluminous file is also a huge undertaking. We note that this problem of repeating fields could be avoided entirely if the normalized record types were directly transformed into the physical file structures.

Now that the record structure has been defined, the analyst draws a record layout showing the placement of each field within the physical record. The data type and length for each data field are also specified at this time. The data dictionary entry for the data elements provides this information. If the documented data type is not available in the programming language to be used, the analyst may choose to store the field as characters. For example, a field containing a date type may be indicated as six characters with a description given as YYMMDD. A date field designed in this fashion allows dates to be placed in ascending order or compared without manipulating the field contents. The issue of how to record the next century must

FIGURE 13-23   **The layout sheet for physical record design**

FILE NAME: COURSE-GRADE				DATE: 11/30/93		
Field Name	SESSION-DATE	COURSE-#		STUDENT-ID	STUDENT-NAME	
		DEPT-#	ASSIGNED-COURSE-#		LAST	FIRST
Data Type	D YYYYMMDD	C	C	C	C	C
Position	0-7	8-11	12-14	15-23	24-38	39-48
Field Name	STUDENT-NAME INITIAL	GRADE				
Data Type	C	C				
Position	49	50-51				
Field Name						
Data Type						
Position						

also be studied. If the date January 3, 2000, were stored as 000103, it would precede the date December 23, 1999 (represented as 991223), in numerical order. Consequently, the analyst chooses YYYYMMDD as the format for all date fields. The record layout sheet for the COURSE-GRADE file record is given in Figure 13-23. Record layout sheets are similarly prepared for the COURSES-TAUGHT and COURSE-LIST files. The blocking factor for each file is also specified in conjunction with the record layout.

Step 6: Select File Access, File Organization, and Storage Medium

Now the analyst must specify the physical design by selecting the appropriate mode of file access, file organization, and storage medium. In the opening section, the terms file access, file organization, and file storage medium were explained independently of each other. In fact, these three factors are intimately related. To make these decisions, the analyst reviews the system requirements for response time, file size, future growth, and processing requirements. The table in Figure 13-24 summarizes the relationships between these factors. If the system will be on-line, then disk storage will be the file medium. As explained earlier, indexed sequential file organization offers a suitable compromise between the need for sequential processing of

FIGURE 13-24   **The relationships among file access, file organization, and file storage medium**

STORAGE MEDIUM	FILE SIZE	FILE ACCESS MODE	FILE ORGANIZATION	RESPONSE TIME (for random access)
Disk	Limited by Disk Size	Sequential	Sequential	Impractical
			Indexed Sequential	Good
	Limited by Disk Size	Direct	Indexed Sequential	Good
			Direct (Hashing)	Superior; fastest access
Magnetic Tape	Unlimited; simply add another tape reel	Sequential	Sequential	Not possible

the data records and the retrieval of records at random. Because the future is uncertain, even a system that presently requires only sequential processing may be converted to an on-line system at some future date. Thus, indexed sequential file organization is a safe bet and is most likely to be chosen. Certain special cases require the fastest possible response time. In that event, direct file organization will be needed. If the file will be too voluminous for disk storage, then magnetic tape must be considered. However, with hard disk storage ranging up to 50 billion bytes and the increasing demand for on-line systems, disk storage is the most popular medium today.

For our sample data files, the analyst selects indexed sequential file organization and disk storage medium. The creation of class lists will employ sequential access of the COURSES-TAUGHT and COURSE-GRADE files and direct access (via indexes) of the DEPARTMENT-CODE file. Inquiries regarding class enrollment will be answered on-line using direct access.

Step 7: Determine the File Conversion Procedures

If the proposed information system will replace an existing computer system, the analyst must plan the conversion of current computer files to the new physical files. A computer program must be written to read the old files and produce the new ones. This program is added to the list of programs to be implemented. If the existing data records are contained in manually recorded files, the analyst will also plan this conversion procedure. The data entry method has already been considered during the Analysis phase. The conversion tasks are formally planned during the Design phase and carried out during the Implementation phase (see Chapter 17).

Step 8: Design the File Controls

As discussed earlier, controls must be imposed on the files. The analyst documents the backup procedures to be followed and indicates the storage site for each backup. Log files are specified for the updating programs. In the event of hardware failure, file recovery procedures must be available. The final documentation of these procedures will be delayed until the Implementation phase, but the preliminary plans are drafted here. Because the STUDENT, COURSE-TAUGHT, and COURSE-GRADE files are crucial to the operation of the university, the backups will be stored at a secure site in a building several miles off-campus. As an extra precaution, the analyst plans to send copies of the master files in a locked case to a bank, which will store them in the vault at no charge. While it would be unusual for all university buildings to be destroyed, the Computing Center Director believes that an ounce of prevention is worth a pound of cure. If these files were ever lost, student transcripts could not be produced. Under the existing system, paper records offer no such backup options since their duplication would be expensive, time-consuming, clumsy, and impossible to handle efficiently. The computer files will provide a convenient way of ensuring continuity despite catastrophic loss.

Control fields should also be incorporated in the files to guarantee that no data records or data fields have been lost or incorrectly stored in the file. Such problems may occur due to erroneous data transmission, hardware failure, or a bug in the software. The control fields serve to ensure that processing has been performed on the entire file without data input error. Either record totals or aggregate totals for an individual data field can be placed into a special record, at the head or end of a file or as a separate control file. A *record total* is simply the count of how many records the file contains. Each time a record is added or deleted, the record total changes accordingly. A *data field total* is the summation of all the values for that field in the file. Since the computation may cause the sum to exceed the existing field length, typically the leftmost digits are dropped. This simple summing technique can be used on any data field, ensuring that not a single bit has been dropped from the records. The analyst now incorporates the necessary control fields for our sample physical file design.

Step 9: Choose the Secondary Keys for the Files

When the file has been stored within a data base system, it is possible to select some nonkey fields by which the records can be retrieved. As stated earlier, these nonkey fields will be called secondary keys. To provide for quick retrieval of the group of records that match the value specified for the nonkey field, the analyst can direct the data base system to build indexes for each secondary key. Such indexes occupy substantial disk space but greatly assist the speedy retrieval of records by secondary keys. For example, it will be very desirable for the users to retrieve records from the STUDENT file by the student's name, stored in the STUDENT-NAME field. Consequently, the analyst identifies STUDENT-NAME as a secondary key and adds this requirement to the list of programming tasks. The retrieval of data records by a secondary key should be planned during the design of the physical files. For conventional file systems, the analyst must decide on appropriate measures to allow such retrieval.

Step 10: Compute the File Storage Requirements

The amount of disk capacity required for each file must be computed. In order to compute the file storage requirements accurately, it is necessary to know the track capacity of the disk storage unit that will be used for the file. The size of the block and the number of bytes per block also affect the number of blocks that can be written on the disk track. Because each physical record will be separated by an interrecord gap, the blocking factor and record size are chosen to minimize this wasted space.

To illustrate the computation of disk storage for a file, the IBM 3380 Disk Storage Unit will be adopted as the storage device for our example. An excerpt from the IBM 3380 Track Capacity Table is shown in Figure 13-25. The capacities for the tracks differ depending on the choice of format. In the **count-data format**, each block contains a subblock containing its relative address on the disk track. The first block on the track has the relative address 0, the second block the address 1, and so on. The count-data format is used for sequential files. In the **count-key data format**, the block contains two subblocks: the count subblock (identical to that given in the count-data format) and the key subblock. The *key subblock* contains the primary key of the last record in the block. The count-key format is used for the indexed sequential file organization to allow the system to search a track until the block containing the record with the desired key is located. As you will recall, the indexed sequential method uses a set of indexes to locate the track containing the desired record. Because the records are written in sequential order by ascending key, the indicated track can then be searched to locate the block containing the desired record.

For our sample STUDENT file, suppose that 3,500 students are presently enrolled at the college each year. After a student graduates, the student's records will be archived. The analyst's initial estimate of the file size is 14,000 records (3,500 students times 4 years). But the registrar's office points out that some students take five years to graduate, while a few students drop out for a year and then return. The decision is then made to archive a student's record either after graduation or after an absence of two years. The new estimate is 20,000 records: 3,500 students times 5 years plus 2,500 records for students who drop out and return later. This is a rough estimate but obviously sufficiently large to accommodate the actual file size.

Count-Data Format		Count-Key Data Format		Blocks Per Track
Data Subblock (bytes)		Data Subblock (bytes)		
Minimum	Maximum	Minimum	Maximum	
23,477	47,476	23,221	47,220	1
15,477	23,476	15,221	23,220	2
11,477	15,476	11,221	15,220	3
9,077	11,476	8,821	11,220	4
7,477	9,076	7,221	8,820	5
6,357	7,476	6,101	7,220	6
5,493	6,356	5,237	6,100	7
4,821	5,492	4,565	5,236	8
4,277	4,820	4,021	4,564	9
3,861	4,276	3,605	4,020	10
3,477	3,860	3,221	3,604	11
3,189	3,476	2,933	3,220	12
2,933	3,188	2,677	2,932	13

FIGURE 13-25

Excerpt from the IBM 3380 Track Capacity Table   This device has 1,770 cylinders and 15 tracks per cylinder.

Reprinted by permission of International Business Machines Corporation

To better illustrate the computation to be performed, let us consider a file with the following physical characteristics:

File length: 20,000 records

Type of record: Fixed length

Record length: 600 bytes

Blocking factor: 5 records per block

Data format: Count-key data

Physical device: IBM 3380 Disk Storage Device

There are two values to be obtained: (1) how many tracks the file will use and (2) what percentage of the disk storage unit the file will occupy. Since the blocking factor chosen is 5, the total number of bytes in the physical record is computed as

$$\text{Bytes per block} = \text{Blocking factor} \times \text{Total bytes per record}$$
$$= 5 \times 600 = 3,000$$

By referring to Figure 13-25, the analyst finds that 12 blocks, each containing 3,000 bytes, can be written on a track. Therefore,

$$\text{Logical records per track} = \text{Blocking factor} \times \text{Blocks per track}$$
$$= 5 \times 12 = 60$$

Next, the analyst computes the number of tracks required for the file.

$$\text{File size (in tracks)} = \frac{\text{Total number of logical records}}{\text{Logical records per track}}$$
$$= \frac{20,000}{60}$$
$$= 333.33 = 334 \qquad \text{(Always round up.)}$$

The IBM 3380 Disk Storage Unit has 15 tracks for each cylinder and a total of 1,770 cylinders. Given this information, the number of cylinders required for the sample file is computed as follows:

$$\text{File size (in cylinders)} = \frac{\text{File size (in tracks)}}{\text{Tracks per cylinder}}$$
$$= \frac{334}{15}$$
$$= 22.27 = 23 \qquad \text{(Always round up.)}$$

Finally, the analyst computes the percentage of the disk unit occupied by the file:

$$\text{Percentage of disk storage unit} = \frac{\text{File size (in cylinders)}}{\text{Total cylinders on disk}} \times 100$$
$$= \frac{23}{1,770} \times 100$$
$$= .013 \times 100 = 1.3\%$$

By estimating the percentage of the disk storage unit to be occupied by a new file, the project analyst can be certain that there is sufficient disk space available for the file. Serious problems in the future are thereby avoided. If the new file will occupy a large percentage of the disk unit, the analyst can recommend acquiring more disk capacity in order to permit sufficient space for the future growth of existing files. Knowing the size of the file also lets the analyst judge whether magnetic tape should be considered as the storage medium. However, the need to reference data records in an on-line system means that the file must be stored on a disk storage unit.

Saving Millions by Inventory Control

When Mervyn's department store needed to develop a new inventory management system, the vice president of MIS, Vivian Stephenson, turned to CASE tools. By using KnowledgeWare, Inc.'s ObjectView development tool, the company launched its Planned Store Inventory (PSI) program last February on a Sequent Computer System. Using the new client/server system, PC users download raw data from the mainframe into their ObjectView-based application, which transforms the data into a format recognized by a modeling application on the Sequent computer. The IBM mainframe, meanwhile, continues to draw data that is updated daily from Mervyn's stores via a satellite connection. So far only 26 percent of the store's inventory is computerized but eventually the system will handle 75 percent of the goods.

In addition to saving millions of dollars, Mervyn's PSI program also figures out exactly what merchandise is needed in particular stores, and when. Before the retailer installed the PSI system, manual proce-dures were still required in order to determine what items should be shipped to the retail outlets. Users obtained data from the mainframe computer and then pulled out their calculators to make the final decision about shipment of goods.

The new precision merchandising translates into more sales and higher customer satisfaction because it increases the chances that consumers will find what they want to buy. "Having the right merchandise in the right stores at the right time sounds simple, but it's difficult to execute," Stephenson said.

Not everything is up to par. The system still lacks the sophisticated security and control features found in the mainframe world. Although Mervyn's has not experienced problems, the client/server system is not considered up to mainframe standards.

Source: Halper, Mark, "Department Store Tackles Inventory Stockpiles," *Computerworld*, September 17, 1993, pp. 79–80. Copyright 1992/93. Reprinted with permission from *Computerworld*.

SUMMARY

The foundation of physical file design is the logical data design described in Chapter 12. One objective of physical file design is to use the file storage medium efficiently by minimizing the amount of blank space caused by the interrecord gaps. Other objectives of physical file design are minimal redundancy of data fields, adequate response time by the system, support for programming tasks yet to be designed, and flexibility for future additions to the files.

In order to design physical files, additional technical concepts are needed. A record format represents the physical organization of the data fields for the records of a file located on a storage medium. A record type or record template portrays the data fields logically but does not show their actual arrangement on a storage medium. A file is a collection of the occurrences of logical records. A physical record or block contains one or more logical records written as a physical unit on a storage medium. The number of logical records contained within a physical record is the blocking factor for the file. A physical record is always followed by an area of blank space, the interrecord gap. A primary key is a field (or group of fields) that uniquely identifies each record in a file. A secondary key is a field that may be used to retrieve records from a file. The two most popular file storage mediums are magnetic disk and magnetic tape.

Two types of record lengths are possible for a physical record: fixed length records and variable length records. Although variable length records are useful in certain situations, they complicate the programming task and are not supported by some file processing software. The two types of file access methods are sequential access and direct access.

File organization is the method by which records are arranged on the file storage medium for retrieval. The three most popular file organization techniques are sequential, indexed sequential, and direct. In sequential file organization, records are physically arranged on the storage medium, one after another. Indexed sequential file organization also arranges the records for a file in sequential order by the primary key, but permits any record to be retrieved directly by indicating its primary key. This direct retrieval is possible by means of a set of indexes that indicate the location of records according to their primary keys.

Direct file organization permits the records on a file to be retrieved in any order without the creation of indexes. Each file record is stored within a bucket, after its primary key is used to compute the bucket's relative address. This computation is performed according to a procedure called hashing. Seven types of files were defined: master files, transaction files, archive files, table files, intermediate files, log files, and backup files.

Ten steps were proposed for the construction of the physical file design. In step 1, the analyst decides whether a data base system (and thus, files designed for the data base) or a conventional file system should be used. In step 2, the logical data design is reviewed to ensure that no data elements have been omitted. In step 3, the system requirements for response time, future file growth, and processing operations are studied. The relationship of the system's data to other existing systems is also inspected. In step 4, the files are designated and a rough sketch of the file contents is obtained by refining the logical data design. In step 5, the choice of fixed or variable length records is made, the record layout is written, and the blocking factor is defined. In step 6, the physical design of the file is further specified by the selection of the file access method, the file organization technique, and the file storage medium. The file conversion procedures for existing data files are outlined in step 7. In step 8, the file controls are specified. The indexes for secondary keys are stipulated in step 9. Finally, in step 10, the file storage requirements are computed. Although each activity has been specified as an independent step, the analyst is always aware of all aspects of the physical file design. The result of one step may influence or define the outcome of another step.

TERMS

archive file
backup file
block
blocking factor
bucket
count-data format
count-key data format
cylinder
data base
division-remainder method
field
file
file access method
    direct
    sequential
file organization
    direct
    indexed sequential
    sequential
file storage medium

fixed length record
grandparent-parent-child method
hashing
intermediate file
interrecord gap
log file
logical record
master file
physical record
record format
record type
relative address
response time
secondary key
table file
tracks
transaction file
variable length record

QUESTIONS

1. Define the terms logical record and physical record.
2. What is meant by the blocking factor? What purpose does it serve?
3. Explain the terms primary key and secondary key.
4. What are the advantages and disadvantages of indexed sequential file organization?
5. Why would you choose direct file organization over indexed sequential organization for a file?

6. What are the disadvantages of conventional file design compared to files for a relational data base?

7. Explain how the logical file design functions as the basis for the physical file design.

8. Describe the grandparent-parent-child method for backing up files.

9. An analyst decides that magnetic tape should be the file storage medium. What access methods and file organization techniques are available for this file?

10. In the discussion of the sample data set, the COURSE-GRADE file was selected to be an indexed sequential file. Why was direct file organization not chosen for this file?

11. The physical design of the COURSE file has these specifications:

> File size: 27,000 records
>
> Record length: 1,740 bytes
>
> Blocking factor: 3
>
> Data format: Count-Key Data format

Compute the file storage requirements for this file when stored on the IBM 3380 Disk Storage Unit. Show the number of tracks, number of cylinders, and the percentage of the IBM 3380 Disk Storage Unit required for this file.

12. The College of Business Administration employs clerk-typists in the Office Services Organization to prepare course material, research papers, and other documents required by the business faculty. All work is accomplished by means of word processing software on a network of personal computers. All document files are located on the network's hard disk and each Friday are backed up on magnetic tape. The backup files are stored in the Computing Services office, just across the hall from the Office Services Organization. Because of the high demand for typing at mid-term and final exam times, the Office Service Organization is sometimes too busy to backup its files and skips the backup procedure in order to meet the faculty's deadlines.
   a. What is wrong with this backup procedure?
   b. What backup procedures do you recommend?

PROJECTS

1. Visit the administrative data processing department at your local college or university. Document the file access method, file organization, and storage medium in use for the student registration files (the student data file, course registration file, and other files needed for student information). Explain the reasons for the choices made by the data processing department.

2. Reread the case study on the Campus Bookstore (Chapter 7) and make the appropriate physical design choices for the file that will contain the textbook orders received from the instructors. What is the best choice for file access method, file organization, and storage medium? Justify your choices.

REFERENCES

Date, C. J. *An Introduction to Database Systems*, 5th ed. Reading, MA: Addison-Wesley, 1990.

Elmasri, Ramez, and Shamkant B. Navathe. *Fundamentals of Database Systems.* Redwood City, CA: Benjamin/Cummings, 1989.

Excelerator/IS Application Guide. Rockville, MD: Intersolv, Inc., 1989.

Kroenke, David M., and Kathleen A. Dolan. *Database Processing*, 3rd ed. Chicago: Science Research Associates, 1988.

McFadden, Fred R., and Jeffrey A. Hoffer. *Data Base Management*, 3rd ed. Menlo Park, CA: Benjamin/Cummings, 1991.

CHAPTER 14

Design Principles and Output Design

Objectives

In this chapter, we will discuss the design of information system outputs. The following topics are covered:

- The human–machine boundaries for an information system
- Six basic principles that guide the design of system inputs and outputs
- The steps required for designing system outputs
- The types of media available for computer outputs
- The characteristics of the output that affect the choice of medium: usage, volume, quality, cost, frequency, number of copies, and distribution

INTRODUCTION

After the Analysis phase has been completed, the design of the programs and the computer files is specified in the Design phase. However, before such work can take place, the foundation for the programs should be established by specifying the input/output designs for the data that will enter and leave the system. The problem of input/output design is how to present data to human eyes and ears in the best possible way. To answer this question, this chapter covers four major topics:

1. The definition of good design
2. The human factors that affect design
3. The principles of good design
4. The eight steps of output design

Steps 1, 2, and 8 of the eight-step design process are applicable to both inputs and outputs. Because design factors differ between inputs and outputs, steps 3 through 7 are explained in this chapter only for output design. The design of inputs is covered in Chapter 15.

Some decisions about input design directly affect the output design. For example, the choice of user–machine dialogue (discussed in Chapter 15) will determine how the user obtains the system outputs, such as reports or on-line queries. To maintain consistency for the user, the design of the inputs should be carried over into the design of the outputs. Thus, if the customer for a business is called *client* on the input screen, the report listing all customers with overdue accounts should use the same terminology, *client* rather than *customer*. Although it is possible to design inputs and outputs independently of each other, their design attributes must coincide. Even a few minor differences in design characteristics can confuse the users and prevent them from maintaining operational efficiency for the firm. As we stressed in previous chapters, the user participates throughout the input/output design process. Because the analyst will be designing the portions of the system immediately visible to the user, the users' preferences and criticisms must be sought.

WHAT IS GOOD INPUT/OUTPUT DESIGN?

When something is wrong, we often blame the problem on bad design. If our desk height is just a bit low, the lamp casts shadows on our papers, and the chair is lumpy with no support for our back, we notice these problems rather quickly. If, instead, we experience the comfort of a well-designed desk, chair, and lamp, all positioned correctly, these ideal conditions are simply accepted and we proceed to work with no thought for our surroundings. We plainly expect good design in our environment, so the faults of bad design jar and disturb us. The same is true with computer inputs and outputs for human eyes and ears. If their design is good, the users perform their tasks more easily and make fewer mistakes. They are probably not even aware of how good design enhances their productivity. But given poorly designed screens and reports, the users will grumble and complain. The *user interfaces* (also called *human interfaces*) of an application are these visible system inputs and outputs, which require the utmost care to ensure user satisfaction and productivity in the work place. Interfaces operate at the boundary between humans and machines. The interfaces enable data to be transported across the boundary by transforming its representation from human-readable to machine-readable form—that is, computerized data—or the reverse transformation (see Figure 14-1).

The primary goal of input/output design for human interfaces to the system is to assist the users in their tasks. Hence the interfaces must be designed with human limitations in mind. In the early days of computing, this goal was seldom satisfied. Because computer hardware was very expensive compared to the cost of human resources, the emphasis was on promoting the efficiency of the computer programs. Today, the situation has changed dramatically. As the cost of computer resources has declined, hardware and software capabilities have increased tremendously. This turnabout means that the programmer must design human interfaces for the users, not for the efficiency of the programs or the ease of programming. Naturally, we still have certain trade-offs between computer hardware and the demands of software, primarily with on-line systems. However, in general, the golden rule is "Do unto the users what fits them best and let the computer take care of itself."

How does this general principle translate into good design? There are several guidelines for designing human interfaces. After a design is created, it should be critiqued by the users and, if possible, trial runs should be scheduled to allow hands-on evaluation of the designs. As in the Analysis phase, the users appraise the merits of a report or screen design. Because

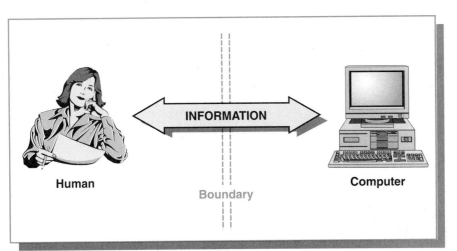

INFORMATION

Human

Boundary

Computer

FIGURE 14-1

The user interface
The user interfaces are the visible system inputs and outputs that cross the boundary between humans and computers.

the users will be the ones who must constantly interact with those designs, they should have the power to approve or reject them. Involving the users at this critical stage taps their business expertise to assist the design process toward a successful conclusion.

Because the requirements for input and output designs differ substantially, we will discuss each type separately. To begin, we present an overview of human characteristics that affect these designs.

HUMANS VS. COMPUTERS

Humans have certain innate capabilities that are taken for granted. They excel at language and pattern recognition. Our language skills can be demonstrated by considering three groups of words [Rubenstein and Hersh, 1984]:

> The quick red fox jumped over the lazy brown dog.
>
> The old flower cost the sad blood.
>
> Asked shoe dog happy the the.

The first is an acceptable English sentence, the second is puzzling but has a correct sentence structure, and the third group of words fails to fit any sentence structure and has no meaning whatsoever. Even children as young as three or four will find that the third group of words is nonsense. For a computer to arrive at the same conclusions requires a long, complicated program that performs grammar checking, such as Grammatik. By analyzing the lines for grammatical structure, Grammatik can determine that the first and second word groups are grammatically correct but will reject the third as a sentence. Grammatik will note that it is unusual to end a sentence with "the." However, it does not address whether the second or third line makes sense; that is not the job of a grammar checker. A more complex program would be needed to analyze the meaning of each line.

Pattern recognition is another strong point of humans. We can look at patterns and immediately recognize circles, squares, and rectangles even at a young age. A toddler can quickly stack toy blocks, whereas a robot must painstakingly recognize each surface of the blocks and methodically stack them under the control of a complex computer program. Another example of pattern recognition is the manner in which we read. Using our pattern recognition skills, we can easily guess at a misspelled word. We may not even detect misspelled words in a document because we mentally correct the erroneous letters. When the computer "reads" a document, it does so letter by letter, with great precision. The spelling checkers are able to detect misspellings and suggest other words; however, to reject a correct spelling of an incorrect word requires a different type of program, such as Grammatik. For example,

> Their is there book.

is a meaningless sentence caused by misspelled words. A spell checker would find all the words to be correctly spelled, while a grammar checker would detect the errors. Yet we immediately see that something is very peculiar about the sentence, although we may have to read it aloud in order to recast it as "There is their book."

The placement of words in context allows us to quickly read textual information without pausing to observe misspelled words. People are good at inferring structure from examples, especially in the domain of languages. But details such as punctuation can be confusing in computer interfaces. In a study of the Query-By-Example system, a significant number of errors resulted from incorrect underlining, confusing "greater than" with "greater than or equal to," and forgetting periods [Thomas, 1976]. Fully 50% of the errors in a study of IQL, another query system, included problems such as having to translate "over 50" to "51 or more" [Gould and Ascher, 1974]. When the computer conventions for using a commonplace word or symbol vary from the customary usage, people may find them troublesome and a source of many errors.

Humans are not good at processing vast amounts of data. Therefore, condensation of data in tables or graphs helps us to analyze large amounts of data. In addition, humans are liable to make errors. Because people are fallible and may key in the wrong data, it is always best to minimize the number of characters to be written or keyed by people. For example, using 34912 is preferable to typing a 15-digit number such as 34912-67081-96511, since a single wrong keystroke can result in an error.

Moreover, we have a limited short-term memory—our memory of recent events. Shown a list of a hundred unrelated items and told to remember them all after one rapid reading, most people cannot recall more than a dozen items. Similarly, memorizing 15-digit numbers is a difficult or even impossible task. But our memory capacity for information stored over long periods is much greater. We can recall hundreds of events in our lives, know many people by name, and continue to master new concepts. This capacity is nonetheless limited. The computer can assist us by offering the capability of "remembering" information at any time. After recording the information on a secondary storage device, the computer can be used to refresh our memory by retrieval of the desired data.

Because of our memory limitations, consistency is important for humans. We want to know that a particular symbol, say the asterisk (*), always means the same thing in this system and all the other systems with which we interact. If an asterisk has various meanings in the different programs in use, very likely we will misuse the symbol and experience frustration in our interaction with the computer programs. Consequently, standardization of the interfaces is important.

Humans also fail to accomplish all but the simplest computational tasks or data processing activities with any degree of reliability. How many of us can add up 20 columns of ten-digit numbers correctly in an instant, create hundreds of invoices without error, and in a matter of minutes scan thousands of accounts for those overdue by more than 30 days? We know that we are incapable of performing these tasks rapidly and accurately without the assistance of machines. That is why computers have proved so valuable in the data processing area.

These differences between humans and computers are summarized in Figure 14-2, which also includes the design implications of human limita-

FIGURE 14-2   The characteristics of humans and computers

Characteristic	Human	Computer	Implications for Design
Language skills	Good	Poor; requires complex programming. True understanding is not given.	Use an available natural language query system, if desired. Inadvisable to build an in-house natural language system.
Pattern recognition	Good	Poor; requires complex programming	Unless using proven software, do not employ pattern recognition by the computer program.
Short-term memory	Limited	Vast	Do not expect the user to remember many detailed instructions. Use the computer to assist the user. Standardize conventions and user interfaces.
Long-term memory	Good but may be imprecise	Vast	Same as for short-term memory.
Computational skills	Poor	Superior	Assign all computational work to the computer program.
Accuracy level	Poor	Superior	Build checks against human error. Minimize the data to be entered by the user. Design screens for ease of use by the user.
Cultural Bias	Culturally determined	None	Documents and screens scan from left to right, top to bottom. Use terms from work environment.

tions. All of these remarks point to the conclusion that the use of the computer should assist us in our shortcomings and supply us with the capabilities that we lack. Therefore, in the design of programs, the unique characteristics of humans should not be forgotten.

PRINCIPLES OF GOOD DESIGN

There are six basic principles of good input/output design which can be summarized as $U^2H^2C^2$:

User involvement

Users first, computers last

minimize Human efforts

remember Human limitations

Convention standardization

Cultural bias

(see Figure 14-3). The importance of user involvement, the first U principle, was discussed in the previous section. The analyst should consult the user throughout the design of the human interfaces to increase the user's satisfaction with the system. Ideally, the user should be able to view the designs and test them by actual usage prior to their adoption into the system. The second U principle states that the design choices must be made to create the best design for the user rather than the easiest design for the programmer to code. The internal workings of the computer are not the user's problems. The human interfaces must be formulated to assist the user, regardless of the

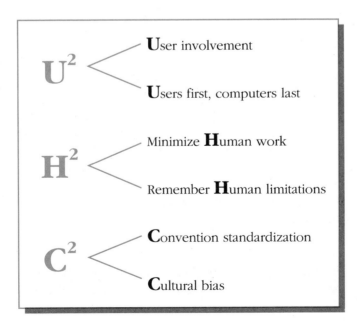

FIGURE 14-3
The principles of good design: $U^2H^2C^2$

difficulties posed to the programmer. However, if the system processing will be severely degraded by this principle, compromises may be necessary.

The first H principle states that, wherever possible, we should minimize the user's interaction with the computer. This statement translates into the avoidance of manual data entry in order to reduce the incidence of error. The user should never key data that can be retrieved from an existing computer file and should never be asked to enter a value that can be computed by the information system. The number of keystrokes required of the user should also be minimal. For example, using the zip code to identify a client's city and state is more appropriate than having the user enter this information. The city and state values can be retrieved from the ZIP CODE table and displayed for the user. When internal codes must be created for such data elements as customer identification numbers, they must be carefully designed to allow for future growth but avoid excessive length.

The second H principle stands for remembering the human limitations of the users as discussed in the previous section. Because humans are prone to error, checks should be placed in the system to prevent the entry of erroneous data. The types of edit checks to be performed are discussed in conjunction with input design in Chapter 15. Care must be taken to avoid overwhelming the user with too much detail that cannot be quickly assimilated. Although the use of different colors for computer displays would seem highly desirable, putting too many colors in a screen display confuses the viewer. For the same reason, screens should not be cluttered with too much information; the human short-term memory and pattern-recognition capabilities will become overpowered. If screens are layered beyond three levels, the user may also find the system difficult to handle. Customer inquiries are frequently performed with time pressures, and it may be difficult for the user to switch screens. The system should be designed to help the user as much as possible so that screens can be easily called up and the link between screens is evident to the user.

Next come the two C principles of good design. The first C principle stands for the conventions that must be imposed on the information system. These conventions should be standardized. If other systems already have established conventions, the designer should adopt these standards rather than introduce new ones. Standardization assists the user by eliminating the need to remember many operating procedures. For example, if the key F1 summons the help feature in the firm's other information systems, the designer should adopt this same convention for the new system. The conventions inherent within the system software should also be adopted rather than introducing new and confusing procedures.

The final C principle stands for the incorporation of existing cultural biases. One such bias is the scanning of data from left to right, top to bottom. Screens, forms, and any data representations should follow this preferred pattern as illustrated in Figure 14-4. Another bias is the preference to treat

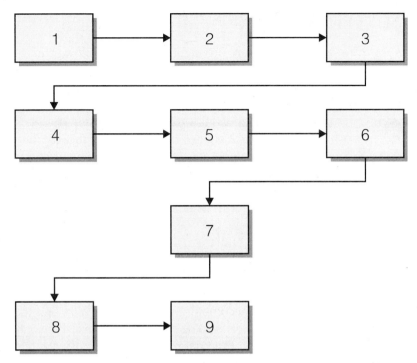

FIGURE 14-4
The culturally preferable arrangement of information Left to right, top to bottom scan.

the computer as an impersonal object. Consequently, messages from the computer should not attempt to imitate human dialogue but express information neutrally. Other biases may be present due to the work environment. Terms common to the work place should be employed rather than the expressions preferred for the general public. The users' own likes and dislikes should be considered in the design of the human interfaces, because this is the place where they interact with the system. To summarize, the analyst must be cognizant of the users' strengths and weaknesses and design the human–machine interfaces accordingly. Providing for user involvement and testing of the input/output designs ensures that user satisfaction and good designs will result.

> **Warning**
> Although it is tempting to write funny or personalized error messages, you should simply inform the user about the problem in a brief but precise message. Lengthy messages telling the user what's wrong at the computer terminal are daunting; a simple message is all the user wants or needs.

OUTPUT DESIGN IN EIGHT STEPS

As shown in Figure 14-5, there are eight steps to be followed in the preparation of output designs for an information system. Step 1 considers the identification of which input and output data flows must be designed for human eyes and ears. In order to do so, we locate the boundaries of the system and mark the data that will flow directly to or from the system users or the external entities. Step 2 defines the contents of the outputs. Step 3 defines what purposes the output data serves for the organization. Step 4 selects the output medium and processing method. A brief description of the various media available for output data is presented. Step 5 designs the data formats. Step 6 specifies any forms that must be used in conjunction with the output data. Step 7 indicates the controls to be imposed on the data. Step 8 obtains the formal approval of the user for the final design.

Even though these tasks are presented as separate steps, in the design process most of these steps are really interdependent. The sequential ordering of these steps is done only to facilitate our discussion. The decision in one step may affect the outcome of the other steps. Although the user's approval is considered the final step, as a matter of course the analyst consults with the user throughout the design process. Because the designs of inputs and outputs involve some inherently different considerations, we will concentrate first on output design and save the discussion of input design for the following chapter.

FIGURE 14-5

Output design in eight steps

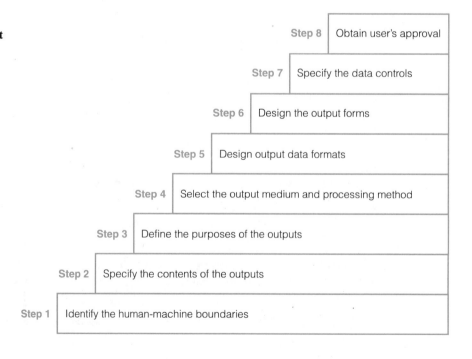

Step 8 | Obtain user's approval

Step 7 | Specify the data controls

Step 6 | Design the output forms

Step 5 | Design output data formats

Step 4 | Select the output medium and processing method

Step 3 | Define the purposes of the outputs

Step 2 | Specify the contents of the outputs

Step 1 | Identify the human-machine boundaries

Step 1: Identify the Human–Machine Boundaries

During the Analysis phase, the systems analyst prepared a model of the proposed information system represented by data flow diagrams, the associated data dictionary, and the complete set of process descriptions. To initiate the design of the input/output data, the analyst turns to the data flow diagrams and the data dictionary. In step 1, the analyst determines which inputs and outputs cross the boundary from the human users to the computer information system. Before the design of screens, reports, and other documents can begin, it is necessary to define which data flows originate from or flow to persons who will act on them—that is, to decide what interfaces must be designed for the system. In step 2, the contents of these data flows will be specified.

The **human–machine boundary**, which is found by examining the data flow diagram, is the point where the individual and the computer interact by the exchange of information. Everything inside the boundary will be computerized. Every data flow crossing the boundary is an input or output that must be designed. Since the external entities lie outside the boundaries of the system, any data flows sent to or received from external entities cross the human–machine boundary and are marked for design tasks. Figure 14-6 shows the model of the proposed system for Dr. Washington's medical office (Chapter 8) with the human–machine boundary outlined. The inputs and outputs to be designed (called the *net inputs* and *net outputs*) are marked with a bullet at the point of crossing the boundary. As indicated on the data flow diagram, seven outputs are produced by this system: SCHEDULED APPOINTMENT, PATIENT RECALL, 3RD PARTY IN-VOICE, MEDICAL INFO AND CHARGES, PATIENT INVOICE, MEDICAL SUPPLY ORDER, and MEDICAL SUPPLY PAYMENT. Each output must be designed for effective use by the medical and accounting staff as well as by the patient, third-party carrier, and medical supplier.

Another example is furnished by the Campus Bookstore information system (presented in Chapter 7) which must service the requests from instructors regarding their textbook orders. The response to such requests is a system output generated from information residing in computer files that are not directly readable by humans. The information system must provide the requested data in a format that can be viewed by human eyes or ears. It should also be noted that some system outputs are produced in a medium that is not discernible by humans. For example, a payroll system may need to supply payroll information in machine readable form to the Internal Revenue Service. Although the data will be produced only in machine readable form, the data nonetheless cross the boundary from the information system to an external entity outside the system. All these outputs are noted by the analyst on the data flow diagram for the new system.

In conjunction with the identification of the net inputs and outputs, the analyst decides how many programs will constitute the information system.

FIGURE 14-6   The proposed system for Dr. Washington's office   Inputs and outputs that cross the human–machine boundaries are marked with bullets.

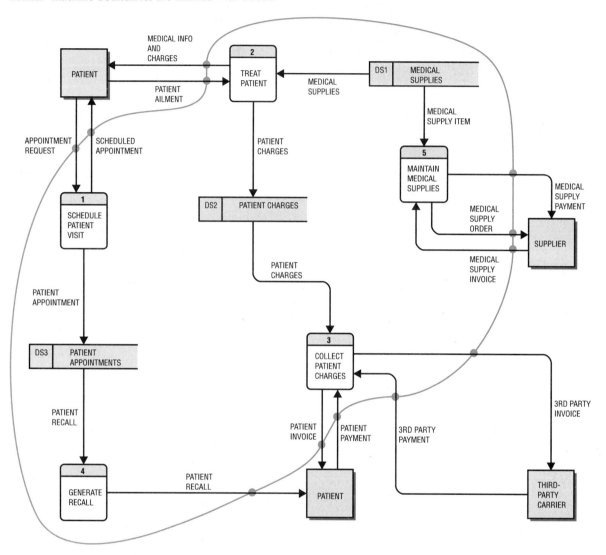

Small information systems may consist of only one program. It is also possible that individual programs will be linked together to be called up by the same menu or master selection procedure. First, the analyst groups together the processes performing a single major activity by drawing a line about them. Second, each major activity is defined as *on-line, batch,* or *manual.* As a rule, those activities to be performed at scheduled intervals are classified as suitable for batch program processing, while an activity triggered by an event or transaction is better handled by on-line processing.

The type of applications most suitable for batch mode have two characteristics:

1. A large number of records on a single file must be processed by the program.
2. The processing is required only at specified time intervals.

Examples of batch processing are the preparation of a weekly payroll, the annual W-2 forms for employees, the renewal notices for magazines, and the utility bills sent by gas and electric companies. Today on-line systems are the preferred mode for transaction processing, such as recording a customer's purchase of a product or a student's course registration. Processing that is performed in response to individual events, such as a customer's inquiry about a telephone bill (an external event) or a manager's request for more information about the quarterly sales figures (an internal event), is also best executed by means of an on-line program. On-line processing has become increasingly important as computer information systems have raised customers' expectations for prompt responses to any questions.

Exceptions to this general preference for on-line processing still exist. For example, if a paycheck has been issued for an incorrect amount, the employee's request for a new paycheck is commonly remedied by a check for a cash advance rather than a newly calculated paycheck. The controls necessary for financial processing limit the processing of paychecks to fixed periods. However, on-line processing can be used both to cancel the erroneous paycheck and to issue a new check for the cash advance.

Sometimes processing has the outward appearance of an on-line system even though the data are merely captured for later processing. The automated teller machine (ATM) provides such an example. Withdrawals and deposits to a bank account are processed on-line to separate files established only for the ATM system. Separate files for the ATM transactions are maintained in order to print the ATM user's correct balance on the transaction slip. The next day, the official accounts for the ATM users are updated by processing the ATM transactions that occurred the day before. This processing is performed in batch mode. One reason for this delay is that deposits can be accepted only after the cash or check deposits have been verified. Thus, the ATM system is a mixture of batch and on-line processing.

Certain tasks may remain manual. Sometimes this is due to cost considerations; other times, it may be due to the nature of the task. An example is the annual counting of the physical items in a retail store. Merchandise inventory totals are then entered into the computer information system in order to adjust the values stored there. Despite the use of an automated system, it is still necessary to determine manually the actual quantity of each merchandise item present in the inventory. Shoplifting, mistakes in sales records, and theft by employees may cause the physical inventory to differ from the computer's figures for the inventory on hand. Accordingly, some manual tasks may remain in the system.

Step 2: Specify the Contents of the Outputs

During the Analysis phase, the systems analyst prepared the definition of each data flow by specifying its contents in the data dictionary. If the data dictionary has not been fully specified, the analyst must remedy this situation before proceeding with the next step. The data type and length of the data elements must be defined so that the actual data representation can be formulated in step 5. For example, the data record PATIENT INVOICE required for Dr. Washington's information system (discussed in Chapter 8) is defined by an Excelerator data dictionary entry in Figure 14-7. Each data element contained within this data record is also defined by its own data dictionary entry to indicate its data type and length.

The analyst also reviews the data dictionary for completeness by verifying that the outputs can indeed be produced by the specified input data. If a CASE tool is not available, each output definition must be inspected to ensure that the corresponding input data will enter the system and be available to produce the desired outputs. We will now describe how the CASE tool Excelerator helps the analyst in performing this verification. This analysis is assisted by the use of the indicator **Base** or **Derived** to describe each data element in the data dictionary. As shown in Figure 14-8, the data dictionary entry for the data element INVOICE NUMBER has its length as four

FIGURE 14-7

The data dictionary entry for the data flow PATIENT INVOICE

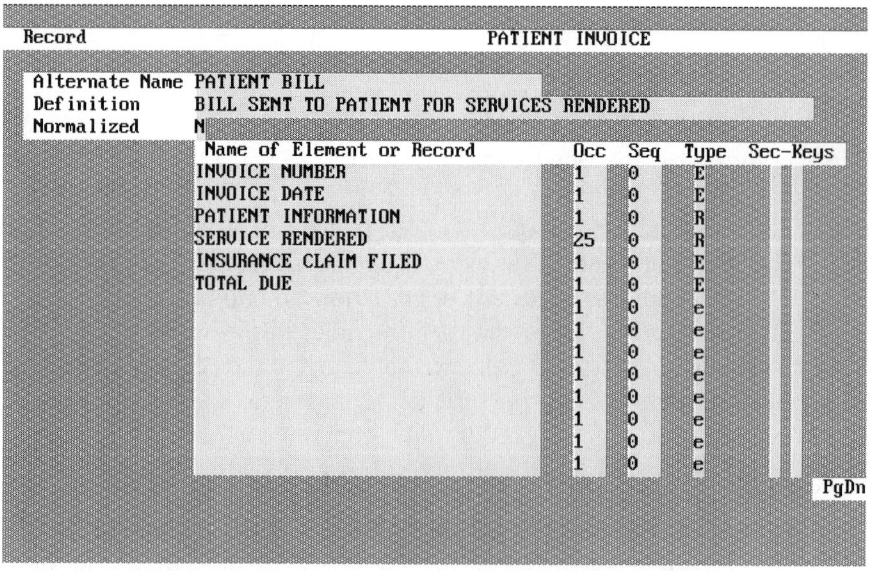

Screen shots produced using INTERSOLV's Excelerator solution for Requirements Analysis and Design.

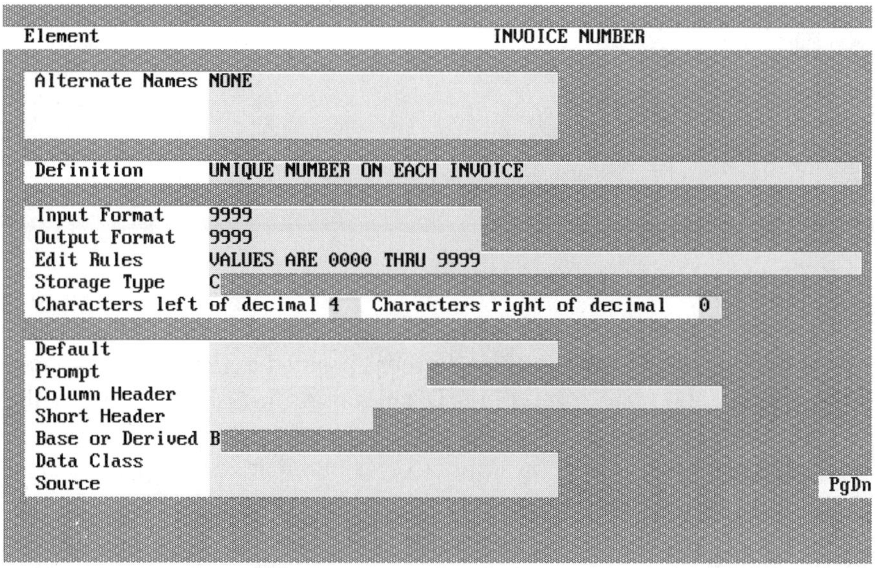
Element INVOICE NUMBER

Alternate Names NONE

Definition UNIQUE NUMBER ON EACH INVOICE

Input Format 9999
Output Format 9999
Edit Rules VALUES ARE 0000 THRU 9999
Storage Type C
Characters left of decimal 4 Characters right of decimal 0

Default
Prompt
Column Header
Short Header
Base or Derived B
Data Class
Source
PgDn

Screen shots produced using INTERSOLV's Excelerator solution for Requirements Analysis and Design.

FIGURE 14-8
The data element INVOICE NUMBER for the data record PATIENT INVOICE

characters, its data type as C for character, and its origin as B for Base. Because INVOICE NUMBER has been marked B for Base, the element cannot exist as an element on an output data flow from a process unless it has also entered the process. If a data element is marked D for Derived, the element must exist on the output data flow of at least one process but not be present on the input data flow to that same process. A Derived data element is created by the manipulations or computations performed by one of the processes in the data flow diagram. If Excelerator is employed as the CASE tool, the ANALYSIS module can be used to find any missing data entries as well as any data elements that violate the rules regarding Base and Derived data elements. By executing the checking features available in the ANALYSIS module, the analyst can ensure that the data dictionary is consistent and complete. This means that the data elements necessary to generate the desired outputs are represented by the system inputs. Other cross-checks of the data records, data elements, and data stores can be performed. Similar analysis capabilities are found in other CASE tools.

Step 3: Define the Purposes of the Outputs

The purpose of a system output will affect its design. By fully understanding the function of the output, the analyst can select the most appropriate output medium and format. Outputs may be designed for either external or internal use. An external document is one that will be received by a person or organization outside of the firm. Internal documents are those sent to individuals within the firm, typically managers. A system output has one of the following functions:

1. To provide information
2. To serve as a turnaround document
3. To act as archival storage

INFORMATIONAL OUTPUTS

Information is supplied either as reports, responses to queries, or the recording of transactions. Reports are further classified as *detail* reports, *summary* reports, and *exception* reports. Detail reports furnish the details of the information required. All information is displayed in its raw form rather than according to certain selection criteria or as summarized information. An example of a detail report is the listing of all sales transactions for the month. Summary reports present summaries of the data such as quarterly reports, which display sales totals per product for that quarter; see Figure 14-9. Another example is the report tabulating how many students with the status of undergraduate, graduate, and special category are enrolled for the current term at a university. A third example is a report listing the grade point average for each student at midterm time. Exception reports display information according to selected criteria. For example, the list of customers with payments more than 60 days overdue is an exception report. A report showing the students with GPAs 3.5 and over for the previous academic term is another example of an exception report.

Queries are requests for information from the existing computer files. The response to queries may be a lengthy report or a short one-line answer.

FIGURE 14-9   **A sample summary report**

QUARTERLY SALES REPORT

PRODUCT NUMBER	PRODUCT DESCRIPTION	APRIL	MAY	JUNE	QUARTERLY TOTALS
A210349	MOUSE	$135,037	$136,217	$144,837	$416,091
A215590	5¼″ DISK DRIVE	$102,035	$106,215	$100,203	$308,453
A234809	3½″ DISK DRIVE	$169,634	$167,669	$175,346	$512,649
A244499	200M HARD DRIVE	$785,663	$727,695	$715,468	$2,228,826
A250832	100M HARD DRIVE	$155,681	$154,984	$163,041	$473,706
A345260	386 MICROCOMPUTER	$199,216	$194,561	$201,431	$595,208
A377903	486 MICROCOMPUTER	$111,031	$114,393	$123,668	$349,092
TOTALS		$1,658,297	$1,601,734	$1,623,994	$4,884,025

Short queries are often answered by screen displays. The ways of formulating queries will be discussed in Chapter 15.

Transactions are the act of doing business and must be recorded. The flow of a transaction typically causes the creation of several outputs. A customer order will require the recording of the transaction. In turn, the invoice to the customer requesting payment will be created and sent to the customer. In addition, a copy of this invoice will be filed as a historical record in the information system.

TURNAROUND DOCUMENTS

A **turnaround document** is a two-part paper document that serves both as an output and later as an input to the system. Figure 14-10 illustrates a typical turnaround document, which serves as the invoice to the customer. To ensure that the payment is recorded properly, the customer is asked to return the top portion of the sheet with the payment. The returned portion then reenters the system as an input. Turnaround documents are typically created by the use of printed forms.

ARCHIVAL STORAGE

Periodically, the firm may remove some or all data records from a computer file to a place for safekeeping, that is, for **archival storage** of the data records. Removing the records from the current file shortens the time it takes to process records, since fewer records remain to be scanned. Examples of information that must be archived are financial and medical records. If the data will no longer be altered, then a read-only data medium such as optical disks may be selected. Using laser technology, an **optical disk** records data at densities far greater than conventional magnetic disks. Since the recording is permanently burned into the disk, the medium is called read-only memory (ROM). The most popular optical disk system is a **CD-ROM** (compact disk/read-only memory) that is used in conjunction with microcomputers. However, the most common medium for archival storage remains magnetic tape.

Step 4: Select the Output Medium and Processing Method

A *medium* is the physical material on which the data are recorded. The *format* of the data is the way in which data are represented on the chosen medium. If desired, the output data may be provided to the user on more than one output medium. For example, the user may call up information at a computer terminal and then decide to print this information rather than only viewing it on the screen. Similarly, output data supplied on microfiche may also be available in conventional printed documents, if the need exists for both types of media.

FIGURE 14-10

A turnaround document The customer returns the top portion of the invoice with the payment and keeps the bottom portion as a record of the transaction.

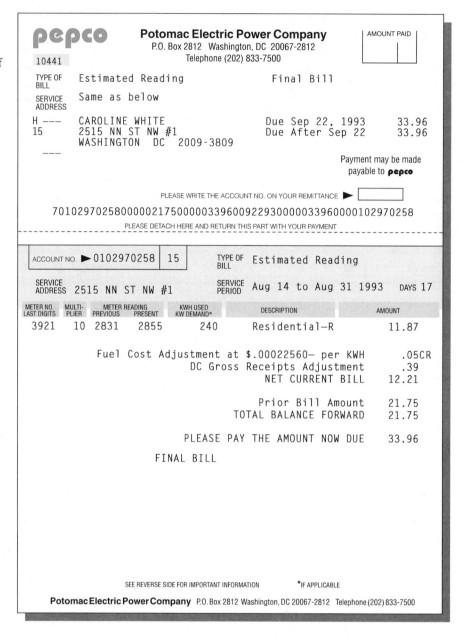

OUTPUT MEDIA

A list of storage media is given in Figure 14-11. The analyst must determine the best medium for the output data by weighing its cost together with its suitability in performing the required system functions. Each medium offers its own set of advantages and disadvantages. Since output devices are typically discussed in an introductory computer information system course, we shall review these devices only briefly.

FIGURE 14-11
Storage media for outputs

Storage Medium	Output Device
Printed documents	Printers: line, serial, or page
Microfilm or microfiche	COM (computer output to microfilm or microfiche)
Screen displays	Computer screens
Voice output	Voice synthesizers
Magnetic tape or disk	Magnetic tape or disk devices
ROM (read-only memory) disks	Optical disks and CD-ROM

Hard Copy   The most common medium for computer output remains paper. The computer output printed on paper is known as **hard copy**. Frequently, multi-ply computer paper is used so that one copy can be retained by the firm while other copies are distributed to other locations, as needed. Invoices are typically sent as paper documents and reports are delivered to management on paper. Paper has serious disadvantages. As the number of paper documents increases, it becomes progressively more difficult to store and retrieve information.

Various types of printers exist for producing hard copy. They are classified as either *impact* or *nonimpact* printers and further categorized as *serial, line,* or *page* printers. The quality and speed of printing vary according to the type of printer but also differ widely within each category. Printing multiple copies by using multi-ply computer paper requires an impact printer. Line printers and serial printers are typically impact printers, where the characters are printed by type bars striking against the paper. A **line printer** strikes all the characters of a line in apparent simultaneity whereas a **serial printer** prints only one character at a time. Line printers are substantially faster and more costly than serial printers. A **page printer** is a nonimpact printer that creates an entire output page at one time by means of a laser beam or an electrostatic charge. Page printers are the fastest and most suitable for voluminous outputs. Because the cost of page printers is very high, they are not widely used unless the application requirements demand high-speed printing. Laser printers for personal computers are much less expensive (often less than $1,500) but also much slower devices (4 to 10 pages per minute).

COM   As an alternative to paper, some firms have turned to COM, computer output to microfilm or microfiche. **Microfilm** is a roll of photographic film that records information in reduced size. **Microfiche** stores many pages on a single sheet of film. Special readers are required in order to view documents stored on microfilm or microfiche. Both textual and graphical displays can be placed on microfilm or microfiche. When compared to printed output, the COM method reduces storage space and costs and offers output speeds 10 to 20 times faster than either line or serial printers. Computer-assisted retrieval (CAR) equipment provides simple loading and retrieving of specific pages from microfilm. The two main disadvantages of microfilm or microfiche are their high cost and the user's need for special devices in order to view the data.

Some retailers have used microfiche to store the catalog of spare parts for its products. Before using the microfiche reader, the clerk for Customer Services examines the index to the microfiche catalog and identifies which microfiche contains the information for the customer's appliance. The appropriate microfiche is then pulled from the stack and the diagram of the device is examined to find the part number for the repair to be performed. If paper were chosen as the storage medium, the clerk would be thumbing through a huge catalog to find information. Rather than reprinting a voluminous catalog, these retailers update the information on parts for new products easily, by simply issuing additional microfiches plus a new index to the set of microfiches containing the information on parts.

Screen Displays   Depending on the application, outputs may be provided as screen displays at the user's terminal or microcomputer. The response to a user's query can be simply placed on the screen for viewing. The disadvantages of screen output are its lack of permanence and the small face of the screen. There is no hard copy for the user to consult later; once the information leaves the screen, it must be recalled for further examination. The screen is a small area and typically contains only 25 output lines and 80 character positions per line. To study a lengthy table of information entails constant flipping between screens, which may be frustrating and unsatisfactory.

Voice Output   Voice output is another possibility for output data. Voice messages are transitory—they exist only temporarily, at the moment they are spoken. Users may not understand a message the first time and may require the message to be repeated. Those users who don't require a second listening may be quite annoyed by its repetition. Voice output has been found to be successful when coupled with machines such as the information service supplied by telephone companies. Today, most telephone companies offer directory assistance (given by the 555-1212 telephone number) furnished by a human operator with the help of the computer. For example, when we ask for the telephone number of the ABC Company the operator responds by obtaining the alphabetized listing with ABC Company on the computer screen and then selecting that name. The computer then "speaks" the telephone number and repeats it once. All the digits 0 through 9, have been recorded by a human operator and stored in digital form within the computer's storage, and the computer simply chooses which digits to issue as voice output. Voice mail is also delivered in spoken form. Because the user can ask for the voice mail message to be repeated, the transistory nature of speech is overcome. However, many users still prefer textual information.

Other Media   The output data may be placed on a secondary storage device for subsequent display on screens or for transmission to other sites. Magnetic tape, disk, and diskettes are popular storage media for data. As mentioned earlier, *optical disk storage devices* have become widely used for high volume data. Such disks can be used to store text, data, and sounds represented as digitized patterns. Most optical disk devices are unable to alter data after it has been written on the disk. Consequently, they are known as *read-only memory* (ROM) devices or *write once, read-many* (WORM) devices. Because the storage capacity of optical disks greatly exceeds that offered by magnetic diskettes, they are often used to store semipermanent data that are changed only periodically rather than modified frequently. Examples are indexes to periodicals issued on optical disks on a fixed schedule such as monthly or bi-monthly. The indexes can be quickly searched by the associated program to provide information to the researcher. Another example is the placement of the entire Merriam-Webster's Ninth Collegiate Dictionary on a CD-ROM. The "reader" of the dictionary can scan its entire contents, including sound and illustrations, on the computer using special equipment.

SELECTION FACTORS FOR THE OUTPUT MEDIUM

As shown in Figure 14-12, seven factors influence the choice of medium for the system's outputs: usage, volume, quality, cost, frequency, requirement for multiple copies, and distribution. As always, there is a trade-off between these factors. Frequently, the characteristics of the output may rule out one medium. If the output is voluminous, microfilm or microfiche may be considered. However, if the purpose of the output is the transmittal of invoices to customers, paper may be the sole possibility. For hard copy, the analyst must ensure that an appropriate printer is available or will be acquired, so that the hard copy can be produced on time. Electronic transmission of outputs should also be considered.

Usage   Usage means the ways in which the output data will be processed by the users. Examples of system outputs are the orders sent to publishers by a bookstore, the listing of books not yet delivered, the tabulation of

Usage	Frequency
Volume	Multiple copies
Quality	Distribution
Cost	

FIGURE 14-12
Seven factors for selection of the output medium

unsold textbooks in stock five weeks after the academic term has begun, the class lists distributed by the university to the instructors, and the tabulation of student enrollment delivered to the president of the college. Each of these outputs has a different use. By understanding the proposed use of a system output, the analyst can better design the medium and the format for this information.

Volume   The quantity of data to be processed greatly influences the choice of medium. If the volume of a single output document is high, then high-speed printers—line or page printers—may be the best choice. Otherwise, too much time is required to produce the document. For high volume output, microfiche is a convenient and relatively inexpensive medium compared to the costly printing and distribution of bulky paper documents.

  The overall length of an output should be estimated so that cost figures can be based on both frequency and length. For paper documents, the output's length is measured in the number of pages required. If screens will be used for output, the total number of screens needed to display the information in a suitable format is an important design criterion.

Quality   Quality refers to the characteristics of the printed document or screen display provided for the output. For example, if a report is first printed on a line printer in all capital letters and then produced on a laser printer with upper and lower case letters, the first report is of poor quality compared to its second version. While the line printer is useful for voluminous reports, its printing quality cannot match that of a laser printer, which uses upper and lower case characters. Similarly, the use of color on reports may be beneficial and, if used judiciously, can heighten the quality of the document. The quality needed for a report depends on its usage. Delivering a summary report to the president of the firm may call for high quality documents with color display, whereas the manager who requires a listing of monthly sales commissions for routine review will be satisfied with line printer quality.

Cost   As always, cost can be a decisive factor in selecting the medium for the system's outputs. If the volume of the system's outputs is low, it is difficult to justify expensive equipment. For example, although the use of microfiche is convenient for many purposes, its high cost is prohibitive unless high volume requirements for output exist.

Frequency   How often the output must be issued defines its frequency. An output may be required either hourly, daily, weekly, monthly, yearly, or sporadically. The output's frequency rate is important in estimating the costs for its production. Scheduling the computer to create the required outputs must also be considered. If a report will be issued daily at 8:00 A.M., the computer schedule must have sufficient time available to execute the programs that produce the desired output.

Multiple Copies The analyst must determine if multiple copies are needed. Several methods for creating multiple copies are available. The computer output could be reproduced off-line by reproduction methods such as photocopying. For fewer copies, multi-ply paper, either layered with carbons or chemically treated paper, can be used directly on an impact printer to create the necessary number of copies. Although the computer could be used to create multiple copies by printing the output more than once, this is usually the least desirable choice because it ties up the printer and, to some extent, the computer. The number of pages together with the number of copies required influences the choice of copying method. Finally, the output could be designed so that forms are placed side by side, allowing the computer to print two or more forms across the page width. Bursting (separating at perforations) the printed output must be estimated as a cost for multiple copies. Automatic bursters should be employed for large volume output.

Distribution   "Who receives the output?" is the question to be answered for distribution. The nature of those who use the outputs will affect the medium choice as well as the format design. If the output goes to a customer, it is important to project the firm's image favorably. The entire document must be placed on suitable forms rather than blank paper. In contrast, if a report will be used by a manager and then discarded the next day, the expense of high quality forms most likely should be avoided.

SELECTION OF PROCESSING METHOD

The *processing method* refers to the way in which the system will produce the output for the user. Either batch or on-line processing methods can be employed. An on-line processing system offers immediate response to the user's request for information. In batch processing the desired information is delayed until the required program has been executed, usually at fixed time intervals. Because both methods offer advantages and disadvantages, the analyst again faces a trade-off situation. The user's desire for a rapid response to a request must be balanced against the cost and hardware requirements of on-line processing. In addition, some information is best supplied as routine reports issued periodically by a batch processing operation. Quarterly reports and yearly summaries are examples of outputs most appropriately produced by a batch processing system.

Queries for small amounts of information are often best handled by means of on-line processing. For example, questions from customers regarding orders or invoices require the system to furnish information to the user who must answer these inquiries. Today such questions are typically answered immediately because the user is able to instantaneously access the customer's account data and obtain the information to reply promptly to these queries. This promptness is only possible when the system permits on-line queries. A basic requirement for on-line queries is a suitable query language that allows the user to indicate in a simple fashion exactly what information is requested from the data files. Such information requests are serviced by providing for unstructured queries in a language easily mastered by the user. A query language such as Query-By-Example gives the user the flexibility to retrieve information for decision making without the need to formulate the exact questions for system outputs months before the system is ready for use. Thus, we see that the design of the human–computer dialogue (discussed in Chapter 15) also affects the design of outputs.

Step 5: Design the Output Data Format

As part of the required steps in the Analysis phase, the contents of the outputs were described completely by their corresponding entries in the data dictionary. In step 4 of the output design, the analyst decided on the medium in which the output will be represented. Now the analyst is confronted with the design of the actual data representation for screens and reports. Such questions as "Where should the data values appear on a page or screen?" or "What headings should be provided for the data?" need to be answered.

The guidelines for allocating data and identifying information on documents or screens have already been given within the $U^2H^2C^2$ principles. As mentioned earlier, the scan should be from left to right and top to bottom, and the labels assigned to the data should mirror the terms used in the work place. Some general rules for the design of screens and reports are listed in Figure 14-13. Most importantly, as we have stated before, recall that the output representation is formulated for the benefit of the users rather than for the ease of programming. This remark must always be tempered by any special considerations for retrieval time and processing constraints. An example is the time taken to display a screen with graphical data. If the processing power of the computer is insufficient to present the display within a reasonable time, the analyst may choose to employ a different type of display. Alternatively, the message "PLEASE WAIT" may be presented until the display is complete.

A second rule is to avoid clutter. If information is jammed into a screen without sufficient blank space, the user will find it difficult to read and

FIGURE 14-13

General rules for the design of screens and reports

1. Design for the user, not the programmer.
2. Do not clutter the space.
3. Organize the format to visually scan left to right, top to bottom.
4. Arrange the data into groups for easy recognition.
5. Label the output fields.
6. Color the output screens selectively.

understand the data values. The third rule was mentioned earlier: Arrange the data so that the user's eye scans left to right and top to bottom. Fourth, place the data into appropriate groups so the user can better recognize relationships among the data. Fifth, identify all output fields with terms meaningful to the user. Sixth, employ color selectively on the screens to enhance the data display. Be sparing, since too much color is distracting and can obscure the information to be conveyed to the viewer.

In order to plan the output design, the analyst may choose to sketch the layout on a form such as that shown in Figure 14-14. The general layout of the headings and data values is entered on the form, which then serves as a guide to the programmer. Another approach is to use a CASE tool (for example, Excelerator) or other software (such as a spreadsheet or data base management system) to sketch the general layout on a computer screen. Many CASE tools also provide for the generation of COBOL code corresponding to the output format. Because the data dictionary contains the complete description of the data elements, the analyst merely indicates the placement of any descriptive text and the data values on the screen. Excelerator also permits the modification of the data description for any elements during the output design procedure.

Another choice for data representation is the graphical depiction of the data. When data are represented visually, more information may be conveyed to the viewer. For example, when the increase in sales for a particular product occurs, a graph showing the steady rise in sales makes this fact immediately visible to the manager. Instead of hunting through pages of data, the manager quickly can see that a product has gained substantial sales. An example of a graph for daily sales data for the month of May is shown in Figure 14-15. This graph also shows the daily sales data for the previous May so that the manager can compare the current sales with historical data.

FIGURE 14-14   A sample layout sheet for output design

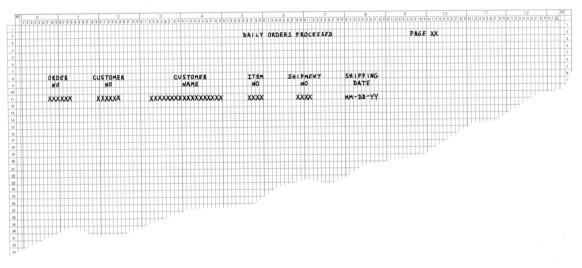

FIGURE 14-15
A graph of sales data for product A210349
This graph compares the daily sales in May for 1992 and 1993.

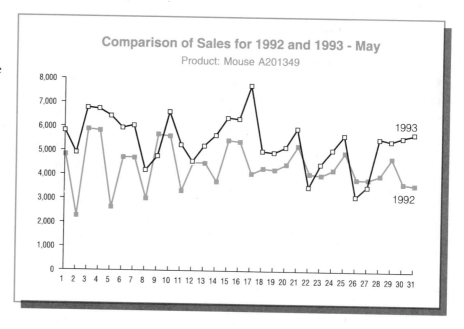

Step 6: Design the Output Forms

Even though much data will be entered and retrieved via screen displays, some data may require forms for printed outputs. Forms may be either preprinted or printed simultaneously with the output data. An example is a paycheck voucher form, as shown in Figure 14-16. The design layout of an output form follows the same principles stated earlier for data outputs. Special software to aid in designing forms may be obtained. Alternatively, CASE software may be used to design the overall layout of the form. The advantage of CASE software is the use of the data dictionary for the creation of the data fields. Each time a data element name is entered, the appropriate data length can be retrieved from the corresponding data dictionary entry and the dummy character string displayed on the screen. In this way, there can be no discrepancy between the length allocated for the data field and its assigned definition in the data dictionary.

Step 7: Specify the Data Controls

System outputs also require safeguards in order to prevent unauthorized use. A major concern is the enforcement of the privacy laws that require the release of confidential data only to authorized persons. Branches of the military, as well as private firms, wish to safeguard confidential information. In private businesses, highly valued information must be safeguarded against theft. Finally, any financial data or data regarding material goods should be secured against loss due to theft. For outputs, several approaches to controlling data are summarized in Figure 14-17. First, secure access to information so that only those authorized can enter the system and request

FIGURE 14-16   An example of a paycheck voucher   The paycheck is electronically deposited in the employee's account and the paycheck voucher is sent to the employee's mailing address.

BUREAU OF ECONOMIC ANALYSIS

20230   FORM AD-334 USDA (REV. 3/85)

SOCIAL SECURITY NO.	PAY PERIOD DATE	P/P	T&A CONTACT POINT	ACCT STAT	ORGANIZATIONAL STRUCTURE	PERSNL OFFICE	PAY PLAN	GR.	STEP
999 99 9999	MO 06 DA 28 YR 93 MO 07 DA 11 YR 93	13	53 11	0010 07 03	1500 53 04 03 0000	1702	GS	07	02

SALARY	RATE	TYPE EMPL.	SCD FOR LEAVE	RET DEDUCTIONS THIS APPOINTMENT
22 636 00	PA	F/T	06 17 91	184 18

STATEMENT OF EARNINGS AND LEAVE

EARNINGS AND DEDUCTIONS

CODE	ITEM DESCRIPTION	HOURS 1ST WK	HOURS P/P	HOURS YR. TO DATE	AMOUNT 1ST WK	AMOUNT P/P	AMOUNT YR TO DATE
01	REGULAR TIME	32 00	63 00	1 073 00	347 20	683 55	11 232 65
21	OVERTIME OVER 4C	10 00	10 00	82 50	162 80	162 80	1 304 70
44	CASH AWARD					650 00	650 00
61	ANNUAL LEAVE		8 00	48 00		86 80	503 36
62	SICK LEAVE		1 00	31 00		10 85	323 27
66	OTHER LEAVE	8 00	8 00	48 00	86 80	86 80	499 92
75D2	RETIREMENT @ .80%					6 94	100 46
75 15	THRIFT SAV-FERS TAX DEF					26 04	328 44
	*AMT BASED ON 868.00						
	75% G , 25% C						
76	SOCIAL SECURITY (OASDI)					104 21	899 87
77	FEDERAL TAX EXEMPTS S02					240 04	1 586 79
78	ST TAX DC EXEMPTS S01					102 08	889 37
83	FEHBA - ENROLL COD UN1					18 52	273 64
97	MED. HOSP. INS. (HITS)					24 38	210 45

****	GROSS PAY					1 680 80	14 513 90
****	NET PAY	ROUTING NO		054001204		1 158 59	10 224 88

BOND ACCOUNT

AUTH NO	DENOM-INATION	DEDUC-TION	BALANCE AVAIL.	NO. ISSUED	ISSUE DATE

YEAR TO DATE LEAVE STATUS

TYPE	ACCRUED	USED	BALANCE	PROJECTED USE OR LOSE	PT. HRS UNAPP	MAX. C/O
ANN	52.00	40.00	36.00	2400 0		
SICK	52.00	25.00	59.00			LEAVE CATEG
COMP				4		REMARKS

SAL CHNG-$ 21906.00PA TO$ 22636.00

NAME AND ADDRESS

|ılıllllıııılılıllıllıııllıl|
CAROLINE M WHITE
2515 NN STREET NW #1
WASHINGTON, DC 20009-3824

FIGURE 14-17
Four controls for output data

> Access Controls
>
> Distribution Controls
>
> Division of Labor
>
> Control Totals

outputs. Second, issue outputs to the proper recipients only. Third, divide the various computer tasks among personnel so no one has full control over the data processing operation. Finally, verify that the output data truly reflect the input data, for instance by comparing output data totals with input data totals. These four data controls—access controls, distribution controls, division of labor, and control totals—are discussed next.

ACCESS CONTROLS

Access controls restrict who can use the computer system and, thus, who can enter or receive data from the system. Three access control methods are password schemes, device authorization tables, and safeguards for communication lines. We note that both input and output data require the imposition of access controls. To avoid repetition, this topic is covered in conjunction with input design (see Chapter 15).

DISTRIBUTION CONTROLS

Printed documents or displays should be available only to those who need to view them. Reports containing sensitive information must be delivered only to authorized persons. The use of a routing slip coupled with the requirement for signatures on delivery may safeguard such documents. In particular, financial documents (such as checks) or authorization of product shipments must be carefully controlled so that theft will not occur. Such documents require printed forms that are sequentially numbered. The actual printing of checks or other sensitive documents should be performed in a controlled environment where the output is available only to those authorized to deliver them to the designated destinations. In addition, the system must be designed to restrict access to the commands that cause financial or confidential information to be printed, displayed, or transmitted to other locations.

DIVISION OF LABOR

The primary safeguard against computer theft is to prevent anyone from assuming autonomous control over a computer program. As shown in Figure 14-18, the programming task, the preparation of data, and the execution of a program are separate activities that should be performed by different persons. A *division of labor* prevents any single individual from altering a

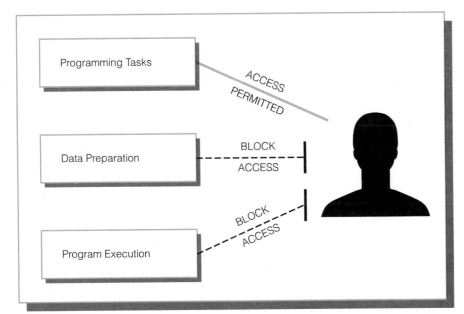

FIGURE 14-18
The division of labor
Allowing one person to
have more than two roles
invites misuse of data.

program, submitting data, and camouflaging theft of money or goods. Ideally, no one should know all the details required to process an unauthorized transaction. Operationally, no one should be allowed to perform all the tasks for a system. This means that computer programmers are not permitted to execute the applications that they have written or to prepare the data for processing by these programs. By eliminating the programmer's access to such programs, we erect barriers that prevent programmers from manipulating these programs for illegal monetary gain. As an additional safeguard, computer programming personnel should be rotated to other programs periodically to avoid exclusive control over sensitive programs.

In the same fashion, computer operators should be periodically assigned to different shifts or, in a company with more than one mainframe or computer network, transferred at intervals. Neither operators nor programmers should be allowed to prepare input data for programs. By dividing the tasks, we make sure no individual exercises complete control over the entire system. These safeguards are designed to reduce the time available for illegally manipulating a given program. The rotation of personnel offers a new person the opportunity to view the program and its outputs and, thus, detect any misuse of the program. An additional precaution is to separate the function of writing checks from the department that authorizes the checks, thereby preventing complete control from being vested in one individual.

CONTROL TOTALS

It is possible to ensure that data have been processed correctly by the imposition of **control totals**, which can be computed for the input data and then compared to the totals calculated for the same data given as output.

These control totals serve as an additional check that the data were handled properly. As discussed in Chapter 13, an example of a control total is the count of the input records processed; after processing is completed, the input record count is compared to the number of output records. If the totals are the same, the data processing has been faithfully performed. Aggregate totals for individual data fields may also be used (see Chapter 13). These control totals are also imposed on manually prepared data as a cross-check between the manual forms and the data records created by the data entry program. Control totals should be verified prior to the distribution of the system outputs.

Step 8: Obtain the User's Approval

Although the system has many facets, the systems analyst must remember that the users will interact with the system primarily through its inputs and outputs. These points of interaction with the system are the interfaces for those who will actually use the system and who must cope with its shortcomings. These interfaces include the screen displays, the printed reports, and the procedures required by the system. Consequently, it is important that the systems analyst continue to involve the user in the design of the system inputs and outputs. To properly design the flows to and from the system, the analyst must understand how the system's inputs originate and what manual processing is performed by the users with the outputs of the existing system. For example, if the report on outstanding accounts payable is now manually scanned to identify those invoices that are older than 30 days, the analyst must delve further to find out how this information is being used. The information on the report should be arranged in the best possible way to assist the users in their tasks. Mere replication of the existing reports for the new system is usually insufficient to meet the users' needs. New reports should be designed as required by the users for the performance of their work.

User involvement also means that the user should review the output formats to see if a more suitable organization of the data is needed. The user may also wish to include other information not previously provided by the old system. The presentation of mock paper documents and screen outputs for approval by the user helps to ensure that no detail is overlooked. The use of a CASE tool or another software package (such as Lotus 1-2-3 or dBASE IV) to quickly create sample inputs or outputs makes the design process a dialogue between the analyst and the user. By seeing sample input and output designs, the user is better able to judge what is wrong with the design. Any criticisms can then be used to modify the design and create new samples for review by the user. This process continues until the user is satisfied with the design formats. This refinement process with rapid exchange of ideas and computer sample designs is a form of *prototyping* (discussed in Chapter 2).

A Case Study in Mismanagement

In this book, good design principles plus controlled coding and testing procedures are presented as the path to a good, working system. Not all firms follow these guidelines. Since there are lessons to be learned from mistakes, let us consider the case of Empire Blue Cross and Blue Shield, the nation's largest nonprofit health insurer. "Empire lost tens of millions of dollars over the last decade through a series of management mistakes that drove the company into financial crisis and undermined its dominance of New York's health care system." Although some problems can be blamed on a bungled health maintenance organization, poor service, and the legal obligation of a nonprofit insurer not to reject the sickest applicants, the core of its problems is a series of computer fiascos that has spanned nearly two decades.

"Empire's inability to build a computer system that could keep track of millions of claims, the heart of any insurance company's business, has cost it millions of dollars and fostered a reputation for poor service." Because of computer problems dating back to the mid-1970s, "Empire was compelled to write off $50 million that had gone uncol-

lected or unbilled. One glitch involved a computer system that could not understand bills of $100,000 or more. For example, a $103,000 charge would be interpreted as only $3,000 and the smaller amount billed to the client. That failure alone occurred 29 times and cost Empire $3 million." The information system for Healthnet, a health maintenance organization established by Empire, originally could not keep track of the complex formula used to calculate payments to doctors who participated in the Healthnet plan. Within two years, the computer system had to be abandoned and another system installed. The problems are not over. A new system for handling claims, costing $17 million, is 18 months overdue and not expected until later this year. Regardless of the other mistakes made, the error-ridden computer information systems have clearly contributed to Empire's dismal financial state.

Source: Fritsch, Jane, and Baquet, Dean, "Big Health Insurer's Path to Crisis Is a Case Study in Mismanagement," *New York Times*, March 29, 1993. Copyright © 1993 by The New York Times Company. Reprinted by permission.

SUMMARY

This chapter discusses the general principles of input/output design and presents several examples of output designs. Before the design of inputs and outputs can begin, the analyst must define the boundaries of the system where human interfaces are required. The user interfaces of an application are those system inputs and outputs that cross these boundaries from the human's view to the computer's internal representation. Most system interfaces are visible representations of data, but some are stored in a form not discernible by humans. Good input/output design is perceived by the users mainly by the absence of negative design features that impair efficiency and productivity. Since humans and computers have different capabilities, the analyst must design user interfaces that use the computer's power to supplement human shortcomings.

The six fundamental principles of good design are expressed as $U^2H^2C^2$: User involvement; Users first, computers last; minimize Human efforts; remember Human limitations; Convention standardization; and Cultural bias. First, because users are directly affected by the interface designs, they should be involved throughout the design activity and give the final approval to the designs. Second, the design features should be formulated for the users rather than the ease of programming. Third, the burden of entering data or interpreting computer outputs should be placed on the computer. In particular, the time and effort required to enter data should be minimized in order to prevent human error. Fourth, the analyst should remember human limitations and design the interfaces to make the computer an assistant to the users. Fifth, conventions for the information system should be standardized. Finally, the designs should incorporate conventions due to cultural bias. For example, the scan of input screens or output displays should be left to right, top to bottom in the United States.

Eight steps were presented for output design. In step 1, after marking the boundaries of the system, the data flowing outside the system to persons or other external entities are recognized as outputs requiring the formulation of appropriate designs. In step 2, although the contents of the outputs were specified during the preparation of the data dictionary, additions may be made during the output design activity. In step 3, by knowing the purpose of the outputs, the analyst can select the most suitable data medium and processing method and design the data representation appropriately. A system output is created for one of the following reasons: (1) to provide information, (2) to serve as archival storage, or (3) to function as a turnaround document. Seven selection factors influence the choice of the output medium: usage, volume, quality, cost, frequency, requirement for multiple copies, and distribution. Typically, since no output medium will be completely satisfactory with regard to all these factors, a trade-off decision must be made.

In step 5, layout forms or software (such as a CASE tool, spreadsheet, or data base management system) are employed to assist the analyst in designing the output data formats. In step 6, the forms needed for the system outputs are designed. In step 7, output controls are designed to prevent the unauthorized use of output data and to verify that the correct processing of the input data has been accomplished. Four controls for outputs were presented: access controls, distribution controls, division of labor, and control totals. In step 8, the user's approval for the designs is requested.

TERMS

access controls	line printer
archival storage	microfiche
Base data element	microfilm
CD-ROM disk	optical disk
control totals	page printer
Derived data element	serial printer
hard copy	turnaround document
human-machine boundary	

QUESTIONS

1. What is meant by *human–machine boundary*?

2. Why should the users be involved in the design of the system's inputs and outputs?

3. A principle of good design is to minimize human efforts. Why is this beneficial?

4. How do the limitations of human memory affect the design of human interfaces?

5. Name the steps in output design.

6. Define a turnaround document and give two examples.

7. Define archival storage.

8. List the three reasons for producing a system output.

9. Define detail report, summary report, and exception report.

10. What is meant by hard copy? What devices are available to create hard copy?

11. What are the advantages and disadvantages of microfiche and microfilm?

12. When is voice output an appropriate medium for output data?

13. What are the seven factors that influence the choice of output medium?

14. Queries for small amounts of information are often best handled by means of on-line processing. Justify this statement.

15. What controls would you recommend for a payroll system that accepts manually prepared time sheets, performs data entry to transfer the data from the forms to magnetic disk, and prints the paychecks on preprinted forms?

16. What advantages are provided by the use of a CASE tool in creating the design of a report?

17. The monthly statement for a checking account is shown in Figure 14-19. Criticize the output format of this statement and explain how its design could be improved.

18. If you do not use an ATM card, ask a friend who does to assist you with this question. Take the ATM card and attempt to withdraw a small amount of money at your local ATM. Since we wish the transaction to fail, when asked to indicate the type of account, choose the wrong type (savings rather than checking or vice versa). This transaction will be

FIGURE 14-19

The monthly statement for a checking acount

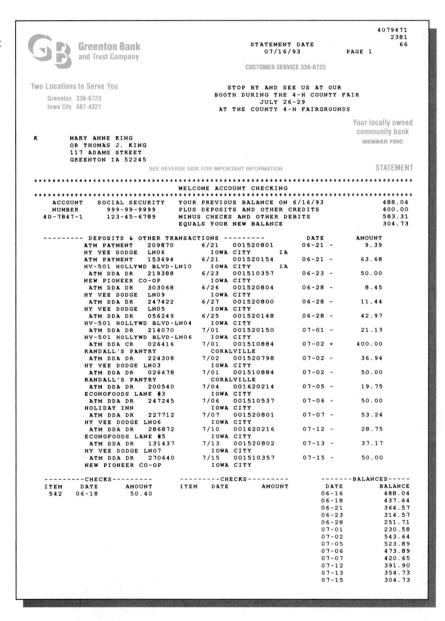

rejected by the ATM after all the transaction information has been entered.

   a. What output message was displayed by the machine? If an output slip was issued by the ATM, what message was given?

   b. Criticize the messages issued by the ATM for this incorrect transaction. Were the messages meaningful to the ATM user? Explain how you could improve on these messages, or justify their appropriateness.

PROJECTS

1. Visit your local bookstore and inquire about ordering a book that is not in stock. Ask how the sales personnel determine whether a book is in stock. If possible, view the computer screens, microfiche, or reports referenced by the sales clerk to answer this question.

   a. Describe the procedure now in use. Include in your description the storage medium and data format of the outputs used to find out what books are in stock.

   b. Could the design of the output data be improved in terms of the medium and data format? Explain.

2. Make an appointment to meet with the manager of a local restaurant to discuss what information is desired for the operation of the restaurant.

   a. What information is presently desired by the manager but unavailable?

   b. Design a report that supplies one set of the desired information. Make a mock-up representation using a CASE tool, a spreadsheet, or a data base management system such as dBASE IV.

REFERENCES

Bailey, Robert W. *Human Error in Computer Systems.* Englewood Cliffs, NJ: Prentice-Hall, 1983.

Brill, Alan E. *Building Controls into Structured Systems.* New York: Yourdon Press, 1983.

Duleavey, Mary Pat. "Electronic Dictionaries for the 21st Century." *The New York Times,* Sept. 6, 1992, p. F8.

Gould, John D., and Robert N. Ascher. "Query by Non-programmer." Presented at the 82nd Annual Convention of the American Psychological Association, New Orleans, August 30 to September 3, 1974.

Martin, James. *Design of Man–Computer Dialogues.* Englewood Cliffs, NJ: Prentice-Hall, 1973.

Morse, Alan, and George Reynolds. "Overcoming Current Growth Limits in GUI Development." *Communications of the ACM,* 36(4), April 1993, pp. 73–81.

Rubenstein, Richard, and Harry Hersh. *The Human Factor.* Bedford, MA: Digital Press, 1984.

Schutzer, Daniel. *Business Decisions with Computers.* New York: Van Nostrand Reinhold, 1991.

Thomas, John C. *Quantifiers and Question-Asking.* Research Report RC5866, IBM Watson Research Center, February 18, 1976.

Wu, Margaret S. *Introduction to Computer Data Processing*, 2nd ed. New York: Harcourt Brace Jovanovich, 1979.

CHAPTER 15

Input Design

Objectives

After completing this chapter, you will have gained an understanding of the following topics:

- The types of input media available for computer inputs
- The steps required for designing system inputs
- The controls needed for input data
- The types of human–machine dialogues possible for the overall system design
- The charting of human–machine dialogues

INTRODUCTION

In this chapter, we will discuss the design of the system inputs. Because some matters relate only to output design, that topic was treated separately in Chapter 14. Despite this division, we must remember that design issues are truly interrelated. This chapter is divided into two parts. The first part describes the steps taken to design the inputs that cross the boundary between human and computer. As in Chapter 14 we offer eight steps as guidelines for the input design tasks. The issues relating to input data controls appear as step 6 and the specifications of data codes are discussed in step 5 in conjunction with the design of data formats. The second part deals with the problem of human–computer dialogues. The six factors to consider before designing such dialogues are explained. The two types of dialogues, program-controlled and user-controlled, are defined. Then the design of human–computer dialogues is demonstrated with several examples. Finally, a technique for charting screen dialogues is described.

INPUT DESIGN IN EIGHT STEPS

As shown in Figure 15-1, there are eight steps to be followed in the preparation of input designs for an information system. Step 1 considers the identification of the input and output data flows that must be designed for

FIGURE 15-1
The eight steps of input data design

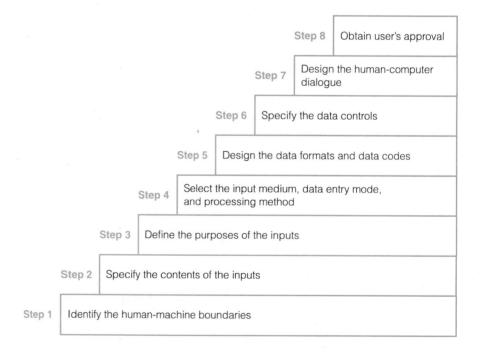

Step 8 | Obtain user's approval

Step 7 | Design the human-computer dialogue

Step 6 | Specify the data controls

Step 5 | Design the data formats and data codes

Step 4 | Select the input medium, data entry mode, and processing method

Step 3 | Define the purposes of the inputs

Step 2 | Specify the contents of the inputs

Step 1 | Identify the human-machine boundaries

human eyes and ears. In order to do so, we locate the boundaries of the system and mark the data that will flow directly to or from the system users or the external entities. Step 2 defines the contents of the inputs. Step 3 defines the purposes of the input data in the information system. Step 4 selects the input medium, data entry mode, and processing method. The various input media available for input data will be briefly described. Step 5 creates the formats for the data. The representation of data elements by coded fields will be discussed here. Step 6 decides what controls to impose on the input to ensure its integrity, avoid human errors, and prevent misuse. Step 7 formulates the way in which the user and the machine will interact, that is, the human–machine dialogue. Here we examine the options for the human–machine dialogue, the means by which the user communicates with the computer system. Step 8 obtains the user's formal approval of the final design.

We wish to remind you that input/output design activities are really executed as a single activity. The sequential ordering of these steps is done only to facilitate our discussion. These eight steps are explained individually but in reality steps 2 through 7 are interrelated activities. The decision in one step may affect the outcome of the other steps.

Step 1: Identify the Human–Machine Boundaries

As we discussed in Chapter 14, the analyst must determine the **human–machine boundary** in order to know which data flows must be designed. Figure 15-2 shows the level 0 data flow diagram for the Campus Bookstore (discussed in Chapter 7). The inputs and outputs traveling to or from the external entities are marked with bullets; the line connecting these bullets denotes the human–machine boundary for this system. The inputs to be designed are the TEXTBOOK ORDER, RETURNED BOOKS PAYMENT, TEXTBOOK SHIPMENT, USED TEXTBOOK, TEXTBOOK INFORMATION REQUEST, and TEXTBOOK INQUIRY. Further examination of these inputs shows us that the bookstore must accept the input RETURNED BOOKS PAYMENT in the format chosen by the external entity PUBLISHER OR DISTRBUTR. Since the bookstore is not large enough to dictate how this input should be delivered, it must be able to handle the externally-defined documents that convey the needed information to its system. A firm that is the primary or sole buyer of goods from a supplier may have the market clout to specify the format and medium of data transmitted by these interdependent companies; huge automobile manufacturers such as General Motors or Chrysler can dictate how information regarding ordering, billing, and payments will be exchanged. Since the Campus Bookstore is too small to receive any concessions from its suppliers, it must accept information as prepared by its suppliers, and then transform the data into a format and medium suited to its computer information system.

FIGURE 15-2 **The data flow diagram for the Campus Bookstore** The inputs and outputs to be designed are marked with a bullet where they cross the boundary.

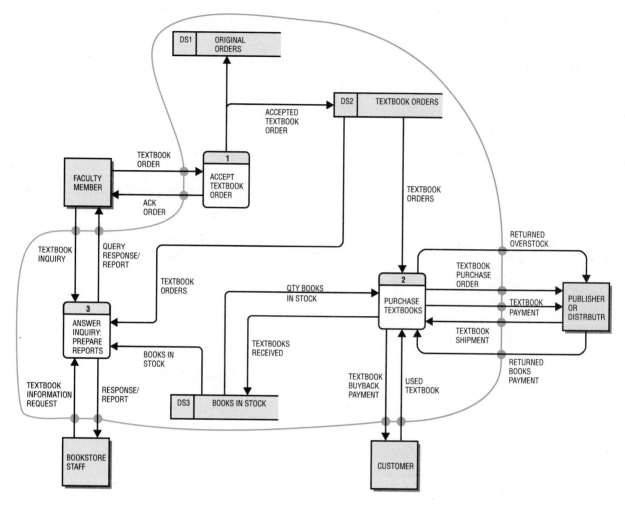

Step 2: Specify the Contents of the Inputs

As discussed in Chapter 14, the analyst reviews the data dictionary for completeness before entering the Design phase. The analyst must verify that the outputs can indeed be produced by the specified input data. If a CASE tool is not available, each output definition must be inspected to ensure that the corresponding input data will enter the system and be available to produce the desired outputs. When employing a CASE tool (such as Excelerator), the analyst invokes the ANALYSIS module and requests that this verification be performed. As explained in Chapter 14, this analysis is assisted by the use of an indicator, Base or Derived, for each data element.

Step 3: Define the Purposes of the Inputs

Before selecting a storage medium and format for the data, it is important to know what purposes are served by the input data. The origin of the data elements must be known as well as their use within the information system. For example, a payroll system is ordinarily dependent on input data that provides information regarding hours worked, vacation time, and sick time incurred by each employee. For a payroll system, the basic problem is to bridge the boundary between the people who supply the input data and the computer that must process the data. During the investigation of the existing system, the analyst will have discovered how the data are currently collected. By understanding the origin of the data, the analyst can decide whether to change the collection method by redesigning the time sheet forms or installing new machines such as time clocks or other devices to collect the data.

In our study of a physician's office (Chapter 8), the action of the physician who treats a patient during an office visit provides the basic input data to the billing system. The data collection process must capture this information from the physician in some fashion so that the data can enter the computer system. This data input serves two purposes: first, the data supply the diagnostic information required for preparing the patient's insurance claim; second, the data provide the treatment details necessary for the patient invoice. By understanding the role of the individual data elements for the patient's visit, the analyst can properly define the output record PATIENT INVOICE. Moreover, in order for the patient's payment to be processed as a system input, it must be received by the office together with the patient's name and identification number. Since the analyst understands the purpose of the invoice and the invoice's eventual payment by the patient, the output form will be designed as a two-part turnaround form such as shown in Figure 15-3. The top part, displaying the patient's name, address, identification number, and invoice number, will be returned with the patient's payment, while the bottom portion, listing the detailed billing information, will be retained by the patient.

Step 4: Select the Input Medium, Data Entry Mode, and Processing Method

In this step, the analyst chooses the input medium and the mode of entry for the data. In addition, the data processing method is defined as either on-line or batch mode. The term **input medium** indicates the physical substance that contains the input data prior to their entry into the information system. Examples of media are paper forms, magnetic strips such as those on credit cards and bank cards, and the computer screen used in combination with the keyboard. The term *data entry mode* denotes whether the input data are sent to the computer immediately at the time of its creation or after some

FIGURE 15-3

The patient invoice as a two-part form

```
                              STATEMENT
                    HIGHLAND INTERNAL MEDICINE
                          1920 Highland Circle
                         Greenton, Illinois 60699
                            (708) 999-7810

                                               Page No.    1


    Henry W. Lyons                        Acct. #   3192
    1818 Pleasant Ave.                    Date:      07/01/93
    Greenton IL  60699
                                         Amount Enclosed: _____

                                         Check Number:    _____

                   RETURN THIS PORTION WITH YOUR PAYMENT

    Date      Patient  Description of Transaction     Doctor   Amount  Ins
    --------------------------------------------------------------------------
    02/17/93  Karen    EGD with biopsy               Stangl    490.00
       PAID BY                 INS:   441.00 Patient:  49.00   490.00-
    02/17/93  Karen    Colonoscopy                   Stangl    520.00
       PAID BY                 INS:   468.00 Patient:  52.00   520.00
    03/02/93  Karen    Office/Oth outpt visit, EST, Le Hall     26.00
       PAID BY                 INS:    23.40 Patient:   2.60    26.00-
    06/05/93  Henry    Office/Oth outpt visit, EST, Le Hall     21.00
       PAID BY                 INS:    18.90                    18.90-
    06/05/93  Henry    Strep screen                  Hall       12.00
       PAID BY                 INS:    10.80                    10.80-


    _____

                       Account Balance:             3.30

                       Insurance Pending:             .00        *

                       Total Due From Patient:       3.30


    |                                                                    |
    |        ** PAYMENT DUE UPON RECEIPT, THANK YOU **                   |
    |                                                                    |


    Next Appointment :

    | CURRENT |  31 - 60 |  61 -90  |  91 - 120 |  121 - UP |          |
    |   3.30  |     .00  |     .00  |      .00  |      .00  |          |

    HIGHLAND INTERNAL MEDICINE                              2774
```

delay. Computer processing of the data may occur at once or later for either entry mode. In delayed entry, the values for the input data are obtained either by manually keying information, which is then transferred to magnetic tape or disk, or by receiving the data in a medium that the computer can read directly without manual intervention. This second type of input is called data in **computerized form**.

The choice of medium for input data is affected by the form of data entry: (1) the keying of the data by a human operator or (2) the direct entry of the data into the computer because the data already exist in computerized form. In the second case the data will be captured in computerized form at the point of origin, that is, the source. This method is also known as **source data automation**. We will first briefly discuss the types of media and then describe the immediate and delayed processing modes of operation possible for data input.

INPUT MEDIUM

The most popular method of data entry is the keying of data on a conventional keyboard, cash register, or specially designed register. In addition to keying the input data, various other media can be used to provide input data directly to the computer. Since input media are usually presented in an introductory course, their characteristics are reviewed only briefly. The types of input media are listed in Figure 15-4.

Punched Cards   Formerly the most popular input medium, punched cards are rarely used now except for a few large batch systems.

Magnetic Ink Character Recognition (MICR)   Since the available characters are limited, only the banking industry uses this medium and character set. A sample bank check with MICR characters is displayed in Figure 15-5.

Preprinted Characters   Optical character recognition (OCR) devices are able to recognize printed text in almost all type fonts. A font is an assortment of type, all of one size and style. Prestige Elite is an example of a type font. Two fonts designed especially for optical character recognition devices in order to minimize scanning errors are the OCR-A and OCR-B fonts shown in Figure 15-6.

Handwritten Characters   Forms can be completely handwritten and then scanned by OCR readers. A form filled by handwritten characters is

FIGURE 15-4
Various input media

Punched cards

Magnetic ink character recognition (MICR)

Preprinted characters

Handwritten characters

Mark sense recording

Magnetic strips

Bar codes

Electronic data interchange (EDI)

Voice input

Voice messages

Touch-tone telephone

Fax input

Magnetic tape or diskettes

FIGURE 15-5   **Magnetic ink character recognition (MICR) as an input medium**

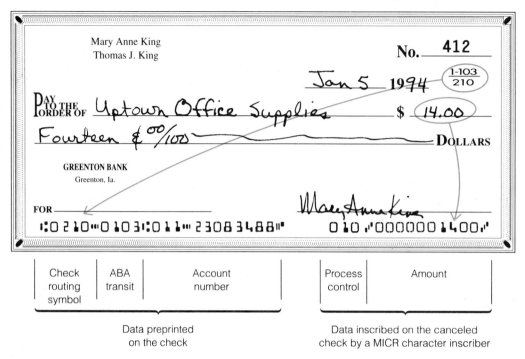

shown in Figure 15-7. The characters must be carefully printed to meet the standards required by the input device or they will not be accepted by the computer as input data.

Mark Sense Recording   When a small amount of data will be entered on a form, mark sense recording is a favored option. Mark sense forms must be specially printed according to rigorous standards in order to be successfully read by the optical reader. Examinations with multiple choice questions are typically administered with mark sense forms.

Magnetic Strips   Magnetic strips are used on the back of ATM cards and credit cards to carry the account number in machine readable form. The cards also have data embossed on the card so that the account number can be imprinted on paper forms using a manually operated device.

FIGURE 15-6

Two optical character recognition (OCR) fonts

OCR – A	OCR – B
ABCDEFGHIJKLMNOPQRSTUVWXYZ	ABCDEFGHIJKLMNOPQRSTUVWXYZ
abcdefghijklmnopqrstuvwxyz	abcdefghijklmnopqrstuvwxyz
0123456789	0123456789

FIGURE 15-7 **A sales slip recorded with handwritten characters to be read by an OCR device**

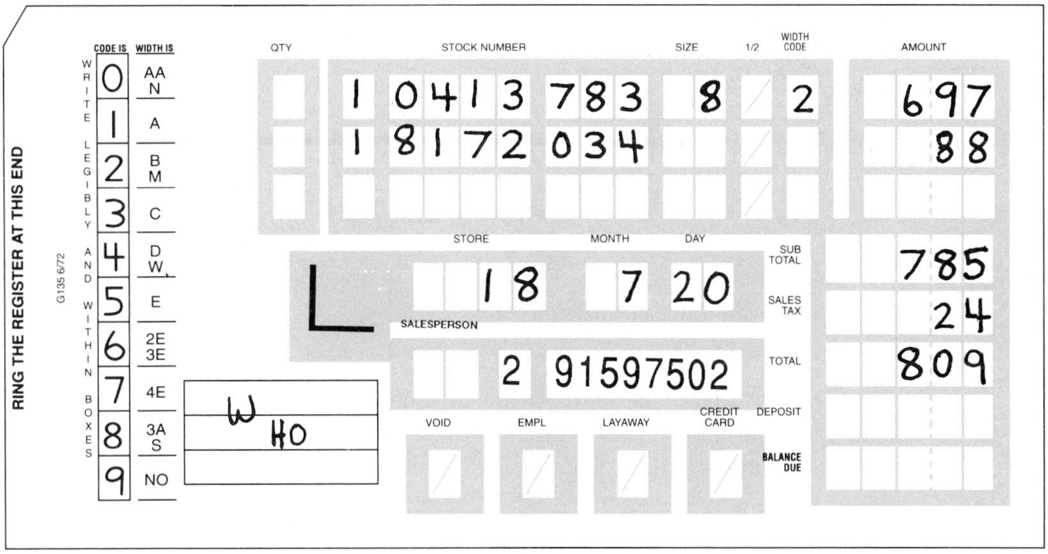

Bar Codes   Bar codes are now used for a variety of applications including grocery stores, magazines, boxed shipments, and documents. One major advantage is that the code can be read regardless of its orientation to the scanner; it is not necessary to align the code for it to be scanned correctly. The bar code for a grocery product is shown in Figure 15-8. Bar codes may be read either by hand-held light pens or stationary laser readers.

Electronic Data Interchange (EDI)   When information is passed electronically from computer to computer over a network, the transmission is called *electronic data interchange (EDI)*. For example, bills of lading and invoices can be transmitted electronically between customers and suppliers. With just-in-time production techniques, which minimize the time between orders and delivery, EDI is the preferred method of data transmission. EDI can be implemented on computers of any size, from mainframe to PC.

Voice Input   Voice recognition systems can identify a limited vocabulary of words spoken by selected individuals. The device is programmed to recognize the enunciation of the speakers. Voice input frees the workers' hands to perform other tasks simultaneously with the capture of data. For instance, workers can sort packages while issuing the label information as voice input.

Voice Messages   In this case, no recognition of the voice patterns is required. The voice message is stored by the computer in digitized form and replayed as vocal output. The individual words contained within the voice messages are not recognized or stored as data. A voice message requires a

FIGURE 15-8

The bar code for a grocery product

large amount of storage compared to the same information represented in textual form.

Touch-Tone Telephone   A touch-tone telephone allows the entry of data. Each key transmits a tone which can be received by the computer and stored as a character. Each tone is entered one at a time.

Fax Input   Documents may be transmitted by fax machines and received by the computer. The documents are stored for viewing by the user but the data on the document may not be directly interpretable by the computer.

Magnetic Tape or Diskettes   Data can be transferred from one computer facility to another by recording the data onto magnetic tape or diskettes. This storage medium is compact, easily transported, and relatively inexpensive for large amounts of data.

COMPARISON OF INPUT MEDIA

The representations of input data described above, except for faxed documents and voice messages, permit the data to be directly transmitted to the computer without the necessity of keying in the data. Data values present in faxed documents or voice messages typically cannot be manipulated or processed by the computer program. The image of the faxed document can be viewed by the user and stored in its entirety on magnetic tape or disk. When the immediate data entry mode is used, processing delays due to data preparation activities are avoided. In addition, if on-line processing is also used, the processing program can promptly reject any data that fail to meet its criteria.

Sometimes additional data must be transcribed onto the source documents so that all the necessary data can be read by a computer input device. An example is the check processing system in the banking industry. Although the checks have been imprinted with certain information, the amount of the check must be inscribed before the check can be processed by the system. A combination of methods can also be used. For example, the sales transaction at a retail store could automatically accept the account number from the magnetic strip on the customer's charge card, scan the bar codes on the merchandise items, and offer the option of manual entry of sales data by the cash register keys.

When selecting an input representation, the systems analyst must be aware of the wide range of options available. When volume of data is high, speed is important, and accuracy is sought, one of the computerized forms may be the best choice. The higher costs for computerized input media often prevent their adoption unless adequate financial benefits offset this disadvantage. It should be noted that the presentation of the data in computerized form does not automatically signify that on-line processing must be used.

TYPES OF DATA ENTRY MODE

As we discussed earlier, the two methods for transferring input data to the computer are: delayed entry or immediate capture of the data in computerized form. When the data are not available in a form suitable for direct input to the computer, delayed processing is necessary. For example, the keying of data is used as a data entry method when (1) data must be transformed from written documents into computerized form (**delayed data entry**) or (2) information was keyed by the operator at the time of data origination and thus captured in computerized form (**immediate data entry**). In the first case, if data have been recorded on forms, they must be transformed into a medium suitable for entry into the computer program. The data will be converted into computerized form on magnetic tape or disk by operators who manually key the data under the control of specialized data entry programs. Because the data are *transcribed* from their original source, there is a high likelihood that errors will be introduced during the transcription process. To prevent such errors, data are often keyed twice. The second set of transcribed data is compared to the first set of transcribed data. Any discrepancies are flagged and must be resolved by the data entry operators.

Delayed data entry is commonly found in **batch processing** systems where data are collected on paper documents and then grouped in batches for processing. Before processing can take place, the data must be transcribed into computerized form. Magazine subscription renewals and production of payroll checks are two examples of batch processing applications where data are typically transcribed for data entry into the computer processing programs. Because the originator of the data is no longer present, it may be difficult to resolve any data errors in the source documents.

Figure 15-9 illustrates the use of delayed data entry for a customer placing a subscription renewal. The customer mails the subscription renewal form to the magazine publisher. The office accumulates the renewal forms until a certain time, say the first day of the month. Then the renewal notices received up to that time are transcribed to magnetic disk by data entry operators. After the transcription has been completed, the renewal notices are processed as a batch by the computer program, the customer

FIGURE 15-9   An example of delayed data entry

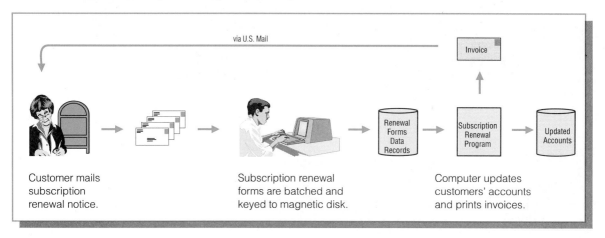

via U.S. Mail

Invoice

Renewal
Forms
Data
Records

Subscription
Renewal
Program

Updated
Accounts

Customer mails
subscription
renewal notice.

Subscription renewal
forms are batched and
keyed to magnetic disk.

Computer updates
customers' accounts
and prints invoices.

accounts are updated, and the set of invoices is prepared for mailing to the subscribers.

In contrast to the time lag required to convert data from paper forms to a computer medium, immediate data entry captures information directly at its source without requiring any additional steps to convert the data to computerized form. Either the data can be entered via keying and directly transmitted to the computer, or the data can be stored in a medium that can be read at a later time by a computer input device. Frequently, we associate immediate data entry with on-line processing of the data. However, it is also possible to use immediate data entry but schedule the actual computer processing of the data for a later time. For example, a retail shoe store could require all sales slips to be handwritten according to the requirements for optical character recognition devices, which read characters printed by hand (see Figure 15-7). The data are thus captured in computerized form because no further action is needed to prepare the data for the computer.

Figure 15-10 illustrates two applications where data are captured via keying. In Figure 15-10a, the airline reservation system uses immediate data entry. The airline clerk records the data at the time the customer requests a reservation, which is immediately recorded by the computer system. This mode of operation is called **real-time processing** because the data are captured and processed immediately. A second name for this mode of operation is **on-line processing** because the reservation is recorded in the data files while the operator is *on line*—directly connected—with the system.

The second application (Figure 15-10b) shows a sales transaction where delayed data entry takes place. The sales clerk uses a combination of cash register keys, a bar code scanner, and a magnetic strip reader to capture the transaction data. Instead of being sent immediately to the computer for processing, the data are recorded on a magnetic tape held within the cash

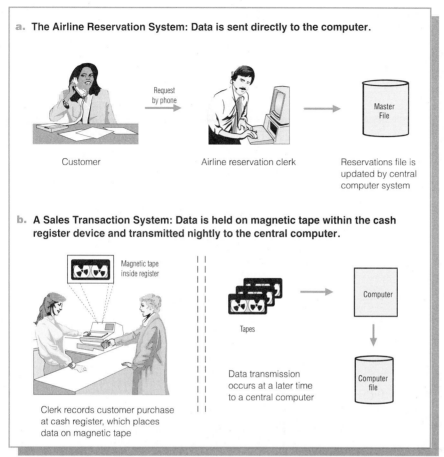

a. **The Airline Reservation System: Data is sent directly to the computer.**

Request
by phone

Customer   Airline reservation clerk   Master
File

Reservations file is
updated by central
computer system

b. **A Sales Transaction System: Data is held on magnetic tape within the cash
register device and transmitted nightly to the central computer.**

Magnetic tape
inside register

Tapes

Computer

Data transmission
occurs at a later time
to a central computer

Computer
file

Clerk records customer purchase
at cash register, which places
data on magnetic tape

FIGURE 15-10

**Two modes of data
entry via keying**

register. Each night, the data recorded on the magnetic tapes in the store's cash registers are transmitted over phone lines to the retail chain's central computer. Computer data processing occurs the next morning after all the data from the branch stores have been received and batched together in a disk file. This type of processing combines immediate data entry with batch processing, and thus delays the actual processing of the data.

Step 5: Design the Data Format

The contents and medium of the input data were defined in earlier steps. In this step, the analyst prepares the visual representation of the data and its associated data entry screens or forms. The rules for allocating data and identifying information on documents or screens were stated in Chapter 14 within the $U^2H^2C^2$ principles: The scan is left to right, top to bottom; computed values are not entered by the user; and the amount of data to be keyed is kept at a minimum.

To sketch the input data form, a standard grid form may be employed (see Figure 15-11). Another approach is to design the screen or form by

FIGURE 15-11   **A standard layout form for input designs**

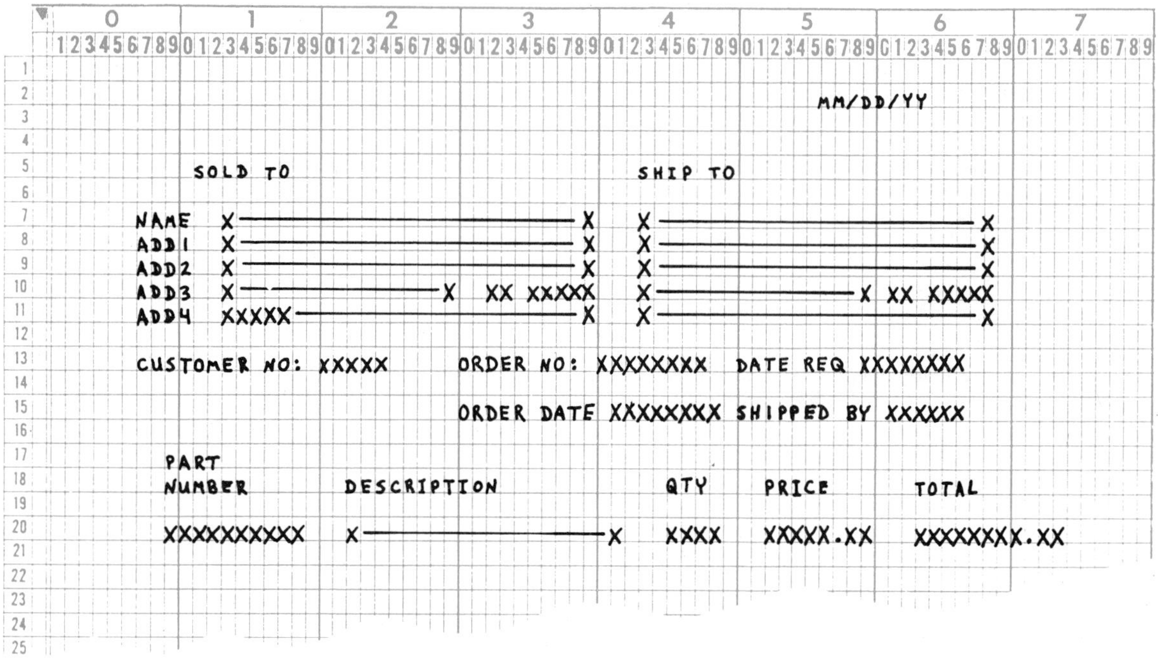

using a CASE tool (such as Excelerator) or software (such as a data base management system or spreadsheet) to lay out the format. In addition to permitting the analyst to quickly paint screens and alter designs, CASE tools can also be used to generate the program code in COBOL for these designs. Because the data dictionary has described each data element, the analyst can indicate the descriptive text on the screen and use the prompts to select the corresponding data elements.

> ### Warning
> Good screen design is more of an art than a science. Try to keep the screen as simple as possible and to incorporate features that assist the user whenever possible. A glitzy design with flashing lights and rainbow colors may show off your computer skills but is not very helpful to most users.

If a data element will be represented as a coded value, the code table should be designed at this junction in the life cycle. If the code table already exists, such as the U.S. zip code table, this step can be omitted. Codes should be designed to allow for future growth. When a code is allotted a range of values from 000 up to 999, no more than 1000 items can be associated with the code. However, too long a coded value becomes cumbersome. Each time the code is recorded manually or keyed into the computer, there is a possibility of human error. The longer the coded value, the greater the probability of error. Choosing a code that allows for two billion values when only 2,000 values are needed today sets the stage for excessive data errors.

Codes should also be designed for ease of use. Although a code designed to include cryptic abbreviations as a memory aid would appear to be highly desirable, the codes may prove to be overlong and incomprehensible to the user. The use of alphabetics should be restricted to designate major categories with numerical values assigned to indicate subcategories. It is best to ban the letters O and I from the codes to avoid confusing them with the numbers 0 and 1. The general structure of the code is also important. For example, the assignment of different leading code numbers to checking and savings account numbers enables banks to immediately recognize the type of account. Moreover, the information system should be designed so that the users are aware of general structures but do not need to memorize any code values. As stated by the second H principle in Chapter 14, the limitations of the human users must be foremost in our minds during the design activities.

Step 6: Specify the Data Controls

The addition of data controls is necessary to prevent erroneous data from entering the system, safeguard the data from unauthorized use, and provide the means to trace the path of the input data through the system. Such controls are implemented as edit checks, audit trails, and access controls. Each type of data control is explained in the following sections. In addition, the controls discussed in Chapter 14—division of labor and control totals— also apply to input data.

EDIT CHECKS

As input data is received by the system, the data are edited to detect any deviations from expected values. Four types of edit tests may be performed: data type testing, table or file lookup testing, range testing, and check digit verification.

Data Type Test   If numerical values must be entered, a check can be performed to ensure that all characters are numerics. When an alphabetic character is detected, a error message such as PLEASE REENTER, DATA MUST BE NUMERIC can be issued. Similarly, if a data value must be alphabetic, the program can reject any numeric characters for this field.

Table or File Lookup Test   When a data value corresponding to a value in a table or file is entered as input, the program can verify that a match is found. If there is no matching value, an error condition is reported by an appropriate message such as PLEASE REENTER ACCOUNT NUMBER, NO SUCH ACCOUNT LOCATED ON FILE.

Range Tests   Range tests verify that the input data values occur within specified limits. If $200 is entered as an hourly wage, but hourly wages range from $4.50 to $50.00 at the firm, the range test rejects this value and requests that the user reenter an appropriate value. In some cases, an override feature is desirable. If the entry says 20 units were produced for the day and the acceptable range is 200 to 350, an error message such as ONLY 20 UNITS ENTERED, IS THIS CORRECT (Y/N)? allows the operator to force the program to accept the low number. Because unforeseen events and variations happen, override provisions are highly desirable.

Check Digit Verification   When a data value is assigned, such as a nine-digit value for a customer account number, an additional digit called a *check digit* may be attached to create a ten-digit value. The **check digit** is derived by applying an arithmetic formula to the original number. When the number is received as input data, the same formula can be applied to verify the correctness of the number. The recommended method for computing check digits is based on two numbers known as the **weights** and the **modulus**. The computation is performed as follows:

1. Each digit in the original number is multiplied by the corresponding digit in the weights.
2. The resulting products are summed.
3. The sum is divided by the modulus to obtain the remainder.
4. The check digit is calculated by subtracting the remainder from the modulus.
5. The check digit is appended to the original number.

Figure 15-12 demonstrates the application of these steps for the number 25140296. The check digit for the number is computed using the weights 987654321 and the modulus 11. To compute the check digit, the 1 in the weights is not used. The weights are aligned so that the unit position in the original number is multiplied by the weight 2, the tens position digit is multiplied by the weight 3, and so on. The sum of the resulting products, 136, is divided by the modulus 11, yielding a remainder of 4. Finally, the remainder of 4 is subtracted from the modulus 11, to produce the check digit of 7. The check digit is appended to the original number to form the data value

251402967

Whenever that number enters the system as input data, the same computation can be performed but with the weight 1 assigned to the check digit. If the number has been entered correctly, the remainder will be zero. A nonzero remainder indicates that the value was entered incorrectly and must be reentered. The modulus 11 may result in a remainder of 0 or 1 and the corresponding check digits of 10 and 11. To avoid the use of two digits for the check digit, an alphabetic character can be used. Another approach is to eliminate any code values that result in a two-digit check digit. For

FIGURE 15-12

The calculation and verification of a check digit   The weights 987654321 and the modulus 11 are used to compute the check digit for the number 25140296.

CREATION OF THE CHECK DIGIT

1. Multiply the digits of the original number, 25140296, by the corresponding digit in the weights. Note that the weight 1 is not used here.

original number $\longrightarrow$	2	5	1	4	0	2	9	6
weights $\longrightarrow$	9	8	7	6	5	4	3	2
products $\longrightarrow$	18	40	7	24	0	8	27	12

2. Sum the products.

   $18 + 40 + 7 + 24 + 0 + 8 + 27 + 12 = 136$

3. Divide the sum by the modulus.

   $136 \div 11 = 12$ with remainder of 4

4. Compute the check digit by subtracting the remainder from the modulus.

   Check digit $= 11 - 4 = 7$

5. Append the check digit to the original number.

   251402967

VERIFICATION OF DATA VALUE

1. Multiply the digits of the data value by the corresponding digit in the weights. The weight 1 is now employed.

amended number $\longrightarrow$	2	5	1	4	0	2	9	6	7
weights $\longrightarrow$	9	8	7	6	5	4	3	2	1
products $\longrightarrow$	18	40	7	24	0	8	27	12	7

2. Sum the products.

   $18 + 40 + 7 + 24 + 0 + 8 + 27 + 12 + 7 = 143$

3. Divide the sum by the modulus.

   $143 \div 11 = 13$ with a remainder of 0

4. Since the remainder is zero, the number was entered correctly. If the remainder is other than zero the number is incorrect.

ERROR DETECTION   To illustrate the detection of an error, assume that the number was entered as 254102967. The verification of the number will yield 146 as the sum of the products. Dividing 146 by 11 gives 13 with remainder 3; since the remainder is not zero, the value is found to be in error.

modulus 11, this means about 9% of the possible numbers will be excluded, not a serious restriction. Other choices of a weight and modulus are possible. The modulus 11 with weights of 987654321 is one of the most popular because it detects 100% of all transcription errors except for 5% of all random errors. Because of the computation required to create the check digit and then to verify proper entry of the coded value, check digits are typically restricted to critical codes such as account numbers and product numbers.

THE AUDIT TRAIL

An **audit trail** is a means whereby individual transactions can be traced through the system. The audit trail serves two purposes. First, it permits management or auditors to follow selected transactions through the system, step by step. By tracing a transaction through the system, the auditors can verify that record-keeping is accurate and fraud has not occurred. Second, the detection and correction of errors is aided by the audit trail. If the master files have become corrupted due to hardware or software error, tracing the original information via the audit trail enables the correct information to be placed in the system. An audit trail for a computer system should always be planned for financial or critical data.

Figure 15-13 illustrates an audit trail through a simplified order processing and invoicing system operating in on-line mode. A file of before- and after-images of the data records and a transaction log supplies the audit trail for each customer order and invoice. A before-image is the data record's representation prior to the execution of the update operation; an after-image is the record's appearance after updating has been accomplished. For an on-line system, the transaction log registers the date and time of the transaction and the person performing the update operation. Each order is represented by the original data which are entered via on-line entry, the various lines on control reports, the invoice, and the delivery note. Details of a single order can be obtained from the various records retained by the system as historical data in order to provide an audit trail. Storing this additional information makes it possible to determine if an order has been filled and where and how errors entered the system.

ACCESS CONTROLS

Protection against unauthorized entry to data files or programs is provided by access controls that are incorporated into the system. It is important to ensure that only authorized individuals store or access data in the computer files. Access controls are implemented by password schemes, device authorization restrictions, and safeguards for communication lines. Each method is discussed in this section.

Password Schemes   Password schemes require the user to enter an assigned identification code and a **password**—a set of characters known only

FIGURE 15-13   **The audit trail in a simplified on-line order processing system**

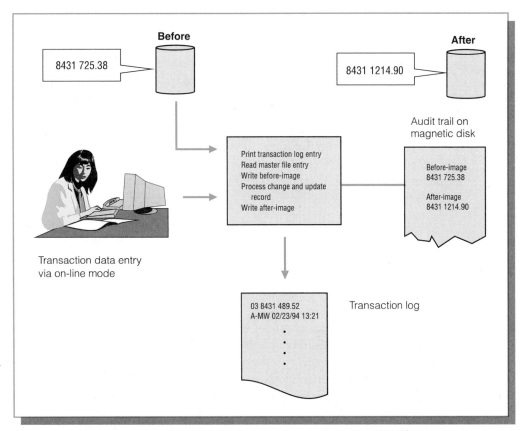

Source: Senn, James A., *Analysis and Design of Information Systems* 2/E, McGraw-Hill (1989), p. 665. By permission of McGraw-Hill, Inc.

to the individual user—in order to gain access to a particular portion of the information system. Special identification codes can be designated in order to restrict the user's operations to read only, write only, or a combination of read/write operations as well as limit the files that can be viewed or altered. To maintain secrecy, passwords should never be displayed by the system either on the screen or in printed form. Many times, when users are allowed to create their own passwords, they choose commonly used words or a familiar name. Such words are the first to be tried by those attempting to break into a system. Since hackers have been know to program break-ins into computer networks by submitting each word in the dictionary as a password, a meaningless string of characters or a string of digits is preferable to a word in the dictionary. Since a person's social security number is present on many documents, it is not a good choice for a password. A suggested choice is to link two birth dates of close relatives (not the user's own birth date) to form a 12-digit number as the password.

Strict controls over users' passwords should be enforced. Ideally passwords should be changed regularly to maintain their secrecy. Upon termination of employment, an employee's identification code and password should be removed from the system immediately. Security enforcement measures for sensitive information should include the ejection of the user from the system after three failed attempts to enter the correct password. In addition, the system should promptly delete the user's identification code, forcing the user to reapply for permission to enter the system. This two-step procedure should prevent the breaking of passwords by repetitive attempts. The system also should not offer a universal identification code easily guessed by a hacker, such as USER or SYSTEM. The problem with issuing new passwords at regular intervals is that users worry about forgetting the passwords and thus will be very likely to record this valuable information on paper or even tape it onto the computer monitor. In turn, this means the physical site itself must be secured from unauthorized entry.

Device Authorization   Access controls for individual terminals are also important. One possibility is the placement of restrictions on terminals according to their physical location. For example, only terminals in the business office would be assigned the access rights to financial information so that only operators at these terminals would have the capabilities of altering and creating financial records. No checks would be printed except by directions given at these terminals. Other terminals could be given the capability to view financial information but remain restricted from the entry of data to the files or from receiving any output via screens or printers. By careful design, the capabilities of each terminal can be limited in order to minimize the opportunities for unauthorized access to confidential information.

Safeguards for Communication Lines   Because data may be transmitted to or from computers over communication lines, it is important to safeguard important data in transit. To assure the security and confidentiality of the data, the data can be transformed to a different representation. We say that the data are encoded or *encrypted*. The process is known as **data encryption**. The encrypted data are then sent over the communication lines secured from eavesdroppers on the line. When received, the data are decoded to the original form for processing. Alternatively, the signals on the communication lines may be altered or *scrambled* by electronic means. In either case, data are unrecognizable while traveling over the communication lines. If the information system is receiving encrypted data, it must be prepared to decode the data prior to processing.

Sensitive data should be accessible only from hard-wired terminals or work stations, and sent only over leased telecommunication lines or protected by a dial-back procedure for terminal connections. In a *dial-back procedure* after the initial phone connection is made with the system, the computer (or computer operator) verifies that the phone number calling is on its list of acceptable data sources; then it disconnects and dials back before accepting any data into the system.

Step 7: Design the Human–Computer Dialogue

In this step, the analyst decides how the users will direct the computer to execute operations. This interaction will be a dialogue that will both convey commands to the computer and also transmit information to the users. Because this topic is so extensive, its discussion will be deferred to the next section.

Step 8: Obtain the User's Approval

To ensure that the user can review the input designs sufficiently, it is recommended that the analyst supply mockups of the initial designs for approval. If screen designs are involved, ideally the user should be able to test them by entering data. After the user discovers any shortcomings in the designs, the analyst can quickly change the formats to reflect the user's preferences. This exchange between the user and the analyst continues until the user has approved the designs.

HUMAN–COMPUTER DIALOGUES

The computer performs tasks according to the commands issued by the computer user. These commands and the computer's responses constitute a **human–computer dialogue** that spans the boundary between the user and the machine. Both input and output data are transported across this boundary by means of the user–machine dialogue. The design of the dialogue determines the ease with which the user interacts with the computer. A well-designed dialogue not only helps the user to perform efficiently but also minimizes the opportunity for human error. Various types of dialogues are possible.

The Human Design Factors

The design of the dialogue is influenced primarily by the characteristics of the users. A particular dialogue may be appropriate for one group of users but woefully unsuitable for other users. By understanding the users' traits, the analyst will be equipped to compose a dialogue that can be used effectively. As shown in Figure 15-14, the users' characteristics to be assessed are: frequency of use, computer skills, educational level, training level for the system, type of operator (active or passive), and the environment.

FREQUENCY OF USE

A user who will perform the designated steps repeatedly throughout the day needs a different dialogue from the user who only occasionally executes the task. Infrequent use means that the user will have difficulty in remembering the steps required for the task. If a person queries the data base only once a month, the particular skills needed for that task may become rusty in the

FIGURE 15-14
The users' character-istics that affect the design of human–computer dialogue

Frequency of use
Computer skills
Educational level
Training
Active or passive operator
Environment

interim. In that case, each time the user performs the task is almost com-parable to the very first time. An example is the sales clerk who can easily ring up routine sales and returns but, when confronted with an unusual sales return, must call the manager to be shown the steps of a process that is rarely executed.

COMPUTER SKILLS

If users have programming experience or possess substantial computer knowledge, the computer is seen as a tool rather than an unknown quantity. Users who have the ability to read technical manuals and understand pro-cedures also possess the capability to master more complicated tasks. How-ever, given the proliferation of software for personal computers, inconsis-tent user interfaces may cause difficulty for even highly sophisticated users.

EDUCATIONAL LEVEL

Highly educated users are likely to view the difficulties of a computer in-formation system as puzzles to be solved rather than formidable tasks. How-ever, bad design makes even the most intelligent users irritable as they search for the elusive keystrokes needed to communicate with the com-puter. As a general rule, gear the type of directions and the interface design to the average ability of the intended users. Do not expect computer ge-niuses who will remember and follow any amount of intricate details.

TRAINING

The amount of training required depends on the tasks to be performed and the design of the system. Some systems are designed for people with no training; others require extensive training. For example, automated teller machines (ATMs) are designed to be used by people with no formal training. The available banking functions are typically limited to withdrawals, depos-its, bill payments, and account balance status reports. Loan applications, transfers of funds between banks, exchange of foreign currency, and other banking functions are not available at the ATMs. Because the number of functions is severely restricted, the ATM dialogue can be less complex than that required for a system offering more banking functions.

ACTIVE OR PASSIVE OPERATOR

There is a substantial difference between a task that requires the user to formulate a dialogue and one that merely requests a reply to a pre-established dialogue. The ATM dialogue shown in Figure 15-15 repeatedly asks the user to respond to predetermined questions. The responses from the user are limited to either keying a few digits or pressing a single button in response to the computer's direction. In contrast, the query procedure for a data base management system may be designed to allow the user to formulate the entire query in a specified format. If the dialogue is flexible, the user is allowed much freedom to form a wide variety of queries—but the burden of formulating the query falls on the user. Regardless of the dialogue design,

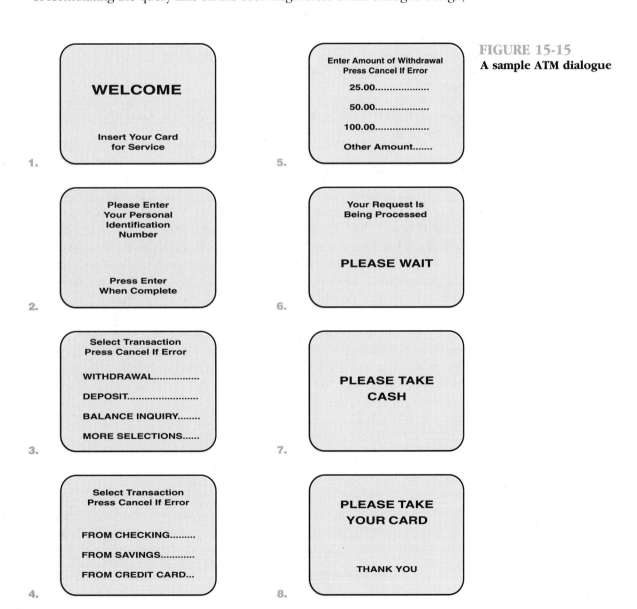

FIGURE 15-15
A sample ATM dialogue

complex queries may prove too difficult for the casual or untrained user. Types of dialogues will be discussed more fully in the next section.

ENVIRONMENT

The environment in which the user functions will affect the system design. An example is the airline reservation system where inquiries are typically received by telephone. The service representative must respond quickly or the customer will become impatient. Where speed is a prime consideration, the system must be carefully designed to assist the user in this regard. An additional consideration is the choice between separate personal computers and terminals controlled by central, shared computers. While graphical user interfaces (described later) are very popular, they are not economically feasible in the latter environment.

Types of Dialogues

There are two basic types of dialogues: *program-controlled* dialogues and *user-controlled* dialogues. Both types are popular since they fulfill the needs of users with differing characteristics.

PROGRAM-CONTROLLED DIALOGUE

In a **program-controlled dialogue**, the program guides the dialogue by asking the user to respond to various choices. Although the user has the ability to select different paths in the dialogue, the options available are limited to a fixed set of commands, which are displayed on the screen for the user's selection. Program-controlled dialogues provide the users with specific choices and lead them through each task completely. The user does not have to memorize details but only has to understand a general pattern of action. An ATM offers program-controlled dialogue. The set of ATM screens for a cash withdrawal were displayed in Figure 15-15. The user merely supplies information in response to the questions from the ATM program. This type of dialogue requires more operations to be executed by the computer program. If many users are on-line with queries to a central computer, response time could slow beyond acceptable bounds.

USER-CONTROLLED DIALOGUE

In a **user-controlled dialogue** (also called **command-driven dialogue**), the user initiates the dialogue and enters the commands to request tasks to be performed by the program. The correct form of the command must be entered by the user or the system will not perform the command.

The airline reservation system is an example of a user-controlled dialogue. As shown in Figure 15-16, the operator has typed

A17NOVLAXORD500P

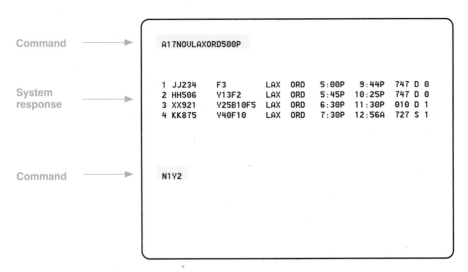

Command

A17NOVLAXORD500P

System
response

```
1 JJ234    F3         LAX  ORD   5:00P   9:44P  747 D 0
2 HH506    Y13F2      LAX  ORD   5:45P  10:25P  747 D 0
3 XX921    Y25B10F5   LAX  ORD   6:30P  11:30P  010 D 1
4 KK875    Y40F10     LAX  ORD   7:30P  12:56A  727 S 1
```

Command

N1Y2

FIGURE 15-16

A command-driven
system: The airline
reservation system

to request the display of all flights from Los Angeles (LAX) to O'Hare Airport in Chicago (ORD) leaving after 5:00 P.M. on November 17. The system replies with the requested display. The third column shows the space available on each flight. To request one seat in tourist class on the flight leaving the Los Angeles airport at 5:45 P.M., the reservations clerk types

N1Y2

to indicate need (N) for one seat (1) in tourist class (Y) on the second flight listed (2).

This information system does not provide any assistance to the operator by displaying labeled boxes to complete. If the airline clerk does not know the exact syntax of the command, nothing will be accomplished. The design of the airline reservation system is based on thorough operator training and a minimal set of keystrokes. Since the system is used by hundreds of operators at the same time, the environment was a decisive factor in the design of this user interface. A more user-friendly interface would lengthen the response time and delay the customers.

Another example of user-controlled dialogue is the disk operating system (DOS) for the IBM personal computer (PC). In Figure 15-17, the user intended to enter the command to copy the file ch10.pix to a diskette by typing

copy ch10.pix a:

but made a keying mistake by omitting the colon. Notice that the user must know the exact format of the command, understand how to include the parameter for the file being copied, and remember the command word of "copy." The DOS system replied with the message

1 file(s) copied

FIGURE 15-17

A dialogue in the disk operating system (DOS) for an IBM PC

```
C:\TEMP>dir *.pix

 Volume in drive C is 8555-W81
 Volume Serial Number is 2501-09CE
 Directory of C:\TEMP

CH10     PIX      2771  07-07-93    1:50p
CH10B    PIX     27824  07-07-93    1:52p
10WP6    PIX      2275  07-21-93   10:05p
10HIJ    PIX      2447  07-21-93   10:07p
        4 file(s)        35317 bytes
                      15519744 bytes free

C:\TEMP>copy ch10.pix a
        1 file(s) copied

C:\TEMP>copy ch19.px a:
File not found - CH19.PX
        0 file(s) copied

C:\TEMP>copy file ch10.pix a:
Too many parameters

C:\TEMP>
```

Courtesy of International Business Machines Corporation.

but the file ch10.pix was copied with the name A into the same directory on the hard disk. Because the user could see that the file had not been copied to the diskette on the A: drive, the message is attempted again as

    copy ch19.px a:

This time the message

    File not found - CH19.PX

    0 file(s) copied

tells the user that the file was not copied. The user tries again but decides to alter the format of the command by typing

    copy file ch10.pix a:

This time the command is correct except for the added word "file." The system displays the error message

    Too many parameters

The user's commands will continue to be rejected by the system or produce unintended results until the precise command format is keyed by the user.

Design of Human–Computer Dialogues

As we have discussed in the previous section, the analyst must decide on either program-controlled or user-controlled dialogue for the information system. Except in rare instances, such as the airline reservation system, the designer will choose to implement a program-controlled dialogue. This option provides the users with the maximum assistance and places the burden on the designer to lead the users through the tasks to be executed. To design a program-controlled dialogue, the designer must also decide on another option. How should the dialogue be presented to the user? Should the dialogue be *driven by menus* or have a *graphical user interface*?

MENU-DRIVEN DIALOGUES

A **menu-driven dialogue** provides interaction between the computer and the user by the use of menus. A **menu** is a screen displaying the options available to the users at that point in the information system. A sample menu for a firm's Sales Activities System is displayed in Figure 15-18. This opening menu provides three choices: (1) sales transaction, (2) sales tracking, or (3) sales reports. The bottom of the screen indicates the additional choices available to the user, exiting the system or changing the active date. Once an option is selected by keying the appropriate digit, another menu is displayed. Choices on the second menu cause a third menu to appear that offers the task specified by the user (see Figure 15-19). The time it takes to reach the desired menu may make frequent users impatient.

Rather than layered menus, *pull-down* menus or *pop-up* menus can be used. Both types are submenus that appear out of the main menu portion of the screen. Microsoft WINDOWS and WINDOWS applications are examples of software that employs pull-down menus. A pull-down menu for a spread-

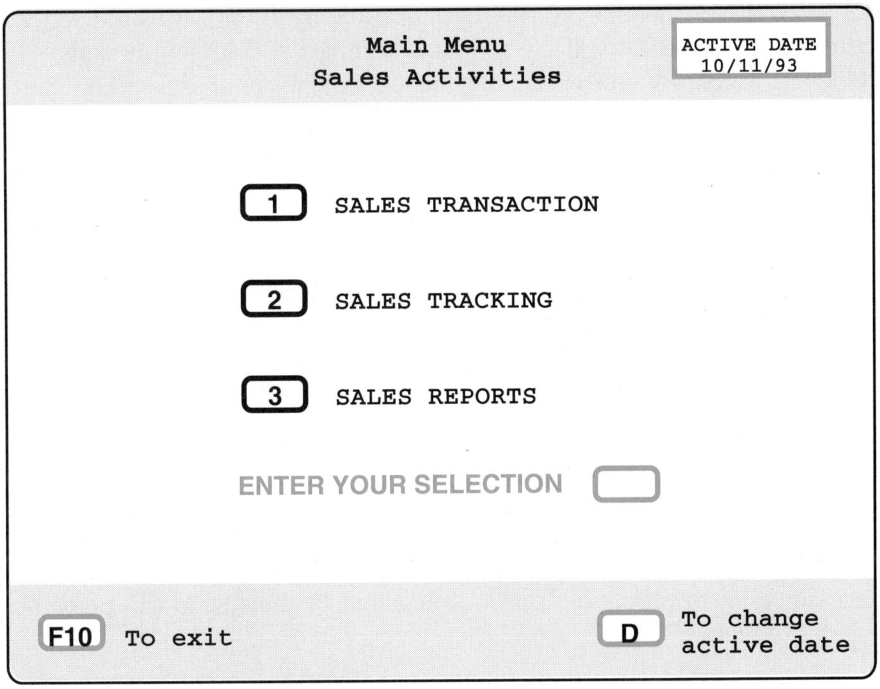

```
                  Main Menu              ┌─────────────┐
               Sales Activities          │ ACTIVE DATE │
                                         │  10/11/93   │
                                         └─────────────┘


            ┌───┐
            │ 1 │    SALES TRANSACTION
            └───┘


            ┌───┐
            │ 2 │    SALES TRACKING
            └───┘


            ┌───┐
            │ 3 │    SALES REPORTS
            └───┘


         ENTER YOUR SELECTION   (       )



  ┌─────┐                          ┌───┐   To change
  │ F10 │  To exit                 │ D │   active date
  └─────┘                          └───┘
```

FIGURE 15-18

A sample menu

FIGURE 15-19

A menu system with three layers

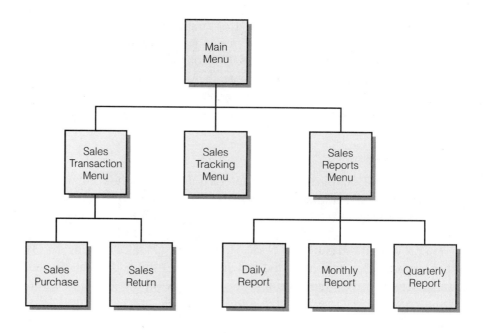

sheet application is depicted in Figure 15-20. The pull-down menu is activated by clicking with the mouse on the desired function from the menu options at the top of the screen. The commands shown in gray cannot be invoked at this time since they are inappropriate in the sequence of commands executed thus far.

Menu-driven systems are especially suitable for users who will use the system on a casual basis. If the system is complex and some functions are seldom invoked, a menu system may be a good choice. Because the menu-driven system prompts the user through the steps required to perform a function, seldom executed functions can still be easily performed.

In designing the screens for menus, the designer must remember not to clutter the screen with too much information. For example, presenting 12 options on a conventional menu (such as shown in Figure 15-18) will delay the infrequent user's work since all 12 options must be read before a selection is made. Menu items should bear self-explanatory titles. If there are too many options to be placed on a single screen, a hierarchical set of menus can be designed, grouping related submenus as a single option. Although submenus can be constructed to any depth, traversing more than three levels of submenus becomes frustrating to the user. Instead, an option to reach deeply nested functions directly should be provided. Since the user work stations do not need graphical capabilities, the conventional menu-driven system saves on hardware costs. The major drawback to menus is the necessity to move through a set of screens before the system can perform the desired task.

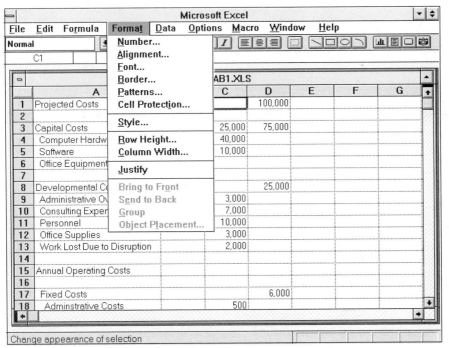

FIGURE 15-20

A pull-down menu in a spreadsheet

Screen shot reprinted with permission from Microsoft Corporation.

COMMAND-DRIVEN DIALOGUES

Command-driven dialogues have been discussed in the section on user-controlled dialogues. In that section, the airline reservation system and the disk operating system (DOS) on the IBM PC were shown as examples of command-driven dialogues.

GRAPHICAL USER INTERFACES

Graphical user interfaces are program-controlled dialogues based on icons; they were first introduced with the Macintosh computer. An *icon* is a small graphical image that represents a program function. Brief descriptive names placed with each icon help the user recall what system functions are available. Interaction with the computer is primarily performed by pointing to the icons on the screen with a mouse and selecting the function by clicking on the mouse, rather than using the keyboard. Figure 15-21 shows a menu displaying icons for the WINDOWS operating system. Application programs designed especially for execution under WINDOWS will display the user's current options on a bar at the top of the screen. After an option is chosen, a pull-down menu displays the choices for that option, as in Figure 15-20. The visual display of such information continually assists the users in selecting and performing the tasks required.

FIGURE 15-21
The WINDOWS menu with icons representing the programs available The user selects the program to be run by pointing to the icon with the mouse and then clicking on the mouse.

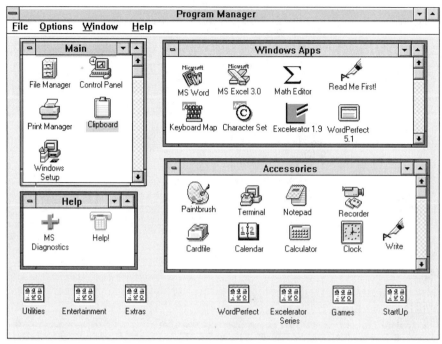

Screen shot reprinted with permission from Microsoft Corporation.

Although WINDOWS, OS/2, and the Macintosh are popular, not all users like using the mouse and the graphical user interface. Many users prefer the keyboard and conventional menus. For some users, constant use of the mouse can be more fatiguing than the keying operations required by traditional systems.

Charting the Dialogue

When designing the screens for an information system, the analyst must not only design each individual screen but must link these screens together for access by the user. Since a typical information system requires many possible screens—perhaps, even hundreds of screens—for selection by the user, it is necessary to document the paths to these screens. "Which screen leads to another screen?" is the question to be answered by this documentation. Some screens may allow the user to move forward or backward to other screens. Other screens may repeat themselves as many times as necessary for the particular function being performed. Fortunately, a technique exists to chart the screen dialogue.

A **dialogue tree** maps the connection between the various screens and the messages between the user and the computer. Arrows indicate that a screen will lead to the linked screens. A two-way arrow means that the screens lead to each other in either direction. Most dialogues are designed to allow the user to return to the previous screen by depressing a designated key. The tree is read by tracing a path from the top of the tree (labeled START) downward through branches on the tree. A path will not traverse all branches but follows the dialogue to its final termination. The tree structure is useful for charting menu-driven dialogues.

Figure 15-22 shows the dialogue tree design for the ATM cash withdrawal discussed previously. The dialogue tree has multiple branch points.

FIGURE 15-22   A dialogue tree for ATM withdrawal screens

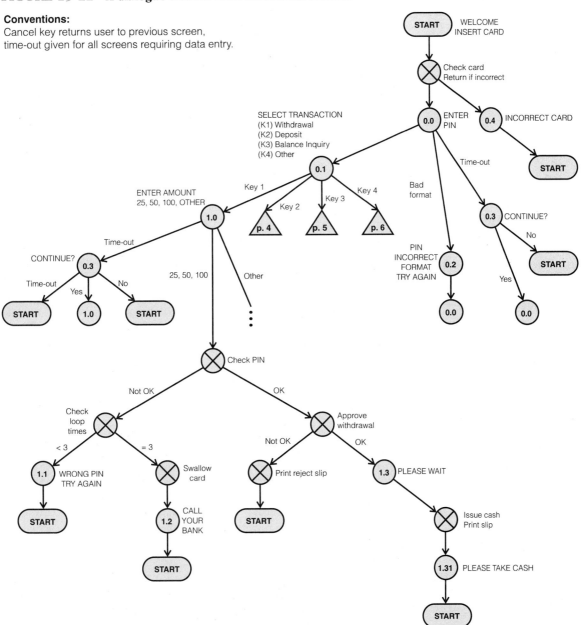

At each fork, the user replies by depressing the appropriate key. The use of previously displayed screens is possible and is indicated by writing the appropriate screen number within the circle. The ATM dialogue tree includes the following information:

1. The user is allowed to cancel the transaction at any point in the dialogue tree unless the transaction is being processed.
2. The number imprinted on the bank card is checked to verify that it meets the criteria for a bank number. If unacceptable, the user is returned to the START screen.
3. If the personal identification number (PIN) is not entered with the correct number of digits, the PIN is rejected. The user is asked to repeat the entry of the PIN number. This path is given by the nodes START, 0.0, and 0.2, ending in the return to 0.0.
4. The PIN is checked only after all the information required for the transaction has been entered. If the PIN is incorrect, the user is allowed only two more attempts to enter a correct PIN. After the third attempt, the card is retained by the machine.
5. The path for a successful withdrawal transaction is given by the screens 0.0, 0.1, 1.0, 1.3, and 1.31. After the transaction has been completed, the user is returned to the START screen.

DIALOGUE TREE CONVENTIONS

Although dialogue trees are constructed rather freely, certain conventions have been used in this text. Because no standard set of conventions has been adopted, differing symbols and conventions will be found in other texts. The conventions observed in constructing the ATM dialogue tree are displayed in Figure 15-23. We will now explain each convention shown in this figure as well as the notation for diagramming loops.

Screens   Screens are indicated by a number within a circle, called a node. Because of space limitations, only a sketch of the dialogue contained within the screen is shown to the right or left of the node.

Actions   Actions are shown by a circle containing an X. The actions performed are written to the right or left of the node.

Screen Numbers   Each screen is numbered uniquely. Additional digits are added to the screen's identifying number in order to assign successive screens. For example, the screen number 1.2 signifies that it occurs after screen 1.0. The screen node numbered 1.21 means that it will be displayed after screen 1.2. A screen may be reused by simply assigning the same number to a node.

Connections   Nodes are connected by lines with arrows indicating the direction of the flow. When choices are made by the user, the lines are labeled with the appropriate selections.

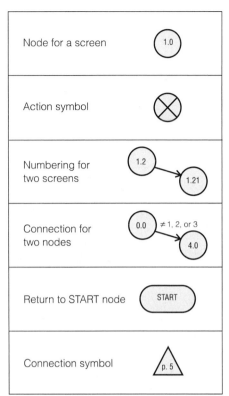

FIGURE 15-23
The symbols used in dialogue trees

Start Node   The return to the START node is indicated by an oval labeled START.

Connection to Other Pages   Because dialogue trees quickly become complex, it is often desirable to continue a path on another page. A triangle with the page number is used to show the continuance of the path on another page.

Loops   Dialogues frequently allow the user several tries to enter a data value. After a fixed number of tries, the system may reject any further attempts and return to the opening menu. This limitation is typically imposed on sensitive data where hit-or-miss guesses should be discouraged. For example, the attempt to enter the PIN number in the ATM dialogue is limited to three trials. After the third failure, the bank card is retained by the ATM machine and the user is told to CALL YOUR BANK. Whenever possible (without cluttering the chart), outline the loop by drawing a dashed line encompassing all the nodes within the loop. In the case of the ATM dialogue, the loop is difficult to mark in this way since the PIN number is not checked until all the transaction information has been obtained from the user.

In order to illustrate these conventions, a sample dialogue tree showing only the screen dialogue is presented in Figure 15-24. The number within a

FIGURE 15-24

A dialogue tree that shows the organization of the user screens in the dialogue between the user and the computer

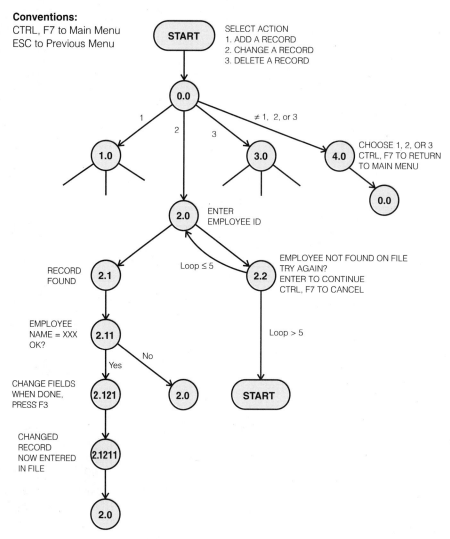

circle indicates the number assigned to the individual screen. A short description of the screen is placed adjacent to the circle. The dialogue tree begins with the word START and leads immediately to the screen node labeled 0.0. The menu displayed for screen 0.0 is shown to the right. This screen asks the user to select from options of adding, deleting, or changing a record on the employee file. To return to the main menu, the user presses the CTRL and F7 keys simultaneously. The convention of keying CTRL with F7 has been written to the left of the START node.

Because of space limitations, only the path for record modification has been illustrated. After the user keys 2 to select "CHANGE A RECORD" the system displays screen 2.0, with the dialogue

ENTER EMPLOYEE ID

Two paths lead from this screen. The left branch leads to another screen node, which displays the message RECORD FOUND followed by the screen dialogue (labeled 2.11) which asks if this EMPLOYEE NAME is the one desired by the user. When the correct record is found, the remaining portion of this branch (2.121 and 2.1211) shows the dialogue between the user and the system to modify the located record. The right branch leads to screen 2.2,

EMPLOYEE NOT FOUND ON FILE

TRY AGAIN?

ENTER TO CONTINUE, CTRL–F7 TO CANCEL

The Right Choice for Input Design

When examining the issue of input design, the system's goals must always be in the forefront. For many firms, a new information system can yield the high returns, thereby placing the firm competitively ahead. Jordan's Furniture, a $70 million business in Avon, Massachusetts, demonstrated the value of innovative technology when it created a computerized receiving system. Inventory is now made available to customers just 20 minutes after it has been unloaded from delivery trucks at Jordan's three stores. The reason for this speed is the computerized receiving system. In addition, the new system has reduced inventory errors by 90%. But the competitive edge in customer services was really acquired by maintaining five years of customer data on-line so that Jordan's superior customer service cannot be rivaled by other firms.

The night before a truck comes in, the receiving staff prints out bar codes for the incoming merchandise. When the truck arrives, bar-code stickers are immediately placed on the furniture. The codes are then scanned as furniture is received, stacked and stored in the warehouse, and the scanned information is transmitted to the central computer. Terminals throughout the store allow the sales force to find out if an item is in stock or on order, the arrival dates of merchandise, and prices. Customers are more satisfied because they can inquire about what is happening with the store's stock and have confidence in the information supplied by the salespeople via the computer.

The cost savings of the new system are not known, but the fact that Jordan's Furniture survived a recessionary economy in 1991–1992 is proof enough of its value for Chief Executive Officer Steven J. Gaskins. "When we put computers in in 1977, none of our competitors knew what a computer was," he observed. And the firm does not intend to rest on its laurels. Plans are already underway to shorten the response time and eliminate errors from the bar-code scanners by acquiring radio frequency scanners.

Source: Kelly, David A., "From Truck to Customer in 20 Minutes," *Computerworld*, January 11, 1993. Reprinted with permission from David A. Kelly.

The analyst should check whether standards exist at the computer center for drawing dialogue trees. If no standards have been specified, the analyst should adopt the above conventions. Because dialogues can quickly become complex, continue branches on additional pages whenever necessary. Before implementing any screen designs, establish conventions for keys to be used to cancel actions or return to previous menus.

SUMMARY

This chapter deals with the two design issues of system inputs and human–computer dialogues. The tasks required for input design have been arranged in a sequence of eight steps. In step 1, the analyst identifies the inputs to be designed by locating the boundaries of the information system. In step 2, the analyst specifies the contents of the input data flows by describing the data elements. In step 3, the analyst defines the roles of the input data within the information system. In step 4, the analyst decides on the input medium, data entry mode, and processing method. Either delayed or immediate data entry into the computer information system may be chosen together with either on-line or batch processing mode. The input medium is selected to match the system requirements. In step 5, the analyst designs the representation of the data and its associated data entry screens or forms. If a data element will be represented as a coded value, the code table will be designed at this time.

In step 6, the data controls—edit checks, audit trails, access controls, division of labor, and control totals—are specified. Four edit checks can be performed on data values: data type tests, table or file lookup tests, range tests, and check digit verification. A data value may be appended with a check digit which is used to verify the value when it enters the system as input. An audit trail should be incorporated to facilitate tracing individual transactions through a system. Access controls are supplied by password schemes, device authorization restrictions, and safeguards for communication lines (data encryption and dial-back procedures). Division of labor and control totals were covered in Chapter 14.

In step 7, the analyst defines the human–computer dialogue, which allows the exchange of commands and information between the users and the information system. In step 8, although the users have been consulted throughout these steps, the analyst now formally requests their approval for the final input designs.

As indicated by step 7, the analyst must formulate the overall framework in which the user will direct the computer to perform its tasks. The user's directions and the computer's responses constitute a human–computer dialogue that crosses the human–machine boundary. Input and output data are also transferred across the boundary by means of this dialogue. The form of the human–computer dialogue should be chosen to facilitate the user's work and fit the user's particular attributes. The user's characteristics to be considered are: frequency of use (how often the user executes the tasks); computer skills; educational level; training level desired (how many hours of training are needed for efficient user performance); active or passive operator; and the user's environment.

Human–computer dialogues are classified as either program-controlled or user-controlled. In a program-controlled dialogue, the program offers the users a set of actions from which to select the desired action. An example of a program-controlled dialogue is the ATM machine. In a user-controlled dialogue, the user enters the commands to indicate which task should be executed by the system. If the command is incorrectly specified, the task will not be performed. The DOS operating system for the IBM PC provides an example of a user-controlled dialogue.

A popular form of a program-controlled dialogue is a menu-driven system. A menu is a screen displaying the options available to the users at that point in the information system. After selecting an option, a submenu can appear to allow the user to select a more detailed choice. Although submenus can be layered to any depth, it is advisable to limit them to three levels. Pull-down menus, which are submenus displayed directly over a portion of the main menu, are useful in preventing too many layers. Graphical user interfaces (GUIs) are the final example of human–computer dialogue. The design of dialogues is aided by the construction of a dialogue tree, which indicates each possible path through the system. The dialogue tree diagrams the user's commands and the corresponding replies from the computer in a structure similar to a decision tree.

TERMS

audit trail	input medium
batch processing	menu
check digit	menu-driven dialogue
command-driven dialogue	modulus
computerized form	on-line processing
data encryption	password
delayed data entry	program-controlled dialogue
dialogue tree	real-time processing
graphical user interface (GUI)	source data automation
human–computer dialogue	user-controlled dialogue
human–machine boundary	weights
immediate data entry	

QUESTIONS

1. Briefly describe the eight steps for input design.
2. What is the difference between delayed data entry and immediate data entry?
3. What are the advantages of on-line processing?
4. What documentation from the Analysis phase is required for the design of the human interfaces?
5. The ATM dialogue with the user requires many screens. This use of multi-layered screens violates the recommendation that menu-driven systems have only three screens nested three deep at most. Justify the ATM's use of screens that are more than three levels down.
6. Explain the purpose of the audit trail.
7. What is meant by a graphical user interface? Give two examples of a GUI.
8. Why was the airline reservation system designed as a command-driven system rather than as a program-controlled system?

PROJECTS

1. Visit a local record store that sells LP records, tapes, and CDs for all types of music. Observe how a sales transaction is recorded at the register so you can describe the interface that captures the data values for each sales transaction. If an automated system is in place, you may use the operating procedures now in place to fulfill this project. Perform the following design activities to document the input design for the sales data created during the sales transactions.
   a. Create the data dictionary entry for the data record containing the data elements created during the sales transaction and the entries for the data elements within this data record.
   b. Specify the means to identify uniquely the various types of merchandise sold in the store. For example, what codes identify the recordings of Beethoven's Fifth Symphony conducted by Leonard Bernstein on LP, CD, or cassette?
   c. Is the method of data capture delayed or immediate?
   d. Indicate the method of processing the sales transaction data in order to update the quantity on hand in the inventory file.

2. Arrange an appointment with the placement director at your college in order to study the recording of students who register for interviews. If your college does not have a placement office, call the director of human resources at a local firm. For this project, we are concerned only with recording the basic information about a student or candidate for employment: name, address, date of birth, academic background, and other pertinent information.

    a. Describe the input medium and mode in use for recording this information.

    b. Obtain any forms used for manually recording this information. Create a data dictionary record that represents the information to be stored in the files for each student or applicant.

    c. What method of recording this information do you recommend for a computer information system that handles these data elements? Justify your choice.

3. Ruth Hwong has opened a tutoring service for college students in a variety of subjects. Ms. Hwong will match the students in need of academic help with a student who is willing and able to tutor. Each potential tutor must register by providing the following information: name, address, phone number, and the number or title of each course that the student can cover. A maximum of eight courses may be recorded. Since Ms. Hwong is familiar with computers, she wants to design an information system to help her match tutors with students. She will have each student fill out a form and then enter the information in the computer information system. To help her, you are asked to do the following tasks.

    a. Create the data dictionary entry for the data record containing the information for each tutor as described above. Also create the data dictionary entries for each data element found within the data record for the tutor information.

    b. Design the TUTOR INFORMATION form to be used by Ms. Hwong to initially capture the pertinent information for each tutor.

    c. Design the screen that will be used for entering the data from the TUTOR INFORMATION form. If possible, use a CASE tool for designing the screen.

4. An airline reservation screen was presented in Figure 15-20. The ABC airline has now decided that its reservation clerks cannot master a command-driven information system and has asked you to design a menu-driven system. Design the screen or set of screens necessary to perform the inquiry for all flights leaving Los Angeles (LAX) around 5:00 P.M. for O'Hare airport (ORD) in Chicago. Assume that you must begin with an opening menu that allows the reservation clerk to choose the function to perform the inquiry for flights scheduled to depart about 5:00 P.M. from LAX to ORD.

REFERENCES

Bailey, Robert W. *Human Error in Computer Systems.* Englewood Cliffs, NJ: Prentice-Hall, 1983.

Brill, Alan E. *Building Controls into Structured Systems.* New York, NY: Yourdon Press, 1983.

Elmer-DeWitt, Philip. "The Machines Are Listening." *Time,* August 10, 1992, p. 45.

Hicks, James O., Jr. *Management Information Systems*, 3rd ed. Minneapolis/St. Paul: West, 1993.

Martin, James. *Design of Man–Computer Dialogues.* Englewood Cliffs, NJ: Prentice-Hall, 1973.

Rubenstein, Richard, and Harry Hersh. *The Human Factor.* Bedford, MA: Digital Press, 1984.

Schutzer, Daniel. *Business Decisions with Computers.* New York, NY: Van Nostrand Reinhold, 1991.

Stahl, Bob. "Principle of 'Least Astonishment' Can Polish Up Interface Design." *Computerworld*, September 15, 1986, pp. 61–70.

CHAPTER 18

Hardware Selection and Program Design

Objectives

The Design phase includes the selection of the hardware and software platforms and the preparation of the program design. In this chapter, we will explain:

- The step-by-step procedure for the selection of the physical computer system

- The reasons for program design specifications prior to the actual coding of the program

- The program design methodologies of structured design and Warnier–Orr diagrams

- How to transform the data flow diagrams prepared in the Analysis phase into the program design represented by the diagrams called structure charts

INTRODUCTION

The activities of the Analysis phase produce an abstract model of the proposed information system by using the technique of data flow diagrams. Now, in the Design phase, we are concerned with specifying how to translate that model into the computer programs still to be coded. Before entering the coding stage, we must carefully formulate plans for the program code as well as the hardware platform on which the program code will be executed. As shown in Figure 16-1, the specifications created by the Analysis phase are supplied to the Design phase in order to define (1) the hardware and software requirements, (2) the program and data file design, and (3) the training guidelines. First, the analyst must draft the requirements for the computer hardware and its peripheral equipment, such as secondary storage devices or communication equipment, as well as those for the software needed to build the system. Although no absolute rules can be provided for selecting new hardware, general guidelines will be presented in this chapter. After the hardware and software specifications have been determined, the acquisition of these resources can proceed.

The second major objective of the Design phase is the formulation of the program design. Although a model of the proposed information system was already developed using data flow diagrams supplemented by the data dictionary and process descriptions, this model does not provide the detailed

FIGURE 16-1

The activities of the Design phase

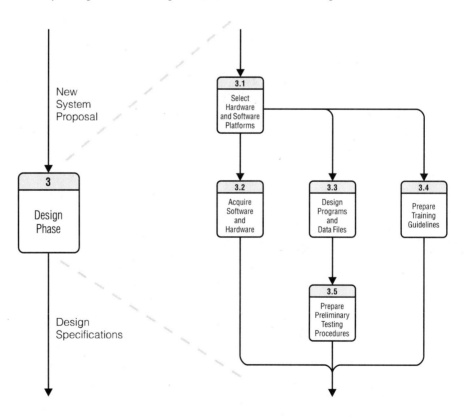

specifications for the writing of the program code. In the Design phase, the program designers will formulate an abstract representation of the program before the actual coding takes place. To create this abstraction, the analyst will use a tool such as *structured design*, which depicts the program design by means of diagrams known as *structure charts*. Another popular methodology for program design is *Warnier–Orr diagrams*. Describing the program at a logical level above the physical code allows changes in the design to be made more easily. In doing so, the structure of the program becomes visible to the designer and any necessary modifications can be incorporated. Once the information system has been implemented as a set of detailed program statements, it becomes difficult and expensive in both time and money to change the design. After the logical program design has been formulated, the programmers write the detailed program code by following the specifications documented by the conventions of the particular design methodology. After the program design is completed, preliminary plans are drafted for the testing of the program code.

A related question here is: Who really designs the program, the analyst or the programmer? The answer is determined by the firm's own preference. At some firms the analyst performs this role, while at other organizations the programmer is assigned this responsibility. In the discussion of this topic, it does not matter to whom the task has been given. The important point is that program design must be a separate task; we cannot simply move directly from analysis activities to writing the program code. If time is not spent designing the program on an abstract level, the problems found later in the system will return to haunt the computer staff. Delineating the program carefully ensures that good program coding can be written and testing will proceed to a successful conclusion. Future maintenance burdens are also eased. Without the design documentation, any future changes to the system will require intensive study of the program code, a time-consuming and often fruitless task. Creating a higher level specification based on sound design principles allows the information system to be more easily modified without the introduction of programming errors.

In this phase, we also design the data files (see Chapters 12 and 13). Since the model of the system is already in hand, the training guidelines can be drawn up. The type of system—on-line or batch—directly influences the training requirements. Typically, preliminary schedules for training and testing procedures are prepared prior to exiting the Design phase.

SELECTION OF HARDWARE AND SOFTWARE

Although hardware and software are often discussed as two separate entities, we know that the computer cannot function without its associated software. Consequently, in the selection of hardware, the analyst must always be aware of the relationship between computer hardware and the software, including both the systems software (e.g., the operating system) and the commercial software available for the computer. Moreover, the choice of software is ordinarily far more important than the physical computer hardware. If the hardware cannot be efficiently used by the computer professionals and the end-users, then its value will be greatly diminished. Primarily, the focus should be on selecting the software which will allow the most efficient and productive use of the computer hardware. However, the selection of a software application package is closely bound to the choice of hardware. If only a few software packages are marketed for a particular computer while another computer has access to a wealth of commercial application packages, then clearly the chosen hardware will limit the packaged software to be considered for the system. Since the topic of packaged software selection was discussed in Chapter 2, the following discussion will concentrate on the acquisition of the computer system.

The Factors in Hardware Selection

Nine factors to consider in selecting hardware are listed in Figure 16-2. Six of the factors concern hardware capacity: memory size, processing speed, input/output channels, equipment for human interfaces, secondary storage capacity, and communication components. When evaluating the hardware, we must consider three additional features: systems software, available commercial software, and the vendor (reputation and quality of service). In the following discussion, the basic assumption is that a new hardware system will be acquired. Many times, the current hardware will be adequate for the

FIGURE 16-2   Computer hardware selection criteria

Hardware Features

Primary Memory Size

Processing Speed

Number of Channels
    Input, Output, and Communications

Equipment for Human Interfaces

    Screen Displays

    Printers

    Other Input/Output Devices

Secondary Storage Capacity

Communication Components

PLUS

Additional Criteria

Systems Software

Available Commercial Software

Vendor Reputation and Service

proposed information system. The processing requirements for the new system will determine whether to implement a new computer system or upgrade some current hardware components.

HARDWARE FACTORS

Since computers range in size from microcomputers to minicomputers to mainframes, the analyst must first estimate the processing requirements of the system. The system's processing requirements must be matched to the hardware so that the right choice can be made. In general, these processing requirements are specified by the following factors: throughput, response time, file storage requirements, on-line processing, types of input/output devices needed, printing capacity, and data communication requirements (see Figure 16-3). Since this list differs somewhat from the hardware items listed in Figure 16-2, the problem for the analyst lies in determining if the hardware features meet the needs specified for the system.

The first factor, **throughput**, is defined as the total amount of work that can be accomplished within a fixed time period. An example of system throughput is the number of transactions processed per minute for an on-line processing system. Although the computer's internal processing speed (measured in arithmetic operations per second) and the size and speed of its primary memory directly affect its capacity for throughput, mere examination of only these hardware ratings is insufficient. The system's throughput is also limited by the speed of the computer's secondary storage and input/output devices as well as the available systems software, especially the operating system. In the same way, the response time for an information system is not merely a product of the computer's internal processing speed. **Response time** is the time elapsed from the submission of a job until the user is notified of its completion, for example, by a message on the display screen.

File storage requirements are a major concern for the selection of a computer system. The forecast for secondary storage requirements is given by adding together the total file storage estimate, the space required for the

Throughput

Response Time

File Storage

On-Line Processing

Input/Output Devices

Printing Capacity

Data Communications

FIGURE 16-3

The processing requirements for an information system

systems software, and that needed for the firm's computer programs. During the physical file design step, the size of the files, future file growth, and the amount of disk space for any file indexes were estimated. The space required for the operating system and other systems software plus the firm's own programs must also be estimated. The total amount projected for files and programs is then used to check that sufficient disk capacity will be provided by the computer systems under consideration. It is always wise to purchase excess capacity rather than the minimal storage capacity required at the moment. As the volume of business grows, more disk storage invariably will be needed. The transfer rate — the time required to read or write data to the device — is also important since it will affect the overall efficiency of the computer system.

The requirement for magnetic tape subsystems or other devices for backup purposes must also be considered. It is crucial that adequate backup on the files be maintained. If suitable devices for backup operations are not available, these computers may be eliminated from consideration.

If we examine the issue of on-line processing, we see that the number of terminals possible for a particular computer is dependent on several hardware factors as well as software features. The capabilities for data communications, the number of channels, the computer's internal processing speed, and the appropriate systems software are factors that must be present in order to successfully implement an on-line information system. The systems software is especially important. If the operating system is unable to support the number of terminals planned for the information system, the proposed application cannot be implemented on that computer.

The types of input/output devices available with the computer are also important factors in the selection of the system. Although many types of input/output devices are available, the hardware interface required for a particular device may not be present on all computers. Even if this interface is available, the computer's input/output devices (including the secondary storage devices) must be correctly balanced with regard to data transfer rates. The internal hardware specifications of the computer must be reviewed to ensure that proper balancing of the input/output devices is performed. Thus, the overall configuration must be studied in addition to the availability of the desired input/output devices.

Printing capacity may be another prime consideration. For example, if it has been determined that the fastest type of laser printers should be employed in order to process the firm's printed output within an acceptable time frame, then computers unable to supply such printing capacity must be eliminated from consideration.

Data communication capabilities are typically a major concern for any computer today. An important specification is the maximum number of terminals that can be placed on-line with adequate response time. This restriction on the computer must be greater than or equal to the number of terminals projected for the new system. If these two numbers are exactly equal, problems may result when the system must be expanded to more terminals in the future. Finally, the ability to communicate with other types of computers, even those from other manufacturers, must also be reviewed. In this regard, the analyst should ensure that computers presently used in-house will be able to communicate with the new computer system.

SOFTWARE FACTORS

The decision to select a particular computer is directly influenced by the software available for that system. In particular, the operating system is a key component in realizing efficient use of the computer. If the systems software associated with the computer does not supply the software features necessary for the information system or future projected systems, then the superiority of hardware features must be weighed against the lack of appropriate software to support the firm's operations. In the same way, the systems software essential for the development of in-house software must be available. Appropriate programming language support and data base tools should be procurable. More generally, the future needs of the organization must be examined. No computer system will last forever. It is necessary to foresee the eventual conversion to a new system. Will this conversion be aided by the choice of computer system made today, or will serious problems arise due to lack of foresight? Because the conversion to a new computer system is costly, planning must encompass future needs as well as present requirements.

THE CHARACTERISTICS OF THE VENDOR

Finally, the characteristics of the vendor should be reviewed. The natural path for hardware upgrading is to continue with the same hardware manufacturer in order to avoid excessive conversion costs. **Upward compatibility** of computer systems means that, when hardware capacity must be expanded, the existing programs can be moved to a larger system without coding changes. The transition to a new computer is ordinarily more easily accomplished with an upgrade to a system provided by the same manufacturer when upward compatibility is available. If the manufacturer does not facilitate this upward mobility, then the firm will face major conversion problems at some point in the future. Problems may also be encountered if the firm deals with a computer produced by a manufacturer who is financially weak and faces the possibility of bankruptcy. If the manufacturer leaves the marketplace, the support services necessary for the computer system as well as the possibility of upgrading in the future will be lost. Finally, the vendor's reputation regarding service is an important factor to be considered in acquiring a computer system. Discussion with the vendor's current customers is helpful in rating the vendor's performance in meeting its obligations.

The Steps in Selecting Computer Hardware

The eight steps proposed for the selection of a computer system are summarized in Figure 16-4. The actual procedure will vary depending on the projected hardware costs and the need to purchase software application packages. As we have said, a general rule is that hardware selection is secondary to the choice of suitable, effective software to solve the firm's problem. The reasoning behind this statement is that the acquisition of adequate hardware is a relatively straightforward process, since there exist many comparable choices; however, substantial differences typically exist among software packages and systems software. Since good software is crucial to the firm's overall vitality, software must be chosen first, and only then, hardware.

STEP 1: SPECIFY EXTERNAL SOFTWARE REQUIREMENTS

In this first step, the analyst is interested in the external software requirements for the system: the software to be supplied from sources outside the firm. If a software application package will be purchased, the software rather than the hardware becomes the overriding consideration. Here, the motto "Software First, Hardware Second" is clearly appropriate. But we must realize that the software available for the computer system also affects the development of in-house applications. Having little or no supplementary software could curtail the firm's future plans. We must also understand that the choice of programming language is affected by the compilers associated with the installed computer system. Even if the availability of a fourth generation language is not important today, future needs may develop. It is important to note that more flexibility for future growth is given by a computer system that has attracted an array of software vendors and their products.

FIGURE 16-4

The steps in selecting the computer hardware

1. Specify external software requirements.
2. State the minimal hardware requirements.
3. Issue the request for proposal (RFP).
4. Study the proposals.
5. Perform benchmarks.
6. Select the best computer system.
7. Determine the mode of acquisition: rent, lease, or purchase.
8. Negotiate the contract.

STEP 2: STATE THE MINIMAL HARDWARE REQUIREMENTS

As we have already discussed, the minimal hardware requirements for the proposed information system must be defined. In doing so, the analyst describes the hardware specifications that must be met by a computer system in order to be considered for adoption.

STEP 3: ISSUE THE REQUEST FOR PROPOSAL (RFP)

Now that the hardware and software specifications are known, the analyst creates a detailed statement of these requirements. The firm then issues these specifications to computer manufacturers, turn-key vendors, resellers or leasing firms, requesting them to bid on the proposed system. A *turn-key vendor* is a firm that supplies and maintains both application software packages and the computer platforms on which they may be executed. The firm's request for bids is known as the **request for proposal (RFP)**. The RFP includes the general specifications of the information system that will be implemented on the hardware rather than merely listing the hardware details. The firm hopes to ensure that, by fully understanding the problem, each vendor will be able to submit a suitable bid. Those vendors who believe that their computer systems match the proposal's specifications will reply with a bid that describes the hardware system and its cost. Some vendors will choose not to bid on the system, either because they do not have a suitable system or because they do not find it financially worthwhile to engage in the time-consuming bidding process.

    Vendors are reliable sources of information on their individual hardware systems. They know the best ways to configure their hardware to accomplish the various tasks required by a firm. The vendor's sales and technical personnel are also able to draw on past experiences with other users of their computer equipment in order to assess the hardware needs of the firm. Such information and the complete technical specifications of computer systems are usually unavailable to the analyst except from these sources.

STEP 4: STUDY THE PROPOSALS

Once the bids have been received, a detailed study is performed. Further questions may be raised with individual vendors. Representatives from the vendors are likely to call on the firm to explain their proposals. At this point, the analyst should eliminate any proposals that do not fully meet the stated requirements.

    The computer systems proposed by the vendors may vary substantially in hardware specifications. It is the analyst's job to understand these differences, evaluate the proposed systems, and determine their appropriateness for the problems to be solved. To aid the analyst's decision, it may be profitable to study the detailed comparisons of computer systems and their attributes that are published annually by the consulting firms that specialize in this area. Some information may also be obtained from trade journals.

STEP 5: PERFORM BENCHMARKS

A **benchmark** is a special program designed to measure the performance of the computer system by performing operations typical of the actual processing required by the computer installation. Several benchmark programs are executed so that the performance level for the various functions commonly required for the users' workload can be measured. The capabilities of the data storage devices, the speed of processing transactions, and the compatibility of the internal computational methods are some operations that are usually evaluated by the use of benchmark programs. Because the benchmarks cannot be executed without the assistance of the systems software, the associated software is indirectly appraised by these benchmarks. In addition, benchmarks may be written to test the effectiveness of the systems software in performing certain tasks such as the handling of concurrent processing by input/output devices. It is important to note that the vendor's claims for hardware performance are meaningless without the corresponding overall processing speeds.

The set of benchmarks is executed on all the computers under consideration by the firm. Processing times for the benchmarks are compared for the different computers. As shown in Figure 16-5, it is possible that there will be no clear winner for all the benchmarks. Instead, one computer may have the best times for some benchmarks, while another computer is superior for other benchmarks. The benchmark results must be weighed in accordance with the job mix at the users' organization.

FIGURE 16-5

A comparison of the benchmark results

Benchmark: (measured per minute)	Computer 1	Computer 2	Computer 3
Transactions processed	30	35	25
COBOL arithmetic statements	395	378	324
Data base queries	65	57	62
Sample payroll checks	52	49	75
COBOL compiled statements	100	90	92
VSAM data retrieval of records	103	115	130
Total Times	**746**	**726**	**711**

STEP 6: SELECT THE BEST COMPUTER SYSTEM

Armed with the knowledge of appropriate trade-offs, the analyst selects the best choice for the organization. The benchmarks serve as guidelines in this selection process. As mentioned earlier, since one computer may surpass other computers on some but not all benchmarks, the results of the benchmarks must be evaluated in light of the installation's job mix. But the benchmarks serve only as guidelines and do not dictate the final choice. As we have said, the analyst must consider more than the hardware capabilities demonstrated by the benchmark results. The capabilities of the systems software and the commercial software packages available for a particular computer must be appraised. The vendor's long-term stability and its reputation for customer services are two other important factors to be assessed during the selection process. The analyst must weigh all the different attributes of each contending computer system in order to select the best choice for a particular installation's work.

> ### *Warning*
> Although microcomputers are prevalent on campus, another hardware choice may be the right one. Remember that choosing the most appropriate hardware for an information system requires experience and knowledge of available hardware. Don't make any quick calls, especially if your range of experience is limited; take time to study the options.

STEP 7: DETERMINE THE MODE OF ACQUISITION

When acquiring computing power, the firm is faced with several options. As indicated in Figure 16-6, a basic question is whether the computer should be located in-house or outside computing services should be contracted with companies dedicated to supplying computer hardware and software ser-

In-House Computing: Acquisition Methods
Rental
Lease
Purchase

Alternatives to In-House Computing
Service Bureaus
Outsourcing

FIGURE 16-6
The options for computer hardware acquisition

vices. If the firm chooses to acquire its own computer, it must also decide on the mode of acquisition. Computers may be purchased, rented, or leased from the manufacturers or from firms that specialize in the leasing of computers. The acquisition method affects the mode of payment for the system. The right method for the organization is dependent on two factors: (1) the projected life of the computer system at the firm and (2) the payment method most appropriate for the organization at the time of acquisition.

Because a computer is simply a machine, it faces the same problems as other machines. Parts of the computer may simply wear out. As the computer ages, it will become increasingly difficult to find replacement parts. Since computers are part of a rapidly changing technology, the computer experiences obsolescence in a relatively short time compared to other machines. Even if the computer is still operative, new computers with greater capabilities will become available and may even cost substantially less than the older computer. Despite conversion costs, the firm may gain financially by changing computer systems. The analyst also knows that the firm's computing needs are likely to increase in the years to come. The problem of the firm is how to best deal with the uncertainties of the future. Thus, the issue of rental, lease, or purchase as the means to acquire the computer system is directly affected by the firm's desire to avoid obsolescence, minimize costs, and facilitate the procurement of increased computing power whenever needed in the future. The additional factor of the firm's own financial picture also affects the payment method.

Rental   Computer *rental* rather than leasing is defined to be the use of the computer for only a short period of time, often a few months or a year. The arrangement allows the user or the supplier to cancel the agreement with short notice, often 30 to 60 days prior to the return of the computer. Payment is made on a monthly basis. The advantage to rental is that the organization is able to quickly change to another computer system. This flexibility for change is useful when plans have been made to acquire a new computer system that is not yet ready for delivery. By renting on a short-term basis, the firm can retain the current system but is able to move quickly to the new hardware without incurring high financial penalties. Rental agreements are favored by firms with older computer systems that will soon be replaced by new systems. If older hardware equipment is rented, special care should be taken with the rental contract so that adequate guarantees of maintenance as well as restrictions on downtime are incorporated.

Lease   A *lease* is an arrangement to use the computer system for a long period of time, typically from two to seven years. The payment schedule is fixed and does not change during the leasing period. Because the user does not have the option of cancelling at short notice, the financial provisions are more favorable. At the end of the leasing period, the computer system remains the property of the computer vendor.

Because the computer system has not been purchased, the user can avoid technical obsolescence by acquiring a new system at the end of the leasing period. A leasing arrangement with the computer manufacturer usually allows for the upgrading of the computer without penalties. However, when new equipment is installed, the payments may be increased.

Leasing is a popular method of computer acquisition. It ensures that the firm can easily install new equipment without undue financial loss for the changeover required in the midst of technological advances. However, it is important that the break-even point for leasing versus purchase arrangements be determined. If the leasing period is too long, a purchase agreement is preferable. A rule of thumb is that the leasing of a computer for more than five years is not cost effective. In general, the system should be purchased if its lifetime exceeds five years.

Purchase   The purchase of a computer means that the title to the computer is transferred to the purchaser. The advantage of a purchase agreement is financial. Since leasing costs over an extended period of time will ordinarily exceed the initial purchase price of a computer, the firm saves money by buying the equipment outright. Because the firm owns the computer, it can depreciate the computer hardware over time. This is not possible with the leasing option. Consequently, there are tax advantages to the purchase arrangement.

The disadvantages of purchasing instead of leasing are inherent in the ownership of equipment. The firm now becomes wholly responsible for the maintenance of the computer hardware. The firm must decide whether to retain a staff able to perform computer maintenance or negotiate a maintenance agreement with the supplier, usually the manufacturer. Both avenues have proved popular, depending on the size of the firm. If contracted with the supplier, the maintenance charges are determined on a yearly basis with payments due monthly. Maintenance costs normally increase each year. When monthly maintenance charges are paid to an outside firm, they are tax deductible as a business expense.

As discussed earlier, computer technology is still experiencing rapid change. Improvements in technology have continued to lead to new computers that cost substantially less than previous computers. Thus, after five years of ownership, the value of the computer hardware will be much lower. During that five-year period, equipment upgrades are likely to be necessary because of increased demands for both faster processing and more computing capacity. If the firm must replace a computer that was purchased rather than leased, it loses most of its investment in the present hardware. However, the ability to deduct these losses from taxes overcomes some financial disadvantages of the purchase option. For that reason, purchasing remains a popular option.

STEP 8: NEGOTIATE THE CONTRACT

A formal contract is negotiated between the users' organization and the seller or leaser of the computer hardware. The required performance level of the hardware may be written into the contract. For example, the capability to process a specific number of transactions per minute or the ability to respond to a data base inquiry within a given time may be a provision of the contract. If the computer fails to meet these requirements, the contract may be voided or penalties exacted from the vendor. A specific limit to interruptions in computer operations due to hardware or vendor-supplied software failures may be inserted into the contract. Heavy penalties for lengthy hardware downtime may also be written into the contract with the vendor's concurrence.

The contract becomes a legally binding document made between the users' organization and the supplier of the hardware or software. Despite a carefully constructed contract with penalty provisions, the analyst knows that the organization rather than the vendor will suffer the most from disruption in services. Thus, primary consideration must be given to the procurement of reliable hardware and software from a responsible and trustworthy vendor.

Alternatives to In-House Systems

There are two alternatives to the acquisition of an in-house system: *service bureaus* and *outsourcing*. **Service bureaus** are companies that operate computer facilities and perform computer processing for other firms. Typically, the user's data is transmitted to the service bureau and the results returned via telecommunication lines. The software that performs the data processing is often supplied by the service bureau. Some service bureaus also offer the complete handling of the raw data, transforming it into computer input, executing the processing, and returning the completed output. Accounting and payroll are two common operations performed by service bureaus. Alternatively, the user may elect to create custom programs for processing and employ the service bureau as the source of computing power rather than acquire an in-house computer.

Users gain financial advantages from the use of service bureaus. An in-house computer facility means incurring expenses for highly paid, trained staff plus the cost of computer equipment. If the firm's work load does not justify the costs of maintaining a computer facility, service bureaus provide an attractive option, particularly for smaller firms. However, since microcomputers have gained in power and software application packages are more readily available, small firms are more frequently turning to their own in-house solutions.

Outsourcing is the operation of the computer facility by an outside firm that supplies such services. With this option, the users' firm engages the outsourcing firm to establish and maintain the computer facility located at the users' site. All the users' processing needs are usually met by the outsourcing firm. The computer professionals are employees of the outsourcer, rather than of the firm itself.

Firms adopt the outsourcing approach to achieve financial savings. Since the outsourcing firm is dedicated to computer applications, its expertise in hardware and software is high. Because of the outsourcer's familiarity with computing issues, the firm can concentrate on its own objectives without expending resources to sustain its employees' knowledge in the computing arena. The outsourcer may develop new information systems (or acquire commercial application packages) as needed by the firm as well as maintain the existing systems. The cost of computing services is fixed by contract.

The major disadvantage arises when the firm needs to create strategic systems of its own. Since the outsourcing firm has contracts with many firms, it typically wishes to develop application software that can be sold to more than one firm. By its nature, a strategic system should be designed to gain a competitive advantage in the marketplace and, thus, should be developed exclusively for a single company. Primary interest in the development of new strategic applications also rests with the managers of the users' firm rather than the outsourcer. This conflict between the firm's objectives and the outsourcing firm is the primary concern regarding the establishment of outsourcing. Nonetheless, outsourcing has been adopted, even by some major firms.

DESIGNING THE PROGRAMS

The second major objective of the Design phase is the accomplishment of the program design. Because the Analysis phase has produced a somewhat detailed model of the proposed information system, it is tempting to think that we could simply begin to code the programs. Since the data flow diagrams do not display the program structure, however, and also omit the handling of most error conditions and input/output operations, more detailed information is needed to guide the programmer in the writing of the program code. For this reason, we introduce a model for program design which serves as the link between the data flow diagrams and the actual programs, which must still be coded as a series of program statements. As we mentioned earlier, there are two popular diagramming techniques for depicting program designs. The first, *structured design*, is based on the use of diagrams called *structure charts*. A second technique called *Warnier-Orr diagrams* provides a different type of diagram for expressing the program's logic. Because structure charts are more widely used, we will concentrate primarily on that methodology.

The aims of program design are the production of suitable documentation to guide the programmers in the coding of high quality programs. *High quality programs* are those that are found to contain few errors during testing and later during production use. The program structure should help to prevent the introduction of any new errors by the program maintenance process. In order to achieve this goal, errors should be *localized* within a particular range of program code rather than allowed to affect other program areas, usually without the programmer's knowledge. A second but equally important objective is the provision of program documentation that will facilitate the maintenance of the programs in the future. Since maintenance activities constitute a large percentage of the system's costs, it is essential to produce clearly stated documentation of the program's logic so that necessary modifications can be made by the maintenance programmers without difficulty.

Structured Design

The basic premise of **structured design** is the use of *top-down design* to create the program structure. **Top-down design** means that the program will be expressed in a hierarchical framework of *modules*. A **module** is a self-contained set of contiguous program statements that performs its task independently of other modules. Since the program tasks are divided into separate modules, a module calls on other modules to execute particular tasks rather than duplicating another module's code. A module represents a subroutine, a separate program, or a COBOL paragraph in the PROCEDURE division. There is only one entrance and one exit from the program coding for a module. The use of a GO TO statement to jump into a module is forbidden. Modules are limited in size, usually to the 55 lines (for a printed page) or the maximum possible on a computer screen (typically 25), so that the programmer can easily view the module's logic. Smaller modules are preferred because they minimize the impact of any program modification to a particular module. Structured design is a methodology for defining the relationships between the modules, the data and control information passed between them, and the individual tasks to be performed by each module.

STRUCTURE CHARTS

A **structure chart** is a graphical representation of the program modules and their relationship to each other within a hierarchical structure. Let us examine the simple structure chart in Figure 16-7. This structure chart illustrates the different symbols used to depict its various components. A *module* is represented by a rectangle labeled with the module's name. If the module represents program coding available on the installation library, it is drawn as a rectangle with additional vertical lines at each side. In Figure 16-7, module C is depicted as a subroutine available from the library.

The link between two modules is shown by a line with an arrow pointing toward the called module. This link is known as a *connection*. A **connection** indicates that the top module (the *parent*) commands its subordinate module (the *child*) to perform its specified task. A parent module is also known as a **manager module** because it directs its subordinate

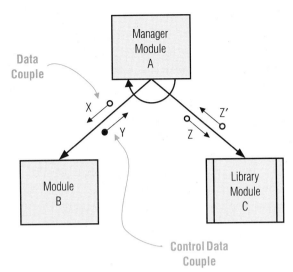

FIGURE 16-7

A sample structure chart   The curved arrow indicates a loop: the repetition of B and C.

modules to execute their tasks. The modules that accomplish the detailed processing are found at the lowest level of the structure chart.

The passing of data between the modules is designated by the appearance of a **couple**, which is depicted by an arrow in the direction of the flow. The circle on the arrow shaft indicates the type of data being passed. An open circle designates data to be processed by the receiving module, while a shaded circle signifies *control data*. The data item name is placed adjacent to the couple. Here the term *data item* signifies either a single data element or a group of elements. A data item is either data to be processed by the receiving module or *control data* that give information about a condition discovered by the sending module. **Control data** provide information that is used by the receiving module for decision making. For example, if a module is responsible for reading a data record from the file, then it also sends control data to signal when the end of the file has been reached. The receiving module then decides on the course of action depending on the information given in the control data. Another name for a control data item is a **switch** or **flag**. The repetitive execution of a set of subordinate modules, that is, a *loop*, is shown by drawing a curved arrow below the manager module.

In Figure 16-7, we see module A, the controlling module, with its two subordinate modules, B and C. Module A is called the manager module since it directs modules B and C to do the work. Modules B and C are called *worker modules*. When module A calls on module B, it passes data item X downward to B; the action is depicted by the couple pointing towards B. Module B performs its specific task and returns the flag Y to A, to indicate that a particular condition has been detected. Module A then calls on module C to perform its assigned job, passing data item Z downward. After C completes its work, it sends data item Z' to A.

Each module must send and receive the minimum amount of data required to perform the tasks. Therefore, module B requires the data item X in order to perform its task; otherwise, A would not send X down to B. X does not contain any data that are not absolutely required for the processing done in module B. Similarly, the return of the data flag Y is essential to module A. Before A can continue its work by calling C, it must know the contents of the flag Y. Likewise, C needs the data item Z to execute its job and the data item Z′ is required by A to complete its work. Modules B and C function independently of each other. They do not share data or statements. Any data required by a subordinate module must be passed to it by the manager module. The data to be sent to or from a module are dependent on its task. Although not shown in Figure 16-7, more than one couple can be sent to or from a module.

Strictly speaking, modules may be executed in any order. More practically, a structure chart is ordinarily drawn so that the order of execution is from left to right. Exceptions to this rule involve modules that must be called by more than one manager module; in that case, left to right ordering may impair readability. An example of this type of connection is shown in Figure 16-8. Both modules B and C call on module E to perform its task for them. To avoid the crossing of lines, module E is placed between modules F and G. The lower level modules are called by module B in the order D, E, and F. Module C calls on its worker modules in the order G and E. The execution order of the worker modules is specified by the module descriptions for B and C.

COUPLING

The term *couple* indicates the data that are passed to and from modules. As stated earlier, an objective of structured design is to reduce the number of problems caused by program statements that are related to each other.

FIGURE 16-8

A structure chart where left to right order is inappropriate The couples are omitted to simplify the diagram.

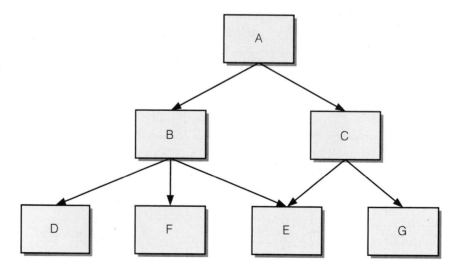

Therefore, each module should be independent of the other modules except for the linkage provided by the data transmitted between modules. The more data passed between modules, the more likely that a change in one module will affect other modules. **Coupling** measures the degree of independence between two modules. The term *loosely coupled* describes modules that are insulated from changes coming from the outside world. Thus, whenever a module is modified, the impact on other modules can be quickly determined by examining the couples sent and received by the modified module.

Consider the module VERIFY STUDENT-ID shown at the left of Figure 16-9. Its calling module EDIT STUDENT DATA sends the entire record (STUDENT-RECORD) to its subordinate module, which needs to verify only that the field STUDENT-ID is valid. Transmitting unnecessary data fields to the module VERIFY STUDENT-ID is risky, for any changes made in the record format may cause the subordinate module to behave improperly. Thus, these two modules are said to be *closely coupled.* Instead, as shown on the right-hand side of Figure 16-9, the modules should be *loosely coupled* by sending only STUDENT-ID to the subordinate module.

COHESIVENESS

A module is said to be *cohesive* if it performs only one function. By restricting the operations performed by a module, the analyst controls the effects of modifications to the code, once again localizing the changes to a particular module rather than scattering them throughout the program. Three factors help to determine the **cohesiveness** of a module: its name, its description, and its coupling.

The proper naming of a module assists in establishing its cohesiveness. Although top level modules—manager modules—will have broad names,

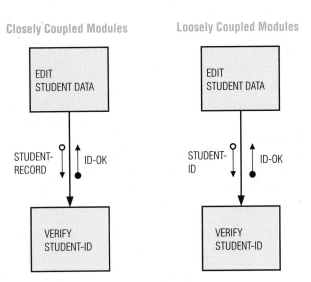

Closely Coupled Modules   Loosely Coupled Modules

FIGURE 16-9

Close Coupling vs. loose coupling The closely coupled module VERIFY STUDENT-ID receives the entire STUDENT RECORD; to obtain loosely coupled modules, only the field STUDENT-ID is sent.

module names should describe only one task. Examples are VALIDATE STUDENT-ID, COMPUTE GROSS-PAY, and PRODUCE PAYCHECK. Even though the module PRODUCE PAYCHECK will undoubtedly call on many other modules to perform various tasks, its name indicates only one main function. Examples of modules with poor cohesion are CHECK STUDENT-DATA AND ENROLL STUDENT, COMPUTE ANNUAL-DATA AND PRINT BILLS, and ACCEPT AND EDIT TIMESHEETS. Each of these modules really performs two functions rather than only one. Some poorly defined modules with low cohesiveness are not so easy to spot and may appear with deceptively simple or misleading names. For example, if the module EDIT TIMESHEET also creates the gross pay for each employee, you know something is wrong! If the structure chart is misleading, it is always possible to examine the process descriptions themselves to find out if more than one function is performed by the module. Such study is, however, time-consuming and difficult because of the search of detailed statements. Consequently, the software developer is entrusted with the responsibility of drawing an accurate structure chart with appropriately named modules and couples.

Coupling also affects the cohesiveness of the module. If a worker module receives a control flag that indicates the operations to be performed, the module is likely to have weak cohesion. Since the control flag selects which tasks will be performed, the receiving module must have more than one function. However, the return of a control flag from a module does not affect its cohesiveness. Modules linked by only a single input or output are likely to be strongly independent and, thus, cohesive modules.

THE CONVERSION OF A DFD TO A STRUCTURE CHART

Although the model of the proposed system was fully documented in the Analysis phase, some essential factors have been omitted from consideration. In the interest of clarity, the design of many error paths, control information, most repetitions (loops), decisions regarding flows, details of input/output operations, and the program structure itself have been ignored. But if all these details are left to the discretion of the programmer, key design decisions may adversely affect the overall efficiency of the program. As discussed previously, the data flow diagrams (DFDs) and process descriptions are insufficient to act as the guidelines for the construction of the physical program code. Instead, the program structure inherent within a data flow diagram can be transformed into a structure chart, which can then be refined to reflect the additional details necessary for preparing the program code.

The transformation of a DFD to a structure chart is based on the fact that the fundamental structure of any system is given by the following three steps:

1. Get data (input).
2. Process data.
3. Put data (output).

The structure chart must show how these three basic system operations interact with each other. In Figure 16-10, a structure chart has been drawn to illustrate the structure of any system by displaying these basic functions as individual modules. This structure chart provides the view of a simple system. More complex systems require more than one input or output module as manager modules.

In deriving the structure chart from its related data flow diagram, we must differentiate the DFD processes according to their primary functions. Figure 16-11a shows the main portion of a simplified data flow diagram. The central process of the data flow diagram is labeled PROCESS DATA. The processes leading to this central process are responsible for creating the "Good Input" data which will be transformed into the "Output." As shown, the capturing of the good input data typically consists of several processes in sequence called an **input stream**. These processes obtain the raw input data and perform editing operations in order to create the "Good Input." The central process takes the "Good Input" and produces the solution, which is the system output. In order to send the "Output" to the outside world, a succession of output processes first format the data and then display the solution as the final output. The group of processes that produce the final output is known as the **output stream**.

In Figure 16-11a, only one process has been shown to perform the transformation of the good input data into the solution. If only one process lies between the input and output streams, it is called the *central transform*. If a group of processes is found, they are called the *transaction center* and will be grouped under a manager module bearing this name. The trick in deriving a structure chart from a data flow diagram is to identify the central transform or transaction center on the DFD. Each process on the DFD will appear as a module on the derived structure chart. Additional modules will be given to supplement the DFD processes. The structure chart derived for the data flow diagram in Figure 16-11a is displayed in Figure 16-11b.

The detailed explanation of the procedure to derive a structure chart from a DFD is somewhat long. Since the easiest way to gain an understanding of the process is to actually see the two diagrams side by side, we will

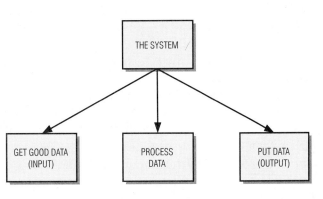

FIGURE 16-10

The basic components of a system shown as a structure chart

FIGURE 16-11 **Two representations of an information system** The main portion of a DFD (a) is transformed into a structure chart (b).

a. **The general form of a DFD**

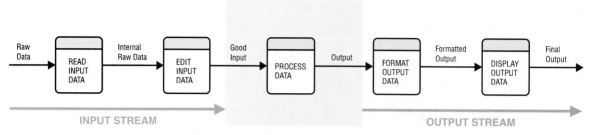

b. **The structure chart for the DFD in part a**

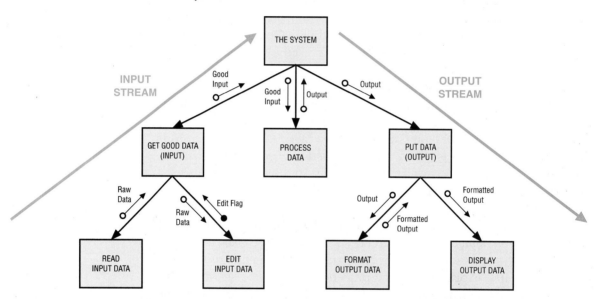

first discuss an example; its full explanation will be deferred to the next section. In Figure 16-12, the data flow diagram for a simplified order processing system at a catalog store is shown. The central transform is identified as process 2. In Figure 16-13, the top module of the structure chart has been assigned the name of the system. On the next level, the module on the left, GET CUSTOMER ORDER, represents the means by which the input data INITIAL-ORDER is obtained for processing. At the right, PRINT ORDER is the manager module that directs the set of processes by which the system emits the order. The middle process, COMPLETE ORDER INFO, accepts the input INITIAL-ORDER and issues the output COMPLETED ORDER, which must then be processed by the output stream for printing and transmission to the Order Department. Although it has not been shown, the module COMPLETE

FIGURE 16-12   The simplified DFD for a batch order processing system

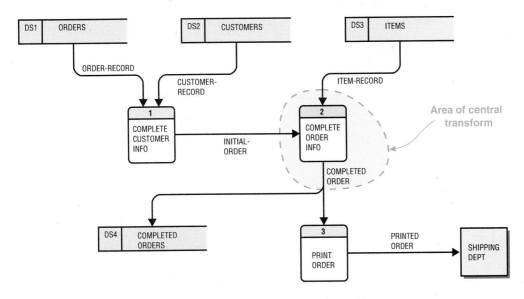

FIGURE 16-13   The structure chart derived for the DFD in Figure 16-12   The flag EOF indicates when end of file occurs on the CUSTOMER file.

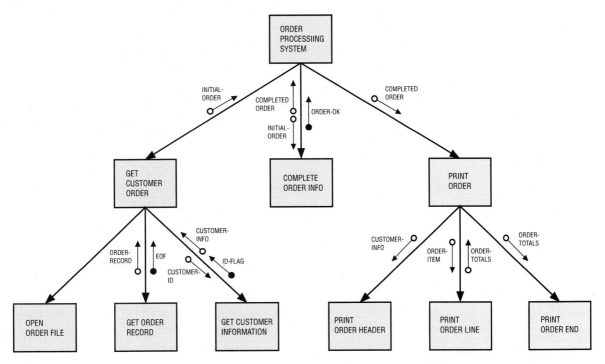

ORDER INFO will also call on its subordinate modules in order to accomplish its function. As you examine these two diagrams, you should consider the similarities existing between them and also note that new modules, not found on the DFD, now appear on the structure chart. Physical details such as PRINT ORDER HEADER are now necessary to guide the writing of the program code.

DRAWING STRUCTURE CHARTS

Since data flow diagrams represent a hierarchical partitioning of the proposed system into successively refined levels, they bear a resemblance to the diagramming technique given by structure charts. The data flow diagrams show *what* the system does, while the structure charts are designed to show *how* the system will be implemented by computer programs. Because of the similarities between the two diagramming techniques, guidelines exist for converting the data flow diagrams into structure charts. Although the procedure is not a strictly mechanical conversion, most data flow diagrams can be easily altered into their corresponding structure charts.

The first step for this conversion is to identify the central transform or transaction center of the DFD. Processes leading *to* the central transform or transaction center perform input processing while those leading *away* from this central processing accomplish output processing. Examples of input processes are given by these process names: ACCEPT EMPLOYEE TIMESHEET, VALIDATE ACCOUNT NUMBER, and EDIT PAYROLL DATA. Output processes similarly focus on the output data rather than the creation of new data, as in PRODUCE MONTHLY REPORT, PREPARE PAYCHECK, and FORMAT INVOICE.

The **central transform** is a central process whose function is to transform its input data into output data. In other words, the central transform is a process that changes or adds data to its input(s) in order to create its output(s). Thus, we often find that one or more data elements of its output(s) will be derived by the process's operations. As you will recall from Chapters 14 and 15, *base data elements* simply enter and exit the process; they are renamed only because new knowledge has been gained about them. Such processes usually can be eliminated as possible transform centers. Instead, we typically look for a process that creates new data elements from its input(s). For example, the process COMPUTE PAYCHECK receives the input data necessary to derive the values of such data elements as GROSS PAY, NET PAY, and FICA; these newly formed values called *derived data elements* are issued from the process on its output data flows. Other examples of central transforms are processes with names such as COMPLETE ORDER INFORMATION, ENROLL STUDENT IN CLASS, and ALTER SCHEDULE.

To illustrate a central transform, Figure 16-14 contains a simplified DFD, which will be converted into a structure chart. This DFD has two input legs while the output stream has only one output leg. In Figure 16-15a, the same DFD appears with labels on the processes and data flows. The first input leg

FIGURE 16-14   **The outline of a DFD with a central transform**   All labels and external entities are omitted to simplify the diagram.

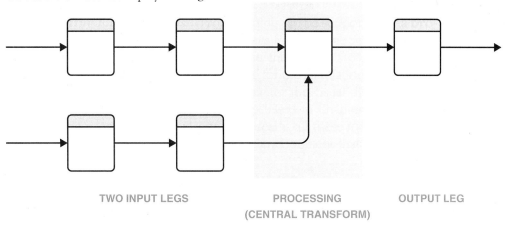

TWO INPUT LEGS   PROCESSING   OUTPUT LEG
                            (CENTRAL TRANSFORM)

is formed by processes P1 and P2, and the second input leg is composed of processes P3 and P4. The output stream contains only a single process P6. Process P5 is identified as the central transform. The corresponding structure chart appears as Figure 16-15b. The top module is simply called THE SYSTEM. The central transform, process P5, is represented as a module which receives the input data C and F and returns the data G to its parent module, THE SYSTEM.

Because the process P5 must receive the inputs C and F, we have created two modules, GET C and GET F, to supply these two inputs to the top module. The top module can then send these data items, C and F, to the module P5: MAKE C AND F INTO G. Thus, the input legs are changed into two legs within the structure chart. The input leg for GET C is built on two modules, GET B and P2: MAKE B INTO C. The module GET B receives the input data B and sends it to the module GET C, which then sends it to the module labeled P2: MAKE B INTO C. Since module GET B needs the data B, its two subordinate modules work to provide B. The module GET A supplies data item A to the module GET B which then sends it to the module P1: MAKE A INTO B. Because the process P1 does, in fact, make A into B, the module returns the data item B to its manager module. A similar decomposition takes place for the module GET E, which relies on its worker modules to furnish the data item E.

The output stream is represented on the structure chart in a similar fashion. The output stream contains the different processes by which the output G is transformed into the final output data H. Thus, the output stream on the structure chart is headed by the manager module, OUTPUT G. Process P6 in the DFD output stream becomes the worker module labeled P6: MAKE G INTO H. Because the data item H must still be transformed into the final output to be sent to the external entity, the module OUTPUT G calls on the module PUT H to create the final output H. This latter module (PUT H)

FIGURE 16-15   The derivation of a structure chart from a DFD with a central transform

a. The DFD in Figure 16-14 with processes and data flows labeled

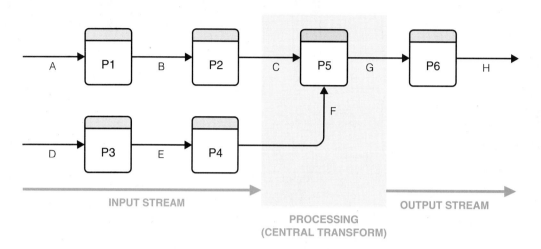

b. The structure chart derived
from the DFD in part **a**

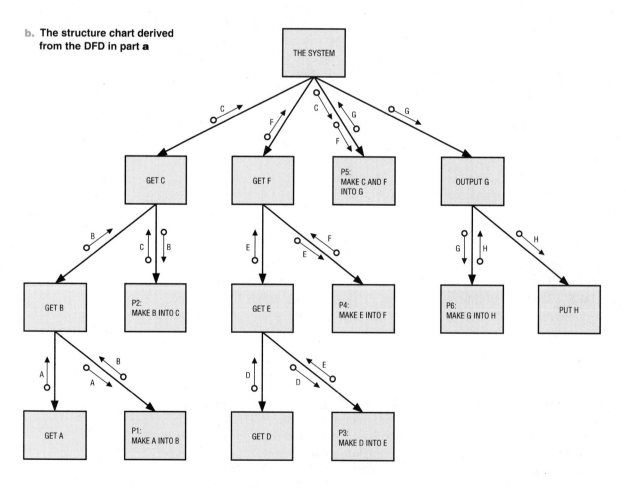

is the concluding task, which delivers the system output to the outside world. However, this module may call on worker modules to format the data and carry out related output tasks.

A **transaction center** is a group of processes that lies between the input and output streams. The presence of a transaction center in the data flow diagram, rather than a single central transform process, alters the conversion procedure slightly. Figure 16-16a shows a DFD with a transaction center containing the processes QQ, RR, SS, and WW. In Figure 16-16b, all four processes have been converted into worker modules called by the manager module labeled TRANSACTION CENTER (MAKE B INTO G). The process PP, which accepts A and creates B, has been placed under a manager module (GET B) that provides data item B for the top module. Similarly, the output stream begins with the manager module OUTPUT G that receives G, sends G to module XX that returns H, and then sends out H to its worker module labeled PUT H.

Finally, you may ask what happened to all those levels of DFDs that were drawn to document the information system in more detail. The DFD given by explosion of a process is placed under its corresponding module when converted into a structure chart. In Figure 16-17a, the explosion of process P2 is represented by the DFD with processes 2.1, 2.2, and 2.3. The derivation of the structure chart now locates these processes as worker modules under the module corresponding to P2 in Figure 16-17b. The input data flows and output data flows that appear on the DFD are represented by couples on the structure chart.

DESIGN THE MODULES

Now that the program structure has been defined by the structure chart, it is necessary to describe the operations to be performed by each module. If the structure chart is closely related to the data flow diagram and the DFD processes were fully described in the project dictionary, it will be relatively easy to specify the modules corresponding to the processes given on the DFD. However, the details of input and output processing will require additional work.

Modules are usually defined in *pseudocode*. **Pseudocode** is similar to structured English but is more closely related to actual program code. Whereas the process descriptions for a DFD avoid controls and flags, they are now included in the module descriptions. Pseudocode statements do not conform to the syntax of any particular programming language but allow a freer format. The pseudocode statements serve to guide the programmer in the writing of the code. Each DFD process description is translated into pseudocode with the addition of control-type statements and input/output statements.

Each module must be specified in sufficient detail so that the programmer can write the program code to perform its function. Most of the inputs

FIGURE 16-16   **The derivation of a structure chart from a DFD with a transaction center**

a. An outline of a DFD with a transaction center

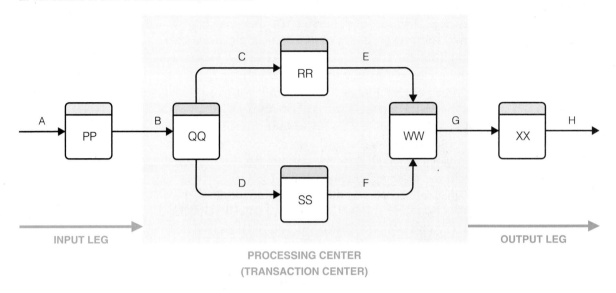

b. The structure chart for part a

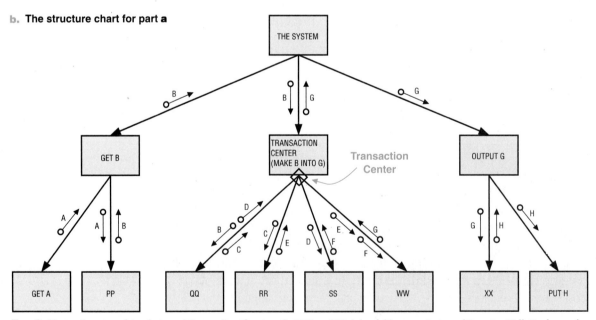

Tom DeMarco, *Structured Analysis and System Specification,* © 1979, p. 320. Adapted by permission of Prentice Hall, Englewood Cliffs, NJ.

a. A DFD with an exploded process

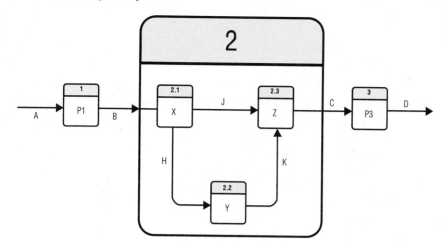

FIGURE 16-17
Converting a leveled DFD to a structure chart

b. The structure chart derived for the leveled DFD

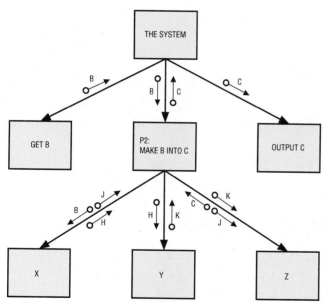

Tom DeMarco, *Structured Analysis and System Specification,* © 1979, p. 318. Adapted by permission of Prentice Hall, Englewood Cliffs, NJ.

and outputs to the module should be fully described by the data dictionary entries already in existence. Descriptions of control data will need to be added to the data dictionary. The function of the module should be stated in a simple sentence that establishes the relationship between the module's inputs and outputs. Each module should be appropriately named to indicate its function.

To assist in the documentation of the modules, the CASE tool Excelerator can explode a module to create a module description very similar to that provided for primitive process descriptions associated with the DFDs. In Excelerator, a module is described by the use of three separate screens. As shown in Figure 16-18, the opening screen allows for the specification of the couples that flow to or from the module. Data items named on the couples are known as input or output parameters. For the module description displayed in Figure 16-18, the Input Parameters are defined as the data item SEARCH-CUSTOMER-ID and the Return Values are given as ID-FLAG. The second screen is not relevant to us here; it deals with the control of the project rather than the documentation of the module. The third screen given for this module appears in Figure 16-19. The pseudocode for the module is entered on the screen in the same fashion as performed for primitive process descriptions.

Sometimes designers choose to employ flowcharts to document the module's logic. If flowcharts are used, they should conform to the requirements for structured programming (discussed in Chapter 17). Since most CASE tools do not provide for the use of flowcharts, it is preferable to use pseudocode.

PACKAGING THE DESIGN

Packaging the design refers to the refinement of the program design to meet the physical requirements of the system, such as the computer configuration, operating system, programming language, secondary storage capacity, and response time. Since the theoretical structure of the program will

FIGURE 16-18

The opening screen in Excelerator for the explosion of a module

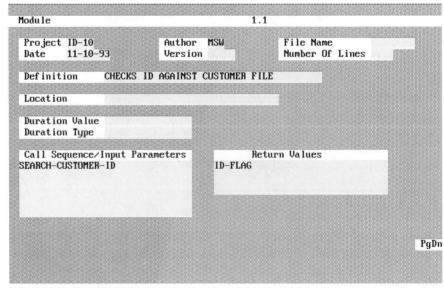

Screen shots produced using INTERSOLV's Excelerator solution for Requirements Analysis and System Design.

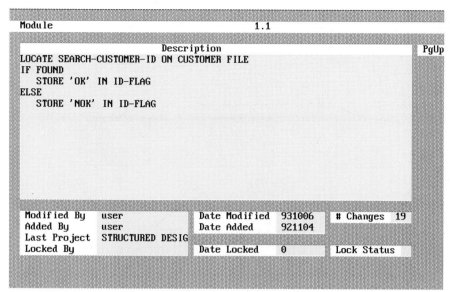

FIGURE 16-19

The final Excelerator screen for the explosion of a module

Screen shots produced using INTERSOLV's Excelerator solution for Requirements Analysis and System Design.

be implemented in a particular physical environment, it is necessary to fine tune the final programs so they perform efficiently. Recall that the designer has aimed for a program structure that is easy to maintain and straightforward to code. This ideal design must now be compromised to mesh with the realities of the physical world.

First, consider how the program has been broken into many separate modules. A parent module causes its child module to be executed by issuing a call to the module. Such calls consume primary storage and program execution time. Whenever a child module consists of only one line, its execution requires several more instructions, because the module must be called by its parent. If the parent module is called by its own parent, additional instructions must be performed. Consider the structure chart shown in Figure 16-20. Because the bottom module ACCUMULATE LINE COUNT is several levels down, several calling sequences must be performed before the computer instructions in this module are executed. All these calls increase the program's running time. In addition, this bottom module occurs within a loop. The module ACCUMULATE LINE COUNT will be called for every line printed by the program. Hence the program will expend a proportionally high amount of CPU time, over and over again, in order to reach this bottom module so that only a few lines of code can be executed. Under these circumstances, the basic questions in packaging the design are: What modules should be combined, and what modules should retain their independence from other modules?

Some experts argue that these decisions should be delayed until after the program has been coded. Ed Yourdon, an expert on systems analysis and

FIGURE 16-20

A structure chart with loops The curved arrow signifies a loop.

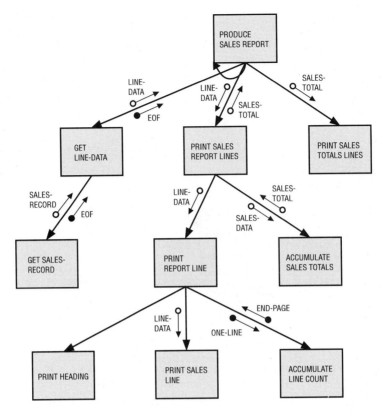

design methods, has said "It is easier to make a working system efficient than to make an efficient system work" [DeMarco, 1979, p. 313]. While that statement is certainly true, the reworking of an existing program is not a simple task. At the outset, it is wise to combine modules that are really too small to stand alone. For example, consider the computation of NET-PAY by a separate module that receives GROSS-PAY and TOTAL-DEDUCTIONS (see Figure 16-21). The module consists of a single program statement:

COMPUTE NET-PAY AS GROSS-PAY MINUS TOTAL-DEDUCTIONS.

Should this statement be placed in a separate module? Its parent module can easily incorporate this statement and eliminate the need to call a subroutine that performs only one statement. Since this statement seems fixed and unlikely to change due to business conditions, the answer is "yes."

Common sense tells us that a single line module is undesirable except in unusual circumstances. Consequently, we recommend some initial smoothing of a program's structure charts and then additional refinement after a working system has been built. As hardware has gone down in cost and up in power, the trade-off between program efficiency and program readability has come to favor saving human labor over sparing the machine. The use of strictly independent modules (that is, loosely coupled and highly cohesive modules) typically reduces the time required for the testing activ-

FIGURE 16-21   **A structure chart with the module COMPUTE NET PAY**

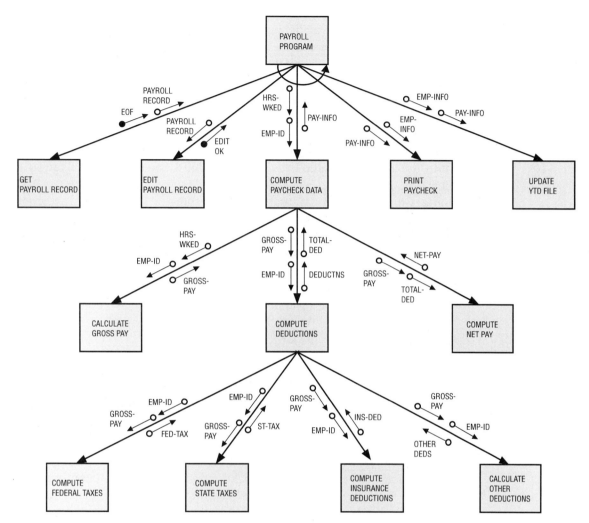

ities and thus reduces human effort. Nonetheless, the recommendations of structured design sometimes need to be bypassed in order to achieve realistic program designs.

The packaged design includes the input/output designs and physical file descriptions (explained in Chapters 13, 14, and 15). If CASE tools were used, the program code for these designs may have already been produced for transfer to the programming staff.

ADVANTAGES AND DISADVANTAGES OF STRUCTURE CHARTS

Structure charts offer several advantages. First, they allow the evolution of the program design to occur as a step-by-step process based on the diagramming techniques used in the Analysis phase. The system components described by the data flow diagrams, process descriptions, and data dictionary are directly incorporated into the logical program design. Second, the use of manageable, well-defined information in the form of modules and couples enables the system design to be controlled. Third, the hierarchical arrangement of modules creates a program structure that is well-organized and manageable. Fourth, good module design ensures that errors and future changes will be localized and thus more manageable.

Structure charts also have some disadvantages. First, the diagrams quickly become unwieldy and unreadable. The numerous flags and data passed between modules clutter the chart and make it difficult to understand fully the interrelationship between the modules. Second, the details regarding system processing requirements (such as weekly, monthly, or yearly processing) are omitted until the final packaging occurs. It would be better if such details could be documented as an integral part of the program design. Third, many CASE tools do not assist the designer in restructuring the data flow diagram into a structure chart. Under these circumstances, there is no convenient way to show the linkage between the DFD processes and the structure chart's modules; the process descriptions given for the DFD processes cannot be simply moved over to serve as the basis for the module descriptions. The designer must repeat many steps in order to completely document the structure charts.

Warnier–Orr Diagrams

The technique of Warnier–Orr diagrams was originated by Jean-Dominique Warnier and adapted by Ken Orr. **Warnier–Orr diagrams** are organized about the outputs required by the system. The system outputs are defined to be any data flowing outside the system but also include the data files, screen displays, and other output data not usually designated as system outputs. Because Warnier–Orr diagrams offer certain features not found in structure charts, some designers prefer to use this diagramming technique. Since the Warnier–Orr methodology focuses on the data structures that enter and leave the system, it is called a **data-driven methodology**. This approach is based on the belief that data structures are subject to change more frequently than the processes within the organization. By contrast, a method that concentrates on how processes transform the data flowing through the system, such as structured analysis and design (data flow diagrams and structure charts), is known as a **process-driven methodology**.

In a Warnier–Orr diagram, a program structure or data structure is presented as a hierarchical arrangement placed horizontally on the page. Braces denote the beginning of a group of items on the same level. This type of diagram may be used to depict organizational structures, data structures, computer programs, or manual procedures. Each named item on the diagram is called a *parent* or a *child*. The basic principle is that a parent can have many children but a child can have only one parent.

Figure 16-22 shows the sample output CUSTOMER ORDER in the form of a Warnier–Orr diagram. The output is divided into three groupings or records called Order header, Order item, and Order end. A brace encloses each group of data elements for three major categories. Since the number of order items can vary from 1 to N, the notation (1,N) is placed under the data name Order item. All the data elements contained within each record are immediately visible to the reader. Successive braces group together the data items located on each level of the data structure. The parent Customer order has three children: Order header, Order item, and Order end. In turn, these subrecords also have children. For example, the subrecord Order item has the children designated Item number, Item description, Quantity ordered, Item price, and Total item cost.

The program structure is displayed in the same style as the data structures. For example, the simplified order processing system represented by the structure chart in Figure 16-13 is now displayed as a Warnier–Orr diagram in Figure 16-23. However, the operations for processing an order

FIGURE 16-22 The sample output CUSTOMER ORDER shown in a Warnier–Orr diagram

- Customer order
  - Order header
    - Order number
    - Order date
    - Customer ID
    - Customer name
    - Customer address
      - Customer street address
      - Customer city
      - Customer state
      - Customer zip
  - Order item (1,N)
    - Item number
    - Item description
    - Quantity ordered
    - Item price
    - Total item cost
  - Order end
    - Order cost
    - Sales tax
    - Shipping charges
    - Total order cost

Denis Connor, *Information System Specification & Design Road Map*, © 1985, p. 125. Adapted by permission of Prentice-Hall, Englewood Cliffs, NJ.

FIGURE 16-23   The Warnier–Orr diagram for a simplified order processing system

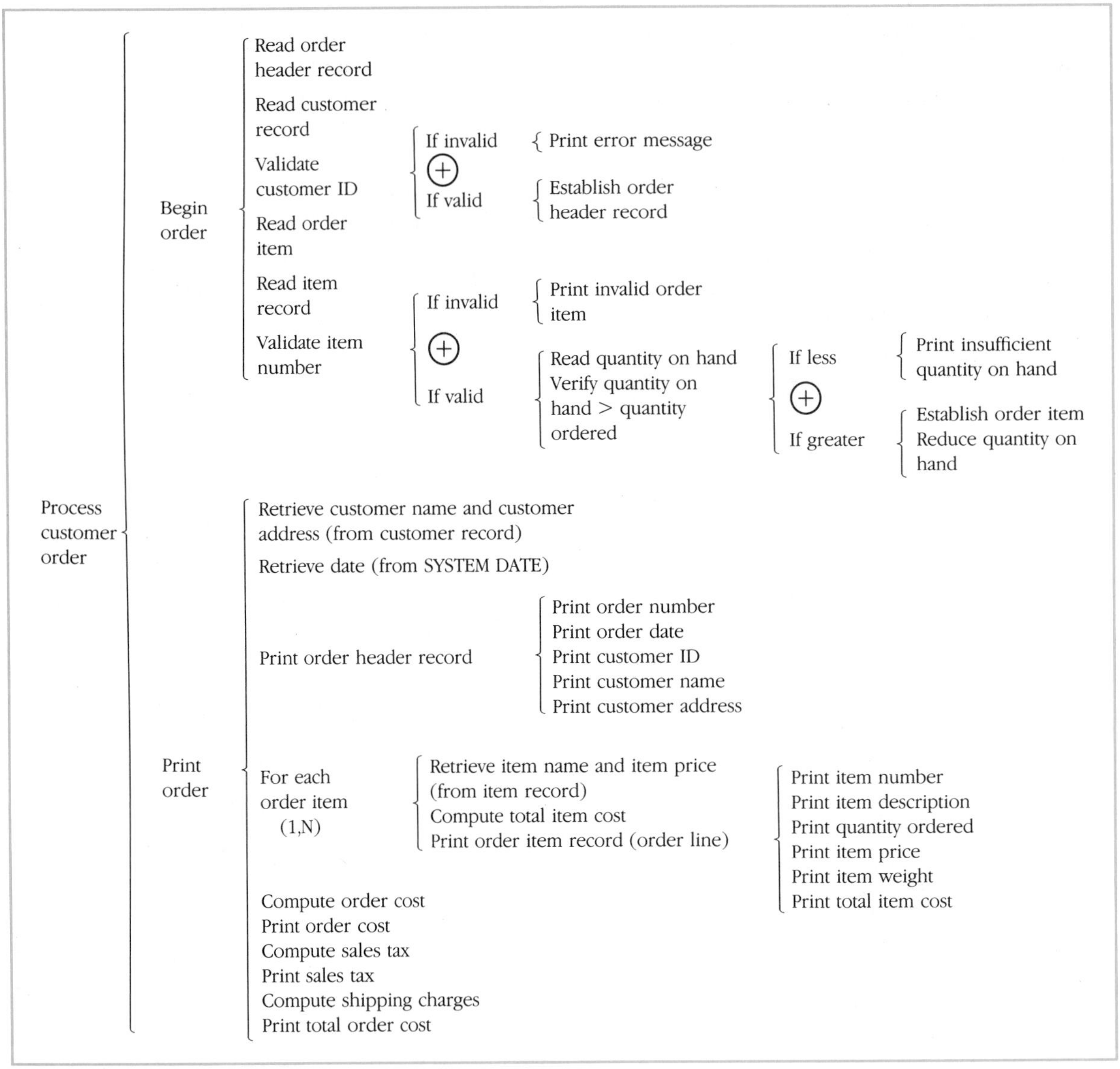

Denis Conner, *Information Systems & Design Road Map*, © 1985, p. 126. Adapted by permission of Prentice-Hall, Englewood Cliffs, NJ.

do not follow the same sequence. The diagram is read from left to right. Braces delineate the successive levels of detailed statements. The top process is labeled Process customer order and is the parent of two processes, Begin order and Print order. A detailed description of these processes proceeds to unfold as we continue to read from left to right. For example, the process Begin order is described by a set of statements. When a statement needs more detail, a brace is given to provide more statements. If we read

Moving Down from Mainframes, Up to PCs

In the "good old days," life was simpler because the choice of hardware was somewhat clearer. There were small, medium, and large computers, with the large ones known as mainframes. Then personal computers (PCs) entered the marketplace and everyone discovered that desktop computers could do all sorts of wonderful things, to the delight of end-users especially. Today, the harnessing of the PCs into client/server networks has begun to push the mainframes out the door of corporations. In client/server computing, the *server*, a powerful computer much less expensive than a mainframe, controls the actions for a network of users' PCs. Upon demand, the *server* fetches data from the corporate data base for the users' PCs, called the *clients*. Using their desktop computers, the users analyze the data as needed and can work together on a project by sharing information.

Down-sizing from mainframes to client/server networks yields great savings because reduced hardware costs are coupled with savings on personnel since mainframe computing staff is no longer needed. For example, one major construction firm replaced its mainframe computer with a network of personal computers in 1991. The reason for the changeover was a projected 50% decrease in its computer expenditures. However, some information managers were uneasy.

Their apprehension was caused by the lack of some essential software for client/server networks. The new computing networks need software to control both the powerful computer acting as the server and the client PCs. Instead of the single-user software commonly available for PCs, client/server packages must work for groups as well as individuals. And, unlike the existing mainframe software, they must have the "user-friendly" features that make PCs so popular—graphics and easy-to-use procedures.

Because creating this type of software is exceedingly difficult, client/server computing continues to lack the "right" software. And companies want more than the capability to do the same old tasks for less money. They are demanding client/server systems that provide quick access to corporate information and analytical processing for lower-echelon personnel, thereby allowing decision making to move downward in the organizational structure.

Some firms are also reaping the benefits of faster and more accurate data processing. At another major corporation, PCs all over the world were linked to a server running financial software. All employees assume responsibility for their own budget analysis activities and enter the financial data directly in the computer. Because the data-entry step performed by keypunch personnel has been eliminated, financial reporting time has decreased from six days to only two days.

Client/server computing is not without problems. Resistance has come from the mainframe staff who worry that their jobs will be terminated. In addition, the software must be "safe." Since the corporate data base is critical for the firm's daily operations, it must be protected by software that prevents break-ins by unauthorized personnel, automatically produces periodic backups of data, and safeguards against system crashes. Software vendors are working hard to fill this gap.

For more information, see Evan I. Schwartz, "Finally, Software That Slays Giants," *Business Week*, March 15, 1993, pp. 96–98 the statement Validate item number, we can obtain the complete description of this statement by following the bracketed statements across the page. The symbol $\oplus$ indicates that one of the conditions will be true. The notation (1,N) indicates that the bracketed statements to the right will be executed up to N times. The Warnier–Orr diagram provides both the overall program structure and the step-by-step description for the program. Such detailed information is not displayed directly on a structure chart but will appear in the module descriptions written in pseudocode. Consequently, Warnier–Orr diagrams provide a more complete display of the program specifications without the need to flip between the diagrams and their associated module descriptions.

SUMMARY

The two major activities in the Design phase are (1) the selection and acquisition of the computer system and (2) the creation of the program design. Although a model of the proposed information system was formulated in the Analysis phase, it does not adequately show the structure and logic of the programs that must be implemented. Consequently, program specifications are provided at a logical design level according to a particular program design methodology, such as structured design or Warnier–Orr diagrams. The program designer may be either the analyst or the programmer, depending on the installation's preference.

Frequently, hardware and software are viewed as two separate issues. However, since the hardware has no value without software, the availability of the desired software is the prime factor in determining the selection criteria of the computer system. The operating system, systems software, data base management systems, and application software are among the software items to be weighed before selection of the computer hardware. The selection of the computer system is based on six hardware features: primary memory size, processing speed, channel capacity, equipment for human interfaces, secondary storage capacity, and communication components. In conjunction with the hardware, the firm should also study various software and vendor characteristics.

Eight steps for the selection of the computer system were discussed: (1) determine the software to be acquired from outside sources; (2) state the hardware requirements; (3) issue the RFP (request for proposal); (4) study the proposals received from the vendors; (5) perform benchmarks; (6) select the best computer system; (7) decide on the acquisition mode: rent, lease, or purchase; and (8) negotiate the contract. A benchmark is a special program designed to measure the performance of the hardware with regard to a particular function performed at the computer installation. Alternatives to in-house computing are service bureaus and out-sourcing.

Designing the programs is the second major activity of the Design phase. Structured design is a methodology for program design based on the diagrams called structure charts. By following general guidelines, the designer can derive the structure charts for the information system from the data flow diagrams that depict the logical model. The program will be defined as a hierarchy of individual modules, where each module has a single entrance and a single exit. A module is a self-contained set of contiguous program statements that performs its task independently of other modules.

The conversion of a DFD to a structure chart was described. The premise for this derivation is that one fundamental structure underlies every program: Get data; process data; put data. Thus, the DFD is analyzed to find the central process (or set of processes) that actually transforms the data and does not simply perform input/output processing for the outside world. The DFD processes that perform only input processing are grouped together as the input stream. Similarly, the processes that accomplish only output processing form the output stream. The process or group of processes that lie between the input and output streams are called the central transform or transaction center, respectively.

The structure chart is then derived from the DFD. Since DFDs omit the handling of most error conditions and read/write activities in order to avoid overly complex diagrams, new processes will be introduced on the structure chart. The lower levels of DFDs are also converted to structure charts and connected to the module corresponding to the DFD process from which they were exploded. The operations of each module must be described in pseudocode. After the structure charts have been drawn, it is necessary to modify the program design for the physical features of the computer hardware and software. Before implementing the program, operational efficiency should be considered during the step known as packaging the design.

An alternative to structure charts, the Warnier–Orr methodology, is a data-driven methodology that concentrates on the data structures that enter and leave the system. This approach is based on the belief that an organization's data structures will change more frequently than its processes. Because the interrelationship between the procedural statements and the data structures is expressly stated, Warnier–Orr diagrams facilitate the writing of the program code.

TERMS

benchmark	coupling
central transform	data-driven methodology
cohesiveness	flag
connection	input stream
control data	manager module
couple	module

continued

outsourcing	structure chart
output stream	structured design
packaging the design	switch
process-driven methodology	throughput
pseudocode	top-down design
response time	transaction center
request for proposal (RFP)	upward compatibility
service bureau	Warnier–Orr diagrams

QUESTIONS

1. Software is the primary consideration in the selection of the computer hardware. Justify this statement.

2. List the steps for the selection and acquisition of the computer hardware.

3. What is the RFP and how is it used in the selection process for computer equipment?

4. What is a benchmark? Why should benchmarks be performed on the computer systems under consideration by the firm?

5. Create a table that lists the advantages and disadvantages of the three acquisition modes for computer hardware: rental, leasing, and purchase.

6. What are the two alternatives to in-house computing? What are the advantages and disadvantages of each alternative?

7. Define structure chart, couple, connection, manager module, and control data.

8. Explain coupling and cohesiveness in structure charts.

9. The logical model of the proposed information system given by a set of data flow diagrams cannot be used directly for the writing of the program code. Explain this statement.

10. Why should the modules in the structure chart be independent of each other? How does this independence affect the program coding and future modifications to the coding?

11. What are the drawbacks to the use of structure charts for program design? What are their advantages?

12. What purposes are served by the step called packaging the design?

13. Explain what is meant by process-driven and data-driven methodologies.

14. What are the advantages and disadvantages of Warnier–Orr diagrams for program design?

PROJECTS

1. The modules in the accompanying partial structure charts are too closely coupled and possibly lack cohesiveness. Redraw these structure charts so that the modules are loosely coupled and highly cohesive. To assist you in this exercise, appropriate data elements and data records have been identified for each structure chart.

    a. Examine Figure 16-24. The vendor record is called VENDOR-RECORD. The flag RECORD-RETRIEVE indicates that the module should retrieve the next vendor record. VENDOR-ID is the data element containing the vendor's identification number.

    b. Examine Figure 16-25. The report ending contains the following data elements: TOTAL-SALES, TOTAL-DIV-A, and TOTAL-DIV-B.

    c. Examine Figure 16-26. The data record STUD-REQUEST contains STUDENT-ID, STUDENT-NAME, COURSE-NUMBER, DATE-OF-SEMESTER, INSTRUCTOR-ID, and INSTRUCTOR-NAME. The flag CLASS-FULL indicates whether the class has already reached maximum enrollment and the student cannot be enrolled in the class.

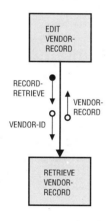

FIGURE 16-24

FIGURE 16-25

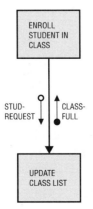

FIGURE 16-26

FIGURE 16-27   The DFD for the cooperative education office

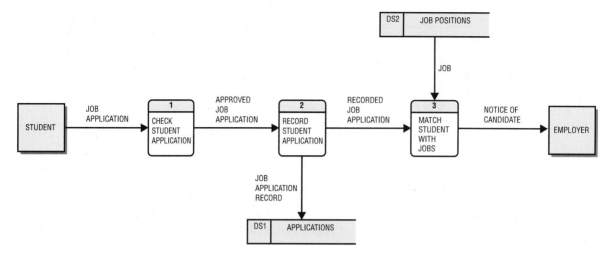

FIGURE 16-28   The DFD for a simplified scheduling system

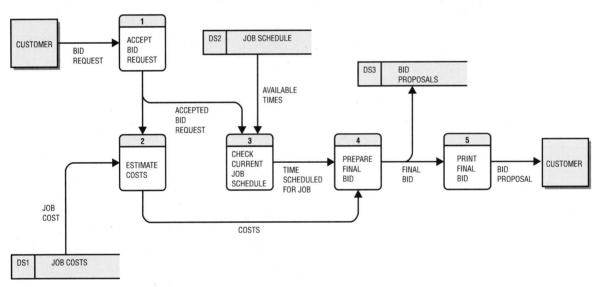

2. Draw the structure chart corresponding to the data flow diagram specified.

   a. Figure 16-27 contains a DFD of a simplified information system for the cooperative education office at a university. The student submits an application for a cooperative education position and is then matched with a potential employer. The system notifies the employer when a student has the proper credentials for its available cooperative education position.

b. Figure 16-28 displays a DFD for a simplified scheduling system. The firm receives a request to submit a bid for a job. It then estimates the costs for the job and determines if its current job schedule allows the firm to fulfill the job's requirements. Finally, the firm prepares the final proposal containing the bid for the job.

REFERENCES

Connor, Denis. *Information System Specification and Design Road Map.* Englewood Cliffs, NJ: Prentice-Hall, 1985.

DeMarco, Tom. *Structured Analysis and System Specification.* Englewood Cliffs, NJ: Prentice-Hall, 1979.

Deposito, Joseph, Jamey Marcum, and Doug White. *Que's Computer Buyer's Guide.* Carmel, IN: Que Corporation, 1991.

Gane, Chris, and Trish Sarson. *Structured Systems Analysis.* Englewood Cliffs, NJ: Prentice-Hall, 1979.

Page-Jones, Meilir. *The Practical Guide to Structured Systems Design*, 2nd ed. Englewood Cliffs, NJ: Yourdon Press, 1988.

Senn, James A. *Analysis and Design of Information Systems*, 2nd ed. New York: McGraw-Hill, 1989.

PART VI

The Implementation, Installation, and Post-Implementation Review Phases

CHAPTER 17

The Final Phases of the Life Cycle

Objectives

This chapter explains the activities in the last three phases of the systems development life cycle (SDLC), that is, the Implementation, Installation, and Post-Implementation Review phases. After completing this chapter, you will understand the following material:

- The techniques recommended for the implementation activities of programming, testing, and debugging

- How to conduct a structured walkthrough

- What steps should be taken to ensure the development of a high quality software product

- The activities performed during the Installation phase in order to provide a smooth transition to the new system

- Why and how the project efforts and the software product should be reviewed in the Post-Implementation phase

INTRODUCTION

As shown in Figure 17-1, the last three phases of the systems development life cycle are the Implementation, Installation, and Post-Implementation Review. The major activities of these final phases are described in the following sections. The first section describes the Implementation phase, which contains the activities for converting the abstract representation of the new system into an operational system. Programmers will study the design specifications provided by multiple diagrams and documents and then create the program coding that will embody the new system. The programs are then tested in order to remove any defects from the code before the new information system is installed.

The second and third sections explain the characteristics of software quality as well as the standards and procedures recommended for the production of high quality software. A software quality assurance program is recommended to impose these requirements in order to raise the quality of the software product to the highest possible level.

The fourth section deals with the Installation phase of the project. This phase involves the changeover from the existing system to the now-finished

FIGURE 17-1

The final three phases of the SDLC: Implementation, Installation, and Post-Implementation Review

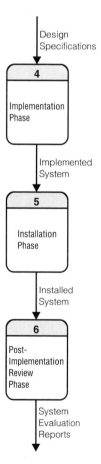

new system. Careful planning is required to ensure that no problems arise during installation. The activities of the Installation phase include the conversion of old files to new formats, the training of the users to operate the new system, the installation of the new system, and the termination of the old system.

The last section discusses the final phase of the systems development life cycle, the Post-Implementation Review phase. The software development work just completed and the job performance of the software developers are examined to gather information that can help to improve the software development process. The new system, now operational, is also studied to see how well the system meets the users' expectations. Any dissatisfaction with the project outcome is viewed as an opportunity to learn ways to improve the methods for future software development. At this time, maintenance activities are scheduled to enhance the system features as requested by the users.

The Gantt chart in Figure 17-2 shows the scheduling of the major activities. Naturally, any overlap of activities is dependent on the details of an individual project. As shown in the Gantt chart, coding activities must be completed before testing can begin. Since the coding of a large system can

FIGURE 17-2   A Gantt chart for the final three phases of the SDLC

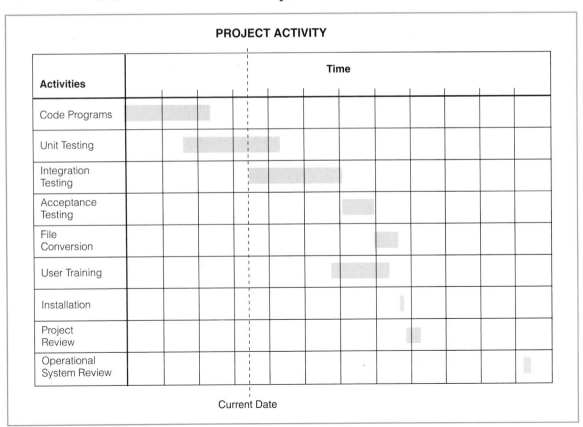

be divided into sections, it is possible that some sections may be tested while coding continues on other portions of the system. The overlap of user training with systems testing, as diagrammed here, is sometimes possible. Note that file conversion and user training must be accomplished prior to system installation. The Gantt chart also indicates that the two major activities performed for the Post-Implementation Review phase are executed independently of each other.

THE IMPLEMENTATION PHASE

Now we have finally reached the point where the design of the information system can be transformed into an operational system. Up to this point, we have only created a theoretical view of the system by representing its specifications and then refining this model into a program design. The conversion of the design into physical program code arrives at last. Unless the Implementation phase activities are successfully carried out, the system is merely a "paper tiger."

In this section, we will explain the major steps in the traditional life cycle approach to systems implementation—coding and testing. These activities are supported by certain techniques for controlling the systems development process and aiding the programmers in their work. Thus, this section is composed of three subsections designated as structured walkthroughs, programming, and software testing. If an alternate approach to systems implementation has been selected, the activities of programming and testing will be replaced or eliminated according to the steps required for that strategy. The effect of alternative approaches (such as software packages, CASE tools, and prototyping) on the life cycle steps was presented earlier in Chapter 2.

Although the Implementation phase is only one portion of this chapter, the coverage of this phase does not reflect the proportion of time and costs allocated within the SDLC. As shown in Figure 17-3, coding and testing typically require 65% of the traditional SDLC while the earlier activities of

FIGURE 17-3

The efforts allocated to the SDLC activities

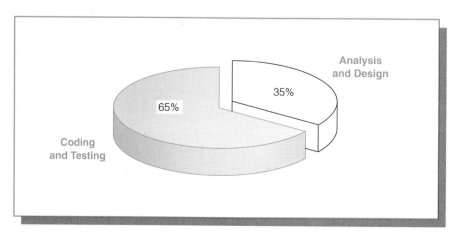

Analysis and Design

35%

65%

Coding and Testing

analysis and design occupy only 35%. As mentioned in previous chapters, the cost of correcting errors increases rapidly as the system moves through the phases in the life cycle. Once the system is operational, the cost is extremely high. Therefore, the importance of the early phases of Preliminary Investigation, Analysis, and Design cannot be emphasized enough.

Structured Walkthroughs

As the software development project progresses along the stages in the life cycle, the project manager is constantly striving to guide the undertaking to a successful conclusion. As discussed in Chapter 5, a project milestone is the end point of a major activity and is marked by one or more tangible outputs called deliverables. The task of the project manager is to ensure that the deliverables passing to the next project stage are complete, accurate, and of high quality. If the next major activity begins with insufficient or incorrect information, the software developers will be seriously handicapped. The outcome of the project, in turn, will become highly questionable. The project manager guards against these uncertainties by instituting formal inspections of the deliverables so that any errors or deficiencies will be detected before the next major activity takes place. Identifying problems early not only prevents serious consequences but means the problems can be corrected more easily. These formal inspections are called *formal technical reviews*. A **structured walkthrough** is a formal technical review performed according to a particular set of conventions. Typically, structured walkthroughs are held to review program design or coding.

THE PARTICIPANTS

The structured walkthrough is performed by a peer group in conjunction with the originator of the deliverable to be reviewed. The deliverable under review is also called the *product*. The person responsible for the deliverable is known as the *author*. For a project activity performed by several individuals, the project leader may serve as the author. The *customer* is the person who requested that this particular deliverable be produced. The peer group consists of the customer and software personnel who have the same capabilities as the author but do not work under the author's direction. As shown in Figure 17-4, the review team consists of the author, the customer, the moderator, a small group of the author's peers, and the technical secretary. All team members are treated as equals in status during the walkthrough session.

The customer is asked to participate in the review process to assure that all of the customer's criteria have been met. For programming activities, the customer is usually the systems analyst; for the program design, a different systems analyst may play the role of the customer; for the information systems model, the customer is typically a representative of the users' group. When the design of the program is reviewed, the programmers responsible for implementing the design also attend the walkthrough both in order to learn about the design and also to join in its scrutiny.

FIGURE 17-4

**The team for a struc-
tured walkthrough**

Participants	Author
	Customer
	Moderator
	Peers
Non-participant	Technical Secretary

The review meeting is chaired by a *moderator*. The moderator functions as the meeting's leader, keeps the discussion on target, and ensures that follow-up measures are taken. This person should have high levels of technical expertise as well as good interpersonal skills. Because all members of the team will be engaged in the critique, the meeting should also have a *technical secretary* with sufficient technical skills to record the session. The technical secretary merely records the meeting and does not function as a participant. The team should be limited in number, so that participants will be at ease in talking openly and freely.

Because the purpose of the structured walkthrough is to assist the author in improving the product, criticism can be more freely given without the presence of the management. Otherwise, the author's peers are likely to be reluctant to point out errors or omissions in the product, fearing that their criticisms will harm their colleague's professional reputation. The walkthrough's sole function is to improve the software product by examining the details of the system components or its overall design. The evaluation of project personnel is not included as an activity here and should be performed as a completely separate task.

THE FORMAT OF THE WALKTHROUGH

Prior to the review meeting, the material to be reviewed should be sent to all participants for study. For a program module, this documentation consists of the module specification, the compilation listing, and any other material that describes the module's code. Previous study of the review material is required to avoid the unnecessary wasting of time at the meeting. The walkthrough is ordinarily scheduled to last about 60 to 90 minutes.

By its very name, a walkthrough means that the author will *walk* the participants *through* by giving a step-by-step explanation of the program unit under discussion. For a program module, the author describes the logic by first defining the overall program structure expressed by its logical groupings; this means that the work performed within each major division of the program will be described as an entire unit. The author then proceeds to explain the coding, line by line. As the code is followed along, the participants ask questions or offer suggestions for improvements.

The errors detected by the reviewers are recorded by the meeting's technical secretary. If too many defects are uncovered, the moderator may choose to adjourn the meeting so that the author can reexamine the product, repair the defects, and reschedule the walkthrough on the revised product. Because finding the best approach for error removal may require lengthy discussions, the author, working with the programming leader, is entrusted to find the optimum way of removing the defects.

Since all of us are prone to human error, the moderator must maintain an atmosphere conducive to comments without blame or personal criticism of the author. Despite the criticisms given at the meeting, the author should never feel personally attacked or humiliated. The exchange of ideas must take place at a professional level among equals. The author's own merits are not under review; only the author's work is subject to comment. The moderator must be alert to the interaction among the participants and direct the discussion solely to the technical problems of the matter under review. If the product is poorly constructed or the session deteriorates into bickering and blaming, the moderator must terminate the walkthrough to avoid further detrimental effects on the team interaction. The programming leader must then resolve the situation prior to the scheduling of a second walkthrough.

THE ERROR LOG

During the walkthrough, the technical secretary records in an **error log** any errors detected. In order to facilitate the error removal process, a suitable form should be employed for recording these errors. Figure 17-5 shows a

INSPECTION CONTROL SHEET

PROJECT: ______________________

MODULE/COMPONENT: ______________________

SESSION DATE: ______________________

MODERATOR: ______________________

AUTHOR: ______________________

INSPECTION TEAM MEMBERS:

NO.	REVIEW POINT	DISPOSITION	APPROVAL
1			
2			
3			
4			
5			
6			
7			
8			
9			
10			

COMMENTS:

☐ ACCEPT AS IS ☐ REVISE ☐ REVISE AND REDO WALKTHROUGH

FIGURE 17-5
An Inspection Control Sheet

sample Inspection Control Sheet for this purpose. Each error is numbered sequentially and then briefly described. The reviewers receive a copy of this summary to review for any discrepancies. After the walkthrough, the errors listed on the form are studied by the author. Some items listed may actually be suggestions about better ways of writing the coding, rather than true errors. If the time required to adopt such improvements is too long, the author may recommend that the suggestions be incorporated at a later time or simply ignored. The author, in conjunction with the programming team leader, determines the disposition of each error. Additional discussions may be held with the walkthrough's participants in order to obtain more advice on how to repair the defects. After the errors have been corrected, the Inspection Control Sheet is appropriately annotated by the author and then reviewed by the programming leader. Depending on the extent of revisions, the program code may be subjected to another walkthrough to ensure its correctness.

Programming

The programming activity for a project must be planned with several factors in mind. The success of the Implementation phase is dependent on the programming language selected as well as other aspects, such as the organizational structure of the programmers, the programming environment, and any standards imposed on the program code (such as structured programming and coding style). A selected group of programming issues will be discussed later under the category of modern programming practices. The topic of coding style will be covered in a separate subsection. Although all these matters are really decided long before the programming activity begins, because they primarily affect the Implementation phase it is appropriate to discuss them here.

> ### Warning
> The programmer's adage is, "Coding is easy; thinking is hard!" Despite time pressures, it always pays to reflect on program design before writing the coding. Because testing does not prove a program to be correct, it is important to conceptualize the program before coding begins. After coding begins, it is costly to modify the program design to correct design errors.

SELECTING THE PROGRAMMING LANGUAGE

The choice of the programming language may be crucial to the success of the project. Walston and Felix [1977] have shown that the amount of effort per line of code is relatively independent of the level of the source language.

This means that the amount of time required to produce 100 lines of tested COBOL code is roughly equivalent to that required to write and test 100 lines in a fourth-generation language. Since a 4GL program is much more powerful, perhaps ten times or more than COBOL, the gains in productivity are great. Although a study by Boehm showed that the choice of the programming language (FORTRAN versus Pascal) for a small software product was not a major factor in outcome or productivity, he concluded that the choice of programming language is a "more significant factor in developing more complex and ambitious software products" [1981, p. 661]. In addition, many computer scientists believe that the features of the programming language itself directly affect the quality of the code produced by a programmer.

Besides the productivity gains provided by programming languages of higher levels, the choice of the programming language is affected by several other factors. As shown in Figure 17-6, these factors are the developmental mode, the features provided by the programming language, the portability desired for the final software product, the previous experience of the programmers, and the programming support environment. As always, there may exist a trade-off between the possible choices. One programming language may be considered far better in one aspect while another is clearly superior elsewhere. Since the overall productivity of the project will be affected by the chosen language, all factors must be weighed before a final decision is made.

Developmental Mode   The approach chosen for developing a project—its **developmental mode**—affects the choice of programming language. The traditional life cycle approach is usually associated with a third-generation language. The use of prototyping for the development mode means that a fourth-generation language or suitable CASE tools must be employed. Naturally, it is also possible to select a fourth-generation language for a project produced under the traditional SDLC guidelines. If a software application package is selected as the developmental mode and it requires modifications, the language of the package's source code will automatically dictate the choice of the programming language to be used for these revisions. With the traditional SDLC approach, the programming language should be selected according to the factors discussed in the following subsections.

Developmental Mode
Language Features
Portability
Programming Experience
Programming Environment

FIGURE 17-6
The factors in choosing a programming language

Programming Language Features   The primary concern is that the programming language fit the application's requirements. If the project consists of several programs, different programming languages could be selected in order to appropriately meet the needs of each type of program. If the programming language does not offer the features appropriate for the application or fails to provide satisfactory performance of the necessary functions, it will seriously handicap the implementation effort and decrease the efficiency of the final system. For example, a fourth-generation language may be a superior choice for a data processing application. But the same 4GL may be unsuitable for an application containing both heavy file processing and computational activities because it fails to provide the features necessary for the mathematical functions required by the program. If this language is chosen despite its deficiencies, the resulting program may be many times more inefficient than one coded in a mathematically-oriented language.

Portability of the Language   A programming language exhibits **portability** when it can be used on several different types of computers. For example, COBOL is almost universally available on computers of various types and manufacture. This means that a COBOL compiler can be purchased or leased for these computers. Because of differences between the language specifications for COBOL from one computer to the next, modifications may be necessary before a COBOL program can be executed on another hardware platform. Depending on the exceptions to the standard COBOL specifications published by the American National Standards Institute, COBOL programs typically can be transported to another hardware configuration with only minor difficulties. However, if many nonstandard provisions were employed, the difficulty of moving to another computer increases.

Programming Experience   Typically, an organization will write all or almost all of its programs in a particular programming language. By doing so, the firm ensures that its programmers will always have a high level of expertise in the selected programming language. To switch to another programming language means that programmers will lack the same high level of proficiency for at least one and perhaps several projects. Training costs will also be incurred. Consequently, most organizations choose to standardize and use a single programming language.

Because productivity gains are anticipated with higher order languages, such as moving from a third-generation language to a fourth-generation language, the costs may be offset by the benefits reaped. In addition to the training costs, the firm must also be willing to accept any higher project costs stemming from a slowdown in the coding and testing activities for the new programming language. If the firm decides to allow the use of several programming languages, implementation costs will increase due to additional training time and the need to acquire and upgrade compilers for more than one language. Since the introduction of a new programming language may seriously affect the costs and time required for the project, it must not be undertaken without managerial approval.

Programming Environments   Programming can be supported by a **programming environment** that includes tools for language processing and program testing. These tools include those that support communication between the project team members, provide for the simulation of the target machine on the existing hardware, and allow for the visual display of step-by-step program execution. CASE tools (discussed in Chapter 2) also contribute to the programming environment. Ideally, all these tools should be integrated to form a software development environment that supports the systems development life cycle.

A selection of support tools for a software engineering environment is listed in Figure 17-7. Programming is supported by an *editor*, which provides for the creation of the source code. A *structured editor* lends more assistance to the programmer by checking for most syntax errors during the actual entry of the code. More sophisticated editors may guide the creation of the program code by providing the programmer with a choice of code components from a menu or set of icons. The editor thus limits the choices to those that are syntactically correct and prompts the programmer to supply the next item.

A *CASE workbench* is a collection of software tools that support the SDLC phases by assisting in various tasks. Among the typical components of a CASE workbench are checking facilities for the analysis and design models, data dictionary facilities, form generation tools, and code generators. To assist the programmer in debugging the program code, the testing support tools may include software that visually displays the program execution. At any point during the program's execution, the programmer can halt the program and examine the contents of the program variables. Such a testing support tool is shown in Figure 17-8, where a COBOL program is displayed by using the programming tool called COBOL Animator. The highlighted code statement

Features	Tools
Programming support	Editor Structured editor CASE workbench
Testing support	Visual display of program execution Examination of data contents during program execution
Documentation	Document preparation systems

FIGURE 17-7

Some tools for a software development environment

FIGURE 17-8

A COBOL program-
ming support tool

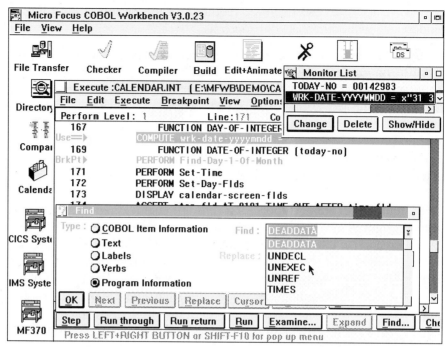

Computer screen photograph of Micro Focus COBOL Workbench® used with permission of
Micro Focus, Inc.

indicates where the program has been halted. The execution is displayed on
the screen and the programmer looks for the source of the program error
by stepping through the program statements. By requesting the contents of
selected variables, the programmer quickly acquires more information, so
that the location of the program error can be pinpointed. In Figure 17-8, the
programmer has decided to request the COBOL Workbench to execute a
Find operation in order to locate DEADDATA, which are the data no longer
used by the program.

The production of the extensive documentation required for the life
cycle phases may be supported by special document preparation systems
associated with the CASE tools or other support tools. Documentation tools
aid the project team in producing reports and other detailed information
according to the standards imposed by the organization. The error logs,
testing logs, and other reporting requirements are also facilitated by the use
of appropriate documentation tools.

MODERN PROGRAMMING PRACTICES

Modern programming practices consist of several procedures that were
developed in the 1970s to improve programming productivity. The specific
practices include structured design notation (such as structure charts, explained in Chapter 16), structured walkthroughs for program design and
code, the chief programmer team and the program librarian (Chapter 5),

top-down program design, and structured programming. Several studies have shown that these practices increase programmer productivity and reduce maintenance costs. Only the last two procedures still require explanation.

Top-Down Program Design   The practice of **top-down program design** means that the program is constructed as a hierarchy of components, each of which represents a single major function. Each component is then refined into a set of hierarchical parts. The process of refinement continues until the final components (known as *modules*) are sufficiently small to be coded within a small number of coding lines, usually fewer than 50 lines. Each module must be self-contained and must function independently of any other module. As discussed in Chapter 16, top-down design is used in the creation of structure charts, which graphically display the program design.

Splitting the program into a hierarchical framework of smaller independent modules reduces the complexity of the program by representing it as a set of manageable parts. In doing so, the thousands of coding lines necessary for a large program are partitioned into small coding sections, each of which can be wholly contained within the mind's eye of the average programmer. Because each module performs a single function independently of the other modules, the debugging of the code now becomes the debugging of independent subsystems. Since the tracking of errors will be performed only within small, well-defined program areas, the debugging of the program has been simplified. After the individual modules have been validated, they are combined to form an integral system. Testing of the integrated system is also necessary to ensure that the modules interact without error.

Structured Programming   In the late 1960s, the use of the GO TO statement in programs was found to be undesirable. As shown in Figure 17-9, a program with GO TO statements requires the programmer to trace its logic from one program section to another. The switching between coding in widely scattered program sections strains the programmer's mental ability to follow the logic and to recall the modifications to the variables in all parts of the program. Since the logical flow of the program forms an intricate pattern of paths, this type of code is known as "spaghetti code."

Today, the GO TO statement is viewed as an invitation to coding errors. **Structured programming** formalizes this viewpoint by forbidding the use of the GO TO statement in programs. Originally, only three basic control **constructs**—sequence, selection, and iteration—were used to write structured programs. Since a fourth construct, multiple selection, has now been designed, it too may be included within a structured program. Because any program can be expressed by means of only the three basic constructs, the GO TO statement can be eliminated. By doing so, structured programming increases programming productivity through reducing coding errors and the time required to detect and remove these errors. Because structured

FIGURE 17-9

Program coding with GO TO statements The programmer must track the logic through intricate paths as the program flow jumps to different locations in "spaghetti code."

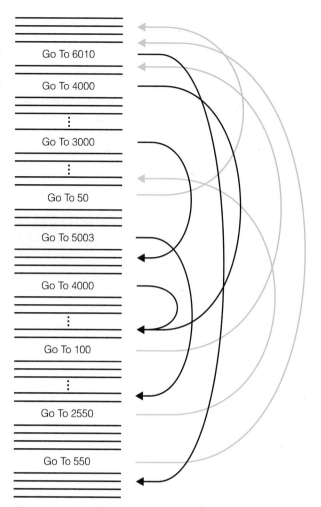

programs are easier for programmers to understand, they have the added benefit of lower maintenance costs. In addition, structured programming is associated with program structures created by stepwise refinement, which represents an early top-down design strategy.

The three basic control structures (also called constructs) for structured programming are diagrammed in Figure 17-10. Because structured programming permits the use of the multiple selection structure, this control structure is also included in this figure. Note that each construct has only one entrance and one exit. These four control structures have been discussed earlier in conjunction with structured English (see Chapter 11).

The **sequence construct** provides for the sequential flow of program statements. The **selection construct** allows the selection of a path based on the single condition stated. The selection construct is expressed by means of an IF-THEN-ELSE statement. The **iteration construct** supports the repetition of a set of statements until a particular condition becomes true. Many programming languages use the DO-WHILE statement to express the itera-

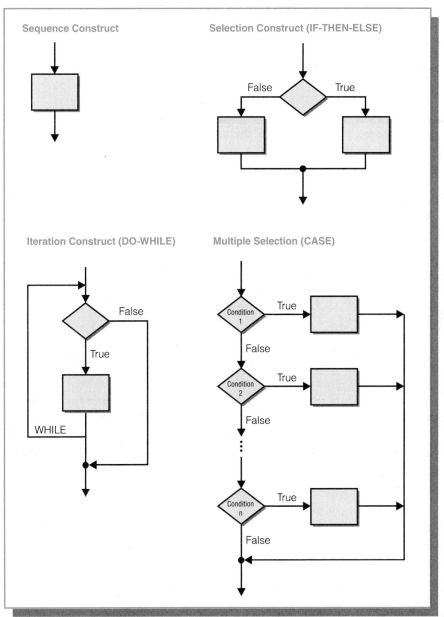

FIGURE 17-10

The control structures for structured programming

tion construct. A DO-WHILE statement causes the specified condition to be tested. If true, the statements contained within the range of the DO-WHILE statement are executed. If false, the statement immediately following the end of the DO-WHILE statement is executed. In COBOL, the iteration construct is provided by the PERFORM-UNTIL statement.

The **multiple selection construct** is embodied by the CASE statement, which permits several conditions to be tested in the order of appearance. As soon as a condition is found to be true, its corresponding group of statements is selected. If none of the conditions is true, the path expressed for the OTHERWISE condition is selected. [*Note:* The CASE construct is not available in the COBOL '74 version but was implemented as the EVALUATE verb in COBOL '85.]

As shown by the control structure diagrams, a structured program always flows in a sequential pattern and will not jump to any program statements in other program areas. The program can always be read one line after another, without flipping back and forth to other pages. The selection, multiple selection, and iteration constructs require that the logical activity be grouped into units. This arrangement into logical sections provides *chunks* of information to be read by the programmer. Instead of reading the coding word by word in isolated lines, the programmer is able to study and remember the information as a series of chunks. This mode of processing information is called *chunking* by psychologists. Top-down design also causes the program to be created in chunks, because the program is divided into subordinate, simpler pieces that are successively refined until smaller and more manageable items are obtained.

CODING STYLE

Programming is a craft dependent on the individual skill of the programmer. The use of appropriate standards imposes principles on the individual programmer who has merely average ability. Four programming conventions are generally imposed on the coding of programs: structured programming, adherence to an "open" programming style, suitable indentation, and comments. These requirements assist the programmer during the development of the final program and greatly improve the maintainability of the code after the program is in production. Structured programming has been discussed in the previous section. We will now briefly discuss the other three items.

Open Programming Style   The adherence to an **open programming style** means that the programmer does not try to be clever and efficient at the expense of clarity. The basic principle for programming is the infamous KISS rule: Keep It Simple, Stupid. Simplicity is far more valuable than tricky, clever code, which soon becomes unintelligible even to its creator. If the code is not straightforward but clever and devious, reading the code during maintenance activities will be difficult and prone to misinterpretation. While there are some occasions where the writing of tight, fast code is truly necessary, in general it is more desirable to produce clear, easily understood code that can be quickly comprehended by both its author and the maintenance programmer.

An example of devious code is the use of the same variable for two different purposes, as when a programmer uses the variable HRS-WORKED first to represent the total time worked by an employee and later to store the number of hours allocated for an employee for the following month's work schedule. While such usage eliminates one location from the total memory locations required for the program, it usually leads to confusion during the debugging of the program and later during maintenance activities. Similarly, clever tricks for data manipulation or computation typically obscure the program logic and pave the way for serious coding errors.

Another convention is that all variables should be declared explicitly. Such practice prevents confusion and aids in the reading of the program. The way in which the program statements are formatted also affects the program's readability. Multiple statements should never appear on the same line. Placing each statement on a separate line and using proper indentation makes the program more readable. Complicated conditional statements should be avoided, and dense nesting of conditional statements should not be used. Further, conditional statements should be stated in a positive way rather than by the equivalent negative statement. Parentheses should be used to clarify logical or arithmetic statements. Since there are preferred coding styles for expressing program logic, the programmer is advised to study a book on programming style such as Kernighan and Plauger [1978].

Suitable Indentation   A style for indentation is associated with the practice of structured programming. Statements of the type called IF-THEN-ELSE, DO-WHILE, or CASE are indented as shown in Figure 17-11. Indenting the statements in a suitable fashion makes the program readable. Instead of searching for the end of the DO-WHILE loop, the programmer immediately sees what statements are within its scope; thus, the program logic can be more easily grasped by the reader. In the same way, the logic embodied by the DO-WHILE, IF-THEN-ELSE, and CASE statements becomes more evident to the programmer during the reading of the program if suitable indentation is employed. Because indentation is a somewhat burdensome requirement for the programmer, a CASE tool that reformats the coding lines into the proper indentation style is invaluable. In doing so, the coding becomes more readable with little effort on the part of the programmer.

Comments   The purpose of comments is to assist the reader in understanding the program. A program with good comments strategically placed within the coding statements provides invaluable documentation. In order for comments to be quickly distinguished from the program code, they should be indented or surrounded by blank lines. Good comments provide insight into the code and do not simply paraphrase the coding lines. Rather than describing each coding line, a comment should explain the purpose of an entire block of code. Figure 17-12 illustrates a good comment that provides an overview of the program.

While the general consensus is that comments are absolutely necessary for good program code, erroneous comments are worse than none at all. Moreover, the problem of updating comments to match the altered program code is a perpetual nuisance. If the programmer changes the program code and fails to alter the corresponding comments, the comments are useless or, even worse, contribute to the misunderstanding of the program.

FIGURE 17-11   Rules for preferred coding indentations

DO-WHILE Statement

All statements within the scope of a DO-WHILE statement are indented.

```
DO WHILE .NOT. EOF
     TOTAL = TOTAL + EMP-PAY
     READ EMPLOYEE-RECORD
ENDDO
```

IF-THEN-ELSE Statement

All statements within the scope of IF-THEN and also under the ELSE portion are indented as shown.

```
IF EMPLOYEE-HRS > 40 THEN
     OVERTIME-HRS = EMPLOYEE-HRS − 40
     TOTAL-PAY = 40 * EMPLOYEE-HRS + OVERTIME-HRS * 1.5 * EMPLOYEE-HRLY-WAGE
ELSE
       TOTAL-PAY = EMPLOYEE-HRS * EMPLOYEE-HRLY-WAGE
ENDIF
```

CASE Statement

Statements within the range of each individual CASE statement are indented.

```
SELECT CASE FOR X
     CASE (X = 0)
        Y = Z * D
     CASE (X > 0)
        Y = Z * X + 3.1416
     OTHERWISE
        Y = 5.907 * (X + Z)
ENDCASE
```

In essence, good comments are like other forms of documentation: The comments can quickly become incorrect due to changes in the code. Management must allow sufficient time to update both the code *and* the comments. Programmers must be encouraged to insert appropriate comments and be rewarded for this practice. On the other hand, if the chosen programming language is a fourth-generation language which will be interpreted, rather than compiled and executed, program execution is very likely

FIGURE 17-12
**Code documentation
given by a lengthy
comment**

```
TITLE:              SUBROUTINE NGON

PURPOSE:            THE PURPOSE IS TO CONTROL THE DRAWING OF NGONS

SAMPLE CALL:        CALL NGON (KNOW, IX, IY, KN)

INPUTS:             KROW      = IS THE LINE ON THE TABLE WHERE THE
                                NEXT LINE OF OUTPUT WILL BE PRINTED.
                    IX        = X-COORDINATE OF THE LEFT END OF THE
                                BOTTOM SEGMENT
                    IY        = Y-COORDINATE OF THE LEFT END OF THE
                                BOTTOM SEGMENT
                    KN        = IS THE NUMBER OF THE LAST NGON

OUTPUTS:            KROW      = IS THE INCREMENTED ROW COUNTER
                    KN        = IS THE INCREMENTED NGON COUNTER

SUBROUTINES REFERENCED:       1.)  DBNGON
                              2.)  ALPHA
                              3.)  ROWCOL

PERTINENT DATA:
      KROW IS CHECKED TO SEE IF THE TABLE IS FULL. IF IT IS THEN REPNT IS
      CALLED TO REFRESH THE SCREEN AND PUT UP A NEW TABLET. THE NGON
      COUNTER (KN) IS INCREMENTED AND THE POINTER ARRAY PO IS WRITTEN
      TO THE DISPLAY FILE.

      A PROMPT IS THEN ISSUED FOR THE NUMBER OF SIDES AND THE ORIENTATION
      OF THE NGON WITH RESPECT TO THE X-AXIS. THE ARRAY 'NG' IS LOADED AND
      WRITTEN TO THE OBJECT FILE.

      THEN ROUTINE DBNGON DOES THE ACTUAL DRAWING. IT REQUIRES THE
      NUMBER OF SIDES, THE LENGTH OF A SIDE, THE ORIENTATION, AND THE
      COORDINATES OF THE STARTING POINT AND IPEN.

AUTHOR:    M. WRIGHT

AUDITOR:   D. CURRIE

DATE:      8/15/93

MODIFICATIONS:

      9/29/93 D. C.
      CHANGES MADE TO ALLOW TABLES TO BE BUILT FOR REPNT.

      10/7/93 R.P.S.
      ADD ERROR CHECKING COMMON 'SPECIAL' AND ERROR HANDLING.
```

Source: Pressman, R., *Software Engineering: A Practitioner's Approach* 3/e, McGraw-Hill (1992), p. 536. By permission of McGraw-Hill, Inc.

to be lengthened by extensive use of comments. A suitable compromise between comments and execution time must be sought.

Software Testing

Testing has two basic objectives: (1) to detect and remove coding and design errors and (2) to determine whether the system performs its tasks according to the user's specifications. As shown in Figure 17-13, these objectives can be labeled as *verification* and *validation* respectively. **Software verification**

FIGURE 17-13

**The objectives of soft-
ware testing**

Verification	Does the product do without error what the programmers think it should do?
Validation	Does the product do what the users want it to do?

stands for the removal of any coding and design errors from the program. For this task, the programmers perform various tests to verify that the program will execute the test data and produce the desired outcome.

The second purpose, **software validation**, is the fundamental questioning of the program's performance to determine if, in fact, it does what the users originally asked for. Because the programmers ordinarily view the software from a technical standpoint rather than in terms of the operational functions required by the users, the programming staff may be wholly satisfied with the system in these areas. Their concern is to follow the program design specifications and to implement them as an error-free system. If the program specifications are flawed, routine testing by the programmers is unlikely to discover these design problems. Although the program may be technically error-free, it may not satisfy the needs of the users. Discrepancies may exist in the program design. Operational aspects of the system, such as the forms to be employed or the user interfaces, may prove unsatisfactory to the user. The users may find that the system fails to meet their own objectives because of such deficiencies. System validation is a broader and more encompassing task than mere debugging of the program code.

Although the purpose of software testing is to prove that the programming system is free of all defects, this is an impossible goal. As Pressman [1992, p. 597] states, "Testing cannot show the absence of defects, it can only show that software defects are present." And, as all programmers know, the likelihood of a defect in the program coding is 100%. The crux of the problem is then how to pursue an impossible ideal. Because humans are imperfect, they produce imperfect software. So why do we perform testing at all? By thorough testing, we strive to locate most of the coding errors caused by human fallibility. Otherwise, no defects will be removed and the error-ridden coding will be completely unusable.

Because testing must be extensive, the testing stage may even account for as much as 40% of the total effort for some projects. Since the detection of errors confirms that the programmer was less than perfect, testing may be viewed as a tedious and unrewarding activity. As in egoless programming (see Chapter 5), *egoless testing* means that finding errors in the program code is not counted against the individual programmer. The search for an error is viewed as a positive action, rather than a faultfinding, ego-bruising activity. A programmer who cannot quickly track down a coding error should feel no loss of professional status on seeking the assistance of other project members. The successful detection and removal of program bugs can be a rewarding enterprise rather than a frustrating task that leads only to self-depreciation.

TESTING AND DEBUGGING

A *test* is defined as the execution of a program to detect the existence of an error, that is, a defect or **bug** in the program. The term **debugging** means the process by which the defect is located and then removed from the program by suitable modification of the code. After the bug is removed, testing must be repeated to guarantee that the error was successfully eliminated and no other bugs were introduced by the program modifications.

Testing requires that a programmer create sample data to test the various paths of a program. It is impractical to test all possible combinations of paths through a program, because the number of combinations may range into the thousands. Therefore, the programmer must select among the paths and assume that other paths are included by such tests. Commonly, the upper and lower bounds of a loop will be tested as well as selected values that fall within the loop. For example, if a module will be executed for any integer values of a customer's age that are greater than or equal to 25 but less than 65, testing might be performed for the following set of values: 0, 10, 24, 25, 26, 35, 60, 64, 65, 66, and 75. If the programmer has established error messages for special cases (such as a negative number), then test data would also include these values. Other "good" values that would be used by the module to compute "good" output values may also be incorporated in the test data. After the test is performed, the programmer will verify that the erroneous input values were rejected by the module and the expected output values from the "good" input data were produced.

If a test causes the program to terminate improperly or to produce erroneous output, the programmer must search for the program bug. Debugging is a skill acquired by experience. Programmers usually acquire this skill the hard way, by making errors and mentally cataloging them. The search for a bug usually begins by examining the code for common types of errors. Prior to executing a test, additional print statements are often inserted in order to display the contents of key variables. This information can then be used to follow the execution flow of the program. For elusive bugs, a recommended practice is to read the coding, statement by statement, and manually compute the values of the variables after each statement is executed. Finally, a wise programmer knows when to seek help. Many times, a programmer may be baffled by the program code and fail to detect the bug despite many frustrating hours spent examining the code. Enlisting a team member to help read the code can speed the debugging process. Sometimes, the mere act of talking to another computer-wise software person can somehow trigger the programmer's mind to suddenly see the error.

THE "DIVIDE AND CONQUER" TESTING STRATEGY

If the program is sufficiently small, it can be tested as a single unit. However, as discussed in Chapter 16, a large program should be formulated in the top-down fashion illustrated in Figure 17-14. A large programming system is composed of several *subsystems*, and each subsystem contains one or more *program segments*. In turn, each program segment represents an integrated collection of other program segments or of program units that interact in order to fulfill the segment's functions. The decomposition of a program segment continues until each program segment on the lowest level is represented by a collection of *program units*. A program unit or **unit module** is defined as a portion of program code that receives input(s) and creates output(s) independently of other program units in the program segment. By its design, a program unit can be tested without the need for the execution of other program units.

Figure 17-15 displays the structure chart of a large programming system, corresponding to the diagram in Figure 17-14. The top box is labeled SYSTEM CONTROL MODULE and represents the program coding that will cause the lower modules to be executed in order to fulfill the system's functions. Each module on the next level is labeled SUBSYSTEM CONTROL MODULE; the subsystem modules contain the program coding to call on their subordinate modules to perform the required tasks. Each subordinate module on the lowest level is labeled UNIT MODULE. The dashed line drawn about a group of modules indicates the modules that compose an entire program

FIGURE 17-14   **The top-down structure of a large programming system**

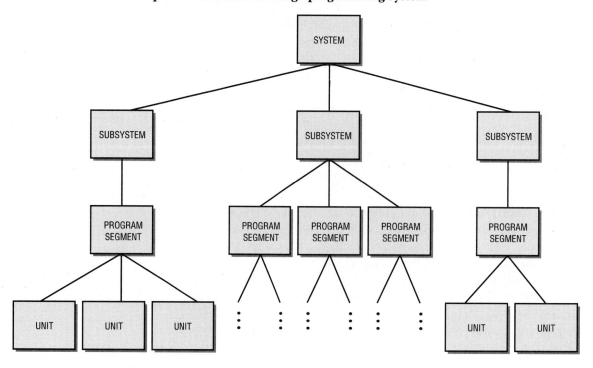

FIGURE 17-15   The structure chart of a large programming system

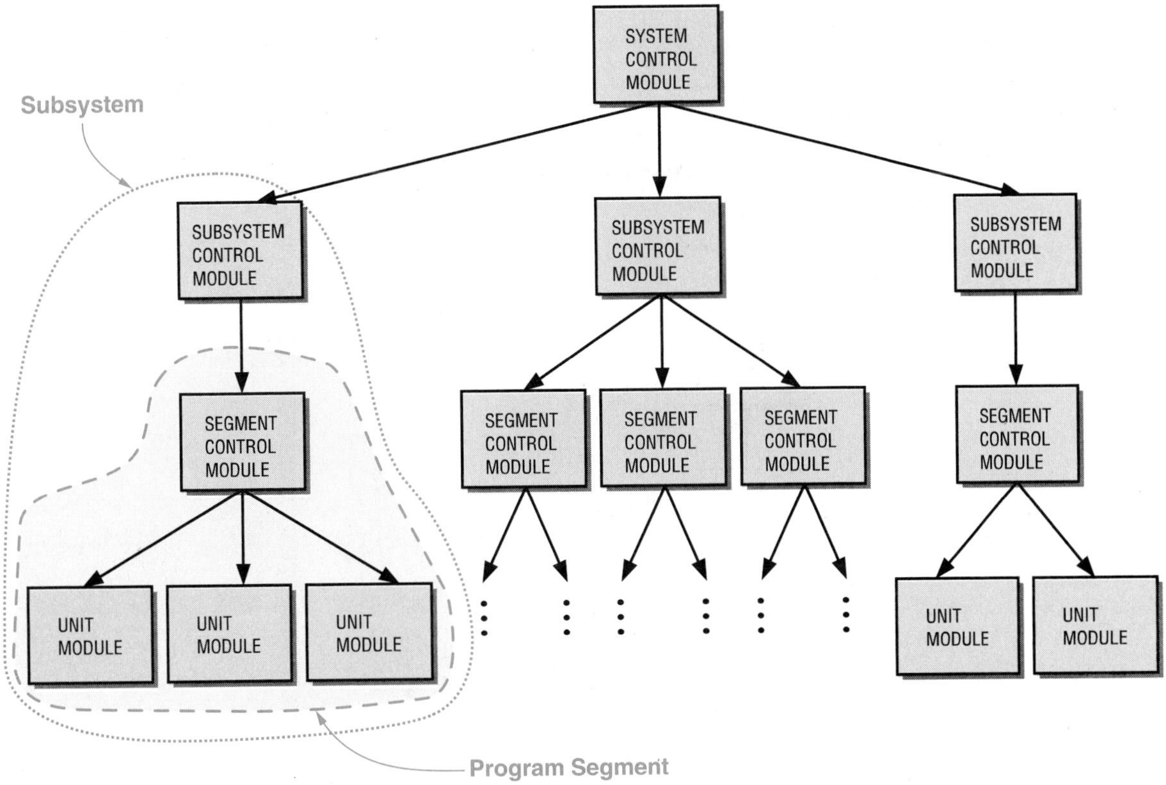

segment; the related set of modules embodying a subsystem is encircled by a dotted line. A unit module is equivalent to a worker module, and a control module is another name for a manager module (see Chapter 16).

The recommended testing procedure is to test the system by dividing it into its logical components: subsystems, program segments, and units. The smallest components are tested first, then each successive level of components is tested, until the unified system has been tested. As illustrated in Figure 17-16, there are five stages in testing. First, each program unit is tested individually. Because the program units are tested independently, detection of errors in the program segments is simplified. This first stage is called *unit testing.*

Second, after the units have been *integrated* into the next level of their program segments, testing of the program segments commences. Integration of higher level program segments follows, and segment testing continues until all segments have been thoroughly tested. Third, the segments are integrated into the program subsystems for testing. Although the subsystems were designed as independent components, they must be integrated eventually to create the final system. Consequently, testing of the subsystems addresses both the proper functioning of each individual subsystem and the interfaces between the subsystems. The output data from a subsystem must be carefully checked for correspondence to the receiving subsystems' re-

FIGURE 17-16

The stages of testing

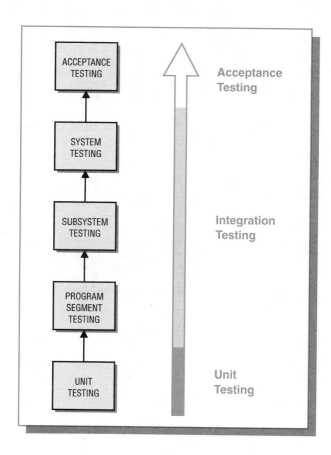

quirements. Fourth, the subsystems are integrated to create the complete system, which is then tested in its entirety. Because the components are gradually integrated to form larger components, the second, third, and fourth stages are known as **integration testing**.

In the final stage, testing is performed to validate the system's performance for the user. Actual production data are employed in order to prove that the system is ready for operational use. The users often submit the data to be used for the acceptance tests and investigate the resulting outputs to determine the system's capabilities. In conjunction with acceptance testing, the users examine the human–machine interfaces, the training manuals, the manual procedures, and other system details that affect their work. The system must demonstrate that it meets the performance requirements of the users. Since the users are testing to decide whether they will approve the system for installation, this final stage is called **acceptance testing**.

APPROACHES TO TESTING

While the objective of testing is easily understood, the difficulties in thoroughly testing the system in a way that facilitates the detection of defects remain. The upward progression from program modules, segments, and subsystems to the testing of the complete system is the accepted testing plan. However, the testing scheme must also specify what tests should be executed and the sequence of these tests. The various techniques commonly used are

Top-down testing

Bottom-up testing

Thread testing

Performance testing

Black-box testing

Because of its size and complexity, a large system will typically be tested with a mixture of these techniques. Different techniques may be employed at different steps in the testing process. Regardless of the approach chosen, testing of the unit modules is always performed independently of any other modules.

Top-Down Testing   In **top-down testing**, the program modules are gradually integrated from the top down. The main module, which calls on the individual modules to perform their tasks, will be executed during all the testing to be performed. This type of module is known as a **driver** or **control module**. Because testing will be performed incrementally from the top down, *program stubs* must be substituted for all untested lower level modules except for the one module to be tested. A program stub is a simple component that masquerades as the component that it replaces. In order to permit the control program to function correctly, each stub must contain enough code to accept input data and produce the same outputs as the actual component. However, the stub really does not perform any manipulation or computation of the data. Previously tested coding for any lower level modules is, of course, put in place for each test run. Untested modules are then integrated into the program structure in either a *depth-first* or *breadth-first* manner as explained next.

Figure 17-17 pictures a control module, MP, with its subordinate modules. The boxes shown with dashed lines indicate stubs rather than actual modules. In the *depth-first* approach, the integration of modules proceeds from the top down by following a single control path to its lowest module. A control path is indicated by its line projecting downward from the control module. For example, the control module MP will be integrated with the module M1 and M4, then M5 is added, and finally M9 and M10 are inserted. As stated earlier, the modules M9 and M10 are tested independently prior to integration. Testing is performed after each step in which a program stub is replaced by its corresponding module. In *breadth-first* testing, the modules are integrated one by one, moving across an entire level horizontally. In this example, breadth-first integration would mean that modules M1, M2, and M3 are integrated before the next level of modules is added.

FIGURE 17-17

Top-down integration using the depth-first approach MP is the main control module. The solid lines indicate the modules already integrated.

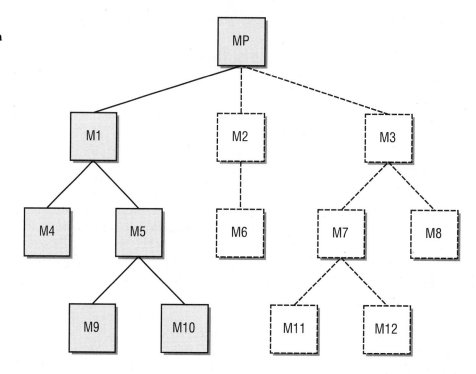

Top-down integration may impose serious limitations on the testing possible, due to the use of program stubs. Because program stubs only simulate the behavior of a component, they have restricted capabilities. Since it is impractical to provide for the full range of input data accepted by the actual component, a stub has only limited functioning. Consequently, the testing of various paths, by necessity, must be confined to selected test data rather than the full range of tests needed to verify the integrated modules. Because top-down testing does not allow for adequate testing of lower level components, bottom-up testing is recommended for low level modules.

Bottom-Up Testing In **bottom-up testing**, the program is integrated from the bottom modules upward until the final system has been constructed. No program stubs are involved. After the lowest modules have been independently tested by the use of drivers written especially for that purpose, integration testing begins. In Figure 17-18, bottom-up integration is illustrated by the same system used for top-down integration. The untested modules have been connected by dashed lines. The set of modules grouped together for testing is called a *cluster*. Testing of the unit modules in a cluster occurs first. Since integration proceeds from the bottom up, modules M5, M9, and M10 (cluster 1) have already been integrated and tested as a unit. Similarly, the modules M7, M11, and M12 (cluster 2) have also been integrated and tested already. We observe that modules M4, M6, and M8 will be

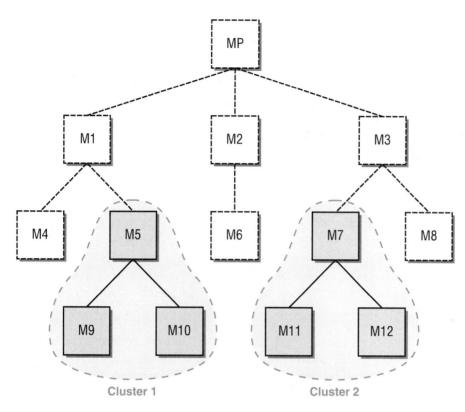

FIGURE 17-18
Bottom-up integration

tested prior to integration testing of their respective clusters. Integration testing then continues as follows:

1. Integration testing of M1 and M4 with cluster 1 (M5, M9, and M10)
2. Integration testing of M2 with M6
3. Integration testing of M3 with M8 and cluster 2 (M7, M11, and M12)

The control module MP will be tested only after all its lower modules have been integrated and tested.

Because the top modules are tested last, a module called a **test driver** must be written to control the execution for each set of modules to be tested. The test driver simulates the modules' environment by obtaining the input data for the modules and receiving their output data. Test drivers also produce the outputs in readable form so that they can be inspected for any discrepancies. After the testing has been completed for a cluster, the driver is replaced by its corresponding control module prior to the next integration step.

The bottom-up approach avoids the difficulty of program stubs. All testing can be performed as needed on the integrated program segments without restrictions on what they can be expected to do. However, testing of the interfaces between the modules on the same level delays the uncovering of incompatibilities between subsystems. When such defects are found, correction may require substantial redesign and rewriting of the program structure. To remedy this shortcoming, a combination of top-down and bottom-up testing may be used for large systems.

Thread Testing   Real-time systems pose special problems in testing. Time-dependent events will affect the interaction between modules. Such events are almost impossible to simulate during testing. Inputs may be sent from sensing devices or keyboards rather than computer data files, adding to the testing control problems. Outputs may be sent to control lines, other computers, or users' terminals rather than recorded in a tangible, easily inspected medium. An additional problem is the testing of the software's actions for the handling of hardware faults.

Thread testing of a real-time system begins by thorough testing of independent modules. After the individual components have been tested, the effects of external events are mapped through the system. Each path or *thread* is then tested. Complete testing of all combinations of threads is an impossibility, because the maximum number of combinations formed by the inputs and outputs is too large.

Performance Testing   Some systems may require additional testing of performance levels—**performance testing**. For example, a sales transaction system may be designed to handle up to 1,000 transactions per second. Unless the system is tested for such high performance requirements, it will be unknown whether these standards were incorporated into the system. Rather than testing merely for the specified performance levels, *stress testing* determines the maximum capacity of the system. When the maximum performance levels are known, safeguards can be incorporated to prevent system failure due to overload. This information is also useful in future planning, as the demands on the system increase over time. For example, if the sales transaction system proves able to handle up to 2,000 transactions per second, the fear of system failure will be alleviated. Once the maximum capacity of the system has been determined, plans for future overloads can be formulated.

Black-Box Testing   When testing is accomplished by the same person who wrote the code, an innate bias is present. Since the author of the code knows its internal logic, tests can be designed to navigate the program paths effectively in as many combinations as possible. The upper and lower boundaries of loops will be checked, the error messages invoked, and other fine details of the program code confirmed. Since the code's author has in-depth knowledge of the program's structure, this testing may be quite successful in verifying the program logic. However, such *white-box testing* fails to examine the specific functional requirements of the code.

Black-box testing (also called *independent testing*) is a technique to overcome the built-in bias of the programmer. In this testing approach, after the code has been tested and debugged to the original programmer's satisfaction, it is turned over to another software staff member for further testing. This person does not study the program logic but concentrates on the tasks to be performed by the code. As illustrated in Figure 17-19, the program code is simply a *black box* that receives inputs and issues outputs. Test data are drawn up to exercise the program code in order to see if the specified inputs will, in fact, produce the desired outputs. Because this approach treats the program code without examination of its internal workings, it is called black-box testing.

Independent testing must be conducted in such a fashion that programmers do not resent the detection of their errors by outsiders. Therefore the testing of someone else's code should be viewed as simply another way to achieve defect-free software. Errors found by black-box testing should be considered "just another error," not some criticism of the coder who failed to find the error by standard testing procedures. The routine exchange of program code for testing among all team members transforms the embarrassment of program errors into a means to learn and share programming knowledge. Alternatively, black-box testing may be assigned to a separate group of computer professionals, who are not members of the project team. For more information about testing, consult the comprehensive book by Glenn Myers [1979] which is still pertinent today.

SOFTWARE QUALITY

The implicit goal of each software project is the development of a high quality software product. Towards that end, many standards are imposed on its development during every phase of the life cycle. We can define *software quality* within a software product as the fulfillment of the users' request by the best-designed software, which meets all the project standards and has high adaptability for the future. As illustrated in Figure 17-20, this definition can be summarized by the acronym **PAR**, for present usability, adaptability for future needs, and revisability. These three components represent the major qualities desired for the software product. The quality of each component depends on the value of its many subfactors.

Present usability indicates that the software product as it currently exists does what it is supposed to do and does it very well indeed. The quality of present usability is measured by the software product's performance, efficiency, reliability, correctness, and security (abbreviated as

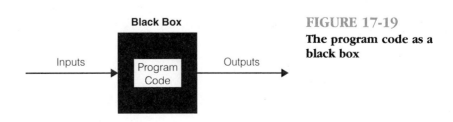

FIGURE 17-19
The program code as a black box

FIGURE 17-20

The characteristics of software quality

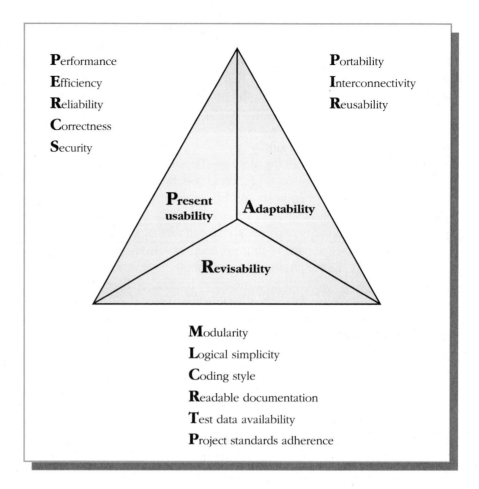

Performance
Efficiency
Reliability
Correctness
Security

Portability
Interconnectivity
Reusability

Present usability

Adaptability

Revisability

Modularity
Logical simplicity
Coding style
Readable documentation
Test data availability
Project standards adherence

PERCS). High quality levels for these characteristics are indicated by affirmative answers to the following questions:

Performance   Does it meet the performance requirements for those tasks?

Efficiency   Does it do the job in the most efficient way, that is, does the program execute as well as it can on the existing hardware?

Reliability   How reliable is the software? The degree of software reliability is indicated by the mean time between any software failures (MTBF) and the severity of these failures.

Correctness   Is the software correct, that is, does it do what the users want it to do?

Security   Is the system secure from outside errors? Can the system recover without loss of data if power failure occurs? Does the system safeguard itself against erroneous input data?

Adaptability for future needs denotes three traits necessary for high quality software: portability, interconnectivity, and reusability. The description of these qualities follows.

Portability	The system can be used on another computer with little or no difficulty.
Interconnectivity	The system can be interfaced with other hardware, as needed, in the future.
Reusability	The system has been developed so that some modules can be reused for other systems.

The final quality to be evaluated for the software product is its **revisability**, that is, the ease with which the programming system can be altered for requirements that arise in the future. Any software product will require some revisions to meet future needs of the firm, to improve its features for the users' operations, and to move to new hardware platforms. The quality of revisability is an inherent goal of the entire software development process. Among the program characteristics that affect revisability are

Modularity of the program

Logical simplicity of the program design

Coding style: comments, straightforward code, and well-chosen variable names

Complete and highly readable documentation of program design, program modules, and testing procedures

Availability of previously used test data

Adherence to project standards

Because no common understanding exists with regard to what high quality software really is, it is difficult to measure the quality of a software product. To earn a high rating on one software factor, the software developer may have emphasized that characteristic at the expense of another trait. This factor does no harm if a factor is irrelevant to the product under development. For example, the possibility of transferring a software product designed for a microcomputer to the organization's mainframe is highly unlikely, so the product can completely lack portability.

THE SOFTWARE QUALITY ASSURANCE PROGRAM

A **software quality assurance (SQA)** program is a set of procedures and standards imposed on the software development process to ensure the development of high quality software. As listed in Figure 17-21, besides software testing, these activities are: modern software practices and tools, formal technical reviews, controls for software testing, standards enforce-

FIGURE 17-21

The activities in a software quality assurance program

Software testing

Modern software practices and tools

Formal technical reviews

Controls for software testing

Standards enforcement

Change control

Project management techniques

Project record keeping

ment, change control, project management techniques, and project record keeping.

Obviously, everyone wants to produce high quality software, but—as we know too well—many developers fail to do so. The reason is that many organizations never implement the procedures necessary to achieve this outcome. Because added procedures translate into higher costs, managers are often reluctant to impose software quality assurance practices on the development process. Analysts and programmers usually believe that they are already performing well and, like many workers, they are reluctant to conform to new procedures. Since any SQA program requires detailed record keeping, the entire effort may be viewed as simply another boondoggle that delays rather than aids the software development process. Further, before an SQA plan can be implemented, a structured development methodology must be adopted. Since some firms still practice the art of programming without formal structured techniques, training costs must be incurred before any SQA program can be initiated. In addition, the introduction of an SQA program may be deferred by management because of reluctance to assume the initial costs and doubt that such programs are truly effective. However, as stated by Sommerville [1992, p. 591], "It is (reasonably) assumed that a well-planned, managed process is more likely to lead to high quality products." The delay in initiating the SQA program only postpones the benefits of such procedures and standards.

Modern Software Practices and Tools

Because the development of high quality software begins with the development of precise and accurate specifications to be followed by a good program design, an SQA program must impose the requirement for modern software practices and tools. These practices and tools include data flow diagrams, data dictionary, process descriptions, structure charts, structured programming, structured walkthroughs, project management, and software tools for the analysis, design, and programming stages.

Formal Technical Reviews

A **formal technical review** is a meeting held to control and assist the software development process. Several types of formal technical reviews are employed during a project. *Structured walkthroughs*, discussed earlier in this chapter, are one type of formal technical review designed to detect errors or omissions in the design or code. A **management review** is intended to monitor the project's progress and provide checkpoints on plans, costs, and schedules. Such reviews are performed at the project's major checkpoints. A **quality review** is used to inspect the quality of work performed by an individual or a team. Unlike a detailed walkthrough, a quality review may be concerned with broader issues such as whether the project specifications are fully met by the program design. Either the specifications, design, code, or documentation may be examined for completeness and correctness.

Controls for Software Testing

Even though thorough testing is absolutely essential to an SQA program, it alone cannot guarantee the high quality of the software product. All the SQA procedures are required in order to achieve this goal. In addition, software testing is diminished in value if proper controls are not placed on its performance. Each test and its accompanying test data should be logged. After each stage of testing has been completed, a formal technical review of the testing performed thus far should be conducted. Test data should be cataloged so that they can be used for future testing activities.

Standards Enforcement

Standards enforcement means that established standards for the software development process must be strictly maintained. This requires the formal documentation of these standards in a standards manual; the creation of such a manual is a time-consuming and difficult process. Figure 17-22 provides examples of areas in which project standards should be documented. The design of appropriate forms for each activity is also necessary. For example, a structured walkthrough must have a standard way to report the errors uncovered and the actions taken to remedy them.

If the software product will be developed for an outside contractor, the contractor may impose different standards on the developmental process. An inspection of the project at its milestones should then include a check that these external requirements have been met. The adherence to standards ensures that the minimal quality criteria will be achieved. The introduction of appropriate CASE tools can assist the software developers in maintaining the project standards. When the software developers formulate specifications, design, or code using a common tool, the CASE tool itself will force

FIGURE 17-22

Examples of project standards

Activity	Standards requirement (to be formalized by the organization)
Formal technical reviews	Review form Meeting format
Change control	Change control form Change review procedure
Programming	Naming conventions Structured programming standards Requirements for comments Documentation format Structured walkthrough: meeting format and review form
Testing	Test data documentation and storage Report format for testing results

the documentation to contain a minimal body of information produced in the same format. Thus, standards are automatically established by this commonality.

Change Control

Change control means that the introduction of specification changes is formally controlled by management. Although changes are almost inevitable for projects requiring months or years to complete, each specification change during the Implementation phase potentially can introduce new errors into the program code. When specification changes occur, the programmer is obliged to incorporate new logic into the program. Subject to the pressure of project deadlines, the refinement of the program design to reflect such changes is frequently omitted, and changes are incorporated only in the program code. The necessary revisions somehow must be quickly incorporated into an already well-defined program design. Extensive code modifications will eventually make the original program design irrelevant, since it no longer reflects the actual programming specifications. Even the logical framework of the programming system may be seriously affected by these changes. As more and more changes are made, the project can grind to a standstill as the programmers constantly modify the code to include the latest changes and rerun the same tests to verify these coding changes.

To prevent this situation, formal procedures must be established to record each change request, estimate its effect on the project, and then select those modifications that must be incorporated prior to installation. The remainder of the requested changes can be retained for possible inclusion after the project is satisfactorily completed. A similar change control mechanism is recommended after the software product has been installed and enters the software maintenance phase.

Project Management Techniques

Project management techniques enable management to forecast, schedule, and control the project's tasks. A by-product of effective project management is the development of *software metrics*. A software metric is any measurement describing any aspect of a software product, including its developmental process and its documentation. An example of a software metric for a software system is the total number of coding lines produced for the system. Another example is the total person-months required for its development. The purpose of collecting software metrics for an information system is to gain information that will aid us in the development of other systems. The measurements of the software product are entered into a data base so that future projects can benefit from this information. As discussed in Chapter 5, retaining historical data from other projects allows us to adjust the COCOMO model for forecasting the effort and time needed to develop software products. Software metrics are also used in determining the effect of various practices on software products. For example, the effectiveness of CASE tools for software development can be rated by evaluating the number of errors found in the system after it is placed in production.

Project Record Keeping

Project record keeping is a primary requirement for any SQA program. Procedures that are not properly documented can have little impact on the software development process. For example, a structured walkthrough is very helpful in discovering defects, but without proper follow-up there can be no assurance that the recommendations of the review meeting were implemented. While record keeping can be burdensome, the use of standard forms (mentioned under project standards) can reduce the time spent on this task. The standardized formats on such forms help the project manager and team members produce these materials more quickly and review them efficiently at later stages in the project.

THE INSTALLATION PHASE

The Installation phase arrives only after the Implementation phase has been successfully completed. The final system now stands ready to be delivered to the users. The principal objective of the Installation phase is to replace the existing system by the newly created system in a smooth, trouble-free manner. In order to accomplish this objective, three activities must be performed:

File conversion

User training

System installation

As depicted in Figure 17-23, the activities of file conversion and user training theoretically can proceed in parallel; both must be accomplished prior to the system's installation. Depending on the project, it is also possible that user training can be scheduled in parallel with the last weeks of testing. However, because some system details affecting the users' interaction with the system might be altered during the testing stage, training should be scheduled as late as possible.

FIGURE 17-23

The Installation phase

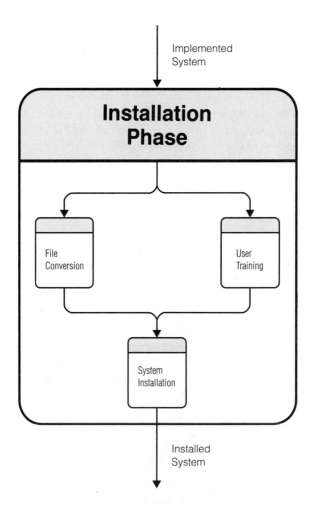

File Conversion

If different file formats will be required by the new system, existing files must be converted to the new formats. Similarly, if a data base management system will be installed, the current files must be transformed. The plans for file conversion were established much earlier, usually at the end of the Design phase, when file formats were frozen in place. As mentioned previously, the programs to perform the file conversion task must be written and tested together with the implementation of the system programs. If possible, the conversion of the files should be scheduled for a time when the system can be halted while the new system is installed. Otherwise, the converted files will be out-of-date as soon as the existing system adds, modifies, or deletes a record from its files. If it is impossible to close down the system, it is necessary to arrange for the updating of both new and old files until the new system installation takes place.

Since the new system cannot be installed until the files are converted, the timing of the file conversion process is crucial to a trouble-free installation. The time needed to convert the files must be estimated carefully and the file conversion task scheduled just prior to the introduction of the new system. It is best to choose a period when the files will undergo little or no updating. For example, files for accounting systems are most easily converted immediately after the close of the fiscal year. As the next fiscal year begins, all updating can be performed on the converted files by using the newly installed system.

User Training

Prior to formal user training, the system documentation for the users must be available in final form. User training manuals and reference guides should also be produced for the system. Depending on the type of system to be installed, either formal training sessions or on-the-job instruction will be scheduled for the users. Although the plans for user training were developed earlier in the life cycle, the actual training should not occur too soon. One reason is that training too far in advance may simply be forgotten by the user. Because the user must continue to work with the existing system until the new system is installed, it is unfair to assume that the user will recall the details of the new system when weeks or even months have passed since the training sessions. Second, if training was accomplished long before the final system is installed, any changes in the users' procedures, forms, or interfaces will require repetition of this instruction. The users may now become confused by the presentation of conflicting information. Third, once the system is available for actual practice, the users must be given the opportunity to interact with the system's interfaces prior to installation. Consequently, training is listed here as an activity in the Installation phase. The actual scheduling is dependent on the project manager.

System Installation

The selection of the file conversion schedule and procedures will depend, to a large extent, on the choice of installation method. There are four possible modes for system installation: (1) direct cutover, (2) parallel operation with single cutover, (3) parallel operation with phased-in cutover, and (4) pilot system conversion. These methods are depicted in Figure 17-24.

DIRECT CUTOVER

The **direct cutover** installation method simply halts the use of the existing system and immediately begins the operation of the new system. The old sys-

FIGURE 17-24

The four conversion methods

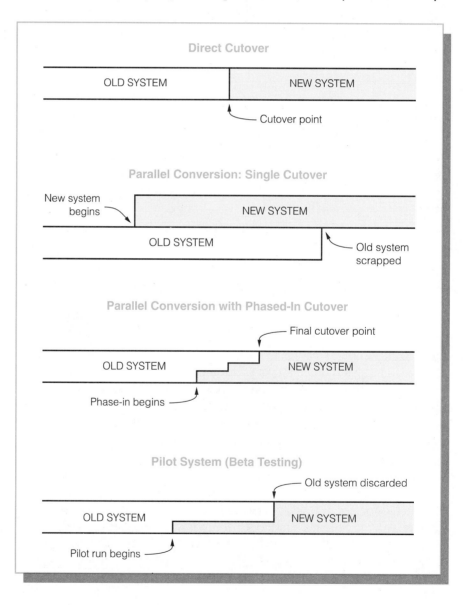

tem just ceases activity as of a stated moment. All future processing is then performed by the new system. The direct cutover method poses the highest risk and gives no umbrella of protection in the event of major software failure.

Once the new system is operational, it is extremely difficult to return to the old system. If mistakes are found in the new system, they must be circumvented until the defects can be removed. Because of the high cost of returning to the old system, only extreme circumstances would force a firm to adopt this course of action. Reversion to the previous system rarely occurs, but when it does it can be both extremely expensive and chaotic for the unfortunate firm.

PARALLEL CONVERSION WITH SINGLE CUTOVER

In order to avoid the risks of direct cutover conversion, the firm may choose **parallel conversion**: operating both the old and new systems simultaneously for an interim period. Because all processing is performed in parallel, the data files are up-to-date and a cutover can be made to the new system at any given time. After the new system has proved itself, the old system is abandoned.

One form of this conversion method is termed **parallel conversion with single cutover**. Since the two systems are executed concurrently during the transition period, the work required of the users increases. No benefits from the new system can be realized until this double effort is discontinued. But the availability of the old system furnishes complete security to the firm's operations. If major software problems materialize, it is a simple matter to stop the new system and continue operations using only the old system.

Parallel conversion is most often chosen when an organization is switching from manual procedures to a computer system. The workers continue to record data manually but also use the new computer system. Periodic inspections are performed to ensure that the two systems remain synchronized. There is a major disadvantage to the continuation of the old system. Workers can easily become confused because of the constant switching between two different sets of procedures.

The parallel running of two computerized systems poses similar problems. If the same computer terminals are used for both systems, the user will be obliged to process the data using the old procedure and the new one as well. Because the user often deals with double entry of the data without hard copy, errors are very likely to occur. When transactions are recorded in one system but not in the other, the two systems quickly become out of phase. Thus, the apparent security offered by parallel running may be illusory.

PARALLEL CONVERSION WITH PHASED-IN CUTOVER

In **parallel conversion with phased-in cutover**, both the old and new systems operate simultaneously, but the installation of the new system and the removal of the old system are accomplished in a piecemeal fashion. The cutover is performed either by functional area, by geographical location, or by some other criterion. For an initial period, both the old and new systems operate in their entirety simultaneously within the selected phase-in division. For example, a hospital information system may be developed to handle outpatient scheduling, inpatient registration, and patient billing. The choice of parallel conversion with phased-in cutover may be made to provide added assurance regarding the new system's quality. First, the outpatient scheduling subsystem is installed in parallel operation with the old system. After a period of time, management drops the old system for outpatient scheduling. Next, the inpatient registration subsystem is installed in parallel operation with the old system. As confidence increases, the cutover for inpatient registration will also be made. Finally, the same procedure is followed for the patient billing subsystem.

The advantage to this method is, once again, the ability to test the new system in production while limiting the consequences of major software problems. If any serious defects are detected, it is only necessary to switch to the old system in one functional area rather than cope with difficulties in the entire system. The disadvantage to this method lies with the difficulties inherent in allowing two different systems to perform processing at the same time. If the new system is unable to interface with the old system in other functional areas, this conversion method cannot be adopted. The disadvantages of parallel running are also present with this method. High costs of dual operation, possible confusion for the system users, and additional work efforts are incurred. The advantage offered is the same as for parallel running—high security in the event of major software errors in the new system.

PILOT SYSTEM CONVERSION METHOD

A variation of parallel conversion with phased-in cutover is known as the *pilot system* conversion method. In this method, the new system is installed in its entirety at one location, say a division of the firm, while the remainder of the firm continues to use the old system. Suppose a firm develops a sales system that includes an ordering system, a billing system, and a sales forecasting system to be used for all the products it manufactures. Before the system is installed throughout the firm, a pilot study of the software's reliability is desired. The system can be installed via the direct cutover method at only one division, while the old system continues to operate at the other divisions of the firm. The new system will then be thoroughly tested in actual production. Final testing of software that is accomplished by operational use is known as **beta testing**. After the software has proved reliable, it will then be installed for use throughout the entire firm.

The problems with the pilot system conversion method stem from the difficulties in operating two different systems that may not always interact with complete compatibility. If data formats conflict or other system aspects cause extra work or confusion for the users, this method may add considerable cost and effort to the project as well as losing the goodwill of the users. When the old and new systems can be used in parallel without such conflict, this method provides the means for uncovering further software defects prior to full installation. Thus, additional security is furnished by beta testing.

Transition to the New System

Three major concerns for the transition to the new system are (1) approval of future modifications to the system, (2) transfer of ownership to the users, and (3) termination of the old system. First, as the project team moves the system to completion, the users may now find that some features have been omitted or designed unsatisfactorily. All these matters suddenly become apparent to the users because the system design is finally visible to them. If the requested changes are incorporated, the system will be delayed. Indeed, the 99% complete system may remain just that. The worst nightmare of project managers is the inability to wrap up a project; if a project is always undergoing change, it can never be installed as a working system. As we discussed earlier, rather than constantly postponing the project completion date to include the desired modifications, these requests should be held for future maintenance and considered after the system is operational. Naturally, there are exceptions to this rule, but in general it is best to defer changes. Otherwise, the "99% complete" syndrome will take over and the system may never be ready for installation.

The second concern in transition—ownership—arises because up to this point the users and project team members have worked closely together to build the new system. Now the software developers must recognize that the operational system belongs to the users. The responsibility of the project team was the building of the best possible system that fulfills the users' requirements. At this point, the project team must teach the users the system's capabilities and limitations as well as the day-to-day operational procedures. Once accomplished, the transfer of ownership marks the end of the software developers' relationship to the project. Although maintenance activities may require the efforts of computer professionals, the users now own the system.

The third issue in transition is closure: The old system must be explicitly terminated at the time agreed on. Sometimes users are reluctant to master the operational details of the new processing system and would prefer to continue the old system. They may delay the actual cutover date by simply not using the new system. In particular, manual systems are apt to be perpetuated by the users. One way to abolish the old system is to remove its documentation from the users' shelves and relegate the old computer programs to archival storage. Other materials related to the old system, such as old forms, can be discarded. If these steps are an integral part of the installation procedure, the new system will be installed unequivocally.

THE POST-IMPLEMENTATION REVIEW PHASE

After the information system has been successfully installed, the last phase of the systems development life cycle, the Post-Implementation Review phase, is entered. As shown in Figure 17-25, this phase has two major purposes: (1) the evaluation of project performance and (2) the review of the final system.

Evaluation of the Project

The review of the activities carried out for the project is conducted by management immediately after the system has been installed. The review is conducted by a committee composed of representatives from management,

FIGURE 17-25

The Post-Implementation Review phase

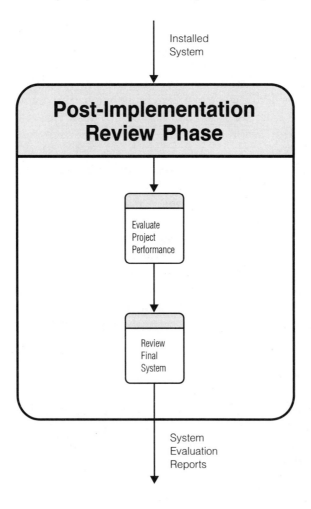

Installed System

Post-Implementation Review Phase

Evaluate Project Performance

Review Final System

System Evaluation Reports

the project manager, and selected software personnel. Each project represents the opportunity for management to learn from its mistakes and to improve the way in which it develops software products. During the Post-Implementation Review phase, the knowledge acquired from the software development project is summarized and documented. Schedule slippage, technical problems, the effectiveness of new tools, and the dynamics of team interaction are examples of topics considered by the Review Committee. The committee should also focus on ways to avoid or overcome project difficulties.

The schedule and person-months estimated for the project are compared to the actual figures. Justifications for the discrepancies between the two figures are presented. If sufficient data are now available, the firm's time and effort estimation model should be adjusted to match the reality of project development activities. As discussed in Chapter 5, the time and costs incurred for the project plus other project information are stored in the historical data base at this time.

Review of the Completed System

The review of the completed system is usually scheduled for three to six months after the Installation phase has been completed. This time lapse permits the users to become familiar with the system; the necessary hard data regarding system performance also emerge after some months of use. As shown in Figure 17-26, the review process asks three questions:

1. Does the system do the job intended?
2. How well does the system do this job?
3. What maintenance projects should be authorized at this time?

The output of the system review process is a report, which states the findings and actions of the review committee.

The first question is primarily answered by the users. Only they can tell if the system meets their original specifications. Features not initially requested but now seen as desirable should be listed as possible maintenance projects. Management also had certain objectives to be met by the system. The system's accomplishments are examined to see if the goals have been met. The cost/benefit analysis for the project is reviewed in order to deter-

---

Evaluation of past efforts

Does the system do the job intended?

How well does the system do this job?

Plans for Future Work

What maintenance projects should be authorized?

FIGURE 17-26
The system evaluation process

Phone Glitches and Software Bugs

On June 26, 1991, an alarm rang inside the control room at C&P Telephone's main building in Baltimore. Dozens of error warnings from the company's main computer were streaming to terminals to notify technicians of a major problem. Red lights appeared on the big board that shows the status of switching hubs scattered around the Washington–Baltimore region. As the error messages scrolled faster and faster across computer screens, it became apparent that the system was going down. All four main computers had failed by the end of the day. Phone service for six million people was disrupted.

That same day, nearly identical computer breakdowns occurred in San Francisco, Los Angeles, and Pittsburgh. The complex call-routing computer system known as Signalling System 7 (SS7) was shut down because of the deluge of maintenance messages. The massive failure began when an electronic circuit board malfunctioned. The cause of the malfunction was apparently somewhere in the SS7 software program or in the way it interacted with other equipment. As a temporary measure, C&P officials ordered the software changed immediately to ignore the maintenance messages. A string of failures then occurred in late June and early July.

The equipment involved in all the breakdowns had been supplied by DSC Communications Corporation, located in Plano, Texas. In the end, DSC Communications discovered the source of the system's collapse: Three faulty instructions in a computer program several million lines long. The character 6 had been typed instead of the letter D. The errors were inadvertently introduced earlier in the year in the course of making a few minor changes in the signalling software. Because the alterations were judged to be insignificant, the standard policy of extensive testing on new or revised computer programs was simply waived by the company officials. Bypassing their own regulations proved to be a costly mistake for the firm, C&P Telephone Company, and the millions who depended on their telephones. The hard-earned lessons are easy to recite but tempting to ignore:

> Any change, no matter how small, can be in error.
>
> Don't violate the software quality assurance program, regardless of your confidence in your own ability—you, too, are human and make errors!

But the lessons for the telephone companies were not yet over. On September 17, 1991, power outage at two American Telephone and Telegraph (AT&T) switching stations in New York City blocked more than five million calls in and out of New York and paralyzed the air traffic control systems at the city's three major airports. The cause of this breakdown was the failure of AT&T technicians to notice alarms that signalled the automatic changeover to batteries at the power plant. Six hours later, an operator finally heeded the warnings but the generator had already failed and the batteries were almost completely drained. Investigation of the incident found that workers had violated company procedures by failing to inspect the equipment when the phone switching system converted to its own power. Had they done so, they would have immediately heard the alarms in the bay that houses the equipment. Visual indicators on the control center's main console also would have told them that the system

needed their intervention. The conclusion by AT&T's president for business communications services is that "errors in judgment" were made. The automatic system worked but its weakest component—the people element—failed. As AT&T discovered, rules alone do not assure us of error-free operations. Enforcement of the rules is necessary!

For more information, see "A.T.&T. Employees Missed Breakdown," by Edmund L. Andrews, *New York Times*, September 19, 1991; "Phone Glitches and Software Bugs," *Science News* 140(7), August 24, 1991, p. 127; "Disconnected, Part 2," *Time* 138(2), July 15, 1991, p. 51; "How a Typo Toppled the Phone Network," *Business Week*, December 9, 1991, p. 44

mine the accuracy of the cost estimates. Management also investigates whether the projected benefits have truly materialized.

The second question relates to how well the system achieves its objectives. First, the overall performance of the system is examined. The day-to-day operations are inspected to see if the anticipated work place benefits have been realized. If not, proposals are made to improve the system to achieve these benefits. The user's interaction with the system is studied in order to determine what flaws exist in the human interfaces. The error rate for any manual processing, such as data input via the keyboard, should be reviewed. If input error rates are abnormally high, system features may require redesign. Second, the software defect rate is scrutinized. Programming errors are classified by date of occurrence, type, severity, and time required for repair. Similar information is maintained on design errors. Given this information, management can assess the quality of the software and decide how to improve the current software development procedures.

Finally, the list of modifications proposed for the system receives action at this time. Even a brand-new system must be maintained to incorporate enhancements and remove programming and design defects. Since large systems take months or years to complete, new features may be required to meet the organizational needs developed over this lengthy period of time. Before maintenance can begin, the users' requests should be ranked by priority. Time and effort requirements must also be estimated for each task. The need to build a new system rather than perform maintenance is an option to be discussed at this time. However, management is usually loathe to begin such work so soon after installation. Instead, authorization is typically given for a selected group of modifications to the system. These tasks are then scheduled appropriately.

SUMMARY

The activities of the final three phases of the systems development life cycle—Implementation, Installation, and Post-Implementation Review—were discussed in this chapter. Up to this point in the life cycle, the new system has been a mere abstraction, represented by diagrams, algorithms, and other descriptions. During the Implementation phase, the abstract becomes reality via the work of programming, testing, and debugging.

A structured walkthrough is a formal inspection of one of the project deliverables in order to detect any errors or omissions prior to the next step in the project. The review team consists of the moderator, the author, and a group of the author's peers. The author of the software deliverable "walks" the participants through the material. A person with a technical background serves as the technical secretary and does not participate in the discussion.

Long before programming begins, the programming language for the project is selected. The language choice is influenced by the factors of developmental mode, the matching of the language features to the application type, portability, the language skills of the programmers, and the programming environment desired for the project. The programming standards imposed for the project should include those commonly known as modern programming practices: top-down program design, structured programming, and coding style conventions of "open" programming style, appropriate indentation, and descriptive comments.

Software testing has the objective of removing defects from the software product. The process by which defects are removed from the program coding is called software verification. The process by which the programming system is shown to meet the users' specifications is known as software validation.

A test is the execution of a program in order to find the presence of a defect, or bug. Testing establishes the presence or absence of particular errors but not the absence of *all* errors. Debugging is the process by which the program is modified to eliminate the known bugs. After a program has been altered in any way, it is essential to perform the test again to ensure that the detected bug has been successfully removed and that no other bugs were introduced by the changes in the code.

The "divide and conquer" testing strategy tests a large program by a series of steps. A program is constructed as a set of subsystems where each subsystem is composed of one or more logical divisions called program segments. In turn, a program segment is a collection of one or more smaller program segments or program units. A program unit is a self-contained independent body of program code with one entrance and one exit. Each unit is tested independently of the other modules. The tested units are then integrated into program segments, each of which is tested separately. Successive integration testing of program segments continues until the subsystems have been formed. After all subsystems have been tested, they are integrated to form the final system. Testing is also necessary upon the system as a whole. After the software developers judge the system to be debugged, the users perform additional tests to ensure that the system meets their specifications; this testing is called acceptance testing. The five testing approaches are top-down testing, bottom-up testing, thread testing, performance testing, and black-box testing.

A software quality assurance (SQA) program is a recommended procedure for assuring that the quality of the resulting software product is high. The definition of software quality was summarized as PAR: present usability, adaptability, and revisability. A software quality assurance program dictates that the software development process include the following activities to assure the end result of high quality software: modern software practices and tools, formal technical reviews (which include structured walkthroughs), software testing, standards enforcement, change control, project management techniques, and appropriate project record keeping.

The system is formally installed during the Installation phase. The existing files must be converted and the users trained prior to the installation. Basically, there are four methods of converting from the old system to the new one: direct cutover, parallel conversion with single cutover, parallel conversion with phased-in cutover, and pilot system conversion. In making the transition to the new system, the project schedule must include the formulation of plans for future system modifications, the transfer of system ownership to the users, and the unequivocal termination of the old system.

Finally, in the Post-Implementation Review phase, the software development activities and the software product are evaluated. The review of the software development activities is performed immediately after installation. Three to six months after installation, the software product is assessed for the quality of its overall design and functional performance. The redesign of system features is considered at this time. The list of proposed changes is inspected and authorization given to those required. The system now enters its maintenance phase.

TERMS

acceptance testing	direct cutover
beta testing	driver
black-box testing	error log
bottom-up testing	formal technical review
bug	integration testing
change control	management review
constructs	modern programming practices
iteration	open programming style
multiple selection	PAR: present usability, adapt-
selection	ability, revisability
sequence	parallel conversion
control module	phased-in cutover
debugging	single cutover
developmental mode	performance testing

continued

portability	structured programming
programming environment	structured walkthrough
quality review	test driver
software quality assurance (SQA)	thread testing
	top-down testing
software validation	top-down program design
software verification	unit module

QUESTIONS

1. What are the major activities of the Implementation phase? How may these activities be scheduled to overlap if appropriate for a project?

2. List the major activities of each phase:
a. Installation
b. Post-Implementation Review

3. Answer the following questions regarding the activity known as structured walkthrough.
a. What is its purpose?
b. Who are its participants?
c. What follow-up is performed afterward?

4. Management should not be represented at structured walkthroughs. What are the reasons for this restriction?

5. What factors affect the choice of the programming language for the project?

6. Explain the programming techniques known as top-down program design and structured programming.

7. When is it appropriate for an organization to choose a different programming language for a software development project rather than the sole language in use over the last five years?

8. Define the following terms: testing, debugging, top-down testing, bottom-up testing, and black-box testing.

9. List the advantages and disadvantages of top-down testing and bottom-up testing.

10. Present usability, adaptability, and revisability are the three major characteristics of high quality software. Explain each of these terms as applied to the quality of a software product.

11. Why is a software quality assurance program necessary?

12. What is the role of change control in producing a high quality software product?

13. **a.** Explain what is meant by the conversion methods called direct cutover and parallel conversion with single cutover

   b. What are the advantages and disadvantages of these two methods?

14. A review of the new system is performed several months after the system has been installed. Why can't this review be scheduled as soon as the system is operational? Explain fully.

PROBLEMS

1. Consider the programming languages with which you are most familiar. If you are not trained in any programming languages, answer this question for COBOL and Pascal. Consult references on programming languages, if necessary.

   a. Explain the advantages and disadvantages of the programming languages you know.

   b. Many firms face high maintenance costs for aging applications written in COBOL. Some firms spend as much as 50% of their effort on maintenance activities. Assuming that the traditional mode of developing software applications will continue to be followed, what programming language do you recommend for the development of data processing applications? Why?

   c. What alternatives should be considered in order to reduce maintenance costs? Specify any developmental mode, software tools, or other techniques you recommend to achieve this goal.

2. Instead of building its own inventory system, the ABC Company has decided to purchase a software package from a well-known vendor. The present system is based on manual operations and paper forms. What conversion approach do you recommend? Why?

3. You have been hired as a consultant for the Super-Furniture Company to improve the quality of the software produced by the firm's software professionals. At present, the data processing center relies on the programmers to test their own coding. All programs are written in BASIC, the only language known by the first few programmers the firm hired. The version of BASIC in use lacks the control structures of CASE or DO-WHILE. It includes an IF-THEN statement but the ELSE clause is missing. Consequently, structured programming is impossible and the programmers employ GO TO statements freely. No structured techniques such as data flow diagrams or structure charts are in use. Project managers track projects carefully by written memoranda sent to their supervisors. Periodic team meetings determine the status of each individual's assignment. Otherwise, programmers work individually and seldom interact during a project. All coordination of the work effort is accomplished solely by the project manager, dealing with each project member in isolation.

a. What problems does this firm have in trying to impose standards for software development?

b. What steps must be taken before a software quality assurance program can be established?

PROJECTS

1. Arrange to visit the manager of a local supermarket to discuss the bar code checkout system used at the store. Discuss with the manager how the system was installed, what problems were encountered initially, and any difficulties experienced later on. Find out what other features are desired by the manager in order to facilitate the work at the store. Prepare a short report summarizing your discussion with the supermarket manager. Include a description of the conversion approach taken by the supermarket for installing the bar code system. If the manager is not aware of the historical details of the bar code system, ask how a new system might be installed such as hand-held computers to record on-shelf inventory data as the merchandise is counted.

2. Consider the following project to record and compute the class grades for the instructors in the Information Systems curriculum. Assume that the program specifications set an upper bound of 500 students per class. Other limits per individual student record are shown in the accompanying table.

Type of Grade	Maximum Number
Homework assignments	35
Quizzes	20
Midterm exams	5
Final exam	1

Prepare a list of test cases based solely on these limits for data fields per student. Explain how and why you limit the number of test cases to be performed.

3. Visit the data processing center at your college and determine whether a software quality assurance program is in operation. If so, prepare a brief report describing the measures taken to ensure a high quality software product. If no SQA program is in effect, document how the center attempts to verify that a program is free from defects.

REFERENCES

Boehm, Barry. "Developing Small-Scale Application Software Products: Some Experimental Results." *Proceedings of IFIP 8th World Computer Congress,* October 1980, pp. 321–326.

Boehm, Barry. *Software Engineering Economics.* Englewood Cliffs, N.J.: Prentice-Hall, 1981.

Knuth, Donald E. "Structured Programming with *Go To* Statements." *Computing Surveys* 6(4), December, 1974, pp. 261–301.

Kernighan, B., and P. Plauger. *The Elements of Programming Style,* 2nd ed. New York: McGraw-Hill, 1978.

Myers, Glenn J. *The Art of Software Testing.* New York: Wiley, 1979.

Pressman, Roger S. *Software Engineering: A Practitioner's Approach,* 3rd ed. New York: McGraw-Hill, 1992.

Sommerville, Ian. *Software Engineering,* 4th ed. Reading, MA: Addison-Wesley, 1992.

Walston, C. E., and C. P. Felix. "A Method of Programming Measurement and Estimation." *IBM System Journal* 16(1), 1977, pp. 54–73.

Index

661